HORA

THE ODES

Bk III 13 O fons Bandusiae.
IV 7 Diffugere nives

HORACE
THE ODES

Edited with Introduction,
Revised Text and Commentary by
KENNETH QUINN
(formerly Professor of Classics, University of Toronto)

Bristol Classical Press

Cover illustration: Horace as a fairly young man. Detail
from the relief on the *Ara Pietatis Augustae* of the second
quarter of the first century A.D.; Villa Medici, Rome

First published by Macmillan Education Ltd in 1980

This edition published in 1996 by
Bristol Classical Press
an imprint of
Gerald Duckworth & Co. Ltd
The Old Piano Factory
48 Hoxton Square, London N1 6PB

A catalogue record for this book is available
from the British Library

ISBN 1-85399-513-4

Printed in Great Britain by
Booksprint, Bristol

Contents

Acknowledgements

The editor and publishers wish to thank the following who have kindly given permission for the use of copyright material:

Harold Ober Associates Inc. for an extract from *Roman Women* by John Balsdon;

Oxford University Press for an extract from *The Roman Revolution* by Sir Ronald Syme.

Preface

I began my first commentary on the *Odes*, for my own use as a teacher, more than thirty years ago; it was a collation of existing commentaries and essentially exegetical; I have been adding to it and revising it ever since. That Horace was a poet who was exciting for what he had to say was a conviction which came to me gradually. Stimulated originally by my reading of Pasquali's monumental *Orazio lirico*, it attained a new urgency and clarity with the publication, just over twenty years ago, of Eduard Fraenkel's *Horace*. Since Fraenkel we have all had to revise our ideas about Horace.

Few of those who write or talk today about Horace can accept the nineteenth-century view of him (reflected by commentators such as T.E. Page and James Gow) as a poet who is fascinating for the precision and the complexity of his style but who had not much to say. The present commentary sets out from the assumptions that Horace is a major poet, and that the *Odes* are a body of work which those who care about poetry can be brought to recognise and enjoy as poetry that works very much as English poetry today works. Like my commentary on Catullus, the present commentary attempts to reconstruct the hypothesis upon which each of the odes rests. My object has been, once again, to discuss each poem as a structural and poetic whole making the kind of sense a poem can be expected to make to the attentive, responsive reader.

A different poet has meant different ways of doing things without preventing adherence to the same general plan. With Horace there is more to explain: to keep explanation related to the text, I have grouped notes on the problems of interpretation of a single passage under a single lemma (sometimes running over several lines) in place of the line-by-line commentary adopted in my Catullus. The goals I set myself have been brevity and clarity. The publisher was anxious to have a book roughly the same size as Page. There seemed little point in mere summary of the material gathered and the points discussed in the commentary of Nisbet and Hubbard: I assume the teacher who uses my book will have his Nisbet-Hubbard by him to consult if he wants (for example) to know more about the Greek models upon which Horace drew, or more about the history of a problem of exegesis. Within the accepted limitation of size I have tried to build up a critical interpretation of the thought and the syntactical and rhetorical structure of each ode as that structure unfolds

in the text. This has meant entering often upon areas commonly regarded
as controversial. I felt there was no alternative but would like to hope
that what is said will be found acceptable as a clearly stated basis for
agreement or constructive dissent.

Books on Horace are numerous and articles on individual odes
innumerable. The case was very different with Catullus, where often there
was not more than an article or two in English that could be pointed to.
I have therefore contented myself with a brief critical bibliography
(Introduction Section 8), as a starting point for independent study.

K.Q.
Toronto, March 1979

Introduction

1 LIFE

Horace tells us more about himself than any other Roman poet; in addition, we possess a short biographical note (it runs into about eighty lines in a modern printed text), usually attributed to Suetonius, which provides additional facts and some of the anecdotes which circulated about Horace a hundred years or so after his death.* He was born on 8 December 65 BC (Suetonius 71R; cf. *Odes* 3. 21. 1, *Epodes* 13. 6, *Epist.* 1. 20. 27-8) at Venusia, a town on the borders of Apulia and Lucania (*Sat.* 2. 1. 34-5); he asks us to imagine his infancy as spent on the slopes of Mt Voltur (*Odes* 3. 4. 9) within sound of the waters of the river Aufidus (*Odes* 4. 9. 2, cf. 3. 30. 10). Apulia provides the setting for boyhood memories (e.g., *Sat.* 1. 6. 71-5: the hulking centurions' sons on their way to school), and the basis for local loyalties — he likes to think of himself as the boy from Apulia who made good (*Odes* 3. 30. 10-14). His upbringing helped also to shape attitudes which lasted throughout his life. His father, a freed slave (*Sat.* 1. 6. 6 and 45-6), was some kind of local official (Horace calls him a *coactor, Sat.* 1. 6. 86, which Suetonius 1-5R takes to mean *exactionum coactor,* or 'tax collector', reporting as an alternative a story that he was a *salsamentarius*); he had as well some kind of small farm (*Sat.* 1. 6. 71). Ambitious for his son, Horace's father brought him to Rome, to see that he was taught by the best teachers (*Sat.* 1. 6. 76-82) and to instil in him, if we may believe Horace, the moral attitudes which came to characterise his writing (*Sat.* 1. 4. 105-26). Presumably, it was also his father who found the money for Horace, when he had completed his introduction to literary studies at the hands of 'basher Orbilius' (*Epist.* 2. 1. 70-71 *plagosus Orbilius*) — a teacher, incidentally, who is included in Suetonius' list of *clari professores (Gram.* 9) — to study philosophy at Athens (*Epist.* 2. 2. 41-5). The period was the mid-forties; Cicero's son Marcus (for whom Cicero wrote his *De Officiis*) must have been among Horace's fellow students; Horace, however, attached himself, we gather, to the Academy, then presided over by Theomnestus — his enthusiasm for Epicureanism (*Odes* 1. 34. 1-2) presumably came later, most likely when

*The *Lives of the Poets* are printed in vol. 2 of the Loeb Suetonius; the best modern text (with Italian commentary) is that of A. Rostagni, *Svetonio de Poetis e Biografi minori,* 1944; the Latin text of the Life of Horace is also to be found in Klingner's edition.

he returned to Italy and came under the influence of Virgil — while
Marcus Cicero studied under the Peripatetic Cratippus. Like the young
Cicero, Horace joined the army of Brutus when the latter arrived in Athens
after the assassination of Julius Caesar; we are told by Plutarch (*Brut.* 24)
that Brutus (then a man of about forty) also attended Theomnestus'
lectures and this may have had something to do with Horace's decision to
throw in his lot with the tyrannicide. He experienced the rout of Philippi
(*Epist.* 2. 2. 46-52; see on *Odes* 2. 7), though we need not take too
seriously his claim that he commanded an entire legion with the rank of
military tribune (*Sat.* 1. 6. 48, Suet. 6-7R).

The course of events during the next few years is unclear. Some time
after Philippi, Horace returned to Italy, taking advantage of an amnesty
extended by Octavian to those who had fought against him (Suet. 7R);
his father's farm had been confiscated (*Epist.* 2. 2. 50-51); his father was
presumably dead; he obtained a post in the Roman Treasury (Suet. 8R
'scriptum quaestorium comparavit'); his title seems to have been *scriba
quaestorius* (perhaps best rendered as 'secretary in the Treasury'; eight
years or more later we find him still a member of the guild of *scribae*
(*Sat.* 2. 6. 36-7). Meanwhile he had begun to write: looking back on his
beginnings years later, he claims 'paupertas impulit audax ut versus
facerem', meaning perhaps that being hard up had given him the courage
to try his hand at writing and possibly also sharpened his tongue. He can
hardly have hoped to make money by his verse (there were no publishers
in Augustan Rome prepared to pay money for the verses of a promising
young poet), but no doubt he hoped to find a patron. In this he succeeded.
Some time in the winter of 38-37 (according to the most likely inter-
pretation of *Sat.* 2. 6. 40-46), he was introduced to Maecenas, first by
Virgil, then by Varius (*Sat.* 1. 6. 54-5; for Varius, see on *Odes* 1. 6); after
a lapse of several months he was accepted as a member of Maecenas' circle
(*Sat.* 1. 6. 61-2 'revocas nono post mense iubesque / esse in amicorum
numero'; *amicus* in this context is a euphemism for *cliens*; cf. *Sat.*
2. 6. 41-2); his journey to Brundisium as part of the suite of Maecenas
(*Sat.* 1. 5) seems to have followed shortly afterwards.

It was to prove a relationship that mellowed with time into something
closer to friendship on equal terms (see on *Odes* 1. 1), though even after
fifteen years or more Horace still found it necessary to assert his indepen-
dence (*Epist.* 1. 7). From Maecenas Horace acquired his small farm in the
Sabine hills, which Horace continued to visit regularly, both as a source of
relief from the turmoil of Rome (*Sat.* 2. 6) and for the return it permitted
to the simple way of life which he had known as a boy and which now
seemed to him ideally suited to his temperament and a symbol of all that
he valued in the traditional Roman way of life. The role he finds congenial
is that of the proprietor of a small estate. Unlike Tibullus (or the *mercator*
whom he satirises in *Odes* 1. 1. 11) he does not dream of working the
land with his own hands — a way of life rejected with contempt by the
intellectual Sallust as fit only for slaves (*Cat.* 4 'non fuit consilium agrum
colundo aut venando, servilibus officiis, contentam aetatem agere'): he

prizes the simple, easy relationships with those around him (*Sat.* 2. 6. 65-76, *Odes* 3. 18) and a communion with nature which is idyllic and pastoral in its overtones (*Odes* 1. 17, 3. 13) rather than that of the modern connoisseur of natural beauty; it is a way of life that is escapist as well as traditional, with the world of nature an almost conscious conspirator (*Odes* 2. 3).

Immersed in this way of life, which becomes for him the objective correlative of an ideal whose roots are moral as well as poetic, Horace devoted himself to poetry and the role of ironic observer of the human comedy to the exclusion of all other honours and rewards. In the last decade of his life, an easy intimacy grew up between him and Augustus (Suet. 9-40R); however, offered an appointment by Augustus as his personal secretary, he refused (Suet. 18-25R) and in his writings he is careful to keep the relationship more formal (*Epist.* 1. 13 and 2. 1) than his relationship with Maecenas. He died 27 November 8 BC a few weeks after Maecenas and was buried on the Esquiline alongside his patron (Suet. 71-79R).

He only occasionally mentions his personal appearance. His description of himself as 'corporis exigui, praecanum' (*Epist.* 1. 20. 24, where he adds the comment that he was 'solibus aptum, irasci celerem, tamen ut placabilis essem') is supported by *Sat.* 2. 3. 308-9; cf. *Epist.* 1. 4. 15-16 'me pinguem et nitidum bene curata cute vises, / cum ridere voles, Epicuri de grege porcum' and Suet. 53-61R.

2 WORKS

The thirty years of Horace's writing life fall into three decades: a decade of experiment from his return to Italy after Philippi until about the time of the battle of Actium (roughly 40-30 BC); the decade after Actium, comprising his finest work; and a decade of declining creative and imaginative powers (roughly 23-13 BC); during the last years of his life Horace seems to have abandoned writing altogether.

His initial ambitions as a writer were limited. He began with loosely structured, discursive verse essays in hexameters which he called 'Conversations' (*Sermones*), an adaptation of the genre traditionally known as *satura*, first given literary form by Lucilius. In the space of about 100 lines, he argued ethical and literary questions, usually from an individual point of view which was forcefully maintained. He expected, he tells us, little difficulty in doing better than the originator of the genre by avoiding Lucilius' slipshod methods of composition. The claim was more presumptuous than it sounds today, for Lucilius had become something of a classic, and Horace's criticism of his style evoked considerable opposition. The *Epodes* likewise have a model, but this time the model is Greek, the iambic poetry of Archilochus, who wrote in the eighth or seventh century BC. The Greek poet provides the metrical form and a way of writing (verse used as a medium of personal invective), but the themes are Roman and the debt to Catullus clear, though never acknowledged; unlike the verse of Archilochus and Catullus, the *Epodes* fail to convey any feeling of personal involvement;

they are literary exercises, of limited interest in themselves as experiments in the new Roman tradition of personal poetry, of considerable interest as Horace's first step towards the formula which was to lead to the *Odes*.

To the seven or eight years after the battle of Actium belongs Horace's most ambitious and permanent contribution to poetry. *Odes* 1-3, comprising 88 poems, were, it seems, published together in 23 BC (see on *Odes* 2. 10).

In the third decade of his writing life Horace returned to the form of the verse essay, clearly in the frame of mind of one who felt his vein of talent exhausted. Round about 20 BC he published a collection of what purport to be letters. The *Epistles* are of course no more real letters than the *Sermones* are real conversations. A new formal elegance takes the place of the cultivated casualness of the *Satires*. Horace no longer has to appear to be talking off the cuff; the years of experience which produced the *Odes* lead to a new precision of statement in the *Epistles* also.

Following Virgil's death in 19 BC, Horace emerges as Rome's leading poet. In 17 BC he was commissioned to compose a choral hymn for the Secular Games, which heralded the start of a new century. This is the *Carmen Saeculare*, a kind of transposition into the public mode of the Sapphic stanza which it is interesting to compare with Horace's use of the Alcaic stanza in the Roman Odes. Three long hexameter epistles, all about poets and poetry, belong also to this third decade. That which stands first in our modern editions, the open letter to Augustus on the state of poetry (*Epist.* 2. 1) is perhaps a year or so later than the *Carmen Saeculare*, the Epistle to Florus (*Epist.* 2. 2) belongs about 19 BC. The date of the third, the Epistle to the Pisos, more often referred to as the *Ars poetica,* is uncertain. Once believed Horace's latest work, it is now thought to belong along with the other literary epistles. If so, Horace's last work represents a return to lyric poetry. A fourth short book comprising fifteen odes appeared about 13 BC, a decade after the publication of *Odes* 1-3. Some are poems attempting, but not achieving, the old manner (the best are the Spring Ode 4. 7 and the fine dramatic monologue 4. 13). Others are frankly laureate writing (4. 4, 4. 5, 4. 14); while still avoiding full commitment to the position of laureate (see his eloquent disclaimer in 4. 2), Horace faces the challenge of praising the military achievements of Augustus' stepsons with considerable skill; the concluding praises of Augustus himself strike a less grandiloquent level, but the theme is handled with disarming grace and simplicity. One or two poems (4. 8, 4. 9) can only be regarded as makeweights. One feels Horace knew his limitations and that his decision to abandon lyric poetry after *Odes* 1-3 was the right one. The very competence of *Odes* 4 (with one or two exceptions) underlines the poverty of invention.

3   THE ODES

Horace's *Odes* have been compared to Bach's *Well-tempered Clavier*. The comparison is justified by the monumental character of Horace's achievement and places the collection in the light in which Horace himself saw it (see on *Odes* 3. 30), but it misrepresents by implication the dry, incisive directness of these subtle poems. The formula is that of the *Epodes*: fresh artistic creation within the metrical form and conventions of an existing genre. In the *Odes* it is the Greek lyric poets of the seventh century BC, especially Alcaeus, who provide the Greek model, but that model is made the vehicle of Roman themes, the attitudes expressed are those of a very distinctive personality moulded by a culture as remote from the culture of Sappho and Alcaeus as that which produced Virgil is remote from that of Homer.

The *Odes* are set in the everyday life of a society which had recreated, in Italy and in Latin, the ideals and cultural values of the Greek-speaking Hellenistic world. In place of the simple, lyric directness of Sappho and Alcaeus (the natural expression of a society which possessed neither the cultural nor the syntactical sophistication to express complex attitudes), Horace's lyric poetry expresses the thoughts of a mind accustomed to a wry detachment, however firm Horace's commitment to the attitudes expressed or implied. The *Odes* are a demonstration that poetry which is neither didactic nor ostensibly serious in tone can be the expression of a philosophy of life. The context most often is that of everyday social life in that section of urban society which had the leisure to devote itself to a life of wine, women and song. To make these themes the basis for a Roman recreation of the traditional forms of erotic and sympotic lyric is in itself to set up an ironic tension between theme and form. Horace's Epicurean detachment is as remote from the emotional naiveté of Sappho and Alcaeus as it is remote from the openly passionate involvement of Catullus. To point to greater complexity is not in itself, of course, to prove greater poetic success. The simple, intense emotions of early Greek lyric match the simple syntactical perfection with which they are expressed and the culture of which they are the product. The use to which they are put by Catullus necessitates a reassessment of forms such as epigram and lampoon till then considered too slight and too ephemeral to be taken seriously. In the *Odes* the poet's speaking voice is more mannered, more elaborately precise. At the same time Horace's verse represents a creative re-fusion of traditions hitherto considered distinct — ancient Greek personal lyric on the one hand and the assertively non-lyric conversational direct-ness (appropriate to the forms he adopted) of Catullus on the other.

What Horace owes above all to Catullus is his ironic stance. The *Odes* are a challenge to the reader to admit that Catullan *urbanitas*, the style of conversation improved upon, can be made the medium of a new, more serious kind of poetry. The traditional themes of wine, women and song are handled with a graceful detachment: the verse is too well-mannered to question openly the values threatened by that detachment; Horace prefers the role of the observer of the human comedy to that of the stern-voiced moralist.

The range of themes which lend themselves to such treatment is neces-sarily limited, and on the more conventionally moral issues (the wrongness of the single-minded pursuit of material wealth, the larger issue of one's duties to the State) Horace sometimes speaks out more plainly, not always

with equal success. Here the moral insight is abstract — an argument
sketched out to defend a way of life, not the intuitive appraisal of a
situation. The worst failures seem to occur when Horace is trying hardest.
The Roman Odes (3. 1-6) in particular have been harshly criticised. Con-
demnation has too often sprung, however, from misappraisal. An ode like
2. 14 has been read as a moralising sermon instead of as a dramatic mono-
logue. The Roman Odes have been dismissed on the basis of a paraphrase
of content, their lyric structure and the reservations implied by complexity
of tone and syntax have been ignored. The characteristic structure of lyric
is the image. To read images for their content (as, for example, in the first
four stanzas of 3. 1 or the opening lines of 2. 18) is to read poetry as if it
were prose rhetoric (decoding the images into statement, instead of sur-
rendering to their evocative power), to isolate content from form and to
remain insensitive to the resonances touched off and the frames of refe-
rence opened up by the subtly-placed loaded word (e.g., the Roman over-
tones of *imperium* and *triumpho* in Stanza 2 of 3. 1) or the exquisitely
precise phrase.

4   SYNTAX AND STYLE

The *Odes* depend for their success upon the delicate handling, with just the
right mixture of approving and ironic attitudes, of themes that are both
traditional and everyday. Only occasionally does Horace permit himself a
more open lyric stance. The basic formula is that of a collaboration between
a complex metrical unit (the 4-line stanza) and a complex syntactical unit —
the sentence which frequently extends over several lines, or even several
stanzas, sometimes setting up an elaborate hierarchy of clause dependent
upon clause, or of appositional expansion following appositional expansion.
Traditional rhetorical structures, above all the tricolon crescendo (see on
1. 8. 1-7), add a further basis of structure. The diction is seldom exalted,
always precise, measured, invariably compact, frequently complex. At the
same time the characteristic syntactical structures of contemporary prose are
avoided. For the logical architecture of the periodic sentence is substituted
the sentence that explores an image, or a series of images, in a context of
precisely stated qualification or appraisal. The effect is to keep the images
under conscious control, the poet's speaking voice constantly stating, or
implying, the appropriate evaluation. The points of coincidence of metrical
unit (stanza-end) and syntactical unit (sentence-end) maintain a carefully
balanced counterpoint. Coincidence of stanza-end and end of sentence is
sufficiently frequent to establish a basic pattern, departure from which
can be felt as a significant variation of tempo (as when a sentence straddles
several stanzas) or dramatically effective: a sentence ending, not just in
mid-stanza but in mid-line, can thus accentuate a logical transition (e.g.,
3. 1. 37), a transition from one image to another (e.g., 2. 5. 9), or even
the transition from narrative to set speech (e.g., 3. 3. 18). Without the
metrical pattern to hold the whole together, such transitions would be
felt as intolerably abrupt (as they seem to those who read the verse as

prose); within the verse structure they permit an economy in the use of
connecting words and formulae which contributes much to the polyseman-
tic compression (meaningful word following meaningful word) of Horace's
style.

5   THE HISTORY OF THE ODES

Horace's *Odes* constitute one of the landmarks in the line of development
from lyric poetry as song to poetry which gives lyric expression to complex
thought. Their influence upon the development of modern lyric is thus
enormous, if most often indirect and unacknowledged. In the Renaissance
Horace was, along with Pindar, the recognised model. Ronsard set out
consciously to rival both. But if the Renaissance poets and their successors
set out to recapture the form, the spirit too often eludes them: the
attitudes expressed are more direct, more simply passionate; the delicacy
of Horatian irony is fundamentally alien to the spirit of the Renaissance.
In the late sixteenth and the seventeenth centuries the reflective, meditative
tone and the elaborate syntax necessary to sustain complex patterns of
thought find their expression in the sonnet, a form originally devised by
Petrarch in the fourteenth century, which becomes, in the hands of the
great English masters of the form, the ideal transposition into English of
the form and manner of the short Horatian ode. The ode comes to be
felt as a grander form, deploying a simpler rhetoric (whether it be the
public rhetoric of Andrew Marvell's 'Horatian Ode upon Cromwell's Return
from Ireland' or the passionate rhetoric of the great nineteenth-century
Romantic odes of Keats and Shelley); to sustain such sublimity of tone
the 4-line rhyming stanza (which in English tends to suggest the ballad,
or the forms of popular verse) is discarded in favour of more elaborate
structures. Throughout the eighteenth century Horace continued to be
popular: the English Augustan age found his personality congenial; there
was a ready response to the formal elegance of his verse. But it was the
Horace of the *Satires* and *Epistles* whom eighteenth-century poets respon-
ded to most strongly and sought to emulate. The *Odes* came to be prized
for their turn of phrase, rather than the subtle fabric of their thought — a
process which had already begun in antiquity. A reputation so founded, on
what Tennyson was to call Horace's 'jewels five words long' (compare
Quintilian's famous *felicissime audax* and Petronius' *curiosa felicitas*), rather
than on the impact of complete poems and the pressure of feeling Horace's
use of language is designed to convey, naturally led those who expected
more of poetry to take Horace lightly, regarding him as an interesting
pioneer rather than one of the great masters of lyric form. The Romantic
movement, by the emphasis it gave to imagination and spontaneity at the
expense of structural strength and subtlety of technique, deepened the
alienation. Because of that alienation, the fact that English lyric poetry
in the twentieth century has returned to modes of expression and thought
remarkably like those of Horace is seldom recognised. The return is not,
however, an accident: it represents a reorientation of the tradition, in which

the meditative stance and the measured seriousness of the poet's speaking voice have re-emerged as the shaping influences in a natural reaction against the excesses of Romanticism. Because Horace's *Odes* are now largely unknown to those who use English at the creative level, there is a tendency to accept as definitive the Romantic dismissal of a poet whom all writers and readers of poetry today who can read him in the orginal Latin find more exciting and congenial than they had expected.

6   METRES

The following table shows the metres employed by Horace in the *Odes*. The individual metres are discussed in the Commentary at their first occurrence.

Name	Total	Book 1	Book 2	Book 3	Book 4
Alcaics					
See on 1.9	37	10	12	11	4
Sapphics					
See on 1.2	25	9	6	7	3
Greater Sapphics					
See on 1.8	1	1			
Asclepiads					
(a) See on 1.1	3	1		1	1
(b) See on 1.3	12	4		6	2
(c) See on 1.6	9	4	1	2	2
(d) See on 1.5	7	4		2	1
(e) See on 1.11	3	2			1
Archilocheans					
(a) See on 1.4	1	1			
(b) See on 1.7	2	2			
(c) See on 4.7	1				1
Hipponacteans					
See on 2.18	1		1		
Ionics					
See on 3.12	1			1	

Of the 103 Odes, 78 are written in 4-line stanzas (37 in Alcaics, 25 in Sapphics, 9 in Asclepiads (c), 7 in Asclepiads (d)). The syntactical structure of the poems written in distichs likewise suggests, more often than not, a 4-line rather than a 2-line unit. With the exception of 4. 8, all the Odes consist of multiples of four lines. (For a fuller discussion and for 'Meineke's canon', see 1. 1 Introduction.)

7 TEXT

Something like three hundred Horatian manuscripts have survived, the
oldest dating from the ninth and tenth centuries. Of these, some twelve
to fifteen are regarded by modern scholars as fundamental to the establish-
ment of the text of the *Odes*. In only one or two cases is a passage of any
length to be despaired of (see on 4. 8), plainly corrupt (e.g., 3. 14. 11) or
widely held suspect (e.g., 1. 23. 5-6, 3. 4. 9-10). Variations between diffe-
rent manuscripts which seriously affect the sense (e.g., 3. 24. 4) are not
numerous; minor variants (e.g., 2. 5. 16 *petet/petit*, 2. 13. 23 *discretas/
descriptas*) are more frequent. Cases where conjecture is commonly re-
sorted to are likewise, apart from obvious repairs, not numerous (e.g.,
1. 25. 20 *Euro* in place of *Hebro*, 2. 13. 15 *Thynus* in place of *Poenus*,
3. 20. 8 *illa* in place of *illi*). There are modern scholars who would revise
the traditional text more drastically, to admit variant readings and con-
jectures which seem to them mistakenly discarded or neglected, or who
question the accepted text on the grounds of sense or Horatian usage. In
all these matters, as in the matter of punctuation and that of the division
(or not) of odes written in monostichic and distichic metres into 4-line
stanzas, Wickham's Oxford text of 1901 (revised by Garrod in 1912) must
be regarded as less than satisfactory. Klingner's Teubner text, first issued in
1939, shows better judgement in the choice of readings.

8 BIBLIOGRAPHY

Texts
WICKHAM , E. C. and GARROD, H. W., *Q. Horati Flacci Opera* (Oxford
    Classical Texts series, 1912, frequently reprinted).
KLINGNER, F., *Horatius, Opera* (Teubner series, 1939, 3rd edition 1957).
    See Section 7.

Commentaries
The best commentary is that of R. G. M. Nisbet and M. Hubbard,
published by Oxford University Press. The commentary on *Odes* 1
appeared in 1970, that on *Odes* 2 in 1978.
    For a characteristically forthright critical appraisal of the *Odes* by the
senior of the two editors (and reflecting the attitude adopted in the
commentary), see Nisbet's chapter on Horace in J. P. Sullivan's *Critical
Essays on Roman Literature* (London, 1962).
    For *Odes* 3, recourse may usefully be had to the edition with English
translation, running commentary and brief notes by G. Williams (Oxford,
1969).
    The following older editions may still be found useful. The commentary
is in all cases grammatical and exegetical rather than critical:

GOW, James (Cambridge, 1896). The best in this group, though occasionally
    wrongheaded.
PAGE, T. E. (Macmillan, 1895). The most widely used edition in English
    schools throughout the present century.

SHOREY, P. and LAING, G. J. (Chicago, 2nd edition 1910; reprinted 1960).
Widely used in American colleges.
WICKHAM, E. C. (Oxford, 1877). Brief commentary, often good, on more
scholarly lines than Gow and Page.

The specialist will find much of value in the monumental editions of
Richard Bentley (Cambridge, 1711) and J. C. Orelli (Berlin, 4th edition 1886).
Among twentieth-century editions in languages other than English, the
most important are:

KIESSLING, A. and HEINZE, R. The 7th edition of Kiessling's commentary
on the *Odes*, published in 1930, represents a complete recasting; for
many years the standard commentary; in German.
TESCARI, O. (Turin, 1936, 3rd edition 1948). Based on the commentary
of Kiessling-Heinze, but including a much wider range of illustrative
parallels; in Italian.

Books on Horace
CAMPBELL, A. Y., *Horace, A New Interpretation* (London, 1924). The first
of a series of twentieth-century reinterpretations of Horace in English.
Vigorous, readable, rather old-fashioned.
COLLINGE, N. E., *The Structure of Horace's Odes* (Oxford, 1961). An
attempt at systematic thematic analysis. Somewhat mechanical.
COMMAGER, S., *The Odes of Horace, A Critical Study* (New Haven, 1962).
An interpretation of the *Odes* based on twentieth-century critical
methodology. Valuable for the precision of the procedures adopted
rather than perceptive.
FRAENKEL, Eduard, *Horace* (Oxford, 1957). The best book on Horace in
English, the work of a veteran scholar valuable for the sensitivity of its
insights as well as for the authority of its interpretations. Selective in its
approach (virtually nothing on Horace's love poetry).
WEST, D., *Reading Horace* (Edinburgh, 1967). Bright and stimulating, but
superficial.
WILKINSON, L. P., *Horace and His Lyric Poetry* (Cambridge, 1945). A
useful, scholarly introduction, often sensitive and perceptive, if some-
what conventional.

Those able to read Italian will find G. Pasquali's *Orazio lirico* (Florence,
1920; reprinted 1964) invaluable.
A special number on Horace of the journal *Arion* was published in 1970
(vol. 9, numbers 2-3); it attempts a representative range of contemporary
critical opinion.
The volume edited by C. D. N. Costa in the *Greek and Latin Studies*
series published by Routledge (London, 1973) contains interesting material
of varying quality, as does the review by G. Williams of the present state
of Horatian studies in the *Greece and Rome New Surveys in the Classics*
series: *Horace* (Oxford, 1972).
For any systematic study of the *Odes*, the *Concordance* by L. Cooper
(Washington, 1916; reprinted 1961) is indispensable.

The Odes

BOOK 1

1

Maecenas atavis edite regibus,
o et praesidium et dulce decus meum:
sunt quos curriculo pulverem Olympicum
collegisse iuvat, metaque fervidis
evitata rotis palmaque nobilis   5
terrarum dominos evehit ad deos;
hunc, si mobilium turba Quiritium
certat tergeminis tollere honoribus;
illum, si proprio condidit horreo
quidquid de Libycis verritur areis;   10
gaudentem patrios findere sarculo
agros Attalicis condicionibus
numquam demoveas, ut trabe Cypria
Myrtoum pavidus nauta secet mare;
luctantem Icariis fluctibus Africum   15
mercator metuens otium et oppidi
laudat rura sui: mox reficit rates
quassas indocilis pauperiem pati;
est qui nec veteris pocula Massici
nec partem solido demere de die   20
spernit, nunc viridi membra sub arbuto
stratus, nunc ad aquae lene caput sacrae;
multos castra iuvant et lituo tubae
permixtus sonitus bellaque matribus
detestata; manet sub Iove frigido   25
venator tenerae coniugis inmemor,
seu visa est catulis cerva fidelibus,
seu rupit teretes Marsus aper plagas.
Me doctarum hederae praemia frontium
dis miscent superis; me gelidum nemus   30
Nympharumque leves cum Satyris chori
secernunt populo, si neque tibias

Euterpe cohibet nec Polyhymnia
Lesboum refugit tendere barbiton;
quodsi me lyricis vatibus inseres,   35
sublimi feriam sidera vertice.

2

2

1   Iam satis terris nivis atque dirae
    grandinis misit pater et rubente
    dextera sacras iaculatus arcis
        terruit urbem,

2   terruit gentis, grave ne rediret   5
    saeculum Pyrrhae nova monstra questae,
    omne cum Proteus pecus egit altos
        visere montis,

3   piscium et summa genus haesit ulmo,
    nota quae sedes fuerat columbis,   10
    et superiecto pavidae natarunt
        aequore dammae;

4   vidimus flavom Tiberim retortis
    litore Etrusco violenter undis
    ire deiectum monumenta regis   15
        templaque Vestae,

5   Iliae dum se nimium querenti
    iactat ultorem, vagus et sinistra
    labitur ripa Iove non probante u-
        xorius amnis;   20

6   audiet civis acuisse ferrum,
    quo graves Persae melius perirent,
    audiet pugnas vitio parentum
        rara iuventus.

7   Quem vocet divum populus ruentis   25
imperi rebus? prece qua fatigent
virgines sanctae minus audientem
    carmina Vestam?

8   cui dabit partis scelus expiandi
Iuppiter? Tandem venias precamur   30
nube candentis umeros amictus
    augur Apollo;

9   sive tu mavis, Erycina ridens,
quam Iocus circum volat et Cupido;
sive neglectum genus et nepotes   35
    respicis auctor,

10   heu nimis longo satiate ludo,
quem iuvat clamor galeaeque leves
acer et Marsi peditis cruentum
    voltus in hostem;   40

11   sive mutata iuvenem figura
ales in terris imitaris almae
filius Maiae patiens vocari
    Caesaris ultor,

12   serus in caelum redeas diuque   45
laetus intersis populo Quirini,
neve te nostris vitiis iniquum
    ocior aura

13   tollat: hic magnos potius triumphos,
hic ames dici pater atque princeps,   50
neu sinas Medos equitare inultos
    te duce, Caesar.

3

1   Sic te diva potens Cypri,
        sic fratres Helenae, lucida sidera,
     ventorumque regat pater
        obstrictis aliis praeter Iapyga,

2   navis, quae tibi creditum   5
        debes Vergilium: finibus Atticis
     reddas incolumem precor
        et serves animae dimidium meae.

3   Illi robur et aes triplex
        circa pectus erat, qui fragilem truci   10
     conmisit pelago ratem
        primus, nec timuit praecipitem Africum

4   decertantem Aquilonibus
        nec tristis Hyadas nec rabiem Noti,
     quo non arbiter Hadriae   15
        maior, tollere seu ponere volt freta.

5   Quem mortis timuit gradum
        qui siccis oculis monstra natantia,
     qui vidit mare turbidum et
        infamis scopulos Acroceraunia?   20

6   Nequiquam deus abscidit
        prudens oceano dissociabili
     terras, si tamen inpiae
        non tangenda rates transiliunt vada.

7   Audax omnia perpeti   25
        gens humana ruit per vetitum nefas:
     audax Iapeti genus
        ignem fraude mala gentibus intulit;

8   post ignem aetheria domo
            subductum macies et nova febrium   30
        terris incubuit cohors
            semotique prius tarda necessitas

9   leti corripuit gradum;
            expertus vacuum Daedalus aera
        pinnis non homini datis;   35
            perrupit Acheronta Herculeus labor.

10   Nil mortalibus ardui est:
            caelum ipsum petimus stultitia neque
        per nostrum patimur scelus
            iracunda Iovem ponere fulmina.   40

4

1   Solvitur acris hiems grata vice veris et Favoni
      trahuntque siccas machinae carinas,
   ac neque iam stabulis gaudet pecus aut arator igni
      nec prata canis albicant pruinis;

2   iam Cytherea choros ducit Venus imminente Luna,   5
      iunctaeque Nymphis Gratiae decentes
   alterno terram quatiunt pede, dum gravis Cyclopum
      Volcanus ardens visit officinas.

3   Nunc decet aut viridi nitidum caput impedire myrto
      aut flore, terrae quem ferunt solutae;   10
   nunc et in umbrosis Fauno decet immolare lucis,
      seu poscat agna sive malit haedo;

4   pallida Mors aequo pulsat pede pauperum tabernas
      regumque turris: o beate Sesti,
   vitae summa brevis spem nos vetat inchoare longam;   15
      iam te premet nox fabulaeque Manes

5   et domus exilis Plutonia; quo simul mearis,
        nec regna vini sortiere talis
     nec tenerum Lycidan mirabere, quo calet iuventus
      nunc omnis et mox virgines tepebunt.   20

5

1   Quis multa gracilis te puer in rosa
          perfusus liquidis urget odoribus
            grato, Pyrrha, sub antro?
             cui flavam religas comam

2   simplex munditiis? Heu quotiens fidem   5
          mutatosque deos flebit et aspera
            nigris aequora ventis
             emirabitur insolens,

3   qui nunc te fruitur credulus aurea,
          qui semper vacuam, semper amabilem   10
            sperat, nescius aurae
             fallacis; miseri, quibus

4   intemptata nites; me tabula sacer
          votiva paries indicat uvida
            suspendisse potenti   15
             vestimenta maris deo.

6

1   Scriberis Vario fortis et hostium
     victor Maeonii carminis alite,
     quam rem cumque ferox navibus aut equis
       miles te duce gesserit;

2   nos, Agrippa, neque haec dicere nec gravem   5
          Pelidae stomachum cedere nescii
          nec cursus duplicis per mare Ulixei
             nec saevam Pelopis domum

3   conamur, tenues grandia, dum pudor
          inbellisque lyrae Musa potens vetat   10
          laudes egregii Caesaris et tuas
             culpa deterere ingeni.

4   Quis Martem tunica tectum adamantina
          digne scripserit aut pulvere Troico
          nigrum Merionen aut ope Palladis   15
             Tydiden superis parem?

5   Nos convivia, nos proelia virginum
          sectis in iuvenes unguibus acrium
          cantamus vacui, sive quid urimur,
             non praeter solitum leves.   20

7

1   Laudabunt alii claram Rhodon aut Mytilenen
        aut Epheson bimarisve Corinthi
      moenia vel Baccho Thebas vel Apolline Delphos
        insignis aut Thessala Tempe;

2   sunt quibus unum opus est intactae Palladis urbem   5
        carmine perpetuo celebrare et
      undique decerptam fronti praeponere olivam;
        plurimus in Iunonis honorem

3   aptum dicet equis Argos ditisque Mycenas:
        me nec tam patiens Lacedaemon   10
      nec tam Larisae percussit campus opimae
        quam domus Albuneae resonantis

4   et praeceps Anio ac Tiburni lucus et uda
     mobilibus pomaria rivis.
     Albus ut obscuro deterget nubila caelo   15
     saepe Notus, neque parturit imbris

5   perpetuos, sic tu sapiens finire memento
     tristitiam vitaeque labores
     molli, Plance, mero, seu te fulgentia signis
     castra tenent seu densa tenebit   20

6   Tiburis umbra tui: Teucer Salamina patremque
     cum fugeret, tamen uda Lyaeo
     tempora populea fertur vinxisse corona
     sic tristis adfatus amicos:

7   'Quo nos cumque feret melior fortuna parente,   25
     ibimus; o socii comitesque,
     nil desperandum Teucro duce et auspice Teucro —
     certus enim promisit Apollo

8   ambiguam tellure nova Salamina futuram;
     o fortes peioraque passi   30
     mecum saepe viri, nunc vino pellite curas:
     cras ingens iterabimus aequor.'

                         8

1   Lydia, dic, per omnis
     te deos oro, Sybarin cur properes amando
     perdere, cur apricum
     oderit campum patiens pulveris atque solis,

2   cur neque militaris   5
     inter aequalis equitet, Gallica nec lupatis
     temperet ora frenis?
     Cur timet flavum Tiberim tangere? Cur olivum

3   sanguine viperino
       cautius vitat neque iam livida gestat armis   10
     bracchia, saepe disco,
       saepe trans finem iaculo nobilis expedito?

4   Quid latet, ut marinae
       filium dicunt Thetidis sub lacrimosa Troiae
     funera, ne virilis   15
       cultus in caedem et Lycias proriperet catervas?

9

1   Vides ut alta stet nive candidum
        Soracte nec iam sustineant onus
          silvae laborantes geluque
            flumina constiterint acuto?

2   Dissolve frigus ligna super foco   5
        large reponens atque benignius
          deprome quadrimum Sabina,
            o Thaliarche, merum diota;

3   permitte divis cetera, qui simul
        stravere ventos aequore fervido   10
          deproeliantis, nec cupressi
            nec veteres agitantur orni.

4   Quid sit futurum cras, fuge quaerere, et
        quem Fors dierum cumque dabit, lucro
          adpone; nec dulcis amores   15
            sperne puer neque tu choreas,

5   donec virenti canities abest   _green tine_
        morosa: nunc et campus et areae
          lenesque sub noctem susurri
            conposita repetantur hora,   20

6   nunc et latentis proditor intumo
gratus puellae risus ab angulo
    pignusque dereptum lacertis
      aut digito male pertinaci.

10

1   Mercuri, facunde nepos Atlantis,
qui feros cultus hominum recentum
voce formasti catus et decorae
    more palaestrae,

2   te canam, magni Iovis et deorum   5
nuntium curvaeque lyrae parentem,
callidum quidquid placuit iocoso
    condere furto;

3   te, boves olim nisi reddidisses
per dolum amotas, puerum minaci   10
voce dum terret, viduus pharetra
    risit Apollo;

4   quin et Atridas duce te superbos
Ilio dives Priamus relicto
Thessalosque ignis et iniqua Troiae   15
    castra fefellit;

5   tu pias laetis animas reponis
sedibus virgaque levem coerces
aurea turbam, superis deorum
    gratus et imis.   20

11

Tu ne quaesieris, scire nefas, quem mihi, quem tibi
finem di dederint, Leuconoe, nec Babylonios
temptaris numeros. Ut melius, quidquid erit, pati,
seu pluris hiemes seu tribuit Iuppiter ultimam,
quae nunc oppositis debilitat pumicibus mare   5
Tyrrhenum. Sapias, vina liques, et spatio brevi
spem longam reseces; dum loquimur, fugerit invida
aetas: carpe diem quam minimum credula postero.

12

1   Quem virum aut heroa lyra vel acri
       tibia sumis celebrare, Clio?
       quem deum? cuius recinet iocosa
           nomen imago

2   aut in umbrosis Heliconis oris   5
       aut super Pindo gelidove in Haemo,
       unde vocalem temere insecutae
           Orphea silvae

3   arte materna rapidos morantem
       fluminum lapsus celerisque ventos,   10
       blandum et auritas fidibus canoris
           ducere quercus?

4   Quid prius dicam solitis parentis
       laudibus, qui res hominum ac deorum,
       qui mare ac terras variisque mundum   15
           temperat horis,

5   unde nil maius generatur ipso
           nec viget quidquam simile aut secundum?
           Proximos illi tamen occupavit
                Pallas honores   20

6   proeliis audax; neque te silebo,
           Liber, et saevis inimica virgo
           beluis, nec te, metuende certa
                Phoebe sagitta;

7   dicam et Alciden puerosque Ledae,   25
           hunc equis, illum superare pugnis
           nobilem, quorum simul alba nautis
                stella refulsit,

8   defluit saxis agitatus umor,
           concidunt venti fugiuntque nubes   30
           et minax, quod sic voluere, ponto
                unda recumbit.

9   Romulum post hos prius an quietum
           Pompili regnum memorem an superbos
           Tarquini fasces dubito an Catonis   35
                nobile letum;

10   Regulum et Scauros animaeque magnae
           prodigum Paulum superante Poeno
           gratus insigni referam camena
                Fabriciumque —   40

11   hunc et incomptis Curium capillis
           utilem bello tulit et Camillum
           saeva paupertas et avitus apto
                cum lare fundus;

12   crescit occulto velut arbor aevo   45
           fama Marcelli; micat inter omnis
           Iulium sidus velut inter ignis
                luna minores.

13   Gentis humanae pater atque custos,
          orte Saturno, tibi cura magni   50
          Caesaris fatis data: tu secundo
             Caesare regnes;

14   ille seu Parthos Latio imminentis
          egerit iusto domitos triumpho
          sive subiectos Orientis orae   55
             Seras et Indos,

15   te minor latum reget aequos orbem:
          tu gravi curru quaties Olympum,
          tu parum castis inimica mittes
             fulmina lucis.   60

13

1   Cum tu, Lydia, Telephi
          cervicem roseam, cerea Telephi
          laudas bracchia, vae meum
             fervens difficili bile tumet iecur;

2   tum nec mens mihi nec color   5
          certa sede manet, umor et in genas
          furtim labitur, arguens,
             quam lentis penitus macerer ignibus;

3   uror, seu tibi candidos
          turparunt umeros inmodicae mero   10
          rixae, sive puer furens
             inpressit memorem dente labris notam.

4   Non, si me satis audias,
          speres perpetuum dulcia barbare
          laedentem oscula, quae Venus   15
             quinta parte sui nectaris imbuit:

5   felices ter et amplius
           quos inrupta tenet copula nec malis
         divolsus querimoniis
           suprema citius solvet amor die.   20

14

1   O navis, referent in mare te novi
         fluctus: o quid agis? fortiter occupa
           portum; nonne vides, ut
             nudum remigio latus

2   et malus celeri saucius Africo   5
         antemnaeque gemant ac sine funibus
           vix durare carinae
             possint imperiosius

3   aequor? Non tibi sunt integra lintea,
         non di quos iterum pressa voces malo;   10
           quamvis Pontica pinus,
             silvae filia nobilis,

4   iactes et genus et nomen inutile,
         nil pictis timidus navita puppibus
           fidit. Tu, nisi ventis   15
             debes ludibrium, cave;

5   nuper sollicitum quae mihi taedium,
         nunc desiderium curaque non levis,
           interfusa nitentis
             vites aequora Cycladas.   20

15

1   Pastor cum traheret per freta navibus
    Idaeis Helenen perfidus hospitam,
    ingrato celeris obruit otio
        ventos ut caneret fera

2   Nereus fata. 'Mala ducis avi domum   5
    quam multo repetet Graecia milite
    coniurata tuas rumpere nuptias
        et regnum Priami vetus:

3   heu heu, quantus equis, quantus adest viris
    sudor, quanta moves funera Dardanae   10
    genti; iam galeam Pallas et aegida
        currusque et rabiem parat.

4   Nequiquam Veneris praesidio ferox
    pectes caesariem grataque feminis
    inbelli cithara carmina divides;   15
        nequiquam thalamo gravis

5   hastas et calami spicula Cnosii
    vitabis strepitumque et celerem sequi
    Aiacem: tamen heu serus adulteros
        crines pulvere collines.   20

6   Non Laertiaden, exitium tuae
    genti, non Pylium Nestora respicis?
    urgent inpavidi te Salaminius
        Teucer, te Sthenelus sciens

7   pugnae, sive opus est imperitare equis,   25
    non auriga piger; Merionen quoque
    nosces; ecce furit te reperire atrox
        Tydides melior patre,

8   quem tu, cervus uti vallis in altera
visum parte lupum graminis inmemor,   30
     sublimi fugies mollis anhelitu,
        non hoc pollicitus tuae.

9   Iracunda diem proferet Ilio
matronisque Phrygum classis Achillei:
     post certas hiemes uret Achaicus   35
        ignis Iliacas domos.'

16

1   O matre pulcra filia pulcrior,
quem criminosis cumque voles modum
     pones iambis, sive flamma
        sive mari libet Hadriano.

2   Non Dindymene, non adytis quatit   5
mentem sacerdotum incola Pythius,
     non Liber aeque, non acuta
        sic geminant Corybantes aera,

3   tristes ut irae, quas neque Noricus
deterret ensis nec mare naufragum   10
     nec saevos ignis nec tremendo
        Iuppiter ipse ruens tumultu;

4   fertur Prometheus addere principi
limo coactus particulam undique
     desectam et insani leonis   15
        vim stomacho adposuisse nostro;

5   irae Thyesten exitio gravi
stravere et altis urbibus ultimae
     stetere causae, cur perirent
        funditus inprimeretque muris   20

6   hostile aratrum exercitus insolens.
      Conpesce mentem: me quoque pectoris
        temptavit in dulci iuventa
          fervor et in celeres iambos

7   misit furentem; nunc ego mitibus   25
      mutare quaero tristia, dum mihi
        fias recantatis amica
          opprobriis animumque reddas.

17

1   Velox amoenum saepe Lucretilem
      mutat Lycaeo Faunus et igneam
        defendit aestatem capellis
          usque meis pluviosque ventos;

2   inpune tutum per nemus arbutos   5
      quaerunt latentis et thyma deviae
        olentis uxores mariti,
          nec viridis metuunt colubras

3   nec Martialis haediliae lupos,
      utcumque dulci, Tyndari, fistula   10
        valles et Usticae cubantis
          levia personuere saxa.

4   Di me tuentur, dis pietas mea
      et musa cordi est: hic tibi copia
        manabit ad plenum benigno   15
          ruris honorum opulenta cornu;

5   hic in reducta valle Caniculae
      vitabis aestus et fide Teia
        dices laborantis in uno
          Penelopen vitreamque Circen;   20

6   hic innocentis pocula Lesbii
      duces sub umbra, nec Semeleius
        cum Marte confundet Thyoneus
          proelia, nec metues protervum

7   suspecta Cyrum, ne male dispari   25
      incontinentis iniciat manus
        et scindat haerentem coronam
          crinibus inmeritamque vestem.

18

Nullam, Vare, sacra vite prius severis arborem
circa mite solum Tiburis et moenia Catili.
Siccis omnia nam dura deus proposuit neque
mordaces aliter diffugiunt sollicitudines.
Quis post vina gravem militiam aut pauperiem crepat?   5
Quis non te potius, Bacche pater, teque, decens Venus?
Ac ne quis modici transiliat munera Liberi,
Centaurea monet cum Lapithis rixa super mero
debellata, monet Sithoniis non levis Euhius,
cum fas atque nefas exiguo fine libidinum   10
discernunt avidi. Non ego te, candide Bassareu,
invitum quatiam nec variis obsita frondibus
sub divum rapiam. Saeva tene cum Berecyntio
cornu tympana, quae subsequitur caecus Amor sui
et tollens vacuum plus nimio Gloria verticem   15
arcanique Fides prodiga, perlucidior vitro.

19

1   Mater saeva Cupidinum
        Thebanaeque iubet me Semelae puer
      et lasciva Licentia
        finitis animum reddere amoribus.

2   Urit me Glycerae nitor   5
         splendentis Pario marmore purius,
      urit grata protervitas
         et voltus nimium lubricus adspici.

3   In me tota ruens Venus
         Cyprum deseruit nec patitur Scythas   10
      et versis animosum equis
         Parthum dicere nec quae nihil attinent.

4   Hic vivum mihi caespitem, hic
         verbenas, pueri, ponite turaque
      bimi cum patera meri: 15
         mactata veniet lenior hostia.

20

1   Vile potabis modicis Sabinum
      cantharis, Graeca quod ego ipse testa
      conditum levi, datus in theatro
         cum tibi plausus,

2   clare Maecenas eques, ut paterni   5
      fluminis ripae simul et iocosa
      redderet laudes tibi Vaticani
         montis imago.

3   Caecubum et prelo domitam Caleno
      tu bibes uvam: mea nec Falernae   10
      temperant vites neque Formiani
         pocula colles.

21

1
    Dianam tenerae dicite virgines,
    intonsum pueri dicite Cynthium,
       Latonamque supremo
        dilectam penitus Iovi:

2
    vos laetam fluviis et nemorum coma,   5
    quaecumque aut gelido prominet Algido
       nigris aut Erymanthi
        silvis aut viridis Gragi,

3
    vos Tempe totidem tollite laudibus
    natalemque, mares, Delon Apollinis   10
       insignemque pharetra
        fraternaque umerum lyra –

4
    hic bellum lacrimosum, hic miseram famem
    pestemque a populo et principe Caesare in
       Persas atque Britannos   15
        vestra motus aget prece.

22

1
    Integer vitae scelerisque purus
    non eget Mauris iaculis neque arcu
    nec venenatis gravida sagittis,
       Fusce, pharetra,

2
    sive per Syrtis iter aestuosas   5
    sive facturus per inhospitalem
    Caucasum vel quae loca fabulosus
       lambit Hydaspes.

3   Namque me silva lupus in Sabina,
          dum meam canto Lalagen et ultra   10
          terminum curis vagor expeditis,
             fugit inermem,

4   quale portentum neque militaris
          Daunias latis alit aesculetis
          nec Iubae tellus generat, leonum   15
             arida nutrix.

5   Pone me pigris ubi nulla campis
          arbor aestiva recreatur aura,
          quod latus mundi nebulae malusque
             Iuppiter urget,   20

6   pone sub curru nimium propinqui
          solis, in terra domibus negata:
          dulce ridentem Lalagen amabo,
             dulce loquentem.

23

1   Vitas inuleo me similis, Chloe,
          quaerenti pavidam montibus aviis
             matrem non sine vano
             aurarum et siluae metu.

2   Nam seu mobilibus veris inhorruit   5
          adventus foliis seu virides rubum
             dimovere lacertae,
             et corde et genibus tremit.

3   Atqui non ego te tigris ut aspera
          Gaetulusve leo frangere persequor: 10
             tandem desine matrem
             tempestiva sequi viro.

24

1   Quis desiderio sit pudor aut modus
    tam cari capitis? praecipe lugubris
    cantus, Melpomene, cui liquidam pater
        vocem cum cithara dedit:

2   ergo Quintilium perpetuus sopor   5
    urget, cui Pudor et Iustitiae soror
    incorrupta Fides nudaque Veritas
        quando ullum inveniet parem?

3   Multis ille bonis flebilis occidit,
    nulli flebilior quam tibi, Vergili;   10
    tu frustra pius, heu, non ita creditum
        poscis Quintilium deos.

4   Quid si Threicio blandius Orpheo
    auditam moderere arboribus fidem
    num vanae redeat sanguis imagini,   15
        quam virga semel horrida

5   non lenis precibus fata recludere
    nigro conpulerit Mercurius gregi?
    durum, sed levius fit patientia
        quidquid corrigere est nefas.   20

25

1   Parcius iunctas quatiunt fenestras
    iactibus crebris iuvenes protervi
    nec tibi somnos adimunt amatque
        ianua limen,

2   quae prius multum facilis movebat   5
           cardines, audis minus et minus iam:
           'Me tuo longas pereunte noctes,
               Lydia, dormis?'

3   In vicem moechos anus arrogantis
           flebis in solo levis angiportu   10
           Thracio bacchante magis sub inter-
               lunia vento,

4   cum tibi flagrans amor et libido,
           quae solet matres furiare equorum,
           saeviet circa iecur ulcerosum,   15
               non sine questu,

5   laeta quod pubes hedera virenti
           gaudeat pulla magis atque myrto,
           aridas frondes hiemis sodali
               dedicet Euro.   20

26

1   Musis amicus tristitiam et metus
           tradam protervis in mare Creticum
             portare ventis, quis sub Arcto
               rex gelidae metuatur orae,

2   quid Tiridaten terreat, unice   5
           securus. O quae fontibus integris
             gaudes, apricos necte flores,
               necte meo Lamiae coronam,

3   Piplei dulcis, nil sine te mei
           prosunt honores; hunc fidibus novis,   10
             hunc Lesbio sacrare plectro
               teque tuasque decet sorores.

27

1   Natis in usum laetitiae scyphis
pugnare Thracum est: tollite barbarum
    morem verecundumque Bacchum
       sanguineis prohibete rixis;

2   vino et lucernis Medus acinaces   5
immane quantum discrepat; inpium
    lenite clamorem, sodales,
       et cubito remanete presso.

3   Voltis severi me quoque sumere
partem Falerni? Dicat Opuntiae   10
    frater Megyllae, quo beatus
       volnere, qua pereat sagitta.

4   Cessat voluntas? Non alia bibam
mercede. Quae te cumque domat Venus,
    non erubescendis adurit   15
       ignibus, ingenuoque semper

5   amore peccas. Quidquid habes, age,
depone tutis auribus. A miser,
    quanta laborabas Charybdi,
       digne puer meliore flamma!   20

6   Quae saga, quis te solvere Thessalis
magus venenis, quis poterit deus?
    Vix inligatum te triformi
       Pegasus expediet Chimaera.

28

Te maris et terrae numeroque carentis harenae
  mensorem cohibent, Archyta,

pulveris exigui prope litus parva Matinum
  munera, nec quicquam tibi prodest

aerias temptasse domos animoque rotundum   5
  percurrisse polum morituro.

Occidit et Pelopis genitor, conviva deorum,
  Tithonusque remotus in auras

et Iovis arcanis Minos admissus, habentque
  Tartara Panthoiden iterum Orco   10

demissum, quamvis clipeo Troiana refixo
  tempora testatus nihil ultra

nervos atque cutem morti concesserat atrae,
  iudice te non sordidus auctor

naturae verique. Sed omnis una manet nox   15
  et calcanda semel via leti.

Dant alios Furiae torvo spectacula Marti,
  exitio est avidum mare nautis;

mixta senum ac iuvenum densentur funera, nullum
  saeva caput Proserpina fugit.   20

Me quoque devexi rabidus comes Orionis
  Illyricis Notus obruit undis.

At tu, nauta, vagae ne parce malignus harenae
  ossibus et capiti inhumato

particulam dare: sic, quodcumque minabitur Eurus   25
fluctibus Hesperiis, Venusinae

plectantur silvae te sospite, multaque merces,
unde potest, tibi defluat aequo

ab Iove Neptunoque sacri custode Tarenti.
Neglegis inmeritis nocituram   30

postmodo te natis fraudem conmittere? Fors et
debita iura vicesque superbae

te maneant ipsum. Precibus non linquar inultis,
teque piacula nulla resolvent;

quamquam festinas, non est mora longa; licebit   35
iniecto ter pulvere curras.

29

1   Icci, beatis nunc Arabum invides
gazis et acrem militiam paras
non ante devictis Sabaeae
regibus horribilique Medo

2   nectis catenas? Quae tibi virginum   5
sponso necato barbara serviet?
Puer quis ex aula capillis
ad cyathum statuetur unctis

3   doctus sagittas tendere Sericas
arcu paterno? Quis neget arduis   10
pronos relabi posse rivos
montibus et Tiberim reverti,

4   cum tu coemptos undique nobilis
         libros Panaeti Socraticam et domum
            mutare loricis Hiberis,   15
               pollicitus meliora, tendis?

30

1   O Venus regina Cnidi Paphique,
         sperne dilectam Cypron et vocantis
            ture te multo Glycerae decoram
               transfer in aedem;

2   fervidus tecum puer et solutis   5
         Gratiae zonis properentque Nymphae
         et parum comis sine te Iuventas
            Mercuriusque.

31

1   Quid dedicatum poscit Apollinem
         vates? quid orat de patera novum
            fundens liquorem? Non opimae
               Sardiniae segetes feracis,

2   non aestuosae grata Calabriae   5
         armenta, non aurum aut ebur Indicum,
            non rura quae Liris quieta
               mordet aqua taciturnus amnis.

3   Premant Calenam falce quibus dedit
         Fortuna vitem, dives ut aureis   10
            mercator exsiccet culillis
               vina Syra reparata merce,

4
    dis carus ipsis, quippe ter et quater
    anno revisens aequor Atlanticum
        inpune: me pascunt olivae,   15
           me cichorea levesque malvae.

5
    Frui paratis et valido mihi,
    Latoe, dones et precor integra
        cum mente nec turpem senectam
          degere nec cithara carentem.   20

32

1
    Poscimus, si quid vacui sub umbra
    lusimus tecum, quod et hunc in annum
    vivat et pluris, age dic Latinum,
        barbite, carmen,

2
    Lesbio primum modulate civi,   5
    qui ferox bello tamen inter arma,
    sive iactatam religarat udo
        litore navim,

3
    Liberum et Musas Veneremque et illi
    semper haerentem puerum canebat   10
    et Lycum nigris oculis nigroque
        crine decorum:

4
    o decus Phoebi et dapibus supremi
    grata testudo Iovis, o laborum
    dulce lenimen mihi cumque salve   15
        rite vocanti!

33

1 Albi, ne doleas plus nimio memor
 inmitis Glycerae, neu miserabilis
 decantes elegos, cur tibi iunior
  laesa praeniteat fide:

2 insignem tenui fronte Lycorida   5
 Cyri torret amor, Cyrus in asperam
 declinat Pholoen; sed prius Apulis
  iungentur capreae lupis,

3 quam turpi Pholoe peccet adultero.
 Sic visum Veneri, cui placet inparis 10
 formas atque animos sub iuga aenea
  saevo mittere cum ioco;

4 ipsum me melior cum peteret Venus,
 grata detinuit compede Myrtale
 libertina, fretis acrior Hadriae 15
  curvantis Calabros sinus.

34

1 Parcus deorum cultor et infrequens,
 insanientis dum sapientiae
  consultus erro, nunc retrorsum
   vela dare atque iterare cursus

2 cogor relictos. Namque Diespiter 5
 igni corusco nubila dividens
  plerumque, per purum tonantis
   egit equos volucremque currum,

3   quo bruta tellus et vaga flumina,
       quo Styx et invisi horrida Taenari   10
           sedes Atlanteusque finis
               concutitur. Valet ima summis

4   mutare et insignem attenuat deus
       obscura promens: hinc apicem rapax
           Fortuna cum stridore acuto   15
               sustulit, hic posuisse gaudet.

                           35

1   O diva, gratum quae regis Antium,
       praesens vel imo tollere de gradu
           mortale corpus vel superbos
               vertere funeribus triumphos —

2   te pauper ambit sollicita prece   5
       ruris colonus; te dominam aequoris
           quicumque Bithyna lacessit
               Carpathium pelagus carina;

3   te Dacus asper, te profugi Scythae
       urbesque gentesque et Latium ferox   10
           regumque matres barbarorum et
               purpurei metuunt tyranni,

4   iniurioso ne pede proruas
       stantem columnam neu populus frequens
           ad arma, cessantis ad arma   15
               concitet imperiumque frangat;

5   te semper anteit saeva Necessitas,
       clavos trabalis et cuneos manu
           gestans aena nec severus
               uncus abest liquidumque plumbum;   20

6   te Spes et albo rara Fides colit
          velata panno nec comitem abnegat,
            utcumque mutata potentis
               veste domos inimica linquis

7   (at volgus infidum et meretrix retro   25
          periura cedit, diffugiunt cadis
            cum faece siccatis amici
               ferre iugum pariter dolosi):

8   serves iturum Caesarem in ultimos
          orbis Britannos et iuvenum recens   30
            examen Eois timendum
               partibus Oceanoque rubro.

9   Heu heu, cicatricum et sceleris pudet
          fratrumque: quid nos dura refugimus
            aetas? quid intactum nefasti   35
               liquimus? unde manum iuventus

10   metu deorum continuit? quibus
          pepercit aris? O utinam nova
            incude diffingas retusum in
               Massagetas Arabasque ferrum.   40

36

1   Et ture et fidibus iuvat
          placare et vituli sanguine debito
       custodes Numidae deos,
          qui nunc Hesperia sospes ab ultima

2   caris multa sodalibus,   5
          nulli plura tamen dividit oscula
       quam dulci Lamiae, memor
          actae non alio rege puertiae

3 mutataeque simul togae.
  Cressa ne careat pulcra dies nota,   10
 neu promptae modus amphorae
   neu morem in Salium sit requies pedum,

4 neu multi Damalis meri
  Bassum Threicia vincat amystide,
 neu desint epulis rosae   15
   neu vivax apium neu breve lilium.

5 Omnes in Damalin putris
  deponent oculos, nec Damalis novo
 divelletur adultero
   lascivis hederis ambitiosior.   20

37

1 Nunc est bibendum, nunc pede libero
 pulsanda tellus, nunc Saliaribus
  ornare pulvinar deorum
   tempus erat dapibus, sodales.

2 Antehac nefas depromere Caecubum   5
 cellis avitis, dum Capitolio
  regina dementis ruinas
   funus et imperio parabat

3 contaminato cum grege turpium
 morbo virorum, quidlibet inpotens   10
  sperare fortunaque dulci
   ebria. Sed minuit furorem

4 vix una sospes navis ab ignibus
 mentemque lymphatam Mareotico
  redegit in veros timores   15
   Caesar ab Italia volantem

5   remis adurgens, accipiter velut
           mollis columbas aut leporem citus
              venator in campis nivalis
                  Haemoniae, daret ut catenis   20

6   fatale monstrum. Quae generosius
           perire quaerens nec muliebriter
              expavit ensem nec latentis
                classe cita reparavit oras,

7   ausa et iacentem visere regiam   25
           voltu sereno fortis et asperas
              tractare serpentes, ut atrum
                corpore conbiberet venenum

8   deliberata morte ferocior,
           saevis Liburnis scilicet invidens   30
              privata deduci superbo
                non humilis mulier triumpho.

38

1   Persicos odi, puer, adparatus,
           displicent nexae philyra coronae,
           mitte sectari, rosa quo locorum
              sera moretur.

2   Simplici myrto nihil adlabores   5
           sedulus curo: neque te ministrum
           dedecet myrtus neque me sub arta
              vite bibentem.

BOOK 2

1

1   Motum ex Metello consule civicum
bellique causas et vitia et modos
     ludumque Fortunae gravisque
         principum amicitias et arma

2   nondum expiatis uncta cruoribus,   5
periculosae plenum opus aleae,
     tractas et incedis per ignis
         suppositos cineri doloso.

3   Paulum severae musa tragoediae
desit theatris: mox ubi publicas   10
     res ordinaris, grande munus
         Cecropio repetes coturno,

4   insigne maestis praesidium reis
et consulenti, Pollio, curiae,
     cui laurus aeternos honores   15
         Delmatico peperit triumpho.

5   Iam nunc minaci murmure cornuum
perstringis auris, iam litui strepunt,
     iam fulgor armorum fugacis
         terret equos equitumque voltus;   20

6   audire magnos iam videor duces
non indecoro pulvere sordidos
     et cuncta terrarum subacta
         praeter atrocem animum Catonis.

7   Iuno et deorum quisquis amicior   25
     Afris inulta cesserat inpotens
        tellure, victorum nepotes
           rettulit inferias Iugurthae:

8   quis non Latino sanguine pinguior
     campus sepulcris inpia proelia   30
        testatur auditumque Medis
           Hesperiae sonitum ruinae?

9   qui gurges aut quae flumina lugubris
     ignara belli? quod mare Dauniae
        non decoloravere caedes?   35
           quae caret ora cruore nostro?

10   Sed ne relictis, Musa procax, iocis
     Ceae retractes munera neniae;
        mecum Dionaeo sub antro
           quaere modos leviore plectro.   40

                        2

1   Nullus argento color est avaris
     abdito terris, inimice lamnae
     Crispe Sallusti, nisi temperato
        splendeat usu.

2   Vivet extento Proculeius aevo   5
     notus in fratres animi paterni;
     illum aget pinna metuente solvi
        Fama superstes;

3   latius regnes avidum domando
     spiritum quam si Libyam remotis   10
     Gadibus iungas et uterque Poenus
        serviat uni;

4   crescit indulgens sibi dirus hydrops
             nec sitim pellit, nisi causa morbi
               fugerit venis et aquosus albo   15
                  corpore languor.

5   Redditum Cyri solio Prahaten
             dissidens plebi numero beatorum
               eximit Virtus populumque falsis   20
                  dedocet uti

6   vocibus, regnum et diadema tutum
             deferens uni propriamque laurum,
               quisquis ingentis oculo inretorto
                  spectat acervos.

3

1   Aequam memento rebus in arduis
             servare mentem, non secus in bonis
               ab insolenti temperatam
                  laetitia, moriture Delli,

2   seu maestus omni tempore vixeris,   5
             seu te in remoto gramine per dies
               festos reclinatum bearis
                  interiore nota Falerni.

3   Quo pinus ingens albaque populus
             umbram hospitalem consociare amant   10
               ramis? quid obliquo laborat
                  lympha fugax trepidare rivo?

4   Huc vina et unguenta et nimium brevis
             flores amoenae ferre iube rosae,
               dum res et aetas et sororum   15
                  fila trium patiuntur atra:

5 cedes coemptis saltibus et domo
 villaque flavos quam Tiberis lavit,
  cedes et exstructis in altum
   divitiis potietur heres;   20

6 divesne prisco natus ab Inacho
 nil interest an pauper et infima
  de gente sub divo moreris,
   victima nil miserantis Orci;

7 omnes eodem cogimur, omnium   25
 versatur urna serius ocius
  sors exitura et nos in aeternum
   exilium inpositura cumbae.

4

1 Ne sit ancillae tibi amor pudori,
 Xanthia Phoceu: prius insolentem
 serva Briseis niveo colore
  movit Achillem,

2 movit Aiacem Telamone natum   5
 forma captivae dominum Tecmessae,
 arsit Atrides medio in triumpho
  virgine rapta,

3 barbarae postquam cecidere turmae
 Thessalo victore et ademptus Hector   10
 tradidit fessis leviora tolli
  Pergama Grais.

4 Nescias an te generum beati
 Phyllidis flavae decorent parentes;
 regium certe genus et penatis   15
  maeret iniquos;

5   crede non illam tibi de scelesta
       plebe delectam neque sic fidelem,
       sic lucro aversam potuisse nasci
              matre pudenda: 20

6   bracchia et voltum teretesque suras
       integer laudo — fuge suspicari
       cuius octavum trepidavit aetas
              claudere lustrum.

                         5

1   Nondum subacta ferre iugum valet
       cervice, nondum munia conparis
              aequare nec tauri ruentis
                     in venerem tolerare pondus:

2   circa virentis est animus tuae   5
       campos iuvencae, nunc fluviis gravem
              solantis aestum, nunc in udo
                     ludere cum vitulis salicto

3   praegestientis. Tolle cupidinem
       inmitis uvae: iam tibi lividos   10
              distinguet Autumnus racemos
                     purpureo varius colore;

4   iam te sequetur (currit enim ferox
       aetas et illi quos tibi dempserit
              adponet annos); iam proterva   15
                     fronte petet Lalage maritum,

5   dilecta, quantum non Pholoe fugax,
       non Chloris albo sic umero nitens
              ut pura nocturno renidet
                     luna mari Cnidiusve Gyges,   20

6 quem si puellarum insereres choro,
  mire sagacis falleret hospites
   discrimen obscurum solutis
   crinibus ambiguoque voltu.

6

1 Septimi, Gadis aditure mecum et
  Cantabrum indoctum iuga ferre nostra et
   barbaras Syrtis, ubi Maura semper
   aestuat unda:

2 Tibur Argeo positum colono   5
  sit meae sedes utinam senectae,
   sit modus lasso maris et viarum
   . militiaeque;

3 unde si Parcae prohibent iniquae,
  dulce pellitis ovibus Galaesi   10
   flumen et regnata petam Laconi
   rura Phalantho.

4 Ille terrarum mihi praeter omnis
  angulus ridet, ubi non Hymetto
   mella decedunt viridique certat 15
   baca Venafro,

5 ver ubi longum tepidasque praebet
  Iuppiter brumas et amicus Aulon
   fertili Baccho minimum Falernis
   invidet uvis;   20

6 ille te mecum locus et beatae
  postulant arces: ibi tu calentem
   debita sparges lacrima favillam
   vatis amici.

7

1
> O saepe mecum tempus in ultimum
> deducte Bruto militiae duce,
>   quis te redonavit Quiritem
>   dis patriis Italoque caelo,

2
> Pompei, meorum prime sodalium,   5
> cum quo morantem saepe diem mero
>   fregi coronatus nitentis
>   malobathro Syrio capillos?

3
> Tecum Philippos et celerem fugam
> sensi relicta non bene parmula,   10
>   cum fracta virtus et minaces
>   turpe solum tetigere mento;

4
> sed me per hostis Mercurius celer
> denso paventem sustulit aere,
>   te rursus in bellum resorbens   15
>   unda fretis tulit aestuosis.

5
> Ergo obligatam redde Iovi dapem
> longaque fessum militia latus
>   depone sub lauru mea nec
>   parce cadis tibi destinatis;   20

6
> oblivioso levia Massico
> ciboria exple, funde capacibus
>   unguenta de conchis; quis udo
>   deproperare apio coronas

7
> curatve myrto? quem Venus arbitrum   25
> dicet bibendi? non ego sanius
>   bacchabor Edonis: recepto
>   dulce mihi furere est amico.

8

1   Ulla si iuris tibi peierati
    poena, Barine, nocuisset umquam,
    dente si nigro fieres vel uno
        turpior ungui,

2   crederem: sed tu simul obligasti   5
    perfidum votis caput, enitescis
    pulchrior multo iuvenumque prodis
        publica cura.

3   Expedit matris cineres opertos
    fallere et toto taciturna noctis   10
    signa cum caelo gelidaque divos
        morte carentis;

4   ridet hoc, inquam, Venus ipsa, rident
    simplices Nymphae ferus et Cupido
    semper ardentis acuens sagittas   15
        cote cruenta;

5   adde quod pubes tibi crescit omnis,
    servitus crescit nova nec priores
    inpiae tectum dominae relinquunt
        saepe minati;   20

6   te suis matres metuunt iuvencis,
    te senes parci miseraeque nuper
    virgines nuptae, tua ne retardet
        aura maritos.

9

1   Non semper imbres nubibus hispidos
manant in agros aut mare Caspium
    vexant inaequales procellae
        usque, nec Armeniis in oris,

2   amice Valgi, stat glacies iners   5
mensis per omnis aut Aquilonibus
    querqueta Gargani laborant
        et foliis viduantur orni;

3   tu semper urges flebilibus modis
Mysten ademptum nec tibi vespero   10
    surgente decedunt amores
        nec rapidum fugiente solem.

4   At non ter aevo functus amabilem
ploravit omnis Antilochum senex
    annos nec inpubem parentes   15
        Troilon aut Phrygiae sorores

5   flevere semper. Desine mollium
tandem querelarum et potius nova
    cantemus Augusti tropaea
        Caesaris et rigidum Niphaten,   20

6   Medumque flumen gentibus additum
victis minores volvere vertices
    intraque praescriptum Gelonos
        exiguis equitare campis.

10

1   Rectius vives, Licini, neque altum
semper urgendo neque, dum procellas
cautus horrescis, nimium premendo
   litus iniquum:

2   auream quisquis mediocritatem   5
diligit, tutus caret obsoleti
sordibus tecti, caret invidenda
   sobrius aula.

3   Saepius ventis agitatur ingens
pinus et celsae graviore casu   10
decidunt turres feriuntque summos
   fulgura montis;

4   sperat infestis, metuit secundis
alteram sortem bene praeparatum
pectus: informis hiemes reducit   15
   Iuppiter, idem

5   submovet; non, si male nunc, et, olim
sic erit: quondam cithara tacentem
suscitat Musam neque semper arcum
   tendit Apollo.   20

6   Rebus angustis animosus atque
fortis adpare, sapienter idem
contrahes vento nimium secundo
   turgida vela.

11

1   Quid bellicosus Cantaber et Scythes,
    Hirpine Quincti, cogitet Hadria
        divisus obiecto, remittas
            quaerere nec trepides in usum

2   poscentis aevi pauca. Fugit retro   5
    levis iuventas et decor, arida
        pellente lascivos amores
            canitie facilemque somnum;

3   non semper idem floribus est honor
    vernis neque uno luna rubens nitet   10
        voltu: quid aeternis minorem
            consiliis animum fatigas?

4   Cur non sub alta vel platano vel hac
    pinu iacentes sic temere et rosa
        canos odorati capillos,   15
            dum licet, Assyriaque nardo

5   potamus uncti? Dissipat Euhius
    curas edacis: quis puer ocius
        restinguet ardentis Falerni
            pocula praetereunte lympha?   20

6   quis devium scortum eliciet domo
    Lyden? eburna dic age cum lyra
        maturet, in comptum Lacaenae
            more comam religata nodum.

12

1   Nolis longa ferae bella Numantiae
    nec durum Hannibalem nec Siculum mare
    Poeno purpureum sanguine mollibus
        aptari citharae modis

2   nec saevos Lapithas et nimium mero   5
    Hylaeum domitosque Herculea manu
    Telluris iuvenes, unde periculum
        fulgens contremuit domus

3   Saturni veteris, tuque pedestribus
    dices historiis proelia Caesaris,   10
    Maecenas, melius, ductaque per vias
        regum colla minacium.

4   Me dulcis dominae Musa Licymniae
    cantus, me voluit dicere lucidum
    fulgentis oculos et bene mutuis   15
        fidum pectus amoribus,

5   quam nec ferre pedem dedecuit choris
    nec certare ioco nec dare bracchia
    ludentem nitidis virginibus sacro
        Dianae celebris die.   20

6   Num tu quae tenuit dives Achaemenes
    aut pinguis Phrygiae Mygdonias opes
    permutare velis crine Licymniae
        plenas aut Arabum domos,

7   cum flagrantia detorquet ad oscula   25
    cervicem aut facili saevitia negat
    quae poscente magis gaudeat eripi —
        interdum rapere occupat?

13

1   Ille et nefasto te posuit die,
         quicumque primum, et sacrilega manu
             produxit, arbos, in nepotum
                 perniciem opprobriumque pagi;

2   illum et parentis crediderim sui   5
         fregisse cervicem et penetralia
             sparsisse nocturno cruore
                 hospitis; ille venena Colcha

3   et quidquid usquam concipitur nefas
         tractavit, agro qui statuit meo   10
             te, triste lignum, te caducum
                 in domini caput inmerentis.

4   Quid quisque vitet, numquam homini satis
         cautum est in horas: navita Bosphorum
             Thynus perhorrescit neque ultra   15
                 caeca timet aliunde fata;

5   miles sagittas et celerem fugam
         Parthi, catenas Parthus et Italum
             robur: sed inprovisa leti
                 vis rapuit rapietque gentis.   20

6   Quam paene furvae regna Proserpinae
         et iudicantem vidimus Aeacum
             sedesque discretas piorum et
                 Aeoliis fidibus querentem

7   Sappho puellis de popularibus,   25
         et te sonantem plenius aureo,
             Alcaee, plectro dura navis,
                 dura fugae mala, dura belli;

8   utrumque sacro digna silentio
       mirantur umbrae dicere, sed magis   30
          pugnas et exactos tyrannos
            densum umeris bibit aure volgus.

9   Quid mirum, ubi illis carminibus stupens
       demittit atras belua centiceps
          auris et intorti capillis   35
            Eumenidum recreantur angues?

10   quin et Prometheus et Pelopis parens
       dulci laborem decipitur sono
          nec curat Orion leones
            aut timidos agitare lyncas.   40

14

1   Eheu fugaces, Postume, Postume,
       labuntur anni nec pietas moram
          rugis et instanti senectae
            adferet indomitaeque morti —

2   non si trecenis quotquot eunt dies,   5
       amice, places inlacrimabilem
          Plutona tauris, qui ter amplum
            Geryonen Tityonque tristi

3   conpescit unda, scilicet omnibus,
       quicumque terrae munere vescimur,   10
          enaviganda, sive reges
            sive inopes erimus coloni.

4   Frustra cruento Marte carebimus
     fractisque rauci fluctibus Hadriae,
          frustra per autumnos nocentem   15
               corporibus metuemus Austrum;

5   visendus ater flumine languido
     Cocytos errans et Danai genus
          infame damnatusque longi
               Sisyphus Aeolides laboris;   20

6   linquenda tellus et domus et placens
     uxor, neque harum quas colis arborum
          te praeter invisas cupressos
               ulla brevem dominum sequetur;

7   absumet heres Caecuba dignior   25
     servata centum clavibus et mero
          tinguet pavimentum superbo,
               pontificum potiore cenis.

                         15

1   Iam pauca aratro iugera regiae
     moles relinquent, undique latius
          extenta visentur Lucrino
               stagna lacu platanusque caelebs

2   evincet ulmos; tum violaria et   5
     myrtus et omnis copia narium
          spargent olivetis odorem
               fertilibus domino priori;

3   tum spissa ramis laurea fervidos
     excludet ictus. Non ita Romuli   10
          praescriptum et intonsi Catonis
               auspiciis veterumque norma:

4   privatus illis census erat brevis,
           commune magnum; nulla decempedis
               metata privatis opacam   15
                  porticus excipiebat arcton

5   nec fortuitum spernere caespitem
           leges sinebant, oppida publico
               sumptu iubentes et deorum
                  templa novo decorare saxo.   20

16

1   Otium divos rogat in patenti
           prensus Aegaeo, simul atra nubes
           condidit lunam neque certa fulgent
               sidera nautis,

2   otium bello furiosa Thrace,   5
           otium Medi pharetra decori,
           Grosphe, non gemmis neque purpura ve-
               nale nec auro.

3   Non enim gazae neque consularis
           submovet lictor miseros tumultus   10
           mentis et curas laqueata circum
               tecta volantis.

4   Vivitur parvo bene, cui paternum
           splendet in mensa tenui salinum
           nec levis somnos timor aut cupido   15
               sordidus aufert.

5   Quid brevi fortes iaculamur aevo
           multa? quid terras alio calentis
           sole mutamus? patriae quis exsul
               se quoque fugit?   20

6   Scandit aeratas vitiosa navis
           Cura nec turmas equitum relinquit,
           ocior cervis et agente nimbos
                ocior Euro.

7   Laetus in praesens animus quod ultra est   25
           oderit curare et amara lento
           temperet risu: nihil est ab omni
                parte beatum.

8   Abstulit clarum cita mors Achillem,
           longa Tithonum minuit senectus: 30
           et mihi forsan, tibi quod negarit,
                porriget hora.

9   Te greges centum Siculaeque circum-
           mugiunt vaccae, tibi tollit hinnitum
           apta quadrigis equa, te bis Afro   35
                murice tinctae

10   vestiunt lanae: mihi parva rura et
           spiritum Graiae tenuem Camenae
           Parca non mendax dedit et malignum
                spernere volgus.   40

17

1   Cur me querelis exanimas tuis?
           nec dis amicum est nec mihi te prius
                obire, Maecenas, mearum
                     grande decus columenque rerum.

2   A, te meae si partem animae rapit   5
           maturior vis, quid moror altera,
                nec carus aeque nec superstes
                     integer? ille dies utramque

3   ducet ruinam. Non ego perfidum
       dixi sacramentum: ibimus, ibimus,   10
           utcumque praecedes, supremum
               carpere iter comites parati;

4   me nec Chimaerae spiritus igneae
       nec si resurgat centimanus Gyges
           divellet umquam: sic potenti   15
               Iustitiae placitumque Parcis.

5   Seu Libra seu me Scorpios adspicit
       formidolosus pars violentior
           natalis horae seu tyrannus
               Hesperiae Capricornus undae,   20

6   utrumque nostrum incredibili modo
       consentit astrum: te Iovis inpio
           tutela Saturno refulgens
               eripuit volucrisque Fati

7   tardavit alas, cum populus frequens   25
       laetum theatris ter crepuit sonum:
           me truncus inlapsus cerebro
               sustulerat, nisi Faunus ictum

8   dextra levasset, Mercurialium
       custos virorum. Reddere victimas   30
           aedemque votivam memento:
               nos humilem feriemus agnam.

18

Non ebur neque aureum
    mea renidet in domo lacunar,

non trabes Hymettiae
    premunt columnas ultima recisas

Africa neque Attali   5
    ignotus heres regiam occupavi

nec Laconicas mihi
    trahunt honestae purpuras clientae,

at fides et ingeni
    benigna vena est pauperemque dives   10

me petit: nihil supra
    deos lacesso nec potentem amicum

largiora flagito,
    satis beatus unicis Sabinis.

Truditur dies die   15
    novaeque pergunt interire lunae:

tu secanda marmora
    locas sub ipsum funus et sepulcri

inmemor struis domos
    marisque Bais obstrepentis urges   20

submovere litora,
    parum locuples continente ripa;

quid quod usque proximos
    revellis agri terminos et ultra

limites clientium   25
    salis avarus? pellitur paternos

in sinu ferens deos
    et uxor et vir sordidosque natos.

Nulla certior tamen
    rapacis Orci fine destinata   30

aula divitem manet
    erum: quid ultra tendis? aequa tellus

pauperi recluditur
    regumque pueris, nec satelles Orci

callidum Promethea   35
    revexit auro captus; hic superbum

Tantalum atque Tantali
    genus coercet, hic levare functum

pauperem laboribus
    vocatus atque non vocatus audit.   40

19

1   Bacchum in remotis carmina rupibus
    vidi docentem, credite posteri,
        Nymphasque discentis et auris
            capripedum Satyrorum acutas.

2   Euhoe, recenti mens trepidat metu   5
    plenoque Bacchi pectore turbidum
        laetatur, euhoe, parce Liber,
            parce gravi metuende thyrso.

3   Fas pervicacis est mihi Thyiadas
    vinique fontem lactis et uberes   10
        cantare rivos atque truncis
            lapsa cavis iterare mella,

4   fas et beatae coniugis additum
    stellis honorem tectaque Penthei
        disiecta non leni ruina   15
            Thracis et exitium Lycurgi.

5   Tu flectis amnis, tu mare barbarum,
           tu separatis uvidus in iugis
               nodo coerces viperino
                   Bistonidum sine fraude crinis;   20

6   tu, cum parentis regna per arduum
           cohors gigantum scanderet inpia,
               Rhoetum retorsisti leonis
                   unguibus horribilique mala;

7   quamquam choreis aptior et iocis   25
           ludoque dictus, non sat idoneus
               pugnae ferebaris; sed idem
                   pacis eras mediusque belli;

8   te vidit insons Cerberus aureo
           cornu decorum leniter atterens   30
               caudam et recedentis trilingui
                   ore pedes tetigitque crura.

20

1   Non usitata nec tenui ferar
           pinna biformis per liquidum aethera
               vates neque in terris morabor
                   longius invidiaque maior

2   urbis relinquam. Non ego, pauperum   5
           sanguis parentum, non ego, quem vocas,
               dilecte Maecenas, obibo
                   nec Stygia cohibebor unda:

3   iam iam residunt cruribus asperae
           pelles et album mutor in alitem   10
               superne nascunturque leves
                   per digitos umerosque plumae.

4   Iam Daedaleo notior Icaro
     visam gementis litora Bosphori
          Syrtisque Gaetulas canorus   15
               ales Hyperboreosque campos;

5   me Colchus et qui dissimulat metum
     Marsae cohortis Dacus et ultimi
          noscent Geloni, me peritus
               discet Hiber Rhodanique potor.   20

6   Absint inani funere neniae
     luctusque turpes et querimoniae;
          conpesce clamorem ac sepulcri
               mitte supervacuos honores.

BOOK 3

1

1   Odi profanum volgus et arceo.
     Favete linguis: carmina non prius
          audita Musarum sacerdos
               virginibus puerisque canto.

2   Regum timendorum in proprios greges,   5
     reges in ipsos imperium est Iovis,
          clari Giganteo triumpho,
               cuncta supercilio moventis.

3   Est ut viro vir latius ordinet
     arbusta sulcis, hic generosior   10
          descendat in Campum petitor,
               moribus hic meliorque fama

4   contendat, illi turba clientium
             sit maior: aequa lege Necessitas
                  sortitur insignis et imos,   15
                       omne capax movet urna nomen.

5   Destrictus ensis cui super inpia
             cervice pendet, non Siculae dapes
                  dulcem elaborabunt saporem,
                       non avium citharaeque cantus   20

6   somnum reducent. Somnus agrestium
             lenis virorum non humilis domos
                  fastidit umbrosamque ripam,
                       non Zephyris agitata Tempe.

7   Desiderantem quod satis est neque   25
             tumultuosum sollicitat mare
                  nec saevus Arcturi cadentis
                       impetus aut orientis Haedi,

8   non verberatae grandine vineae
             fundusque mendax, arbore nunc aquas   30
                  culpante, nunc torrentia agros
                       sidera, nunc hiemes iniquas:

9   contracta pisces aequora sentiunt
             iactis in altum molibus; huc frequens
                  caementa demittit redemptor   35
                       cum famulis dominusque terrae

10   fastidiosus; sed Timor et Minae
             scandunt eodem quo dominus, neque
                  decedit aerata triremi et
                       post equitem sedet atra Cura.   40

11   Quodsi dolentem nec Phrygius lapis
             nec purpurarum sidere clarior
                  delenit usus nec Falerna
                       vitis Achaemeniumque costum,

12   cur invidendis postibus et novo   45
       sublime ritu moliar atrium?
            cur valle permutem Sabina
                divitias operosiores?

                        2

1   Angustam amice pauperiem pati
       robustus acri militia puer
            condiscat et Parthos ferocis
                vexet eques metuendus hasta,

2   vitamque sub divo et trepidis agat   5
       in rebus; illum ex moenibus hosticis
            matrona bellantis tyranni
                prospiciens et adulta virgo

3   suspiret, eheu, ne rudis agminum
       sponsus lacessat regius asperum   10
            tactu leonem, quem cruenta
                per medias rapit ira caedes.

4   Dulce et decorum est pro patria mori:
       mors et fugacem persequitur virum
            nec parcit inbellis iuventae   15
                poplitibus timidoque tergo;

5   virtus repulsae nescia sordidae
       intaminatis fulget honoribus
            nec sumit aut ponit securis
                arbitrio popularis aurae;   20

6   virtus recludens inmeritis mori
       caelum negata temptat iter via
            coetusque volgaris et udam
                spernit humum fugiente pinna.

7   Est et fideli tuta silentio   25
            merces: vetabo, qui Cereris sacrum
               volgarit arcanae, sub isdem
                   sit trabibus fragilemque mecum

8   solvat phaselon: saepe Diespiter
            neglectus incesto addidit integrum;   30
               raro antecedentem scelestum
                   deseruit pede Poena claudo.

3

1   Iustum et tenacem propositi virum
            non civium ardor prava iubentium,
               non voltus instantis tyranni
                   mente quatit solida neque Auster,

2   dux inquieti turbidus Hadriae,   5
            nec fulminantis magna manus Iovis:
               si fractus inlabatur orbis,
                   inpavidum ferient ruinae;

3   hac arte Pollux et vagus Hercules
            enisus arcis attigit igneas,   10
               quos inter Augustus recumbens
                   purpureo bibet ore nectar;

4   hac te merentem, Bacche pater, tuae
            vexere tigres indocili iugum
               collo trahentes, hac Quirinus   15
                   Martis equis Acheronta fugit,

5   gratum elocuta consiliantibus
            Iunone divis: 'Ilion, Ilion
               fatalis incestusque iudex
                   et mulier peregrina vertit   20

6   in pulverem, ex quo destituit deos
mercede pacta Laomedon, mihi
    castaeque damnatum Minervae
        cum populo et duce fraudulento;

7   iam nec Lacaenae splendet adulterae   25
famosus hospes nec Priami domus
    periura pugnaces Achivos
        Hectoreis opibus refringit,

8   nostrisque ductum seditionibus
bellum resedit: protinus et gravis   30
    iras et invisum nepotem,
        Troica quem peperit sacerdos,

9   Marti redonabo; illum ego lucidas
inire sedes, discere nectaris
    sucos et adscribi quietis   35
        ordinibus patiar deorum.

10   Dum longus inter saeviat Ilion
Romamque pontus, qualibet exsules
    in parte regnanto beati;
        dum Priami Paridisque busto   40

11   insultet armentum et catulos ferae
celent inultae, stet Capitolium
    fulgens triumphatisque possit
        Roma ferox dare iura Medis;

12   horrenda late nomen in ultimas   45
extendat oras, qua medius liquor
    secernit Europen ab Afro,
        qua tumidus rigat arva Nilus;

13   aurum inrepertum et sic melius situm,
            cum terra celat, spernere fortior   50
               quam cogere humanos in usùs
                   omne sacrum rapiente dextra,

14   quicumque mundo terminus obstitit,
            hunc tanget armis, visere gestiens,
               qua parte debacchentur ignes,   55
                   qua nebulae pluviique rores.

15   Sed bellicosis fata Quiritibus
            hac lege dico, ne nimium pii
               rebusque fidentes avitae
                   tecta velint reparare Troiae: 60

16   Troiae renascens alite lugubri
            fortuna tristi clade iterabitur
               ducente victrices catervas
                   coniuge me Iovis et sorore;

17   ter si resurgat murus aeneus   65
            auctore Phoebo, ter pereat meis
               excisus Argivis, ter uxor
                   capta virum puerosque ploret.'

18   Non hoc iocosae conveniet lyrae:
            quo, Musa, tendis? desine pervicax   70
               referre sermones deorum et
                   magna modis tenuare parvis.

4

1   Descende caelo et dic age tibia
            regina longum Calliope melos,
               seu voce nunc mavis acuta,
                   seu fidibus citharave Phoebi.

2   Auditis? an me ludit amabilis   5
       insania? audire et videor pios
          errare per lucos, amoenae
             quos et aquae subeunt et aurae.

3   Me fabulosae Volture in Apulo
       nutricis extra limina Pulliae   10
          ludo fatigatumque somno
             fronde nova puerum palumbes

4   texere, mirum quod foret omnibus,
       quicumque celsae nidum Aceruntiae
          saltusque Bantinos et arvum   15
             pingue tenent humilis Forenti,

5   ut tuto ab atris corpore viperis
       dormirem et ursis, ut premerer sacra
          lauroque conlataque myrto,
             non sine dis animosus infans;   20

6   vester, Camenae, vester in arduos
       tollor Sabinos, seu mihi frigidum
          Praeneste seu Tibur supinum
             seu liquidae placuere Baiae;

7   vestris amicum fontibus et choris   25
       non me Philippis versa acies retro,
          devota non extinxit arbor
             nec Sicula Palinurus unda;

8   utcumque mecum vos eritis, libens
       insanientem navita Bosphorum   30
          temptabo et urentis harenas
             litoris Assyrii viator;

9   visam Britannos hospitibus feros
       et laetum equino sanguine Concanum,
          visam pharetratos Gelonos   35
             et Scythicum inviolatus amnem.

10   Vos Caesarem altum, militia simul
      fessas cohortes abdidit oppidis,
          finire quaerentem labores
              Pierio recreatis antro,   40

11   vos lene consilium et datis et dato
      gaudetis, almae. Scimus, ut inpios
          Titanas immanemque turbam
              fulmine sustulerit çaduco

12   qui terram inertem, qui mare temperat   45
      ventosum et urbis regnaque tristia,
          divosque mortalisque turmas
              imperio regit unus aequo.

13   Magnum illa terrorem intulerat Iovi
      fidens iuventus horrida bracchiis   50
          fratresque tendentes opaco
              Pelion inposuisse Olympo;

14   sed quid Typhoeus et validus Mimas
      aut quid minaci Porphyrion statu,
          quid Rhoetus evolsisque truncis   55
              Enceladus iaculator audax

15   contra sonantem Palladis aegida
      possent ruentes? — hinc avidus stetit
          Volcanus, hinc matrona Iuno et
              numquam umeris positurus arcum   60

16   qui rore puro Castaliae lavit
      crinis solutos, qui Lyciae tenet
          dumeta natalemque silvam,
              Delius et Patareus Apollo.

17   Vis consili expers mole ruit sua,   65
      vim temperatam di quoque provehunt
          in maius, idem odere viris
              omne nefas animo moventis:

18   testis mearum centimanus Gyges
     sententiarum, notus et integrae   70
       temptator Orion Dianae
         virginea domitus sagitta;

19   iniecta monstris Terra dolet suis
     maeretque partus fulmine luridum
       missos ad Orcum; nec peredit   75
         inpositam celer ignis Aetnen,

20   incontinentis nec Tityi iecur
     reliquit ales, nequitiae additus
       custos; amatorem trecentae
         Pirithoum cohibent catenae.   80

5

1   Caelo tonantem credidimus Iovem
     regnare: praesens divus habebitur
       Augustus adiectis Britannis
         imperio gravibusque Persis.

2   Milesne Crassi coniuge barbara   5
     turpis maritus vixit et hostium
       — pro curia inversique mores! —
         consenuit socerorum in armis

3   sub rege Medo Marsus et Apulus,
     anciliorum et nominis et togae   10
       oblitus aeternaeque Vestae,
         incolumi Iove et urbe Roma?

4   Hoc caverat mens provida Reguli
     dissentientis condicionibus
       foedis et exemplo trahenti   15
         perniciem veniens in aevum,

5　　　si non periret inmiserabilis
　　　　captiva pubes: 'Signa ego Punicis
　　　　　　adfixa delubris et arma
　　　　　　　　militibus sine caede', dixit,　　　　　　20

6　　　'derepta vidi, vidi ego civium
　　　　retorta tergo bracchia libero
　　　　　　portasque non clausas et arva
　　　　　　　　Marte coli populata nostro;

7　　　auro repensus scilicet acrior　　　　　　25
　　　　miles redibit; flagitio additis
　　　　　　damnum: neque amissos colores
　　　　　　　　lana refert medicata fuco

8　　　nec vera virtus, cum semel excidit,
　　　　curat reponi deterioribus;　　　　　　30
　　　　　　si pugnat extricata densis
　　　　　　　　cerva plagis, erit ille fortis

9　　　qui perfidis se credidit hostibus,
　　　　et Marte Poenos proteret altero
　　　　　　qui lora restrictis lacertis　　　　　　35
　　　　　　　　sensit iners timuitque mortem;

10　　hic unde vitam sumeret inscius,
　　　　pacem duello miscuit: o pudor!
　　　　　　o magna Carthago probrosis
　　　　　　　　altior Italiae ruinis!'　　　　　　40

11　　Fertur pudicae coniugis osculum
　　　　parvosque natos ut capitis minor
　　　　　　ab se removisse et virilem
　　　　　　　　torvus humi posuisse voltum,

12　　donec labantis consilio patres　　　　　　45
　　　　firmaret auctor numquam alias dato
　　　　　　interque maerentis amicos
　　　　　　　　egregius properaret exul;

13   atqui sciebat, quae sibi barbarus
          tortor pararet; non aliter tamen   50
            dimovit obstantis propinquos
               et populum reditus morantem,

14   quam si clientum longa negotia
          diiudicata lite relinqueret
            tendens Venafranos in agros   55
               aut Lacedaemonium Tarentum.

6

1   Delicta maiorum inmeritus lues,
          Romane, donec templa refeceris
            aedisque labentis deorum et
               foeda nigro simulacra fumo;

2   dis te minorem quod geris, imperas;   5
          hinc omne principium, huc refer exitum;
            di multa neglecti dederunt
               Hesperiae mala luctuosae.

3   Iam bis Monaeses et Pacori manus
          inauspicatos contudit impetus   10
            nostros et adiecisse praedam
               torquibus exiguis renidet;

4   paene occupatam seditionibus
          delevit urbem Dacus et Aethiops,
            hic classe formidatus, ille   15
               missilibus melior sagittis.

5   Fecunda culpae saecula nuptias
          primum inquinavere et genus et domos:
            hoc fonte derivata clades
               in patriam populumque fluxit;   20

6   motus doceri gaudet Ionicos
       matura virgo et fingitur artibus
          iam nunc et incestos amores
             de tenero meditatur ungui;

7   mox iuniores quaerit adulteros   25
       inter mariti vina neque eligit
          cui donet inpermissa raptim
             gaudia luminibus remotis,

8   sed iussa coram non sine conscio
       surgit marito, seu vocat institor   30
          seu navis Hispanae magister,
             dedecorum pretiosus emptor.

9   Non his iuventus orta parentibus
       infecit aequor sanguine Punico
          Pyrrhumque et ingentem cecidit   35
             Antiochum Hannibalemque dirum,

10   sed rusticorum mascula militum
       proles, Sabellis docta ligonibus
          versare glaebas et severae
             matris ad arbitrium recisos   40

11   portare fustis, Sol ubi montium
       mutaret umbras et iuga demeret
          bubus fatigatis, amicum
             tempus agens abeunte curru:

12   damnosa quid non inminuit dies?   45
       aetas parentum peior avis tulit
          nos nequiores, mox daturos
             progeniem vitiosiorem.

7

1   Quid fles, Asterie, quem tibi candidi
     primo restituent vere Favonii
          Thyna merce beatum,
               constantis iuvenem fide

2   Gygen? Ille Notis actus ad Oricum   5
     post insana Caprae sidera frigidas
          noctis non sine multis
               insomnis lacrimis agit;

3   atqui sollicitae nuntius hospitae,
     suspirare Chloen et miseram tuis   10
          dicens ignibus uri,
               temptat mille vafer modis;

4   ut Proetum mulier perfida credulum
     falsis inpulerit criminibus nimis
          casto Bellerophontae   15
               maturare necem refert,

5   narrat paene datum Pelea Tartaro,
     Magnessam Hippolyten dum fugit abstinens,
          et peccare docentis
               fallax historias movet   20

6   frustra: nam scopulis surdior Icari
     voces audit adhuc integer. At tibi
          ne vicinus Enipeus
               plus iusto placeat cave;

7   quamvis non alius flectere equum sciens   25
     aeque conspicitur gramine Martio
          nec quisquam citus aeque
               Tusco denatat alveo,

8   prima nocte domum claude neque in vias
        sub cantu querulae despice tibiae   30
            et te saepe vocanti
                duram difficilis mane.

8

1   Martiis caelebs quid agam kalendis,
        quid velint flores et acerra turis
        plena miraris positusque carbo in
            caespite vivo,

2   docte sermones utriusque linguae?   5
        Voveram dulcis epulas et album
        Libero caprum prope funeratus
            arboris ictu;

3   hic dies anno redeunte festus
        corticem adstrictum pice dimovebit   10
        amphorae fumum bibere institutae
            consule Tullo.

4   Sume, Maecenas, cyathos amici
        sospitis centum et vigiles lucernas
        perfer in lucem; procul omnis esto   15
            clamor et ira;

5   mitte civilis super urbe curas —
        occidit Daci Cotisonis agmen,
        Medus infestus sibi luctuosis
            dissidet armis,   20

6   servit Hispanae vetus hostis orae
        Cantaber sera domitus catena,
        iam Scythae laxo meditantur arcu
            cedere campis;

7   neglegens, ne qua populus laboret,   25
           parce privatus nimium cavere et
           dona praesentis cape laetus horae,
               linque severa.

9

1   Donec gratus eram tibi
             nec quisquam potior bracchia candidae
          cervici iuvenis dabat,
              Persarum vigui rege beatior.

2   'Donec non alia magis   5
             arsisti neque erat Lydia post Chloen,
          multi Lydia nominis
              Romana vigui clarior Ilia.'

3   Me nunc Thressa Chloe regit,
             dulcis docta modos et citharae sciens,   10
          pro qua non metuam mori,
              si parcent animae fata superstiti.

4   'Me torret face mutua
             Thurini Calais filius Ornyti,
          pro quo bis patiar mori,   15
              si parcent puero fata superstiti.'

5   Quid si prisca redit Venus
             diductosque iugo cogit aeneo,
          si flava excutitur Chloe
              reiectaeque patet ianua Lydiae?   20

6   'Quamquam sidere pulcrior
             ille est, tu levior cortice et inprobo
          iracundior Hadria,
              tecum vivere amem, tecum obeam lubens.'

10

1   Extremum Tanain si biberes, Lyce,
    saevo nupta viro, me tamen asperas
    porrectum ante foris obicere incolis
        plorares Aquilonibus:

2   audis, quo strepitu ianua, quo nemus   5
    inter pulcra satum tecta remugiat
    ventis et positas ut glaciet nives
        puro numine Iuppiter?

3   Ingratam Veneri pone superbiam,
    ne currente retro funis eat rota: 10
    non te Penelopen difficilem procis
        Tyrrhenus genuit parens.

4   O quamvis neque te munera nec preces
    nec tinctus viola pallor amantium
    nec vir Pieria paelice saucius   15
        curvat, supplicibus tuis

5   parcas, nec rigida mollior aesculo
    nec Mauris animum mitior anguibus:
    non hoc semper erit liminis aut aquae
        caelestis patiens latus.   20

11

1   Mercuri — nam te docilis magistro
    movit Amphion lapides canendo —
    tuque testudo resonare septem
        callida nervis,

2 nec loquax olim neque grata, nunc et   5
  divitum mensis et amica templis:
  dic modos, Lyde quibus obstinatas
   adplicet auris,

3 quae velut latis equa trima campis
  ludit exsultim metuitque tangi   10
  nuptiarum expers et adhuc protervo
   cruda marito:

4 tu potes tigris comitesque silvas
  ducere et rivos celeres morari;
  cessit immanis tibi blandienti   15
   ianitor aulae

5 Cerberus, quamvis furiale centum
  muniant angues caput eius atque
  spiritus taeter saniesque manet
   ore trilingui;   20

6 quin et Ixion Tityosque voltu
  risit invito; stetit urna paulum
  sicca, dum grato Danai puellas
   carmine mulces.

7 Audiat Lyde scelus atque notas   25
  virginum poenas et inane lymphae
  dolium fundo pereuntis imo
   seraque fata,

8 quae manent culpas etiam sub Orco:
  inpiae — nam quid potuere maius? —   30
  inpiae sponsos potuere duro
   perdere ferro;

9 una de multis face nuptiali
  digna periurum fuit in parentem
  splendide mendax et in omne virgo   35
   nobilis aevom,

10   'Surge' quae dixit iuveni marito,
           'surge, ne longus tibi somnus unde
           non times detur; socerum et scelestas
               falle sorores,   40

11   quae, velut nactae vitulos leaenae,
           singulos eheu lacerant: ego illis
           mollior nec te feriam neque intra
               claustra tenebo.

12   Me pater saevis oneret catenis,   45
           quod viro clemens misero peperci,
           me vel extremos Numidarum in agros
               classe releget:

13   i pedes quo te rapiunt et aurae,
           dum favet nox et Venus, i secundo   50
           omine et nostri memorem sepulcro
               scalpe querelam.'

                              12

1   Miserarum est neque amori
        dare ludum neque dulci
        mala vino lavere, aut exanimari metuentis
        patruae verbera linguae.

2   Tibi qualum Cythereae   5
        puer ales, tibi telas
        operosaeque Minervae studium aufert, Neobule,
        Liparaei nitor Hebri,

3   simul unctos Tiberinis
        umeros lavit in undis,   10
        eques ipso melior Bellerophonte, neque pugno
        neque segni pede victus,

4   catus idem per apertum
            fugientis agitato
            grege cervos iaculari et celer arto latitantem   15
            fruticeto excipere aprum.

13

1   O Fons Bandusiae, splendidior vitro,
            dulci digne mero non sine floribus,
                cras donaberis haedo,
                    cui frons turgida cornibus

2   primis et venerem et proelia destinat   5
            frustra, nam gelidos inficiet tibi
                rubro sanguine rivos
                    lascivi suboles gregis:

3   te flagrantis atrox hora Caniculae
            nescit tangere, tu frigus amabile   10
                fessis vomere tauris
                    praebes et pecori vago.

4   Fies nobilium tu quoque fontium
            me dicente cavis inpositam ilicem
                saxis, unde loquaces   15
                    lymphae desiliunt tuae.

14

1   Herculis ritu modo dictus, o plebs,
            morte venalem petiisse laurum
            Caesar Hispana repetit Penatis
                victor ab ora.

2   Unico gaudens mulier marito   5
           prodeat iustis operata sacris
           et soror clari ducis et decorae
              supplice vitta

3   virginum matres iuvenumque nuper
           sospitum; vos, o pueri et puellae   10
           iam virum exspectate, male ominatis
              parcite verbis.

4   Hic dies vere mihi festus atras
           exiget curas: ego nec tumultum
           nec mori per vim metuam tenente   15
              Caesare terras.

5   I pete unguentum, puer, et coronas
           et cadum Marsi memorem duelli,
           Spartacum siqua potuit vagantem
              fallere testa,
                               20

6   dic et argutae properet Neaerae
           murreum nodo cohibere crinem;
           si per invisum mora ianitorem
              fiet, abito:

7   lenit albescens animos capillus   25
           litium et rixae cupidos protervae;
           non ego hoc ferrem calidus iuventa
              consule Planco.

15

1   Uxor pauperis Ibyci,
             tandem nequitiae fige modum tuae
           famosisque laboribus;
             maturo propior desine funeri

2   inter ludere virgines   5
           et stellis nebulam spargere candidis.
       Non, siquid Pholoen satis,
           et te, Chlori, decet. Filia rectius

3   expugnat iuvenum domos,
           pulso Thyias uti concita tympano: 10
       illam cogit amor Nothi
           lascivae similem ludere capreae;

4   te lanae prope nobilem
           tonsae Luceriam, non citharae decent
       nec flos purpureus rosae   15
           nec poti vetulam faece tenus cadi.

16

1   Inclusam Danaen turris aenea
       robustaeque fores et vigilum canum
       tristes excubiae munierant satis
           nocturnis ab adulteris,

2   si non Acrisium virginis abditae   5
       custodem pavidum Iuppiter et Venus
       risissent: fore enim tutum iter et patens
           converso in pretium deo.

3   Aurum per medios ire satellites
       et perrumpere amat saxa potentius   10
       ictu fulmineo; concidit auguris
           Argivi domus ob lucrum

4   demersa exitio; diffidit urbium
       portas vir Macedo et subruit aemulos
       reges muneribus, munera navium   15
           saevos inlaqueant duces;

5   crescentem sequitur cura pecuniam
maiorumque fames; iure perhorrui
late conspicuum tollere verticem;
    Maecenas, equitum decus,   20

6   quanto quisque sibi plura negaverit,
ab dis plura feret; nil cupientium
nudus castra peto et transfuga divitum
    partis linquere gestio,

7   contemptae dominus splendidior rei,   25
quam si quidquid arat inpiger Apulus
occultare meis dicerer horreis,
    magnas inter opes inops.

8   Purae rivos aquae silvaque iugerum
paucorum et segetis certa fides meae   30
fulgentem imperio fertilis Africae
    fallit sorte beatior;

9   quamquam nec Calabrae mella ferunt apes
nec Laestrygonia Bacchus in amphora
languescit mihi nec pinguia Gallicis   35
    crescunt vellera pascuis,

10   inportuna tamen pauperies abest
nec, si plura velim, tu dare deneges;
contracto melius parva cupidine
    vectigalia porrigam,   40

11   quam si Mygdoniis regnum Alyattei
campis continuem; multa petentibus
desunt multa; bene est cui deus obtulit
    parca quod satis est manu.

17

1   Aeli vetusto nobilis ab Lamo —
       quando et priores hinc Lamias ferunt
         denominatos et nepotum
           per memores genus omne fastus

2   auctore ab illo ducit originem,   5
       qui Formiarum moenia dicitur
         princeps et innantem Maricae
           litoribus tenuisse Lirim

3   late tyrannus — cras foliis nemus
       multis et alga litus inutili   10
         demissa tempestas ab Euro
           sternet, aquae nisi fallit augur

4   annosa cornix; dum potes, aridum
       conpone lignum; cras genium mero
         curabis et porco bimenstri   15
           cum famulis operum solutis.

18

1   Faune, Nympharum fugientum amator,
       per meos finis et aprica rura
       lenis incedas abeasque parvis
         aequus alumnis,

2   si tener pleno cadit haedus anno   5
       larga nec desunt Veneris sodali
       vina creterrae, vetus ara multo
         fumat odore.

3   Ludit herboso pecus omne campo,
       cum tibi nonae redeunt Decembres;   10
       festus in pratis vacat otioso
          cum bove pagus;

4   inter audacis lupus errat agnos,
       spargit agrestis tibi silva frondes,
       gaudet invisam pepulisse fossor   15
          ter pede terram.

19

1   Quantum distet ab Inacho
          Codrus pro patria non timidus mori,
       narras et genus Aeaci
          et pugnata sacro bella sub Ilio:

2   quo Chium pretio cadum   5
          mercemur, quis aquam temperet ignibus,
       quo praebente domum et quota
          Paelignis caream frigoribus, taces.

3   Da lunae propere novae,
          da noctis mediae, da, puer, auguris   10
       Murenae: tribus aut novem
          miscentur cyathis pocula commodis:

4   qui Musas amat imparis,
          ternos ter cyathos attonitus petet
       vates; tris prohibet supra   15
          rixarum metuens tangere Gratia

5   nudis iuncta sororibus.
          Insanire iuvat: cur Berecyntiae
       cessant flamina tibiae?
          cur pendet tacita fistula cum lyra?   20

6   Parcentis ego dexteras
           odi: sparge rosas; audiat invidus
       dementem strepitum Lycus
           et vicina seni non habilis Lyco;

7   spissa te nitidum coma,   25
           puro te similem, Telephe, Vespero
       tempestiva petit Rhode;
           me lentus Glycerae torret amor meae.

20

1   Non vides, quanto moveas periclo,
       Pyrrhe, Gaetulae catulos leaenae?
       Dura post paulo fugies inaudax
           proelia raptor,

2   cum per obstantis iuvenum catervas   5
       ibit insignem repetens Nearchum —
       grande certamen, tibi praeda cedat,
           maior an illa.

3   Interim dum tu celeris sagittas
       promis, haec dentis acuit timendos,   10
       arbiter pugnae posuisse nudo
           sub pede palmam

4   fertur et leni recreare vento
       sparsum odoratis umerum capillis,
       qualis aut Nireus fuit aut aquosa   15
           raptus ab Ida.

21

1   O nata mecum consule Manlio —
seu tu querelas sive geris iocos
    seu rixam et insanos amores
        seu facilem, pia testa, somnum —

2   quocumque lectum nomine Massicum   5
servas, moveri digna bono die
    descende Corvino iubente
        promere languidiora vina.

3   Non ille, quamquam Socraticis madet
sermonibus, te negleget horridus;   10
    narratur et prisci Catonis
        saepe mero caluisse virtus:

4   tu lene tormentum ingenio admoves
plerumque duro, tu sapientium
    curas et arcanum iocoso   15
        consilium retegis Lyaeo,

5   tu spem reducis mentibus anxiis
virisque et addis cornua pauperi
    post te neque iratos trementi
        regum apices neque militum arma;   20

6   te Liber et si laeta aderit Venus
segnesque nodum solvere Gratiae
    vivaeque producent lucernae,
        dum rediens fugat astra Phoebus.

22

1   Montium custos nemorumque virgo,
     quae laborantis utero puellas
     ter vocata audis adimisque leto,
          diva triformis,

2   imminens villae tua pinus esto,   5
     quam per exactos ego laetus annos
     verris obliquom meditantis ictum
          sanguine donem.

23

1   Caelo supinas si tuleris manus
     nascente Luna, rustica Phidyle,
          si ture placaris et horna
               fruge Lares avidaque porca,

2   nec pestilentem sentiet Africum   5
     fecunda vitis nec sterilem seges
          robiginem aut dulces alumni
               pomifero grave tempus anno.

3   Nam quae nivali pascitur Algido
     devota quercus inter et ilices   10
          aut crescit Albanis in herbis
               victima, pontificum securis

4   cervice tinguet; te nihil attinet
     temptare multa caede bidentium
          parvos coronantem marino   15
               rore deos fragilique myrto;

5   inmunis aram si tetigit manus,
            non sumptuosa blandior hostia
               mollivit aversos Penatis
                   farre pio et saliente mica.   20

24

1   Intactis opulentior
            thesauris Arabum et divitis Indiae
           caementis licet occupes
               Tyrrhenum omne tuis et mare publicum,

2   si figit adamantinos   5
            summis verticibus dira Necessitas
           clavos, non animum metu,
               non mortis laqueis expedies caput.

3   Campestres melius Scythae,
            quorum plaustra vagas rite trahunt domos,   10
           vivunt et rigidi Getae,
               inmetata quibus iugera liberas

4   fruges et Cererem ferunt
            nec cultura placet longior annua
           defunctumque laboribus   15
               aequali recreat sorte vicarius;

5   illic matre carentibus
            privignis mulier temperat innocens
           nec dotata regit virum
               coniunx nec nitido fidit adultero,   20

6   dos est magna parentium
            virtus et metuens alterius viri
           certo foedere castitas,
               et peccare nefas, aut pretium est mori.

7   O quisquis volet inpias   25
           caedis et rabiem tollere civicam,
       si quaeret pater urbium
           subscribi statuis, indomitam audeat

8   refrenare licentiam,
           clarus postgenitis, quatenus, heu nefas,   30
       virtutem incolumem odimus,
           sublatam ex oculis quaerimus invidi;

9   quid tristes querimoniae,
           si non supplicio culpa reciditur,
       quid leges sine moribus   35
           vanae proficiunt, si neque fervidis

10   pars inclusa caloribus
           mundi nec Boreae finitimum latus
       durataeque solo nives
           mercatorem abigunt, horrida callidi   40

11   vincunt aequora navitae,
           magnum pauperies opprobrium iubet
       quidvis et facere et pati
           virtutisque viam deserit arduae?

12   Vel nos in Capitolium,   45
           quo clamor vocat et turba faventium,
       vel nos in mare proximum
           gemmas et lapides aurum et inutile,

13   summi materiem mali,
           mittamus, scelerum si bene paenitet: 50
       eradenda cupidinis
           pravi sunt elementa et tenerae nimis

14   mentes asperioribus
           formandae studiis; nescit equo rudis
       haerere ingenuus puer   55
           venarique timet, ludere doctior,

15   seu Graeco iubeas trocho
            seu malis vetita legibus alea,
        cum periura patris fides
            consortem socium fallat et hospites   60

16   indignoque pecuniam
            heredi properet; scilicet inprobae
        crescunt divitiae, tamen
            curtae nescio quid semper abest rei.

                        25

1   Quo me, Bacche, rapis tui
            plenum? quae nemora aut quos agor in specus
        velox mente nova? quibus
            antris egregii Caesaris audiar

2   aeternum meditans decus   5
            stellis inserere et concilio Iovis?
        Dicam insigne, recens, adhuc
            indictum ore alio. Non secus in iugis

3   exsomnis stupet Euhias
            Hebrum prospiciens et nive candidam   10
        Thracen ac pede barbaro
            lustratam Rhodopen, ut mihi devio

4   ripas et vacuum nemus
            mirari libet. O Naiadum potens
        Baccharumque valentium   15
            proceras manibus vertere fraxinos,

5   nil parvum aut humili modo,
            nil mortale loquar: dulce periculum est,
        o Lenaee, sequi deum,
            cingentem viridi tempora pampino.   20

26

1   Vixi puellis nuper idoneus
      et militavi non sine gloria,
          nunc arma defunctumque bello
              barbiton hic paries habebit

2   laevom marinae qui Veneris latus   5
      custodit: hic, hic ponite lucida
          funalia et vectis et arcus
              oppositis foribus minacis.

3   O quae beatam diva tenes Cyprum et
      Memphin carentem Sithonia nive,   10
          regina, sublimi flagello
              tange Chloen semel arrogantem.

27

1   Inpios parrae recinentis omen
      ducat et praegnans canis aut ab agro
      rava decurrens lupa Lanuvino
          fetaque volpes,

2   rumpat et serpens iter institutum   5
      si per obliquom similis sagittae
      terruit mannos: ego cui timebo
          providus auspex,

3   antequam stantis repetat paludes
      imbrium divina avis imminentium,   10
      oscinem corvum prece suscitabo
          solis ab ortu.

4
    Sis licet felix, ubicumque mavis,
    et memor nostri, Galatea, vivas
    teque nec laevos vetet ire picus   15
        nec vaga cornix;

5
    sed vides, quanto trepidet tumultu
    pronus Orion? ego quid sit ater
    Hadriae novi sinus et quid albus
        peccet Iapyx;   20

6
    hostium uxores puerique caecos
    sentiant motus orientis Austri et
    aequoris nigri fremitum et trementis
        verbere ripas!

7
    Sic et Europe niveum doloso   25
    credidit tauro latus et scatentem
    beluis pontum mediasque fraudes
        palluit audax.

8
    Nuper in pratis studiosa florum et
    debitae Nymphis opifex coronae   30
    nocte sublustri nihil astra praeter
        vidit et undas;

9
    quae simul centum tetigit potentem
    oppidis Creten, 'Pater — o relictum
    filiae nomen pietasque' dixit —   35
        'victa furore,

10
    unde quo veni? levis una mors est
    virginum culpae! vigilansne ploro
    turpe conmissum an vitiis carentem
        ludit imago   40

11
    vana, quae porta fugiens eburna
    somnium ducit? meliusne fluctus
    ire per longos fuit an recentis
        carpere flores?

12   Siquis infamem mihi nunc iuvencum   45
dedat iratae, lacerare ferro et
frangere enitar modo multum amati
    cornua monstri.

13   Inpudens liqui patrios penates,
inpudens Orcum moror; o deorum   50
siquis haec audis, utinam inter errem
    nuda leones!

14   Antequam turpis macies decentis
occupet malas teneraeque sucus
defluat praedae, speciosa quaero   55
    pascere tigris!

15   "Vilis Europe", pater urget absens,
"quid mori cessas? potes hac ab orno
pendulum zona bene te secuta
    laedere collum;   60

16   sive te rupes et acuta leto
saxa delectant, age te procellae
crede veloci, nisi erile mavis
    carpere pensum

17   regius sanguis dominaeque tradi   65
barbarae paelex".' Aderat querenti
perfidum ridens Venus et remisso
    filius arcu;

18   mox ubi lusit satis, 'Abstineto'
dixit 'irarum calidaeque rixae,   70
cum tibi invisus laceranda reddet
    cornua taurus;

19   uxor invicti Iovis esse nescis;
mitte singultus; bene ferre magnam
disce fortunam: tua sectus orbis   75
    nomina ducet.'

28

1   Festo quid potius die
       Neptuni faciam? prome reconditum,
    Lyde, strenua Caecubum
       munitaeque adhibe vim sapientiae:

2   inclinare meridiem   5
       sentis et, veluti stet volucris dies,
    parcis deripere horreo
       cessantem Bibuli consulis amphoram?

3   Nos cantabimus invicem
       Neptunum et viridis Nereidum comas;   10
    tu curva recines lyra
       Latonam et celeris spicula Cynthiae;

4   summo carmine, quae Cnidon
       fulgentisque tenet Cycladas et Paphon
    iunctis visit oloribus;   15
       dicetur merita Nox quoque nenia.

29

1   Tyrrhena regum progenies, tibi
    non ante verso lene merum cado
       cum flore, Maecenas, rosarum et
          pressa tuis balanus capillis

2   iamdudum apud me est: eripe te morae,   5
    ne semper udum Tibur et Aefulae
       declive contempleris arvom et
          Telegoni iuga parricidae,

3   fastidiosam desere copiam et
           molem propinquam nubibus arduis,   10
               omitte mirari beatae
                   fumum et opes strepitumque Romae.

4   Plerumque gratae divitibus vices
           mundaeque parvo sub lare pauperum
               cenae sine aulaeis et ostro   15
                   sollicitam explicuere frontem:

5   iam clarus occultum Andromedae pater
           ostendit ignem, iam Procyon furit
               et stella vesani Leonis
                   sole dies referente siccos;   20

6   iam pastor umbras cum grege languido
           rivomque fessus quaerit et horridi
               dumeta Silvani caretque
                   ripa vagis taciturna ventis;

7   tu civitatem quis deceat status   25
           curas et urbi sollicitus times,
               quid Seres et regnata Cyro
                   Bactra parent Tanaisque discors?

8   Prudens futuri temporis exitum
           caliginosa nocte premit deus   30
               ridetque, si mortalis ultra
                   fas trepidat; quod adest memento

9   conponere aequos; cetera fluminis
           ritu feruntur, nunc medio alveo
               cum pace delabentis Etruscum   35
                   in mare, nunc lapides adesos

10   stirpisque raptas et pecus et domos
           volventis una, non sine montium
               clamore vicinaeque silvae,
                   cum fera diluvies quietos   40

11   inritat amnis. Ille potens sui
      laetusque deget, cui licet in diem
        dixisse 'Vixi'; cras vel atra
           nube polum pater occupato

12   vel sole puro, non tamen inritum   45
      quodcumque retro est efficiet, neque
        diffinget infectumque reddet
           quod fugiens semel hora vexit.

13   Fortuna saevo laeta negotio et
      ludum insolentem ludere pertinax   50
        transmutat incertos honores,
           nunc mihi nunc alii benigna:

14   laudo manentem; si celeris quatit
      pinnas, resigno quae dedit et mea
        virtute me involvo probamque   55
           pauperiem sine dote quaero;

15   non est meum, si mugiat Africis
      malus procellis, ad miseras preces
        decurrere et votis pacisci,
           ne Cypriae Tyriaeque merces   60

16   addant avaro divitias mari:
      tunc me biremis praesidio scaphae
        tutum per Aegaeos tumultus
           aura feret geminusque Pollux.

30

Exegi monumentum aere perennius
regalique situ pyramidum altius,
quod non imber edax, non Aquilo impotens
possit diruere aut innumerabilis
annorum series et fuga temporum.   5

Non omnis moriar multaque pars mei
vitabit Libitinam; usque ego postera
crescam laude recens, dum Capitolium
scandet cum tacita virgine pontifex;
dicar, qua violens obstrepit Aufidus   10
et qua pauper aquae Daunus agrestium
regnavit populorum, ex humili potens
princeps Aeolium carmen ad Italos
deduxisse modos. Sume superbiam
quaesitam meritis et mihi Delphica   15
lauro cinge volens, Melpomene, comam.

BOOK 4

1

1   Intermissa, Venus, diu
        rursus bella moves? parce, precor, precor:
    non sum qualis eram bonae
        sub regno Cinarae. Desine, dulcium

2   mater saeva Cupidinum,   5
        circa lustra decem flectere mollibus
    iam durum imperiis; abi,
        quo blandae iuvenum te revocant preces.

3   Tempestivius in domum
        Paulli purpureis ales oloribus   10
    comissabere Maximi,
        si torrere iecur quaeris idoneum:

4   namque et nobilis et decens
        et pro sollicitis non tacitus reis
    et centum puer artium   15
        late signa feret militiae tuae,

5   et quandoque potentior
             largi muneribus riserit aemuli,
         Albanos prope te lacus
             ponet marmoream sub trabe citrea.   20

6   Illic plurima naribus
             duces tura lyraque et Berecyntia
         delectabere tibia
             mixtis carminibus non sine fistula;

7   illic bis pueri die   25
             numen cum teneris virginibus tuum
         laudantes pede candido
             in morem Salium ter quatient humum.

8   Me nec femina nec puer
             iam nec spes animi credula mutui   30
         nec certare iuvat mero
             nec vincire novis tempora floribus —

9   sed cur heu, Ligurine, cur
             manat rara meas lacrima per genas?
         cur facunda parum decoro   35
             inter verba cadit lingua silentio?

10   nocturnis ego somniis
             iam captum teneo, iam volucrem sequor
         te per gramina Martii
             campi, te per aquas, dure, volubilis.   40

                                    2

1   Pindarum quisquis studet aemulari,
         Iulle, ceratis ope Daedalea
         nititur pinnis, vitreo daturus
             nomina ponto:

2 monte decurrens velut amnis, imbres 5
  quem super notas aluere ripas,
  fervet inmensusque ruit profundo
   Pindarus ore,

3 laurea donandus Apollinari,
  seu per audacis nova dithyrambos 10
  verba devolvit numerisque fertur
   lege solutis,

4 seu deos regesque canit, deorum
  sanguinem, per quos cecidere iusta
  morte Centauri, cecidit tremendae 15
   flamma Chimaerae,

5 sive quos Elea domum reducit
  palma caelestis pugilemve equomve
  dicit et centum potiore signis
   munere donat, 20

6 flebili sponsae iuvenemve raptum
  plorat et viris animumque moresque
  aureos educit in astra nigroque
   invidet Orco.

7 Multa Dircaeum levat aura cycnum, 25
  tendit, Antoni, quotiens in altos
  nubium tractus: ego apis Matinae
   more modoque,

8 grata carpentis thyma per laborem
  plurimum, circa nemus uvidique 30
  Tiburis ripas operosa parvos
   carmina fingo.

9 Concines maiore poeta plectro
  Caesarem, quandoque trahet ferocis
  per sacrum clivum merita decorus 35
   fronde Sygambros,

10   quo nihil maius meliusve terris
        fata donavere bonique divi
        nec dabunt, quamvis redeant in aurum
            tempora priscum;   40

11   concines laetosque dies et urbis
        publicum ludum super inpetrato
        fortis Augusti reditu forumque
            litibus orbum.

12   Tum meae, si quid loquar audiendum,   45
        vocis accedet bona pars et 'o sol
        pulcer, o laudande' canam recepto
            Caesare felix.

13   Teque, dum procedis, 'Io Triumphe',
        non semel dicemus, 'Io Triumphe',   50
        civitas omnis dabimusque divis
            tura benignis.

14   Te decem tauri totidemque vaccae,
        me tener solvet vitulus, relicta
        matre qui largis iuvenescit herbis   55
            in mea vota,

15   fronte curvatos imitatus ignis
        tertium lunae referentis ortum,
        qua notam duxit, niveus videri,
            cetera fulvos.   60

3

1   Quem tu, Melpomene, semel
                nascentem placido lumine videris,
            illum non labor Isthmius
                clarabit pugilem, non equos inpiger

2 curru ducet Achaico   5
    victorem, neque res bellica Deliis
  ornatum foliis ducem,
    quod regum tumidas contuderit minas,

3 ostendet Capitolio,
    sed quae Tibur aquae fertile praefluunt 10
  et spissae nemorum comae
    fingent Aeolio carmine nobilem.

4 Romae, principis urbium,
    dignatur suboles inter amabilis
  vatum ponere me choros,   15
    et iam dente minus mordeor invido.

5 O testudinis aureae
    dulcem quae strepitum, Pieri, temperas,
  o mutis quoque piscibus
    donatura cycni, si libeat, sonum, 20

6 totum muneris hoc tui est,
    quod monstror digito praetereuntium
  Romanae fidicen lyrae;
    quod spiro et placeo, si placeo, tuum est.

4

1 Qualem ministrum fulminis alitem
  (cui rex deorum regnum in avis vagas
    permisit, expertus fidelem
      Iuppiter in Ganymede flavo)

2 olim iuventas et patrius vigor   5
  nido laborum propulit inscium
    (vernique iam nimbis remotis
      insolitos docuere nisus

3   venti paventem), mox in ovilia
         demisit hostem vividus impetus,   10
            nunc in reluctantis dracones
               egit amor dapis atque pugnae,

4   qualemve laetis caprea pascuis
         intenta fulvae matris ab ubere
            iam lacte depulsum leonem   15
               dente novo peritura vidit,

5   videre Raetis bella sub Alpibus
         Drusum gerentem Vindelici. Quibus
            mos unde deductus per omne
               tempus Amazonia securi   20

6   dextras obarmet, quaerere distuli,
         nec scire fas est omnia; sed diu
            lateque victrices catervae
               consiliis iuvenis revictae

7   sensere, quid mens rite, quid indoles   25
         nutrita faustis sub penetralibus
            posset, quid Augusti paternus
               in pueros animus Nerones.

8   Fortes creantur fortibus et bonis;
         est in iuvencis, est in equis patrum   30
            virtus neque inbellem feroces
               progenerant aquilae columbam;

9   doctrina sed vim promovet insitam
         rectique cultus pectora roborant;
            utcumque defecere mores,   35
               indecorant bene nata culpae.

10   Quid debeas, o Roma, Neronibus,
         testis Metaurum flumen et Hasdrubal
            devictus et pulcer fugatis
               ille dies Latio tenebris   40

11   qui primus alma risit adorea,
          dirus per urbis Afer ut Italas
                ceu flamma per taedas vel Eurus
                    per Siculas equitavit undas;

12   post hoc secundis usque laboribus   45
          Romana pubes crevit et inpio
                vastata Poenorum tumultu
                    fana deos habuere rectos,

13   dixitque tandem perfidus Hannibal:
          'Cervi, luporum praeda rapacium,   50
                sectamur ultro quos opimus
                    fallere et effugere est triumphus:

14   gens, quae cremato fortis ab Ilio
          iactata Tuscis aequoribus sacra
                natosque maturosque patres   55
                    pertulit Ausonias ad urbis,

15   duris ut ilex tonsa bipennibus
          nigrae feraci frondis in Algido,
                per damna, per caedis ab ipso
                    ducit opes animumque ferro;   60

16   non hydra secto corpore firmior
          vinci dolentem crevit in Herculem
                monstrumve submisere Colchi
                    maius Echioniaeve Thebae:

17   merses profundo, pulcrior evenit;   65
          luctere, multa proruet integrum
                cum laude victorem geretque
                    proelia coniugibus loquenda.

18   Carthagini iam non ego nuntios
          mittam superbos: occidit, occidit   70
                spes omnis et fortuna nostri
                    nominis Hasdrubale interempto.'

19   Nil Claudiae non perficient manus,
            quas et benigno numine Iuppiter
                defendit et curae sagaces   75
                    expediunt per acuta belli.

                                    5

1   Divis orte bonis, optume Romulae
            custos gentis, abes iam nimium diu:
            maturum reditum pollicitus patrum
                sancto concilio, redi,

2   lucem redde tuae, dux bone, patriae.   5
            Instar veris enim voltus ubi tuus
            adfulsit populo, gratior it dies
                et soles melius nitent.

3   Ut mater iuvenem, quem Notus invido
            flatu Carpathii trans maris aequora   10
            cunctantem spatio longius annuo
                dulci distinet a domo,

4   votis ominibusque et precibus vocat
            curvo nec faciem litore dimovet,
            sic desideriis icta fidelibus   15
                quaerit patria Caesarem.

5   Tutus bos etenim rura perambulat,
            nutrit rura Ceres almaque Faustitas,
            pacatum volitant per mare navitae,
                culpari metuit fides,   20

6   nullis polluitur casta domus stupris,
            mos et lex maculosum edomuit nefas,
            laudantur simili prole puerperae,
                culpam poena premit comes.

7   Quis Parthum paveat, quis gelidum Scythen,   25
       quis Germania quos horrida parturit
       fetus incolumi Caesare? quis ferae
              bellum curet Hiberiae?

8   Condit quisque diem collibus in suis
       et vitem viduas ducit ad arbores;   30
       hinc ad vina redit laetus et alteris
              te mensis adhibet deum:

9   te multa prece, te prosequitur mero
       defuso pateris, et Laribus tuum
       miscet numen, uti Graecia Castoris   35
              et magni memor Herculis.

10   'Longas o utinam, dux bone, ferias
       praestes Hesperiae' dicimus integro
       sicci mane die, dicimus uvidi,
              cum sol Oceano subest.   40

                            6

1   Dive, quem proles Niobaea magnae
       vindicem linguae Tityosque raptor
       sensit et Troiae prope victor altae
              Phthius Achilles,

2   ceteris maior, tibi miles inpar,   5
       filius quamvis Thetidis marinae
       Dardanas turris quateret tremenda
              cuspide pugnax —

3   ille, mordaci velut icta ferro
       pinus aut inpulsa cupressus Euro,   10
       procidit late posuitque collum in
              pulvere Teucro;

4   ille non inclusus equo Minervae
       sacra mentito male feriatos
       Troas et laetam Priami choreis   15
          falleret aulam,

5   sed palam captis gravis, heu nefas, heu
       nescios fari pueros Achivis
       ureret flammis, etiam latentem
          matris in alvo,   20

6   ni tuis flexus Venerisque gratae
       vocibus divom pater adnuisset
       rebus Aeneae potiore ductos
          alite muros:

7   doctor argutae fidicen Thaliae,   25
       Phoebe, qui Xantho lavis amne crinis,
       Dauniae defende decus Camenae,
          levis Agyieu.

8   Spiritum Phoebus mihi, Phoebus artem
       carminis nomenque dedit poetae: 30
       virginum primae puerique claris
          patribus orti,

9   Deliae tutela deae, fugacis
       lyncas et cervos cohibentis arcu,
       Lesbium servate pedem meique   35
          pollicis ictum,

10   rite Latonae puerum canentes,
       rite crescentem face Noctilucam,
       prosperam frugum celeremque pronos
          volvere mensis.   40

11   Nupta iam dices 'Ego dis amicum,
       saeculo festas referente luces,
       reddidi carmen docilis modorum
          vatis Horati.'

7

1   Diffugere nives, redeunt iam gramina campis
       arboribusque comae;
    mutat terra vices, et decrescentia ripas
       flumina praetereunt.

2   Gratia cum Nymphis geminisque sororibus audet   5
       ducere nuda choros;
    inmortalia ne speres, monet annus et almum
       quae rapit hora diem.

3   Frigora mitescunt Zephyris, ver proterit aestas,
       interitura, simul   10
    pomifer autumnus fruges effuderit, et mox
       bruma recurrit iners;

4   damna tamen celeres reparant caelestia lunae;
       nos ubi decidimus
    quo pius Aeneas, quo dives Tullus et Ancus,   15
       pulvis et umbra sumus.

5   Quis scit an adiciant hodiernae crastina summae
       tempora di superi?
    Cuncta manus avidas fugient heredis, amico
       quae dederis animo.   20

6   Cum semel occideris et de te splendida Minos
       fecerit arbitria,
    non, Torquate, genus, non te facundia, non te
       restituet pietas.

7   Infernis neque enim tenebris Diana pudicum   25
       liberat Hippolytum
    nec Lethaea valet Theseus abrumpere caro
       vincula Pirithoo.

8

Donarem pateras grataque commodus,
Censorine, meis aera sodalibus,
donarem tripodas, praemia fortium
Graiorum, neque tu pessuma munerum
ferres, divite me scilicet artium 5
quas aut Parrhasius protulit aut Scopas,
hic saxo, liquidis ille coloribus
sollers nunc hominem ponere, nunc deum;
sed non haec mihi vis, nec tibi talium
res est aut animus deliciarum egens: 10
gaudes carminibus; carmina possumus
donare, et pretium dicere muneri.

Non incisa notis marmora publicis,
per quae spiritus et vita redit bonis
post mortem ducibus, non celeres fugae 15
reiectaeque retrorsum Hannibalis minae
non incendia Karthaginis inpiae
eius qui domita nomen ab Africa
lucratus rediit clarius indicant
laudes quam Calabrae Pierides, neque 20
si chartae sileant quod bene feceris,
mercedem tuleris. Quid foret Iliae
Mavortisque puer, si taciturnitas
obstaret meritis invida Romuli?
Ereptum Stygiis fluctibus Aeacum 25
virtus et favor et lingua potentium
vatum divitibus consecrat insulis.
Dignum laude virum Musa vetat mori,
caelo Musa beat. Sic Iovis interest
optatis epulis inpiger Hercules, 30
clarum Tyndaridae sidus ab infimis
quassas eripiunt aequoribus ratis,
ornatus viridi tempora pampino
Liber vota bonos ducit ad exitus.

9

1 Ne forte credas interitura quae
  longe sonantem natus ad Aufidum
   non ante volgatas per artis
    verba loquor socianda chordis:

2 non, si priores Maeonius tenet   5
  sedes Homerus, Pindaricae latent
   Ceaeque et Alcaei minaces
    Stesichorique graves Camenae,

3 nec, siquid olim lusit Anacreon,
  delevit aetas; spirat adhuc amor   10
   vivuntque conmissi calores
    Aeoliae fidibus puellae.

4 Non sola comptos arsit adulteri
  crinis et aurum vestibus inlitum
   mirata regalisque cultus   15
    et comites Helene Lacaena,

5 primusve Teucer tela Cydonio
  direxit arcu, non semel Ilios
   vexata, non pugnavit ingens
    Idomeneus Sthenelusve solus   20

6 dicenda Musis proelia; non ferox
  Hector vel acer Deiphobus gravis
   excepit ictus pro pudicis
    coniugibus puerisque primus.

7 Vixere fortes ante Agamemnona   25
  multi; sed omnes inlacrimabiles
   urgentur ignotique longa
    nocte, carent quia vate sacro.

8   Paulum sepultae distat inertiae
         celata virtus; non ego te meis   30
             chartis inornatum silebo
                 totve tuos patiar labores

9   inpune, Lolli, carpere lividas
         obliviones: est animus tibi
             rerumque prudens et secundis   35
                 temporibus dubiisque rectus,

10   vindex avarae fraudis et abstinens
         ducentis ad se cuncta pecuniae,
             consulque non unius anni,
                 sed quotiens bonus atque fidus   40

11   iudex honestum praetulit utili,
         reiecit alto dona nocentium
             voltu, per obstantis catervas
                 explicuit sua victor arma.

12   Non possidentem multa vocaveris   45
         recte beatum; rectius occupat
             nomen beati, qui deorum
                 muneribus sapienter uti

13   duramque callet pauperiem pati
         peiusque leto flagitium timet,   50
             non ille pro caris amicis
                 aut patria timidus perire.

                         10

O crudelis adhuc et Veneris muneribus potens,
insperata tuae cum veniet pluma superbiae
et quae nunc umeris involitant, deciderint comae,
nunc et qui color est puniceae flore prior rosae,

mutatus, Ligurine, in faciem verterit hispidam,   5
dices 'Heu', quotiens te speculo videris alterum,
'quae mens est hodie, cur eadem non puero fuit,
vel cur his animis incolumes non redeunt genae?'

11

1   Est mihi nonum superantis annum
      plenus Albani cadus, est in horto,
      Phylli, nectendis apium coronis,
         est hederae vis

2   multa, qua crinis religata fulges;   5
      ridet argento domus, ara castis
      vincta verbenis avet immolato
         spargier agno;

3   cuncta festinat manus, huc et illuc
      cursitant mixtae pueris puellae,   10
      sordidum flammae trepidant rotantes
         vertice fumum.

4   Ut tamen noris, quibus advoceris
      gaudiis, Idus tibi sunt agendae,
      qui dies mensem Veneris marinae   15
         findit Aprilem,

5   iure sollemnis mihi sanctiorque
      paene natali proprio, quod ex hac
      luce Maecenas meus adfluentis
         ordinat annos.   20

6   Telephum, quem tu petis, occupavit
      non tuae sortis iuvenem puella
      dives et lasciva tenetque grata
         compede vinctum.

7   Terret ambustus Phaethon avaras   25
     spes et exemplum grave praebet ales
     Pegasus terrenum equitem gravatus
          Bellerophontem,

8   semper ut te digna sequare et ultra
     quam licet sperare nefas putando   30
     disparem vites: age iam, meorum
          finis amorum

9   (non enim posthac alia calebo
     femina), condisce modos, amanda
     voce quos reddas; minuentur atrae   35
          carmine curae.

                    12

1   Iam veris comites, quae mare temperant,
     inpellunt animae lintea Thraciae,
     iam nec prata rigent nec fluvii strepunt
          hiberna nive turgidi.

2   Nidum ponit Ityn flebiliter gemens   5
     infelix avis et Cecropiae domus
     aeternum opprobrium, quod male barbaras
          regum est ulta libidines.

3   Dicunt in tenero gramine pinguium
     custodes ovium carmina fistula   10
     delectantque deum, cui pecus et nigri
          colles Arcadiae placent.

4   Adduxere sitim tempora, Vergili.
     Sed pressum Calibus ducere Liberum
     si gestis, iuvenum nobilium cliens,   15
          nardo vina merebere.

5   Nardi parvus onyx eliciet cadum
        qui nunc Sulpiciis accubat horreis,
        spes donare novas largus amaraque
           curarum eluere efficax.   20

6   Ad quae si properas gaudia, cum tua
        velox merce veni: non ego te meis
        inmunem meditor tinguere poculis,
           plena dives ut in domo.

7   Verum pone moras et studium lucri   25
        nigrorumque memor dum licet ignium
        misce stultitiam consiliis brevem:
           dulce est desipere in loco.

13

1   Audivere, Lyce, di mea vota, di
        audivere, Lyce: fis anus; et tamen
           vis formosa videri
              ludisque et bibis inpudens

2   et cantu tremulo pota Cupidinem   5
        lentum sollicitas: ille virentis et
           doctae psallere Chiae
              pulcris excubat in genis;

3   inportunus enim transvolat aridas
        quercus et refugit te, quia luridi   10
           dentes, te quia rugae
              turpant et capitis nives.

4   Nec Coae referunt iam tibi purpurae
        nec cari lapides tempora, quae semel
           notis condita fastis   15
              inclusit volucris dies;

5   quo fugit venus, heu, quove color, decens
    quo motus? quid habes illius, illius,
        quae spirabat amores,
            quae me surpuerat mihi,   20

6   felix post Cinaram notaque et artium
    gratarum facies? Sed Cinarae brevis
        annos fata dederunt,
            servatura diu parem

7   cornicis vetulae temporibus Lycen,   25
    possent ut iuvenes visere fervidi
        multo non sine risu
            dilapsam in cineres facem.

14

1   Quae cura patrum quaeve Quiritium
    plenis honorum muneribus tuas,
        Auguste, virtutes in aevum
            per titulos memoresque fastus

2   aeternet, o qua sol habitabilis   5
    inlustrat oras, maxime principum?
        Quem legis expertes Latinae
            Vindelici didicere nuper,

3   quid Marte posses: milite nam tuo
    Drusus Genaunos, inplacidum genus,   10
        Breunosque velocis et arces
            Alpibus inpositas tremendis

4   deiecit acer plus vice simplici;
    maior Neronum mox grave proelium
        conmisit immanisque Raetos   15
            auspiciis pepulit secundis,

5   spectandus in certamine Martio
        devota morti pectora liberae
            quantis fatigaret ruinis,
                indomitas prope qualis undas   20

6   exercet Auster Pleiadum choro
        scindente nubis, inpiger hostium
            vexare turmas et frementem
                mittere equum medios per ignis.

7   Sic tauriformis volvitur Aufidus,   25
        qui regna Dauni praefluit Apuli,
            cum saevit horrendamque cultis
                diluviem meditatur agris,

8   ut barbarorum Claudius agmina
        ferrata vasto diruit impetu   30
            primosque et extremos metendo
                stravit humum sine clade victor,

9   te copias, te consilium et tuos
        praebente divos; nam tibi quo die
            portus Alexandrea supplex   35
                et vacuam patefecit aulam,

10   Fortuna lustro prospera tertio
        belli secundos reddidit exitus
            laudemque et optatum peractis
                imperiis decus adrogavit.   40

11   Te Cantaber non ante domabilis
        Medusque et Indus, te profugus Scythes
            miratur, o tutela praesens
                Italiae dominaeque Romae;

12   te fontium qui celat origines   45
        Nilusque et Hister, te rapidus Tigris,
            te beluosus qui remotis
                obstrepit Oceanus Britannis,

13   te non paventis funera Galliae
duraeque tellus audit Hiberiae,   50
    te caede gaudentes Sygambri
      conpositis venerantur armis.

15

1   Phoebus volentem proelia me loqui
victas et urbis increpuit lyra,
    ne parva Tyrrhenum per aequor
      vela darem. Tua, Caesar, aetas

2   fruges et agris rettulit uberes   5
et signa nostro restituit Iovi
    derepta Parthorum superbis
      postibus et vacuum duellis

3   Ianum Quirini clausit et ordinem
rectum evaganti frena licentiae   10
    iniecit emovitque culpas
      et veteres revocavit artis,

4   per quas Latinum nomen et Italae
crevere vires famaque et imperi
    porrecta maiestas ad ortus   15
      solis ab Hesperio cubili.

5   Custode rerum Caesare non furor
civilis aut vis exiget otium,
    non ira, quae procudit ensis
      et miseras inimicat urbis;   20

6   non qui profundum Danuvium bibunt
edicta rumpent Iulia, non Getae,
    non Seres infidique Persae,
      non Tanain prope flumen orti;

7   nosque et profestis lucibus et sacris   25
      inter iocosi munera Liberi
          cum prole matronisque nostris
              rite deos prius adprecati

8   virtute functos more patrum duces
      Lydis remixto carmine tibiis   30
          Troiamque et Anchisen et almae
              progeniem Veneris canemus.

Commentary

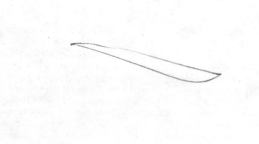

Book One

1. 1

Introduction: A poem to H.'s patron, introducing the collected edition of his poems — a relaxed, discursive epistle (more in the manner of H.'s hexameter verse than that of the poems which follow), in which H.'s ambition to be ranked among the great lyric poets is put on the same level as the obsessions of ordinary men. In a society where only slaves and professional soldiers were subjected to fixed conditions of employment, the clear-cut distinction we make between job and pastime hardly existed; the way those with whom H. associated spent their lives was very much a matter of personal decision and the freedom to follow one's enthusiasms correspondingly greater. All the same, to see poetry equated with the traditional Roman careers (politics, the army, commerce), or even with such socially acceptable pursuits as hunting and victory at the Olympic games, would have surprised many. H.'s opening poem is as much a challenge as an apology. Cf. the change of tone when he returns to the same theme in 4.3.

For the presentation copy of *Odes* 1-3 offered to Augustus, see *Epist.* 1.13; for the date, 2.10I.

Structure: After the opening address to H.'s patron (lines 1-2), a series of examples of the things that give men pleasure in life (lines 3-28) leads up to H. and his own personal obsession (lines 29-34). If H. can win the stamp of approval from his patron, his delight will know no bounds (lines 35-6).

With the exception of 4.8 (the text of which is suspect on other grounds) all of the odes consist of multiples of four lines. Of 103 poems, 78 are written in metres based on a 4-line stanza (Alcaics, Sapphics, Asclepiads c and d); 16 of the remaining 25 are in couplets, 9 in single-line metres. (The individual metres will be discussed as they occur.) It is commonly held that these 25 odes are also composed in 4-line stanzas, 4.8 being emended to bring it into line with this principle — the so-called *lex Meinekiana* (after J. Meineke's edition of 1834, in which this arrangement was adopted).

Odes composed throughout in endstopped stanzas (or syntactically complete blocks of four lines) are the exception rather than the rule (3. 9, 4. 12). In this respect the *Odes* differ markedly from most modern poetry in stanzaic form. It is clear, none the less, that H. was sensitive to the structural possibilities of concidence (or its absence) of metrical unit and syntactical unit. The end of the stanza coincides with the end of a sentence (or with a distinct syntactical pause — e.g., the end of a clause) sufficiently often for the absence of coincidence to be felt. Syntactical enjambment (the syntactical unit spilling over into the middle of the first line of the stanza following, e.g., as in 1. 5. 4-5) is not uncommon and always striking. In a longer poem, the spill-over of the sense from one stanza to the next builds up easily identifiable blocks of sense serving as a key to the rhetorical structure of the poem. Considerable variety in the effect obtained is permitted by the range of syntactical possibilities (no pause at all at the stanza-end, light pause, end of sentence and stanza-end coincide). The odes written in couplets seem in most cases to be likewise composed in 4-line stanzas, with coincidence (or its absence) at the stanza-end a significant structural feature. They are accordingly printed in 4-line stanzas in the following pages; an exception is 2. 18. In the odes written in single-line metres, analysis along these lines does not seem profitable and these odes are printed here without division into stanzas. Individual cases are considered in the section on Structure following the Introduction to each ode.

Metre: Asclepiad (a):

$$\underline{\quad}\ \underline{\quad},\ \underline{\quad}\ \cup\cup,\ \underline{\quad}\ \wedge\ \underline{\quad}\ \cup\cup,\ \underline{\quad}\ \cup\bar{\cup}$$

This is the basic Asclepiad line, used in all the odes written in Asclepiad metres, either exclusively or combined with glyconic and other metres to form couplets or quatrains. The only other odes written exclusively in Asclepiad (a) are the concluding ode of Book 3 and 4. 8. The various combinations are dealt with at their first occurrence.

The first nine poems in Book 1 are all in different metres; the other poems in Asclepiads in this group are 1. 3 (Asclepiad b), 1. 5 (Asclepiad d) and 1. 6 (Asclepiad c). Of 34 poems in Asclepiads, the highest concentration is to be found in the group 1. 1-24 (ten poems in Asclepiads); next comes the group 3. 7-16 (six poems in Asclepiads); of the 15 poems in Book 4, seven are in Asclepiads.

1-2] Six of the first seven odes are addressed to public figures: 1. 1 to Maecenas (the poet's patron and chief adviser to Augustus); 1. 2 to Augustus; 1. 3 to Virgil (Rome's leading poet, known to be engaged on his great national epic); 1. 4 to Sestius (*consul suffectus*, 23 BC, the year of publication of *Odes* 1-3); 1. 6 to Agrippa (Augustus' commander-in-chief and official deputy); 1. 7 to Plancus (senior *consularis* at the time of publication of *Odes* 1-3). The order is clearly planned. After 1. 7, the next ode addressed to a real person is 1. 18 (to Varus) and with this poem begins a second, more loosely connected series of odes for personal friends: 1. 18 to Varus; 1. 20 to Varus; 1. 22 to Fuscus; 1. 24 to Virgil; 1. 26 in honour of Lamia; 1. 29 to Iccius; 1. 33 to Albius [Tibullus?]. — **Maecenas]** The initial vocative suggests conversational directness (cf. 1. 8. 1, 1. 29. 1, 1. 33. 1); it is also the position of honour (cf. 1. 10. 1), particularly here, where the name of the poet's patron begins the collection; a purely honorific vocative is usually postponed; the *Epodes*, *Satires* 1 and *Epistles* 1 similarly begin with an address to Maecenas. — **atavis ... regibus]** The order is *pater, avus, proavus, abavus, atavus*; cf. 3. 29. 1 and *Sat.* 1. 6. 1-2 'Non quia, Maecenas, Lydorum quidquid Etruscos / incoluit finis, . . .'. — **o et]** Hiatus (not uncommon after exclamatory o). — **praesidium]** The word used of the protection extended by a *patronus* to his *clientes*; see, e.g., Cicero *de Orat.* 1. 18. 1 'praesidium clientibus atque opem amicis porrigentem atque tendentem'; here figuratively of the *patronus* himself; it had become traditional for the great figures of the later Republic to include poets and intellectuals among those to whom they extended their protection and to whom their table was open as regular guests; H. begins his collection by emphasising his relation to his *patronus*; it is largely due to Maecenas that the word *patronus* came to acquire its eighteenth-century sense of 'patron'; for H.'s attempt to redefine the relationship, see *Epist.* 1. 7. — **dulce decus]** Repeated in more emphatic form 2. 17. 4; cf. 1. 32. 13. — **meum]** With both nouns.

3-28] The argument which now follows is to be taken as H.'s half-serious defence (addressed to the sympathetic ear of his patron) of his chosen way of life. The manner (easygoing, colloquial) suggests the *Satires* and *Epistles* more than the denser, terser dignity of the lyric Horace; similarly, the tone is closer to satire than the more delicate irony of the *Odes*; cf. the use made of similar material in 3. 1. 5-16.

3-6] **sunt quos]** For the formula cf. 1. 7. 5. — **curriculo]** 'racing chariot' (*OLD* 5) rather than 'race-track' (*OLD* 4); the context probably revives the affective overtones of the word (a diminutive of *currus*). — **pulverem Olympicum collegisse]** = 'to have raised a cloud of dust at the Olympic games'; *pulverem* cancels the evocative force of *Olympicum*; H. is not satirising chariot racing, but making the point that what can seem only a disagreeable experience to the outsider is exhilarating for the man for whom chariot racing is a passion (the wealthy Roman who chooses to take part in the famous Olympic games); cf. 2. 16. 34-5; for the disagreeable side of sport cf. 1. 8. 1-12; **collegisse]** the perfect perhaps fixes on the charioteer at the moment after the race, but the use of the perfect infinitive (with little or no perfective or aoristic force) is a mannerism of Augustan poetry. — **metaque evitata]** The phrase functions as a noun-equivalent, serving, along with *palma nobilis*, as subject of *evehit*; by a common idiom noun + past participle express what we should express as an abstraction ('the rounding of the turning post') on the model of *ab urbe condita* (= 'from the foundation of the city'), etc.; to have avoided collision with the *meta* means one has secured the inner position at the turn and hugged the *meta* while turning — a manoeuvre courting disaster if misjudged, or if the other drivers crowd you in, and therefore exhilarating if successfully executed. — **fervidis rotis]** The iron rims, i.e., become hot to the touch; cf. *Aen.* 11. 195 'ferventisque rotas', Ovid *Ars* 3. 396. —

palmaque nobilis] The palm of victory: *nobilis*, the term conventionally applied to the victor (= our 'hero'; cf. 1. 8. 12, 1. 12. 27) is transferred to the garland of palm leaves which symbolises victory; cf. 4. 2. 17-18. — **terrarum dominos]** The stars of the Olympic chariot race are already lords of the earth; an exciting race crowned with victory makes them feel like gods — and, therefore, 'lords of the earth' in a different sense; the sentence, i.e., imposes, as it progresses, a reassessment of the denotation of *terrarum dominos*; Latin idiom avoids the double-barrel relative clause (our 'there are those whom . . . and whom . . .'), preferring to express the second idea as an independent statement ('and victory raises them . . .'); the grammatical status of *terrarum dominos* is that of an appositional expansion of a direct object of *evehit* (e.g., *eos*, often omitted when unemphatic); some take *terrarum dominos* as an ornamental expansion of *deos*, but this gives weak sense.

7-10]   One man gets his excitement from political success, another from success in business. — **hunc . . . illum . . .]** sc. *iuvat*; failure to recognise the appositional status of *metaque . . . deos* has led to strained interpretations of these lines. — **si mobilium . . . honoribus]** Cynicism about politics was to be increasingly the note of the Augustan age; see on 3. 1. 14-16; 'mobilium turba Quiritium' suggests the demagogue exhilarated by the support of the mob at election time, rather than a member of the great families, who tended to regard the senior magistracies as their ancestral right; **certat tollere]** visual, suggesting the unruly support of the mob, clamouring for victory for their candidate rather than abstract ('vie with one another'); **tergeminis honoribus]** the traditional *cursus honorum*, the offices of aedile, praetor and consul (NH revive the interpretation of the ancient commentator Porphyrio, 'reiterated applause'). — **illum . . . areis]** The speculator in grain who has cornered the whole of the Lybian corn harvest; H. represents him as exhilarated — not by the deal he has just pulled off, but by the sight of the grain stacked in his warehouse (thus equating him with the miser who gloats over his accumulated wealth); cf., for the corner in grain, 3. 16. 25-8, *Sat.* 2. 3. 87; for the miser and his granaries piled high with corn, *Sat.* 1. 1. 46-53; as in the previous examples, H. is not arguing that different pursuits interest different men, but concentrating in each case on that which makes the man who has chosen that pursuit most happy (the excitement of the race and the victory, the excitement of the election, the pleasure the speculator gets from contemplating his full warehouse); **verritur]** the grain is swept together after threshing.

11-18]   Further examples: the small-time farmer and the overseas trader. — **gaudentem . . . sarculo]** Cf. Tibullus' picture of himself in 1. 1; if this is what a man enjoys, nothing will shift him. — **Attalicis condicionibus]** 'the promises of an Attalid' (Attalus I of Pergamum and his successors, especially Attalus III); see on 2. 18. 5. — **numquam demoveas]** 'you'd never shift'; the so-called 'ideal' second person singular. — **trabe Cypria]** Cyprus was well known as a shipbuilding centre; for *trabs* = 'ship', cf. Catullus 4. 3. — **Myrtoum mare]** The western part of the Aegean S of Euboea (after the island Myrto); H., as is appropriate to the lyric manner (in which the characteristic rhetorical structure is the clear-cut image, not the argumentative abstraction), prefers to particularise. — **pavidus nauta]** 'a timorous sailor', the sea not being his element; *nauta* = 'one who travels by sea', not necessarily a sailor by profession (cf. *viator*, one who travels by land); cf. 1. 28. 23, so 4. 5. 19 'navitae'. — **luctantem . . . Africum]** 'the SW wind in its fight with waves of the Icarian sea'; the *mare Icarium* (after the island Icaros) lay to the E of the *mare Myrtoum*; see on 4. 2. 3-4; cf. 3. 7. 21; for the idea of a storm as a fight between contending forces cf. 1. 9. 10-11; *Icariis fluctibus* is dative. — **mercator]** The overseas trader who travels the seas to bring back cargoes from Greece and the Middle East; in the Roman world, a large-scale entrepreneur, often rich, several times the butt of H.'s irony (cf. 1. 31. 11, 3. 1. 26, 3. 24. 36-40, 3. 29. 57-61). — **metuens]** Strictly temporal, 'while he is afraid'. — **otium . . . rura sui]** i.e., the countryside around the small town where he has a country estate. — **mox . . . pati]** When he retires to his estate, he finds he cannot adapt to the simple way of life (18 'indocilis pauperiem pati') which had seemed so attractive a prospect at the height of the storm — he misses the exhilaration of the life at sea (and the way of life of a prosperous *mercator*); cf. 2. 16. 1-4; **reficit rates quassas]** 'he refits his battered ships'; **pauperiem]** the simple life which H. constantly extols (not 'poverty'); cf. 3. 2. 1, 3. 29. 56; contrast 1. 12. 43, 1. 18. 5, 3. 16. 37.

19-22]   **est qui]** Resumes the construction of 3 'sunt quos'; we come now to the man for whom enjoying life means taking things easy. — **Massici]** A Campanian wine; cf. 2. 7. 21,

3. 21. 5. — **partem . . . de die**] 'to break into the day'; a long noon siesta is meant; cf.
2. 7. 6-7. — **nunc . . . sacrae**] For such picnics and their Epicurean background, see 2. 31;
viridi sub arbuto] the arbutus is an evergreen tree or shrub with attractive flowers and
berry-like red fruit; cne variety is called the strawberry tree; **membra stratus**] An
accusative dependent on a past participle (occasionally a present, etc., indicative passive)
as though it were the direct object of a deponent verb is a common mannerism of
Augustan verse; for the construction in Catullus, see Quinn on Catullus 64. 64; most
likely, it owed its popularity to association with the accusative of respect dependent on
an adjective (4. 2. 60 'cetera fulvos', etc.), though the two constructions are historically
distinct (the latter a pure Grecism, the former probably an archaism); other examples 1.
2. 31, 2. 7. 7-8, 2. 11. 15, 4. 8. 33, 4. 11. 5; with a finite verb, 2. 13. 38); **aquae . . .
sacrae**] i.e., the point where a spring gushes forth to form a stream (cf. 2. 3. 11-12, 2.
11. 18-20, 3. 13); such springs were commonly worshipped as the seat of a nymph or
other divinity.

23-8]   **multos castra iuvant**] *iuvant* picks up 4 'iuvat', with which the series began, for the
most paradoxical case of all: there are men who like war — lots of them; the modern
reader is perhaps surprised to see the soldier in such company, but the mood of the
Augustan age was to play down war, except as a necessary defence of national interest
(3. 2, 3. 5); *castra iuvant* stresses the glamour of active service (cf. 1. 7. 19-20). —
lituo . . . sonitus] i.e., the excitement of the sounds of battle; the *lituus* was a curved
horn used by cavalry formations, the *tuba* a straight horn used by infantry formations.
— **bellaque . . . detestata**] If men like war, the mothers of those who fight do not; the
thought seems characteristically Roman; cf. Catullus 64. 348-9, *Aen.* 8. 556, 9. 473-502,
11. 147; contrast *Epodes* 16. 8 'parentibusque abominatus Hannibal'; **matribus**] dative
of the agent; **detestata**] past participle of a deponent verb used passively (a mannerism
of Augustan verse); cf. 2. 6. 11. — **manet . . . plagas**] Last in the series comes the hunter
who stays out all night, thoughts of his young wife dispelled by the excitement of the
chase; for *manet* = 'pass the night' add *Sat.* 1. 5. 37 'In Mamurrarum lassi deinde urbe
manemus' to the examples in *OLD* 2a; for the idea cf. *Sat.* 2. 3. 234-5 'In nive Lucana
dormis ocreatus, ut aprum / cenem ego'; Cicero *Tusc.* 2. 40 'Pernoctant venatores in
nive' (as an example of acquired endurance); for Jove as the weather god, see on 1. 2. 2;
cf. 2. 3. 23; **tenerae**] the primary sense in H. is 'young' (cf. 1. 21. 1, 3. 24. 52, etc.); the
senses 'loving' and 'needing protection' are probably also present as overtones; for young
wives, see 2. 5I; **seu . . . fidelibus**] the hunter's dogs have started a deer and he is prepared
to spend all night tracking it down; **seu . . . plagas**] the boar, i.e., has broken free from
the net set to trap it and must be pursued; **teretes**] the basic sense seems to be 'round',
'smooth', hence 'thin', 'strong'; **Marsus**] H., as usual, particularises, locating his wild boar
in the territory of the Marsi, a mountainous region to the E of Rome famous for its
soldiers (2. 20. 18, 3. 5. 9).

29-34] H. likes introducing himself at a key point in the rhetorical structure of an ode;
cf. 1. 5. 13, 1. 7. 10, 1. 16. 22, 1. 31. 15, 4. 1. 29; here he depicts himself as the enthu-
siast whose obsession is as natural and as forgivable as the next man's. — **doctarum . . .
frontium**] = 'the ivy garlands which grace literate brows', i.e., recognition as a poet; the
ivy garland is associated with Bacchus (along with Apollo, the god of lyric poetry; see on
3. 25. 1) and is the traditional symbol of the poet (cf. *Eclogues* 7. 25, etc.); possibly,
poets in Augustan Rome actually wore such garlands while performing their works (much
as guests at a drinking party wore garlands; see on 1. 38), at any rate on such occasions
as those implied in *Epist.* 1. 19. 40-41 and 2. 2. 91-6; **praemia**] suggests some kind of
recognition was necessary before one could assume the garland of ivy; contrast 3. 30.
15-16, where the garland of bay leaves is the symbol of victory or success (as in athletic
etc. contests), and this seems to be the sense also in *Epist.* 2. 2. 96. cf. Lucretius 1.
929-30 (= 4. 45); *doctarum* (unlike, i.e., the 'unlearned' brows of athletes, etc.,) implies
the taste and mind well stocked with the work of his predecessors expected of an
ancient poet rather than erudition. — **dis miscent superis**] Cf. 6 'evehit ad deos'. —
gelidum nemus] The glade and the cave are traditional poetic haunts, perhaps evoking
the supposed pastoral origins of poetry; see on 2. 1. 39 and 3. 4. 40, also 4. 3. 11; cf.
Epist. 2. 2. 77; **gelidum**] 'cool', not 'chilly'. — **Nympharumque . . . chori**] The order of
H.'s symbols of poetic activity suggests a progressive retreat from reality into the fanciful;
for the Nymphs and Satyrs (both pastoral symbols) cf. 2. 19. 3-4; see also 1. 4. 5-6, 4. 7.
5-6 (for the Nymphs), 3. 4. 25, 4. 3. 15, 4. 14. 21 (for the dancing). — **secernunt populo**]

Cf. 3. 1. 1. − si . . . barbiton] The trappings of poetry just listed only cut off H. from the common herd (i.e., produce in him a state of exhilaration like that of the charioteer in the middle of the race) provided the Muses do not deny inspiration; for the *tibia* and the *barbitos* (= *lyra*) see on 1. 12. 1-2; for Euterpe and Polyhymnia see on 1. 12. 2 Clio; **Lesboum barbiton]** i.e., lyric poetry in the tradition of Sappho and Alcaeus; cf. 3. 30. 13; *tendere*, 'tune' (in preparation for playing).

35-6] For H., writing lyric (provided inspiration is not denied him) is in itself the intensest of pleasures and its own reward. But he wants others to think his work good, too − above all his patron: if Maecenas puts him on the same level as the great lyric poets of the past, his happiness will know no bounds. For the transition from modest understatement to cautious expression of hopes for lasting fame cf. Catullus 1. 9-10. − **quodsi me]** The emphasis falls this time on *quodsi* not on *me* (contrast 29 and 30 *me*). − **lyricis vatibus]** The lyric poets of ancient Greece; the list drawn up by the Hellenistic scholar Aristarchus contained nine names: Pindar, Bacchylides, Sappho, Anacreon, Stesichorus, Simonides, Ibycus, Alcaeus and Alcman; see Pfeiffer, *History of Classical Scholarship*, vol. 1, 205; **vatibus]** the old Roman word is revived to stress the inspired or prophetic power of the poet; cf. 1. 31. 2, etc.; overtones of irony seem nearly always detectable in H.'s use of the word (2. 6. 24, 2. 20. 3, 3. 19. 15); cf. *Epist.* 1. 7. 11 'vates tuos'. − **inseres]** i.e., add to the official list (or 'canon'); the future implies a judgement following perusal of *Odes* 1-3, now offered for the first time in collected form by H. to his patron; contrast the more confident note of 3. 30 and the assertion of acknowledged success in 4. 3. 13-15. − **sublimi . . . vertice]** H. will hold his head so high it will bump against the stars; an adaptation of a Greek proverb expressing joy re-establishes the easy, colloquial tone on which H. normally speaks to his patron.

1. 2

Introduction: After an urbane introductory poem to Maecenas, a laureate poem in honour of Augustus: long may he reign! Despite H.'s attempt in Stanzas 1-6 at something pitched on a subtler key than open flattery, the second half of the ode has to be accepted on its own terms as a rhetorical set piece, to be admired for the ingenuity with which the flattery is conveyed; the expression of true feeling is almost excluded by the ritual nature of the occasion (cf. the flattery of a formal eighteenth-century dedication to a royal patron), as is all sustained or intense effort of the poetic imagination. In any case, H., if not quite the deferential flatterer ironically depicted in *Epist.* 1. 13, has not reached the easy intimacy with Augustus of *Odes* 4. 5 or *Epist.* 2. 1.

Structure: Stanzas 1-3 constitute an appropriately elaborate statement of the minor theme, 'we Romans have been warned enough'; Stanzas 4-5, at first sight a variation on Stanza 3, deftly introduce the theme of unreasonable, destructive anger, which is reintroduced in more pointed form in Stanza 6. Lines 25-30 provide the transition to the major theme, 'what god can we look to help us in our plight?' (See below on these lines.) There can be only one answer, of course, but the formal rhetoric of the ode requires the rejection of three possible candidates (Apollo, Venus, Mars) before we reach the obvious choice − the god Mercury, whom we know as Augustus: long may he reign! (See below on lines 30-52.)

Metre: Sapphics

$$or \quad \underline{\quad}\underline{\quad} \cup \underline{\quad}\underline{\quad} \, \underline{\quad}\underline{\quad} \, \underline{\quad}\underline{\quad} \wedge \cup \cup \underline{\quad}\underline{\quad} \cup \underline{\quad}\underline{\quad} \, \cup \underline{\quad}\underline{\quad} \Big\} \; ter$$

$$\underline{\quad}\underline{\quad} \cup \underline{\quad}\underline{\quad} \, \underline{\quad}\underline{\quad} \, \underline{\quad}\underline{\quad} \cup \wedge \cup \underline{\quad}\underline{\quad} \cup \underline{\quad}\underline{\quad} \, \cup \underline{\quad}\underline{\quad}$$

$$\underline{\quad}\underline{\quad} \cup \cup \underline{\quad}\underline{\quad} \, \cup \underline{\quad}\underline{\quad} \quad \text{(Adoneus)}$$

In H.'s practice, syllable 4 of lines 1-3 is always long and there is always a caesura after syllable 5 or 6 (the latter, rare in *Odes* 1-3, is common in *Odes* 4 and *CS* − 6 cases in Book 1, 1 in Book 2, none in Book 3, 22 in Book 4, 19 in *CS*).

Elision after syllable 5 in lines 1-3 occurs only in 2. 4. 10, 2. 16. 26, 3. 27. 10, 4. 11. 27.

Synaphaea is usual (a line ending with a vowel, i.e., is not normally followed by a word beginning with a vowel in the next line of the same stanza); exceptions: 1. 2. 41, 1. 12. 6, 1. 12. 7, 1. 12. 25, 1. 12. 31, 1. 22. 15, 1. 25. 18, 1. 31. 5, 2. 2. 6, 2. 16. 5, 3. 11. 29, 3. 11. 50, 3. 27. 10, 3. 27. 33 (none of these involves a short syllable); elision at line-end occurs in 2. 2. 18, 2. 16. 34, 4. 2. 22, 4. 2. 23; word division at line-end occurs in 1. 2. 19, 1. 25. 11, 2. 16. 7.

1-4] We Romans have had enough warning; in a more moralistic context, H. would call upon his fellow-countrymen to mend their ways; here the occasion imposes a different rhetoric: divine assistance must be invoked (lines 25-30). Jove (the sky god and god of the weather in general — see 2. 6. 17-18, 2. 10. 15-17, 3. 10. 8) is in particular the god of the thunderbolt, with which he strikes terror into man and beast, as in *Georgics* 1. 328-34, *Aen.* 7. 140-2; cf. 1. 3. 40, 1. 12. 59-60, 1. 16. 11-12, 1. 34. 5-12. 3. 2. 29-32, 3. 3. 6, 3. 4. 74-5. Here the protracted stormy weather and the lightning which strikes the shrines are combined as equally portentous. Lucretius had given an elaborate explanation of thunder, lightning and thunderbolts (6. 96-534). In 1. 34 H. affects to have been converted from such misguided rationalism. The mood of the Augustan age was for a revival of religious beliefs (see 3. 6); not even Lucretius had objected to the use by poets of traditional imagery (2. 655-60). The image of the hand of Jove striking down the guilty from the sky was hard to resist; here Jove uses his thunderbolt as a portent (striking down buildings as a warning of the more direct action which will come if the warning is not heeded); Roman poets and historians alike are much given to the recording of such warnings; e.g., the detailed catalogue (following the assassination of Caesar) in *Georgics* 1. 466-88; cf. Tibullus 2. 5. 71-9, Ovid *Met.* 15. 779-99, Dio 45. 17. Note the -*is* alliteration in lines 1-2. — **Iam satis**] Emphatic, as in *Sat.* 1. 1. 120, 1. 5. 13, *Epist.* 1. 7. 16. — **terris**] = **in terras**; the dative in place of *in* or *ad* with the accusative is a frequent mannerism of the high style in Augustan verse. — **misit**] 'Has hurled'. — **rubente dextera**] Turns the conventional personification into a vivid image; cf. 3. 3. 6 'fulminantis magna manus Iovis'. — **sacras arcis**] Probably, the two summits of the Capitoline hill (the *arx* proper and the temple of Jove); for Jove to strike his own shrines is a particularly dire warning. — **iaculatus**] Cf. *Aen.* 1. 42, Ovid *Am.* 3. 3. 35. — **urbem**] Rome.

5-8] The focus shifts from warning of divine anger to apprehension of cataclysm. H. now sets the events of 1-4 in a context of myth and cosmic significance. The assertion that they are evidence of divine anger thus assumes the status of a poetic truth — not demanding acceptance with simple-minded literalness, but the expression none the less of ideas seriously held. — **terruit gentis**] The repetition for solemn effect; cf. 21 and 23 *audiet*, and 2. 14. 1, 4. 13. 1-2; **gentis**] the nations of the earth. — **saeculum Pyrrhae**] Pyrrha represents the classical version of the myth of universal flood. — **nova monstra questae**] Introduces an ironical note as a corrective to the grandiloquence of 1-4 and the solemnity of the repeated *terruit*; the *nova monstra* are the events specified in lines 7-12; H. focuses on the chaos of the flood (excluding Pyrrha's subsequent role, along with Deucalion, in repeopling the earth when the flood had subsided; for a full account, see Ovid *Met.* 1. 253-312); *questae* demythologises the legend by introducing a notion of realistic, everyday pathos. — **omne cum ... egit ... haesit**] When *cum* follows the principal clause ('inverted *cum*') the clause virtually acquires the status of an independent statement (*cum* = *et tum*, as *qui*, etc., often = *et ille*, etc.); a feature of the high style, though not confined to verse; cf. 1. 25. 13; **Proteus**] better known as the prophet who could change his shape, was also the guardian of Neptune's seals (see *Georgics* 4. 387-95); the hint of irony is intensified by the juxtaposition of Pyrrha and Proteus; we are to imagine Proteus driving his charges ('omne pecus egit') across the swollen waters of the flood on a sightseeing expedition (seals would not normally have the opportunity to visit mountain peaks); for *visere* cf. Catullus 11. 10 'Caesaris visens monimenta magni'; a freer use of the infinitive is characteristic of the common style of Augustan verse.

9-12] The ironical note continues in lines 9-10 (H.'s picture of the order of things subverted is not aimed at stressing the terror or the pathos of the events depicted) and is followed by a key-modulation in lines 11-12 into something closer to true pathos. — **piscium et**] The order (hyperbaton) belongs to the high style. — **summa ulmo**] The particularisation ('on top of a tall elm') heightens the irony; cf. Ovid *Met.* 1.296 'Hic summa piscem deprendit in ulmo'. — **et superiecto ... dammae**] Rhythm and word order end the 12-line sentence with an appropriate flourish; **pavidae dammae**] the deer is the symbol of the harmless, timorous animal; cf. 1. 32.

13-16] The first person *vidimus* comes as a sharp corrective to H.'s increasingly whimsical exploration of myth. As 19 'Iove non probante' makes clear, H. speaks no longer of portents (Stanza 1) or of cataclysm (Stanzas 2-3), but of the consequences of the unreasoning, destructive pursuit of revenge, no more than hinting as yet at the misguided division of Roman against Roman of which he will speak more plainly in Stanza 5. Father Tiber turning against his own city in response to the unreasonable

complaints of his wife (her sons, after all, became the founders of Rome) is the symbol
of the uxorious Mark Antony in revolt against his own country. (The translation 'flood'
for both the cataclysmic inundation of Stanzas 1-3 and the overflowing Tiber of
Stanza 4 links the two in the English reader's mind in a way which obscures the
rhetorical structure of the Latin: one is a manifestation of divine punishment, the other
of repressensible *violentia*.) H. need not have in mind any particular recent flood (it
would be odd if Tiber had waited 700 years to avenge his wife); more likely, we are to
think of periodic floods, from that at the time of the exposure of Romulus and Remus
onwards (Livy 1. 4. 4) — a persistent, brooding anger not sanctioned by Jove. The
historical foreshortening involved was no doubt more acceptable to H.'s contemporary
audience than to us (see on 3. 3. 37-44). — **Vidimus**] Gnomic, = 'we Romans have
seen' (i.e., more than once). — **flavom Tiberim**] The river is 'muddy' (because in flood;
cf. 1. 8. 8); but the context draws out also the sense of 'flaxen-haired Father Tiber' (cf.
1. 5. 4 'flavam comam'). — **retortis . . . undis**] 'his waves thrown back by the bank on
the Etruscan side'; the Tiber, i.e., instead of swinging SW (its normal course) spills NE
between the Capitoline and the Palatine hills into the Forum; **litore**] = *ripa*, *OLD* 1 c;
the sense of the passage has from time to time been oddly misunderstood from anti-
quity onwards. — **deiectum**] Supine. — **monumenta regis templaque Vestae**] The temple
of Vesta, said to have been built by Numa; *monumenta* and *templa* refer to the same
complex of buildings, seen from a different point of view; Ilia had been a Vestal Virgin
before her seduction by Mars; for *monumenta* see on 3. 30. 1-2.

17-20] Ilia (= Rea Silvia), the legendary mother of Romulus and Remus, was seduced by
Mars; H. makes her the wife of Tiber (according to other forms of the legend she was
the wife of the river Anio), presumably on the strength of the story that she was thrown
into the Tiber following the (supposed) death of her children; cf. 3. 3. 30-33, 3. 9. 8;
contrast Livy's drily sceptical version (1. 3. 11-47). — **Iliae querenti**] Dative with
iactat. — **dum . . . iactat . . . labitur**] There is a strong tendency in all forms of classical
Latin to prefer the historical present in *dum*-clauses where the sense is 'whilst' (perhaps
for greater vividness, perhaps also to distinguish such clauses from those where the
sense is 'until', in which the actual occurrence of the event is stressed); *iactat* suggests
the literal sense ('throws himself around'), while the figurative sense is drawn out by the
dative *Iliae querenti* and by *se ultorem* ('vaunts himself to complaining Ilia as her avenger');
vagus] 'spreading in all directions'; often of rapid or violent motion (unlike English
'wandering'); chosen here to intensify the conflict between the naturalistic picture of
the Tiber in flood and the fanciful picture of the god taking drastic action as a result of
his wife's complaints. — **uxorius**] Pejorative, as in *Aen.* 4. 266-7 'pulchramque uxorius
urbem / exstruis'; the division *u* / *xorius* is a traditional licence of the Sapphic stanza
(see above on Metre); cf. Catullus 11. 11-12 'ulti / mosque Britannos'.

21-4] Parallel to Stanzas 4-5, as is pointed to by the anaphora of 13 *vidimus*, 21 *audiet*
(each the first word in its stanza), but the shift from perfect to future brings a sterner
note. — **audiet, audiet**] Like *vidimus*, refers to an indefinite number of occasions; for
the repetition, see on 4-5 *terruit*. — **acuisse ferrum**] i.e., to have armed themselves for
war; **ferrum**] the Latin idiom in such cases is to prefer the singular (the citizens having
one sword each), unlike English, which prefers the plural ('sharpen their swords'). —
quo . . . Persae . . . perirent] The Parthians are regularly referred to by H. (with no more
than tenuous historical justification) as *Persae* or *Medi* (cf. 51 *Medos*); the obstacle which
the Parthians represented to Roman hegemony in the East is thus made to seem of the
same order as the threat to Greek civilisation represented by the Persian invasions of the
fifth century. The defeat of Crassus at their hands at Carrhae in 53 was conventionally
held an abiding disgrace (see on 3. 5), their more recent successes over the forces of
Mark Antony (see on 3. 6. 9-12) ⟶ther proo⟨ tha⟩ the menace must finally be quelled;
the need for a final decisive victory is a recurring theme, clearly reflecting official prop-
aganda at the time of publication of *Odes* 1-3; 'the swords which had been better (i.e.,
more properly) turned against the Parthians' are those which Antony turned against his
fellow-Romans. — **audiet pugnas**] 'will hear of battles', *OLD* 8. — **vitio parentum rara
iuventus**] The internecine slaughter of the Civil Wars will mean that the population of
Rome in the next generation will be much reduced; H. thinks only of the old Roman
families (not of the flood of aliens to Rome); *parentum* = *parentium*.

25-30] The central stanza of the poem and the turning point from minor to major theme.
The assumption that only a god can save Rome and the suggestion in Stanza 11 that

Augustus is that god depend heavily on the mythical context built up in Stanzas 1-5 and the accompanying mode of thought, which provide a rhetorical structure within which gods can plausibly be appealed to, so that the only question becomes 'to which god do we turn?'

The tempo now becomes more urgent; the triple question *quem? . . . prece qua? . . . cui? . . .* (anaphora in asyndeton) suggests a tricolon crescendo, but the third member 'cui . . . Iuppiter', which might be expected to occupy the whole stanza, is cut short, as though interrupted by the sudden direct entreaty 'tandem venias precamur'. — **quem . . . divum**] Probably *divum* is better taken as genitive plural; **vocet**] deliberative subjunctive, like 26 *fatigent.* — **ruentis imperi rebus**] = 'to bolster the fortunes of state on the verge of collapse; *imperi* = the organised structure of government; *rebus* is dative of advantage. — **minus audientem Vestam**] Praying for the State was one of the duties of the Vestal Virgins; **minus audientem**] perhaps 'less and less', but more likely = less than she did before the wrong done Ilia (another example of historical foreshortening — see on 13-16). — **carmina**] Their ritual entreaties: *carmen* = any formally structured (hence normally metrical) discourse. — **cui dabit partis . . . Iuppiter**] 'to whom will Jove assign the role . . .'; whereas mortals are uncertain what to do, Jove's intervention is certain (contrast the indicative *dabit* with the subjunctives *vocet* and *fatigent*); i.e., Rome's destiny, is assured and Jove the agent of destiny (see on 3. 4. 53-64); only the identity of her saviour remains in doubt; **scelus**] that the Civil Wars represent the working out of an ancestral curse is a recurring theme in Augustan poetry; see on 3. 6. 1-4; **expiandi**] though the Civil Wars are over, the burden of guilt remains and must be expiated (a reference to Augustus' policy of moral and religious reform); cf. 2. 1. 4-5.

30-52] The elaborate syntactical structure is the vehicle of a subtly contrived rhetorical structure. Apollo's aid is first solicited (lines 30-32); the possibility is next raised that Venus (legendary mother of Aeneas and the divine ancestor of the Julian house into which Augustus had been adopted) may prefer to assume the task (lines 33-4); or perhaps Mars has taken pity on his descendants (35-40); or perhaps our saviour will turn out to be Mercury, disguised as Caesar; if so 'serus in caelum redeas' etc. (41-50). After 33 'sive tu mavis', we expect an apodosis parallel to 30 'tandem venias precamur'; similarly after 35-6 'sive . . . respicis'. In fact, however, the prayer is no longer for the god's coming (which is now taken for granted) but for his long-continuing presence on earth.

Simultaneously, the role of Rome's saviour shifts from expiation of ancestral guilt (29 'partis scelus expiandi') to revenge for the murder of Julius Caesar. By 49 *tollat* the transition to prayers for the long life of a saviour already here on earth has been effected. Protocol excluded explicit address of Augustus as a god (though his divine ancestry through Julius was officially recognised), but obliquely worded compliments in which divinity was assumed or tactfully foreshadowed were not discouraged, and almost obligatory in a formal address such as the present. The complex sentence in which the situation shifts as the sentence develops, so that what could not be plainly asserted is in the end asserted after all, was a recognised rhetorical strategy, wholly acceptable here where no real deception is intended — the discerning reader is interested in how H. will get away with saying what has to be said with appropriate subtlety.

30-40 **nube candentis umeros amictus**] 'his shining shoulders clothed in cloud', as he descends in an epiphany from Olympus; cf. *Il.* 5. 186 νεφέλη εἰλυμένος ὤμους '; for the syntax see on 1. 1. 21-2 'membra stratus'; Apollo was very much to the fore in Augustan religious reforms; for a story circulated by his enemies of Augustus at a dinner party dressed as Apollo, see Suetonius *Aug.* 70. — **augur**] Cf. *CS* 61 'augur . . . Phoebus'. — **Erycina**] As protectress of her temple at Eryx in Italy (named after Venus' brother). — **ridens**] Venus is regularly represented as smiling; see on 3. 27. 67. — **quam Iocus circum volat**] As in Roman wall-painting. — **neglectum genus**] The misfortunes of Rome are proof of Mars' neglect. — **respicis**] 'have regard for'; cf. 1. 15. 22. — **auctor**] Mars, the father of Romulus and Remus and thus of the Roman race. — **nimis longo satiate ludo**] i.e., even Mars, whose appetite for war is traditional (cf. 1. 28. 17), may tire of the protracted bloodshed of the Civil Wars and come to Rome's assistance; **satiate**] elaborate vocatives of this kind (in prose a relative clause would be normal) are a traditional mannerism of the high style of verse; cf. 2. 3. 4, 2. 6. 1, 2. 7. 2, etc. — **quem iuvat**] Almost 'though you take pleasure in'. — **Marsi peditis**] A correction of the *Mauri peditis* of the MSS; for the Roman legionary of rustic stock, see on 3. 6. 37-44; cf. 2. 20. 17-18, 3. 5. 9.

41-4] sive mutata figura] The assistance of Apollo, Venus or Mars is speculative and in the future; a fourth possibility is that the god is already here, having provisionally taken on human shape; for the device of arriving, as if spontaneously or by accident, at a predetermined goal, see on 3. 11. 25 and 3. 27. 25. — **iuvenem]** The word for a man in full possession of his bodily faculties, especially in a heroic context (Catullus 64. 4 'lecti iuvenes' of the Argonauts, *Aen.* 1. 627 of Aeneas and his men); any age, therefore, between 17-18 and 40 or so; Augustus (two years younger than H.) was turning 32 at the time of Actium, in his early forties at the time of publication of *Odes* 1-3 (his relative youthfulness compared with the other leaders in the Civil Wars is of course an obvious distinguishing characteristic); when too old for active service, one passes from the status of *iuvenis* to that of *senex*, whereas *vir* (of a grown man) is virtually free from limitations of age; in the common style of Augustan verse, *adulescens*, the ordinary prose word for 'young man', is avoided (not used by either H. or Virgil), *iuvenis* being used instead; the translation 'young man' of *iuvenis* is sometimes, therefore, appropriate (e.g., 1. 6. 18, 4. 4. 24, perhaps 1. 25. 2, 3. 9. 3), but is often apt to mislead; the translation 'a youth' is almost always misleading (though the use of the English word 'youth' in the sense of grown men has become part of the cant of heroic rhetoric in certain contexts — it is the nation's youth which dies in battle, etc; for this sense H.'s word is *pubes* (3. 5. 18, 4. 4. 46); similarly, the translation 'youth' of *iuventus* and *iuventas* (see on 3. 4. 50, 2. 11. 6); when H. means 'a youth', he says *puer*; see Austin on Cicero *Cael.* 1. 2; for *puer*, see on 1. 5. 1. — **ales]** Mercury is always represented as the winged god (because of his winged sandals). — **imitaris]** Present of the deponent, not future active; the saviour, in other words, is perhaps already here; H., so to speak, makes an inspired guess. — **almae filius Maiae]** *filius* is nominative because the phrase operates as a condensation of 'tu qui es filius' etc., not as a vocative; only names and phrases which are regarded as part of the actual form of address are treated as vocative; for qualifiers of an imperative or 2nd-person subjunctive, etc. the nominative is preferred (cf. 45 'serus redeas', 46 'laetus intersis'); there is naturally room for choice either way, though phrases like 37 'satiate' are obvious poetic artificialities. — **Caesaris ultor]** i.e., the youth (he was then 19) who came to the fore as the avenger of the murder of his adoptive father is perhaps the man chosen by Jove to save Rome; note that the hypothesis of the poem requires the assumption that the crisis threatening to engulf Rome still threatens, but it is beginning to be realised that Augustus is the heaven-sent saviour.

45-8] serus redeas] i.e., instead of becoming a god, Augustus is to rejoin the gods (a more extravagant compliment); cf. the discreet references to Augustus' apotheosis in 3. 3. 11-12, 3. 25. 6; see also 3. 2. 21-4. — **Quirini]** Originally a Sabine deity, later identified with Romulus (as in 3. 3. 15). — **iniquum]** = 'in disgust'. — **ocior . . . tollat]** Romulus, according to an account which Livy 1. 16. 2 reports with proper scepticism, was 'sublimem raptum procella' (a traditional fate); *ocior*, though in form a comparative, frequently = simply 'swift'; perhaps a guarded reference to Augustus' serious illness of 23 BC which forced him to relinquish the consulship.

49-52] A final laureate stanza. **pater]** = *pater Populi.* — **princeps]** The title was officially conferred in 28 BC. — **Medos]** See on 22 *Persae.* — **equitare]** The Parthians were cavalrymen. — **inultos]** 'unpunished'; the adjective is formed from the past participle (treated as passive; cf. 1. 1. 25) + *in*; cf. 2. 1. 26, where the meaning is 'unavenged'. — **te duce]** Cf. 1. 7. 27 'Teucro duce'. — **Caesar]** Emphatic position.

1. 3

Introduction: After Maecenas (1. 1) and Augustus (1. 2), Virgil, who first introduced H. to his patron (*Sat.* 1. 6. 54-5). A farewell poem (Virgil is off to Greece) with some thoughts on foreign travel and misplaced human ingenuity in general. Virgil again in 1. 24 and 4. 12.

The propemptikon or *bon voyage* poem commonly struck a disapproving or a cautionary note — reproaching a friend for heartlessness in deserting you, or warning him of the dangers that lie ahead; cf. 3. 27. Here, one suspects it is more a case of one poet showing another what he can do by grafting a mock-solemn diatribe against the wrongness of progress (a favourite theme of the elegists) on to a propemptikon.

The voyage cannot be that which Virgil embarked on in 19 BC and which ended in his death; whether an earlier journey is referred to, or a project which was abandoned, there is no way of telling.

Structure: The propemptikon proper (Stanzas 1-2) takes the form of an elegantly worded request to the ship which is to convey Virgil; the diatribe against the foolhardiness of the first navigator (Stanzas 3-6) ends on a fine note of moral indignation, which prepares the way for the denunciation of human enterprise in general (Stanzas 7-9); the poem concludes with a resounding climax in Stanza 10.

Metre: Asclepiad (b); the first of twelve odes in which a glyconic

$$\underline{\quad}\ \underline{\quad},\ \underline{\quad}\ \cup\cup,\ \underline{\quad}\ \cup\,\bar{\cup}$$

alternates with the basic Asclepiad line

$$\underline{\quad}\ \underline{\quad},\ \underline{\quad}\ \cup\cup,\ \underline{\quad}\ \bigwedge\ \underline{\quad}\ \cup\cup,\ \underline{\quad}\ \cup\,\bar{\cup}$$

— the metre of 1. 1; the others are 1. 13, 1. 19, 1. 36, 3. 9, 3. 15, 3. 19, 3. 24, 3. 25, 3. 28, 4. 1, 4. 3. Though the metrical pattern is thus the distich, the syntactical organisation of these odes and the fact that all conform to Meineke's canon suggest the basic structural unit is the 4-line stanza, and they are commonly printed accordingly (so Teubner, not *OCT*); on Meineke's canon, see 1. 1M.

1-8] Virgil's ship, like countless others, both before it (no doubt) and after, is a living creature — if not able to speak, like Catullus' *phaselus* (Catullus 4), at any rate able to listen and act on instructions; cf. the ship in 1. 14. — **Sic regat**] *sic* imposes a restriction on the wish expressed, as in our 'So help you God!'; H.'s wish for a good voyage is conditional on the ship's handing over Virgil safe and sound to terra firma at the conclusion of the voyage; the ship is thus treated as a person to whom a friend has been entrusted for safekeeping; *sic* = 'to this end', therefore, more than 'on this condition', but the lines are designed as a witty expression of H.'s affection for his friend rather than as the expression of an entreaty to be taken seriously; for the construction cf. 1. 28. 25; see Quinn on Catullus 17. 5; for very different wishes in a propemptikon, see *Epode* 10. — **diva potens Cypri**] The Venus marina of 3. 26. 5, 4. 11. 15; cf. 1. 5. 16; Cyprus was the most famous of her homes; with the genitive cf. 1. 5. 16. — **fratres Helenae**] Castor and Pollux, familiar as protectors of those at sea (cf. 1. 12. 25-32, 4. 8. 31-2). — **lucida sidera**] Either in their role as the constellation Gemini, or as the phenomenon of St Elmo's fire (described as *stellae* by Seneca *NQ* 1. 1. 13 and Pliny *NH* 2. 101), apparently referred to by Cinna ('lucida cum fulgent summi carchesia mali') and perhaps a commonplace of the propemptikon; for Castor and Pollux, see on 3. 3. 9. — **ventorumque pater**] Aeolus. — **regat**] = 'take command of', i.e., 'watch over'. — **obstrictis**] 'kept confined' by Aeolus in their mountain dungeon as in *Aen.* 1. 52-86. — **Iapyga**] Iapyx is a nor'westerly, the ideal wind for a ship sailing from Brundisium across the Adriatic (about 95 km of open sea) to the gulf of Corinth (ESE to the coast of Epirus, then SSE along the coast); cf. 3. 27. 20. — **creditum debes**] The language of accountancy: Virgil has been deposited with the ship, which is therefore responsible for safekeeping and surrender on the instructions of the depositor (for an interesting echo, see on 1. 24. 11-12). — **finibus Atticis reddas**] Attic territory comes within a few km of the Isthmus of Corinth; Virgil will disembark at Corinth and continue his journey by land (or take ship again on the other side of the Isthmus; cf. Propertius 3. 21); the total distance Rome—Athens is about 1600 km, less than a quarter of it by sea. — **animae dimidium meae**] 'he who is half my *anima*' (as we say, 'without whom life is not worth living'); cf. 2. 17. 5; in *Sat.* 1. 5. 41-2 H. speaks of Virgil and other friends as 'animae qualis neque candidiores / terra tulit, neque quis me sit devinctior alter'.

9-16] **Illi ... erat**] 'that man had heart of oak and triple-plated bronze about his *pectus*'; a rewording of traditional material describing stoutness of heart, perhaps also a witty allusion to the hull of the trireme which was to take Virgil (a VIP in a man of war?) — very unlike the frail craft of lines 10-12; cf. the *aerata triremis* of 3. 1. 39; see also 2. 16. 21; **pectus**] according to the Epicureans, the site of the intelligence as well as the emotions; hence often 'mind' as much as 'breast' or 'heart'; cf. 2. 10. 15, etc.; denunciation of the inventor of a practice considered nefarious is a traditional commonplace; cf. Tibullus 1. 10. 1, etc.; it is used here as a variation on the equally familiar commonplace in which the first ship to sail the seas is denounced (Ovid *Am.* 2. 11. 1, etc.); as a further variation, the courage (however misguided) of the first navigator, rather than his moral turpitude, is stressed — a more tactful approach in the present case, the moral point being held over till Stanza 6; cf. 3. 24. 36-44. — **praecipitem Africum**] 'the sou'westerly hurtling down upon him'; cf. 1. 1. 15. — **decertantem Aquilonibus**] = 'fighting it out with one northerly after another', i.e., as in a cyclone when the wind keeps shifting; cf. 1. 9. 10 'ventos deproeliantis'. — **tristis Hyadas**] 'the grim Hyades'; seven stars of the constellation Taurus, traditionally associated with rain. — **Noti**] Notus, or Auster, is the southerly, described as the chief 'arbiter Hadriae' because the Adriatic is exposed to the south. — **Hadriae**] a traditionally stormy sea; also 1. 33. 15, 2. 14. 14, 3. 3. 5, 3. 27. 19.

17-20] The first sailor is imagined on his first voyage. — **Quem ... gradum**] 'What approach of death did he fear?', i.e., when was he ever afraid if not now? — **siccis oculis**] i.e., without shedding tears of terror; the Greeks and Romans wept more frequently and held weeping less shameful than we do. — **monstra natantia**] cf. Europa in 3. 27. 25-8. — **Acroceraunia**] 'the Headlands of Thunder', noted for storms and shipwrecks, in Epirus, and in Virgil's path, therefore, if he followed the usual course to the east; cf. Gyges in 3. 7. 5.

21-4 H. moves on from the courage of the first sailor to make a moral point, the impiety of navigation; the note of witty overstatement which we sense in the preceding lines now becomes apparent. — **Nequiquam**] More emphatic than *frustra*; only here and 1. 15. 13 and 16; *frustra* five times in the *Odes*. — **abscidit**] 'separated off' (land and sea having been mixed in the primeval chaos); cf. Ovid *Met*. 1. 23 'Nam [deus] caelo terras et terris abscidit undas'. — **prudens**] 'in his wisdom'. — **dissociabili**] 'incompatible'. — **transiliunt**] 'leap (lightly) over'; cf. 1. 18. 7.

25-8] The denunciation of navigation in Stanzas 3-6 is used as a springboard for the even more sweeping denunciation of progress in Stanzas 7-9 in preparation for the climax of Stanza 10. H. approaches here the kind of wit of which Ovid was to make himself the past master; the polemical, moralising note of, e.g., Tibullus 1. 10 is thus absent — **Audax omnia perpeti**] = 'able to endure all ordeals undaunted'; *perpeti* is emphatic, 'to endure to the end'; this use of an infinitive to extend and define an adjective, as in Greek, is common in the Odes. — **gens humana**] *gens* = 'nation', 'race' (cf. 28 *gentibus*), *genus* 'tribe', 'offspring'. — **ruit ... nefas**] All forms of progress towards civilised life are thus represented as sinful and forbidden by the gods. — **Iapeti genus**] Prometheus, who stole fire from the gods and is represented by Aeschylus as a benefactor of mankind condemned to suffer by a jealous Zeus, is here represented as an impudent thief whose gift to mankind brought only harm; cf. 1. 16. 13-16.

29-33] **post ignem subductum**] 'after the theft of fire'; cf. *ab urbe condita*, 'after the foundation of the city'; see on 1. 1. 5-6 — **macies ... gradum**] i.e., mankind, which had hitherto been healthy and as good as immortal, now became subject to all our present ills; **incubuit**] 'fell upon'; **semotique ... leti**] 'and the slow necessity of death, till then a remote contingency'.

34-40] The logic of the concluding lines dispels any lingering thought that H. means us to take them seriously: Daedalus' attempt at flight is treated as another instance of human presumption, on the same footing as Hercules' descent to the underworld (to kidnap Cerberus) — the last of the Twelve Labours and a symbolic defiance of death itself. — **expertus ... aera**] 'Daedalus essayed the empty air'; cf. 2. 20. 13, 4. 2. 2-4. — **perrupit**] The final syllable counts as long (lengthening in arsis); cf. 1. 13. 6, 2. 6. 14, 2. 13. 16, 3. 5. 17, 3. 16. 26, 3. 24. 5 — all 3rd person singulars. — **Herculeus labor**] This use of the adjective instead of the genitive of a proper name is a feature of the high style; cf. 1. 4. 17, 1.34. 11, 3. 1. 7, 4. 2. 9, etc. — **Nil ... est**] = 'Nothing is beyond us mortals'; what in a different context would sound like praise is given an ironical twist. — **caelum ... petimus**] Equates the sin of Daedalus with the assault on Olympus by the Giants and Titans (see on 3. 4. 42-68). — **iracunda fulmina**] 'his angry thunderbolts' = 'the thunderbolts Jove resorts to when angry' (transferred epithet); for the thunderbolt of Jove, see on 1. 2. 1-4.

1. 4

Introduction: The first of H.'s spring odes (cf. 4. 7, 4. 12). Winter is over, life is coming back into the world; it is a time for joy; death is never far away, let us make the most of life before it is too late.

The coming of spring is a familiar theme of Hellenistic poetry; among Roman parallels the closest are Lucretius 1. 1-16 and 5. 737-47 (the latter, like *Odes* 4. 7, is a description of the cycle of the seasons, beginning with spring).

Structure: Stanzas 1-2 describe the spring scene — first, the real, everyday world (Stanza 1), then a fancifully stylised picture of the world of nature and myth (Stanza 2). Stanzas 3-5 urge joyful celebration (Stanza 3) and, at the same time, willingness to learn the lesson of spring (Stanzas 4-5). For the rhetorical structure of lines 9-17, see on these lines.

Metre: Archilochean (a) (only here in H.). The long lines consist of a dactylic hexameter down to the bucolic diaeresis (i.e., the first four feet), followed by three trochees:

$$\text{\_\_\_} \cup\cup, \text{\_\_\_} \cup\cup, \text{\_\_\_} \wedge\cup\cup, \text{\_\_\_} \cup\cup | \text{\_\_\_} \cup, \text{\_\_\_} \cup, \text{\_\_\_} \bar{\cup}$$

The short lines are iambic trimeters catalectic:

$$\bar{\cup} \text{\_\_\_}, \cup \text{\_\_\_}, \bar{\cup} \wedge \text{\_\_\_}, \cup \text{\_\_\_}, \bar{\cup} \text{\_\_\_}, \bar{\cup}$$

The effect of the movement to and fro between different metrical patterns is perhaps to symbolise the equivocal nature of spring and H.'s reaction to it. Organisation in 4-line stanzas seems clear (see on 1. 3M). There are no elisions.

1-4] *Solvitur*] i.e., it is the time of the spring thaw and preparations for warmer weather ahead; cf. 10 *solutae*, 1. 9. 5 *dissolve*. — **acris**] Balances *grata*. — **grata vice**] Spring, i.e., is merely a new phase (though a welcome one) in a continuing series. — **Favoni**] *Favonius* is the Roman name for Zephyrus, the mild west wind of spring. — **machinae**] 'windlasses'; the ships have been laid up during the winter. — **neque . . . igni**] The cattle and sheep which have been kept inside all winter and are now restive; soon some will be at work (pulling the plough, e.g.), all look forward to fresh pastures; their impatience is shared by the ploughman who has spent the winter by his fireside. — **prata . . . pruinis**] The fields, i.e., which the ploughman is impatient to plough and the animals to graze upon; a last look at winter after the images of restlessness and activity in the preceeding lines.

5-8] We move from the everyday scene to the world of fancy, into which the imagination of the sophisticated observer transposes the rural scene before his eyes; cf. 1. 17. 1-4, 3. 18. 1-4; that world too is a mixture of pleasures and tasks resumed. — **Cytherea Venus**] Venus, as the generative force in nature (the *alma Venus* of Lucretius 1. 1-4), is the presiding goddess of spring (cf. Lucretius 5. 737 'it ver et Venus'); *Cytherea* (after Cythera, an island off the coast of Laconia; cf. 3. 12. 5) shifts the focus, however, from this very Roman Venus to the more glamorous, more frivolous Greek Aphrodite, whose attributes the Roman goddess takes over, at any rate in the literary imagination. — **choros ducit**] 'leads the dancing'; cf. 4. 7. 5-6. — **imminente Luna**] The (full) moon is imagined leaning out of the sky to watch; but Luna is also a goddess, here not directly identified with Diana (see on 3. 22. 2-4; cf. Cicero *Tusc*. 1. 92). — **Nymphis**] Personifications of natural objects — rivers, trees, mountains. — **Gratiae decentes**] The Graces were probably old vegetation goddesses, represented by H. as comely (*decentes*) rather than glamorous figures; in art they appear sometimes naked, sometimes robed; also 1.30. 6, 3. 19. 16, 3. 21. 22, 4. 7. 5; **decentes**] cf. 1. 18. 6 (Venus), 3. 27. 53 (Europa). — **alterno pede**] = 'beat the ground, first with one foot, then the other', in a simple rustic dance, like that in 3. 18. 15-16, as the heavy spondaic rhythm suggests (this line is the only one in the poem to begin with five long syllables); contrast the corrupt sophistication of 3. 6. 21. — **dum . . . officinas**] Vulcan is Venus' husband; he goes off to work while his wife plays — spring represents a mixture of work and pleasure for the divine world also; for the foundry of the Cyclopes (beneath Mt Etna), see *Aen*. 8. 416-53; the rhetorical structure allots *gravis* to *officinas* rather than to *Volcanus* — the word describing those who work in the foundry rather than the foundry itself: 'heavy-footed', 'serious-minded' (unlike the light-footed, frivolous dancers) seem the right connotations; **ardens**] 'blazing' (i.e., with burning eyes and face afire — Vulcan is the god of fire), but also 'keen', *OLD* 3-6; **visit**] of a divine visitation (cf. 3. 28. 15), but also with ironic overtones of a visit of inspection; the variant *urit* has little to commend it; **officinas**] a calculatedly prosaic word, to round off the fantasy.

9-17] The succinct, spare rhetorical articulation of these lines repays attention; the redoubled *nunc decet* creates a sense of urgency; 13 *pallida Mors* explains that urgency and effects a vivid transition to 15-17, which offer (after the plangent *o beate Sesti*) a dry, explicit statement of the need to make the most of life before it is too late (*vitae . . . longam*), followed by the more pathetic, more fanciful *iam . . . Plutonia*. — **Nunc decet**] 'Now's the time'; the time meant is not the moment of the thaw but the spring that lies ahead, as *flore . . . solutae* makes clear; we pass, i.e., to a general statement about spring as a time of joy and thanksgiving. – viridi myrto] The myrtle garland and the gleaming head suggest a party, the spring flowers suggest a picnic (like that in 2. 3 or 2. 11); for the myrtle garland, see on 1. 38. 5 (where it connotes avoidance of fuss and extravagance, cf. 2. 7. 25); being an evergreen, it is always available. – nitidum] i.e., gleaming with hair oil; see on 1. 5. 2; cf. 3. 19. 25. – flore . . . solutae] i.e., spring flowers; the singular flos can have a collective force (OLD 1 b – cf. our 'foliage'); usually qualified by a genitive, here by the relative clause; thus 3. 29. 3 'cum flore rosarum' practically = 2. 3. 14 'flores rosae'; cf. 3. 15. 15, 4. 10. 4; the force of the plural terrae is to suggest the flowers which will soon be springing up everywhere on the orbis terrarum. – nunc et decet] 'now's the time too'. – Fauno] Faunus, a god of the countryside, likely to be present at any time (in the summer, 1. 17. 3, in the late autumn, 3. 18); unlikely that H. has in mind the sacrifice in mid-February mentioned by Ovid Fasti 2. 193 etc.: that is an urban festival and in umbrosis lucis continues to emphasise the rural setting; flore . . . solutae is not consistent with mid-February. – seu poscat . . . haedo] For the animals used in sacrifice, see on 3. 23. 4; lamb being dearer than goat or pork, the sense seems to be 'a lamb, if he insists; a kid, if he is content with that'; the 'modest lamb' of 2. 17. 32 is by contrast with the sacrifice to be expected from Maecenas; in 3. 18. 5 Faunus is promised a haedus; poscat, malit] subjunctive, perhaps, because the circumstances of the sacrifice are indefinite and the god's wishes as yet undetermined. – pallida Mors] Death personified is visualised as looking like the shades of the dead in the underworld (cf., e.g., Aen. 4. 26 'pallentis umbras'). – aequo pede] That Death awaits rich and poor alike is a commonplace of ancient literature; cf. 2. 3. 21-8, 2. 14. 9-12, 2. 18. 32-4; round this trite reflection (strengthened by Epicurean overtones stressing the need to enjoy life while we can) is built one of the most striking passages in the Odes; aequo both of the even, unvarying sound of Death's knock and because Death visits all classes without distinction; cf. 2. 18. 32. – pulsat] Some hold that the ancients kicked at doors instead of knocking; more likely, kicking was reserved for imperious demands for entry; cf. Sat. 1. 1. 10 'Sub galli cantum consultor ubi ostia pulsat'. – tabernas] Single-room apartments in larger structures, hence 'shops', 'hovels'. – regumque turris] 'princes' castles'; regum need not have the common sense 'merchant princes' (as 2. 14. 11 and, probably, 2. 18. 34), turris may refer to real palaces; but the connotations of the phrase easily expand to cover the extravagant mansions of the rich (cf. 2. 15. 1 'regiae moles'), a frequent theme in H. (add 2. 10. 7-8, 3. 1. 45 to references above). – o beate Sesti] The break in mid-line and the formal vocative suggest an impassioned note; L. Sestius, a sound Republican but a minor figure, became consul suffectus upon Augustus' resignation of the consul-ship 1 July 23 BC; clearly, the ode follows odes for Maecenas, Augustus and Virgil for that reason; we thus have a terminus a quo for the publications of Books 1-3; for a terminus ad quem, see on 2. 10. – vitae . . . longam] An appropriate reflection for one entering upon high office; cf. 1. 11. 6, 2. 16. 1; inchoare = especially, 'to begin what may be left unfinished'; cf. Catullus 35. 13 and 18. – iam . . . nox] 'soon night will be upon you'; for the night of death cf. Catullus 5. 5 'Nobis cum semel occidit brevis lux, / nox est perpetua una dormienda'. – fabulaeque Manes] 'the storied Manes' – i.e., of whom so many tales are told; see on 3. 4. 9. domus Plutonia] 'Pluto's unsubstantial house' – i.e., lacking in substance, like everything in the underworld; cf. 4. 7. 16; for the adjectival Plutonia, see on 1. 3. 36; the imagery is conventionally poetic – no belief in the reality of the underworld is implied, rather the contrary; for a moderate statement of contemporary rationalist attitudes, see Cicero Tusc. 1. 10-12 'Dic quaeso: num te illa terrent, triceps apud inferos Cerberus, Cocyti fremitus, traiectio Acherontis, "mento summam aquam attingens enectus siti Tantalus", tum illud quod "Sisyphus versat / saxum sudans nitendo neque proficit hilum"? fortasse etiam inexorabiles iudices, Minos et Rhadamanthus?' etc.; for a more forceful statement, see Lucretius 3; we can assume that for H., as for Lucretius and Cicero, death meant annihilation; the conventional language provides none the less a valid poetic code for the expression of genuine feeling; cf. 2. 3. 25-8, 2. 13. 21-40, 2. 14. 17-20, 3. 4. 69-80.

17-20]   quo simul mearis] Cf. 4. 7. 21 'cum semel occideris'; simul = simul atque as 1. 9. 9, 1. 12. 27, etc. – regna . . . talis] 'you will not draw lots to choose a magister bibendi'; it was his duty to set up the rules for the drinking – the proportion of wine to water, etc.; cf. 2. 7. 25-6; see on 3. 8. 13, 3. 19. 11-12; a symbol of social life and its pleasures; tali are knuckle bones used as dice. – nec . . . mirabere] 'nor will you admire young Lycidas'; for the Greek name, see on 1. 5. 3; it is the name of one of the shepherd singers in *Eclogue* 9; nothing need be inferred about Sestius' personal tastes — everybody admires Lycidas. — **quo . . . tepebunt**] A slackening of the tension which began after the climax at *Plutonia* now becomes more apparent; Lycidas is approaching the ambiguous age where he is equally attractive to both sexes; he is thus perhaps a concluding symbol of change in a poem about change; see on Nearchus in 3.20; cf. Gyges in 2. 5. 20-24 and Ligurinus in 4. 10; **calet . . . tepebunt**] his male admirers are openly passionate, the reaction of the girls will be more discreet — it will be Lycidas' turn to take the initiative; with *calet* cf. 4. 9. 11 'calores'; **iuventus omnis**] = 'all the men' (not 'all the youths' — see on 1. 2. 41).

1. 5

Introduction: The first love poem in the collection. The theme is a frequent one in H.'s love poetry: the battle of the sexes as waged between unequal partners — here inexperienced boy attempting the conquest of a girl experienced in such encounters, well able to cope with the situation as long as it amuses her. With Pyrrha compare Lydia in 1. 8, Barine in 2. 8, Pholoe in 3. 15 and the Gaetulian lioness of 3. 20. Other types are the ageing flirt (Lydia in 1. 25, Chloris in 3. 15, Lyce in 4. 13), the innocent, inexperienced girl (Lydia, apparently, in 1. 13, Chloe in 1. 23, Lalage in 2. 5, Neobule in 3. 12). For more equally matched partners, see 3. 9.
Structure: Lines 1-5 sketch in the situation. The remainder of the ode represents the unwinding of H.'s thoughts as they pass from prediction in the form of two exclamations in asyndeton (5 *quotiens . . .* !, 12 *miseri quibus . . .* !) to reminiscence (lines 13-16).
Metre: Asclepiad (d); the basic Asclepiad line

$$\text{——} \ \text{——,} \ \text{——} \ \cup\cup, \ \text{——} \ \Lambda \ \text{——} \ \cup\cup, \ \text{——} \ \cup\,\bar\cup$$

(the metre of 1. 1) is repeated; a pherecratean

$$\text{——} \ \text{——,} \ \text{——} \ \cup\cup, \ \text{——} \ \overset{\cup}{——}$$

and a glyconic

$$\text{——} \ \text{——,} \ \text{——} \ \cup\cup, \ \text{——} \ \cup\,\bar\cup$$

(the metre of 1. 3. 1, etc.) complete the stanza.
1-5]   A question discreetly sets the stage: the girl is a familiar figure, her latest lover is not (see on 9 *fruitur*). For an opening question as a device of launching a poem cf. 1. 9, 1. 24, 1. 29 (a string of questions), 1. 31, 2. 7, 2. 17, 3. 7, 3. 8, 3. 20, 3. 25, 3. 28, 4. 1; cf. the string of indirect questions in 1. 8. — **multa in rosa**] Rose petals scattered around for their fragrance or forming a bed on which to lie while drinking, etc., are a traditional symbol of luxurious living; the boy, i.e., has spared no expense; see Levens on Cicero *Verrine* 5. 27. 2; cf. 3. 19. 22; in 1. 38. 3, 3. 29. 3 the reference is more likely to garlands of roses, as in 2. 11. 14 and perhaps 1. 36. 15; observe that the description of scene and participants fixes the question as (1) one asked by an observer (not, i.e., the absentee's 'who is kissing thee now?'), (2) one Pyrrha is not expected to answer (she is otherwise engaged). — **gracilis puer**] 'slip of a youth'; *gracilis* suggests slender build, fragility, more than gracefulness; **puer**] where *iuvenis* denotes a man in the full possession of his physical powers (see on 1. 2. 41), *puer* implies youthfulness, often with protective or affectionate overtones (as, e.g., 3. 9. 16); cf. 1. 9. 16, 1. 13. 11, 1. 27. 20, etc.; thus especially of a young slave (1. 29. 7, 2. 11. 18, etc.); like *puella,* occasionally applied with some generosity (see on 4.1. 15). — **perfusus . . . odoribus**] Continues the impressionistic technique of 'multa in rosa' with increased emphasis on extravagance and lack of restraint; both *perfusus* and *odoribus* are pejorative (cf. *Epodes* 17. 23; contrast the neutral *odoratus* of 2. 11. 15, 3. 20. 14); *liquidis* implies the gleam of hair oil (cf. *nitidus* 1. 4. 9, 3. 19. 25); Roman men used scent (2. 3. 13, 2. 7. 23, 3. 14. 17 — especially scented hair oil, 1. 29. 7-8, 2. 7. 8, 2. 11. 15, 3. 20. 14, 3. 29. 4) on social occasions; the exotic provenance of the scent is stressed (2. 7. 8, 2. 11. 16) and expensiveness implied (4. 12. 14-16); cf. Catullus 10. 11 and 13. 11-14; **urget**] 'importunes'; see on 2. 9. 9; the boy, i.e., is courting Pyrrha with confidence and success (see on 9 *fruitur*). — **grato sub antro**] = 'in this attractive grotto'; some kind of artificial cave seems to be implied, conducive perhaps of illusions of an idyllic pastoral background; cf. the caves in *Eclogues* 6. 13 and 9. 41 and the cave where Dido and Aeneas meet, *Aen.* 4. 165; caves similarly provide

a conventional 'pastoral' backdrop for poetic inspiration or performance (see on 2. 1. 39; cf. 3. 4. 40, 3. 25. 2-4); *grato* emphasises the lushness of the scene and perhaps hints that real-life caves are not always romantically attractive. — **Pyrrha**] A Greek name does not necessarily mean a foreigner (Sybaris in 1. 8 is obviously a Roman or Italian of good family; cf. Neobule and Hebrus in 3. 12 — and Catullus' Lesbia); while such names may occasionally conceal the identity of a real person (a mistress of H., e.g., who actually existed, like Catullus' Lesbia or, probably, Propertius' Cynthia), their function more often seems to be (1) to warn the reader that the person spoken of or addressed is to be regarded as typical of a class; they are thus sharply distinguished from those addressees (all men) who are named by their real names and usually historically identifiable; (2) chosen, at least in some cases, as a pointer to character or appearance (Pyrrha = 'yellow-haired', Lalage = 'prattler'), as often in English eighteenth-century literature, occasionally to place of origin (Barine, 'the girl from Bari'); Licymnia in 2. 12 is usually regarded as a special case; nothing can be inferred from such names about social or marital status; many clearly are (or are to be imagined as) *adulterae* (see on 1. 15. 9 *moechos*) rather than *meretrices*; Pyrrha is clearly being courted (not offering her services for payment) in something that will develop into a liaison, from which she will break loose when she is minded to; the situation, i.e., is not unlike that in Tibullus 1. 8. 28-52: Marathus, described as a boy and unbearded, is involved, in his first affair, with an experienced woman called Pholoe, whom Tibullus urges to be co-operative and not ask for gifts; Pholoe is presumably married since the affair is spoken of as a clandestine one; here, the boy's (temporary) open, uncontested possession (10 *vacuam*) suggests Pyrrha is unattached (more the type of Barine, the irresistible, utterly faithless *femme fatale* of 2. 8). — **cui flavam religas comam?**] 'for whom do you bind back your yellow hair?' — as a provocative gesture, and as an assertion of detached control of the situation; Phyllis (2. 4. 14) and Chloe (3. 9. 19) are also described as *flavae*; **religas**] in 2. 11. 24 and 3. 14. 22 binding back the hair is a preparation for action; here smoothing or combing back hair that has perhaps become ruffled seems to be implied; Ovid *Ars* 3. 133-54 on hairstyles (a section beginning with the words 'munditiis capimur') speaks of the active, no-nonsense style, 143 'altera succinctae religatur more Dianae'; **comam**] the whole head of hair (contrast *capilli, crines*). — **simplex munditiis**] Implies the chic conferred by sure, simple taste — and also that the simplicity is an illusion; cf. Propertius 4. 8. 40 'munda sine arte'; Pyrrha, i.e., is not overdressed like Lyce in 4. 13. 13-14; for the appositional expansion spilling over into the following stanza cf. 4. 11. 5.

5-16]   The remainder of the poem consists of a single long sentence, representing the unwinding of the poet's thoughts as he observes the scene. The *puer*'s uncomprehending amazement when Pyrrha unleashes her raging temper is represented by a metaphor in which she becomes the sea, its calm surface, now glistening and inviting, soon to be tossed by storm winds, and the *puer* an innocent young sailor now putting to sea for the first time.

5-8]   Heu = 'Alas!' introducing a reaction of pity, etc., as in 2. 14. 1, 3. 2. 9 *eheu*; *heu* (1. 2. 37, etc.) is the commoner form in the Odes. — **quotiens . . . insolens**] Introduces a carefully phrased prediction: the boy is on the threshold of a liaison which will last for some time — he will have to endure Pyrrha's anger, not once but many times, before the final shipwreck; **fidem . . . flebit**] = 'he will tearfully complain she has broken faith and the gods have turned against him'; i.e., each time she turns on him in a fit of anger; **mutatosque deos**] ironically lends cosmic significance to what we are implicitly invited to see in a different perspective; *mutatos* with both nouns, as often in the *Odes*; for —*que*, see on 2. 19. 28 *mediusque*; **nigris ventis**] storm winds are black; see on 3. 7. 1 *candidi*; **emirabitur**] 'will look upon in utter wonder'; for the unusual, striking polysyllable (a calculated occasional effect of the ironic style) cf. 1. 9. 11 *deproeliantis*, 2. 14. 11 *enaviganda*; **insolens**] 'in his innocence'; the objection of Bentley and others that *insolens* is inconsistent with *quotiens* (we can only be wholly innocent the first time) need not be pressed — as H. goes on to point out, it isn't until you're shipwrecked that you really understand; elsewhere (1. 16. 21, 2. 3. 3, 2. 4. 2, 3. 29. 50) *insolens* = 'insolent', 'arrogant'; perhaps a suggestion here too that to protest the gods have turned against you when a girl loses her temper is presumptuous.

9-12]   We move back out of the metaphor into epithets appropriate to the girl. — **te fruitur**] 'possesses you'; i.e., is Pyrrha's acknowledged lover for the time being; the implication is that the scene of lines 1-4 is not a first, preliminary encounter, but a scene from an early stage in the affair when all is as yet going well. — **aurea**] 'shining like gold', 'resplendent'; an epithet of Venus in *Aen.* 10. 16, applied by Cynthia to herself in her epitaph, Propertius 4. 7. 85; no doubt a reference to the glamorous creature before H.'s eyes; but probably also predicative, 'in your present sunny-tempered mood'. — **vacuam**] 'available', his uncontested mistress; see on 1. 6. 19. — **amabilem**] 'lovable' cf. 2. 9. 13, 4. 3. 14; his love i.e., will turn to hate. — **nescius aurae fallacis**] An unexpected revival of the sea metaphor, in preparation for Stanza 4, 'with no knowledge of how a breeze can deceive' (by turning into a gale — the *nigri venti* of line 7); cf. *Aen.* 5. 850 (Palinurus) 'credam fallacibus auris?'; but *aura* is also the word for 'charm', that which fascinates about a woman; cf. 2. 8. 24; see on 13 *nites.* — **miseri . . . nites**] Grammatically, the statement relates to Pyrrha, but the words used are applicable also to the sea on a sunny day; *miseri*, 'poor', 'wretched', 'unlucky', is the stock epithet of the lover, either in the anguish of unrequited love, or (as here) when tormented by an imperious mistress; cf. 1. 27. 18, 3. 12. 1, Propertius 1. 1. 1; see on 3. 12. 1; the connotations are 'to be pitied', 'getting more than he bargained for', rather than those suggested by English 'wretched'; **quibus nites**] 'whom your radiance attracts' — i.e., Pyrrha's present admirers and prospective victims; cf. Barine in 2. 8. 7-8 on whom all eyes turn when she goes out; *nites*, like *aura*, evokes the mistress-as-goddess cliché; the beloved manifests herself to the lover as a goddess manifests herself to her worshipper, surrounded by a special effulgence and emitting a special fragrance; cf. 1. 19. 5, 2. 5. 18, 4. 11. 5; (of men) 3. 3. 25, 3. 12. 6; **intemptata**] 'unassailed'.

13-16]   The rhetorical structure binds the concluding lines to those preceding by opposing H.'s hard-earned wisdom to the innocence of Pyrrha's present and future victims; the movement of thought is thus from prediction to reminiscence; at the same time the metaphor of the sea once more occupies the foreground; H. is the old sailor (i.e., the experienced lover) who has been shipwrecked in his time (i.e., only just managed to disengage himself from a disastrous love affair), now a cynical realist about such matters; we need not assume H. wants us to think of him as a former lover of Pyrrha (he may simply regard himself as an authority on the type) or as now retired from the pursuit of love as in 3. 26 (not all sailors who have been shipwrecked give up the sea), though the former is the more economical assumption in both cases; of the poems about love immediately following, 1. 13 represents H. as struggling to preserve avuncular detachment, 1. 16 and 1. 17 are not inconsistent with the status of one retired from serious involvement (cf. 1. 6. 19-20); in 1. 19 H. finds himself (to his surprise) passionately in love again. The intricate, balanced word-order of the concluding lines produces a rallentando consistent with the emotional detachment asserted. — **me**] Emphatic; cf. 1. 1. 29, 1. 7. 10, 1. 28. 21, etc. — **tabula votiva**] 'by means of a votive tablet', recording, i.e., the circumstances of the *votum*, with perhaps a picture of the shipwreck; cf. *Sat.* 2. 1. 32 (of Lucilius) 'quo fit ut omnis / votiva pateat veluti descripta tabella / vita senis'. — **sacer paries**] Cf. 3. 26. 4-6, Plautus *Men.* 143 'vidisti tabulam pictam in pariete', Cicero *Verr.* 4. 122 'iis tabulis interiores templi parietes vestiebantur'. — **uvida vestimenta**] Cf. *Aen.* 12. 768 (of an ancient olive) 'servati ex undis ubi figere dona solebant / . . .et votas suspendere vestis'; *uvida* ironically emphasises the promptness of the dedication — **potenti maris deo**] 'to the potent divinity of the sea'; it would be doubly appropriate if H.'s offering had been to Venus marina (as in 3. 26) and some alter *deo* to *deae* to secure this; sedulous avoidance of the obvious point is more consistent, however, with H.'s practice of ending his odes on a low key (cf., e.g., 3. 5. 55-6, 4. 2. 59-60); while *deo* suggest Neptune rather than Venus, it is possible that H. uses the word in the sense 'divinity' (male or female, cf. Greek θεός), like Virgil, apparently, in *Aen.* 2. 632 *ducente deo* (also of Venus); see Austin on the passage in Virgil; Servius quotes Calvus, 'pollentemque deum Venerem'.

1. 6

Introduction: A polite, modestly-worded verse epistle to M. Vipsanius Agrippa (the commander of Augustus' fleet at Actium, appointed his official deputy during Augustus' illness in 23 BC), confessing H.'s total incapacity for epic poetry in any form, and his inability, therefore, to celebrate the feats of arms of the forces under Agrippa's command: the task will have to be left to Varius.

The epic poem celebrating the exploits of a leading statesman or soldier was an exercise in public relations and indeed the only kind of poetic activity, apart from the drama, whose social function was widely recognised. Serious poets naturally regarded such poems as hack work (a debasement of the old Roman tradition of historical epic created by Naevius and Ennius), and the polite disclaimer on grounds of incapacity (*recusatio*) is a common theme (see, e.g., the proemium to *Georgics* 3, Propertius 2. 1). It is not necessary to suppose that Agrippa had invited H. to be his poetic biographer and that 1. 6 is H.'s public refusal: 'I would if I could' is a sufficient compliment if it comes from a poet whose talents are known to lie in other directions, particularly if (as in the present case) the disclaimer is given a place of honour in a strictly limited exclusive series (following poems to Maecenas, Augustus, Virgil and Sestius, preceding an ode addressed to a senior *consularis*). The occasion alluded to in Stanza 1 is probably Agrippa's recent appointment as area commander in the East and the exploits those of the Roman forces under his command in the widely advertised final show-down with the Parthians (see 3. 21).

For Agrippa as a critic of poetry, see his forthright views on the *Aeneid* as reported by Suetonius *Vita Verg.* 205-7R.

Structure: The ode is organised around two related binary oppositions: 1 'Scriberis Vario') ('nos neque haec dicere . . . conamur': 13 'Quis . . . digne scripserit?') ('nos convivia, nos proelia virginum . . . cantamus'). The first (Stanzas 1-3) states the *recusatio* in negative terms, the second (Stanzas 4-5) contrasts the impossibility of adequate treatment of heroic prowess with H.'s own modest themes.

Metre: Asclepiad (c); the basic Asclepiad line —

$$\underline{\quad}\ \underline{\quad},\ \underline{\quad}\ \cup\cup,\ \underline{\quad}\ \bigwedge\ \underline{\quad}\ \cup\cup,\ \underline{\quad}\ \cup\,\bar{\cup}$$

is repeated twice and then followed by a glyconic —

$$\underline{\quad}\ \underline{\quad},\ \underline{\quad}\ \cup\cup,\ \underline{\quad}\ \cup\,\bar{\cup}$$

1-4] **Scriberis Vario**] = 'You will be celebrated by Varius'; the natural interpretation is that Varius' poem (a historical epic) has already been announced; less likely (especially in view of the place of honour alloted the ode) that H. means 'apply to Varius'; L. Varius Rufus, the leading epic poet of the day (Virgil's *Aeneid* is still being written), friend of H. and Virgil (and literary executor of the latter); along with Virgil, he introduced H. to Maecenas (*Sat.* 1. 6. 55, cf. *Sat.* 1. 10. 81); accompanied H. on his journey to Brundisium (*Sat.* 1. 5. 40); *scribere* = 'write about' (cf. 14 *scripserit*), hence in the passive = 'to be written about'; *Vario* is best taken as dative of the agent (an alternative to the ablative with *ab*, rare with finite verbs, a feature of the high style of verse); its function here is perhaps to de-emphasise Varius in favour of *scriberis*. — **fortis . . . victor**] = 'a brave soldier and the conqueror of our enemies'. — **Maeonii carminis alite**] = 'on the wings of epic poetry'; *Maeonii* = like that of Homer, the creator of epic, from Maeonia, the old name of Lydia; (Homer being traditionally born in Smyrna in Lydia); some link *Vario* and *alite*, taking both as ablative, but this is less natural; the reading *aliti* is against the MSS and inelegant. — **quam . . . gesserit**] The phrase looks to the future, either because Agrippa's career is not yet over, or, more likely, because H. has in mind especially the new phase of it which is just beginning; **ferox miles**] = 'the brave forces under your command' (*te duce*, grammatically a modifier of *gesserit*, like *navibus aut equis*, defines the forces meant); collective singular, as in 3. 5. 5. — **navibus aut equis**] Agrippa was, of course, the hero of the naval battle at Actium (see, e.g., *Aen.* 8. 682-4) and Varius' poem would doubtless refer to his exploits in the battle; but his present command (assumed 23 BC) was likely to involve combined operations (maintaining control in the East generally, the coming campaign against the Parthians) and the primary reference here is probably to these; any campaign against the Parthians would naturally involve cavalry.

5-9] H. never writes epic (neither historical epic, nor mythological epic) because he is no good at it. — **nos**] = I; the plural is more formal than the singular (though less formal than in English) but very frequent, stressing one's role as a political or literary, etc., figure (as opposed to the private individual); contrast 1. 1. 29 'me' and 4. 2. 27 'ego'. — **haec dicere**] = 'deal with such subjects in verse'; *dicere* (used, like *canere*, of all forms of verse) preserves the fiction of oral performance (cf. 1. 17. 19, 3. 25. 7-8) as 19 *cantamus* preserves the fiction of lyric performance. — **gravem . . . Ulixei**] = 'the wrath of Achilles and the wanderings of Ulysses'; the subjects of the *Iliad* and the *Odyssey*, i.e., poetry on Homeric themes; **gravem stomachum**] ironic oxymoron — *stomachum* debunks (cf. 1. 16. 16); *gravem* emphasises the consequences of Achilles' stubborn pique; **cedere nescii**] 'unable to relent', i.e., his protracted refusal to help the Greeks (until the death of his friend Patroclus); **duplicis**] 'wily'. — **saevam Pelopis domum**] The 'cruel house of Pelops' (more familiar to us as a repertoire of themes for tragedy) symbolises epic poetry on mythological themes other than those of the Homeric cycle. — **tenues grandia**] *tenues* picks up *nos, grandia* summarises 'neque haec nec gravem . . . domum' to emphasise the basis for his disclaimer ('these are mighty themes and my talent is a slender one').

9-12] The present *conamur* stresses it is H.'s settled practice to avoid epic (not a decision reached in Agrippa's case alone); *tenues grandia* summarises his views on the matter; he now proceeds to give his reasons more fully. — **dum . . . vetat**] i.e., 'unwillingness to make a fool of myself (*pudor*) and lack of inspiration have always prevented me'; according to the usual Latin idiom, the present *vetat* (like the present *conamur*) denotes a state of affairs beginning in the past and still continuing, whereas English prefers the perfect; **inbellisque . . . potens**] 'a Muse whose power is confined to the unmartial lyre'; *inbellis* is best taken as a stock epithet (lyric poetry, i.e., cannot cope with warlike themes), not as implying a deficiency peculiar to H.'s lyric poetry; the lyric poetry of Alcaeus on material themes and H.'s own occasional ventures in the Cleopatra Ode (1. 37) and the Roman Odes (3. 1-6) hardly invalidate the generalisation; polite disclaimers are not meant to be closely scrutinised. — **laudes . . . ingeni**] i.e., 'detract from the glory of your achievements and those of our Emperor by writing bad epic poetry about them' (H. might successfully allude to them in his lyric poetry, but full-scale treatment must be left to Varius); reference to the achievements of Augustus as the theme above all others for epic poetry is *de rigueur* in a *recusatio;* **deterere**] 'blunt'.

13-16] No poet can do justice to heroic deeds. One might take this as harsh criticism of Homer: H., if pressed, would presumably have replied that the qualities of the *Iliad* lie elsewhere (in Homer's humane compassion, his moral insight, his poetic imagination, etc.). We have to remember it is a general who is being addressed. — **Martem . . . adamantina**] i.e., the God of War, presiding over the battle, a stock theme never adequately treated; for *adamantina*, see on 3. 24. 5. — **scripserit**] Picks up 1 *scriberis*, 'could celebrate'. — **pulvere Troico nigrum**] 'black with the dust of the plain of Troy'. — **Merionen**] The charioteer of Idomeneus; cf. 1. 15. 26; why H. singles him out for mention twice is not clear (an allusion to a poem now lost, or as minor figure set against major figure in an impressionistic evocation of scene?). — **ope . . . parem**] In *Il*. 5 Diomede, with the help of Athena, takes on Aphrodite and Ares in single combat, wounding both.

17-20] H. modestly describes his themes as those of sympotic and erotic lyric — the conventional image of the lyric poet in the ancient world before H., and probably pretty much Agrippa's view of the level of seriousness of lyric. Such a description hardly does justice to H.'s own achievements (or even to the odes immediately preceding and following 1. 6), but the etiquette of the occasion prescribes self-depreciation; for some of the occasions when H. tried his hand at encomiastic *lyric*, see 1. 2, 1. 12, 1. 32, 2. 1, 4. 2. — **proelia virginum**] As opposed to the *proelia* of heroes more familiar to Agrippa. — **sectis . . . acrium**] = 'formidable opponents for us men to have to face with their sharpened fingernails'; **sectis**] trimmed to a sharp point (rather than pared and therefore harmless, as some editors); the long pointed nails are cultivated by society beauties as an adornment, of course, but when it comes to a fight they have their uses; **in iuvenes**] with *sectis* (ironically implying the nails are deliberately sharpened for combat) as well as with *acrium*; for the sense of *iuvenis*, see on 1. 2. 41; the *rixae* of Augustan love poetry tend to deal more with male aggression (doors smashed, dresses torn, etc. — see 1. 13. 9-12, 3. 14. 25-6), but H. likes sometimes to view the familiar scene from a fresh perspective (see 3. 12I). — **cantamus**] See on line 1; cf. 1. 22. 10, etc. — **vacui**] Points to H.'s favourite role as detached observer of the human comedy; *vacuus* = 'not paired-off in love', 'unattached' (as Pyrrha in 1. 5. 10 is 'unattached' and therefore available to receive the *puer's* attentions), and thus 'uninvolved'; so 1. 32. 1; cf. H.'s role in 1. 8 and 1. 13 — and his surprise at the return of passion in 1. 19. — **sive . . . leves**] = 'or if I fall in love, no more than customarily foolish'; **sive quid urimur**] the fire is the fire of passion, but the reformulation ('or if a trifle passionate') undercuts the cliché; **non praeter solitum**] i.e., not exceeding the norm of those who fall in love; **leves**] i.e., lacking in *gravitas* (the characteristic Roman virtue); contrast 4. 9. 8.

1. 7

Introduction: An after-dinner conversation (or the like) with a distinguished friend, elegantly reconstructed as lyric — the first half discursive, the second exploiting traditional rhetorical structures (the mythological *exemplum*, the set speech) to extract a moral comment appropriate to the occasion and congenial to H.'s way of life and cast of thought. (See on lines 19-21 for an alternative interpretation.)

L. Munatius Plancus, consul in 42 (the year of Philippi — see on 3. 14. 28) was a senior *consularis* at the time of publication of *Odes* 1-3, in his sixties and very much an elder statesman; it was Plancus who had proposed the title Augustus in the Senate in 27; he was to be censor (along with Paullus Remilius Lepidus) in 22; his last military appointment seems to have been as governor of Syria, about 35 BC. Cicero *Fam.* 10 contains 23 letters from and to Plancus and an open letter (10.8) from Plancus to the Roman people.

Structure: Lines 1-14 set up a formal, extended binary opposition leading into the main theme (the figure sometimes called 'priamel' or preamble); lines 1-9 form a tricolon decrescendo (1 Laudabunt . . .', 5 'sunt quibus . . . ', 8 'plurimus dicet . . . '); 10 'me . . . ' introduces the second arm of the binary opposition which continues until line 14. At line 15 a bridge passage begins unannounced with an abrupt transition from the style of conversation improved upon to something closer to that of traditional lyric; this prepares the ground for the mythical exemplum (lines 21-4) and the formal set speech (lines 25-32) which follows, apparently unconnected with the opening lines but in fact a transposition into a different key of a comparable situation (see on 25-32).

Metre: Archilochean (b); dactylic hexameters alternating with dactylic tetrameters; variation between dactyl and spondee (and therefore in syllable-count) is permitted. The case for arrangement in 4-line stanzas is rather stronger than that for arrangement in couplets. The same metre in 1. 28; cf. 1. 4 and 4. 7.

1-4] See Structure. The tricolon decrescendo provides an elegant restructuring of the relaxed talk of a man who is in a mood to be urbanely ironical at the expense of those who praise the famous cities of Greece. — **Laudabunt alii**] 'Let other praise'; the future indicative expresses a quasi-imperative (as often) rather than a prediction; the point of view of the speaker, and therefore the sense to be attributed to his opening words, are fixed by lines 10-14, when it becomes clear that *alii* is not distributive (= 'some', correlative with 5 'sunt quibus') but = 'others than I' — Italians who affect to prefer the cities of the Greek world to Italy; seven tourist attractions of the Hellenistic world are reeled off in rapid succession. — **claram Rhodon**] *claram* = both 'shining' (bathed in sunshine) and famous; cf. Catullus 46. 6 'Ad claras Asiae volemus urbes'; Rhodes, noted in H.'s day as a centre of learning, was much visited by wealthy Romans anxious to attend the lectures of famous professors. — **Mytilenen**] The principal city of Lesbos. — **Epheson**] Famous for the mysteries. — **bimarisve Corinthi moenia**] Corinth, on an isthmus, has the sea on either side; the walls are probably those destroyed by Memmius in 146 BC. — **Thebas**] Traditionally associated with Dionysus (the scene of Euripides' *Bacchae*). — **Delphos**] Site of the oracle of Apollo. — **Tempe**] The famous 'vale of Tempe'; cf. 1. 21. 9, 3. 1. 24; neuter plural.

5-7] Lines 1-4 dismiss the travel snob, lines 5-7 deal with the culture snob — the poet who is content with traditional hackneyed themes from the Greek-speaking world (instead of writing about the world he lives in, as H. does); the satirical note (H. speaks as a cultural nationalist) becomes more apparent. — **sunt quibus unum opus**] 'there are those whose only concern'; for the construction cf. 1. 1. 3; *unum* is emphatic. — **intactae Palladis urbem**] i.e., Athens; the periphrasis parodies the style of the poetasters derided. — **carmine perpetuo**] 'in never-ending poetry'; more likely one poem after another than one long poem (though Ovid so describes the *Metamorphoses*, *Met.* 1. 4); for *carmen*, 'poetry', rather than 'poem' cf. 3. 28. 13, 3. 30. 13. — **undique decerptam olivam**] An ironic ambiguity, (1) = 'the ubiquitous olive' (the olive, i.e., that grows everywhere in Attica and is therefore available on all sides for weaving a garland), (2) 'the olive picked by all' (i.e., the common reward of all who write on that well-worn theme, the praises of Athens).

8-9] Finally, the long-winded, learned writer of hymns (probably aetiological hymns in the manner of Callimachus and his imitators). — **plurimus**] 'long-winded', 'boring'; for *multus* in this sense, see Quinn on Catullus 112.1; the superlative in this sense perhaps only here; many take = *plurimi*, but this gives weak sense; for the movement from plural to singular cf. 1. 1. 3 'sunt quos . . .', 7 hunc . . .', 9 'illum . . .', 19 'est qui . . .', 23 'multos'. — **in Iunonis honorem**] With both *plurimus* and *dicet*. — **aptum dicet . . . Mycenas**] = 'will sing the praises of Argos and Mycenae'; for *dicet*, see on 1. 6. 5; *aptum equis* and *ditis* represent traditional epithets of Argos and Mycenae (seats of the worship of Hera).

10-14] In H.'s opinion, however, there is no place like Tibur — the scene (as it will appear from lines 20-21) of the dramatic monologue. — **me**] For *me* introducing the second arm of a binary opposition cf. 1. 1. 29, 1. 5. 13, 1. 28. 21, etc. — **nec tam, nec tam**] Introduces a further pair of famous beauty-spots (completing the round dozen); picked up by 12 *quam*. — **patiens Lacedaemon**] Sparta, noted for the sober restraint of its inhabitants. — **Larisae campus opimae**] 'fertile Larissa'; the honorific epithet is again traditional. — **percussit**] 'impressed'. — **domus . . . rivis**] Four scenic attractions in the area around Tibur (Tivoli): (1) the temple of Albunea, said to be the last of the Tiburtine Sibyls (nymphs personifying the springs of sulphurous water below Tivoli); (2) the falls of the river Anio; (3) the sacred wood of Tiburnus (a founding hero of Tibur); (4) the orchards watered by irrigation channels from the Anio (*mobiles* because the water can be redirected from one channel to another at will); for Tibur and its waters, see also 1. 18. 2, 2. 6. 5, 3. 4. 23, 3. 29. 6, 4. 2. 31, 4. 3. 10; there is no certainty that H. had a house at Tivoli (2. 6. 5-6, and *Epist.* 1. 8. 12 are inconclusive; 4. 2. 30-32 and 4. 3. 10-12 perhaps less so; 2. 18 11-14 seem to settle the matter; Suetonius *Vita Horat.* 66 ('domus ostenditur circa Tiburni luculum'), if more than local legend, must refer to a period later than Odes 1-3); Tibur perhaps provided a staging point (Tibur is about 25 km NNE of Rome) on his way to and from his Sabine farm (several km further on into the hills) where he could pass the night with friends — in the present instance, perhaps with Plancus (21 'Tiburis tui' suggests we are to think of Plancus as H.'s host); in any case (if the interpretation of 19-20 is correct) Tibur is the setting of the present monologue.

15-21] The fact that H. and Plancus are relaxing together in Tibur justifies the praise of Tibur as a beauty-spot in 12-14 and permits the general reflection on life which now follows; there is a noticeable rise in the rhetorical level at this point. — **Albus . . . Notus**] 'Just as often a fine southerly sweeps away the clouds from an overcast sky'; i.e., even Notus (a wind more often associated with rain) *can* bring a spell of fine weather; cf. 2. 9 for a similar argument; winds bringing fair weather are 'white', storm winds are 'black'; cf. 3. 7. 1, 3. 27. 19. — **sic**] Both picks up 15 *ut* and serves a deictic function (= 'as you are now doing'). — **sapiens**] = 'if you are sensible'. — **finire . . . labores**] = 'don't forget to keep the anxieties and stresses of life within limits'; i.e., take a break from them occasionally; **finire**] 'set limits to', 'keep within bounds', not 'put an end to'; **memento**] cf. 2. 3. 1; **tristitiam . . . labores**] *tristitia* covers a range of connotations from 'cares', 'anxieties' to the attitude of mind these produce ('depression') and the reaction they produce ('grim determination') to face up to them; *labores* is always a strong word ('toil', 'stresses'); H. is to be imagined, no doubt, as in part flattering Plancus (the statesman and man of action) and in part reacting to his present surroundings (by contrast with which the cares of life are easily exaggerated). — **molli mero**] i.e., by the application of wine, which mellows all things: the usual remedy in the *Odes*, though the word-order here makes the prescription somewhat unexpected (a hint, perhaps, not to take the grandiloquence of the preceding lines too seriously). — **seu te . . . tenent, seu . . . tenebit**] Hard; the best interpretation is 'whether the life of the soldier on active service has a hold on you, or whether you find that the life of retirement in Tibur will not let you go'; i.e., Plancus (though at the moment relaxing in Tibur) has been, is, and may go on being a soldier, or he may decide to stay in Tibur and retire; 'fulgentia signis castra' stresses the glamour and attraction of military service, while simultaneously setting up a symbolic contrast between the soldier's life and the obscurity of retirement ('densa Tiburis umbra tui'); at the time of publication of *Odes* 1-3, Plancus' days of active service were almost certainly a thing of the past, though he might still hope for a proconsular post, but in polite conversation (especially with the great) the Romans were readier than we are to regard flattery as a social obligation which it would be as boorish to deny as it would be foolish to take the flattery seriously; Plancus can thus go on being treated as a soldier long after his campaigning days are over; as it turned out, his appointment as censor settled the matter for him; many assume that 'seu te ... tenent, seu ... tenebit' must mean that Plancus is not at Tibur (but may come in the future); this detroys, however, the obvious parallel with Teucer and makes interpretation of the ode as a consistent whole extremely difficult.

21-4] Teucer, the transposition to the heroic scale of the man of action who knew how to relax, represents the common strategy of proof via mythological *exemplum*; cf. 1. 8. 13-16. — **Salamina ... cum fugeret**] = 'during the period of his exile from his native Salamis and his father'; he was banished by his father after returning from the Trojan War without his brother Ajax. — **tamen**] i.e., despite the 'tristitiam vitaeque labores' of his wanderings as an exile — **uda Lyaeo tempora**] The periphrasis is in the heroic manner, though more mock-heroic ('his wine-steeped temples') than seriously poetic. — **populea ... corona**] i.e., he put on the garland of poplar leaves before making his speech.

25-32] The circumstances of Teucer's speech are left to be inferred from the obvious parallel with H.'s speech to Plancus (*tristis* picks up 18 *tristitiam*), the hints provided by lines 21-2 and the speech itself, especially 32 *cras*; Teucer and his men are relaxing ashore during a break in their wanderings (perhaps only overnight); cf. Aeneas' speech to his men, *Aen.* 1. 198-207 and the Centaur's speech to Achilles, *Epodes* 13. 12-18). — **quo nos cumque**] Tmesis, = 'quocumque nos'; see on 1. 32. 15 — **melior fortuna parente**] = 'a fate kinder to me than my father was'. — **o socii comitesque**] Most editors place a comma after *ibimus*, but the stronger pause, by throwing the vocative into association with 'nil desperandum', gives a more plangent and convincing effect. — **Teucro duce et auspice Teucro**] To speak of oneself by name or in the third person belongs to the rhetoric of the high style; according to the usual idiom, H. adapts the foreign situation to Roman institutions and nomenclature; the reading *auspice: Teucri* (dative) adopted by *OCT* is well-established, but gives an awkward rhythm. — **certus Apollo**] 'Apollo who does not err'; i.e., Apollo at his oracle at Delphi. — **ambiguam Salamina**] i.e., 'a second Salamis, to rival the first'. — **o fortes peioraque passi**] A second, more plangent vocative; cf. Virgil's 'O passi graviora', *Aen.* 1. 199. — **vino pellite curas**] Picks up 19 'molli mero' cf. 1. 18. 3-4. — **cras ingens iterabimus aequor**] A flourish of rhetoric, to end speech and poem, strengthened by the tension between the grandiloquence of *ingens aequor* and the casual, everyday note struck by *iterabimus;* **ingens**] 'huge', 'mighty', a word much favoured by Virgil in the *Aeneid*, asserts the high style; **iterabimus**] a technical term of agriculture, used of ploughing a field a second time (cf. the adverb *iterum*); here context revives the connection with *iter*, 'journey', especially a day's march (as in such phrases as *magnis itineribus*); **aequor**] any flat expanse — most often in verse of the sea (*aequora ponti*), but the latent sense ('plain', etc.) is revived by *iterabimus* (cf. 1. 9. 10-11); for Teucer and his men, crossing the ocean has become as familiar a routine as ploughing a field for the farmer; for H. and Plancus it is the symbol of man's seemingly endless life of toil (18 *vitae labores*), from which no more than temporary respite can be hoped for.

1. 8

Introduction: Like 1. 5, a study in unequal partners. Again it is the boy who is young and easily corrupted, the girl who is experienced. The corruption follows the lines familiar to the reader of Roman comedy: loving Lydia has caused him to lose interest in all else — in particular those manly pursuits conventionally expected of a young Roman of good family. Unlike the typical lover of Augustan elegy, who is more often represented as exposed to the anguish of unrequited love (cf. 1. 33, 2. 9) than as the lover triumphant, Sybaris does not seem to be wasting his time: all points to a total adjustment to a new way of life.

The social background is conveniently summarised by Lily Ross Taylor, *JRS* 1924, 158:

Cicero tells us [*Cael.* 11] that in former times, for a year after the taking of the *toga virilis*, the young *tiro* was trained at Rome in *exercitatio ludusque campestris*. This preliminary training was restored for the young noble by Augustus who felt its importance as a preparation for the military service insisted upon for all who sought political preferment. Indeed, the old *tirocinium* ... seems to have been lengthened from one to two years. The young Roman, who now took the *toga virilis* at the age of fifteen, spent the two years before beginning his active military service in a vigorous course of training at Rome. Augustus was encouraged in his plans for the training of youth by Maecenas, who, in the speech Dio (III, 26) credits him with making after Actium, urged the emperor to provide for all sons of senators and knights (the group that rode on horseback at the *pompa circensis*) instruction in exercises with horse and armour under teachers paid by the state.

Cf. 1. 29, 3. 2. 1-12; for an ironical reversal of the situation, see 3. 12.

Structure: The rhetorical structure sets up an attitude of scandalised reproach:a triple indirect question (2 'cur properes ... ', 3 'cur oderit ... ', 5 'cur neque equitet nec temperet ... ') is followed by a triple direct question (8 'cur timet ... ', 10 'cur vitat neque gestat ... ', 13 'quid latet ... ') — at first establishing a more urgent tempo, then modulating into the mythological exemplum of Stanza 4, which unexpectedly puts matters in a new light. Each set of questions forms a tricolon crescendo (see on lines 1-7); for a similar pattern (on a related theme) cf. 1. 29.

Metre: Greater Sapphic; an Aristophaneus (a normal Sapphic hendecasyllabic line minus the first four syllables):

_____ U U _____ U _____ _____

alternates with a Sapphic hendecasyllable in which a choriamb (_____ U U _____) has been inserted between syllables 4 and 5:

_____ U _____ _____, _____ U U _____, _____ U U _____ U _____ _____

This combination only here in H. If arrangement in 4-line stanzas is assumed (see 1. 1M on Meineke's canon), there is a conflict between metre and syntax until both structures coincide at the end of Stanza 3, thus throwing the final *exemplum* into prominence.

1-7] The tricolon crescendo is H.'s favourite rhetorical figure. Frequently, as here, the formal structure is a triple anaphora in asyndeton (each member beginning with the same word, no conjunctions or connecting particles); often, as here, the third member is double-barrelled; contrapuntal conflict between syntactical structure and metrical structure (line or stanza) is normal, sometimes resolved (as in lines 13-16) in the third member of the tricolon; for the figure (Behagel's 'Gesetz der wachsenden Glieder'), see Fraenkel 351 note 1; other examples include lines 8-16 below, 1. 14. 3-9, 2. 5. 10-20, 3. 25. 1-6. **– Lydia, Sybarin]** For the names, see on 1. 5. 3 *Pyrrha*; Lydia perhaps suggests a foreign girl – a *libertina* or a *meretrix*; Sybaris may be geographical (he will be in that case a Roman citizen, the son of a municipal noble, like Hebrus in 3. 12), but the name is clearly chosen for its connotations of effete, luxurious living (Sybaris is, or has become, a sissy). **– per ... oro]** The MSS vary between 'per omnis te deos oro' and 'per omnis hoc deos vere' (and a combination of these). **– cur properes amando perdere?]** = 'why do you have to ruin Sybaris if you love him?', but the transposition into idiomatic English defuses the oxymoron; the stance adopted is one H. favours, that of the middle-aged detached observer, mildly cynical in attitude, but disposed to indulgence towards lovers' follies (cf. the struggle to maintain that pose in 1. 13); he is aware that fast women are the ruination of innocent young men, but has the sense to realise Lydia acts the way she does because she loves Sybaris, not because she is wicked or morally depraved; he merely registers surprise at the rapidity (*properes*) of Sybaris' decline from the status of fine upstanding young man of good family to that of slacker and sissy. **– cur ... solis]** H.'s second question passes from reproach of Lydia (what is she up to?) to an appeal for help (how does she explain Sybaris' change of attitude to manly pursuits?); the Campus Martius is the place where Sybaris and his fellow-members of Augustus' cadet corps train (cf. Cicero's 'exercitatio ludusque campestris' quoted in Introduction); the cavalry exercises of lines 5-7 and the field athletics of 8-12 may be presumed to take place here; a healthy right-minded young Roman (H. implies) should enjoy the sunshine and not mind the dust and the heat of the sun; **patiens]** = 'he who till now could stand up to'. **– cur ... frenis]** The third question throws into sharper focus the picture of Sybaris before Lydia corrupted him; cf. Tibullus 1. 4. 11-12; **militaris]** i.e., playing the part of a soldier (in his role as a member of the cadet corps); nominative singular; **inter aequalis]** 'along with those of his own age' (and class); **equitet]** 'ride his horse'; **Gallica ... frenis]** i.e., control his mount (a horse imported from Gaul, or of Gallic stock) by pulliing on his bridle (the bit of which is fitted with 'teeth'; cf. 3. 12. 10 'eques ipso melior Bellerophonte'.

8-16] The second series of questions, though comparable in length to the first (9 lines as against 7), is differently laid out: 'cur . . . tangere' introduces a quicker tempo; 'cur . . . expedito' maintains the tempo and a practical down-to-earth realism, the swelling effect of the crescendo being secured by making the second a double-barrelled question; the key modulation at line 13 is thus marked on several levels (mythical past instead of realistic present, more diffuse syntax, a more plangent, less sharply defined line of statement).

8-12] **cur . . . tangere?** Swimming in the Tiber seems to have been a favourite exercise for young Romans; see on 3. 12. 9 'simul unctos Tiberinis umeros lavit in undis'; **flavum** a traditional-sounding epithet ('tawny'; see on 1. 2. 13), when backed up by line 10 acquires less agreeable overtones ('muddy', therefore 'dirty'). — **cur . . . expedito?**] Olive oil suggests, in a Roman context, not sunburn lotion but wrestling (an ancient wrestler anointed himself to make it easier to slip out of an opponent's hold); it thus becomes the symbol of another of the manly pursuits which have become distasteful to Sybaris; **neque . . . bracchia**] 'no longer displays arms (*bracchia*) black and blue from the gear he handles'; **armis**] the general word for 'equipment' of any kind; see on 3. 26. 3; illustrated by 'saepe', etc.; ablative with *livida*; **saepe . . . expedito**] = 'he who was once hailed as a hero for breaking the record for throwing the discus and casting the javelin'; illustrates and explains *armis* (rather as in a hendiadys the first colon may be general and allusive and the second explicit and descriptive); the traditional contests of skill of Greek athletics assume at Rome a more practical, para-military objective; *armis*, therefore, probably includes other forms of weapons drill (one does not normally get bruised throwing the discus or casting the javelin, though one might from the sling used for carrying the latter and perhaps also from transporting *disci*); **trans finem**] i.e., beyond the mark reached by others; **nobilis**] cf. 1. 1. 5.

13-16] **Quid latet?**] 'Why has he gone under cover'; the change of interrogative particle (after 5 *cur*'s) is the first hint of a modulation into a more plangent key; cf. the change of mood in 1. 29. 10; for key modulation, see on 1. 10. 13-16 and 2. 5. 17-20; in Roman love poetry the man who falls in love 'goes out of circulation' (is no longer seen by his friends); cf. Catullus 6 and 55. — **ut . . . Thetidis**] 'as did, they say, the son of Thetis of the sea'; Achilles, son of the sea nymph Thetis; because of the prophecy that he would be killed at Troy, he went off and concealed himself at the court of King Lycomedes of Scyros; with 'marinae filium Thetidis' cf. 4. 6. 6. — **sub . . . funera**] 'when the deaths at Troy impended, a cause for tears'; the phrase = 'when the Trojan War was at hand', but moulds the Iliadic context to H.'s present purpose: not 'fighting' but 'death', not 'glory' but 'tears'; chief among the tears evoked are those of Thetis in *Il.* 18. 35-51 when Achilles' own death was at hand; for the phrase cf. 2. 18. 18. — **ne virilis cultus . . . catervas**] A calculated ambiguity: the primary sense of *virilis cultus* is 'dressing like a man' (the legend was that Achilles dressed as a girl at Scyros, to avoid detection — a disguise penetrated at any rate by the King's daughter Deidamia, who fell in love with him; their son was Neoptolemus); but the secondary sense, 'behaving like a man', is drawn out by context and provides the parallel for Sybaris — he, too, has gone out of circulation (*latet*), preferring to spend his time with the girl he loves to the practice of 'the manly cult'; the *cultus virilis* in this second sense (the tough, simple life of the soldier) is one of Rome's proudest traditions (cf. the speech of Remulus in *Aen.* 9. 603-13); if H. appears to question it here, the parallel of Achilles puts questioning in its proper perspective — Sybaris is passing through a stage any healthy young man has to pass through; like Achilles, he can be relied on to turn out all right (a brave soldier) in the end; H.'s point of view, i.e., is human and sympathetic, not anti-militaristic, though 'in caedem . . . catervas' forces us to face the reality of war; in a different context (3. 2. 1-12) H. will praise the tough, simple life (*angusta pauperies*) of the young soldier on active service; in 1. 29 we see again the detached observer; **in caedum . . . proriperet**] 'snatch off into slaughtering Lycian squadrons'; hendiadys; the Lycians fought on the Trojan side under Sarpedon (the bravest of the Trojan allies).

1. 9

Introduction: A dramatic monologue, with H. in his favourite role as the middle-aged commentator — detached, indulgent — on the human comedy; his companion is a young man on the verge of life (the foil for H.'s worldly wisdom), the scene a country retreat in sight of Mt Soracte on a winter's day following a storm.

The storm and the calm which followed (cold, serene, a time for reflection) symbolise the tempestuous involvement of *iuventus* and the disengagement of middle age. The vehicle of this conversation piece is an elegantly structured poem, the first of H.'s Alcaic Odes, and carefully planned to touch off appropriate echoes of the model H. wishes to invoke. The archaic form encapsulates, however, the complexity of a refined, urbanely subtle intellect.

Structure: Stanza 1 sets the scene; the rest of the poem is built around a series of commands — the first three matter of fact (5 *dissolve*, 7 *deprome*, 9 *permitte*), the remainder forming the structural basis for an expanding pattern of thought (13 *fuge quaerere*, 15 *adpone*, 15-16 *nec sperne*, 20 *repetantur*). Three tightly endstopped stanzas emphasise the metrical pattern — the content conversational, realistic, an occasional rhetorical flourish (the well-chosen word, the sharply chiselled image), but at the same time evoking well-known lines of Alcaeus. Stanzas 4-6 constitute a single sentence, the stanzas no more than lightly endstopped (Stanza 4 spilling over into the heavily charged aphorism of the *donec*-clause, Stanza 6 bound to Stanza 5 by the anaphora 18 *nunc . . . 21 nunc*).

Metre: Alcaics; the commonest metre in the *Odes*, constituting almost one-third of the collection. An opening hendecasyllabic line:

$$\underline{\underset{\cup}{}} \underline{} \cup \underline{} \underline{} \wedge \underline{} \cup \cup \underline{} \cup \bar{\cup}$$

is repeated unchanged and then in abbreviated form:

$$\underline{\underset{\cup}{}} \underline{} \cup \underline{} \underline{} \underline{} \cup \underline{} \bar{\cup}$$

followed by a fourth line made up from the second halves of the previous lines:

$$\underline{} \cup \cup \underline{} \cup \cup \underline{} \cup \underline{} \bar{\cup}$$

In H.'s practice:

(1) In lines 1-3, the opening syllable is normally long.

(2) In lines 1-2, syllable 5 is long and normally followed by a caesura, the effect being to throw into prominence (especially if caesura and syntactic pause coincide) the word preceding or following the caesura.

(3) In line 3, a break between words after syllable 4 occurs only in 1. 26. 11 (unless syllable 4 is a monosyllable linked syntactically to the word following), is unusual after syllable 5 (first instance 1. 9. 11 *deproeliantis* — a variation noticeably less common in *Odes* 1-2), very common after syllable 6; a variation is a polysyllable straddling the line and ending with —*que* which shifts the pause to after syllable 7 (e.g., 1. 27. 3, 3. 4. 19, 43, 47, 55, 63). The effect is often to throw into prominence a word consisting of (or ending in) three long syllables (e.g., 1. 9. 3 *laborantes*, 7 *quadrimum*). In lines 1-3 of the Sapphic stanza (as at the beginning of the Asclepiad lines), words containing three consecutive long syllables are common. Such words are normally precluded from lines 1-2 of the Alcaic stanza by the caesura after syllable 5; a polysyllable, therefore, when it occurs in line 3 can dominate a whole stanza, forming a kind of metrical climax (e.g., 3. 1. 3 *Giganteo*).

(4) In line 3, a double dissyllable at the end of the line is avoided; there are only eight cases in 317 lines; in five of these the first dissyllable is repeated at the beginning of line 4 (e.g., 1. 16. 3-4 'sive flamma / sive mari'; so 1. 26. 7-8, 2. 13. 27-8, 2. 14. 11-12, 2. 19. 7-8).

(5) As in the Sapphic stanza, synaphoea is normal.

1-4]   The opening question (see on 1. 5. 1-5) sketches in the scene and sets the tone (at the level of conversation improved upon). Yet despite the conversational tone and the contemporary scene, words and metre evoke familiar lines of an ode of Alcaeus (338 LP ὕει μὲν ὁ Ζεῦς', etc.), though H.'s scene in fact differs significantly from that of Alcaeus (see on lines 9-12; cf. 1. 37. 1-4). — Vides ut . . .] For *vides* + indirect question cf. 1. 14. 3, 3. 20. 1, 3. 27. 17. — alta . . . Soracte] = 'Mt Soracte rises up shining white and covered in snow'; Mt Soracte (800 metres), about 32 km N of Rome, a prominent landmark, is the scene of Byron's famous 'farewell Horace whom I hated so' in *Childe Harold* Book 3; alta nive] with *candidum* and with *stet* — the snow forms a thick ('deep') blanket of white which rises high in the air; with *stet* ('rises stiff and motionless') cf. 3. 3. 42, 3. 28.

6. – **nec ... acuto**] Soracte might at a pinch be visible from Rome, but the second and
third questions make it clear we are to imagine a rural setting (trees bending under the
weight of snow, streams apparently arrested in midcourse by a hard frost), while the
third question finally brings the scene into sharp focus (there has been a heavy fall of
snow, but the snow has stopped and been succeeded by a night of frost); **nec iam
sustineant onus**] the trees are in leaf, either because there has been an unusually early
autumn snowfall or because they are evergreens (*ilex*, etc.); the snow has lodged in the
branches during the storm; now as the snow thaws (in the sun?) lumps of it fall to the
ground – as though the trees were struggling to keep their load of snow, but let slip
part of it every now and then (*laborantes*, i.e., personifies; cf. 2. 9. 7); **flumina**] small
streams which easily freeze over; no justification for supposing (as some do) that
flumina is a poetic plural and that a freezing-over of the Tiber (a very rare phenomenon)
is meant.

5-8] The natural reaction to the cold is to take steps to get warm. We may suppose, if we
like, that H. and his companion have come outside to admire the view (or have just
reached their destination, perhaps – though lines 6 and 9-12 make that less likely), and
now retreat indoors. – **Dissolve frigus**] 'Dissolve the cold'; cf. 1. 4. 1. – **ligna ...
reponens**] = 'pile up a really good log-fire'; with *reponens* cf. 3. 17. 14 *conpone*. –
benignius deprome ... merum] = Either 'decant a more generous supply of that four-
year-old wine from its two-lugged Sabine jar', or (taking *benignius* as adjectival, *deprome*
as 'bring down' and *Sabina diota* as descriptive ablative instead of ablative of separation)
'bring down a more benign (i.e., 'mellower') wine from the cellar in its two-lugged Sabine
jar'; in either case, the suggestion is that they have been drinking already (pausing perhaps
for a look out of doors) and that a more liberal supply of wine or a wine of better quality
is now called for to offset the cold; for *deprome*, see on 3. 28. 1-4; here the sense 'decant'
seems the more probable; **quadrimum**] a vin ordinaire rather than a wine to make a fuss
about; for wines served on special occasions, see on 3. 21. 1-4 and 1. 20. 1; **Sabina diota**]
further identifies the wine, for our benefit as well as that of Thaliarchus, by its container;
it is a wine from the region of H.'s Sabine farm, like the *vile Sabinum* of 1. 20. 1; **diota**]
only here in the Odes; the usual containers referred to are the *amphora*, the *testa* and
the *cadus*, all large or largish earthenware jars, usually with two handles for transport,
the first either the table *amphora* (equipped with feet, so it could stand on the table and
holding only a few litres – enough for a small party) or a storage *amphora* (capacity
roughly 20-30 litres), the other two normally bulk containers; mention of a *testa* or a
cadus implies a heavy night's drinking by a largish party – though 3. 29. 2 'non ante
verso cado' suggests it was the practice to broach a special wine at a party, leaving what
was left to be drunk later or by the household slaves; **Thaliarche**] 'Lord of the banquet';
one of H.'s punning names (see on 1. 5. 3); since the party is clearly an unpretentious
tête-à-tête, the pretentious title is probably jocular – H., i.e., though the host, expects
the *puer* to wait upon him (cf. 1. 29. 7-8), dignifying him for the purpose with a title
absurdly out of keeping with the unpretentious wine he is to serve (cf. Leuconoe in 1. 11.
6, Lyde in 3. 28. 7); **merum**] describes the wine as it comes from the container, before
being mixed with water (the usual practice).

9-12] In Alcaeus' poem (see on lines 1-4) the storm is raging about those who seek refuge
and comfort from it in warmth and wine. H. in Stanzas 1-2 concentrates on the after-
math; the storm (now alluded to for the first time) is over, a thing of the past, whose
passing confirms one's trust in the power of the gods. – **permitte divis cetera**] 'all else
entrust to the gods'; 'leave all to the gods' is one of the great commonplaces (see, e.g.,
Archilochus 130W 'τοῖς θεοῖς πείθοι᾽ ἅπαντα'); H. revives the commonplace and gives
it an Epicurean flavour by adding *cetera* ('all else', i.e., than warmth and good wine). –
qui ... deproeliantis] 'for as soon as they have calmed the winds fighting it out on the
boiling plain of the sea ... '; in Latin, a continuing relative which is the subject, object,
etc. of a subordinate clause, may play no grammatical role in the succeeding principal
clause; this idiom, though common in formal English until the eighteenth century, is
not possible in modern English; **simul**] = *simul atque*, as often in the Odes; **aequore
fervido deproeliantis**] normal battles are fought on flat land, the winds fight over the
'plain of the sea', which is lashed to fury (literally 'boils') as a result of their contention;
for *aequor*, any flat expanse, whether of land or sea, see on 1. 7. 32; for contending
winds, see on 1. 3. 13. – **nec cupressi ... orni**] Tall trees (the Italian 'mountain' or
'flowering' ash and cypress both attain a height of 25-30 metres), likely to be tossed

in a storm; the storm is that which has just ceased (yesterday's storm?); the trees are there to be pointed to as evidence that it has blown itself out; but the storm is also symbolic (the storm of life, which no longer affects the old); *veteres* with both nouns, as often in the *Odes*.

13-18] Thoughts of the storm now over prompt the question, 'What about tomorrow?' The answer, for H., is 'don't worry about tomorrow, count each day as so much gain' (cf. 1. 11. 8, 3. 29. 41-3). — fuge quaerere] = 'don't ask'; cf. 2. 4. 22; the first of a fresh, more urgent series of imperatives (15 *adpone*, 16 *sperne*, cf. 20 *repetantur*). — Fors] 'Fate' in the vaguest sense, less dramatic than the Fortuna of 1. 34. 14-16 and 3. 29. 49-52. — lucro adpone] The metaphor is from accountancy. — nec dulcis amores ... neque tu choreas] *nec* is best taken as correlative with *neque* (not as connecting 'dulcis amores sperne' with what precedes); we are to imagine H. breaking away from his increasingly philosophical train of reflection, to turn to everyday, practical advice: the ordinary pleasures of life are to be enjoyed before it is too late; it may be felt that the sudden switch does violence to the rhetorical structure; the dramatic setting should, however, be remembered and the role the pleasures in question play in the *Odes*; dulcis amores] = 'the pleasures of love' as in 3. 12. 1-2 'dulci vino', 'the pleasure of wine'; cf. 1. 16. 23; puer] see on 1. 5. 1; choreas] formal group dancing at parties, etc., like that in 4. 1. 25-8; cf. the *chorus* of 2. 5. 21. — donec ... morosa] i.e., 'while you are young and active, not white-haired and short-tempered ('self-centred', 'peevish'), sc., like me'; for *virenti* (the greenness of the young, supple plant) cf. 1. 25. 17-20, 4. 13. 6-10; canities] the symbol of vanished youth and the onset of middle age, as in 2. 11. 15; cf. 3. 14. 25.

18-24] 18 *nunc* ... 21 *nunc* are also correlative, like 15 *nec* ... 16 *neque* ..., the two pairs forming a binary opposition — what should not be rejected (16 *sperne*), what should be actively pursued (20 *repetantur*). The complaint of editors that the winter scene of Stanzas 1-2 has been inexplicably left behind misses the essentially dramatic structure of the ode: it is not a poem about a winter's day, but a poem representing the thoughts of a speaker in that scene; the structure is psychological, not logical, with more than a hint that the speaker is pursuing thoughts of vanished youth as much as giving advice to his companion. — campus et areae] The campus is the Campus Martius of 1. 8. 4, here representing, like *areae*, public places where boy and girl in love can meet (or at any rate see one another) by arrangement ('conposita repetantur hora'). — lenesque ... susurri] = 'whispered conversations at dusk', before the girl must retreat indoors, or close her shutters (as in 3. 7. 29). — repetantur] The subjunctive is a variation on the subjunctives 13 *fuge*, 15 *adpone*, 16 *sperne*. — nunc et latentis ... pertinaci] The complex word order secures a slowing of the tempo at the close, as in 1. 5. 13-16; *et* is intensive, emphasising *latentis*, rather than a delayed conjunction; latentis ... ab angulo] the laugh coming from a corner which betrays the whereabouts of the girl who has concealed herself there and which brings pleasure (*gratus*) to the boy (because it shows the girl is willing to be discovered; cf. 24 *male pertinaci*): boy and girl are playing hide and seek, i.e., at a party or the like; pignusque ... pertinaci] discovery leads to a struggle between boy and girl for the possession of an ornament or a ring which the boy can claim to regard as a pledge (*pignus*) that she loves him; for the studied triviality of the conclusion following grander themes cf. 1. 4. 17-20, 3. 5. 50-56; male pertinaci] the finger puts up no more than a show of resistance; as in lines 21-2, the girl is playing to lose.

1. 10

Introduction: A sophisticated exercise in hymn form, the first of several (cf. 1. 21, 1. 30, 1. 35, 3. 11, and the parody 3. 21). The subject is Mercury and his benefactions of mankind. A fine example of elegantly controlled feeling and the exploitation of traditional form. For other references to Mercury, see 1. 24. 15-18, 2. 7. 13-16, 2. 17. 29-30, 3. 11. 1-24; in 1. 2. 41-9 Augustus is identified with Mercury.

Structure: The five endstopped stanzas support the formal rhetorical structure. Stanza 1, invocation, followed by an initial summary appraisal of Mercury as the civilising god. Stanzas 2-5 are strung together by a common device of hymn form, anaphora of the second person pronoun (5 'te canam', 9 'te ... risit', 13 'duce te', 17 'tu reponis'); this simple structure holds together, not so much a list of the god's attributes, benefactions, etc., as the poet's highly personal explorations of traditional material.

Metre: Sapphics; see 1. 2M; there is a delayed caesura (after syllable 6) in lines 1, 6 and 18.

1-4] H.'s Mercury is the quick-witted, civilised god, a good talker (*facunde*), good at negotiation, not too scrupulous; H. has in mind the Athenian *palaestra* familiar to us from the dialogues of Plato, where Socrates talked and argued with the young men who came to exercise their minds as well as their bodies; cf. the inscription in hexameters (for a statue of Mercury found at Rome, *carm. epig.* 1528) which includes the line 'sermonem docui mortales atque palaestram' (a hexameter) – **nepos Atlantis**] his mother Maia was the daughter of Atlas; cf. 1. 2. 43 'filius Maiae'. – **feros ... recentum**] = 'the crude ways of primitive man'; **recentum**] (= *recentium*) 'freshly created'. – **voce formasti**] 'civilised by giving them the power of speech'; for H.'s view of language as a civilising force, see *Sat.* 1. 3. 99-106. – **catus**] = 'shrewd, witty fellow that you are'; following on *facunde*, the word points to H.'s mildly irreverent, secularising treatment of Mercury. – **decorae more palaestrae**] = 'and the *palaestra*, that elegant institution'; transferred epithet.

5-8] Mercury, the messenger of Jove, the god of the lyre – and the god of thieves. – **nuntium**] Mercury's regular role in epic. – **curvaeque lyrae parentem**] Cf. 1. 32. 13, 3. 11. 1-8. – **callidum ... furto**] *callidum* (masculine) with *condere* (epexegetic infinitive) = 'nimble-witted in covering up any piece of trickery he wished by a witty strategem'; an attempt (not seriously intended to convince) to gloss over an aspect of the Greek Hermes which the Greeks made no bones about.

9-12] A traditional *exemplum* illustrating the attribute of Mercury just mentioned. According to Pausanias, the theft of Apollo's cattle was related in Alcaeus' hymn to Hermes (see Page, *Sappho and Alcaeus* 253); the story also in Hesiod and elsewhere; H.'s version closely resembles that given by the scholiast on *Il.* 15. 256. – **boves ... amotas**] 'unless you gave back the cattle you stole that time'; *reddidisses*, dependent on 'minaci voce dum terret' (treated as a past verb of saying), reports the future perfect indicative of the *oratio recta.* – **dum terret**] 'while he was threatening'; the historic present indicative is usual in *dum*-clauses (with the meaning 'while') where the principal verb is perfect; cf. 1. 22. 10-11. – **viduus pharetra risit Apollo**] = 'burst out laughing on realising he had been deprived of his quiver'; Apollo, i.e., reaches for an arrow to threaten Mercury with and finds Mercury has stolen his quiver while he has been talking; the phrase, especially the *callida iunctura* 'viduus pharetra' forms an elegant, stylising flourish at the conclusion of the realistic vignette.

13-16] A sudden change of key: we pass from charming anecdote to one of the most pathetic episodes in the *Iliad* (*Il.* 24. 333 ff.) – aged Priam threading his way by night through the Greek camp before Troy on a secret visit to Achilles in order to beg back the body of his son Hector; the traditional powers of Hermes as escort of the dead to the underworld are extended to give magical protection to Priam on his journey. The concise, elegantly structured pathos of H.'s evocation of the scene is remarkable; for other examples of key modulation, see on 1. 8. 13-16, 1. 34. 12-16 and 2. 5. 17-20. – **quin et Atridas superbos**] *quin* marks the change of key, *et* emphasises *Atridas*; the 'proud sons of Atreus' are Agamemnon and Menelaus, arrogant at the prospect of victory after the death of Hector. – **Ilio relicto**] The simple, telling phrase (Troy represents protection for the aged king; to leave it is to surround himself with danger). – **dives Priamus**] The wealth of Priam is traditional, but *dives* here evokes the treasure which Priam took with him as a ransom for his son's body. – **Thessalosque ignis**] The camp fires of Achilles' Thessalian Myrmidons. – **iniqua Troiae castra**] 'the camp hostile to Troy'; the simple phrase is full of meaning; *iniqua* implies not only the hostility of an enemy, but the ill luck which had come Troy's way with the death of Hector. – **fefellit**] 'eluded'.

17-20] A formal concluding stanza taking up the role of Mercury as escort of the dead evoked in Stanza 4; for Mercury in this role cf. 1. 24. 15-18. – **laetis sedibus**] The Elysian fields; cf. *Aen.* 6. 638 'devenere locos laetos'. – **reponis**] The preverb *re-* implies, as often, that the action denoted by the verb is right and proper, part of the established order of things. – **virgaque aurea**] The *cadaceus.* – **levem turbam**] Because the *animae* whom Mercury escorts lack physical substance.

1. 11

Introduction: A fragment from a conversation. The situation is not unlike that of 1. 9, except that H.'s companion this time is a girl. Again there is a background of storm, and again the storm is easily recognised as a symbol of life. The first of five odes 8 lines in length; the others are 1. 30, 1. 38, 3. 22 and 4. 10.

Structure: The basic rhetorical structure is constituted by the opening prohibitions 1 'ne quaesieris . . . ', 2-3 'nec temptaris . . . ' and the string of commands in the last 3 lines (6 'Sapias', 'vina liques', 7 'spem reseces', 8 'carpe diem'), the last of which sums up the message of the poem; the two groups are separated by the exclamation 'Ut melius . . . mare Tyrrhenum!' See below on lines 3-6.

The strong pauses (some of them very abrupt) all fall in mid-line, the lines spilling over from one to the next more often than not. H. perhaps aims, within the framework of these very long lines (16 syllables), at an effect comparable to that of Virgilian hexameter.

Metre: Asclepiad (e) (also 1. 18, 4. 10). Each line consists of a normal Asclepiad line expanded by a choriamb following the usual caesura and cut off from the normal second half-line by a further caesura:

$$\underline{\quad}\ \underline{\quad}, \ \underline{\quad}\ \cup\cup\ \underline{\quad}\ \wedge\ \underline{\quad}\ \cup\cup\ \underline{\quad}\ \wedge\ \underline{\quad}\ \cup\cup\ \underline{\quad}\ \cup\,\bar{\cup}$$

1-3] Leuconoe, it seems, is anxious to know what the future holds in store for H. and herself. H. discourages such curiousity. His attitude is the correct Epicurean one: cf., e.g., Cicero *Tusc*. 3. 32 '[Epicurus teaches] satis esse male cum venisset; qui autem semper cogitavisset accidere posse aliquid adversi, ei fieri illud sempiternum malum'. Belief in astrology as revealing the future was widespread and deprecation of recourse to it not confined to Epicureans; see, e.g., Cicero *De Div*. 2. 87 'Ad Chaldaeorum monstra veniamus, de quibus Eudoxus, Platonis auditor, in astrologia iudicio doctissimorum hominum facile princeps sic, opinatur, . . . Chaldaeis in praedictione et in notatione cuiusque vitae ex natali die minime esse credendum. Nominat etiam Panaetium, qui unus e Stoicis astrologorum praedicta reicit. . . . 'cf. Propertius 2. 27. — **ne quaesieris, nec temptaris]** 'stop asking, stop meddling'. — **scire nefas]** 'it's not permitted knowledge' (i.e., not knowledge which is morally wrong, but knowledge which is withheld from human beings by the divine order of things). — **quem mihi, quem tibi]** The words provide a first hint, to be filled out by subsequent hints, of the relationship between H. and Leuconoe (H., i.e., is not this time the outside observer as in 1. 5 and 1. 8, but one of the *dramatis personae*). — **Leuconoe]** A name formed from λευκός and νοῦς, perhaps 'Empty head'; for such names, see on 1. 5. 3 *Pyrrha*. — **Babylonios numeros]** 'Babylonian calculations', Babylonian astrologers being the acknowledged experts at Rome.

3-6] Humbly to endure misfortune with calm acceptance of one's powerlessness except to endure it, is a basic tenet of both Stoics and Epicureans (though in lines 6-8 H. speaks of course as an Epicurean). — **Ut melius . . . !]** 'How much better . . . !' — **pati]** Not 'suffer' but 'endure passively'. — **seu . . . seu . . . etc.]** Some editors subordinate to 6 *sapias*, but this gives a weaker rhythm and obscures the balance between prohibition and command separated by intervening exclamation which seems fairly clearly to constitute the rhetorical structure of the ode. — **pluris hiemes]** 'yet more winters'; one can reckon years by winters as well as by summers, but, as in 1. 15. 35, the perspective is altered — the future is seen as holding in store only suffering and tribulation; added to 'quidquid erit, pati', 'seu . . . Tyrrhenum' seems like excessive pessimism, excluding the prospect of any but the most fleeting happiness (8 'carpe diem . . . '); this is, however, H.'s view — the world around us is a continuous swirl of distractions and discomforts ever threatening the wise man's inner tranquillity; the winter storm now raging round the Etrurian coast is thus a symbol of the ordinary condition of the world (which must continue as long as life itself continues), while H.'s present *tête-à-tête* with Leuconoe represents the brief respite from that storm which one must reach out and grasp before it is too late. — **seu . . . ultimam]** = 'or whether this will be our last'; **Iuppiter]** the weather god as much as the deity who presides over men's destinies; see on 1. 2. 1-4; as in 2 *di*, H. uses the traditional formulae of everyday conversation, not the technical language of the philosopher. — **quae . . . Tyrrhenum]** An unexpected image: the storm expends the force of the sea (*debilitat*) by sending it crashing against the rocks, but the rocks which bar its passage are pumice (not, e.g., granite) — soft rock, subject to erosion by the action of the sea; pumice rocks are, of course, a feature of the Etrurian coast not far, presumably, from where H. and Leuconoe are talking — perhaps within sight), but storm and rocks are probably also symbolic of the human condition; cf. 4. 15. 3.

6-8] **Sapias**] 'Be sensible'. — **vina liques**] 'strain the wine'; a further hint, to fill out the dramatic setting of the monologue; the scene is a party; H. asks the girl to strain the wine so that they can settle down to drinking (cf. the instructions to Thaliarchus 1. 9. 5-8, to Lyde 3. 28. 2); no slaves present, therefore; at the same time, straining the wine symbolises the sort of practical, positive step toward limited happiness which is worth taking (instead of wasting time on the idle fears and speculations of lines 1-3). — **spatio brevi . . . reseces**] = 'prune back hope to fit the space at our disposal'; the ablative is easily understood if not easily classified; hope like a vine is apt to reach out unprofitably unless we control it; the brief space is not so much that of the span of human life as the limited time span within which hopes for the future are sensible. — **dum loquimur . . . invida aetas**] 'while we are talking, greedy time will have fled'; i.e., if we're not careful, it will be too late for us to enjoy ourselves before we've finished talking; cf, Ovid *Am.* 1. 11. 15 'dum loquor hora fugit'; the verb of the *dum*-clause is present, though the clause refers to the future, by an extension of the usual idiom (see on 1. 10. 11). — **carpe diem**] A famous phrase; *carpere*, the word used of plucking fruit or flowers, of a cow chewing its cud, of the hidden fire of love within Dido (*Aen.* 4.2 'caeco carpitur igni') suggests quick, firm movement outwards from a base — here something like 'reach out and grasp the day'; cf. 3. 27. 44, 4. 2. 29, 4. 9. 33; for the idea of making the most of each day as it comes cf. 1. 9. 14-15, 3. 29. 41-3; for 'plucking the flowers of life' cf. Ovid *Ars* 3. 77-8 'carpite florem, / qui nisi carptus erit, turpiter ipse cadet'. — **quam . . . postero**] 'counting as little as possible on its successor'.

1. 12

Introduction: As in 1. 24, 1. 32, 3. 4 and 3. 11, H. begins by representing himself as poised, awaiting the inspiration of the Muse; as in 3. 11, he is uncertain what course inspiration will take, though clear about the sort of poem he wants.

What follows seems, from the point of view of logic, little more than build-up for the song in praise of Augustus in Stanzas 13-15. As in 1. 2. 25-40, candidate after candidate is summarily disposed of until Augustus is arrived at. A reminiscence of Pindar provides the starting point (see below on lines 1-2) and the development of the theme is likewise very much in the manner of Pindar (Fraenkel 291-7 is good on this aspect of the poem). But the ode which results, though competently executed, seems oddly stilted and point-less; in particular, the galaxy of minor Roman heroes in Stanzas 10-11 is too perfunctory to prepare the way adequately for what follows.

Structure: The ode is held together by a series of climactic surges in the manner of Pindar, each concluding at a turning point in the development of H.'s theme. The opening triad of questions ('Quem virum aut heroa . . . ?', 'quem deum?', 'cuius nomen . . . ?') sets this pattern: the third question flows over into the following stanza and is then expanded by the 6-line relative clause 7 'unde vocalem . . . ducere quercus?'. A similar rhetorical structure holds together Stanzas 5-8: H.'s pantheon begins with Jove and an appropriate flourish (lines 13-18): Pallas, Bacchus, Diana, Apollo, Hercules and the Dioscuri follow in rapid succession; then comes a second climactic surge (lines 27-32) while one aspect of Castor and Pollux as protectors of mankind is explored for its imaginative possibilities. In Stanzas 9-12 the rapid tempo is resumed, followed (when we finally arrive at Augustus in lines 46-8) by a third and final climax in Stanzas 13-15. The climactic positions are thus occupied by Orpheus, the Dioscuri Castor and Pollux, and Augustus in a loose rhetorical structure, the symmetry of which is more apparent than real.

Metre: Sapphics; see 1. 2M.

1-12] The ode begins with a clear echo of Pindar *Ol.* 2. 2:

$$τίνα\ θεόν,\ τίν'\ ἥρωα\ τίνα\ δ'\ ἄνδρα\ κελαδήσομεν;$$

The order 'man, hero, god' reverses Pindar's however, and the triple question swells out into a more elaborate structure.

The different musical instruments referred to in the *Odes* symbolise H.'s role as
lyricus — a poet who writes in the tradition of Sappho and Alcaeus, or in the tradition of
choral lyric (Pindar, etc.). The *lyra* consisted of a sounding board of tortoise shell
(*testudo*) with curved arms supporting strings (*fides*); the resultant instrument bore some
resemblance to a modern guitar; originally, there were only four strings; the 7-string lyre
was attributed to Terpander of Corinth (c. 650 BC); referred to simply as *testudo* 1. 32.
14, etc.; also called *barbitos* (1. 1. 34, etc.). The *cithara* (1. 15. 15, etc.) was a lyre with
a large wooden sounding board and straight arms. The *fistula* was a reed pipe, similar to
our flute, usually the symbol of pastoral poetry (1. 17. 10, 4. 12. 10), but in the *Odes*
sometimes performed along with the *lyra* and the *tibia* (3. 19. 19-20, 4. 1. 22-4). The
tibia was, strictly speaking, an instrument more akin in range to the modern oboe than
to the flute; this is the *tibia Berecyntia* (i.e., 'Phrygian') of 3. 19. 18 and 4. 1. 22 (called
'Berecyntia' from the connection with the rites of Cybele; cf. Catullus 63. 22); in the
Odes, however, the term is used generically to include the flute proper (Greek αὐλός,
not to be confused with the *tuba* (1. 1. 23). H. probably declaimed his verse (and
intended it should be so performed by others); anything that we should want to describe
as song would have been incompatible with the dense syntactical structure of the *Odes*;
it is unlikely that he accompanied himself on either the *lyra* or the *tibia* (references to
these instruments being wholly conventional); professional musicians (like Lyde in 2. 11.
21-4), however, undoubtedly did use such instruments and their use seems to have been
a prominent feature of parties. — **lyra vel acri tibia**] = 'to the accompaniment of the lyre
or the shrill flute'; the choice of instruments probably symbolises a choice between the
simpler lyric manner of Sappho and Alcaeus and the more complex, flowing style of
Pindar and choral lyric (cf. 3. 4. 1-4); the former is H.'s usual manner, the latter adopted
only on special occasions, as here; *acri* suggests the flute proper rather than the *tibia
Berecyntia*. — **sumis celebrare**] H. attempts to dramatise the onset of inspiration, asking
us to imagine him impelled to go outside his usual range of themes (as defined 1. 6. 16-20)
for a song of praise, but unaware as yet who is to be the subject of the poem now taking
shape; the variant *sumes* is typical of the confusion in the MSS of present and future (see
on 2. 5. 16). — **Clio**] In post-classical poetry, the Muse of History; H. seems to choose
his Muses (as he does his human characters) on the basis of the general appropriateness
of their names rather than in accordance with any association of a particular Muse with a
particular kind of poetry; thus, he perhaps connected the name Clio with κλείεν); 'to
celebrate'; the other Muses named in the *Odes* are Calliope (3. 4. 2), Euterpe (1. 1. 33),
Melpomene (1. 24. 3, 3. 30. 16, 4. 3. 1), Polyhymnia (1. 1. 33) and Thalia (4. 6. 25). —
cuius recinet . . . Haemo] If this is not mere rhetorical flourish, we are presumably
expected to imagine that the name of the man, hero or god (whichever it is to be) chosen
by Clio as the subject for H.'s poem will reverberate around Mt Helicon or one of the
neighbouring peaks before being conveyed to H.; recinet] cf. 3. 27. 1; the present
recinit, though it has less MS support, deserves consideration; **iocosa imago**] the same
phrase 1. 20. 6; **in umbrosis Heliconis oris**] i.e., the wooded slopes of Mt Helicon (in
Boeotia, one of the haunts of the Muses); with *oris* (= 'regions', not necessarily 'shores')
cf. 1. 26. 4; **super Pindo**] the range dividing Thessaly from Epirus; **gelidove in Haemo**]
a range in Thrace. — **unde**] i.e., from the slopes of the Haemus range. — **temere**] Pell-
mell. — **insecutae Orphea silvae**] Cf. 1. 24. 13-14, 3. 11. 13-14, *AP* 395-6. — **arte materna**]
The mother of Orpheus was the Muse Calliope. — **rapidos . . . lapsus**] Cf. 3. 11. 14. —
blandum et] (= *et blandum*) 'likewise persuasive'; postponement of *et* is a feature of the
high style; cf. 4. 15. 5, etc.; for postponed *-que* see 3. 4. 19. — **auritas**] 'with their ears
pricked up'.

13-21] The obvious starting point for a hymn of praise is Jove; in *Eclogues* 3. 60, e.g.,
Damoetas begins the singing contest with the words 'Ab Iove principium'; Theocritus
begins his encomium of Ptolemy (17. 1) in similar terms. The futures 13 *dicam*, 21
silebo, 25 *dicam*, like the deliberative 34 *memorem* must, if taken seriously, imply that
H. remains uncertain about the subject of his poem until Stanza 13; *dicam*, in that case,
= 'make mention of', rather than 'celebrate'. — **parentis**] Picks up the Homeric descrip-
tion of Zeus as 'father of gods and men'. — **qui res hominum . . . horis**] Cf. 3. 4. 45-8;
variisque . . . horis] 'and regulates the firmament with the changing seasons'. — **unde**]
'from whom' (i.e., in descent by birth). — **nil maius . . . ipso**] Jove, the father of gods
and men, is greater than all his descendants. — **nec viget . . . secundum**] None of the
other gods is Jove's equal when it comes to authority and power. — **Proximos**

occupavit honores] Second only to Jove, however, in respect of the honours paid her,
is Pallas; after these two come the rest; Pallas is the warlike Homeric Athena rather than
the Roman Minerva; for her fame in song cf. 1. 7. 5-6. — **proeliis audax**] Some (including
OCT) take as vocative with *Liber*, but this is forced and unnatural (in 2. 19. 21-8 Bacchus
aids Zeus against the giants, but this is not the usual conception).

21-32] After Jove and Pallas come most of the traditional Roman major gods; notable
omissions are Venus, Mercury and (perhaps most surprising) Mars. — **virgo**] Diana —
metuende ... sagitta] Apollo killed the Pythian serpent and is conventionally represented
as an archer; *metuende* again 2. 19. 8 (of Bacchus). — **dicam et ... Ledae**] Hercules,
Castor and Pollux are heroes who achieved immortality (see on 3. 3. 9); *dicam* picks up
13 *dicam*. — **hunc ... nobilem**] Cf. *Sat.* 2. 1. 26-7 'Castor gaudet equis, ovo prognatus
eodem / pugnis'; *superare* with *nobilem*, 'famous for victory'; for *nobilis* cf. 1. 1. 5, 1. 8.
12; the combination adjective + 'explanatory' (or 'epexetic') infinitive is aimed at repro-
ducing in Latin the allusive compactness of the Greek compound epithet. — **quorum ...
refulsit**] The singular *stella* suggests the reference is to the phenomenon of St Elmo's
fire rather than to the constellation Gemini (see on 1. 3. 2); **alba**] = 'that brings clear
weather'; see on 1. 7. 15. — **defluit ... umor**] The spray 'drains down from the rocks'
against which the sea had been pounding during the storm; for the sea beating against
rocks cf. 1. 11. 5. — **minax ponto unda recumbit**] 'on the open sea the swell subsides'.
— **quod sic voluere**] 'because they (Castor and Pollux) have willed it so'.

33-48] After gods and heroes comes H.'s men. A dozen great names are picked from
Roman history. The order in Stanza 9 is chronological (with a jump from Tarquin to
Cato); in Stanzas 10-11 it seems deliberately haphazard; Stanza 12 brings us up to the
present. The list bears obvious similarities to Virgil's catalogue of Rome's great men in
Aeneid 6. — **post hos prius an ...**] Romulus, the founder of Rome, is an obvious first
choice; but Numa, who brought peace and the rule of law (see Livy's portrait of him,
1. 18), the expulsion of Tarquin and the founding of the free Republic, and the suicide
of the younger Cato (Lucan's hero), which symbolised the final victory of Julius Caesar
in the Civil War, are represented as equally attractive themes; 33 *prius* picks up 13 *prius*
— there no doubt about where to begin was possible (even if Pallas came close to Jove),
here doubt is possible. — **superbos ... fasces**] The symbol of Roman power came in
Tarquin's case to symbolise the overweening arrogance of the monarch. — **Catonis ...
letum**] Cato becomes the symbol of dogged resistance, admirable, however wrongheaded,
for its moral courage; cf. 2. 1. 23-4; he is perhaps slipped in here to make the inclusion of
Marcellus (lines 45-6) seem less strained. — **Regulum ... Fabriciumque**] The list of
Roman minor heroes corresponds to the list of gods in lines 21-5: *referam* corresponds
structurally to 21 *neque te silebo*; for Regulus, see 3. 5. 13-56; the plural *Scauros*
probably = 'that great house, the Scauri', chosen as representative of the great patrician
families to whom Roman history owed so much; the most distinguished were M. Aemilius
Scaurus, cos. 115 and M. Aurelius Scaurus, cos. 108; the reputation of the Scauri of the
late Republic was more equivocal; *Paulum* evokes L. Aemilius Paullus, cos. 219 and 216,
killed in action at the Battle of Cannae ('animae magnae prodigum' = 'who courageously
threw away his life'); *Fabricium* evokes C. Fabricius Luscinius, consul 281 and 278, best
known for the story of his refusal to poison Pyrrhus (Cicero *Off.* 3. 22); none of the
really great Romans of the past is included; **gratus ... camena**] = 'I will offer thanks to
them by giving them a prominent place in my poetry'. — **hunc**] Corresponds structurally
to 26 *hunc*, introducing in both cases the rallentando which precedes the climactic surge
at the end of each section of the poem (see Structure). — **Curium**] M. Curius Dentatus,
consul 290 and 275, victor over Pyrrhus in the Battle of Beneventum; called unkempt
('incomptis capillis') because tradition represented him as a rustic son of the soil
summoned to greatness. — **Camillum**] M. Furius Camillus, dictator 396, the conqueror
of Veii and the 'second founder' of Rome after its capture by the Gauls in 390. —
crescit] The asyndeton *tulit, crescit, micat* puts Marcellus on the same level of impor-
tance as Fabricius, etc. while underlining the difference between them (Fabricius, etc.
were simple farmers whose rise to fame was sudden, the reputation of Marcellus has been
growing steadily, the ascendancy of Caesar over all is manifest). — **Marcelli**] Almost
certainly a reference to the young M. Claudius Marcellus, nephew and son-in-law of
Augustus and clearly marked out as his successor, whose unexpected death in 23 BC
wins him a place of honour in Virgil's pageant of heroes, *Aen.* 6. 860-86; some suppose
the reference must be to the hero of the second Punic War, M. Claudius Marcellus, but

this is to fail to appreciate the special perspective of imperial flattery; Peerlkamp's *Marcellis* (dative plural) is ingenious but uncalled for ('crescit . . . aevo', 'grows like a tree with the unmarked lapse of time', i.e., steadily but imperceptibly, is clearly appropriate to the young Marcellus). — **micat . . . sidus**] While *sidus* might seem to suggest the comet which appeared after the death of Julius Caesar, the reference is clearly to Augustus; the metaphor of the star follows naturally enough on the simile of the tree, the metaphorical star occupying structurally the position occupied by 28 *stella* in the less elaborate climax of the second section of the ode; H. (responsive, as always, to current propaganda) may intend to imply that the comet which marked the apotheosis of Julius has become a star standing over the head of Augustus, symbolising his ascendancy and proclaiming his forthcoming apotheosis; Virgil seems to come close to this in his tableau of Actium, *Aen.* 8. 680-81 (of Octavian) 'stans celsa in puppi, geminas cui tempora flammas / laeta vomunt patriumque aperitur vertice sidus'. — **luna**] Largest and brightest in the night sky; perhaps also a hint (in preparation for Stanzas 13-15) that Augustus derives his glory from Jove as the moon derives its light from the sun.

49-60] We have reached the real subject of the poem by an appropriately devious route. H. concludes with a formal prayer to Jove asking him to protect Augustus, who acknowledges his supremacy. — **Gentis . . . custos**] Picks up lines 13-16. — **orte Saturno**] = 'son of Cronos'; the formal patronymic of ritual style. — **fatis data**] While compatible with the traditional style of ritual, suggests the more philosophical view of human destiny of the *Aeneid*, in which Jove is more the administrator of fate than the all-powerful god of primitive belief. — **secundo Caesare**] Suggests, not the humility of 3. 6. 5, but that Augustus is the chief lieutenant of Jove, his chief commander on earth; this notion is picked up and expanded in lines 53-7. — **Parthos Latio imminentis**] In the *Odes* the Parthians are regularly represented as an enemy who will have to be dealt with before peace is assured; with the exaggeration of 'Latio imminentis' cf. 1. 37. 6-8 (of Cleopatra); here, as elsewhere, H. seems to reflect the official propaganda current at the time of publication of *Odes* 1-3; see Introduction to 3. 5; contrast the mood of 2. 11. 1-5. — **egerit . . . triumpho**] 'will have led before him, reduced to subjection in a just triumph'; *iusto triumpho* with *egerit*. — **subiectos . . . Indos**] Conquest deep into Asia is a possibility that can be thrown out (implying that the victories of Augustus will eventually rival those of Alexander) without implying seriously entertained objectives; see on 1. 29. 9; **subiectos Orientis orae**] = 'those who dwell hard by the edge of the world where the sun rises'; *Orientis* is genitive, *orae* dative; cf. Catullus 11. 2-4; **Seras**] Greek accusative plural (the *a* is short). — **te**] The final stanza begins with a pattern of anaphora in asyndeton built around the personal pronoun (*te . . . tu . . . tu . . .*). a traditional feature of hymns; the normal structure is one of appositional expansion; here the opening *te* is strongly opposed to the following *tu*'s by the change of subject from Augustus (*reget*) to Jove (*quaties, mittes*). — **latum . . . orbem**] = 'will rule justly over the whole breadth of the earth', while Jove confines himself to the traditional roles set out in the concluding lines; the MSS are divided between *latum* and *laetum* (OCT). — **gravi curru**] For the chariot of Jove, see 1. 34. 8-12. — **parum . . . lucis**] For the thunderbolt of Jove, see on 1. 2. 1-4; *castis lucis* is dative with *inimica*.

1. 13

Introduction: Lydia again. Are we to assume she is the Lydia of 1. 8 and the Lydia of 1. 25 (perhaps also the Lydia of 3. 9)? The same type, that is to say, the same representative fiction of H.'s imagination. (There seems little likelihood that the name conceals a 'real' person whose identity might be known to H.'s contemporaries; see on 1. 5. 3 *Pyrrha*.) If so, the shift in perspective is intriguing and, presumably, planned. One thing the corruptress of 1. 8, the infatuated Lydia of 1. 13, the Lydia already no longer as young as she used to be of 1. 25 and the Lydia of 3. 9 whose infatuation with Calais is wearing off have in common is a taste for lovers younger than themselves: Sybaris, Telephus, Calais are all young, their youth insisted upon (cf. 1. 13. 11 *puer*, 3. 9. 16 *puero*; with the Lydia of 1. 25 age is more a relative matter). Whether they belong to the type castigated by H. in 3. 6. 21-32 — the married woman of good family who *iuniores quaerit adulteros* — or to a more modest rank in society there is no telling; the Lydia of 1. 25 at any rate has a husband (see on 1. 25. 9 *moechos*).

In the Pyrrha ode and the Sybaris ode, the emphasis is on the male victim; in 1. 13 we see the relationship from the woman's point of view (she is infatuated, dreams of ever-lasting love); H., as usual, casts himself in the role of the middle-aged observer of the human comedy, but finds it hard for once to maintain that role; it seems a good guess (one confirmed by 3. 9 — if we assume Lydia there is the Lydia of 1. 13) that Lydia was once H.'s mistress (see below on lines 15-16) and that she now confides in H. as one to whom such confidences can safely be made, thereby subjecting H. to an exquisite torture which he must struggle to conceal under a pose of disinterested adviser. H.'s awareness of his own involuntary emotional involvement is expressed with elegant irony.

Structure: Five endstopped stanzas (within each stanza enjambment is usual, or at most a light pause). Stanzas 1-3 are set in the present: Stanza 1 sketches in the hypothesis of the poem; Stanza 2 describes H.'s reaction in detail; in Stanza 3 the focus shifts from H. to the evidence which prompts this jealous reaction. The prediction of Stanzas 4-5 is to be read in the light of this reaction.

Metre: Asclepiad (b); alternating Glyconics and Asclepiads as in 1. 3.

1-4] **Cum**] Picked up by 5 *tum* (though *cum* and *tum* are not correlative in the ordinary sense); repeated confidences (and recurring torture for H.) are implied. — **tu**] Emphatic (Lydia, i.e., is a special case, and H.'s reaction not typical). — **Telephi, Telephi**] The repetition suggests how the name keeps recurring in Lydia's conversation. — **cervicem roseam, cerea bracchia**] 'his pale pink neck, his waxy arms'; with *roseam* cf. 4. 10. 4 and *Aen*. 1. 402 (of Venus) 'rosea cervice refulsit'; *cerea* probably stresses the smoothness of Telephus' skin; both terms are Lydia's, not H.'s, and probably suggest male attractiveness as seen through the protective eyes of a woman in love, and described in terms mildly distasteful to another man; Telephus is no he-man lover, no athletic type, but a mere *puer* (line 11). — **vae**] Mock-heroic, to prepare the way for the ironically literary description of H.'s reaction which follows; cf. 1. 5. 5 *heu*. — **meum . . . iecur**] The liver is in Greek poetry the site of the passion of love (cf. 1. 25. 15 — also ironical); **fervens tumet**] 'boils and swells'; i.e., a violent onset of passion; **difficili bile**] 'with angry bile'; to be taken as a literary pun rather than seriously descriptive of symptoms: the Greek verb χαλεπαίνω, 'I become angry', suggests to H. the adjective χαλεπός, 'difficult'; hence *difficili*.

5-8] H.'s description of his less deep-set symptoms is obviously intended to recall Sappho's famous description of her feelings; Catullus' adaptation of Sappho's lines (Poem 51 — not without hints of urbane, ironic exaggeration) is equally famous; cf. the epigram of Valerius Aedituus quoted Gellius 19. 9. 10 ('verba labris abeunt, / per pectus miserum manet subido mihi sudor', etc.); H.'s mental perturbation and changing colour provide an acceptable echo of Sappho, his furtive tears and the explanation of them are his own and plainly ironic. — **nec mens nec color . . . manet**] = 'my mental faculties are disturbed (i.e., my thoughts are confused), my colour keeps changing' (the blood drains from his cheeks, perhaps alternating with hot flushes); the elegant simplicity of the words is in sharp contrast with the struggle for precise description in Sappho and Catullus; **manet**] agreement with the nearer. — **umor . . . labitur**] *umor* = 'tears'; the metonomy is literary, like the hyperbaton of *et*, but also prepares the way for treating the tears as the external manifestation of fires within in lines 6-7; for tears as evidence of passion cf. 4. 1. 34; **furtim**] because he conceals his tears from Lydia. — **arguens . . . ignibus**] 'proving to what extent I am consumed by slow fires within'; *quam* with *penitus* and *macerer* rather than with *lentis; lentus* is the stock epithet; cf. 3. 19. 28 'lentus amor'. Tibullus 1. 4. 81 'lento me torquet amore', Ovid *Ars* 3. 573 'ignibus hic lentis uretur'; where there is *umor*, in other words, there's fire; the image suggested seems to be that of sap oozing out from a log of greenish wood as the fire licks around it; H.'s tears are thus proof of passion, but his formulation of the idea verges, deliberately, on the absurd.

9-12] H., as he has just explained, is on fire; *uror*, 'burn', a cliché of Augustan love poetry, ostensibly proclaims an actual conflagration. But that which sets H. on fire is not Lydia's beauty but the evidence of her new young lover's ardour. Even in Stanza 2 we might suspect that Lydia is scarcely intended to be listening to H.'s confession (as Thaliarchus has to be imagined as listening to H. in 1. 9, or Leuconoe in 1. 11); the scene sketched in lines 1-8 is not (as in the true dramatic monologue) the actual scene in which the speaker speaks or is overheard voicing his thoughts, but a recurring scene and the poem a synthesis of H.'s reactions to those occasions; 1. 13 works, i.e., like the typical modern poem in which the addressee is merely a formal device permitting concise, effective

organisation of the poet's material; see on lines 13-16 below. — uror] Cf. Tibullus 2. 4.
5, Propertius 2. 3. 44, etc. — and H. himself 1. 6. 19, 1. 19. 5, *Epodes* 11. 4; cf. 3. 7. 11.
— candidos . . . rixae] The loaded language of jealousy: where H. sees evidence of
drunken brawls, the detached observer might see evidence only of passionate love; for
the *rixae amoris*, see Lucretius 4. 1079-83, Tibullus 1. 10. 53 ff.; cf. 1. 6. 17-18. — sive
puer . . . notam] *puer* likewise is H.'s word (and must therefore be accepted with caution
from one who is middle-aged) but is plausible enough (see Introduction); furens] 'in his
madness' (i.e., the madness of passion); memorem notam} = 'a souvenir of his affection'.
13-16]   Non . . . speres] 'If you would only listen enough to me, you wouldn't hope . . . '
But H. knows she is not in a mood to listen to reason; his words of advice, i.e., are only
to soothe his own jealous imagination. — perpetuum] = *eum perpetuum fore*, 'yours for
ever' (the dream of all innocent girls who become infatuated); we may suppose Lydia is
less innocent than it comforts H. to imagine. — dulcia . . . laedentem oscula] 'bruising
those sweet lips of yours like the barbarian he is'. — quae Venus . . . imbuit] Venus is to
be imagined, perhaps, as dipping the lips of those mortals whom she favours — those
women, i.e., whom she chooses to make irresistible — in her own special nectar (the
mysterious drink of the gods, likely to go to the head of mere mortals); Lydia's kisses
at any rate, according to H. (who must be presumed to assert this from personal expe-
rience) have especially intoxicating qualities; apart from confirming the suspicion that
Lydia was once H.'s mistress, the poetic fantasy is aimed at representing, symbolically
and in concrete terms, the elusive quality of feminine charm; see on 1. 5. 11 *aurae* and
Quinn on Catullus 13. 11-12; Ben Jonson's version of the conceit ('Song to Celia') is
well known; for nectar, see also 3. 3. 11-12; quinta parte] perhaps a reference to
Pythagoras' division of the elements into air, fire, water, aether and 'a fifth element'
more perfect than all the rest: thus, 'the purest essence'; many take, however, as 'a fifth
part' (i.e., one part in five, pure ambrosia being too much to expect Venus to part with);
in either case, the wistful memory of a former lover rather than a compliment paid to Lydia.
17-20]   To be thrice blessed is to be unusually blessed; to be more than thrice blessed is
rare luck indeed. But that is the luck lovers need if they are to live happily together until
death do them part. Lydia's chances, i.e., are just about nil. H.'s starting point is his usual
Epicurean view of love as a transitory madness: men and women keep falling in love;
infatuation succeeds infatuation, but love never lasts; cf. the detailed working-out of this
idea in 1. 33. — quos . . . copula] 'whom a bond never broken holds together'. — nec
malis divolsus . . . amor dies] = 'and whom no love torn apart by ill-natured recrimina-
tion will release (i.e., from the bond that holds them together) sooner than their dying
day'; suprema citius die] = 'citius quam suprema die'; cf. Propertius 2. 15. 25 'Atque
utinam haerentis sic nos vincire catena / velles ut nunquam solveret ulla dies'.

1. 14

Introduction: Cited by Quintilian 8. 6. 44 as an example of *allegoria*: 'ut "O navis referent
. . . portum" totusque ille Horatii locus quo navem pro re publica, fluctuum tempestates
pro bellis civilibus, portum pro pace atque concordia dicit'. Quintilian's interpretation,
though occasionally contested, has been generally accepted, despite differences of opinion
about details, and uncertainty about Stanza 5. The ship of state is a common metaphor
in Greek literature and navigation an obvious symbol for political activity (as in 2. 10.
1-4). H.'s starting point is probably Alcaeus 326LP (quoted and so interpreted by
Heracleitus, *Homeric Allegories*; see Page, *Sappho and Alcaeus* 187). But the poem is
perhaps intended to be recognised as well as recalling an actual storm involving the ship
on which Octavian was returning to Italy after Actium. In Suetonius' account, Octavian's
fleet (like the ship in 1. 14) was battered by the storm on two separate stages of its
journey (Suetonius *Aug*. 17. 3):

Ab Actio cum Samum in hiberna se recepisset, turbatus nuntiis de seditione praemia
et missionem poscentium, quos ex omni numero confecta victoria Brundisium
praemiserat, repetita Italia tempestate in traiectu bis conflictatus, primo inter
promunturia Peloponensi atque Aetoliae, rursus circa montes Ceraunos utrubique
parte liburnicarum demersa, simul eius in qua vehebatur fusis armamentis et
gubernaculo diffracto . . . .

Unless Suetonius has used H.'s poem to embroider his description, it is perhaps better to read H.'s poem as a dramatic re-enactment of an actual event, lending that event symbolical significance by giving it a context and a style linking the event with a literary tradition where 'allegorical' (i.e., symbolic) interpretation was well established. It is noteworthy that, as in H.'s propemptikon to Virgil (1. 3), the ship itself is addressed, unlike Alcaeus' ode (which describes a personal experience).

Structure: Lines 1-9 are closely held together by enjambment (all the pauses in mid-line); the tone is urgent and animated. Following 9 *aequor,* the tone becomes more reasoning and argumentative, and (as if to underline the symbolic significance of what is said — whereas 1-9 are more purely descriptive) in lines 9-15 metrical and syntactical structure coincide (except at the end of line 14); in both sections the basic rhetorical structure is the tricolon crescendo (see below on the lines in question). For lines 15-20, see below on these lines.

Metre: Asclepiad (d) (see 1. 5M).

1-9]   The ship is personified (cf. 12 'silvae filia nobilis') and addressed (like Virgil's ship in 1. 3) as though itself capable of taking action: it has been so battered by the waves as to be scarcely seaworthy (7-9 'vix durare carinae possint imperiosius aequor'); now the harbour is in sight, but a fresh storm (1-2 'novi fluctus') threatens; the ship must strain to make port (2-3 'fortiter occupa portum') before it is too late. The possibility of symbolic transfer of all these details to the events of the Civil Wars is obvious, whether we imagine the dramatic moment is the storm that overtook Octavian on his way back to Italy after Actium (so that the 'novi fluctus' symbolise the threats of an uprising among Octavian's troops mentioned by Suetonius) or not; it is not necessary to limit the symbolic significance of the poem to a single occasion; several times, what had been hoped to be a decisive (if bloody) victory was followed by a fresh outbreak of fighting; cf. 2. 7. 15 (the ocean of war which dragged back Pompeus after Philippi). — **referent . . . novi fluctus**] Best taken as a warning of imminent storm (but see below on lines 15-20); **in mare**] i.e., into the open sea. — **quid agis?**] 'what are you doing (that you don't see the danger)?' — **occupa portum**] *occupare* implies action taken to anticipate action by another (getting in first, or acting, as here, before it is too late); cf. 2. 12. 28. — **nonne vides ut . . . ?** See on 1. 9. 1; cf. 3. 20. 1, 3. 27. 17. — **nudum remigio latus**] The first member of a tricolon crescendo (the second is 'et malus . . . gemant', the third 'ac sine funibus . . . aequor'); the urgent, excited tone suggests a separate statement (sc. *sit*), rather than construction with *gemant*, which involves a somewhat artificial zeugma (though cf. 3. 10. 5-7); the ship, i.e., has had its oars sheared off all along one side; *nudum latus* ('naked flank') reinforces the personification; oars were used for manoeuvring a ship in and out of harbour (or on other occasions when sails were useless or inappropriate); a special effort will be called for, even without the storm. — **malus . . . Africo**] = 'the mast that has been damaged by the South-Westerly'; *saucius* further reinforces the personification; **celeri**] 'swift-footed', perhaps rather as we speak of a ship 'running before the wind'. — **antemnaeque**] 'the yards', which carry the sails. — **gemant**] Both with *malus* and *antemnaeque*. — **funibus**] Ropes used to strengthen the hull and hold the timbers in place, either as a permanent feature of construction or (as seems appropriate here) as a makeshift after damage or as an emergency measure in bad weather (as in the voyage of St Paul, Acts 27: 17); the manner of their attachment (bow to stern, beamwise, etc.) is unclear, perhaps varying according to circumstances. — **carinae**] 'the hull'; the plural suggests a complex structure of beams and planks which is likely to disintegrate (cf. such plurals as *viscera, castra,* etc.). — **imperiosius aequor**] i.e., a sea too eager to assume command.

9-15]   A further tricolon crescendo ('Non . . . lintea', 'non di . . . malo', 'quamvis . . . nil . . . fidit'), the second member expanded by the relative clause, the third preceded by the *quamvis*-clause, but welded into the series by the *nil* which picks up the repeated *non*. — **Non . . . lintea, non di**] The obvious, if weak, sense to attach to *non . . . lintea* is that the ship's sails are torn; the repetition in asyndeton of *non di* (sc. *sunt integri*) requires the rather less obvious sense 'you have no sails and no gods left' (or perhaps 'you have no fresh supply of sails or gods in reserve'); i.e., both sails and the painted figurehead of the ship have been destroyed and there is no possibility of replacing them. — **quos . . . malo**] = 'to whom you can turn if danger strikes again'; because the figure-head has been lost the sailors cannot turn to it to save them; in this literal sense, *di* is a generalising plural; the symbolic sense (Rome's gods have deserted her) is obvious and paramount. — **quamvis . . . inutile**] The ship is an aristocrat among ships, built (like the *phaselus* of Catullus 4) of Pontic pine; again the symbolic sense (noble state, proud of its past) is easily extracted; the ancient commentator Acron, one of the more industrious allegory-hunters, points out that Pompey was the conqueror of Mithridates of Pontus, arguing that the ship represents his son S. Pompeius, whom H. would dissuade from once again embarking upon war; **quamvis iactes**] 'however much you boast of'; some punctuate the *quamvis*-clause with 'non di . . . malo', placing a full stop after *inutile*, but this gives a weaker rhythm and rhetorical structure. — **nil . . . fidit**] 'a frightened sailor has no confidence in painted poops'; an ironic aphorism; **pictis**] elaborately decorated (with designs 'picked out' in colour).

15-20] The conclusion seems oddly anticlimactic, even for H., the mildly worded warning against the deceptive waters around the Cyclades hard to reconcile with the urgency of the opening lines. Some assume the allegory is dropped in the final stanza; others that the opening warning 'referent . . . novi fluctus' refers to a future storm, not one now imminent; neither is a convincing solution; nor does the suggestion of Anderson *Class. Phil.* 61, 1966, 84 ff. that the ship is really an ageing flirt compel conviction; an acceptable solution must respect the rhetorical structure: 20 *vites* backs up and interprets 16 *cave* (for the mixture of imperative and subjunctive cf. 1. 11. 6-8 'sapias . . . liques . . . reseces . . . carpe'); the former warns emphatically and colloquially, but in general terms, the latter enunciates a specific warning. — **Tu . . . cave**] 'Unless the winds are in for a laugh, watch out'; probably a colloquial formula, the logic of which is not to be pressed; **nisi debes**] i.e., unless the matter is settled (by fate, e.g.) and there's nothing to be done about it; cf. *AP* 63 'debemur morti nos nostraque'. — **nuper . . . Cycladas**] *quae* must denote the ship (not, i.e., 20 *aequora*), *interfusa* must go with *aequora*; the language of *nuper . . . levis* echoes that of the love poet to his mistress, picking up the personification of the ship as *filia nobilis* (but with the ship as symbol of the state of Rome now to the forefront): 'you who a while ago filled me with anxiety, whom I could no longer endure and who are now my darling, the object of my earnest desire . . . ' (H. alludes apparently to the disenchantment which led him to fight at Philippi — on the Republican side, but against Octavian) and his subsequent return of affection; with *desiderium* cf. Catullus 2. 5; contrast 1. 24. 1; *cura* for 'mistress' is frequent in Roman love poetry; **interfusa . . . Cycladas**] 'avoid the seas that roll around the shores of the glistening Cyclades'; the area was one noted for storms (Livy 36. 43. 1 'est ventosissima regio inter Cycladas'); an example of H.'s studied irrelevance in a concluding image (cf. 3. 5. 50-56, 4. 2. 54-60); the words must none the less contain an intelligible warning — perhaps 'don't venture a passage of the Cyclades; the beauty of the islands is deceptive; these seas are dangerous; get into port before it is too late' (2-3 'fortiter occupa portum'); for the Cyclades cf. 3. 28. 14; the modern reader feels the final stanza should connect the ship with Rome; it has to be remembered that Rome was not a port and that for a Roman the commonest use of ships was for travel in the eastern Mediterranean.

1. 15

Introduction: A kind of epic in miniature, notably more Homeric in tone and content than H.'s usual manner, and the first of several explorations in the *Odes* of a mythical theme (cf. 3. 3. 17-68, 3. 11. 21-52, 3. 27. 25-76, 4. 4. 37-76 — contrast brief mythical *exempla* such as 1. 8. 13-16, 1. 10. 9-12 and 13-16; 1. 7. 21-32 perhaps transitional). Paris, on his way back to Troy with Helen, is stopped at sea by Nereus, who prophesies the war between Trojans and Greeks which will be the outcome of Paris' act.

Paris and Helen are the prototypes of the adulterer (*adulter, moechus*) and the adulteress (*adultera, moecha*); cf. 3. 3. 18-28 and 4. 9. 13-16. In general, H. is more interested in the *moecha* than in her lover. His *moechae* include Lydia in 1. 25, Pholoe in 1. 33, Damalis in 1. 36, Chloris in 3. 15. The type easily shades off into the girl who simply changes partners (e.g., Lydia in 3. 9) and is not easily distinguished from the unattached *demi-mondaine* — hard to identify unless a husband seems precluded by the hypothesis of the poem (e.g., Barine in 2. 8), or by an incidental remark (the reference to Neaera's *ianitor* in 3. 14. 21). Has the Pyrrha of 1. 5 a husband? What is the status of Tyndaris in 1. 17 — is Cyrus her husband or merely the lover from whom H. hopes temporarily to prise her free? In a society where consensual marriage was common, such distinctions are not clear-cut. It is a reasonable, if unprovable, hypothesis that H. is indulgent towards the *demi-mondaine* (whether she has a *vir* or not) even when upbraiding so ruthless a representative of the type as Barine, but harsh on what may be called the 'Sempronia type' (the upper-class *moecha* past her prime — see on 3. 6. 25-32, where H. castigates the type in terms appropriate to the Roman Odes). This at any rate would be consistent with the line taken in *Sat*. 1. 2. For the social reality which the *moecha* represents, see 3. 6. 25-32. The ageing flirt (Lydia in 1. 25, Chloris in 3. 15, Lyce in 4. 13), whether married or not, is naturally a special case.

Structure: Stanzas 1-3 constitute a first statement of theme and a demonstration of H.'s method of handling it: lines 1-5 succinctly set the stage for Nereus' speech (cf. 1. 7. 21-4, 3. 3. 17-18, 4. 4. 36-49), lines 5-8 state the prophecy, lines 9-12 repeat the prophecy in more pathetic terms (the tricolon crescendo 'quantus ... ', 'quantus ... ', 'quanta ... ' is followed by the vivid 'iam galeam Pallas ... parat'). Stanzas 4-8 are an extension of the prophecy, forming a kind of second movement highlighting incidents in the coming war in which Paris will be conspicuous. Stanza 9 rounds the poem off with a general statement about the course of the war.

Metre: Asclepiad (c); see 1. 6M.

1-5] **Pastor**] The emphasis on Paris as 'the herdsman' is as old as Homer (*Il*. 24. 29); cf., in Roman poetry, *Aen*. 7. 363, Ovid *Her*. 5 and 16. — **traheret**] Implies that, if Helen was a ready party to the seduction, her abduction to Troy was against her will. — **perfidus hospitam**] The juxtaposition defines the relevant aspect of Paris' perfidy: he had been a guest in Helen's house at the time of the seduction. — **ingrato ... ventos**] i.e., stilled the winds, so that the fleet was becalmed; *ingrato* because Paris was eager to get Helen home. — **caneret**] The usual word for a formal prophecy. — **fera fata**] 'a cruel prophecy' (*OLD ferus* 7). — **Nereus**] Like other sea gods, Nereus has the power of prophecy; as father of the Nereid Thetis and grandfather of Achilles, he is of course an interested party.

5-8] **Mala ... domum**] The abduction of Helen, the traditional cause of the Trojan War, is spoken of in characteristically Roman terms (for a more cynical formulation, see *Sat*. 1. 3. 107-10); **ducis domum**] evokes the traditional Roman ceremony (*deductio*) in which the groom escorts the bride to her new home following a pretence of forcible abduction (said to perpetuate the memory of the 'rape' of the Sabine Women); cf. 7 *nuptias*; **mala avi**] cf. Catullus 61. 19-20 'Bona cum bona / nubet alite virgo'. — **quam ... milite**] Echoes the formal, archaic language of prophecy. — **coniurata**] Refers to the alliance of Greek cities which sent contingents to Troy — **rumpere**] Verse style prefers the simple infinitive where the more elaborate etiquette of prose requires an accusative and future infinitive. — **nuptias**] Reinforces the notion of marriage implied in *mala ... domum*. — **regnum Priami vetus**] 'Priam's ancient kingdom' was founded by Priam's father Laomedon; for the abduction of Helen as the precipitating factor in Troy's destruction, see on 3. 3. 18-24.

9-12] Stanza 2 prophesies the outbreak of war. Stanza 3 looks to the ensuing suffering; hence the more pathetic tone. — **heu heu**] 'Alas!', an exclamation prophesying disaster; cf. 1. 5. 5; also line 19. — **quantus ... genti**] A formal tricolon crescendo with anaphora in asyndeton; **equis**] the horses are put before the men, not on humanitarian grounds but because (1) the sweat-drenched cavalry horses present a more vivid picture, (2) the expanding structure of the tricolon requires a swell in the level of pathos; **quanta moves funera**] 'what heroes (*quanta*, not *quot funera*) among your own people you are bringing to their death'; for the thought cf. *Aen*. 8. 537-40; with *moves* ('set in motion') cf. 4. 1. 2; with *Dardanae genti* cf. 21 *tuae genti*; **Dardanae**] from Dardanus, son of Zeus and Electra, the ancestors of Laomedon and Priam); H. prefers the noun used adjectivally (=, as often, 'Trojan') to the genitive plural, or the longer forms (*Dardanius*, etc.); cf. 2. 9. 21 'Medumque flumen', etc. — **iam ... parat**] A further, more succinct, more urgent tricolon; the passage evokes the arming of Pallas Athena, the protectress of the Greeks (called *Pallas* or *Minerva* by the Romans) *Il*. 5. 733-47: H. selects the traditional symbols of the goddess (the war helmet, the *aegis*, the chariot), adding zeugmatically an unexpected fourth item to the third member of the tricolon — Pallas' mad rage against the Trojans; the same rhetorical pattern in lines 16-19; cf. the more Roman Minerva of 3. 3. 23; **aegida**] see on 3. 4. 57; **currusque**] poetic plural, as *Epodes* 9. 22; H. elsewhere uses the singular.

13-20]   As the prophecy gains momentum, Stanza 4 spills over into Stanza 5; the resultant complex rhetorical structure is held together by the repeated *nequiquam* in lines 13 and 16 (anaphora in asyndeton) until the abrupt break after 19 *Aiacem*, which throws into emphasis the ironically worded prediction that Paris (represented in lines 13-19 as a cowardly womaniser) will not be able to escape his fate. — **Veneris praesidio ferox**] Homer's Paris is rescued by Aphrodite in a cloud of mist from his duel with Menelaus, and boasts to Helen he will fight again and win, *Il.* 3. 380-440; Paris was Venus' favourite because he chose her in the beauty competition with Minerva and Juno (the 'Judgement of Paris' — a legend not in Homer); cf. 3. 3. 19 'incestus iudex'; **ferox**] 'tough', 'heroic', the word used by Catullus of Theseus in Poem 64; here ironical, implying Paris boasts of his courage before women, but is in fact a coward; allusion to Mark Antony, represented by Augustan propaganda as a coward and a womaniser, is evident. — **pectes caesariem**] For a Roman (though not for a Greek) a symbol of effeminacy; cf. 4. 9. 13; contrast 1. 5. 4. — **grataque . . . divides**] A further symbol of effeminacy; it is playing to women which is shameful rather than lyre-playing in itself (Achilles plays the lyre to Patroclus in his tent, *Il.* 9. 186-91), though once again the value system appealed to is Roman, not Greek; **feminis**] equally with *grata* and *divides*; **divides**] a technical term, the meaning of which is uncertain; the lyre was probably used to accentuate the metrical beat of the lines which the performer declaims as he accompanies himself on the lyre; but a secondary sense, 'playing to each of the women in turn', is perhaps also present (cf. 1. 36. 6). — **thalamo**] The bedroom to which Aphrodite whisked him from the duel with Menelaus; H. implies Paris did not venture into battle again. — **gravis hastas . . . Aiacem**] The same rhetorical pattern as in lines 11-12, here structured as a tricolon crescendo; **gravis**] (1) 'massive', (2) almost 'nasty', 'disagreeable'; **calami spicula Cnosii**] = 'Cretan arrows' (the best); Paris is eventually killed by a poisoned arrow fired by Philoctetes from the bow of Heracles (this story not in Homer); **strepitumque**] the uproar of battle; **Aiacem**] the 'swift-footed son of Oileus' (*Il.* 2. 527), not the better known son of Telamon. — **tamen heu serus**] i.e., fate will catch up with Paris in the end. — **adulteros . . . collines**] (1) An allusion to Hector's taunts before the duel, *Il.* 3. 54-5 ('your lyre will not help you, nor will your hair or your looks when you lie in the dust'); H. adds *adulteros* (cf. 3. 3. 25, 4. 9. 13; see on 1. 25. 9), (2) the vivid *collines* ('smear', i.e., with dust instead of hair oil); Iarbas in *Aen.* 4. 216 represents Aeneas as a second Paris, oily locks and all ('crinemque madentem').

21-32]   As the momentum of the prophecy increases further, Stanza 6 spills over into Stanza 7 which in its turn flows on over into Stanza 8. — **Non . . . respicis**] 'Have you no thought for', i.e., 'have you forgotten'; **Laertiaden**] Odysseus; the first of a string of famous names from the *Iliad*; to each is added an epithet or descriptive phrase in the Homeric manner; **exitium**] because he devised the stratagem of the wooden horse; **tuae genti**] cf. 10 'Dardanae genti'; **Pylium Nestora**] Nestor from Pylos, the wise old man among the Greek leaders. — **urgent**] i.e., 'are out for your blood'. — **Teucer**] For Teucer, see on 1. 7. 19. — **te**] The third in a series of anaphorae (13, 16 *nequiquam*, 21, 22 *non*); some good MSS have *Teucer et* (for the resultant trochee, see on 36 *ignis*). — **Sthenelus**] A minor character, chosen for the evocative force of the name rather than with reference to any particular incident. — **sciens pugnae**] Another Homeric tag (cf. *Il.* 5. 549). — **sive . . . piger**] Sthenelus was the charioteer of Diomede; the more elaborate appositional expansion marks a kind of climax. — **Merionen**] Also a charioteer; see on 1. 6. 15. — **nosces**] 'you will get to know'; the future brings us back to the dramatic moment of Nereus' prophecy, forming a kind of pause between the vivid *urgent* and the even more vivid *ecce furit*. — **ecce furit reperire**] i.e., on the battlefield; with the infinitive cf. 2. 4. 22 'fuge suspicari', etc. — **Tydides**] Diomede, son of Tydeus (one of the Seven against Thebes); cf. 1. 6. 16. — **melior patre**] Again the detail is Homeric (*Il.* 4. 405). — **quem tu . . . anhelitu**] The imaginative amplification which crowns the prophecy corresponds to nothing in Homer and is perhaps wholly H.'s; cf. the timorous fawn of 1. 23. 1-8; **in altera parte**] 'on the other side'; **lupum**] cf. 1. 22. 9-12; **graminis inmemor**] 'with no thought for the grass'; cf. *Eclogues* 8. 2. 'immemor herbarum iuvenca'; **sublimi anhelitu**] = 'with panting head upreared'; a vivid touch to mark the climax of the image and the poem, before the bathetic 'non hoc pollicitus tuae'; some see a reference to the Greek medical expression μετέωρον πνεῦμα, of shallow, panting breath; but (1) heavy, struggling breathing is appropriate to flight, shallow, panting breath to subsequent regain of calm; (2) a visual detail is more likely at the conclusion of the image. — **pollicitus**] Cf.

1. 29. 16 'pollicitus meliora' (also a concluding bathos). — **tuae**] Almost = 'to your girl-friend'; cf. 1. 25. 7.

33-6] A quiet ending is appropriate after the bathos of line 32. It takes the form of a concluding summary of the prophecy: the wrath of Achilles and his withdrawal from the fighting (the subject of the *Iliad*) will postpone the day of Troy's destruction, but Troy will fall and be destroyed by fire. — **Iracunda classis Achillei**] The fleet is identi-fied with its leader; for the ships of Achilles, see *Il.* 2. 771. — **matronisque**] The Trojan mothers (above all Hecuba) whose sons are killed and who are themselves taken captive. — **post certas hiemes**] i.e., the ten years which the Trojan War was fated to last; for an odd variation on this, see *Aen.* 8. 398-9. — **uret Achaicus ignis**] The subject of *Aen.* 2; the opening trochee (permitted by Greek metrical practice), found only here in H. (unless *et* is accepted in place of *te* in line 24), is taken by some as of early composition; others emend (e.g., Pergameas), but the emphatic repetition 'Ilio . . . Iliacas' seems to authenticate the text.

1. 16

Introduction: 'Do what you like with those old verses of mine. I can understand your anger: I used to have a temper too. Now I am all for peace: let's be friends.'

'O matre pulcra' is H.'s urbane version of the 'palinode' — a poem apologising for, or disowning, a previous attack. The most famous is the ode (or odes) written by Stesichorus after being blinded, tradition has it, by Castor and Pollux for a poem attack-ing Helen of Troy; following recantation, his sight was restored (Plato *Phaedr.* 243 a, Isocrates *Helen* 218 e, both quoted by Page *LGS* 62; the surviving fragments suggest two such palinodes; see Bowra, *Greek Lyric Poetry* ² 108-12); H. alludes to Stesichorus in *Epodes* 17. 42-4 — itself an ironic palinode to his old enemy Canidia. Closer to H.'s poem is Catullus 36 — a carefully worded counter-proposal rather than a palinode in any strict sense. But where Catullus' poem shows the poet, in no frame of mind to forgive and forget, engaged in a battle of wits with a mistress while things still rankle on both sides, 1. 16 shows H. in his favourite pose as a love poet — all middle-aged reasonableness, ready to treat the verses which angered the girl as an indiscretion of his younger years which he is willing to disown provided the girl, too, is willing to make appropriate amends: the diatribe against anger, an example of H.'s elegant mock-grandiloquence (cf. 1. 3. 9-40), is directed as much at the girl (who has harboured her anger) as against himself. In 3. 14. 25-8 H. is likewise more disposed than when he was younger to be reasonable when a girl is uncooperative; a decade later he will confess (4. 1. 3-4) 'non sum qualis eram bonae sub regno Cinarae'.

Structure: A succinct opening statement of the hypothesis of the poem (Stanza 1) is followed by a mock-serious sermon on anger as the most uncontrollable of the passions (Stanzas 2-3 state the case with the fullness appropriate to the high style, Stanza 4 adduces a mythical explanation of where anger came from). Lines 17-21 proceed to cite some suitably impressive examples of the consequences of anger. Then at line 22 (in mid-stanza) comes an unexpected reversal of perspective: it is the girl's angry refusal to make things up that H. has been so solemnly deprecating, not his own — H.'s verses are a thing of the past; can't the girl be reasonable, too?

Metre: Alcaics; see 1. 9M.

1-4] **O matre . . . pulcrior**] Possibly Stesichorus' palinode began with some such compli-ment (Helen's mother was Leda; cf. Ovid *Her.* 'pulchrae filia Ledae'); a 'motto line' in that case, like 1. 18. 1; but in the Roman tradition of personal invective in which H. places his poem, the formula has more equivocal overtones; of four examples in Catullus (22. 14, 27. 4, 39. 16, 99. 2) only the last is complimentary; it seems a good guess that we are intended to suspect that H.'s *iambi* began with some such defamatory opening salvo as 'O matre turpi nata longe turpior', and that the present bland reversal, even if, on the face of it, irreproachably conciliatory, is hardly calculated to offer complete satisfaction to the complainant (cf. the verbal recantation at the end of Catullus 42); the tone of urbane mockery which that reading suggests is certainly consistent with the way H.'s poem proceeds, just as it is consistent with H.'s manner to pick up a familiar line, phrase, or idea and give it fresh meaning by applying it to different circumstances (see on 1. 9. 1-4); some have supposed that H.'s *iambi* were directed against the girl's mother (the

Canidia, perhaps, of *Epodes* 8 and 17) — an attractive hypothesis, at first sight (cf. the mother-daughter of 3. 15), but hard to reconcile with the way the poem ends. — **quem . . . cumque . . . iambis**] = 'do what you like with my libellous iambic verses'; **quem . . . cumque**] 'whatever'; for the division ('tmesis') cf. 1. 9. 14; **iambis**] in Catullus, the term denotes verses in the Roman tradition of personal invective, not necessarily in iambic metre, imitated by H. in *Epodes* 4, etc.; no need to suppose a reference here to an actual epode (extant or otherwise); the function of *iambis* here and 24 'in celeres iambos' is more to place H.'s present poem in the tradition of Catullus 36 (thus preparing the way for the talk of destroying poems by fire, etc. which follows); **modum pones**] 'put an end to', 'dispose of'; cf. 3. 15. 2; the future indicative, as often, serves as a polite imperative. — **sive flamma**] As Lesbia in Catullus 36 had vowed she would burn the 'truces iambos' Catullus had written about her; for the double dissyllable *sive flamma*, see 1. 9M. — **sive mari . . . Hadriano**] i.e., the Adriatic, a symbol of storm; so perhaps a stormy end to stormy verses; but tossing into the sea, etc. seems to have been as proverbial as tossing to the winds; cf. 1. 25. 20, Catullus 70.

5-12]   Four forms of frenzied passion: the madness of religious frenzy, the madness of prophetic inspiration, the madness of drunken frenzy, the madness of orgiastic ritual, all described as less destructive of mental equilibrium than passionate anger. As often, H. echoes the commonplaces of moralistic literature: for Cicero on *ira* as a form of madness, see *Tusc.* 4. 74. The very conventional *exempla* so elaborately evoked and the rhetorical flourish of the quadruple *non* (anaphora in asyndeton) is a warning (in the present context) that H. is not wholly serious. — **Dindymene**] Cybele (also known as *Magna Mater*), the 'domina Dindymene' of Catullus 63. 12; cf. 35. 14, 63. 91; after Mt Dindymus in Phrygia; she is represented by Catullus as driving her worshippers mad. — **adytis**] May be read either as locative or instrumental. — **mentem**] Prepares the way for 22 'conpesce mentem'. — **sacerdotum**] The priestess of Apollo, like Virgil's Sibyl in *Aen.* 6. — **incola Pythius**] i.e., the god Apollo when he inspires the priestess as a *praesens deus*. — **Liber**] Bacchus, in his role as the god of drunkenness. — **non acuta sic geminant Corybantes aera**] We pass from divinities who inspire frenzy to the frenzied worshippers of Cybele and Bacchus/Dionysus (the term 'Corybantes' is applied to the worshippers of both divinities, whose wild music drives those who hear it to frenzy; for the music, see Catullus 63. 21-30, 64. 261-4); **geminant**] i.e., 'clash' by bringing the bronze cymbals (*aera*) together with a sharp strident crash (*acuta*); the language is artificially imprecise and allusive in parody of the high style. — **tristes ut irae**] i.e., 'bitter outbursts of anger'; *tristis* 'making sad', rather than 'sad', as often; **irae**] the plural of the abstract noun denotes instances of the abstraction, as often; that 'ira furor brevis est' (*Epist.* 1. 2. 62) is a commonplace, overstated for ironic effect; **ut**] correlative with *sic* and, less directly, with *aeque* (the normal correlative of *aeque* is *ac*; *aeque ut* is rare and unclassical). — **neque, etc.**] *neque*, followed by three *nec*'s corresponds to the quadruple *non* of Stanza 2. — **Noricus ensis**] Noricum, in the Alps, was known for its steel; oddly enough, the first extant occurrence of the phrase is found in H.'s earlier dramatised palinode (*Epodes* 17. 70-71) where Canidia predicts for H. (among other disagreeable deaths) suicide 'ense Norico'. — **saevos ignis**] 'cruel conflagration' (not lightning). — **tremendo . . . tumultu**] Jove descending from the sky, hurling his thunderbolts — the most terrible of warnings to mankind to desist from wickedness; cf. 1. 2. 2-3, 3. 3. 6, etc.; for **ruens**, 'hurtling down', cf. 1. 19. 9.

13-16]   A parody of aetiological myth (a favourite theme of Hellenistic elegists and their Roman imitators). The myth is that recounted by Protagoras in Plato's dialogue (*Prot.* 320 d - 321), in which Prometheus and his brother Epimetheus equip the mortal creatures they have moulded from clay with various attributes; anger, not mentioned by Protagoras, is probably a fanciful addition by H.; for Prometheus, see 1. 3. 27-8. — **fertur, etc.**] The construction is 'Prometheus, coactus addere . . . , et (= etiam) . . . adposuisse'; **principi limo**] 'the primeval clay', from which the human prototype was fabricated; **coactus**] man being a synthetic creature, Prometheus was compelled to find his components where he could (no need to suppose he was compelled by some god to equip man with anger); **particulam undique desectam**] = 'bits clipped from all sorts of creatures'; the singular because only one *particula* from each — an example of the Latin idiomatic preference for the singular where English prefers the plural (cf. such phrases as 'use your heads'); cf. 16 *stomacho*; **insani leonis**] 'of a raging lion'; **vim**] (1) 'attribute', 'characteristic', (2) 'violence'; **stomacho**] the actual organ, traditionally supposed to be the

site of anger (as the liver of love), often therefore as a synonym of anger (as 1. 6. 6).
17-21] **irae**] 'his mad rages', picks up 9 'irae'. — **Thyesten**] Son of Pelops, brother of
Atreus; the feud between them is cited by Cicero *Tusc.* 4. 77 as an example of the evils
to which *ira* leads. — **exitio gravi stravere**] 'laid low in terrible ruin'. — **altis . . . insolens**]
An impressive-sounding generalisation (rather like Catullus 51. 15-16 'otium et reges
prius et beatas perdidit urbes'), if not, from the point of view of historical insight, on a
par with Thucydides' ἀληθεστάτη πρόφασις; the most famous of cities so destroyed
were Troy (Propertius 3. 9. 41-2 'Moenia cum Graio Neptunia pressit aratro/victor')
and Carthage in 146 BC; ploughing over the land symbolised its return to the status of
farmland; cf. 3. 3. 40-41; for this use of *cur* to introduce an indirect question with final/
consecutive force cf. Catullus 10. 11, 14. 5, Livy 7. 9. 2 'Ea ultima fuit causa cur bellum
indiceretur'; **ultimae causae**] 'primary' or 'original cause'; the plural to match *irae* (a
common idiom here overriding that stated above on 14 *particulam*); **hostile . . . insolens**]
no caesura in this line.

22-8]   The sudden 'conpesce mentem' surprises — the reader, encouraged to assume that
the rhetoric of 5-21 is offered as an apology for the anger which produced H.'s *criminosi
iambi*, finds an unexpected reassessment imposed on him, in order to build a fresh, viable
consistency. The denunciation of anger has now to be read as a warning to the girl to
keep *her* anger within reasonable limits. ← **Conpesce mentem**] Something like 'don't
persist in this unreasonable state of mind' — going on being angry about something that
happened a long time ago; *conpesce* suggests *compes*, 'shackle', though probably not
etymologically related; cf. 2. 20. 23; *mens*, 'frame of mind', 'attitude', *OLD* 8. — **me
quoque**] H. is now in a position to say magnanimously 'I used to get all worked up'; for
the *me* at the turning point of an ode, see on 1. 1. 29. — **pectoris fervor**] = 'a boiling
over of the emotions'; *pectus*, according to the Epicurean physiology (Lucretius 3, etc.),
was the site of all mental and emotional activity; 'heart', 'emotions', 'mind' are all
appropriate translations, therefore, according to context. — **temptavit**] 'afflicted', like
a disease; cf. *Georgics* 3. 441 'turpis oves temptavit scabies', *Sat.* 1. 1. 80 'at si condoluit
temptatum frigore corpus'. — **in dulci iuventa**] = 'in the good old days before middle
age overtook me'; *dulci* introduces the appropriate note of regret; cf. 3. 12. 2; for
iuventa, see on 1. 2. 41; H.'s *Epodes* (always called *Iambi* by H.) belong to the time when
he was 25-35. In the year of publication of *Odes* 1-3 H. turned 42; the offending verses
need not have been written more than 5-10 years previously, but H. has learnt to be
sensible and tolerant in the interval (cf. 3. 14. 27-8; for the effect of middle age on out-
look, a common theme in the *Odes*, cf., e.g., 2. 11. 5-8); the girl has yet to learn that
lesson; we can easily suppose that she was 17-20 then, in her twenties now — still young
enough for H. to be anxious to make things up; a clear implication, therefore, of 'in
dulci iuventa' is 'when I was the age you are now'. — **in celeres iambos**] Cf. Catullus 36. 5
'truces vibrare iambos'. — **misit furentem**] The nearest H. comes to recantation: = 'I was
crazy when I wrote those verses, but I was angry'; **misit**] often a strong word ('hurled',
'drove'). — **nunc . . . tristia**] = 'now I am anxious to end our quarrel and make peace';
the *dum*-clause makes it clear H. is speaking of his relationship to the girl, not in general.
— **dum . . . reddas**] Carefully worded, in order to enable the reader to get the situation
in sharp focus: 'provided, now that I have withdrawn my insults, you become my *amica*
and restore me to life'; **fias amica**] practically = 'become my mistress'; the clear impli-
cation is that she was not H.'s mistress before; since H. offers anger as justification for
his *criminosi iambi*, the most likely hypothesis is that she spurned H.'s advances;
recantatis opprobriis] i.e., now that H. has written this poem apologising for them; one
might suppose the apology less than handsome, but the girl must accept the honour done
her in being made the recipient of a palinode as sufficient compensation; **animumque
reddas**] the model of 1. 19. 4 'finitis animum reddere amoribus' suggests the sense
'surrender your heart to me'; the model of 4. 1. 30 'spes animi credula mutui' suggests a
supporting sense, 'return the affection I bear you'; i.e., H. is still interested (or interested
again); he feels he has done the handsome thing, and looks forward to a *quid pro quo*; we
may suspect H. has reason to suspect the girl's anger not unappeasable and that his poem
(like Catullus 36) is intended to be taken as a constructive step forward in a delicate
process of negotiation; cf. the manoeuvring for position in 3. 9.

1. 17

Introduction: An invitation (or possibly a conversation piece — but see on lines 17-20) to a
girl to leave the summer heat of Rome and her husband or lover behind, in order to join
H. on his Sabine farm, where they can picnic in idyllic surroundings under the protection
of Faunus himself. The fact that 1. 16 and 1. 17 are both in Alcaics has encouraged some
to suppose that Tyndaris (= 'daughter of Tyndareus', i.e., Helen) is the unnamed addres-
see of 1. 16.

Contrast the pastoral note of lines 1-12 with the ironic realism of 3. 18; the inhabitants
of this idyllic scene are not the shepherds and shepherdesses of the *Eclogues*; they belong
to the 'real' world of Augustan elegy (cf., e.g., Tibullus 2. 1) with everyday life in Rome
still very much in their thoughts. For the party *en tête-à-tête* (wine and singing to follow)
cf. 3. 28.

Structure: Stanzas 1-3 set the stage. Following the bridge passage 'Di me tuentur ... ', etc.
in lines 13-14, the remainder of the ode takes the form of an elaborate tricolon cres-
cendo, each member introduced by an emphatic, deictic *hic* (anaphora in asyndeton):
14-16 'hic tibi copia manabit ... ' (a single statement); 17-20 'hic in reducta valle ...
vitabis ... et ... dices' (two statements); 21-5 'hic innocentis pocula Lesbii duces ...
nec ... confundet ... nec metues ... ' (three statements, the last flowing over into the
double-barrelled subordinate clause 'ne ... iniciat ... et scindat ... '.

Metre: Alcaics; see on 1. 9M.

1-4]   Stanza 1 establishes the pastoral mood, with no hint of the direction the poem will
take. — **Velox ... Faunus**] i.e., the journey from Arcadia to H.'s Sabine farm is swiftly
accomplished; **Lucretilem**] said by Porphyrio to be a hill in the Sabine country; **Lycaeo**]
a mountain in Arcadia; the two geographical features are no doubt chosen for the simi-
larity in sound (*Luc-*, *Lyc-*); **Faunus**] one of H.'s tutelary deities (cf. 2. 17. 28, 3. 18;
also 1. 4. 11). — **et igneam ... ventos**] i.e., Faunus protects H.'s flocks both from
summer heat and wind and rain of winter; the present invitation is to a summer picnic
(17-18 'caniculae vitabis aestus'); **capellis**] H. has sheep as well as goats on his farm (see,
e.g., 3. 18. 13); the she-goats have a special relevance, however, as will appear in Stanza
2; **usque meis**] emphatic; the protection extended to H. is very special (cf. lines 13-14).

5-12]   Stanzas 2-3 describe the blissful scene on H.'s farm when Faustus is in residence. —
inpune ... mariti] A girl about to spend a country holiday with a man other than her
husband or present lover needs reassurance: hence the emphasis on safety (*inpune*,
tutum per nemus); the *capellae* have strayed from the beaten path but no harm will come
to them; they are married to an unpleasant fellow but he is conspicuous by his absence;
their young enjoy the same miraculous protection as their mothers from the usual
dangers of life; the tableau has a hidden ironic relevance to Tyndaris which does not
fully emerge until Stanzas 5-7; **quaerunt**] the subject is *capellae* (picked up from 3
capellis); **deviae olentis uxores mariti**] an appositional expansion of *[capellae]*, the
implied subject of *quaerunt*; the suggestion of the high style implicit in the periphrasis is
undercut by the content (cf. 1. 25. 14); with *deviae* cf. 2. 11. 21; *olentis mariti*] the
male goat symbolises lust in Roman poetry; it also smells and thus provides a convenient
symbol (when its smell is stressed) for the physically repulsive lecher (cf. Catullus 69. 6).
— **nec ... nec ... lupos**] The first *nec* links *metuunt* (subject *haediliae*) to *quaerunt*,
the second *nec* links *Martialis lupos* to *viridis colubras* (both objects of *metuunt*);
Martialis] sacred to Mars because of the she-wolf who suckled Romulus and Remus;
haediliae] the reading *haedilia* ('goat pens') of inferior MSS may be disregarded; similarly,
the contention of some editors that *Haediliae* is the genitive of a proper name. —
utcumque ... saxa] The sound of his pipe proclaims the arrival of the god; **utcumque**]
frequentative, 'whenever'; cf. 1. 35. 23, 2. 17. 11, 3. 4. 29, 4. 4. 35; **fistula**] ablative
with *personuere*; **Usticae cubantis**] = the slopes of Mt Ustica; the mountain, i.e., is
spoken of as a reclining giantess; Mt Ustica, like Mt Lucretilis, cannot be identified.

13-14]   A bridge passage, marking the transition (at mid-point in the poem) from idyllic
description to invitation. — **Di me tuentur ... cordi est**] A favourite pose, adopted with
varying degrees of seriousness; in 2. 17. 28-30 Faunus saves him from death because of
his poetic gifts; cf. 2. 7. 13-14, 3. 4. 9-28; for the magical immunity H. enjoys as a love
poet, see also 1. 22; divine protection is as much a symbol of the inspired poet as his

lyre; such claims fall outside the domain of prosaic, factual truth; H. undoubtedly
believed none the less in his lyric gift and undoubtedly linked that gift (and the luck it
has brought him) with a way of life of which the Sabine farm is a recurring symbol.

14-16] For the rhetorical structure of lines 14-28, see under Structure. – **hic ... cornu]**
A preliminary assurance, expressed in the traditional language of pastoral, that H.'s
farm will provide in abundance all that Tyndaris can wish for. The basic statement is
'hic tibi copia manabit ad plenum opulenta', 'here a rich supply will flow for you in
abundance'; **benigno cornu]** adds the image of the horn of plenty (Cornucopia), filled
to overflowing; the ablative attaches itself both to *manabit* ('from a kindly horn') and
to *opulenta* (descriptive ablative); **ad plenum]** while linked primarily with *manabit*, can
be felt as attaching itself also to *benigno*; **ruris honorum]** may be taken with *benigno* or
with *opulenta*; however we construe the grammatical allegiances, the sense is not mate-
rially affected; the rich complexity of the syntax reinforces the idea of overflowing
plenty.

17-20] H. abruptly transposes out of the symbolic language of pastoral into the crisper,
more precise style appropriate to an invitation. – **hic ... aestus]** Escape from the mid-
summer heat in Rome is a more positive inducement, perhaps, than description of rural
peace and plenty; cf. H.'s invitation to Maecenas 3. 29. 17-20; **in reducta valle]** cf. 3. 1.
47 'valle Sabina'; *reducta* = 'secluded', 'tucked away'; the same phrase in *Epodes* 2. 11;
Caniculae aestus] cf. 3. 13. 9; **vitabis]** the second person singular of the future indicative,
equivalent as often to an imperative, indicates an invitation; a conversation piece (H.
talking to the girl while showing her around) would more naturally require *vitemus* or
the like. – **et fide Teia ... Circen]** Tyndaris is to entertain H. with her singing, accom-
panying herself on the lyre, like Lyde in 3. 28. 9-16 and 2. 11. 21-4; cf. Phyllis in 4. 11.
34-6; Tyndaris' social status is thus determined; at the same time the eternal triangle
which will form the subject of her song (two very different women in love with one man)
is not devoid of ironic appropriateness to the triangular nature of the occasion proposed
(two very different men in love with one girl – see on lines 24-8); **fide Teia]** i.e., in the
manner of Anacreon of Teos; **dices]** 'celebrate'; see on 1. 6. 5; **laborantis in uno]** =
'struggling under the burden of love for one and the same man' (i.e., Ulysses); with
laborantis cf. 1. 9. 3; *uno* is emphatic, as always; **Penelopen]** the prototype of the
virtuous wife; cf. 3. 10. 11; **vitreamque Circen]** the prototype of the alluring seductress
who ensnares the traveller with her wiles; *vitream* suggests the glitter and radiance appro-
priate to a goddess or divinely lovely woman, but with connotations of impenetrable,
ever-changing mystery; ancient glassware was translucent, but not transparent; see on 3.
13. 1; contrast 1. 18. 16.

21-8] The missing component in a complex ironical pattern now falls into place: Tyndaris
has a husband (or a regular lover) who corresponds to the *olens maritus* of line 7 and to
Penelope in line 20 (like Cyrus, Penelope is the injured party, though the present context
naturally favours Circe); Tyndaris' visit to the farm will make her *devia* like the *capellae*
of line 6, while H. modestly accepts for himself the role of a rustic Circe. – **innocentis
... sub umbra]** H.'s drinking party will be an innocent occasion, unlike those wild parties
at Rome at which Cyrus loses all control of himself; for H. and a girl drinking together
cf. 1. 11. 6, 3. 28. 2-4, 4. 11. 1-2; *innocentis* picks up the emphasis laid in 5 *inpune
tutum*, etc. on the innocuous nature of the occasion; **Lesbii]** a respectable, imported
wine; see on 1. 20. 1; **sub umbra]** i.e., out of the heat of the summer sun. – **nec ...
proelia]** 'nor will Bacchus join with Mars in launching a fight'; i.e., no drunken brawls
(like that in 1. 27 – the sort of thing Tyndaris has to put up with in town) at H.'s picnic.
– **nec metues ... vestem]** Nor will Tyndaris have to fear (as she would if she were seen
flirting with another man in town) that Cyrus will become suspicious and resort to
violence, perhaps bursting in on the party (like Cynthia in Propertius 4. 8. 49-52) or,
more likely, creating a scene while the party is in progress; for a party as a place where
love affairs begin, see 1. 36. 17-20, 3. 19. 25-8, 3. 21. 3; **suspecta]** 'having come under
suspicion'; passive past participle of a deponent verb, as 1. 1. 25 *detestata*, etc.; **male
dispari]** = 'upon you who are too good for the fellow'; with *male* cf. 1. 9. 24; **et scindat
... crinibus]** 'and tear off the garland entwined in your hair'; partygoers habitually
donned a garland of myrtle, etc.; see on 1. 38. 2; **inmeritamque vestem]** 'and tear your
innocent dress'; tearing the girl's dress in a fit of anger is one of the stock items of
lovers' quarrels (*rixae amoris*), in comedy as well as in the elegists.

1. 18

Introduction: An ode for Varus on the pleasures and the dangers of wine, in which H.
   dissociates himself from those who overstep the mark. A curious poem — apparently an
   attempt to break away from the conventions of hymn form, and, as a result, oddly form-
   less; closer syntactically, as well as stylistically, to H.'s hexameter verse.
      For H. on the virtues of wine, see 3. 21, *Epist.* 1. 5. 16-20.
Structure: Lines 1-4, in praise of the vine. Lines 5-11, an expansion of the theme of 1-4,
   quickly passing into a warning against the danger of excessive drinking; we pass from the
   everyday world to the world of myth. Lines 11-16 modulate to an even more impassio-
   nate key for H.'s promise to the god that he will not be among those who surrender to
   excess.
Metre: Greater Asclepiad; see 1. 11M; as in 1. 11, the choriamb is self-contained except in
   the concluding line.
      The long lines are mostly endstopped. The spill-over in 8-9 is normal enough, those in
   3-4 and 10-11 contribute further to the unusual character of this unusual, perhaps experi-
   mental poem.
1-4] The opening line is an adaptation of a line of Alcaeus in the same metre (Alcaeus 342
   LP):

   μηδ'ἕν ἄλλο φυτεύσῃς πρότερον δένδριον ἀμπέλω.

   For such 'motto' lines, see on 1. 9. 1-4; also on 1. 16. 1. The borrowed line is at once
   grafted on to an Italian theme (line 2). Lines 3-4 explain the opening injunction. — **Vare**]
   Traditionally identified as Quintilius Varus, the critic of *AP* 438-44 and the Quintilius of
   Odes 1. 24 — dead at the time of publication of *Odes* 1-3; the identification rests on the
   superscription of one group of MSS and is not older than the fourth century AD. Others
   propose P. Alfenus Varus, consul suffectus in 39 BC, usually supposed to be the Alfenus
   of Catullus Poem 30 (in the same metre) and the Varus of Poems 10 and 22 (probably
   not the Alfenus of *Sat.* 1. 3. 130-32). In either case, Varus is chosen, probably, more as a
   compliment to a personal friend (like Fuscus in 1. 22); contrast Iccius in 1. 29, Albius in
   1. 33, both integrated into the theme of the ode in which they occur. — **sacra**] Because
   of the connection with Bacchus; nothing corresponding to *sacra* in Alcaeus. — **Tiburis**]
   For Tibur, see on 1. 7. 13; Varus is to be presumed to have a villa there. — **Catili**] Catilus,
   or Catillus (*Aen.* 7. 672), is the legendary founder of Tibur. — **Siccis . . . proposuit**] Cf.
   H.'s edict for poets *Epist.* 1. 19. 8-9 'forum putealque Libonis mandabo siccis, adimam
   cantare severis'. — **neque mordaces . . . sollicitudines**] Cf. 1. 7. 17-19 and 31; two poly-
   syllables (*sollicitudines*, the longest word in the poem) end the first section with a
   flourish.
5-11] **Quis . . . crepat?**] The emphasis falls on *gravem* (to be taken with both nouns) and
   crepat ('rattle on at length about'): 'Who harps on the theme of the hardships of military
   life or of being poor when he's had a drink or two?' — **Quis non . . . Venus?**] sc. *crepat*;
   not hymns of praise, but party talk, in which wine and women (if we may believe H.)
   take the place of the cares of life; the variant *increpat* ('finds fault with') is attractive with
   gravem militiam aut pauperiem, unconvincing with line 6; **Bacche pater, decens Venus**] =
   'wine and love' (i.e., drinking and making love); by a common idiom Bacchus and Venus
   symbolise the thing or activity over which they preside (cf. *Ceres* = 'bread' or 'eating
   bread'); here the vocative revitalises the metonomy for poetic effect, the sense required
   being secured by context (*crepat* excludes, e.g., the sense 'songs in honour of'); **decens**]
   a somewhat unexpected epithet of Venus, secures the sense 'free from unseemly excess
   or violence', in preparation for what follows; see on 1. 4. 6. — **ne quis . . . Liberi**] 'lest
   any man overstep the rites of Bacchus, that temperate god'; *munera* in the sense of
   'duties', 'obligations', thus representing drinking as a task imposed by the god which must
   therefore be discharged; to make moderation sound more like a religious obligation,
   Bacchus is represented as himself a moderate god (cf. 1. 27. 3, so that those who drink to
   excess overstep the proper limits of his cult) — an ironic but not wholly implausible
   rationalisation (Bacchus, unlike Jove, *is* in Greek poetry a modest, boyish figure possessed
   of wild, terrifying powers); **transiliat**] as Remus sacrilegiously jumped over the rising

walls of Rome (an association perhaps elicited by the near homonyms *moenia/munera*); **Liberi**] an ancient Italian god, early identified with Dionysus, particularly in his aspect as 'the Liberator' (from care, from rational restraint, etc.). — **Centaurea ... debellata**] The Centaurs started a drunken brawl at the wedding of Hippodamia to the King of the Lapithae; **rixa debellata**] the brawl which became a battle fought to the bitter end; **super mero**] the ablative emphasises the local sense (the battle literally took place over the unmixed wine); for *merum*, see on 1. 9. 8. — **monet ... Euhius**] If Bacchus' severe treatment of the Sithonians alludes to a particular incident, the story is as obscure as that of the Centaurs and Lapithae is familiar; the *cum*-clause which follows suggests no more is intended than appeal to the well-known fact that the Thracians were hard drinkers, an example to others of the misuse of wine (cf. 1. 27. 1-4); *Sithoniis* in that case = 'Thracians', as not uncommonly. — **cum fas ... avidi**] = 'when (sc., as regularly happens), with their appetite for lechery, they make precious little distinction between right and wrong'; the clause states a generalisation; *libidinum* with *avidi* rather than with *exiguo fine* (making lust the basis of decision rather than some more substantial criterion); with the enjambment cf. lines 3-4.

11-16] The poem began on the level of conversation improved upon (H.'s favourite style). The formal, literary rhetoric of lines 5-11 permits the transition to something closer to hymn form in the final section. As often at the turning point of an ode, the focus shifts from general statement to H. himself; see on 1. 1. 29. — **Non ego te invitum quatiam**] Hard; there seems to be a shift from Bacchus as god of wine and drinking to Bacchus (= Dionysus) the god of orgiastic ritual; in both cases the god stands for moderation in circumstances that easily lead to excess; excess in the first case leads to drunkenness, excess in the second to enslavement by the god; thus, 'non ego ... quatiam' =, apparently, 'I will not meddle with the mysteries as an intruder', the initiates being represented as helpless victims selected by the god for enslavement (a view reflecting traditional Roman disapproval of the *Bacchanalia*); *quatiam* probably alludes to ritual procedures such as the waving of the *thyrsus* and the display (by waving them) of various cult objects; to lay hands on these is to lay hands on the god himself. — **candide Bassareu**] 'fair Bassareus' (a traditional cult title of Dionysus). — **nec ... rapiam**] = 'nor (on the other hand) will I expose the secrets of your cult' (by snatching the cult emblems from their place of concealment and openly displaying them; picked up by 16 *arcanique Fides prodiga*; as in the previous clause H. adopts the language and symbolism of the cult; cf. 3. 2. 25-30. — **Saeva ... tympana**] H. invites the god to lead the procession of the initiate himself; the instruments are those associated with the worship in Phrygia of Cybele as well as Bacchus; see, e.g., Catullus 64. 261 ff. (of Bacchus), 63. 21-2 and Lucretius 2. 618 ff. (both of the worship of Cybele); **saeva**] the savage beat of the drums symbolises the savage enslavement by the god of his initiate; cf. 1. 19. 1; **cum Berecyntio cornu**] the Phrygian *tibia*, a kind of oboe (see on 1. 12. 1-2). — **quae ... vitro**] The god's attendants in the procession are also his victims; cf. the symbolic attendants of Fortuna in 1. 35. 17-24; these are not of course the normal retinue of Bacchus, or the usual celebrants of his cult; for the idea that the god's initiates are also his slaves, see Catullus 63 (of Cybele), esp. 74-91; **caecus Amor sui**] 'blind self-love'; **plus nimio**] 'too much by far', 'much too much'; **Gloria**] 'boastfulness', 'vainglory'; **arcanique Fides prodiga**] the final personificatio i is that of the irresponsible blurter-out of secrets; cf. 3. 2. 25-32; **perlucidior vitro**] 'as easily seen through as glass'; ancient glass, while not transparent like modern sheet glass (see on 3. 13. 1), can yet serve as an image for that which cannot conceal.

1. 19

Introduction: H., to his surprise, is in love — not just a flirtatious mood (1. 6. 19-20 'sive quid urimur, non praeter solitum leves'), but the real thing: a direct appeal to the goddess, complete with propitiatory offering, is called for.

The mockery of conventional forms and attitudes, and the self-mockery (H. had thought he was too old for this sort of thing to happen to him — though the confession is not wholly unexpected when we remember the smouldering jealousy of 1. 13) are both evident. The language of the ode is as exaggerated as H.'s reaction (consternation mixed with pleasure) to the discovery that he still has it in him.

The arrangement of H.'s first six love poems (1. 5, 1. 8, 1. 11, 1. 13, 1. 17 and the present ode) is obviously planned; no reason, however, to suppose the order chronological.

Structure: The syntactical structure imposes arrangement in quatrains, not couplets: each quatrain is heavily endstopped; the quatrains follow one another in asyndeton. Within each quatrain, until the concluding line, there are no strong pauses, each statement or word group being connected to that preceding by a conjunction (or, in the case of 5 and 7 *urit*, by anaphora). Apart from 12 'quae nihil attinent', there are no subordinate clauses. The resultant structure is faster-moving and more animated than H.'s usual manner.

Metre: Asclepiad (b) (as in 1. 3).

1-4]   Mater saeva Cupidinum] In Hellenistic art, Aphrodite is escorted by a retinue of *Erotes* ('amorini' — the primary sense here), but the sense 'mother of our desires' is also present and seems in Greek to be the original sense (the personalised plural being an allegorical representation of a poetic plural not originally intended in a personal sense); **saeva]** not an ornamental epithet, but describing the mood in which Venus descends upon H. (contrast 1. 18. 6 *decens*, 3. 21. 21 *laeta*, 3. 27. 67 *perfidum ridens*); H. uses the line again (on a similar occasion) in 4. 1. 5. — **Thebanaeque Semelae puer]** The son of Semele (known also as Thyone — cf. 1. 17. 23) of Thebes is Bacchus; H., presumably, has fallen in love at a party (a recognised risk — cf. 1. 36. 17-20, 3. 19. 25-8, 3. 21. 3). — **iubet]** Agreement with the nearer. — **lasciva Licentia]** 'lecherous License', the frame of mind induced by Venus (= sexual desire) and Bacchus (= drinking — see on 1. 18. 6), is represented as their attendant; cf. the allegorical attendants on Bacchus in 1. 18. 14-16; for the idea, Propertius 1. 3. 14 'hac Amor, hac Liber, durus uterque deus'. — **finitis ... amoribus]** = 'to surrender my heart to a mistress with whom I had broken' (taking the plural *amores* in the common sense of 'girlfriend'); H., i.e., has fallen in love with an old flame whom he has seen at a party; this gives a more sharply focused ironic sense than if we take *amores* as a collective (= 'love-making', as in the title of Ovid's *Amores*), giving the sense 'fall in love again'; with *animum reddere* cf. 1. 16. 28.

5-8]   Urit] See on 1. 13. 9; cf. 1. 6. 19. — **Glycerae]** Cf. 3. 19. 28 'me lentus Glycerae torret amor meae'; Glycera also 1. 30. 3, 1. 33. 2. — **nitor]** See on 1. 5. 13 *nites*; cf. 3. 12. 8 'Liparaei nitor Hebri'; **splendentis ... purius]** Cf. the description of Chloris 2. 5. 18-20; *splendentis* reinforces *nitor*. — **grata protervitas]** *protervitas* implies sexual desire and the ability to arouse desire in others — a quality which here appeals to H.; see on 1. 26. 2 and 2. 5. 15 *proterva*; for a less favourable context cf. 1. 25. 2, 3. 14. 26. — **voltus ... adspici]** = 'her face to gaze at which leads only too easily to surrender'; **lubricus]** perhaps picks up the metaphor of *nitor* (dazzled by Glycera's looks, one cannot help stumbling — losing, i.e., the posture of detached aloofness appropriate to the dominant male); **adspici]** evokes the love-at-first-sight cliché (see on 3. 12. 8-9 'simul ... in undis').

9-12]   In me tota ruens Venus] The goddess of love hurtles down upon H. like Jove himself (1. 16. 11-12 'tremendo Iuppiter ipse ruens tumultu'); Venus' intervention is to be taken at the level of seriousness fixed by the language and imagery of Stanza 2 and by the following context; the infatuation is purely physical — no hint of the tortured mental anguish, or of the hopes for lasting happiness of which we hear so much from Catullus and the Augustan elegists. — **Cyprum deseruit]** In order to give H. her undivided attention (*tota ruens*), Venus has had to abandon the best-known of her shrines, that in Cyprus; cf. 1. 30. 2. — **nec patitur ... attinent]** Traditionally, the onset of love suspends normal activities; thus Neobule in 3. 12. 5-7 abandons her spinning; for H., a poet, the onset of love means he can no longer write on serious themes; the Scythians and Parthians are chosen as representative of major contemporary themes for serious poetry; the Scythians symbolise the threat to Rome's NE frontier (cf. 1. 35. 9, 2. 11. 1, 3. 4. 36, 3. 8. 23, 3. 24. 9, 4. 5. 25, 4. 14. 42); for the Parthians, see on 1. 12. 53 and 3. 51; cf. H.'s disclaimer to Agrippa in 1. 6; **versis equis]** refers to the well-known Parthian cavalry tactic, a feigned retreat followed by a sudden advance and a hail of arrows; **dicere]** 'celebrate', 'write about'; see on 1. 6. 5; **nec quae nihil attinent]** H. can only write about Glycera, all other themes are irrelevant.

13-16] The poem unexpectedly becomes a dramatic monologue; we hear H. addressing his slaves as they prepare for a propitiatory sacrifice to the goddess — a ceremony as fanciful as that which marks H.'s final retirement from the campaigns of love in 3. 26 (or as the dedicatory plaque of 1. 5. 13-16); contrast the sacrifice to Diana in 3. 22. — **Hic, hic ponite]** The same formula in 3. 26. 6. — **vivum caespitem]** Fresh-cut turf, to form an altar. — **mihi**] With *ponite*. — **verbenas**] Greenery to adorn the altar. — **bimi meri**] Wine two years old (i.e., a young wine); wine for sacrifice was not mixed with water. — **mactata . . . hostia**] = 'when the sacrifice has been made, the goddess will arrive in more lenient mood'; cf. 3. 23. 17-20; the animal to be sacrificed is not mentioned (the *pueri* will know what it is).

1. 20

Introduction: A party is in prospect. H.'s guest is his patron Maecenas. As usual, the talk is of the wine to be offered (which fixes the nature of the occasion), not of food. H. is in a position to offer only a local wine, but it has special associations.

No details of place and time. Curiosity therefore about whether the party is to take place at Rome (like the party in *Epist*. 1. 5) or (as in 3. 29) on H.'s Sabine farm is misplaced. (That H. was in a position to receive his patron to dinner in Rome is clear from *Sat*. 1. 6. 111-18, though it is to be assumed that H. was more often a guest at Maecenas' 'parasitica mensa'; for dinner on the Sabine farm, see *Sat*. 2. 6. 65-76.) The ostensible status of the ode is not that of an invitation (as 3. 29 or *Epist*. 1. 5, or, probably, *Odes* 1. 17, 4. 11 and 4. 12) but that of dramatic monologue — a fragment of conversation in which we hear H. talking to his guest, who has already arrived: cf. 3. 8, 3. 28.

A warning of humble fare was not unusual, it seems, when the party was an informal one. Philodemus' invitation to his patron Piso (*Anth. Pal.* 11. 44) is often cited as a model; cf. Catullus 13. The picture of H.'s simple lifestyle is not to be taken too seriously. When entertaining a girl, he is more ostentatious: in 3. 28 he offers a Caecuban wine of 59 BC, in 4. 11 a nine-year old Alban wine; cf. the wine of 65 BC offered Messalla in 3. 21, the *cadus* specially ordered from the merchant offered Virgil in 4. 12, the very special wine he proposes to drink in 3. 14. 17-20 (if he can get it) in honour of Augustus' return from Spain; see below on line 1.

Structure: A flowing opening sentence (Stanzas 1-2) is followed by a brief word of explanation and apology.

Metre: Sapphics (see 1. 2M).

1-8] **Vile Sabinum**] A cheap local wine (see on 2 *ipse*); cf. the four-year old Sabine offered by H. in 1. 9. 7-8; the Sabine wines, the lightest of Italian wines, are recommended for drinking by Galen when seven to fifteen years old. — **potabis**] *potare*, more casual or colloquial than *bibere*, is commoner in H.'s hexameter verse than in the *Odes* (2. 11. 17, 4. 13. 5; *bibere* 11 times in the *Odes*). — **modicis cantharis**] *cantharus*, a cup with handles, large rather than small; cf. 1. 27. 1 *scyphis*; the ordinary word is *pocula* (as in line 12); *modicis* corrects *cantharis* — as we might say, 'a modest spree'; H., i.e., will not be stingy with his wine (like the host of 2. 14. 25-8), but it's not going to be an orgy. — **Graeca testa**] A jar which had held a Greek wine (or one from Magna Graecia), to improve the flavour of the cheap Sabine during the ageing process; contrast 1. 9. 7-8. — **ipse**] The wine is one whose laying-down H. personally superintended, though he probably did not grow it on his own estate (cf. *Epist*. 1. 14. 23 'angulus iste feret piper et tus ocius uva'). — **levi**] The cork is smeared with pitch to protect it while the wine is stored. — **datus plausus**] Clearly, the occasion referred to in 2. 17. 25-6 (Maecenas is greeted with applause on his first appearance following an illness), linked there with H.'s own escape from death when the tree nearly fell on him (see 2. 13. 1-12), similarly commemorated by H. in 3. 8. 9-12. — **theatro**] Probably the theatre built by Pompey (Rome's first permanent theatre); the Theatre of Marcellus was probably not yet built. — **clare Maecenas eques**] 'Maecenas, my distinguished knight'; Maecenas, though descended from Etruscan kings (1. 1. 1, 3. 29. 1), was content to remain an *eques* (i.e., he never sought an office conferring senatorial status) but lent distinction to the humbler order; the best MSS have *care; clare*, the reading of some late MSS, was preferred by Bentley, followed by Klingner (not *OCT*). — **paterni fluminis**] Because the Tiber reaches Rome from Etruria and Maecenas is of Etruscan origin. — **simul et**] 'and simultaneously'; for the delayed *et* see on 1. 12. 11. — **ripae**] Subject with *imago* of *redderet* (agreement with the nearer). — **iocosa imago**] 'the joyous echo'; cf. 1. 12. 3-4; the Theatre of Pompey, in the Campus Martius, is on the N side of the Tiber, the Mons Vaticanus lies on the S and W as the Tiber swings SW at the Capitoline.

9-12] H. does not quarrel with Maecenas' more expensive tastes, he is just not in a position to cater to them; cf. the difference in animals to be sacrificed proposed 2. 17. 30-32. The wines named are wines which someone owning estates in the area S of Rome might offer; for Caecuban see 1. 37. 5, 2. 14. 25, 3. 28. 3, for wine from Cales see 1. 31. 9, 4. 12. 14; they represent the comfortable life style of a man who is well-off, not the ostentation of a man who might import rare or expensive wines from southern Italy or from Greece. — **tu bibes**] Maecenas can drink these wines whenever he feels like it because he has them in his cellar (having grown them, probably, on his own estates); for Maecenas as a producer of famous wines, see Pliny *NH* 8. 170; for this sense of the future indicative cf. 3. 23. 13 *tinguet*; some have found *bibes* hard to reconcile with 1 *potabis* and have been led to emend ('tum bibes', 'tu bibas'). — **mea pocula**] i.e., when H. offers wine to his guests; see on 2 *cantharis*. — **Falernae vites**] Wines from the *Falernus ager* in Campania; cf. 1. 27. 10, 2. 3. 8, 2. 6. 19, 2. 11. 19, 3. 1. 43. — **temperant**] Because they are smooth to drink, unlike H.'s cheap Sabine; but *nec temperant* perhaps in the technical sense 'are not added' (to lesser wines to improve the quality); H., i.e., doesn't propose even to mix a modest Falernian or Formian with his cheap Sabine. — **Formiani colles**] The hills around Formiae, on the coast of Latium; cf. 3. 16. 34; **colles**] i.e., hillside vineyards.

1. 21

Introduction: Instructions to a mixed choir of girls and boys for a hymn in praise of Diana and Apollo, which becomes the hymn, ending with a supplicatory stanza addressed to Apollo alone.

The basis of the ode is simple and traditional: the girls are to sing the praises of Diana, the boys of Apollo. Cf. Catullus 34. In H.'s hymn, however, the plan is executed with a frigid exactness destructive of lyric spontaneity — and then broken for the prayer to Apollo, the mannered syntax of which underlines rather than alleviates the conventional nature of the sentiments expressed. The ode lacks both the personal whimsy and the immediacy of feeling of 3. 22.

Structure: Stanza 1, preliminary instructions to both girls and boys; Stanzas 2-3, more detailed instructions to girls and boys in turn; Stanza 4, prayer to Apollo.

Metre: Asclepiad (d) (see 1. 5M).

1-4] For the mixed choir cf. 4. 6. 31-2; see also on 3. 14. 10. — **tenerae**] = 'young'; see on 1. 1. 26. — **dicite**] 'celebrate'; see on 1. 6. 5. — **intonsum . . . Cynthium**] In line 1 the name of the goddess is put first with no qualifying adjective; in line 2 the name of the god comes last, adjective and noun framing the line. — **Latonamque**] Mother of Diana and Apollo; why the boys (and not the girls) should sing her praises is not clear; she is not mentioned again. — **supremo Iovi**] Dative of agent. — **dilectam penitus**] 'truly and deeply beloved', unlike Jove's numerous paramours; for *dilectam*, see on 2. 5. 17 *dilecta*.

5-8] H.'s Diana here is the huntress goddess of the wilds (= the Greek Artemis) — not the 'diva triformis' of 3. 22 (and Catullus 34). The construction is 'vos (i.e., the girls) laetam . . . coma (sc., tollite laudibus)'. — **laetam . . . coma**] = 'the goddess who rejoices in streams and forest glades'; **coma**] in the sense 'foliage', 'leaves', a conventional metaphor. — **quaecumque . . . Gragi**] The combination 'laetam nemorum coma' is not unpleasing: the strain placed on *coma*, however, as antecedent to the complicated relative clause which follows (specifying representative haunts of the goddess — a regular feature of hymn form) is somewhat excessive and artificial; Mt Algidus is in the Alban hills near Rome (see on 3. 23. 9), Mt Erymanthus in Arcadia; Gragus is a mountainous area in Lycia; **prominet**] 'stand out on', i.e., constitute a prominent feature of; **nigris . . . viridis**] an example of H.'s interest in colour contrast — dark green mountain forests (cf. 4. 12. 11-12), green (lower) slopes.

9-12] The boys (10 *mares*) are asked to extol, not the god, but the vale of Tempe (traditionally associated with Apollo; cf. 1. 7. 4), his birthplace on the island of Delos, and the god's shoulder, famous for the quiver and the lyre. — **Tempe**] Neuter plural accusative. — **insignemque . . . umerum lyra**] The quiver and the lyre are the symbols of Apollo as the avenging god armed with his arrows of pestilence (as in *Il.* 1) and the god of poetry; thus, either the quiver or the lyre adorns his shoulder, according to the role assumed; for the quiver cf. 1. 10. 11-12; for the lyre (the invention of Mercury, half-brother of Apollo through their father Jove), see 3. 11. 1-24; some refer *insignem* to Apollo (making it parallel to *laetam*), taking *umerum* as accusative of respect (or reading

umeros), unnecessary repairs which fail to take account of the mannered artificiality of
H.'s style in this ode.

13-16] The concluding prayer is addressed to Apollo the archer who protects the righteous
as well as punishing the wicked (he presides, e.g., over the victory at Actium, *Aen.* 8.
704-5; cf. Propertius 4. 6. 67-8). — **lacrimosum**] Cf. 1. 8. 14. — **famem pestemque**]
Famine and pestilence are, along with war, the traditional scourges of a nation. — **a
populo et principe Caesare**] Modelled on the traditional Republican formula 'Senatus
populusque Romanus'. — **in Persas atque Britannos**] Praying to the gods to bring mis-
fortune to one's enemies is equally traditional; the phrase contributes further, however,
to the uninspired, laureate note on which the ode concludes; cf. the simple dignity of the
conclusion of Catullus 34. For the Britanni see on 1. 35. 30.

1. 22

Introduction: It is a commonplace of Roman love poetry that the lover enjoys a special
immunity: lovers' oaths when broken do not incur the wrath of Jove (thus Barine in
2. 8 flourishes despite her perjuries); the lover is exempt, too, from the dangers which
threaten the lives of ordinary men (Tibullus 1. 2. 27-8 'Quisquis amore tenetur eat
tutusque sacerque/qualibet'; cf. Propertius 2. 27 and 3. 16. 11-18). The inspired poet
likewise enjoys special protection (3. 4. 9-36, especially 29-36; cf. 2. 7. 13-16, 2. 17.
28-30). The poet whose inspiration is his mistress can be expected, therefore, to enjoy
a quite exceptional degree of protection.

As often in H., a theme is explored for the possibilities it offers: a tree nearly falls on
H. — and he sees himself in the underworld listening to Sappho and Alcaeus; he catches
a distant glimpse, perhaps, of a wolf — and draws appropriately absurd conclusions, the
justification for which is the exquisite, sophisticated irony deployed in relating the
incident and in drawing these conclusions. Not surprisingly, the incident of the wolf is
not included among those escapes from death listed in 3. 4. 25-8 which possess (what-
ever H.'s interpretation of them) some more serious claim to reality. The resultant poem,
in Sapphic stanzas, plays with echoes of two famous poems by Catullus in that metre
(see on lines 5-8 and 23-4).

Structure: The ode consists of three sentences, each two stanzas in length; no strong pauses
in mid-line, the odd stanzas all lightly endstopped.

Metre: Sapphics (see 1. 2M).

1-8] **Integer . . . purus**] 'The man who is whole of life (i.e., whose way of life is characte-
rised by moral integrity) and pure of sin'; impressive language made more impressive by
the double genitive of respect (a Grecism, characteristic of the high style), and hardly
the way one would expect a serious moralist to describe a poet composing a poem to,
or about, his mistress; one might argue (if there were reason to suppose H. serious) that
the moral innocence derives from H.'s idyllic surroundings and the attitude of mind (11
'curis expeditis') in which he gives himself over to a harmless distraction; but perhaps
the opening line, in addition to establishing the appropriate level of irony, contains the
first of a series of echoes of Catullus, who is always quick to protest his moral innocence
(see, e.g., Poem 76, especially 76. 19 'si vitam puriter egi'). — **non eget . . . pharetra**]
Placed before the double *sive*-clause which states the circumstances in which ordinary
mortals may require the unusual weapons specified, the principal clause can only elicit
the reader's somewhat bemused assent. — **Fusce**] Aristius Fuscus, an old and intimate
friend; see *Sat.* 1. 9. 60-78, *Sat.* 1. 10. 83, the addressee of *Epist.* 1. 10. — **sive . . .
Hydaspes**] A tricolon crescendo, postulating three especially dangerous journeys; syntax,
metre and similarity of subject matter (though the places specified are different) inevit-
ably recall Catullus 11. 2-12; as in Catullus, the stanza concludes with a succinctly
evoked image (cf. 'quae loca fabulosus lambit Hydaspes' with Catullus 11. 4 'tunditur
unda'; 11. 7-8 'sive quae septemgeminus colorat / aequora Nilus'); in Catullus the places
are chosen for their remoteness (from Rome and from one another), H.'s places symbolise
danger: the 'sweltering Syrtes' (strictly sandbanks off the coast of modern Libya and
Tunisia) here, as elsewhere, stand for the adjacent desert — an allusion perhaps to a
famous march by the younger Cato from Benghazi to Leptis Magna in 47 BC (the sort of
journey ordinary men, if not Cato, would only undertake armed 'Mauris iaculis', etc.; cf.
2. 20. 15); the 'inhospitable Caucasus' is traditionally a wild and dangerous place (Zeus

chained Prometheus there); the 'fabulosus Hydaspes' is a river of the Punjab, famous as
the site of Alexander's victory in 326 BC; for *fabulosus*, see on 3. 4. 9.

9-12]   Deceptively matter-of-fact after the grandiloquence of lines 1-8. The parallel is exact:
the 'Sabine wood' corresponds to the exotic danger spots of Stanza 2; H., like the travel-
ler there, has wandered off the beaten track ('ultra terminum'); suddenly, danger looms;
he is unarmed (*inermem*), but suffers no harm. The parallel fits at every point, but every-
thing is domesticated in the process; despite the asserted monstrosity in Stanza 4 of the
wolf that run away, the incident adduced is as absurdly inadequate as proof of the
generalisation drawn from it in the preceding stanzas as it is as a justification for the
confident assertion of Stanzas 5-6. — **silva in Sabina**] Cf. 3. 16. 29-30 'silvaque iugerum
paucorum', *Sat.* 2. 6. 3 'paulum silvae', *Epist.* 1. 16. 9-10 'quercus et ilex', etc. — **dum
... Lalagen**] We are to imagine H. working out aloud the lines of a poem in honour of
his mistress; see on 1. 6. 5 *dicere*; cf. the picture of H. totally preoccupied with compo-
sing light verse, *Sat.* 1. 9. 2 'nescio quid meditans nugarum, totus in illis'; *Lalage*
('prattler') also 2. 5. 16; for such names, see on 1. 5. 3 *Pyrrha*; for *dum* with the present
indicative, see on 1. 2. 17. — **curis expeditis**] = 'cares dismissed' (i.e., all other preoccupa-
tions thrown to the winds). — **fugit inermem**] We are perhaps intended to recall the
Greek saying referred to by Socrates in Plato *Repub.* 1. 336 d that if you saw an ememy
before he saw you, you were not left helpless.

13-16]   Wolves were not uncommon in ancient Italy. This one, however, was something
special. — **quale portentum**] In ordinary speech we might say 'a monster the like of which
a man never saw in his life before'; H., in accordance with the conventions of his form
(but in a tone approaching parody), goes on to specify places where the like could not
have been seen. — **neque ... aesculetis**] For 'war-like Daunias' (the ancient Kingdom of
Daunus), see on 3. 30. 11; for the Sabellian stock of the SE and their reputation as
soldiers, see on 3. 6. 37-44; for wolves there cf. 1. 33. 7-8; the SE is still noted for its
oak forests. — **Iubae tellus**] Probably, Juba II of Numidia, later of Gaetulia and
Mauritania — roughly speaking the *Syrtes aestuosae* of line 5. — **leonum arida nutrix**]
The lions of North Africa, i.e., are nothing to the wolf H. saw on his farm; Gaetulia, it
seems, was particularly noted for its lions (cf. 1. 23. 10, 3. 20. 2); **arida nutrix**] oxymoron;
an ancient nurse was normally a wet-nurse who remained as the child's attendant and
confidante through life; cf. the Gaetulian lioness of 3. 20. 2.

17-24]   Wolves cannot harm H., therefore nothing can — neither the rigours of the fog-
bound north nor the sun-scorched, uninhabitable south: Stanzas 5-6 are linked by
anaphora in asyndeton, so as to form an appropriately emphatic rhetorical framework
for H.'s absurd *a fortiori*. — **pigris campis**] Locative ablative without *in*, as regularly in
the common style of Augustan verse; with *pigris* ('thick', 'inert') cf. Lucretius 5. 746
'bruma nives affert pigrumque rigorem'. — **nulla arbor aestiva recreatur aura**] The initial
negative negates the whole proposition (a common idiom) — no trees and no summer
breezes to refresh them either; cf. 3. 10. 11-12 (= 'you're no Penelope and you haven't
an Etruscan father either'). — **malusque Iuppiter**] 'Jove in evil mood'; for Jove as the
sky god, see on 1. 2. 1-4. — **sub curru**] The chariot in which the sun god drives across
the sky each day, getting too close to the earth for human habitation at the mid-point
of his journey. — **dulce ... loquentem**] We expect 'I shall come to no harm', but once
again the lighthearted non-logic of the poem asserts itself, for a final proclamation, not
of H.'s immunity, but of the unshakability of his devotion to Lalage; to cap everything,
a reminiscence of Catullus in which H. goes one better than his original: in his version
of Sappho (also in Sapphic stanzas) Catullus has (51. 4-5) 'spectat et audit / dulce
ridentem'; Sappho, however, in her poem had spoken of the girl's 'sweet voice' as well
as her laughter; H. repairs the omission, placing his 'dulce loquentem' in the final line of
the stanza (the place occupied by Catullus' 'dulce ridentem') to emphasise the point;
'dulce loquentem' picks up, moreover, the name of H.'s mistress (Lalage, the 'prattler').

1. 23

Introduction: Like 1. 13, a study in love that takes account of the girl's feelings as well as
the man's. But whereas the Lydia of 1. 13 is at least experienced enough to take in her
stride and enjoy the *rixae amoris*, Chloe has still to face up to the realities of life instead
of running to seek protection from her mother at the sight or sound of a man. See 3. 11I;
cf. 2. 5 and 3. 12.

Structure: Stanza 1 sets up the hypothesis and provides a first working out of the simile of the frightened fawn. Stanza 2 explores the image of the fawn in more detail. Stanza 3 rejects the analogy. Stanzas 1 and 2 each comprise a single sentence; Stanza 3 is built around the blunt juxtaposition of lines 9-10 and 11-12.

Metre: Asclepiad (d) (see 1.5M).

1-4] The simile of a girl as a young animal is an obvious one, whether it is the shyness of the girl which is illustrated, or her high-spirited friskiness. H.'s starting point seems to be Anacreon (see 2. 5I) — **Vitas]** The sense is fixed by the simile: Chloe doesn't make herself scarce (refuse to meet H.); she shies away at the sight of him, so that they never meet; the simile catches her on the move, looking round anxiously for her mother, with H. observing her from a distance; it is not necessary to suppose the fawn is running away from the lion or tiger of Stanza 3 (a legitimate cause for fear), it merely wants to get back to its mother; cf. the calf of 4. 2. 54-60. — **quaerenti . . . matrem]** The mother is thus not just an elaboration of the image — Chloe too has a mother whom she follows around (lines 11-12); for the innocent girl brought up by a protective mother cf. Catullus' Ariadne, 64. 87-8; **pavidam]** the mother is in a panic because the fawn has strayed out of sight; **montibus aviis]** i.e., the fawn is lost, cannot find its way back. — **non sine . . . metu]** Because it is lost, every sound, even the rustle of the breeze in the trees, alarms the fawn; *non sine metu* is weaker than *pavidam* — the mother is in a panic, the fawn merely jumpy; **aurarum et siluae]** hendiadys; cf. *Aen.* 2. 726-8 'me . . . omnes terrent aurae'; H. adapts the traditional cliché to the pastoral scene; **siluae]** three syllables.

5-8] The image of the fawn is now explored for its imaginative potential — **seu . . . foliis]** 'whether the coming of spring has quivered in leaves easily set in motion'; for Favonius, the warm life-bringing wind of spring, see on 1. 4. 1; the sound of the rustling in the trees is a sign that the *bruma iners* of 4. 7. 12 is over — and enough to make the fawn jump; *inhorruit* suggests the quick, sudden movement of a momentary breath of wind, also the fancy that the sound is that of spring himself shivering (because the winter cold is not yet past); many literal-minded scholars have found fault with this beautiful, evocative phrase (finding it too poetic for H., or objecting that there are no leaves for the wind to rustle in until after spring has come); some of those persuaded of the need to emend have found *vepres* ('thorn-bush', 'briar') *ad ventos* acceptable; those who think more highly of H. as a poet may find it not irrelevant that spring is the season in Roman poetry when the thoughts of man and beast turn to love. — **seu . . . lacertae]** The first *seu*-clause is an expansion and interpretation of 4 'aurarum et siluae metu', the second suggests an alternative cause for alarm; lizards coming out to sun themselves again symbolise the coming of spring; **dimovere]** = 'parted the leaves of'; the sound which accompanies the scuttling of the lizards is what frightens the fawn. — **et corde et genibus]** The heart beats faster, the knees tremble.

9-12] The fawn behaves as though every breath of wind and every scuttling lizard were a lion or a tiger; Chloe's apprehensions are equally groundless. — **Atqui]** 'And yet'; cf. 3. 5. 49, 3. 7. 9. — **non ego te . . . persequor]** The three monosyllables push the image of the fawn aside and shift the focus to H. and Chloe; *non* negates the whole phrase, 'I'm not a tiger or a lion and I'm not pursuing you to crush you to pieces either' (for the idiom, cf. 3. 10. 11-12, 4. 15. 16-20); H., i.e., keeps his distance, detached, only mildly admonishing; for Gaetulian lions cf. 1. 22. 15-16, 3. 20. 2; **frangere]** the infinitive rather than a clause ('ut frangam') is characteristic of the simpler syntax of verse style. — **desine]** See on 2. 9. 17. — **tempestiva viro]** Cf. 3. 19. 27, 4. 1. 9; contrast Lalage in 2. 5. 1-4; for the age at which a girl was considered old enough for marriage, see 2. 5I.

1. 24

Introduction: A lament, addressed to Virgil, consoling him for the death of their friend Quintilius. The only poem (apart from 1. 37, on the death of Cleopatra), in a collection of poems where death is a recurrent theme, which commemorates the death of a contemporary. (The unnamed shipwrecked sailor of 1. 28 hardly falls into this category; see also on 2. 9. 10 *Mysten*.) For Quintilius see on 1. 18. 1.

Structure: In such circumstances, there is little opportunity for originality: the ingenious, or the unexpected, is an offence against taste, especially when the friend who is being consoled is also a poet. All one can hope is that the poem one writes will be felt as a transposition, into the more tightly organised struxtures of poetry, of one's own retreat from grief to stoical acceptance. The last two lines reject the implied answer to the opening question.

Stanzas 1-3 are heavily endstopped, the sentences are short and vigorous. At line 13 the rhythm changes — an elaborately structured sentence (the vehicle of the dominant image of the poem), which spills over into the following stnza. Stanza 1, appeal to the Muse. In Stanzas 2-5 the emotional reaction to Quintilius' death is brought under progressively tighter intellectual control: Stanzas 2-3 come to terms with the reality of Quintilius' death; in Stanzas 4-5 the commonplace that death is final and irrevocable is made the motif that gives fresh vitality to a traditional image, in preparation for the moral commonplace of lines 19-20.

Metre: Asclepiad (c) (see 1. 6M).

1-4]   **Quis . . . capitis?**] 'Why feel shame for unrestrained grief at the loss of one so dear?'; the rhetorical question 'Quis sit pudor aut modus?' is answered in the concluding sentence; the poem thus represents by its structure the movement of the mind from unrestrained grief to acceptance of the inevitable; *pudor*, as often, the shame that restrains (the fear of doing what one will be ashamed of), not the shame which follows action; *modus*, 'limit'; *sit*, potential, 'can there be'; **desiderio**] 'sense of loss'; contrast 1. 14. 18; **tam cari capitis**] in both Greek and Latin, the head symbolises the living human being, as an object of affection, or as one whose status as human being (or, in technical contexts, as citizen) is threatened; cf. 3. 5. 42. — **praecipe . . . Melpomene**] The Muse is appealed to for inspiration; see on 3. 4. 1-4; for Melpomene, see on 3. 30. 16. — **pater**] Jove, father of the Muses (their mother is Mnemosyne).

5-8]   **ergo . . . urget**] The deliberate *ergo* marks the first step toward coming to terms with the fact that Quintilius is dead; *ergo* and *urget* form an alliterative frame; **perpetuus sopor**] a traditional commonplace (cf. 3. 11. 38); the poetic revitalisation of the commonplace possible in a different context (e.g., Catullus 5. 5-6 'nobis cum semel occidit brevis lux, / nox est perpetua una dormienda') is inappropriate here. — **cui . . . parem**] The unparalleled virtues of the deceased are likewise a commonplace of lament; the divinities chosen emphasise the character of Quintilius as a man who would have been ashamed (*Pudor*) of breaking a promise (*Fides*) or telling a lie (*Veritas*); the personification of *Pudor* comes oddly after 1 *pudor*.

9-12]   Stanza 3 introduces Virgil, as Quintilius' closest friend. — **Multis bonis**] The *boni* are those one approves of — one's true friends (as here) or (in a different context) one's political associates. — **Vergili**] For Virgil, see also 1. 3 and 4. 12. — **tu . . .deos**] = 'You ask the gods to give Quintilius back to you, but your appeal to them is misguided: it was not on such terms that you placed him in their care'; **frustra pius**] a wryly ironical oxymoron: to ask the gods to protect a friend shows *pietas* (a proper sense of obligation to the friend, a proper respect for the gods); to ask the gods to restore the friend to life no less so, but the asking back is as idle as the entrusting was unavailing; **non ita creditum**] normally, an object deposited for safekeeping may be claimed back (cf. the terms under which H. entrusts Virgil to the safekeeping of the ship that is to take him to Greece in 1. 3. 5-7); but Quintilius was *non ita creditus* (i.e., the deposit was not subject to surrender on demand, the analogy of human transactions breaks down, the will of the gods is inscrutable; under what circumstances Quintilius was entrusted by Virgil to the gods we can only guess; it would be an odd coincidence (to which nothing points in the text) if he too had been about to undertake a journey by ship, and one could feel the gods had struck a hard bargain; a more likely guess is that Virgil entreated the gods to look after Quintilius during a serious illness and they have done so on their own terms.

13-18]   The poetic level of the ode swells to a crescendo in these lines, but the message is the same as in Stanza 3: death is irrevocable. When Orpheus played his lyre, the very trees of the forests followed him in procession (cf. 1. 12. 7-12). Legend tells too that Orpheus was able to claim back his wife Eurydice from the underworld; Virgil had related that tale in the *Georgics* (4. 453-558); if H. avoids alluding to it here, we can take it he does so out of tact, not forgetfulness. Legends are the stuff of poetry, they provide a special language for talking about experience; the fact that H. questions, by implication, the truth of the legend of Orpheus (as he questions, by implication, the power of the gods) does not prevent him from using that language (he goes on to make poetic use of the legend of Mercury psychopompus); but the death of a close friend is a moment to face the facts of the human condition. — **si moderere**] = 'if you were to play'. — auditam **arboribus fidem**] 'the lyre to which the trees listened'; **árboribus**] dative of agent; **fidem**] a conventional poetic metonomy. — **num . . . imagini?**] 'would blood return to the idle ghost'; **vanae**] the *imago* which is the figment of our idle imagination; **imagini**] the shade of the departed (also called *anima, umbra*) which figures so prominently in poetry about the dead. — **quam . . . gregi**] = 'when Mercury, who is not easily influenced by entreaties that he unlock the gates of death, once and for all (*semel*), with his rod before which men quake, has rounded it (*quam,* antecedent *imagini*) up and included it in his black flock'; **non lenis**] the figure called litotes, in which a negative amounts to a strong affirmative; cf. 1. 25. 16 'non sine questu'; **precibus** equally with *lenis* and *recludere*; **nigro gregi**] the troop of shades which Mercury leads, like a kind of sinister shepherd, to join the numberless dead in the underworld; the image here is the same as in 1. 10. 17-20, but Mercury has become a ruthless, fearsome figure; contrast, e.g., 16 *virga horrida* with the *virga aurea* of 1. 10. 18-19.

19-20] A concluding explicitly moralising motto line, couplet or stanza is an occasional feature of the *Odes*; cf. 4. 12. 28, 1. 3. 37-40, 1. 13. 17-20, 3. 6. 45-8. Death being omnipresent, any consolatory reflection, unless it is to be bizarre or eccentric, must enunciate a commonplace; the art of 1. 24 lies in the poetic skill and taste with which we are prepared for acceptance of the truth, bluntly and compactly stated.

1. 25

Introduction: the first appearance in the *Odes* of one of H.'s favourite types, the ageing flirt. Lydia is not yet a figure of fun, like Lyce in 4. 13 or Chloris in 3. 15; nor is she, like Barine in 2. 8, an old hand at the game of love, but still in her prime, ready for a new generation of lovers. Time is beginning to tell, however; Lydia's popularity is waning. H. adopts a traditional form, the paraclausithyron or serenade by the lover before the locked street door of his mistress, to a new purpose; cf. 3. 10, 3. 26 and the final stanza of 3. 7; see F. O. Copley, *Exclusus Amator*, 1955; cf. Ovid's ageing flirt, *Ars* 3. 69-80. As in 4. 13, it seems more reasonable to suppose the poem intended for performance as a soliloquy or interior monologue (in which the scene observed in Stanza 1 touches off a train of thought that moves first into the past, then into the future) than as an attack in which Lydia is directly addressed. For Lydia see 1. 13I.

Structure: To the four presents 1 *quatiunt*, 3 *adimunt amatque*, 6 *audis* are opposed the futures 10 *flebis* and 15 *saeviet*. Thus, Stanzas 1-2 deal with description of the present scene (the relative clause 'quae prius . . . movebat cardines' glancing for a moment at the past), Stanzas 3-5 with prediction. Within each section the stanzas are lightly endstopped, forming in each case a fast-moving complex sentence.

Metre: Sapphics (see 1. 2M).

At 1. 25 begins a group of Odes in Sapphics and Alcaics, which is broken only at three places by poems in other metres; the actual arrangement is: 25(S), 26(A), 27(A), [28 Archilochean (b)], 29(A), 30(S), 31(A), 32(S), [33 Asclepiad (c)], 34(A), 35(A), [36 Asclepiad (b)], 37(A), 38(S). Cf. the even more regular arrangement of 2. 1-11.

1-8] **Parcius . . . protervi**] The closed windows indicate the (ostensibly) virtuous wife who takes no notice of her ribald admirers (cf. 3. 7. 29-30) — men on their way home from parties, rather than serious aspirants to her affection, who pay tribute to a well-known society beauty by tossing handful after handful (*iactibus crebris*) at her closed shutters, as if hoping she will come to the window (as Asterie is bidden not to in 3. 7. 30): her admirers are not as free with their attentions as they used to be; *parcius* is opposed to 5 *prius*; **iunctas, quatiunt, iactibus**] the alliteration suggests the rattle of stones on wood; **iuvenes**] 'men'; see on 1. 2. 41; **protervi**] see on 1. 26. 2. — **nec tibi . . . limen**] To be taken together rather than as two separate statements; the subject of *adimunt* is still *iuvenes protervi*, but the focus is now on those who are admitted; **somnos adimunt**] ironic euphemism; **amatque ianua limen**] 'and your front door hugs the doorstep'. — **multum facilis movebat cardines**] 'used to turn on thoroughly cooperative hinges'; the hinges take on the character of their mistress (cf. 3. 7. 32 *difficilis*, 3. 10. 11 *difficilem*); the point, however, of the door's cooperation is not merely that it opened readily, but that it connived at a clandestine affair by opening smoothly and silently and thus not waking the lady's husband; H.'s lines rest upon a familiar situation of Roman literature and life and can thus move with succinct economy; *multum* with *facilis* (a colloquialism) rather than with *movebat* (already modified by *prius*). — **audis . . . dormis**] After the ribald passers-by and the successful clandestine callers comes the persistent, unsuccessful admirer; cf. 3. 10; **me tuo**] = 'I who am your devoted lover'; cf. 1. 15. 32 'tuae'; **longas pereunte noctes**] 'all night long on the point of death'; *perire* belongs to the stock *langage galant* of the Roman lover; the plural is probably to be taken as generalising rather than as 'night after night'; **Lydia**] also 1. 8, 1. 13, 3. 9. 6-7.

9-12] Stanzas 1-2 stressed neither Lydia's virtue nor her promiscuity, but that she was in a position to pick and choose (and did). Stanza 3 passes abruptly to the fate that lies in store for her. — **In vicem**] 'In your turn'; H.'s point is not that Lydia will follow in others' footsteps, but that a reversal of roles awaits her: soon, as Lydia's admirers dwindle and her appetite for sex gets out of hand, it will be her turn to take to the streets at night, to suffer the arrogance of those whom till now she has been able to treat with arrogance. — **moechos arrogantis flebis**] 'will lament, with tears in your eyes, the arrogance of lovers', as the lover of lines 6-8 laments her arrogance; *moechus*, like *adulter*, is the lover of a woman who is married or of respectable marriageable status; an affair with a woman who was not of such status did not constitute adultery in Roman law, whether the man was married or not (the great adulterers of classical literature are Paris and Aegisthus — not Agamemnon, since Cassandra was not married); a woman of married (or equivalent) status is presumed, however promiscuous, to have been seduced by her lover; thus Cicero in defending Caelius can argue that the widowed Clodia's promiscuity was so exceptional that the presumption of seduction did not apply (*Cael.* 49 'cum hac si ui adulescens forte fuerit, utrum *adulter* an *amator, expugnare pudicitiam* an *explere libidinem* voluisse videatur?'; cf. ibid. 38); see on 3. 16. 1-8 and 1. 15I; the assertion that the words *moechus*, etc. are often used loosely (= 'lover', 'womaniser', etc.) is erroneous; *moechus, adulter* and the corresponding feminines *moecha* and *adultera* always tell us something about the woman's status, but tell us nothing about the man; *amans* ('lover', the word preferred by the elegiac poets) leaves the question of the woman's status open, *amator* ('womaniser') tends to be pejorative (Cicero in the passage quoted above is content to accept the term, in order to absolve his client from the more serious accusation of adultery); marriage of course covered a range of relationships (see 1. 15I): Lydia might be no more than a *libertina* who has set up house with what we should call a *de facto* husband, but it is a good guess that she belongs to the class castigated by H. in 3. 6. 21-32; her status makes her coming degradation significant and adds point to the obvious echoes of Catullus' Lesbia; **arrogantis**] cf. Chloe's unexpected arrogance in 3. 26. 12. — **anus**] Like *senex*, denotes one who is no longer young (a man or woman in the forties); as in 4. 13. 2 the connotations of English, 'an old woman', are misleading. — **in solo levis angiportu**] 'in a deserted alleyway, a woman of no account'; a clear echo of Catullus 58. 4-5 'nunc in quadriviis et angiportis / glubit magnanimi Remi nepotes'; the fate which Catullus had taunted Lesbia with in a mood of angry rhetoric becomes in H. a study in sombre realism; **solo**] because the lover with whom she has made an assignation has failed to turn up; **levis**] i.e., she who was once a woman of some consequence is now not worth worrying about; **angiportu**] a traditional place of assignation. — **Thracio . . . vento**] = 'while the wind from Thrace rages more fiercely as the moonless nights approach'; she chooses, i.e., dark nights when her faded looks will not show; **bacchante**] the word used of a frenzied female worshipper of Dionysus, suggests that the wind raging in the dark alleyway symbolises the murky, frenzied passion of the ageing nymphomaniac; a wind from Thrace (i.e., a cold, wintry NE wind) is chosen because bacchants are traditionally associated with Thrace; the reference to the *interlunia* (the period between one moon and the next) probably emphasises the sexual connotations; for the word divided between lines cf. 1. 2. 19 and 2. 16. 7.

13-15] Lydia is not a prostitute (or destined to become one), as is frequently asserted, any more than Lesbia was: what drove the one into the streets (if we may believe her angry ex-lover) and will drive the other there is not the wish to make money but an irresistible lust for men. — **cum**] = 'and then' (see on 1. 2. 7. — **quae . . . equorum**] The lust of mares on heat is a traditional topos, its application to Lydia an extreme example of H.'s cruel, sardonic realism; **matres equorum**] high style for 'mares', but, as in 1. 17. 7, the circumlocution is not without point: just as the image of a filly or heifer can dispose us favourably towards a young girl feeling the first stirring of passion (see on 2. 5. 5-9), the image of mares who have already foaled and are drawn again by sexual desire is calculated to repel; **furiare**] 'send mad'. — **iecur ulcerosum**] For the liver as the seat of sexual desire, see on 1. 13. 4; *ulcerosum* suggests the scars of previous attacks; the word is unusual, perhaps a coinage by H. for pejorative effect.

16-20] Lydia's complaint is transposed by H. into an ironically phrased poetical fantasy in which selecting a mistress is spoken of as though it were a matter of no more consequence than selecting material for a garland to wear at a party — some will prefer ivy, some myrtle. — **non sine questu**] Ironical litotes; see on 1. 24. 17 'non lenis'. — **laeta**] 'in joyful mood'; perhaps also a technical term of animal husbandry — cf. *Georgics* 3. 63-4 'superat gregibus tum laeta iuventas, / solve mares'. — **pubes**] The ageing flirt is rendered more pathetic (or absurd) by her passion for *young* lovers; cf. 2. 8. 17 and see on 3. 20. 1-8. — **hedera ... myrto**] 'takes pleasure rather in ivy that is green, and myrtle that is dark'; i.e., some prefer one, some the other (just as some men prefer blondes, some brunettes); but whichever it is, the foliage must be young and its proper healthy colour; for garlands and the materials to make them, see 1. 38; with the image cf. 4. 13. 9-10; the delayed position (hyperbaton) of *atque* is rarer than with *et*; NH prefer to take *pulla myrto* as ablative of comparison (*magis atque* thus = *magis quam*), but this seems rather too ingenious. — **aridas ... Euro**] The dried-out leaves of both the ivy and the myrtle are tossed aside; **hiemis sodali**] a rhetorical flourish to emphasise the concluding rallentando; but the winter wind is an appropriate recipient of withered leaves; **dedicet**] = 'make a present of'; for tossing to the winds cf. 1. 26. 2-3; **Euro**] H., as usual, particularises; the MSS have *Hebro* (*Euro* is a conjecture first found in the Aldine edition of 1501), but tossing to the winter wind is more feasible than tossing in a river in Thrace; the confusion of *v* and *b* (pronounced in post-classical times as a labio-dental fricative almost identical with *v*) is very common in MSS.

1. 26

Introduction: An elegant poem in honour of H.'s friend Lamia. The theme is, in miniature, that of 2. 11 or of 3. 29, 'let's leave the cares of the world behind'; for once, however, instead of urging his views on others, H. speaks for himself; and, whereas an important friend such as Maecenas (3. 29) cannot be expected to take more than a brief respite from the cares of the world, H.'s unconcern can be complete (5-6 'unice securus'). Friends, moreover, can only be expected to seek consolation in wine, women and song: H. has an alternative occupation, poetry, of a new, exciting kind.

   If Lamia is the Aelius Lamia of 3. 17, as seems probable, he shares with Virgil the rare distinction of having two poems addressed to him (Maecenas, the poet's patron, is a special case); for this Lamia, see on 3. 17. 1-8; the Lamia mentioned in 1. 36. 7 is probably his son, as is, perhaps, the Lamia of *Epist.* 1. 14. 6-10. For the suggestion that this was H.'s first poem in Alcaics, see on 8 *coronam*.

Structure: Stanzas 1-2 are held together by the double indirect question 'quis metuatur', 'quid terreat', forming an elaborate syntactical pattern of which the climax is the emphatic 'unice securus'. Lines 6-12 are the poet's appeal to the Muse for inspiration: the opening entreaty 'O quae ... Piplei dulcis' links Stanzas 2 and 3; the concluding justification for the entreaty is structured, in the common manner of addresses to divinities, by the repetition in anaphora of the personal pronoun *hunc*.

Metre: Alcaics (see 1. 9M).

1-6] **Musis amicus**] 'Loved by the Muses', i.e., a poet whose poetry is inspired (not hack work); H.'s favourite role (cf. e.g., 3. 4), but relevant here as an initial statement of claim, in preparation for the request of lines 6-12; linked with the future *tradam*, the phrase assumes something of the status of a proviso (= 'so long as I am visited with inspiration'). — **tristitiam et metus**] For fears of further outbreaks of war on Rome's remote frontiers as a near-obsession of H.'s contemporaries, see on 2. 11. 1-4. — **protervis ventis**] The adjective personifies; in a woman it suggests cheeky independence, in a man high-spirited truculence, easily leading to violence; in a woman *protervitas* is usually regarded as attractive (1. 19. 7, 2. 5. 15), in a man usually deprecated (1. 25. 2, 3. 14. 26); for tossing to the winds as an image denoting disposal of something unwanted cf. 1. 25. 19-20. — **in mare Creticum**] As usual, H. particularises; traditionally, an area of storms, suitably remote from Rome and H.'s present concern; see on 1. 1. 14. — **quis ... orae**] = 'what king strikes terror into the people of the frozen North'; the remote NW is meant (rather than our Arctic); for idea and rhetorical structure cf. 2. 11. 1-4, 3. 29. 25-8; for

H.'s unconcern cf. 1. 19. 9-12. — **quid . . . terreat**] Tiridates was a Parthian princeling supported by Augustus (*Res Gestae* 32. 1 'Ad me supplices confugerunt reges Parthorum Tiridates' etc.), here the symbol of the Eastern ruler in constant danger of being over-thrown by a coup d' état (and the attendant risk of Roman involvement); he seems to have taken refuge in Rome on two separate occasions (one about 30 BC, the other about 26 BC). — **unice securus**] 'supremely unconcerned'; in this colloquial idiom, *unice* = 'more than anyone else' rather than 'uniquely'.

6-10] The Muse is appealed to, to weave a garland for Lamia. The garland need be no more than the present poem, the honour lying, if we assume 1. 26 to be H.'s first poem in Alcaics, in the unprecedented form of the poem. But while several stanzas can perhaps constitute a garland, the word is more often used as the symbol of a collection (cf. the famous 'Garland of Meleager'); 1. 26, moreover, is short and seems to need some subject other than itself. Possibly, H.'s gift to his friend was a modest collection of poems in Alcaics later incorporated in the present more ambitious collection. It is noteworthy that, of the ten poems in Alcaics in Book 1, seven occur in the group 1. 26-37 (see 1. 25M). H. perhaps kept the group virtually intact as an unobtrusive compliment to a friend who had necessarily to take second place to Maecenas. — **fontibus integris**] A familiar symbol of poetic originality, the Muses being traditionally associated with springs (see on 3. 13. 13-16); cf. Lucretius 1. 927-30. — **apricos necte flores**] The sunlit flowers are those which can easily be supposed as growing in the meadows around the spring (as yet untouched by human poet) at which H. has sought inspiration; *apricos* suggests joyful poems rather than poems on such gloomy topics as those alluded to in lines 3-5; the imagery is natural and pictorial, and not to be pressed too closely, as though encoding a message which could be restated logically; for gathering flowers to form a garland as a symbol of innocent, maidenly activity cf. 3. 27. 29-30. — **necte, necte**] The repetition suggests solemn appeal (see on 2. 14. 1); for the rhythm of the double dissyllable, see 1. 9M. — **Piplei dulcis**] 'sweet maiden of Pimplea' (the usual spelling), a place in Pieria near Mt Olympus, the site of the Pierian spring. — **nil . . . honores**] = 'my efforts to honour Lamia are ineffectual unless inspired by you'; cf. 4. 3. 17-24; probably better punctuated (as here) as closely attached to the preceding appeal rather than as a separate statement; **prosunt**] the variant *possunt*, though virtually without MSS authority, is tempting.

10-12] The concluding lines justify H.'s application. — **fidibus novis**] i.e., a new kind of lyric poetry. — **Lesbio plectro**] = lyric poetry in the style of Sappho and Alcaeus (here particularly the latter); cf. 2. 13. 25-40, see on 3. 30. 13-14; the rhythm (a word-break after syllable 4 of line 3 is unparalleled in H. and rare in Alcaeus). — **sacrare**] 'conse-crate'; by making Lamia the recipient of inspired poetry. — **teque tuasque**] The double *-que* (= *et . . . et*) belongs to the high style; cf. 3. 4. 19.

1. 27

Introduction: Like 3. 19, the words of a guest at a party (clearly H. himself, playing, as often, the role of reasonable convivialist) structured as a poem. The most animated of H.'s dramatic monologues. We hear H. deftly pick up interjections, tease one member of his audience for the benefit of the rest. No other ode seems to call to the same extent for acted performance. The party has become wild, the speaker intervenes to reproach his fellow-guests. After a call for calm (lines 6-8), he attempts to defuse the situation by diverting attention to one of the guests, whom he proceeds to tease at length about his latest love affair.

Structure: The scene might be one from comedy, but H. exploits to the full the traditional conventions of verse tragedy and the compression and formal elegance which they permit; the style is highly rhetorical, creating the illusion of speech without imitating it.

Stanzas 1-2 represent the speaker's intervention to prevent the fight which is imminent; four imperatives (2 *tollite*, 4 *prohibete*, 7 *lenite*, 8 *remanete*) grouped in pairs, each pair preceded by a solemn-sounding generalisation, form the structural basis. Stanzas 3-6 represent the speaker in conversation, first with his audience in general, then with one of his fellow-guests. Except for the spillover at the end of Stanza 4, the stanzas are strongly endstopped. The sentences are in the main short and vigorous.

Metre: Alcaics (see 1. 9M). See on lines 3, 15.

1-4] The guests are beginning to hurl cups at one another; H. has to transpose a drunken brawl into something we can take seriously as poetry. Much depends on the persona H. creates for himself. He begins on a note of good-humoured solemnity which might easily collapse into mock-heroic if it did not have the elegant metrical and rhetorical structure to sustain it. − Natis] 'made for'. − in usum laetitiae] 'as an aid to happiness'. − scyphis] large two-handled pottery cups; cf. 1. 20. 2 'cantharis'; instrumental ablative with *pugnare*. − Thracum] 'characteristic of Thracians', 'the sort of thing Thracians do'; for the genitive cf. 3. 12. 1, 3. 13. 13. − tollite] 'away with'. − verecundumque Bacchum . . . rixis] = 'and protect Bacchus, whom such behaviour shames, from brawls and bloodshed'; for Bacchus as a moderate god who disapproves of those who overstep the proper limits, see on 1. 18. 5-11; he is here spoken of, with an irony appropriate to the occasion, as a shy youngster who has to be looked after by brawnier stalwarts when a fight begins; verecundumque] for the delayed caesura, see 1. 9M.

5-8] Stanza 2 reproduces the pattern of Stanza 1: generalisation, followed by exhortation. − vino . . . discrepat] = 'your Persian dagger has absolutely no place at a civilised evening's drinking'; we are not to suppose that H.'s fellow-guests are so armed (or even that the occasional guest is reaching for a knife): H. means that Persians drink armed for a fight and in broad daylight (a practice frowned upon at Rome), civilised men don't; *vino et lucernis* symbolise the typical Greco-Roman symposium (which takes place at night, sometimes all night); cf. 3. 8. 13-15, 3. 21. 21-4; immane quantum] a Grecism on the model of θαυμαστὸν ὅσον, etc.; as in Greek, used paratactically (as a kind of adverbial phrase), not to introduce an indirect question. − inpium] Because an offence against Bacchus. − cubito remanete presso] = 'stay in your place'; at a Roman party the guests reclined, supporting themselves on their left elbows; H.'s fellow-guests are getting up, it seems, to take better aim.

9-10] Voltis . . . Falerni?] H.'s response to a chorus of interjections; severi] position and context suggest taking with *voltis*: H.'s fellow-drinkers, i.e., accuse him of lagging behind and call for strict compliance with the rules laid down by the *magister bibendi* − a neat play upon words permitting H. to apply to the audience a term rendered unexpected by their conduct; partem] = 'my fair share'; see below on 13-14 'Non alia bibam mercede'; some take *severi* with *Falerni*, arguing that *severus* is substituted for *austerus*, the technical term for dry Falernian (as opposed to sweet; see Pliny *NH* 14. 63), the implication being that H. should get down to serious drinking (instead perhaps of trifling with other wines), but this seems weak and over-ingenious.

10-12] A barefaced attempt to ease the tension by diverting attention to a guest in less pugnacious mood than the rest. From this point onwards H. addresses himself to the young man, teasing him at length for the benefit of an appreciative audience. The young man is obviously in love. We may assume the usual symptoms: *pallor, languor, silentium*, inability to concentrate on what is going on around him. In such circumstances, a man's friends took it upon themselves to look into the matter − in case the girl turned out to be a designing hussy or otherwise unsuitable; the lover, for his part, was expected to cooperate, by owning up, producing the girl for inspection , etc., submitting himself to goodnatured teasing from the other members of a group of friends always ready to constitute itself a mutual protection society. See, as poems reflecting different aspects of a familiar social situation, Catullus 6, 10, 55 and 58b, *Epodes* 11. 7-10, *Odes* 1. 8, Propertius 1. 1. 25-39, 3. 25. The conventional, mock-solemn diction is part of the fun. − Opuntiae frater Megyllae] For the periphrasis cf. 3. 9. 14, 3. 12. 8; the implication is that Megylla is better known to H.'s audience than her brother (and herself present; for girls at parties see on 1. 36. 17-20; cf. 3. 14. 21-24). − quo beatus volnere] That love is a physical wound (inflicted by Cupid) is a stock image, always available for revitalisation (cf., e.g., *Aen.* 4. 1-2); here, the oxymoron neatly encapsulates the bitter-sweet anguish of love. − qua pereat sagitta] Continues the image and the stilted, conventional diction ('what arrow' = 'what mistress'; cf. 20 'meliore flamma').

13-14] Cessat voluntas?] = 'Reluctant to tell me, are you?'; the phrase implies that Megylla's brother knows that the rules of the group prescribe confession, is willing to comply but slow about it. − Non . . . mercede] 'These are the only terms on which I drink'; we are no doubt to suppose that one of the guests presses a cup of wine on H., which he makes a show of refusing until Megylla's brother owns up (see on 9-10 'Voltis . . . Falerni' − no need to suppose H. has had nothing to drink); in a performance of the ode before an audience, H. would no doubt make appropriate gestures of refusal.

14-17] **Quae te cumque domat Venus . . . peccas**] Both statements are generalisations: 'whatever girl you fall in love with, she's not one to be ashamed of, you never go off the rails with anyone who isn't free-born'; never *ancillae*, i.e., or *libertinae*, always *ingenuae* (and therefore, probably, *matronae*); to be funny, the compliment should be thoroughly undeserved — either because the reverse is known to the audience to be true, or, more probably, because his age makes the experience he is credited with manifestly implausible; see on 20 *puer*; for a similar kind of leg-pull, see on 2. 4. 13-20; cf. Catullus 6. 1-5; for the tmesis *quae . . . cumque* cf. 1. 6. 3, etc.; with *Venus* ('sexual desire', thus, by a conventional metonomy, 'mistress') cf. 1. 33. 13; **non . . . ignibus**] both the image of fire and the diction are stylised and conventional; **erubescendis**] for the polysyllable straggling the line, see 1.9M; **peccas**] a conventional euphemism of the *langage galant*, revitalised by the ironical oxymoron of 'ingenuo amore peccas'; *peccas* also suggests that Megylla's brother is being complimented as a specialist in adulterous affairs.

17-20] The young man's secret is wormed out of him — and the teasing is redoubled. — **Quidquid habes**] The same phrase (and the same sense) in Catullus 6. 15-16 'quare, quidquid habes boni malique, / dic nobis'. — **tutis auribus**] The safe ears are those of the young man's friends: they won't tell others — but they won't hesitate to tease Megylla's brother themselves; to suppose that the ears are H.'s, conflicts with 10 *dicat* (which seeks an open confession) and rather spoils the joke, though the young man may have been led to suppose his secret was safe with H.; the interpretation desired could be brought out in performance through appropriate stage business. — **A miser**] Mock-pathetic; for *miser*, see on 1. 5. 12. — **quanta laborabas Charybdi**] = 'so that was it, a monster has you in her clutches, and what a monster!' Charybdis, though often paired off with Scylla (the two monsters which presided over the Strait of Messina), is also available as a kind of horror version of the German Lorelei (irresistible and rapacious, rather than mysteriously attractive); **laborabas**] a regular though infrequent idiom, stressing that what is discovered to be the case has been the case all along. — **digne . . . flamma**] The reassurance of lines 16-17 'ingenuo semper amore peccas' turns out to be unfounded; the young man's mistress is a *libertina* or the like; or, if a *matrona*, then a tough proposition (such as the lioness of 3. 20, perhaps); either way, the boy deserved better luck; with *meliore flamma* cf. 1. 33. 13 'melior Venus'; **puer**] like *puella, puer* implies an attitude in the speaker (here ironically protective, cf. 3. 9. 16) rather than an age limit; but the context suggests that Megylla's brother, despite the flattery of lines 14-17, is as much a beginner as the *gracilis puer* of 1. 5.

21-4] **Quae saga . . . , quis magus . . . , quis deus?**] The third member is of a different order from the rest, as though the progression from *saga* to *magus* to some still more potent dealer in magic were abandoned as hopeless; unexpected departure from a familiar rhetorical pattern (here tricolon crescendo) can be as effective as strict adherence; references to the power of witchcraft (to free the victim from infatuation, or invoked by another to ensnare a beloved) are frequent in ancient literature; see, e.g., Dido in *Aen.* 4. 483-93, *Eclogue* 8, Propertius 1. 1. 19-24 and 4. 5; no doubt such practices were widely resorted to; Thessaly and Colchis were reputed to produce the best witches, *magi* usually came from Persia. — **Vix . . . Chimaera**] The original chimaera was part lion, part snake and part goat — a dangerous monster to get in the toils of; it was killed by Bellerophon mounted on Pegasus; the Chimaera who has Megylla's brother in her clutches may prove too much even for them.

1. 28

Introduction: After the most dramatic in form of H.'s monologues, the most ambitious and perhaps the most challenging in the demands it places on the interpreter. For once, the speaker is not H. himself. H. exploits instead the common convention of ancient epitaphs (both actual grave inscriptions and literary imitations of these) by which the deceased addresses the living. His speaker is an unnamed corpse, drowned in a shipwreck, pathetically eager for the ritual handful of dust which releases the dead man's soul from its body for its eternal peace; he addresses in turn the great Tarentine philosopher Archytas (whose tomb is nearby) and a passing traveller. H.'s own escape from death in shipwreck (3. 4. 28) may have suggested to him this unusual combination of traditional material. What seems to have attracted him is the opportunity for ironical exploration of the thoughts that can be presumed to run through the mind of an imagined character poised between life and death. The two halves of the ode are held together by the reversal of attitudes which the second half imposes: what, on an initial reading, we take to be conventional irony (the contrast between Archytas' achievements and the handful of dust that now confines him) turns out to be closer to envy — the contrast remains, but is seen in a fresh perspective from the point of view of a dead man who asks for nothing more than that his soul be so confined, instead of being condemned to range the earth.

Structure: Lines 1-6, opening epigram: the speaker addresses Archytas; syntactical structure, a single sentence. Lines 7-20, increasingly gloomy reflections on immortality. A second long complex sentence (lines 7-15) is followed by a series of loosely structured statements (lines 15-20). Lines 21-22, the speaker reveals his standing in the matter. Lines 23-36, the speaker turns from Archytas to plead with an unnamed *nauta* to perform the ritual act of burial: a short sentence states the dead man's request (lines 23-5); a longer sentence promises rewards (lines 25-9); a series of threats follow (lines 30-34), then a final entreaty — 'it won't take long' (lines 35-6).

Metre: Archilochean (b); see 1. 7M. Though the total number of lines is divisible by four, the syntactical and rhetorical structure seems clearly based on the couplet, not on a 4-line stanza.

1-6] The opening six lines might stand alone as an example of the elegant, witty, ironic manner of Hellenistic literary grave epigram. In H.'s poem they are the starting point for a more elaborate pattern of irony: to the contrast between the wide-ranging achievements of Archytas while he lived and the narrow confines of the grave that holds his remains, is added the contrast between Archytas who attained that last ambition of mortal man — a handful of dust and the peace which the grave brings, and the speaker who has as yet had that denied him. Archytas of Tarentum, a distinguished mathematician, the most eminent of Pythagoras' pupils, a friend of Plato, lived in the first half of the fourth century BC. — **Te cohibent pulveris exigui parva munera**] The handful of dust (cast upon the body of the deceased as part of the rites of burial) which 'confines' or 'hems in' the great Archytas is spoken of with evident irony, but the irony turns out to be that of the envious *anima* of the shipwrecked sailor, condemned to wander aimlessly because it has been denied the 'pulveris exigui parva munera'; cf. the shade of Palinurus in *Aen*. 6. — **maris . . . mensorem**] The resonant rhetoric (note the alliteration of '*maris . . . me*nsorem' and the assonance of ter*rae . . .* hare*nae*') is literally true: Archytas was, among other things, a geometer (= *terrae mensor*), a theoretician (not just a practical surveyor) who concerned himself with such problems as calculating the size and mass of the earth, etc.; he also devised a mathematical procedure for calculating the number of grains of sand in the universe — a task traditionally reckoned impossible; alongside such achievements reference to 'pulveris exigui parva munera', in itself no more than a rhetorically emphatic restatement of a traditional phrase, acquires a fresh component of irony. — **prope litus Matinum**] The meaning of the adjective is uncertain (does it refer to a mountain, a promontory, or some other feature?) but a point on the coast of Apulia is indicated (cf. H.'s reference to himself in 4. 2. 27); a site near Tarentum (which would seem more natural) is not precluded — according to some ancient writers, Apulia extended to the gulf of Tarentum. — **nec . . . prodest . . . morituro**] That a man's achievements while alive avail him nothing when he is dead is one of the great commonplaces — though not H.'s own view of the matter in his prouder moments (see 3. 30. 6-7); here, the commonplace prepares the way for the reflections on the universality of death which follow (lines 7-20) — a subject upon which the speaker is discovered at lines 21-2 to hold an understandably prejudiced view; **aerias temptasse domos**] a phrase that might be used of a hero's bid for immortality (in Homer the gods are regularly described as 'possessing houses on Olympus'); Archytas' assault upon the heavens was, however, an intellectual one ('animo') as an astronomer — and (according to the speaker) demonstrably unsuccessful; **rotundum percurrisse polum**] = 'to have ranged over the whole wide heavens'; **morituro**] ablative with *animo*; the *animus* (to which Archytas owed his achievements) is mortal, the *anima* is not 'destined to die'; emphatic final position.

7-15] It is also a commonplace that even the great figures of the past were overtaken by death. The speaker's list is made up, however, of those who in various ways seemed — temporarily — to have eluded death. In a different context, and speaking in his role as *Musarum sacerdos*, H. offers a more impressive list, 3. 3. 9-16. Here the list is confined to those whose claim to immortality can be dismissed as false or derisory. — **Occidit et**

Pelopis genitor] *et* is emphatic, 'even Tantalus'; while dining with the gods, Tantalus might feel he had achieved immortality (as Archytas might have felt as he encompassed the universe with his intellect), but he was mistaken. — **Tithonusque ... auras**] Tithonus, husband of the goddess of Dawn, *was* granted exemption from death, but not from the normal ageing process, so that he got older and older (and of less interest to his wife); what eventually happened to him is something legend is not clear about; the speaker's 'remotus in auras' ('vanished into thin air') is perhaps H.'s own wry version (adapted to the present occasion) — Tithonus, i.e., though technically immortal (like our old soldiers) eventually just faded away. — **Minos**] The reference is to King Minos' inclusion while alive among those with whom Jove shared his secrets (not to his position as judge of the dead in Hades). — **habentque ... verique**] The son of Panthus is Archytas' own master Pythagoras ('iudice te non sordidus auctor naturae verique'); according to a story often alluded to by ancient writers, Pythagoras, while visiting the temple of Hera at Argos, recognised one of the shields hanging there as the shield he had himself dedicated during his previous incarnation as Euphorbus, son of Panthus, during the Trojan War; the shield was taken down and an inscription found on the back which authenticated Pythagoras' claim; 'so', says the speaker, 'Pythagoras eluded death once, but the second time death has got him'; the cynical, witty tone of this final *exemplum*, if hardly appropriate to a normal rhetorical amplification of the theme 'death takes the famous too', suits admirably the special point of view of the speaker; **Orco**] the dative (instead of the normal preposition and accusative) is characteristic of the high style; contrast 3. 4. 75 'missos ad Orcum'; Orcus in H. seems to be a person, however, rather than a place (cf. 2. 3. 24, 2. 18. 30 and 34, 3. 11. 29, 3. 27. 50, 4. 2. 24) and the dative is perhaps to be felt as a normal dative of advantage; **quamvis ... atrae**] 'even though, by appealing to the evidence of his days at Troy on that occasion when he took down the shield, he had conceded nothing to black death except sinews and skin'; i.e., he had claimed that only his body had died; *quamvis*, when used as a concessive conjunction, is more often constructed with the indicative than the subjunctive; **nervos atque cutem**] an ironical simplification, to be attributed to the speaker rather than to Pythagoras; **non sordidus auctor**] = 'an authority not to be sneezed at'; again we catch the cynical tone of voice of the speaker; **naturae verique**] hendiadys, 'on the true facts about the nature of the world'.

15-20]   The speaker now opposes to these misguided or false claims to immortality his own view of the grim reality of the human condition. — **Sed omnis ... leti**] *nox* and *via* both with *manet*: 'a single night and a road to death, to be trodden once and once only, await us all'; no less a commonplace than those which preceded, coexisting along with the others in the repertoire of tradition; the present formulation has obvious echoes of Catullus 5. 5-6 'nobis cum semel occidit brevis lux, / nox est perpetua una dormienda' and 3. 11-12 'qui nunc it per iter tenebricosum / illud, unde negant redire quemquam'. — **Furiae**] Like Virgil's Allecto, more figures of bloodshed and horror than of vengeance. — **torvo spectacula Marti**] Mars watches over the battlefield as an ordinary upper-class Roman watches a gladiatorial contest; for Mars as a grim, sardonic figure who treats war as a sport cf. 1. 2. 37 — **exitio ... nautis**] 'the greedy sea is the death of sailors'; for *nautis*, see on 23 *nauta*; in this 'double-dative' construction, the first (*exitio*) expresses the end ('final dative', cf. 4. 11. 3), the second (*nautis*) designates the person involved; with *avidum mare* cf. 3. 29. 61 'avaro mari'. — **mixta ... fugit**] A climactic couplet; **Proserpina**] it was her duty to cut off a lock of hair from those about to die; cf. *Aen.* 4. 698-9 and Austin thereon; **fugit**] perfect.

21-2]   An emphatic *me* introduces a turning point in the rhetorical structure; a device H. uses several times (cf. 1. 1. 29, 1. 5. 13, 1. 7. 10, etc.); here, however, an unexpected twist: *me* introduces, not the poet speaking in an apppropriate persona, but a dramatic character, in no way representative of H. himself. — **Me quoque ... obruit undis**] The natural meaning is 'I too was drowned at sea (i.e., like Archytas) — in a November storm', which explains why Archytas' grave is 'prope litus Matinum' and preserves the unity of the poem; what Archytas, the speaker and the man addressed in the remainder of the poem have in common is that they have all been exposed to the perils of travels at sea; the constellation Orion sets in November, hence a southerly storm at that time may be described as 'the raging companion of Orion at his setting'; **rabidus**] cf. 1. 3. 14 'rabiem Noti'; nearly all the MSS have the commoner and more obvious *rapidus*; **Illyricis undis**] presumably he was on his way across the Adriatic (to or, more likely — given the season — from Illyria) when the storm 'overwhelmed him' (*obruit*) and then, some time later, his corpse was washed up on the *litus Matinum* (rather as the corpse of Palinurus was washed ashore, *Aen.* 6. 362); for travel by sea in late autumn see on 3. 7. 5-8.

23-9] Lines 21-2, as well as marking the turning point of the ode, serve as a bridge passage between the first half (in which the addressee is the dead Archytas) and the second half (in which the addressee is an unnamed passing *nauta*. — **At tu, nauta**] It is clear from 27-9 that the *nauta* is not a 'sailor' in our ordinary sense but a *mercator*, one who hopes to profit from his voyage: *nauta*, i.e., = 'traveller by sea' (as *viator* = 'traveller by land'); cf. 3. 4. 30-32; the term can thus include Archytas and the speaker: all three are travellers by sea; one died and was buried; one was drowned and has not been buried; the third is a passing traveller, addressed by the dead man as 'nauta' as, in a normal grave inscription, the passing traveller is addressed by the deceased as 'viator'. — **vagae harenae**] Genitive with *particulam*. — **ne parce dare**] *ne* with the present imperative is poetic syntax; so too is the infinitive with *parce* (cf. 3. 8. 26, 3. 28. 7). — **ossibus**] The corpse is already a skeleton (the dead man, i.e., and the *nauta* are not from the same ship). — **capiti**] The head is singled out as representing more than any other part the individual human being. — **inhumato**] The hiatus following *capiti* is most unusual in that the elided vowel is the same as that which follows. — **particulam**] = the 'pulveris exigui parva munera' of lines 3-4. — **sic**] 'on this condition', i.e., 'provided you do this'; see on 1. 3. 1. — **quodcumque ... Hesperiis**] = 'however much the south-easterly bullies the seas around the Italian coast'; for Eurus cf. 1. 25. 20, 2. 16. 24; **minabitur**] the future probably refers to the journey upon which the *nauta* is about to embark. — **Venusinae ... sospite**] 'may the forests of Venusia take a beating, but no harm come to you'; Venusia, on the border of Apulia and Lucania, was H.'s birthplace; the forests will be those on the slopes of the Apennines above the coastal plain (see on 3. 6. 41-2); for the oak forests of that region, see 1. 22. 14; the area is specified, not as the only one in which the *nauta* may encounter danger, but because it was here that disaster overtook the speaker. — **multaque merces ... Tarenti**] The dead man wishes the *nauta* a prosperous as well as a safe voyage; **unde potest**] = 'from where all profit comes', i.e., the gods; with *unde* cf. 1. 12. 17; **aequo ab Iove**] 'from a favourably disposed Jove'; **Neptuno**] god of the sea, as well as protector of Tarentum (perhaps the *nauta*'s home port).

30-36] The spirits of the dead are conventionally represented in Roman literature as possessed of a new, detached wisdom, inspiring awe in their contacts with the living, if not actual fear; cf., e.g., the shades of Hector and Creusa in *Aen.* 2 (or the shade of Cynthia in Propertius 4. 7); H.'s ineffectual shade, unable to command, forced instead to plead and threaten, is a figure closer to comedy. Contrast the terror inspired by the unburied shade of Polydorus in *Aen.* 3; Virgil's Palinurus in *Aen.* 6 is closer, but still a figure of dignity and pathos. — **Neglegis ... conmittere?**] 'Do you not take into account that the wrong you are doing will one day bring harm to your innocent children?'; to deny burial is a *fraus* (a transgression of divine law); in such cases, the sons are apt to suffer for the sins of their fathers. — **Fors et ... ipsum**] = 'Perhaps it will be your own fate to have rights withheld and to suffer arrogance in your turn'; divine punishment is sure but notoriously slow (cf. 3. 2. 31-2 — unless the offence is so heinous that Jove strikes you down on the spot with his thunderbolt) and unpredictable; if the *nauta* is scoundrel enough to deny the dead man's request, he may be scoundrel enough not to worry what happens to his children; the possibility that he may in his turn be left unburied is, there-fore, put forward as more likely to give him pause; **debita iura**] *debita* is used in its technical sense, 'withheld'; a difficult phrase, variously interpreted. — **Precibus ... resolvent**] = 'My entreaties will be answered, nothing you can do will expiate you'; **precibus**] entreaties lodged with the proper gods, therefore 'curses'; **piacula**] it is one of the most awesome commonplaces of ancient tragedy that no action by an individual can forestall divine retribution: the anger of the gods, once incurred, must run its course. — **quamquam ... curras**] Lines 30-34 are constructed to leave the impression that the dead man threatens too much, as if not himself convinced of the inevitability of divine punishment; the final couplet reinforces this feeling of a pathetic, ineffectual figure nearer to comedy than to tragedy; the words put on the dead man's lips follow traditional formulae, revitalised by the fresh, dramatic context; the passer-by is regularly represented in grave inscriptions as in a hurry; cf., e.g., *Carm. Epig.* 513. 2 'Cur tantum properas? Non est mora dum legis'; but a request to linger long enough to read an inscription and a request for burial are of a different order; **licebit ... curras**] 'when you've cast the dust three times, you can run'; Antigone thus buries her brother, Sophocles *Ant.* 431; syntax

(*licebit* plus subjunctive without *ut*) and diction (*curras*) are colloquial and close to the
style of comedy, as though the dead man were now seeking to ingratiate himself with
the *nauta* more than to threaten him.

1. 29

Introduction: Iccius, like the young Roman subaltern of 3. 2. 1-12, is about to cover him-
self with glory on his first campaign. The immediate theatre of operations is Arabia
rather than Parthia (see on 4 *Medo*); whether the campaign is that of 26-25 BC under
Aelius Gallus, prefect of Egypt, as is commonly supposed, is perhaps doubtful (though
see on 3 *Sabaeae*), since that campaign ended rather too disastrously (according to Dio
53. 29. 4, most of the army perished) for H. to publish, only a year or so after the event,
a poem bubbling with ironic banter at Iccius' expense; see 1. 35I; as always in H.'s more
personal poetry, banter is made the vehicle for seriously-held attitudes to life. Iccius, if
he went at all, survived, to reappear in *Epist*. 1. 12 as manager of Agrippa's estate in
Sicily. See 1. 8I and see on 3. 2. 1-6.

Structure: An opening triad of direct questions (1 'invides?', 2 'paras?', 5 'nectis?') sketches
in the hypothesis of the poem and establishes H.'s attitude. The remainder of the ode
consists of a second triad of questions arranged as a tricolon crescendo (5-6 'quae . . .
serviet?', 7-10 'puer quis . . . paterno?', 10-16 'quis neget . . . cum tu . . . tendis?'), the
third of which introduces a key modulation that brings H.'s treatment of his theme into
the desired perspective. Cf. the structure of 1. 8.

   To emphasise the rhetorical structure, the metrical structure is muted: Stanza 1 spills
over into Stanza 2, which in its turn spills over into Stanza 3; the pause at the end of
Stanza 3 is nominal, the third question of the second series being readily felt as incom-
plete at this point. Of the six questions, four end in mid-line.

Metre: Alcaics; see 1. 9M; see on line 11.

1-5]   **Icci**] The initial vocative suggests urgent, intimate directness; cf. 1. 8. 1, 1. 33. 1, 2.
6. 1. – **beatis . . . gazis**] In the mind of the Roman soldier the thought of loot always
loomed large; Iccius is no exception and his expectations are high, we gather; the East
is regularly represented as full of untold treasures; cf., e.g., 3. 24. 1-2; *beatis* probably
hints as well at the name Arabia Felix, the gateway to the far East, as opposed to
Arabia Deserta to the north; **nunc**] the first hint of the change which has come over
Iccius; **gazis**] the word always conjures up images of oriental wealth and luxury. –
acrem . . . Sabaeae] 'you're planning a tough campaign, are you, for the as yet uncon-
quered kings of Sheba?', i.e., going to give them a rough time; for a curious echo, see
Augustus *Res Gestae* 26. 5 (of the campaign of Aelius Gallus) 'in Arabiam usque in
fines Sabaeorum processit exercitus'; H. teases Iccius, who is obviously a very junior
officer, by talking as though he were commander-in-chief, planning the whole campaign;
the kings of Sheba occupied more or less the territory of the present-day Yemen. –
horribilique . . . catenas] A successful campaign meant prisoners of war (who can be
brought back as slaves), as well as loot and glory; a good general looks ahead – when
the time comes for taking prisoners, it is important to have the chains ready; the 'shaggy
Mede' represents Augustan Rome's Public Enemy Number One, the Parthians (see on 1. 2.
22) – a long way from Arabia, but once you start conquering the East, there's no knowing
where you'll stop.

5-10]   The first two cola of the second triad, while ostensibly backing up the opening
question, quickly place the issues involved in a different perspective, in preparation for
the final ironic reversal of lines 10-16. No doubt many a Roman dreamt of bringing home
a barbarian concubine, torn from the arms of her fiancé; but the most famous case was
Agamemnon and Cassandra. A handsome royal page to pour one's wine is an equally
obvious daydream; but once again an illustrious precedent is to hand – Ganymede,
whisked away to be the cup-bearer of Jove himself. It cannot be said that one must think
of Agamemnon and Cassandra and of Jove and Ganymede, or get the poem wrong. Nor is
it simply that these are natural precedents to think of after the build-up of Iccius in lines
1-5. The two questions seem worded to touch off a controlled association of ideas which
leads the sensitive reader accustomed to the manipulation of a familiar repertoire of
mythical exempla to imagine Iccius casting himself in the absurdly glorious role these
precedents suggest. – **sponso necato**] The phrase places the girl: she had a fiancé, one

easily thinks of him killed in battle — no ordinary slave girl, therefore; for Cassandra's fiancé (Choroebus) and his death, see *Aen.* 2. 341-6 and 402-8; for similar material with more straightforward overtones, see 3. 2. 8-12; see also 2. 4. 13-16. — **Puer quis . . . unctis**] For a *puer* acting as wine steward cf. 3. 19. 10; **ex aula**] places the boy — he is a royal page, trained to act as cup-bearer to a king; cf. Livy 45. 6. 7 'pueri regii apud Macedonas vocabantur principum liberi ad ministerium electi regis'; **capillis unctis**] i.e., sleek and smart in appearance; see on 1. 5. 2; **ad cyathum**] an important utensil in the ritual of a Roman symposium; see 3. 19. 11-12, cf. 3. 8. 13-14; **statuetur**] 'will be stationed'. — **doctus . . . paterno?**] An elliptical phrase designed to challenge the reader's imaginative response; it is a reasonable assumption that the boy was taught to shoot by his father (using his father's bow because he was too young to have a bow of his own), that the arrows were Chinese because this happened in China (a romantic, remote land for a Roman; cf. 1. 12. 55-6), and that the boy was captured in some far Eastern campaign, brought back and trained by his royal master — before being captured again by Iccius; a final, extravagant embellishment of the daydream foisted upon Iccius by H.

10-12] The emphasis placed on the innocent victims of Iccius' ambitions (while the pursuit of loot and glory fades into the background) and the skill with which our sympathy is elicited lay the ground for the carefully articulated ironical reversal which now follows. As in 1. 8. 13-16, a slight formal change is the only hint that the third member of the tricolon is of a different level of seriousness from the other two: after the two confident future indicatives ('quae . . . serviet', 'puer quis . . . statuetur'), the potential subjunctive 'quis neget' marks the modulation to a more resonant key. Unlike 1. 8, the poem ends on a note of direct, abrupt challenge. — **arduis . . . montibus**] Rivers running uphill are the stock example of the figure called *adynaton*, an impossible event, the occurrence of which would indicate a total reversal of the normal order of things; cf. 1. 33. 7-8; the most famous instance of the image of rivers reversed in their course is Euripides *Medea* 410 (often imitated); the familiarity of the cliché heightens the irony: the impossible, it seems, *can* happen; **arduis montibus**] locative (rather than dative for accusative with preposition, as, probably, 1. 28. 10); **pronos**] i.e., streams that till their reversal had been hurtling downwards. — **et Tiberim reverti**] Domesticates the cliché.

13-16] The second member of the tricolon was expanded by an appositional phrase ('doctus . . . paterno'), the third member flows over into the following stanza (cf. 2. 5. 21-4). Iccius is now unmasked: he is not the typical junior officer for whom active service is the natural sequel to training in the *militia equestris* of Augustus, but an enthusiastic disciple of the Stoic philosophers who has exchanged one enthusiasm for another. — **coemptos . . . Panaeti**] i.e., Iccius' personal collection of the works of the distinguished Panaetius; **coemptos undique**] 'snapped up wherever they came on the market'; **nobilis**] idiom and the balance characteristic of H.'s manner link with *Panaeti* (not with *libros*); **Panaeti**] the distinguished Stoic philosopher; he came to Rome about 144 BC and resided there until he became head of the Stoa in 129 BC; his writings do not seem to have been extensive (compared, e.g., with those of Epicurus); perhaps Iccius was a collector who bought every copy he could of the master, rather than a philosopher. — **Socraticam et domum**] Perhaps 'and the Socratic school'; but the ironic context suggests the more literal 'and his Socratic house' (because of the books it contained, the talk that went on there); 'Socratic' in either case = Stoic; cf. *Epodes* 8. 15 'libelli Stoici' 3. 21. 9. — **mutare tendis**] 'are proposing to exchange'; Iccius' departure is not after all imminent, it seems; he is only making preparations; *mutare* = simply 'exchange'; no need to suppose Iccius selling his books to buy breastplates (nothing suggests he is short of money); the emphasis thrown on *tendis* by its delayed final position implies Iccius may yet change his mind; for this sense of *tendere* cf. *Epist.* 2. 2. 57; the echo of 9 *tendere* seems unintentional and (to our modern ear) surprising. — **pollicitus meliora**] The literal translation, 'having promised better things', gives clearly the right sense, though this use of *polliceri* is unusual — obviously no actual verbal undertaking is referred to; by conventional Roman standards, Iccius is doing the right thing, behaving like a man; and yet it is clear that H. wants us to feel it is a pity things have turned out the way they have; no doubt it is Iccius' impulsiveness, his jumping from one excess to another, which H. deplores, not his patriotism; no doubt, too, H., having in his youth thrown over his philosophical studies to join the army of Brutus, is disposed to be indulgent; and yet, as with 1. 8, the modern reader is surprised to find Augustan Rome more tolerant of the questioning of out-and-out militarism in H. and in Virgil than the modern historian would lead him to expect.

COMMENTARY

1. 30

Introduction: An elegantly worded address to Venus and an extended epigram that leaves
more unsaid than said. The goddess's cooperation is asked on behalf of Glycera; H.
sponsors, as it were, an appeal (or appeals) for assistance which Glycera is already making
— with some urgency, or, perhaps, with some frequency (see on 2-3 'vocantis ture multo').
Why? Clearly, Venus is being invoked — not propitiated as in 1. 19. 13-16: Glycera wants
her help, she isn't asking to have her own anguish made more endurable; this must be the
sense of *vocantis*; the elaborately symbolic diction of Stanza 2 points in the same direction.
It all still sounds somewhat mysterious. Is this the Glycera with whom H. has fallen passio-
nately in love in 1. 19 (and with whom he is still stubbornly in love at 3. 19. 28), or the
heartless Glycera who has deserted Albius in 1. 33 — or neither of these? Has she for once
encountered stubborn resistance? If so, who is the recalcitrant lover? An explanation is
suggested below on lines 5-8.
Structure: One of five odes 8 lines long; the others are 1. 11, 1. 38, 3. 22 and 4. 10. Stanza 1
follows, in miniature, the familiar pattern of hymn form (opening vocative, places cited
with which the goddess is associated, prayer); Stanza 2 repeats the message in more
mannered language.
Metre: Sapphics; see 1. 2M.

1-4] H.'s starting point seems to be an epigram by the Alexandrian Posidippus (*Anth. Pal.*
12. 131), in which the aid of Aphrodite is solicited on behalf of a courtesan whose lover
has deserted her. As usual, H. improves on his model; the irony is more deftly deployed,
H.'s own standing in the matter is an active component of the wit. — **regina**] For the
caesura after syllable 6, see 1. 2M. — **Cnidi Paphique**] Cnidos (in Caria) and Paphos (in
Cyprus) are two of the most famous centres of the worship of Aphrodite. — **sperne
dilectam Cypron**] In ancient religious belief, the divinity is potentially present in his
shrine, his actual presence being secured by the ritual enacted; it was left to the Hellenis-
tic poets, as part of their witty, irreverent exploitation of traditional forms, to press the
problem of ubiquity: if Venus is to be in one place, she cannot be in another; her presence
is urgently needed in Rome; she must be induced, therefore, to forsake her beloved
Cyprus; *sperne* (one of H.'s improvements on his model) attributes to the goddess the
frame of mind of the tourist who abandons a favourite resort for another where he hopes
to be made more fuss of; contrast 1. 19. 9-10. — **vocantis te**] The immediate context
requires the sense 'invoke'; but the sense 'invite' is drawn out by 'te transfer in aedem'; *te*,
object of the participle *vocantis*, is also object of the main verb *transfer* (a common
idiom). — **ture multo**] The formula suggests repeated invocation rather than isolated
extravagance; see below on 5-8. — **te ... decoram transfer in aedem**] 'take up residence
in Glycera's elegant shrine' (*aedem*, in the sense 'house', requires the plural); pretty clearly,
however, shrine and place of residence are equated, either because from Venus' point of
view the difference was immaterial, or, more probably, because Glycera's elegant establish-
ment was, in effect, a temple of love; see on 3. 26. 6-8; contrast 4. 1. 9-12.

5-8] The matter-of-fact 'te transfer' of lines 3-4 reinforces the notion of a more or less
permanent change of domicile. Reappraisal of 'vocantis ture te multo' begins to suggest
itself. Our initial assumption that Glycera was in desperate straits is threatened by a less
obvious, wittier sense which our attempts to read the poem as a consistent whole make
increasingly compelling: Glycera's calls upon the goddess's assistance, H. seems to be
suggesting, are so regular an occurrence that Venus would be well advised to abandon her
favourite haunt in Cyprus and take up permanent residence with so hospitable a devotee.
Naturally, when she comes, she will want to bring her retinue with her. Again the idea is
a commonplace of hymnal poetry, rendered witty by the process of irreverent seculari-
sation of the divine which pervades the poem. — **fervidus ... Mercuriusque**] *puer,
Gratiae, Nymphae, Iuventas* and *Mercurius* are all subjects of *properent*; for the delayed
—*que* of *properentque* (= 'properent, properentque'), see on 2. 19. 28; **fervidus puer**]
Cupid can no doubt be described as *fervidus* because of the zeal with which he assists his
mother; but perhaps H. has in mind the more sinister Cupid whose burning gaze sets Dido
on fire with love in *Aen.* 1. 710; cf. 1. 32. 9-10; **solutis Gratiae zonis, Nymphae**] traditio-
nally, members of Venus' retinue; cf. 1. 4. 5-6; for *solutis zonis*, see on 3. 21. 22; **parum
comis ... Iuventas**] a Roman deity of respectable antiquity and antecedents, but here
more the Greek Hebe; 'parum comis sine te' attempts a witty allegorisation of the truth

formulated by Catullus in Poem 86, that good looks without *Venus* do not constitute beauty; with Venus in residence, Glycera need have no worries; **Mercuriusque**] why Mercury — especially in so prominent a place as the concluding line of the poem? undoubtedly the answer attributed to the ancient commentator Acro (commended by NH), that Mercury appears in his role as the god of commercial transactions, is correct — a divine pimp to manage the business side of an establishment run under the patronage of Venus herself; the last word of the poem firmly places Glycera — she is no victim of unrequited love, but a *demi-mondaine* whose business is booming.

1. 31

Introduction: The first, and really the only, occasion in the *Odes* on which H. explicitly assumes the role of *vates* (line 2), to which he had laid tentative claim in 1. 1. 35 and which he can regard (with the passage of time) as assigned to him by common consent in 4. 3. 15, so that he can, half-humorously, in writing to Maecenas style himself 'vates tuus' (*Epist*. 1. 7. 11). For H. the word connotes moral authority, rather than inspiration, or the prophetic stance he assumes as 'Musarum sacerdos' in 3. 1. 3, especially the moral authority of one whose manner of living acts out a philosophy of life which permits him to censure others (cf., e.g., 2. 16. 33-40, 2. 18, 3. 29).

The occasion is the formal dedication of Augustus' splendid new Temple of Apollo on the Palatine on 9 October 28 BC, a ceremony which made Propertius late for a meeting with his mistress (Propertius 2. 31). H. does not ask us to imagine him as participating in the formal dedication, but as adding his personal tribute to the newly installed Apollo. On such an occasion one can suppose the god more than usually attentive to the prayers addressed to him. The things a man prays for are worth taking note of, therefore. H. asks, not as ordinary men might, for rich estates, but the capacity to enjoy what he has in sound health and with intellect unclouded by advancing age.

Structure: The basic rhetorical structure consists of lines 1-3 (opening questions) plus Stanza 5 (the poet's prayer to Apollo which constitutes also his answer to the opening questions). This basic structure is expanded by the quadruple *non* structure of lines 3-8 (what the poet does *not* pray for), which leads into the further expansion of Stanzas 3-4, where the poet's rejection of conventional attitudes is expressed as a binary opposition ('others can . . . , but for *me* . . . ').

Metre: Alcaics; see 1. 9M; in lines 9 and 17 the first syllable is short.

1-3] **Quid . . . vates?**] = 'What does the poet-moralist ask of Apollo on the occasion of the dedication of his temple?'; as *vates*, H. has a special claim on Apollo, the god of lyric poetry (see, e.g., 1. 21. 10, 2. 10. 19-20); particular emphasis was placed on this aspect of Apollo in Augustus' new temple, which was to include a large library where poets could meet and perform their works. — **quid . . . liquorem?**] 'what is his prayer as he pours his libation of new wine from its cup?'; there seems to be an allusion to the ceremony of the Meditrinalia (a festival marking the end of wine-making and involving libations of new and old wine) which fell on 11 October, two days after the dedication of Augustus' temple (so NH); see on Stanza 5; i.e., the prayer H. makes as *paterfamilias* on his Sabine farm at the Meditrinalia will serve as his prayer to Apollo; for the prayer, see on Stanza 5; **patera**] a flat dish used for libations; **novum liquorem**] the freshly-pressed grape juice, too young as yet to qualify as wine; cf. Tibullus 2. 1. 45 'aurea tum pressos pedibus dedit uva liquores'; here a symbol of the new order of things which the dedication of Augustus' temple represents; H., it seems, did not grow grapes on his farm (see *Epist*. 1. 14. 23, quoted on 1. 20. 1-8), but it is easy to imagine him presiding over some simple rustic ceremony, as chief landowner in the district (see *Epist*. 1. 14. 1-3, quoted on 3. 18. 9-12).

3-8] More ambitious men than H. might feel the occasion of the dedication authorised more audacious requests of the god, but for H. the prayer he makes each year is enough. Lines 3-8 deal with the former. — **Non . . . feracis**] 'Not rich-bearing cornfields in fertile Sardinia'. — **non armenta**] 'not herds of cattle'; **aestuosae grata**] the adjectives oppose one another, introducing a note of ironic disparagement (in Calabria the cattle are enough to gladden a farmer's heart, but the heat is terrible; cf. *Epodes*. 1. 27-8). — **non aurum . . . Indicum**] We pass from the rich farmer to the merchant prince in Rome and his elaborate, over-decorated house; cf. 2. 18. 1-2, 3. 1. 45-8. — **non rura . . . amnis**] Not, finally, an expensive country estate in Campania; cf. 2. 15; the Liris divides Latium from Campania, where it flows through the richest and most famous of Italian wine-growing areas; **quieta, taciturnus**] the Liris is slow-flowing, this is peaceful country compared with the wilder Sabine hills of H.'s farm.

9-16] Stanzas 3-4, though syntactically a self-contained section, form an integrated part of the rhetorical structure. A natural sequence of thought in lines 3-8 has led H. to Campania; an equally natural sequence leads him to contrast the growers of a famous Campanian wine with himself; cf. 1. 20. 9-12. – **Premant falce**] 'prune'; the *falx* is a small sickle used for pruning vines (to prevent too rapid growth of the vines and consequent deterioration of the grapes). – **Calenam**] For wines of Cales cf. 1. 20. 9, 4. 12. 14. – **quibus dedit Fortuna**] i.e., good luck to them. – **dives ... merce**] i.e., such wines are only for rich people, such as the importer of Syrian perfumes and spices; for the *mercator*, see on 1. 1. 16; **aureis exsiccet culillis**] ironic juxtaposition – the little golden goblets proclaim sophisticated refinement, but the *mercator* drains them greedily to the last drop; **Syra merce**] H. regularly prefers the shorter gentile form of the proper name to the adjectival form; **reparata**] 'got in return for' (no necessary implication of barter). – **dis carus ... inpune**] Ironical: if the wine-growers are lucky, the *mercator* is luckier still – to be alive; **aequor Atlanticum**] i.e., the mysterious seas beyond the Pillars of Hercules (= the straits of Gibraltar, the western edge of the civilised world where Homer's Ulysses communed with the spirits of the dead), regularly visited by the *mercator* in the course of trade with Spain. – **me ... malvae**] The olives, etc. symbolise H.'s simple, unpretentious way of life; cf. *Sat.* 1. 6. 114-15, *Epist.* 1. 5. 2; no suggestion that he is a teetotaller (or even a strict vegetarian); the ironic bathos undercuts the pretentiousness of the extravagant way of life of the wealthy, and prepares the way for 17 *frui paratis*; for the emphatic *me*, see on 1. 1. 29.

17-20] Lines 2-3 'quid orat ... liquorem' suggest that H.'s prayer is based on a prayer offered at the Meditrinalia. Our information about this ceremony comes from Varro *Ling. Lat.* 6. 21, who is more interested in etymologising (he derives *Meditrinalia* from *mederi*) than with describing ritual. A prayer for long life and good health seems likely enough. H.'s prayer represents his personal version, as Epicurean and poet, of that common aspiration most memorably encapsulated by Juvenal, 'mens sana in corpore sano'. – **Frui paratis dones**] 'Grant me enjoyment of what is at hand'; that the things actually needed for life are readily available ('in promptu') and that the wise man should content himself with these are Epicurean commonplaces; see, e.g., Lucretius 6. 9-10 'ad victum quae flagitat usus / omnia iam ferme mortalibus esse parata'; *frui* in the neutral sense of 'enjoy' – the ability to avail oneself freely of the basic needs of life, rather than the pleasure taken in them, which is assumed. – **et valido mihi et integra cum mente**] = 'without hindrance from either physical or mental infirmity'; the MSS have *at precor*, but the correlative *et ... et* seems clearly right and is generally accepted. – **Latoe**] 'son of Lato' (the Doric form of Leto), the goddess known to the Romans as Latona (1. 21. 3, etc.). – **precor**] Soundness of mind in old age is both rarer than soundness of limb and more precious to H.; *precor* introduces and, as it were, apologises for the more audacious request. – **nec ... carentem**] The second request is parallel to the first syntactically (*degere*, like *frui*, depends on *dones*), and repeats the essence of *integra cum mente* in more personal form; the first *nec* joins *degere* to *frui*, the second *carentem* with *turpem*; *turpem* suggests the humiliation and the physical squalor of the old man who is not *integra cum mente*; *nec cithara carentem* expresses the hope that old age will not deprive H. of his chief passion in life (see 1. 1. 29-34); cf. the wry confession some twenty years later, *Epist.* 2. 2. 55-7 'singula de nobis anni praedantur euntes: / eripuere iocos, venerem, convivia, ludum; / tendunt extorquere poemata: quid faciam vis?'; for *senectam*, see on 2. 14. 3.

1. 32

Introduction: Odes 1. 32 picks up – and rejects – H.'s description of himself in 1. 6. 17-20 as one who merely dabbled with verse on the theme of love in the absence of any serious involvement. Instead, he plans now verse that will last, in the tradition of Alcaeus, and appeals to the lyre of Apollo for inspiration.

The theme is conventional enough; for the appeal to the lyre cf. 3. 11. 3-6 (there des-

cribed as the lyre of Mercury); for the appeal for inspiration cf. 3. 4. 1-4. Only the posi-
tion of the ode surprises. H. can hardly mean that the odes which follow aim at a more
serious treatment of love than, say, 1. 13 or 1. 19; of the remaining poems in Book 1,
only 1. 33 (in Asclepiads) is about love, while 7 poems in Sapphics and 7 in Alcaics
precede (1. 16, 1. 17 and 1. 25 on love themes). The ode is perhaps intended to record
H.'s first perception of himself as a Roman Alcaeus — still a poet of love, with no thought
yet of the deeper themes to come, but a love poet who brings to the theme a new serious-
ness of treatment.
Structure: Stanzas 1-3 form a single syntactical structure leading up to the concluding appeal
to the lyre, the passionate intensity of which still strikes an unexpected note.
Metre: Sapphics; see 1. 2M.
1-5] Poscimus] 'This is my prayer'; the echo of 1. 31. 1 *poscit* can hardly be accidental
(the word is a common one but it occupies a prominent place in each poem); 1. 32 is
perhaps to be taken as following 1. 31 as an additional prayer, H. the poet speaking this
time rather than H. the philosopher-moralist; the plural suggests the poet thinking of him-
self in his role as artist (cf. 1. 6. 17-20) rather than as an individual human being (as in
1. 1. 29-34); the variant *poscimur* ('I am summoned to perform'), as in Ovid *Met.* 2. 143-4
'non est mora libera nobis! / poscimur', etc., though well attested, is too abrupt to be
convincing. — **si quid . . . tecum]** States H.'s entitlement to have his prayer answered — a
common formula, not implying any doubt; cf., e.g., Catullus 76. 19-20 'si vitam puriter
egi, / eripite', etc.; the poet has served his apprenticeship, learned his craft writing verse
about love, but with no real involvement, emotional or artistic; **vacui]** cf. 1. 6. 19
'*cantamus vacui*'; though the qualification added there naturally puts the matter in a
different light from here, the echo helps to define the area of non-involvement (Stanza 3
will make it clear that H. is still thinking of poetry about love); **sub umbra]** i.e., out of
heat of the sun; cf. Tityrus (also a love poet) in *Eclogue* 1. 1; **lusimus]** the stock word for
poetic trifling; cf. *Sat.* 1. 10. 37 'haec ego ludo', Catullus 50. 2 'multum lusimus in meis
tabellis'; especially of love poetry, as 4. 9. 9 'siquid olim lusit Anacreon'; cf. Catullus 68.
17 'multa satis lusi'; **tecum]** personifies — poet and lyre work in collaboration. — **quod
. . . pluris]** = 'good enough to last another year and longer'; with the phrase cf. 1. 11. 4-6;
hunc in annum] 'into this present year'; some of H.'s light verse is still read and looks like
standing the test of time, but H. has put such verse behind him; Bentley, Page and others
take the relative clause with what follows, but this strains the sense of *hunc in annum;* the
order is also less natural; moreover, H.'s modest claim for his light verse probably echoes
Catullus 1. 9-10 'quod . . . / plus uno maneat perenne saeclo'; in H., however, the sub-
junctive is generic, not the expression of a wish. — **age . . . civi]** = 'inspire me to write
poetry in Latin in the tradition of Alcaeus'; for *dic* (the poet's appeal to the Muse for
inspiration), see on 3. 4. 1, cf. 1. 24. 2-3, 3. 11. 7; *Latinum* is opposed to 'Lesbio primum
modulate civi', not to 'si quid . . . lusimus tecum' (H. does not mean, i.e., that till now he has
written in Greek); **carmen]** 'poetry', not necessarily 'a poem' (see on 1. 7. 6); H., i.e., is
not asking for inspiration for a particular poem which then follows as in 3. 4 and 3. 11,
but for inspiration at the moment of turning to a new kind of poetry; **Lesbio . . . civi]** the
'lyre first played by the citizen of Lesbos' symbolises poetry, not just in the metres used
by Alcaeus (he was not the first to use lyric metres — he uses, e.g., the Sapphic stanza,
the metre used by H. in this poem, which owes its name to his great predecessor) but in
the manner of Alcaeus; as in *Epist.* 1. 19. 23-34 H. identifies himself as the successor of
Alcaeus rather than Sappho; cf. 2. 13. 21-8; there is of course no suggestion that H. posses-
sed the actual lyre used by Alcaeus; see on 3. 11. 1-8; *Lesbio civi* stresses the involvement
of Alcaeus in political life; **modulate]** for the sense cf. 1. 24. 14, for the form (part parti-
ciple of a deponent verb used as a passive), see on 1. 1. 25 *detestata*; for the syntax
(vocative appositional expansion instead of relative clause), see on 2. 7. 2.
6-12] qui . . . arma] = 'who, tough soldier though he was, when the fighting eased . . . '. —
sive . . . navim] Refers to Alcaeus' wanderings as an exile from his island home; **iactatam]**
'storm-tossed'; for the idea (hero relaxing before putting to sea again) cf. 1. 7. 21-32; for
Alcaeus the soldier-exile cf. 2. 13. 27-8. — **Liberum et Musas Veneremque]** Celebrated by
the poet of wine and love. — **illi . . . puerum]** Cupid; cf. 1. 30. 5. — **et Lycum . . .
decorum]** i.e., love poems; none of the fragments of Alcaeus refer to homosexual attach-
ments, but he was apparently well-known in antiquity for poetry on this theme; cf.
Cicero *Tusc.* 4. 71 'Fortis vir in sua re publica cognitus quae de iuvenum amore scribit
Alcaeus!'; **nigris oculis]** traditionally reckoned beautiful; cf. Catullus 43. 2, Propertius 2.

12. 23; **nigroque crine**] Lycus no doubt wore his hair long, like Gyges (2. 5. 23-4),
Nearchus (3. 20. 14) and Ligurinus (4. 10. 3); in *nigris* the first syllable counts as long, in
nigro as short, according to the normal rules; to scan the same word both ways in quick
succession is a Hellenistic trick, occasionally imitated by Roman poets.
13-16]   The frivolity of lines 11-12 is carefully calculated (cf. the use made of Lycidas in
1. 4. 19 and of Gyges in 2. 5. 20-24) to emphasise the key modulation and the sudden
seriousness of tone which now follows. − **O decus Phoebi**] The lyre brings honour to
Phoebus as god of poetry (cf. 3. 4. 4, 4. 6. 29), though its invention is ascribed to
Mercury (1. 10. 6, 3. 11. 1-2); for *decus* cf. 1. 1. 2. − **dapibus Iovis**] Cf. 3. 11. 5-6. −
laborum dulce lenimen] 'you who bring sweet comfort to those who struggle'; *labores*
in contexts like this always suggests almost intolerable physical and/or mental stress
(like the 'Labours' of Hercules); cf. 3. 4. 39. − **mihi . . . vocanti**] 'accept the salutation of
one who invokes you in proper fashion'; i.e., 'receive his prayer favourably', 'be propitious
to him'; *cumque* seems to be used as a kind of deprecatory or apologetic enclitic (= 'such
as I am' or 'such as it is') softening a phrase that might otherwise seem to make too
positive an assertion − the force H. perhaps attributed to *cumque* in 'quam rem cumque'
(1. 6. 3), 'quo nos cumque' (1. 7. 25), 'quem criminosis cumque voles' (1. 16. 2), 'quae
te cumque domat Venus' (1. 27. 14); H.'s fondness for separating *cumque* from its relative
suggests further experimentation here with what H. took to be an appropriate archaism;
the absence of the relative has worried commentators; see Fraenkel 170; Lachmann's
medicumque, though favoured by NH, is too highhanded to be plausible.

1. 33

Introduction: Albius' mistress has deserted him and he has been pouring out his grief in
elegiac verse. The consolation H. offers him, that no two people ever stay in love with one
another, is intended less to console than as an ironic, incisive statement of H.'s views on
how the world works, and the proper way to deal with its absurdities in verse. If H.'s
attitude seems light-hearted, we may suspect he did not take Albius' outpourings very
seriously, attributing them to the unreal conventions of elegiac poetry and regarding them,
therefore, as fit subject for well-directed banter.
  Albius is, almost certainly, the poet Tibullus, and, presumably, the Albius of *Epist*. 1. 4
and a personal friend of H; the name Glycera does not occur in his extant poems (see
below).
Structure: Lines 1-4 admonish; lines 5-9 back up the admonishment with a series of examples
from real life which show how the world works; in lines 10-12 H. indulges in some mock-
serious philosophising on the subject; lines 13-16 cite his own case by way of proof. The
strong pauses are at the end of lines 9 and 12.
Metre: Asclepiad (c); see on 1. 6.
1-4]   The subordination of lines 1-4 to 6 *torret* and 7 *declinat* is idiomatic rather than real,
like our idiom in which a conditional clause is followed by a statement of fact ('if you're
interested, I'll be at home tonight'); the *ne* clause is thus closer to a prohibition (less
formal than *ne dolueris*) than a final clause and virtually an independent statement; cf.
2. 4. 1-4, 4. 9. 1; Brink, *Proc. Camb. Phil. Soc.* 1969, 4-6, argues there is always an
ellipse (such as 'hoc dico') in such cases, at any rate in the *Odes*. − **ne . . . memor**] The
appropriate course to take, H. would have us believe, when a mistress walks out on you,
is to do all you can to put her out of your thoughts; Albius instead gives vent to unres-
trained grief; **plus nimio**] more than is tolerable, perhaps more than is good for him. −
inmitis] 'ruthless' or 'relentless' − a strong word representing Albius' view of the matter;
saevae (cf. line 12), like *crudelis*, would imply sadistic enjoyment in inflicting pain. −
Glycerae] = 'sweetheart'; the name, it seems, belies her character; Tibullus' mistress in
the elegies which have come down to us are Delia (accused of betrayal in 1. 5 and 1. 6)
and Nemesis (accused of betrayal in 2. 6); Glycera is H.'s latest mistress in 1. 19 (he is
still in love with her in 3. 19) and the devotee of Venus in 1. 30; for such names, see on
1. 5. 3 *Pyrrha*. − **miserabillis**] Full of self-pity. − **decantes**] 'sing through to the finish'
and therefore bore others; cf. Cicero *de Orat*. 2. 75 'Nec mihi opus est Graeco aliquo
doctore, qui mihi pervulgata praecepta decantet'. − **cur**] 'asking why'. − **iunior
praeniteat**] 'a younger man outshines you'; an unkind cut: in elegy it is always a 'rich
lover' (*dives amator*) who alienates the affections of the poet's mistress; *praeniteat* rams

the point home — she finds her new lover more attractive; for the radiance of the beloved (in the eyes of the lover), see on 1. 5. 13 *nites*. — **laesa fide**] Cf. 1. 5. 5-6.

5-9] The *ronde de l'amour*: A loves B, B loves C. General statment is particularised. The names are all Greek in H.'s (and Tibullus') usual manner, but each girl is sharply delineated: Lycoris has 'a narrow forehead', Pholoe has a sharp temper and is fastidious about her lovers. — **insignem tenui fronte**] In a man, the opposite of receding hair; cf. *Epist.* 1. 7. 25-6 'reddes / . . . nigros angusta fronte capillos'; of a woman, the phrase perhaps implies she wore her hair in a fringe. — **Lycorida**] The name used by Gallus in his elegies for his mistress, the actress Cytheris. — **Cyri torret amor**] = 'is passionately in love with Cyrus'; for the metaphor of fire, see on 1. 13. 8. — **in asperam Pholoen**] Pholoe is a prickly customer, or has at any rate a sharp tongue, as is implied by her remarks about Cyrus; cf. 1. 35. 9; the name recurs in 2. 5. 17 and 3. 15. 7 and also in Tibullus 1. 8. 69 (where Pholoe is unreceptive of the attentions of Marathus). — **declinat**] Cyrus, despite Lycoris' passionate love for him, is falling in love with Pholoe; *declinare* is the word used by Lucretius of atoms which deviate from their normal course (2. 221, etc.). — **sed prius . . . lupis**] The figure called *adynaton* (see on 1. 29. 10-12); **iungentur**] not 'to copulate with', but 'to be mated with' (in a semi-permanent liaison); cf. 11 *iuga aenea*; for the wolves of Apulia, see 1. 22. 13-14. — **quam . . . adultero**] 'than Pholoe would go off the rails with an ugly lover'; the emphasis is on *turpi* — Pholoe has no objection to taking a lover, but she draws the line at Cyrus because she can't stand his looks; for *adultero*, see on 1. 15. 19; **peccet**] the usual word for an extra-marital relationship (1. 27. 17, 3. 7. 19).

10-12] H.'s examples involve couples — men and women who are either married (as Pholoe is married, it appears) or at any rate (like Albius, presumably, and Glycera) involved in a semi-permanent liaison. His argument is that always in such cases one of the partners is in love with his or her mate, the other partner with somebody else. He now proceeds to philosophise on this theme, rather in the manner of Aristophanes in Plato's *Symposium*. — **Sic visum Veneri**] Mock-solemn, 'Venus has decreed it so'; cf. *Aen.* 2. 428 'dis aliter visum' and see Williams on *Aen.* 3. 2. — **placet**] Used of divine ordinances, etc.; cf. 2. 17. 16; but the idea that Venus takes pleasure in acting so is not excluded. — **inparis formas atque animos**] 'shapes ill-matched and temperaments that are incompatible'. — **sub iuga . . . cum ioco**] The brazen yoke is the symbol of partnership in love (cf. 2. 5. 1-2 and 3. 9. 18) — either marriage (here, of those who marry for love, not of arranged marriages as in 2. 5) or else partnership in some kind of stable liaison; it is H.'s settled view that such partnerships are irrational and doomed to failure (cf. 1. 13. 17-20): handsome man falls in love with ugly girl or vice versa (*inparis formas*) and then realises his mistake, or the two just cannot get on (*inparis animos*); either way, one partner loses interest and seeks consolation elsewhere; *formas* is perhaps intended to evoke (and explicitly contradict) the optimistic view attributed to Aristophanes by Plato (*Symp.* 191E) that falling in love is the pursuit of like by like; for the yoke as the symbol of partnership, see on 2. 5. 1; the symbol of the yoke is of course latent in the words *coniunx* and *coniugium*; the yoke is also the symbol of enslavement to a god or a mistress (*OLD* 2 a); cf. 14 *grata compede*; the yoke is bronze because it is a goddess who enslaves; cf. 3. 27. 67 'perfidum ridens Venus'.

13-16] A variation on the emphatic *me* at a turning point in the rhetorical structure of an ode; see on 1. 1. 29. — **melior cum peteret Venus**] A calculated ambiguity: after the personalised Venus of lines 1-12, the primary sense is 'when Venus in more kindly mood was heading in my direction' (for this sense of *melior*, see *OLD* on *bonus* 4 b; for the notion that the goddess seeks out her victim cf. 1. 19. 9 'In me tota ruens Venus'); for *peteret* cf. 3. 19. 27, 4. 11. 21; but while this is the sense elicited by context, the more obvious sense 'when better loving was to hand' (i.e., when a more attractive girl was eager to become my mistress) is equally present and necessary; for *Venus* almost = 'mistress' (but with overtones still of Venus as the goddess who enslaves) cf. 1. 27. 14 'Quae te cumque domat Venus' and Lucretius 4. 1185 'nec Veneres nostras hoc fallit'; see on 4. 13. 5. — **grata compede**] Builds on the ambiguity of the previous line — Myrtale is both H.'s mistress and his enslaver; the peculiarity of the lover is that he welcomes his enslavement; H., however, had a choice: he could have had a mistress with whom things would have gone more smoothly (*melior* in the sense of well-disposed, perhaps also in the sense 'more attractive', or the sense 'more socially acceptable') but he remained enslaved by Myrtale, whose temper showed she had lost interest in him (thus confirming by his own case the argument of Stanzas 2-3); for the girl who turns in anger on her lover and the metaphor of the sea cf. Pyrrha in 1. 5; the phrase *grata compede* is used in a similar context in 4. 11. 23-4. — **detinuit**] The perfect implies that later H. too in his turn lost interest; Myrtale only here. — **libertina**] Places Myrtale but also ironical: it is the *libertina* who enslaves the free H.; for H.'s preference for *libertinae* (as opposed to *matronae*), see his own precepts in *Sat.* 1. 2, cf. *Epodes*14. 15-16 'me libertina nec uno contenta Phryne macerat'. — **fretis . . . sinus**] A final distancing image; **acrior**] 'sharper-tempered', or 'a tougher proposition' (not 'more passionate') as *curvantis* confirms; cf. 3. 9. 22-3 'inprobo iracundior Hadria'. — **curvantis**] 'hollowing out' (with its angry, storm-tossed waters), i.e., eroding the coastline into bays and inlets.

1. 34

Introduction: H., till now something of a backslider in matters of religious observance (he accepted the new scientific explanation of things), has been compelled to change his ways. A clap of thunder out of a clear sky (an impossible event according to the Epicurean materialist explanation of natural phenomena) has caused him to abandon his confidence in an ordered, predictable universe: the truth is that we are at the mercy of wholly arbitrary and unpredictable powers who may strike at any time.

There is general agreement that H.'s recantation of Epicureanism is not wholly serious. We may doubt that he ever was a doctrinaire materialist: *Sat.* 1. 5. 101-3:

> namque deos didici securum agere aevom
> nec, siquid miri faciat natura, deos id
> tristis ex alto caeli demittere tecto

does not, in context, indicate the fervent disciple. What attracted him, and continued to attract him (as his description of himself in *Epist.* 1. 4. 16 as 'Epicuri de grege porcum' suggests), was Epicurus' advocacy of the simple life. But about the meaning of the ode as a whole and the degree of seriousness to attribute to it there is less agreement.

The clue seems to lie in 7 *plerumque*. H. does not assert there is no connection between clouds and thunder: he concedes there is a usual order of things; but that order can at any time be overthrown. Similarly, H. might argue (if logical prose were his medium), the high are not regularly overthrown, the low not regularly exalted; but the normal order of things can be at any time suspended in a particular case, and the wise man must live with the knowledge that disaster can descend upon him as unexpectedly as thunder out of a clear sky. The thunderclap out of a clear sky is thus not so much a refutation of Epicurean physics as a symbol and a warning to a man accustomed to think in symbols. The conclusion implied by the ode, in the language and with the concision appropriate to lyric form, is that Epicurean attempts to eliminate fear of the gods are misguided: we might as well fear the gods since the arbitrary forces they symbolise exist. If the ode begins in an ironical or playful tone, it ends in complete seriousness.

Structure: Three sentences make up the ode, The first (lines 1-5) announces H.'s confession; the second states the reason for his change of view in appropriately poetic terms; the third interprets the symbolical significance of the thunderclap. The turning points are in mid-line.

Metre: Alcaics; see 1. 9M.

1-5]   Parcus deorum cultor] Stingy in his sacrifices to the gods (during the period covered by the following *dum*-clause); i.e., negligent rather than an out-and-out non-believer. — **insanientis . . . erro**] 'while I strayed off-course, learned in a mad philosophy'; *erro* prepares the way for *cursus relictos*; the 'mad philosophy' is Epicureanism; for H.'s acknow-ledged adherence to Epicureanism, see Introduction; like his friend Virgil, he seems in middle life to have come closer to Stoicism (see especially the Roman Odes), though he preferred to think of himself as a member of no school (*Epist.* 1. 1. 13-15); for *dum* + present indicative in a clause referring to the past, see on 1. 2. 17. — **retrorsum vela dare**] i.e., put about, change his tack in order to return to the course from which he had strayed; cf. *Aen.* 3. 686 'dare vela retro'; an ancient ship could not turn 180° about unless the wind changed. — **iterare cursus relictos**] 'to resume the course I had abandoned'; if we are to respect the logic of the poem, H. must be taken to mean that henceforth he will be diligent in his observance of the rites due to the gods; for *iterare*, 'to sail once more', cf.

1. 7. 32; many have found the phrase hard and some favour reading *relectos* (an emenda-
tion originally proposed by Heinsius), but H. means no more than that he had been
following a course (the common course of mankind), had strayed off-course and is now
back on course. — **cogor**] 'forced', by reason (and/or fear), not by any external agency;
the present implies a conclusion only just being reached.

5-8] The phenomenon which caused H. to mend his ways is described in the traditional
language and imagery of poetry. — **Namque . . . plerumque**] Most of the time what we
see and hear is Jupiter parting the clouds with his fiery thunderbolt, to strike down the
guilty or as a warning to mankind; see on 1. 2. 2. — **per purum . . . equos**] What H. heard,
however, was the rumble of thunder out of a clear sky — no clouds, no flash of fire;
naturally, the sound pulled him up short, because Lucretius had taught that this does not
occur (Lucretius 6. 400-401 'numquam caelo iacit undique puro / Iuppiter in terras fulmen
sonitusque profundit'): he takes it perhaps as a personal warning that Jove is on his trail;
tonantis] the traditional ornamental epithet of horses' hooves, here restored to its literal
sense (Jove's horses are actually the cause of thunder), reinforces the point.

8-12] **volucremque . . . concutitur**] 'and the flying car at which . . . reverberate'; lines 8-12
describe, not what H. observed on the occasion in question, but what he now, as an
orthodox *deorum cultor*, believes to be the case; *concutitur* is not historical present but
the present used in general statements; the double relative clause embraces the entire
universe (cf. 3. 4. 45-8); **bruta tellus**] 'the heavy, unresponsive earth', as opposed to the
less substantial fabric of the heavens; **vaga flumina**] 'the rivers in their wandering courses';
invisi . . . sedes] Taenarum is the southernmost point of the Peloponnese; a cave there was
supposed to be one of the entrances to the underworld; **Atlanteusque finis**] Atlas, the
giant-mountain, at the western limit of the known world; for the adjectival form, see on
1. 3. 36 *Herculeus*; for the delayed caesura, see 1. 9M.

12-16] The switch from mock-seriousness to utter seriousness is an example of H.'s trick of
key modulation (see on 1. 10. 13-16). In many societies the sophisticated believer will
sometimes use traditional language and imagery to communicate what could otherwise
only be less effectively communicated; Socrates is thus often represented by Plato as
expressing unconventional, sincere belief in conventional terms. Conscious irony of
expression is compatible with serious belief; its sudden abandonment for simpler, more
telling language when that becomes possible, or more effective, is an obvious rhetorical
device. — **Valet . . . promens**] For the thought cf. 1. 35. 1-4, 2. 10. 13-17, 3. 29. 49-56;
valet] 'is strong enough'; cf. 2. 5. 1; **deus**] the non-specific word bridges the gap between
the Jove of lines 5-12 and the Fortuna of line 15; cf. *Epodes*. 14. 6; the implication for
the sophisticated reader is that all these terms are metaphors for that supreme, arbitrary
power presiding over man's destiny which the Epicureans had sought to exclude. —
hinc] Correlative with 16 *hic*. — **apicem**] The symbol of the absolute ruler; cf. 3. 21.
19-20. — **stridore acuto**] The swish of wings; cf. *Aen*. 1. 397 'stridentibus alis' (of the
swans of Jove); *acuto* suggests 'high-pitched', 'strident' and therefore menacing. —
sustulit] Instantaneous rather than gnomic perfect; so probably also *posuisse*. — **gaudet**]
Fortuna, like Venus in 1. 33. 12, takes positive pleasure in her task.

1. 35

Introduction: A formal hymn in praise of the goddess Fortuna, invoking her protection
for Augustus' forthcoming campaign against Britain as well as for a newly-raised expedi-
tionary force to the Middle East.

Dio mentions plans by Augustus for an expedition to Britain in 34, 27 and 26 BC (49.
38. 2, 53. 22. 5, 53. 25. 2), none of which eventuated; most assume it is the last of these
which is referred to in Stanza 8 and that the expedition to the Middle East is that under
Aelius Gallus in which Iccius is planning to take part in 1. 29; NH toy with 35 BC on the
grounds of metrical peculiarities, but this is implausibly early. Assuming a reference to
the expedition of Aelius Gallus also raises difficulties, however, since, at the time of publi-
cation of *Odes* 1-3, that expedition must have been known to have ended disastrously (see
1. 29I). In this case, as in others, to press the identification of an ode with a particular
historical event is probably unwise: a reading of 1. 35 by H. in 26 BC would no doubt be
taken as referring to campaigns then imminent, or believed to be imminent. When the ode

is published along with the others which made up the collection, it will have a different reception: a new expedition to the Middle East is now imminent, an expedition to Britain still something which is talked about; the ode acquires a fresh topical relevance and is interpreted by its audience in that light. Much the same applies to the Roman Odes (3. 1-6): most likely, they were composed over a period of years; when published together as a group in *Odes* 1-3, they take on a collective relevance to events then imminent. Even when an ode refers explicitly to a particular historical event which is easily identified and remains fresh in the public memory, e.g., 1. 37 on the death of Cleopatra, publication some years after the event permits a degree of historical foreshortening for artistic effect. Normally, poems, unlike letters and other historical documents, have attributed to them the relevance they seem to invite at the time of publication. Thus, 3. 5. 2-4 'praesens divus habebitur / Augustus adiectis Britannis / imperio gravibusque Persis', in its context as one of the Roman Odes addressed to the new generation, will naturally be taken as referring to the situation in 23 BC. Revision by H. of his text to emphasise contemporary relevance may be assumed, and may sometimes be tentatively postulated on formal grounds: Stanzas 9-10 of 1. 35, e.g., rather look as though they had been added afterwards, to emphasise the hopes pinned on (and the luck entreated for) a new generation of soldiers, free from the guilt of internecine strife. By invoking for them the protection of Fortuna (rather than Jove, or Mars) H. perhaps means to wish better luck to their arms than their predecessors enjoyed.

Structure: The ode represents H.'s most sustained exercise in hymn structure. For simpler models cf. 1. 10, 1. 21 and 1. 30. After an opening stanza invoking the goddess, a pattern of anaphora in asyndeton in which the emphatic *te* of line 5 is repeated five times leads up to the prayer of Stanza 8. Stanzas 9-10 break with the formal hymn-structure to express the poet's indignant condemnation of Roman collective guilt, ending in the supplementary prayer of lines 38-40. For the structure of lines 5-16, see on these lines.

Metre: Alcaics; see 1. 9M; the first syllable of lines 15 and 37 is short.

1-4] There are two departures from normal hymn-structure: the goddess is not named in the invocation (nor does her name occur elsewhere in the poem), and only one of her shrines is mentioned, that at Antium, about 80 km S of Rome. The fact that Fortuna is named in the concluding stanza of the poem immediately preceding, though clearly not fortuitous, hardly alleviates the oddity. Presumably, only Antium is mentioned because H. wishes the poem to be understood as addressed to the Fortuna of Antium (not to Fortuna in her temple in Rome itself, or at Praeneste, or the goddess Fortuna more generally). Fortuna is an Italian goddess (a 'bringer' of prosperity, perhaps) of respectable antiquity later identified with the Greek and especially Hellenistic Tyche. − **gratum**] sc. 'tibi'; cf. 1. 30. 2 'dilectam Cypron'. − **praesens**] i.e., actually present in her shrine and on hand to help. − **imo . . . triumphos**] This is the Fortuna of 1. 34. 14-16 who raises up the lowly and casts down the mighty; understandably, as her protection is being invoked, she is spoken of in more favourable terms in this role than in 3. 29. 49-52; **imo tollere de gradu**] 'to raise from the bottom rung'; **mortale corpus**] 'our mortal frame'; **superbos . . . triumphos**] 'to turn proud triumphs into funerals', the triumphal procession symbolising the Roman leader at his moment of greatest glory; cf. *AP* 226 'vertere seria ludo'.

5-16] The recital of the goddess's attributes begins with a somewhat loosely structured tricolon crescendo, in which the first and second members are controlled by 5 *ambit*; the third member is constituted by the multiple subjects of 12 *metuunt* in Stanza 3, which flows over into Stanza 4 to form a first climax at line 16. − **pauper ruris colonus**] The small-scale farmer symbolises the class which had to struggle for existence; cf. 2. 14. 12. − **ambit**] 'solicits your support', 'ingratiates himself upon you', like a candidate for public office. − **te . . . carina**] The phrase suggests the *mercator* or overseas trader (see on 1. 1. 16) rather than the ordinary sailor; where the farmer needs luck to survive, the *mercator* plays for higher stakes; **dominam aequoris**] in art, Fortuna is sometimes represented along with a ship's rudder or prow and the shrine at Antium may have emphasised Fortuna's role as mistress of the seas; but that those who travel by sea are subject to Fortuna is a very obvious reflection; **Bithyna carina**] ships of Pontic pine from shipyards in Bithynia are often referred to; cf. Catullus 4; **lacessit**] 'challenges'; **Carpathium pelagus**] named after Carpathus, an island between Rhodes and Crete. − **te Dacus asper, te profugi Scythae**] The various subjects of *metuunt* are best taken as loosely structured into three groups, forming a minor tricolon crescendo within the major tricolon of which they constitute the third member; the *Dacus* and the *Scythae* stand for the wild tribes of the NE frontier; for the Dacians, see on 3. 8. 18, for the Scythians, see on 1. 19. 10; *asper* implies an enemy not easily dealt with, or quick on the attack (cf. 1. 23. 9, 1. 33. 6, 3. 2. 10); **profugi]** 'quick to retreat' (the opposite of the Dacians), cf. 4. 14. 42. — **urbesque . . . ferox]** The second group represents the 'cities and peoples' of the civilised world, as opposed to the nomad Dacians and Scythians; **ferox]** 'bold', the word used of Theseus in Catullus 64. — **regumque . . . tyranni]** The third group are the high and mighty of this world, those whose power is arbitrary and un-Roman and who have most to fear because they have most to lose; **metuunt tyranni]** oxymoron; tyrants are more often thought of as feared than fearing; cf. 3. 1. 17-21. — **iniurioso . . . frangat]** The expansion of *metuunt* applies only to the members of the third group (only for them is popular uprising the chief and constant fear); *iniurioso* combines the ideas of insult and injury; **columnam]** symbolises the royal palace and the power over the people which it represents; when it is thrown flat, the house falls; cf. 2. 17. 4; **populus frequens . . . concitet]** succinctly evokes the image of revolution (an armed horde calling on those who hang back to join them); the repetition of *ad arma*, first with *frequens* ('rushing to take up arms') and then with *concitet* suggests the repeated cry 'ad arma!' while not formally reporting it.

17-28] After the climactic Stanza 4, the rhetorical pattern of Stanzas 2-3 is resumed in Stanzas 5-6. The praise of Fortuna, while remaining graphic, takes on a symbolic and allegorical character. Stanza 7 follows as a second climax, concluding the long aside which separates the invocation of Stanza 1 from the prayer of Stanza 8.

17-20] **te . . . Necessitas]** The ritual context secures the image of Fortuna preceded wherever she goes by Necessitas (like a Roman magistrate preceded by his lictors); but the wording of the image is obviously designed to encapsulate the philosophical truth that the events we ascribe to Fortuna fall within a framework erected by fate. — **clavos . . . plumbum]** Just as the lictors carry the *fasci*, the symbol of the magistrate's *imperium*, so Necessitas carries the symbols of Fortuna's power; cf. 3. 24. 5-8 (where, however, Necessitas is represented as working on her own, as in 3. 1. 14-16); **clavos trabalis]** large spikes (some have been found as much as 50 cm in length) for fixing the beams of a house, etc. to the pillars which support them; **cuneos]** it appears from Cicero *Tusc.* 2. 23 (a translation of Aeschylus, describing the fastening of Prometheus to the rocks of Caucasus) that *cunei* are some kind of wedge-shaped spikes; **aena]** (three syllables) with *manu*, 'in her hand of bronze'; Campbell's *aenos* is attractive; **severus uncus]** 'the cruel clamp', used for fixing the marble facing to a wall constructed of cheaper material; **liquidumque plumbum]** the lead is poured into the slot in the stone to fix the clamp firmly to it; Necessitas carries the molten lead in some vessel ready for pouring (presumably, the lead was normally heated on the site, but Necessitas is no ordinary workman).

21-8] We come now to the lesser attendants who wait upon Fortuna — and to one of the most perplexing passages in the Odes: the words and phrases used are not difficult, all seems clear except the sequence of thought. — **Spes et Fides]** Both are associated with Fortuna in Roman cult. — **albo velata panno]** 'with her hand wrapped in cloth'; see Livy 1. 21. 4 (on the cult of Fides) '[Numa] sacrarium . . . vehi iussit manuque ad digitos usque involuta rem deivinam facere'. — **rara]** 'uncommon', 'precious'; as often in allegory, the attribute of an abstraction sits uneasily upon its personification. — **colit]** 'attends upon', *OLD* 7. — **nec comitem abnegat]** Must mean 'nor does either Spes or Fides refuse to act as your companion'. — **utcumque linquis]** 'whenever you abandon'. — **mutata veste]** The most natural meaning might seem to be that Fortuna somehow puts on mourning, but why she should then desert those she has till now protected is hard to see; the change of garb must somehow symbolise Fortuna's changed attitude — she, as it were, reveals her hand. — **potentis domos]** *potentis* is best taken as accusative plural. — **at volgus infidum . . . retro cedit]** The best that can be made of this is that the crowd of so-called friends, etc., who throng the houses of the great (23-4 *potentis domos*) while all goes well, instead of attempting to restrain Fortuna and her attendants when they stalk out, or to bar their way, shrink back in fear (*cedo, OLD* 8 'to step aside', 'make way for'); the *meretrix periura* is presumably added to the *volgus infidum* to suggest that it is the company the rich man keeps which Fortuna can no longer endure; the remainder of the stanza in that case fills out the picture of the terrified guests uncertain what to do when Fortuna walks out; the second climax in the preamble ends, like the first, with an image of Fortuna deserting those she had supported; this is not wholly satisfactory (it leaves *mutata veste* inadequately explained), but gives reasonable sense; much confusion has been introduced into discussion of the passage by those who feel Fortuna should not

desert without warning the house she has supported (but this is precisely what Fortuna
does — she is a goddess to be feared, not to be judged by the standards applicable to
human beings), or that Spes and Fides should not follow her when she leaves; or who,
looking for a simple binary opposition between the conduct of Fortuna and the *volgus
infidum*, have been puzzled that they should stay when she leaves. — **diffugiunt . . .
amici**] The rich man's so-called friends drain their cups and flee (their cowardly desertion
of their friend being set in contrast to the majestic departure of Fortuna and her com-
panions); cf. for the idea 2. 8. 18-20. — **ferre iugum pariter dolosi**] The infinitive with
dolosi is hard; perhaps 'evasive about sharing the burden' of misfortune which has fallen
on their friend.

29-32] Having established Fortuna as unpredictable and to be feared, H. is now in an
effective position rhetorically to entreat her protection for Caesar and the expedition to
the East. For speculation about the campaigns referred to, see Introduction — **serves**] Cf.
1. 3. 8. — **iturum**] = 'when he goes'; the formula is sufficiently vague to fit a campaign
which can be talked of as imminent but is still not a matter of the immediate future. —
Caesarem] See on 1. 12. 52. — **in ultimos orbis Britannos**] An echo of Catullus 11. 11-12
'ultimosque Britannos' and 29. 4 'ultima Britannia'; H. picks up the phrase 4. 14. 47-8
'remotis Britannis'; for the Britanni, see also 1. 21. 15, 3. 4. 33, 3. 5. 3; *orbis* is genitive
with *ultimos*. — **iuvenum recens examen**] 'the great army of brave men just now raised';
for *iuvenum* (almost = 'heroes'), see on 1. 2. 41; here, context seems to require the sense
of a new army of young recruits (as opposed to the veterans of the Civil Wars); cf. 3. 2.
1-4; examen] bees suggested to the Roman mind disciplined activity rather than martial
courage; cf. the simile in *Aen.* 4. 402-7 likening Aeneas' men preparing to depart from
Carthage to a swarm of bees; here, H. has perhaps in mind the great mass of recruits in
training for service in the coming campaign. — **timendum . . . rubro**] The army is repre-
sented as 'fit cause for fear' even before it has arrived; *Oceano rubro* denotes what we call
the Persian Gulf and the Indian Ocean as well as the Red Sea.

33-4] Mention of the 'iuvenum recens examen' touches off thoughts of the older generation
and the guilt they share for the bloodshed of the Civil Wars — a recurrent theme in the
Odes; cf. 1. 2. 21-4, 2. 1. 4-5; we are perhaps to think of that generation as having de-
served to be deserted by Fortuna, as the great of Stanza 6 deserved to be deserted because
of their way of life and the comapny they kept. — **cicatricum**] The scars which remind
the older generation of their participation in the internecine strife of the Civil Wars. —
sceleris] Cf. *Epodes* 7. 18 'scelusque fraternae necis'. — **fratrumque**] The third genitive in
the series is of a different order from the preceding two; the sense is not easily pinned
down, comprising both 'we regret what our brothers did' and 'we regret what we did to
our brothers'.

34-40] **quid . . . aetas?**] = 'what crimes did our cruel generation shrink from?'; *refugimus* is
perfect; the first person because H. is speaking of the generation to which he belonged
himself (cf. 36 *liquimus*). — **quid . . . liquimus?**] 'what crime did we not embark upon?'.
— **unde . . . continuit?**] = 'from what acts of crime did the soldiers of our generation hold
back in fear of the gods?'; for neglect of the gods during the Civil Wars cf. 3. 6. 1-4. —
quibus pepercit aris?] = 'what shrines were not desecrated?'. — **O utinam . . . ferrum**] A
final address to Fortuna; *nova incude* symbolises the new generation now under arms;
diffingas . . . ferrum reformulates the theme of 1. 2. 21-2 in more positive terms; **retusum**]
'blunted'; **Massagetas**] A Scythian tribe living to the east of the Caspian; the ode ends on
the optimistic theme of extensive eastern conquest.

1. 36

Introduction: A poem to commemorate a welcome-home party for H.'s friend Numida.
    Both the party and the poem to mark it seem to have been traditional: see NH 401; H.'s
    model is clearly Catullus 9 (in honour of his friend Veranius — also just back from Spain);
    cf. the party in honour of Pompeius, 2. 7. 17-28. Of Numida nothing is known.
Structure: The poem takes the form of a dramatic monologue, increasingly excited in tone.
    Lines 1-9 provide the basic data and set the scene; lines 10-16 are a set of instructions
    aimed at ensuring the success of the party; lines 17-20 predict the way the party will go.
Metre: Asclepiad (b); see 1. 3M.
1-9] H., we gather, is giving the party; we overhear him talking as the guests arrive (cf. 3. 8

and, probably, 1. 20); he explains the details of the sacrifice which precedes the party while the guest of honour and his friend Lamia occupy the centre of the stage. — **Et ture ... debito**] The poem begins with a brief, elegant tricolon crescendo; incense there must be, but a lyre seems to have been something rather special (a pipe at sacrifices was more normal), though no doubt the lyre player would come in useful later; to sacrifice a calf is more than H.'s usual kid or lamb (cf. the fatted calf of 4. 2. 54-60; for the animals used at sacrifices, see on 3. 23. 1-8); **iuvat**] 'I am glad to'; **debito**] the calf, it seems, had been offered as a *votum* for Numida's safe return. — **custodes Numidae deos**] The gods to whom the *votum* had been made; cf. the gods invoked to protect Virgil, 1. 3. 1-2. — **Hesperia ab ultima**] 'from remotest Spain'; Numida had probably been on the Cantabrian campaign in NW Spain (perhaps as a member of the *cohors praetoria* of one of the Roman commanders, like Catullus' friends Veranius and Fabullus when they were in Spain thirty years earlier; for the Cantabri, see on 2. 11. 1-5. — **caris ... Lamiae**] The guest of honour has just arrived, it seems, and is going the rounds of the friends assembled to greet him, being particularly effusive in his greeting of Lamia; cf. the kisses exchanged at the party for Veranius in Catullus 9. 8-9; Roman men were freer with such greetings than we should find normal; not to be so greeted by a friend (or even an acquaintance) amounted to being cut (cf. Catullus 79. 4, Cicero *Sest*. 111); **dividit**] 'distributes'; Klingner's *dividet* is a misprint. — **memor ... togae**] The phrase implies that, though Numida and Lamia were boyhood friends, they have not kept in touch, or seen one another recently — no doubt because Numida went to Spain shortly after assuming the *toga virilis* and Lamia didn't; cf. Cicero's description of the alternative careers open to a young man, *Cael.* 11 (Numida had chosen, i.e., 'statim merere stipendia'); Lamia is presumably the son of the Lamia of 1. 26 and 3. 17, usually identified as L. Aelius Lamia, Augustus' *legatus* in Spain 24-22 BC; it is a sensible guess that he invited Numida to accompany him to Spain and that the son is invited to the party to meet his old friend again (and as a compliment to his father, who is now commander-in-chief in Spain); **actae ... puertiae**] Lamia, it seems, was always the leader of the set or gang to which Numida belonged when both were boys; cf. for the title *rex Epist.* 1. 1. 59-60 'at pueri ludentes "rex eris" aiunt, / "si recte facies"'; *puertiae = pueritiae*; **mutataeque simul togae**] i.e., both put on the *toga virilis* (assumed between the ages of 15 and 17) together, possibly at the same ceremony.

10-16] Instructions for the party which is to follow; cf. 1. 38, 2. 11. 18-24, 3. 14. 17-24. *Cressa ... nota* is best taken as a final clause, and 11 *neu* as correlative with the *neu* in lines 12, 13, 15 and 16, each introducing a jussive subjunctive; the string of *neu*'s has a hint of the mock-heroic, suggesting the light-hearted rhetoric appropriate to a joyous occasion. — **Cressa nota**] = 'let this be a red-letter day'; cf. Catullus 68. 147-8 'si nobis is datur unis / quem lapide illa dies candidiore notat'; the expression, variously explained as referring to a white chalk or to white pebbles, was clearly one the origin of which had been lost. — **neu promptae modus amphorae [sit] **] = 'let there be unlimited supplies of wine'; for *promptae*, see on 3. 28. 2; for *modus* cf. 1. 16. 2. — **neu morem ... pedum**] = 'let the Salic-style dancing never cease'; the dancing, i.e., is going to be pretty heavy-footed stuff, reminiscent of the ancient rites of the Salii; see on 1. 37. 2; contrast 4. 1. 28, which purports to refer to an actual rite; **Salium**] as usual, H. prefers the noun form to the adjectival. — **neu ... amystide**] = 'let not Damalis, that heavy drinker, outdo Bassus when it comes to the Thracian sconce'; Bassus, presumably, is urged not to let the men down; for the Thracians as heavy drinkers cf. 1. 27. 1-4; for teasing of an individual at a party cf. 1. 27. 10-24, 3. 19. 25-8. **neu desint ... lilium**] = 'let's see this isn't a party where the roses, etc. run out'; the celery and the lily are for garlands; the plural *rosae* suggests the use of rose petals to form a kind of carpet (see on 1. 5. 1); for garlands worn at parties, see 1. 17. 27 and 1. 38. 2; for celery cf. 2. 7. 24, 4. 11. 3; *vivax* ('long-lasting') is opposed to *breve*.

17-20] A final fade-out, self-contained (syntax and 4-line stanza coincide for the first time) and at a little distance from the point. For the trick of a sharply-focused concluding image cf. 3. 5. 50-56, 4. 2. 54-60. 'All eyes will be on Damalis, but there will be no prising Damalis free from her new lover.' Damalis is clearly a regular partygoer if such predictions can be made about her. We learnt in Stanza 4 that she is a heavy drinker. We now learn she is a recognised beauty, married (19 *adultero* — see on 1. 25. 9 *moechos*) and not, it seems, at her first lover. — **putris**] lit., 'crumbling', or, as we say, 'melting'. — **novo adultero**] If the poem is going to hang together, the 'new lover' should be some-

body already mentioned; the neatest solution is Numida, called Damalis' lover by anti-
cipation (cf. 1. 33. 9): Damalis, i.e., is bound to fall in love (is perhaps obviously falling
in love) with the young hero back from the wars. — **divelletur**] Even if her other admirers
were to resort to force, it would be no use; cf. 1. 13. 19, 2. 17. 15. — **lascivis . . .
ambitiosior**] Damalis clings closer than ivy to the wall, etc. over which it spreads in
every direction; i.e., once she gets a man in her clutches, there's no escape; the image
graphically conveys Damalis' temperament (no suggestion she has her new lover literally
in her arms); the comparison is commonplace (cf. *Epodes* 15. 5-6), but the unexpected,
learned polysyllable *ambitiosior* rounds off stanza and poem with a flourish, while
lascivis, with a balancing irony, attributes Damalis' emotions to the innocent ivy; the two
epithets are thus elegantly and ingeniously 'transferred'; for the effective use of the un-
expected polysyllable, see Quinn on Catullus 7. 1; the context requires for *ambitiosior*
the literal sense 'spreading round and round' (so Pliny *Nat. Hist.* 5. 15, of the river
Jordan), the commoner figurative senses 'eager to please', 'importunate' subsisting as
overtones; with *lascivis* cf. 4. 11. 23; for love at parties cf. 3. 19. 25-8, 3. 21. 3.

1. 37

Introduction: An ode celebrating the victory over Cleopatra and her death. The mood of
spontaneous joy which dominates the poem is the result of a carefully planned illusion
and depends a good deal on historical foreshortening: the battle of Actium was fought
on 2 September 31 BC; Alexandria was occupied by Octavian's forces eleven months
later; Cleopatra committed suicide, a few days after Antony, on 10 August 30; Octavian
remained in the East (apart from a brief visit to Brundisium just after Actium) for a year
more, returning to Rome on 13 August 29, to celebrate a threefold triumph for his
victories in Illyricum, at Actium and in Alexandria; ostensibly, 1. 37 represents H.'s
reaction to the news of Cleopatra's death (a year after Actium); the concluding stanza
suggests, however, a date closer to Octavian's triumph in 29 (two years after Actium),
or even later, the poem being in fact written, most likely, to commemorate Octavian's
conquest of his most formidable foreign opponent in his hour of triumph — observe
that the last word in the poem is *triumpho*; cf. the compression of events in *Aen.* 8,
where the battle and flight of Cleopatra, her death and the threefold triumph all follow
one another in a closely related sequence. Historical foreshortening is a legitimate device
for artistic or dramatic effect: it allows H. to combine the immediacy of Alcaeus' famous
poem on the death of the tyrant Myrsilos (332 LP):

> νῦν χρὴ μεθύσθην καί τινα πὲρ βίαν
> πώνην, ἐπεὶ δὴ κάτθανε Μύρσιλος.

with the juster, more detached view of Cleopatra expressed in Stanzas 6-8. This third
section of the ode does not blend altogether happily, however, with the earlier sections;
one may suspect it was added (or expanded) when the ode was revised for publication,
to express a more mature judgement than the emotions of the months following Actium
or the actual moment of triumph would have permitted, and also perhaps to reflect the
Emperor's considered view of his old enemy (see on lines 21-32). If so, the resultant
poem is more successful artistically (see Structure) than in the treatment of its theme.
Structure: The poem opens with a short, fast-moving tricolon crescendo (Stanza 1). The
remainder of the ode represents a repetition of the same figure on a more elaborate
scale: lines 5-12, the threat to Rome; lines 12-21, the battle; lines 21-32, death. The
first member of this second tricolon ends with the phrase 10 *quidlibet impotens*, etc.;
in the second member, the corresponding phrase 17 *remis adurgens*, etc. flows over into
the final clause 20 *daret ut catenis*, etc.; the structure of the third member is similar:
participial phrase 25 *ausa et iacentem*, etc. + final clause 27 *ut atrum*, etc., the syntactical
flowering out appropriate to the third member of the series being provided by the parti-
cipial phrase 30 *saevis Liburnis scilicet invidens*, etc. The use of participles as a structural
device suggests H.'s manner in the *Epodes* (e.g., *Epode* 1).
Metre: Alcaics; see 1. 9M.
1-4] 'Now is the time to rejoice . . . '. In Alcaeus (quoted in Introduction), the rejoicing is
for the death of the tyrant Myrsilos; in H.'s adaptation of his model there is no mention

of death (the death of Cleopatra is the subject of lines 21-32, where it is spoken of as a
past event, viewed from the perspective of the moment of triumph). As in 1. 9, H. evokes
Alcaeus but adapts his model to fit a significantly different case (see on 1. 9. 1-4 and 9-12).
The opening recalls as well the opening lines of *Epode* 9: he had asked then 'Quando
repostum Caecubum ad festas dapes / victore laetus Caesare / . . . bibam?'. — **pede libero**]
(1) free from restraint; (2) free from the threat of slavery. — **pulsanda tellus**] Joyful
dance is several times described by H. in terms that suggest heavy-footed celebration; cf.
1. 4. 7, 1. 36. 12, 3. 18. 15-16. — **Saliaribus . . . sodales**] = 'now would be the time,
friends, to offer the gods on their couches a real first-class banquet'; H. proposes in effect
a variation on the *lectisternium*, an ancient ceremony said to have been adopted in 399 BC
and repeated later in times of great national emergency, in which images of the gods were
brought into the streets, placed on *pulvinaria* and served with a feast; what H. proposes is
a ceremony of thanksgiving (not an appeal to the gods to save Rome — they have done
that) and a banquet for the gods on a really sumptuous scale; the phrase *tempus erat*
suggests appropriate action without pressing for it (something like 'now would be a good
time, if ever there was one'); cf., for the phrase, Livy 8. 5. 3, Ovid *Am.* 2. 9.24 and 3. 1.
23; for the imperfect, *Sat.* 2. 1. 6-7 'Peream male, si non optimum erat'; the Salii were famous
for their dinners; see, e.g., Cicero *Att.* 5. 9. 1 'Epulati essemus Saliarem in modum'; cf.
2. 14. 28; the reference to the Salii reinforces the implication of *tempus erat* — H. expects
his friends to celebrate by drinking and dancing; a really sumptuous *lectisternium* would
be equally in order, but is not put forward as a serious suggestion (the official ceremony
to mark the victory over Cleopatra is the triumph referred to in the last line of the ode);
sodales makes the implication clearer — H. speaks as a private individual to his personal
friends, not to or on behalf of the Roman people, assuming (as in 3. 14. 13-28 and 4. 2.
49-60) the role of private citizen, emotionally but not officially involved, who comments
on a public occasion as bystander rather than participant.

5-12] There could be no celebration so long as Cleopatra threatened Rome's very existence.
H. permits himself, for dramatic and rhetorical effect, a good deal of freedom with fact:
for the compression of events see Introduction; there is no reason to suppose that
Cleopatra ever planned the overthrow of Rome itself (cf. 1. 12. 53); reference to Antony
is excluded for obvious reasons (and also on technical grounds — a triumph could only be
celebrated over a foreign enemy). — **antehac . . . Caecubum**] The normal caesura after
syllable 5 is absent; cf. line 14; **depromere**] see on 3. 8. 11; **Caecubum**] see on 1. 20. 9;
patriotism rather than connoisseurship is reflected in the choice. — **cellis avitis**] Suggests
some more elaborate storehouse than the *horreum* of 3. 28. 7; cf. the Caecuban wines of
2. 14. 25-6 which are 'servata centum clavibus'; *avitis* suggests wines of respectable anti-
quity; cf. the Caecuban of 59 BC in 3. 28. 8 and see on 3. 21. 1. — **dum parabat**] 'so
long as she planned'; the imperfect because the pastness of the event is stressed; contrast
1. 2. 17, etc. — **Capitolio**] The symbol of Roman authority; cf. 3. 3. 42, 3. 30. 8, 4. 3. 9.
— **regina**] The common contemporary term for Cleopatra; cf., e.g., Cicero *Att.* 14. 8. 1
(of Cleopatra's departure from Rome) 'Reginae fuga mihi non molesta est'. — **dementis
ruinas**] A compact phrase: the overthrow of Rome is described as 'mad' because it is the
ambition of a woman who is out of her mind (has mad ambitions, not crazy projects in
the sense that they are impossible of fulfilment). — **funus et imperio**] Reverses the order
of 'Capitolio . . . ruinas', to form a chiasmus; *funus et* = *et funus.* — **contaminato . . .
virorum**] = 'with her filthy gang of diseased perverts'; *contaminato* suggests the eunuchs of
Cleopatra's court and the sexual perversions of a licentious East; *turpium morbo* likewise
suggests sexual perversion (cf. Catullus 57. 6 'morbosi pariter' of the relationship between
Julius Caesar and Mamurra) — not venereal disease; *virorum* is ironical; some suggest
turpium is the substantive and *morbo virorum* = 'men only in vice', but this seems over-
ingenious; presumably, H. means Cleopatra's advisers (not those who fought at Actium),
but the language of political vituperation is not to be pressed. — **quidlibet impotens
sperare**] = 'unable to control her ambitions, to which there was no end'; for *impotens*,
see on 2. 1. 26; the phrase is compact, but strained, more in the style of H.'s experiments
with syntax in some of the later epodes. — **fortunaque dulci ebria**] The sweet wine of
success had gone to her head (she had been first the mistress of Julius Caesar, then of
Antony, with a good chance of ruling the world); the first section of the ode ends, as it
began, with drinking (the one the celebration of sane men, the other the intoxication of
a crazed mind); cf. 14 'mentemque . . . Mareotico'.

12-21] The second section of the ode commemorates, with the fast-moving, allusive, imaginative economy of lyric, the victory at Actium. — **minuit furorem**] = 'helped to bring to her senses', but the simplicity and economy of H.'s ironical understatement are untranslatable. — **vix . . . ignibus**] That Octavian attempted to destroy Cleopatra's fleet by fire seems to be historical (see Dio 50. 34-5); that the destruction was almost total is a simplification of propaganda; see, e.g., the account of the battle in Syme, *Roman Revolution* 297. — **mentemque . . . Mareotico**] H. would have us believe that Cleopatra was not only crazy with ambition, but literally drunk at the time of the battle and suffering from hallucinations; **Mareotico**] i.e., 'Mareotic' wine, after Lake Mareotis near Alexandria; probably intended to suggest a barbarous concoction; the normal caesura after syllable 5 is omitted. — **in veros timores**] i.e., the illusory terrors of her hallucinations were displaced by real fears for her life and safety. — **Caesar remis adurgens**] Octavian is naturally represented as leading the pursuit; *remis* economically evokes a close-up in which we see Octavian standing over his men straining at the oars in hot pursuit. — **ab Italia volantem**] Once again H. simplifies and intensifies historical truth to bring out its symbolic significance (a device as legitimate in lyric as in bronze relief, etc.); the actual facts of history and geography are not to be pressed. — **accipiter . . . Haemoniae**] The similes suggest total, detached mastery of the situation and effortless rapidity of pursuit; we are not intended to think of the ruthlessness of the hawk; cf. 4. 4. 9-10; similarly, *mollis* suggests cowardly flight with no offer of resistance; *citus* suggests the *venator* running behind his dogs in hot-footed pursuit; **in campis . . . Haemoniae**] particularises in H.'s usual manner; *nivalis* suggests the snowy peaks of Thessaly for pictorial effect (no suggestion that the plains are covered in snow); *Haemoniae* evokes Achilles. — **daret . . . monstrum**] Distinguished prisoners followed the victorious general in his triumph; thus, Vercingetorix followed in chains behind the chariot of Julius Caesar in his triumph in 46 BC; we are told Cleopatra was invited to a later triumph and was greatly pleased to see her sister Arsinoe, also in chains; Vercingetorix was subsequently executed, Arsinoe released; **fatale monstrum**] = 'this monstrous creature bent upon our destruction'; for *monstrum* cf. 3. 4. 73, 3. 27. 48 and 4. 4. 63; both words belong to the language of vituperation (thus Cicero *Pis.* 9 describes P. Clodius as a 'fatale portentum'); contrast 3. 3. 19 'fatalis iudex'.

21-4] The ungrudging generosity with which H. speaks of Cleopatra's suicide is unexpected after the abuse heaped on her in the preceding lines. The generosity following her death is as much in accord with official attitudes as the abuse while she lived; Plutarch *Ant.* 86 tells us that Octavian, though 'annoyed' at Cleopatra's suicide, admired her nobility (cf. 21 *generosius*) and ordered that she should be buried beside Antony with the honours due to a queen. However, the suspicion that the ode represents a revision and expansion of an earlier poem is hard to resist (see Introduction). — **Quae**] The continuing relative makes a fresh start and is thus free to disregard the gender of *monstrum*. — **generosius**] A prisoner of war became a slave, and could be executed if thought dangerous, or as a lesson to others; Cleopatra had good reason to suppose that the fate of Vercingetorix would be her own. — **quaerens**] Suggests initiative, going out of one's way (not failure). — **nec . . . expavit ensem nec . . . reparavit oras**] Both statements refer to Cleopatra's conduct after the battle: she was not afraid to face the swords of Octavian's troops when they entered Alexandria, nor did she flee after Actium to some place of concealment, but returned to her palace to await the inevitable; **reparavit**] 'took in exchange', i.e., 'went to' (instead of returning to Egypt).

25-8] **ausa . . . serpentes**] Both infinitives are best taken with *ausa, fortis* with what precedes rather than with what follows (as most editors; the *OCT* punctuation, which places a semicolon after *oras*, implying that *ausa = ausa est*, is clearly wrong): 'daring, brave woman that she was, to look calmly on her palace lying in ruins and to take up and hold . . . '; **iacentem**] in fact, the palace does not seem to have been destroyed; NH, therefore, propose 'prostrate in defeat'; it is easier to take the destruction as symbolic rather than historical; **asperas serpentes**] Plutarch speaks of a single snake (an asp); once again H. writes for effect (perhaps with the double snake which served as a symbol of the Egyptian royal house in mind); so Virgil *Aen.* 8. 697 and Propertius 3. 11. 53; *asperas* suggests the angry hiss of the aroused snake. — **atrum venenum**] The poison is both 'black' and 'deadly'. — **corpore conbiberet**] Tradition, ancient and modern, has Cleopatra clasp the asp to her bosom; H. forgoes this realistic touch, as inappropriate to the simple dignity of his concluding image; *conbiberet* implies she did not falter while her body absorbed every drop of the poison.

29-32] **deliberata morte ferocior**] = 'more fiercely proud by having chosen the moment and manner of her death'; an appositional expansion of *conbiberet* (rather than parallel with *ausa*). — **saevis Liburnis . . . triumpho**] The *Liburnae* are the famous small galleys which are supposed to have ensured the victory of Actium by their ability to outsail and outmanoeuvre the larger, clumsier quinqueremes of Cleopatra; cf. *Epodes* 1. 1-2; H. imagines Cleopatra as denying them by her suicide the reward of having her led in Augustus' triumph; *saevis Liburnis* is dative with *invidens*, not ablative with *deduci*; *scilicet* interprets 'deliberata morte ferocior', 'in that by her death she denied . . .'; *privata* = 'stripped of her queenly status'; the infinitive *deduci* is dependent on *invidens* (as in 10-11 'impotens sperare', syntax is strained for the sake of compactness); **superbo triumpho**] in the event, an effigy of Cleopatra was led in Octavian's triumph; NH maintain that *deduci* = 'brought back to Rome' (arguing that for the sense 'led in triumph' *duci* not *deduci* is appropriate; cf. Livy 28. 32. 7) and that *triumpho* = *ad triumphum*; it is no doubt more straightforward sense to have the *Liburnae* denied the honour of conveying Cleopatra to Rome, but this misses the force of the personification — the *Liburnae* want what they were entitled to regard as their reward for victory, to have their enemy led in triumph as Augustus' prisoner.

The whole of the concluding stanza, but especially the last two lines, is one of the finest examples in the *Odes* of H.'s powerful, effective choice of words, arranged in telling order.

1. 38

Introduction: Ostensibly, instructions to the slave who acts as H.'s butler or wine waiter: no elaborate garlands, unpretentious myrtle will be sufficient. But, given the place of the ode in the book, it is hard not to lend H.'s dislike of needless elaboration a wider application.

Structure: One of five odes 8 lines long; the others are 1. 11, 1. 30, 3. 22 and 4. 10.

Metre: Sapphics; see 1. 2M.

1-4] The stanza is arranged in the form of a tricolon crescendo. — **Persicos adparatus**] Persian luxury was proverbial; disparagement of Eastern effeminacy and its manifestations a common theme. — **odi**] 'I despise', 'reject'; cf. 3. 19. 22 (in a context calling for extravagance in similar circumstances). — **puer**] H. addresses his slave; cf. 3. 14. 17; see on 1. 5. 1. — **displicent**] = 'I disapprove of'. — **nexae philyra coronae**] Garlands stitched to a base of bast (lime bark), a process permitting more complicated arrangements; for garlands at parties, see 1. 7. 23, 1. 17. 27, 1. 36. 16, 2. 7. 23-5, 2. 11. 14-15, 3. 14. 17, 4. 1. 32, 4. 11. 3-5; cf. 1. 25. 17-20. — **mitte sectari**] = 'don't keep trying to find'; for *mitte* in this sense with a direct object cf. 2. 20. 24, 3. 8. 17, 3. 27. 74. — **rosa . . . moretur**] = 'the last rose of summer'; for a garland of roses cf. 2. 11. 14-15; for rose petals at parties to form a kind of carpet (a sign of luxury), see on 1. 5. 1.

5-8] **Simplici myrto**] i.e., myrtle by itself. — **nihil . . . curo**] *nihil* should go with *curo*, giving the sense 'I am not in the least interested in . . . '; the proper form of the negative with *adlabores* would be *ne quid*; but for H. to express indifference after the strong stand taken in Stanza 1 is strange; a colloquialism in which the negative appropriate to the subordinate verb is attached by anticipation to the main verb seems more likely; cf. the common use of *nego* in the sense *dico non*, and the occasional use in comedy of *non opus est* in the sense *opus est non*; e.g., Plautus *Merc.* 917 'non opus est intro te ire' (= 'it is essential you don't go in'); cf. Terence *Hau.* 187 'cave faxis, non opus est' ('it's essential you don't); if this idiom can be admitted here, we get the more appropriate sense 'I am particularly anxious that you should not go out of your way to add anything . . .' (*sedulus* with *curo*). — **ministrum**] For a slave as wine waiter cf. 3. 19. 10. — **sub arta vite bibentem**] A bower of vines seems to be intended, dense enough for the leaves to provide shade from the sun; one naturally thinks of H. on his Sabine farm, where the avoidance of elaboration would be appropriate; no suggestion that guests are to be expected; H. enjoying a modest drink by himself symbolises a way of life; note that the last word in the book is *bibentem*.

Book Two

Book 2 is the shortest of the first three and the most uniform: nine of the twenty odes are 24 lines in length; there are two odes 32 lines long, four 28 lines long, four 40 lines long. It is also the most serious in tone of the three books (though the tone is not as openly moralistic as has been maintained by those who have taken dramatic monologues such as 2. 11 and 2. 14 as straight sermons), and the most limited in range; only three odes (2. 4, 2. 5 and 2. 8) have love as their theme.

Of the twenty odes, twelve are in Alcaics, six in Sapphics; there are thus only two poems (2. 12 and 2. 18) not in one or the other of these metres. For the first eleven odes, poems in Alcaics and Sapphics follow one another in strict alternation (an arrangement resembling that of 1. 25-38, but quite different from that of the remainder of Book 1); in the group 2. 13-20, only 2. 16 is in Sapphics; the remainder (with the exception of 2. 18, in Hipponacteans) are all in Alcaics.

2. 1

Introduction: The opening ode of Book 2 is addressed to Asinius Pollio, a leading figure in the contemporary political and literary world. While obviously intended as a formal compliment to Pollio, the ode is very much an introduction to the book which follows: a polarity, rather like that in Catullus 1, is set up between the poet's friend engaged on a serious literary enterprise and the poet's own humble talents. At the same time, with characteristic irony, H. permits himself (as he will do again, on a larger scale, in 4. 2) a sustained passage (lines 17-36) in the high rhetoric of the grand manner for which he professes no capacity; these lines, despite the impassioned note, are perfectly conventional in the sentiments expressed.

Pollio was born in 76 BC and was consul in 40 BC. He fought on Caesar's side and later on Antony's; he quarrelled with Antony, but did not go over to Octavian, withdrawing instead from politics to devote himself to literature. He and his brother had been friends of Catullus (Catullus 12); Virgil's Fourth *Eclogue* is addressed to him; H. named him in *Sat.* 1. 10. 85 among the friends whose judgement about his work he valued. He is credited with the first public library in Rome and with the institution of the *recitatio*. He died AD 4. His *History of the Civil Wars* has not survived.

Structure: Stanzas 1-2 state the theme of Pollio's *History* (a series of accusatives, governed by 7 'tractas, ends with the vivid image of Pollio picking his way through the scene of the recent conflagration). In Stanzas 3-4 the historian is complimented and named. In stanzas 5-6 H. imagines the friends listening to Pollio's account of the battle of Pharsalus – a dramatic, impassioned passage, ending with the resounding 'praeter atrocem animum Catonis'. In Stanzas 7-9 Cato's name leads to thoughts of the fighting in Africa; these thoughts to the reflection 'where have Romans not perished during the Civil Wars?' In Stanza 10 H. pulls himself up short: mourning for the dead is not the business of a love poet.

Metre: Alcaics; see 1. 9M.

1-8] **Motum civicum**] 'Civil unrest'; the chaos, i.e., of the years 60-49 before the fighting began. – **ex Metello consule**] Q. Caecilius Metellus Celer, the husband of the infamous Clodia (the mistress, probably, of Catullus), was consul along with L. Afranius in 60 BC, the year of the political alliance of Pompey, Crassus and Julius Caesar commonly referred to as the First Triumvirate. – **bellique causas et vitia et modos**] The main themes of Pollio's *History* are linked by *-que*, different aspects of a particular theme by *et*; after the *motus civicus* comes the war itself, then the forces of Destiny involved, then the social consequences; **vitia**] the crimes committed; *vitium* is a less emotionally charged synonym of *scelus* or *delictum*; cf. Cicero *de Orat*. 1. 58. 247 'legibus et praemia sunt proposita virtutibus et supplicia vitiis'. — **ludumque Fortunae**] Cf. 1. 2. 37, 3. 29. 49-50; Fortuna is 'chance', the Hellenistic Τύχη; — **gravisque . . . amicitias**] The primary sense is 'the dire consequences (for Rome) of that understanding between distinguished friends'; but a secondary sense, 'the dire consequences (for others) of having friends among the great' readily suggests itself — a guarded reference to the proscriptions: after the three quarrelled, to be known as a supporter of one of the leaders meant proscription by his opponents; with the first sense, *principes* refers to the original alliance; with the second, the reference is more general; for *amicitiae* of political alliances, or the relationship between a political leader and his supporters, see Brunt, ' "Amicitia" in the late Roman Republic', *Proc. Cam. Phil. Soc.* 191 n.s. 2, 1965, 1-20. — **arma**] = 'fighting'; the battles of Pharsalus, Thapsus, Philippi, Actium. — **nondum . . . cruoribus**] 'flecked with gore for which the guilt remains'; though the war is over, the burden of guilt still lies on all who took part; cf. 1. 2. 29-30; this was of course the official view, a keystone in Augustus' policy of moral and religious reform (see on 3. 6. 1-4); for the plural *cruores*, 'drops of blood', cf. *Aen*. 4. 687 'cum gemitu atros siccabat cruores' and Austin thereon. — **periculosae . . . aleae**] = 'a work risky at every point as a throw of dice' — because of the danger of offence to survivors; possibly a reference to Caesar's famous remark 'iacta alea est', made as he crossed the Rubicon (Suetonius *Jul*. 32); for *alea*, 'a risky action', see *OLD* 2; **opus**] 'material', anything which is the result of labour in both the literal sense (e.g., building material) and the figurative sense (a literary work). —**tractas**] 'handle'; like *opus*, in both the literal and the figurative sense. — **incedis**] 'advance', like a man picking his way through the scene of a recent conflagration. — **doloso**] Because the spent ash gives no sign of the fire still smouldering beneath.

9-16] 'May the stage not be long deprived of the talents of one who is also a distinguished figure in the courts and a distinguished ex-soldier.' — **severae musa tragoediae**] *musa* = 'poetic inspiration' (all ancient plays were in verse); *severae*, 'austere', the appropriate epithet for tragedy as opposed to comedy. — **desit theatris**] Pollio's plays were more likely to have been read to an invited audience; stage performances of new plays were not common in the Augustan age, but writing plays was considered (as is clear from H.'s *Ars Poetica*) a very respectable way for the literary amateur to spend his time and the polite fiction that the writer writes for performance is maintained; Pollio is referred to as the leading tragedian of the 30s in *Sat*. 1. 10. 42-3; cf. *Eclogues* 8. 10 'sola Sophocleo tua carmina digna coturno' (though some doubt Pollio is meant); **desit**] more complimentary than *absit*: it implies positive loss; *absit* might also suggest a suspension of performance, whereas *desit* implies performance eagerly looked forward to. — **ubi . . . ordinaris**] Pollio's account of the Civil Wars will put the record straight; *ordinaris* = *ordinaveris*. —**grande munus repetes**] 'you will resume your noble task'. — **Cecropio coturno**] *Cecropio* = 'Athenian' (after Cecrops, the legendary King of Attica); the *coturnus* ('buskin') is the traditional symbol of the tragic actor and thus of tragedy itself. — **insigne . . . triumpho**] As well as being a leading tragedian, Pollio is also a public figure — lawyer, politician and former army commander; these talents, being less relevant to the matter in hand than his literary talents, are dealt with more summarily; **insigne . . . reis**] = 'an outstanding defence lawyer' (the role Cicero always prided himself on); for *praesidium*, see on 1. 1. 2; **consulenti curiae**] it was the practice of the presiding consul to take the advice of Senators in order of seniority; in 23 BC, the date of publication of *Odes* 1-3, Pollio was 53 and a consularis of seventeen years' standing; **Pollio**] the vocative comes almost at the end of the opening panegyric; **Delmatico triumpho**] Pollio was awarded a triumph for his victory over the Parthini in Illyria in 39 BC; it was the climax of his military career and he subsequently retired from public life.

17-24] The switch to graphic statement of the subject matter of Pollio's *History* is intentionally abrupt. Stanzas 5-6 are probably intended to represent H.'s imaginative reaction to a reading by Pollio from his *History* at a *recitatio*. *Iam nunc*, followed by 18 *iam*, 19 *iam* and 21 *iam*, makes it sound as though it were all taking place before H.'s eyes. Pretty certainly the reference is to the battle of Pharsalus (48 BC), at which the advance of Caesar's veterans turned the key cavalry battle into a rout (*Bell. Civ.* 3. 93). — **Iam nunc**] 'Already now'; *OLD* 3 b. — **cornuum**] The *cornu* was a straight horn, the *lituus* or cavalry horn, a curved horn. — **perstringis**] = 'deafen'; the word is also used of dazzling the eyes by bright light; the use of the second person follows the usual idiom by which the Roman writer is represented as doing himself what he describes others doing. — **strepunt**] The *lituus* was shriller than the *cornu*. — **fugacis**] We catch the cavalry at the moment when they turn their horses in flight; cf. 2. 14. 1. — **voltus**] Accusative plural: the look of terror on the faces of the fleeing horsemen. — **audire iam videor**] Cf. 3. 4. 6-7. — **magnos duces**] i.e., Pompey as well as Caesar. — **cuncta terrarum**] More rhetorically effective than 'cunctas terras'. — **atrocem animum Catonis**] H. represents the battle of Pharsalus as decisive (Pompey was murdered shortly afterwards); Cato's resistance (he joined Pompey's followers in Africa) is treated an an example of Cato's dogged spirit rather than as a threat to Caesar's supremacy; Cato committed suicide after Caesar's defeat of the Pompeians at Thapsus in 46 (*Bell. Afr.* 88); *atrocem* suggests the unreasonableness of Cato's extreme stand against Caesar; 1. 12. 35 'Catonis nobile letum' is more generous; Virgil makes Cato a lawgiver among the shades, *Aen.* 8. 670; his death gave impetus to the legend of the uncompromising Stoic; a century later he figures as the high-minded opponent of a despicable Caesar in Lucan's epic; observe that H. confines himself to episodes of the Civil Wars at a decent distance from the present.

25-8] A transitional stanza: mention of Cato evokes memories of the African campaign; reaction to these leads to the rhetoric of 29-36. — **Iuno ... amicior Afris**] The gods were traditionally supposed to abandon doomed cities to their fate; cf. *Aen.* 2. 351-2 'Excessere omnes adytis arisque relictis/di quibus imperium hoc steterat'; we are to imagine a host of minor divinities returning along with a malevolent Juno (in the *Aeneid* the protectress of Carthage and the enemy of Rome) to take vengeance upon the Romans, who, being engaged in *inpia proelia* (line 30), have become vulnerable to attack; for Juno cf. 3. 3. 17-68. — **inulta ... tellure**] 'had retreated from a land he was powerless to defend'; *inulta* = 'unavenged'; contrast 1. 2. 51; **inpotens**] 'powerless', with overtones of ineffectual, angry frustration; see on 1. 37. 10, 3, 30. 3. — **victorum ... Iugurthae**] The Roman dead in the African war are spoken of as sacrifices offered at the tomb of Iugurtha; cf. the human sacrifices offered by Achilles to the dead Patroclus, *Il.* 21. 26-8, and the sacrifices to the dead Pallas promised *Aen.* 10. 517-20 and delivered 11. 81-2; Iugurtha was starved to death in prison at Rome 104 BC.

29-36] The previous stanza provides the impetus for the series of impassioned questions which now follows; cf. *Epodes* 7. 3-4 'parumne campis atque Neptuno super/fusum est Latini sanguinis?', *Aen.* 1. 459-60 ' "Quis iam locus," inquit, "Achate,/quae regio in terris nostri non plena laboris?" ' — **quis ... campus**] As well as in Italy itself (siege of Mutina), the Civil Wars were waged in Greece, the Middle East, Africa and Spain, assuming, within the limits of the Roman world, the status of a global conflict; **Latino**] i.e., not just Roman; cf. 4. 14. 7; see on 3. 6. 37-44; **pinguior**] 'more fertile'. — **sepulcris ... testatur**] 'bear witness by its graves to the unholy battles fought there'; a civil war is necessarily *inpium*. — **auditumque ... ruinae**] As though the collapse of Italy resounded throughout the Middle East; the *Medi* are the Parthians; cf. 1. 2. 21-2; *Hesperiae* = *Italiae*, but emphasises the opposition of West and East; **ruinae**] as though it were the collapse of a physical structure. — **gurges**] Any stormy or agitated stretch of water, the raging of the waters symbolising the human conflict; often little more than the synonym of *fluctus*, but in good writing the movement of the waters is probably always to be visualised. — **quae flumina**] Refers, like 'qui gurges', to the war at sea; a rhetorical flourish, therefore, though rivers such as the Nile can reasonably be said to be not unaware (*ignara*) of the fighting of the Civil Wars. — **Dauniae**] After Daunus, legendary King of Apulia, the region where H. was born and spent his boyhood; usually taken as = 'Italian' (as *Cecropius* = 'Athenian'); more likely, a reference to the ships of Octavian's fleet, or those squadrons of it which were based in Brundisium (in Calabria) and probably largely manned from Apulia; for the contributions of the South East to Roman manpower, see on 3. 6. 37-44; *Dauniae* thus gives heroic, allusive connotation to a statement which is basically meaningful and accurate; cf. 1. 22. 14, 3. 30. 11, 4. 6. 27. — **decoloravere**] The emphatically-placed polysyllable; for the idea cf. Catullus 11. 7-8. — **nostro**] A poem about the Civil Wars ends by emphasising the unity of Italy.

37-40] H. pulls himself up short, a device not uncommon in Pindar; cf. 3. 3. 69-72. —
ne . . . retractes] = 'better not take up afresh themes appropriate to Simonides';
Simonides of Ceos (best known for his epitaph on the Spartan dead at Thermopylae)
was celebrated for his dirges (poems in honour of the dead); *ne* + present subjunctive
amounts to a tactfully-worded prohibition; an explanation or an alternative course of
action usually follows (40 *quaere*); see on 1. 33. 1-4; cf. 4. 9. 1; *retractes* picks up 7
tractas; **relictis iocis**] 'casting persiflage aside'; i.e., abandoning the bantering, ironic
stance which characterises many of the *Odes*, and is occasionally flaunted when
protesting incapacity for laureate poetry; see on 1. 6. 17-20; **Musa procax**] 'my
shameless Muse'; because she does not know her place and attempts themes too big
for her; many punctuate 'ne relictis, Musa, procax iocis'. — **neniae**] See on 3. 28. 16. —
Dionaeo sub antro] Dione was the mother of Venus; as in 1. 6. 17-20 and 3. 3. 69-72,
H. poses as the poet of love; all three passages are naturally examples of Horatian
irony, intended to disarm criticism; poetry is regularly thought of by the Romans as in
origin a pastoral activity; cf. Lucretius' account of the origin of poetry, 5. 1379-1411;
thus Virgil places poetry in an idealised pastoral landscape in the *Eclogues*; the
cave assumes as a result a symbolic role; cf. the cave of the Muses in 3. 4. 40; cf.
2. 19. 1-4, 3. 25. 4; similarly, *nemus*, 1. 1. 30; see also on 1. 5. 3. — **leviore plectro**]
Practically a descriptive ablative with *modos* (= *modos leviores*); contrast 4. 2. 33.

2. 2

Introduction: A curiously unsatisfactory poem based on the Stoic paradox that the wise man
is king; cf. on 4. 9. 34-44.

C. Sallustius Crispus, grandnephew and adoptive son of the historian, was to succeed
Maecenas as Augustus' chief adviser. He is honoured by Tacitus with an extended obituary
(*Annals* 3. 30): while stressing his intellectual qualities, Tacitus notes that 'he was the
complete antithesis of tradition, in that by a way of life of studied refinement he
carried elaborate opulence almost to the point of decadence' ('diversus a veterum
instituto, per cultum et munditias copiaque et afluentia luxu propior').
Structure: Stanza 1, intriguing generalisation. Stanzas 2-4, argument: it is our actions which
bring lasting fame; self-discipline will bring you greater respect and authority than
great riches; wealth is a dangerous self-indulgence; Stanzas 5-6, conclusion: the true
ruler is the man who has learned to turn his back on riches.
Metre: Sapphics; see 1. 2M.
1-4] Hard: 'inimice lamnae, nisi temperato splendeat usu' ('you who would have nothing
to do with *lamna*, if it didn't gleam from use in moderation' — i.e., 'when used
sensibly') is perhaps an adaptation of a phrase employed by Sallustius to justify the
extravagant style in which he lived; while opposed to hoarding, he just can't resist
the gleam of silver, and seeks to excuse himself by arguing that wealth is all right so
long as you use it sensibly (i.e., don't hoard it) — a witty evasion rather than a serious
justification. H.'s answer is going to be (Stanza 4) that the life of luxury is a dangerous
and insidious form of self-indulgence; the way is prepared for this rejoinder by the
conventionally respectable arguments of Stanzas 2-3. — **Nullus . . . terris**] H. counters
Sallustius' defence, which he anticipates (having heard it before), by saying in effect,
'if you'd let the miserly old earth hoard its treasures, you wouldn't be subject to
temptation'; the phrase turns around the usual commonplace of the miser hoarding
his treasure (cf., e.g., *Sat*. 1. 1. 41-2 'quid iuvat inmensum te argenti pondus et auri/
furtim defossa timidum deponere terra'); the inversion is probably *ad hominem* —
Sallustius owned mines himself (we hear of copper mines in the Alps); moreover, if
not an Epicurean, he was no doubt familiar with the Epicurean doctrine that substances
have no colour in the dark (Lucretius 2. 745-8 'Praeterea, quoniam nequent sine luce
colores/esse', etc.). — **lamnae**] Usually taken as 'silver plate'; perhaps a colloquialism, =
'silver coins', and hence 'money' (*OLD* 3); Sallustius' justification in that case is that
there is nothing wrong with money so long as you spent it without extravagance.
5-8] H.'s frontal attack on self-indulgence will come in Stanza 4. He begins obliquely,
citing the case of another distinguished figure in the Imperial court, C. Proculeius, the
half-brother of the Murena who was involved in the conspiracy of 23 BC (see on 2. 10)
and thus the half-brother of Terentia, the wife of Maecenas; according to Porphyrio,

he divided his property among his two brothers left destitute by the Civil Wars. —
extento aevo] Proculeius' lifespan will be extended — the common Roman concept of
immortality as living on in the memory of others; cf. 3. 30. 6 'non omnis moriar';
what will bring Proculeius immortality, however, will be — not spending his wealth on
himself, but giving it away. — **animi paterni**] Either genitive of description (= 'notus
fuisse animi paterni', 'known to feel for them like a father') or genitive of respect
'known for his attitude to them, which was that of a father'). — **metuente solvi**] 'on a
wing that takes care not to come unstuck'; the reference is to Icarus; cf. 2. 20. 13,
4. 2. 2-4; for the construction cf. 3. 11. 10.

9-12] The moralising becomes more specific: Sallustius will do better to bring his
appetite for the luxurious way of life under control. The point is made by appeal to
the well-known Stoic paradox. — **latius regnes**] 'the bounds of your kingdom will be
set wider'; the king ruling over his dominions is the conventional symbol of wealth and
power; but if Sallustius can master his appetite for luxury, he will rule over a mightier
kingdom than if he were to make himself master of Africa and Spain; the comparison is
made easier by the practice of referring to the rich man as *rex* (see on 2. 15. 1 *regiae*). —
avidum . . . spiritum] The stress is on *domando*; with *spiritum* cf. 2. 16. 38. — **remotis
Gadibus**] Cf. 2. 6. 1. — **uterque Poenus**] The inhabitants of the former Phoenician
colonies in Spain as well as Carthage in Africa. — **serviat uni**] = 'tibi serviat uni', 'were
to be your exclusive slave'; like 'Libyam . . . iungas', a hyperbolic case imagined for
the sake of the argument.

13-16] The direct attack on Sallustius now begins: the life of luxury is a disease, as
insidious as hydropsy; yielding to its insatiable demands makes things worse. —
indulgens sibi] It is a symptom of the disease that the victim cannot help himself; he
keeps drinking and the disease keeps getting worse. — **nisi causa fugerit**] 'unless the cause
has been eliminated'. — **albo corpore**] Ablative of separation, like *venis*.

17-24] We pass from the hypothetical king of 9-12 to an actual king, who, despite his
wide dominions, is denied true happiness. Prahates IV was expelled from the throne of
Parthia, then recovered his kingdom in 26 BC. — **Redditum Cyri solio**] = 'restored to
the throne which had belonged to the Persian King Cyrus'; for the King of Persia as the
stock symbol of the happiest man on earth, see 3. 9. 4. — **dissidens plebi**] = 'contrary
to popular opinion'; though an enemy of Rome, Prahates is regarded by ordinary people
with envy as 'beatus Prahates'. — **beatorum**] The final syllable is elided. — **Virtus**] The
Stoic λόγος / ἀρετή, Cicero's 'ratio recta' (*Tusc.* 4. 15. 34). — **falsis . . . vocibus**]
'teaches not to misuse words'; this is what the Stoic philosopher can teach ordinary
people — if they will only listen or observe his example. — **regnum . . . uni**] Virtus
identifies the Stoic sage alone as king; *uni* picks up 12 *uni*. — **propriamque laurum**]
The garland of bay leaves (a common symbol of distinction) which is his and his alone;
as with *diadema* the imagery is drawn from the coronation of the ordinary king; Virtus,
metaphorically speaking, conducts her own coronation. — **quisquis . . . acervos**] = 'the
man who can see piled-up treasure as he passes by and not look back'; not the only
test of Stoic wisdom, but selected so that the rhetorical structure of the ode can lead us
back to where we began.

2. 3

Introduction: A graceful dramatic monologue whose frankly Epicurean sentiments are
in striking contrast with the doctrinaire Stoicism of 2. 2. If 2. 2 is very much *ad
hominem*, 2. 3 is the speaker's response to the charm of his surroundings. Comparison
with Lucretius 2. 14-33 is instructive and probably intended, especially 20 ff.:

> Ergo corpoream ad naturam pauca videmus
> esse opus omnino . . .
> cum tamen inter se prostrati in gramine molli
> propter aquae rivum sub ramis arboris altae
> non magnis opibus iucunde corpora curant,
> praesertim cum tempestas arridet et anni
> tempora conspergunt viridantis floribus herbas.

Cf. 1. 1. 19-22, 2. 11. 13-20.

Structure: Stanzas 1-2, general statement: be moderate in all things. Stanzas 3-4, 'the beauties of the countryside are there for our enjoyment — before it is too late'. Stanzas 5-7, 'the annihilation of death awaits us all'.

Metre: Alcaics; see 1. 9M.

1-4] H.'s starting point is not especially Epicurean; the immediate intellectual context is very possibly Cicero's version of the Aristotelian doctrine of the Golden Mean, *Off.* 1. 90 (published about 43 BC): 'Atque etiam in rebus prosperis et ad voluntatem nostram fluentibus superbiam magnopere, fastidium arrogantiamque fugiamus. Nam, ut adversas res, sic secundas immoderate ferre levitatis est, praeclaraque est aequibilitas in omni vita et idem semper vultus eademque frons.' — **Aequam arduis**] By placing the words at the limits of the opening line and holding *mentem* over to the following line, H. invites taking them in their literal sense ('level', 'steep'), a sense which then subsists at a level just short of the visual — something like 'keep a level head when the going is steep'; cf. 3. 29. 32-3. — **mentem**] 'frame of mind'; cf. 1. 16. 22, 1. 37. 14, etc. — **non secus in bonis . . . laetitia**] 'similarly, when things go well [remember to preserve a frame of mind] restrained from all presumptuous joy' (that optimistic euphoria which does not reckon with the certainty of a reversal of fortune); H.'s point is that one is never happy long; cf. 1. 35, 3. 29. 49-56; to count on happiness is presumptuous; for *insolens*, see on 1. 5. 8; **temperatam**] 'held in check'; *ab insolenti temperatam laetitiam* corresponds grammatically to *aequam,* forming the concluding term of a chiasmus; *in bonis* is the vulgate; *ac bonis*, favoured by Bentley, was revived by Brink, *Proc. Camb. Phil. Soc.* 1971, 17-19 (who describes 'non secus in bonis' as a solecism) and adopted by NH; *temperatam* in that case has to be an appositional expansion of *aequam*; on balance, it seems better to take *non secus* absolutely; H. wishes perhaps to suggest the compression (sometimes as negligent of formal grammar as of logic) of conversational speech.]

4-8] **moriture Delli**] The sonorous *moriture* and the assertion of the high style mark a rise in the level of plangency in preparation for the transition from Stanza 2 to Stanza 3; by the end of Stanza 3 the line of statement will modulate again, from sonorous abstraction to concrete imagery, ending with 'interiore nota Falerni' on a calculatedly frivolous note, a good example of H.'s sureness of touch in exploiting the pathos inherent in an idea without descending to the stridency of rhetoric; for poetic vocatives like *moriture*, see on 1. 2. 37; **Delli**] Q. Dellius, a contemporary of H. and a veteran of the Civil Wars; he changed sides so often M. Valerius Messalla Corvinus called him 'desultor bellorum civilium' (Seneca *Suas.* 1. 7); after going over to Octavian from Antony just before Actium, he seems to have retired from public life to devote himself (like Pollio in 2.1) to writing history; his account of Antony's Parthian campaign, in which he participated, is drawn upon by Plutarch in his life of Antony; H. chose him, no doubt, for the role of the silent actor in his monologue as one who had passed from whole-hearted participation in war and politics to the role of relaxed observer of life. — **seu maestus . . . vixeris**] Provides the opposing figure implied in Stanza 1 to the man who gives himself over to *insolens laetitia*; H. does not say the sensible man must not surrender to *maeror* ('deep, brooding grief'); he speaks as a survivor of bloody civil war who lives amid the threat of renewed war (see 2. 11I); the man who is continually reduced to gloom and despair might as well relax and enjoy himself before it is too late: death is equally inevitable either way; **omni tempore**] 'at every (fresh) crisis'; for *tempus* in this sense, see *LS* 2 a; cf. 2. 7. 1. — **seu te . . . bearis**] 'or whether you cheer yourself up when there's a public holiday'; i.e., make a regular practice of it; the man who relaxes in pleasant natural surroundings is representative of the sensible reaction between the extremes of living 'maestus omni tempore' and giving onself over to 'insolens laetitia'; the sequence of ideas in lines 1-8 is elliptical rather than logical, depending heavily on the emotional incitement of contrasting phrases; the object (as becomes clear in Stanzas 3-4) is less logical proof than rationalisation of the way the speaker and his companion are spending their time; **per dies festos**] when no public business could be transacted; **bearis**] = *beaveris*. — **interiore nota Falerni**] 'with a choice Falernian'; *nota* = what we call the 'vintage' of a wine — the year in which it was harvested; the jars were labelled, it seems, with the names of the consuls of the year; **interiore**] a wine that has had time to age properly; the jars containing wine which had been stored longest would be further back from the entrance to the storeroom than more recent vintages; **Falerni**] a wine from the *ager Falernus* in Campania, one of the best-known Italian wines; see on 1. 20. 10; not, i.e., an expensive imported

wine, but a symbol of moderate self-indulgence; for H.'s fondness for spending a long
afternoon with a friend in suitable surroundings over a jar of wine, see 2. 7. 6-8; cf.
2. 11. 13-17.

9-12] The general statement of lines 6-8 is particularised by an appeal to the scene around
the speaker: a pine tree and a poplar growing so close together their branches interlock,
a stream tumbling down a slope; at the same time he switches from argument (or an
impatient show of argument) to an appeal to what since Ruskin is usually called the
'pathetic fallacy' — the attribution to inanimate nature of animate, quasi-human
characteristics: what is the point, he asks, of this activity of trees and streams if it is
not the result of nature's anxiety to contribute to our pleasure? In Lucretius the picnic
scene was no more than an agreeable setting easily secured; in H. the natural scene
conspires to promote our pleasure. — Quo?] 'To what end?'; picked up by 11 *quid?*,
'why?'; the traditional text has been questioned from time to time by those who have
not appreciated the illusion of conversational urgency (the usual repair being to read
qua for *quo*, which then becomes an anticipation of *huc*, and to eliminate *quid* by
conjecture); see NH. — **pinus ingens**] The pine is massive, the poplar is pale; in accordance
with H.'s usual economy in pairing words, each epithet implies its opposite: the poplar
is slender or frail, the pine is dark and sombre; see on 3. 27. 25. — **umbram . . .
consociare**] 'conspire to extend their shade'; a series of hints secure an animistic image
of tall, swarthy pine and fair, slender poplar locked in embrace as they tower over the
picnic scene, sharing the emotions of the picnickers as well as contributing to their
pleasure. — **amant**] 'take pleasure in'; but because *amare* is used of repeated or habitual
action, the image suggested is of the tree-lovers clasping one another in embrace after
embrace, in the excitement of passion, or as the branches sway in the breeze. —
obliquo rivo] The stream somehow cuts across the speaker's field of vision at an angle,
either because the stream follows a zig-zag course, or because it tumbles down a
hillside. — **laborat fugax**] Also personifies: the stream 'exerts itself', all anxiety to
escape (*fugax*), perhaps from a spring which wells up nearby; cf. the scene in 3. 13.
13-16. — **trepidare**] A word H. likes; cf. 2. 4. 23, 2. 11. 4, 2. 19. 5, 3. 27. 17, 3. 29. 32,
4. 11. 11 and, in a similar context, *Epist.* 1. 10. 21 '[aqua] quae per pronum trepidat
cum murmure rivum'.

13-16] The emphatic deictic *huc* makes it clear that Stanza 3 is to be thought of as the
actual décor; cf. 2. 11. 13 'sub alta vel platano vel hac pinu iacentis', 2. 14. 22 'harum
quas colis arborum'. Even at a picnic a Roman has slaves to fetch and carry at his bidding
(*ferre iube*; cf. 2. 7. 23-5, 2. 11. 18-24). The occasion is to be an elaborate affair by our
standards; scent and rose petals (cf. 3. 14. 17), the standard trappings of a banquet, as
well as wine — a symposium more than a picnic. — **Huc**] Points to the spot where the
wine, etc. are to be put down. — **nimium brevis . . . rosae**] The roses are selected for
their emotive associations: they symbolise the transitoriness and the fragility of all
human enterprises (as well as providing an attractive setting; cf. 1. 5. 1) and prepare
the way for the moral reflections of lines 15-16. — **dum . . . atra**] = 'while you have the
means, are young enough and malignant fate permits'; a tricolon crescendo; the three
sisters are the Parcae, in whose hands lie the distribution of good and evil and human life
itself; they are represented as engaged in spinning the thread of human existence;
Lachesis was said to assign the lot, Clotho to spin the thread, Atropos to sever it; see
Quinn on Catullus 64. 303-22; cf. 2. 6. 9, 2. 16. 39, 2. 17. 16, *Epodes* 13. 15, *CS* 25;
atra] the colour which symbolises death.

17-20] Stanza 5 picks up, in an illustrative tableau, the theme of 4 *moriture*. The details
form a moral backdrop to the picnic scene. H. follows the conventions of Roman wall
painting, etc., in which the details depicted are chosen for their symbolic significance
rather than on any basis of naturalism; drastic foreshortening of distance is common to
bring together into an effective composition objects or persons whose relevance is
thematic, however implausible their presence in a single place or moment of time. —
cedes, etc.] Echoes the Epicurean view of man as the temporary, not the permanent,
owner of his possessions; so *Sat.* 2. 2. 129-32:

> nam propriae telluris erum natura nec illum
> nec me nec quemquam statuit: nos expulit ille,
> . . .
> postremum expellet certe vivacior heres.

cf. 2. 14. 21; the repetition of *cedes* is for pathetic effect; cf. 2. 14. 1, 4. 13. 1 and 17-18.
— coemptis saltibus] The background to the tableau is Dellius' large country estate,
amassed by buying out his neighbours (cf. 2. 15); with *coemptis* cf. 1. 29. 13-14 (an
overtone of extravagance there also); *saltus* connotes rolling country, a mixture of
wooded hills and open pasture; for the sentiment that large estates are no protection
against death cf. *Epist.* 2. 2. 177-9. — domo] Dellius' town house. — villaque] His country
house; a villa on the Tiber (somewhere, i.e., to the NE of Rome) seems to have been
sought after; cf. Cicero *Rosc. Am.* 20 'fundos tres et decem reliquit qui Tiberim fere
omnes tangunt'. — lavit] H. prefers to older by-form of *lavare* in the *Odes*; cf. 3. 4. 61,
3. 12. 2, 4. 6. 26. — heres] Cf. 2. 14. 25-8, 3. 24. 61-2 and *Sat.* 2. 2. 132 (quoted above).
21-4]   The first of two concluding stanzas elaborating the theme of the inevitability of death
for rich and poor alike. The connection with what precedes is psychological rather than
logical, as often in H.'s dramatic monologues. The starting point, that death awaits the
man who worries constantly no less than the man who knows how to relax, is lost sight
of as the speaker's thoughts unwind. In addition to their psychological interest, as an
example of a speaker waxing eloquent, while relaxing over a jar of wine, upon the great
commonplaces of the human condition, the lines earn their place in the poem by their
neatly contrived imaginative structure, in which we pass from the realism of lines 22-3
to the fantasy of lines 25-8. — divesne] Forms a first binary opposition with *pauper,*
prisco natus ab Inacho, 'descended from Inachus of old', forms a second opposition with
infima de gente (the man of humblest birth); the two pairs function as alternative subjects
to *moreris* in the double indirect question 'nil interest divesne . . . an . . .'. — ab Inacho]
A mythical king of Argos; here (as in 3. 19. 1), the symbol of antiquity of aristocratic
lineage; *ab* with *natus* seems to suggest the remoteness of descent; contrast *Sat.* 1. 6. 6
'libertino patre natum'. — sub divo moreris] 'abide a while beneath the open sky of Jove';
life, i.e., is an open pasture in which all are herded while waiting their turn to be offered
in sacrifice to the god of Death; *sub divo* suggests also the contrast with the eternal night
in the underworld that awaits us all; at the same time the phrase cha'lenges us to think
of the rich and noble as no more protected by their possessions than the poor and humble.
—victima] An animal (and hence, by extension, a human being) slaughtered as a sacrificial
offering to a god. — nil miserantis Orci] For Orcus, see on 1. 18. 10); for the idea cf. 2. 14.
6 'inlacrimabilem Plutona'.
25-8]   The metaphor changes: life now becomes a transit camp in which men are assembled
for the journey to eternity; the two images of man as the sacrificial victim and man as the
passenger to eternity are linked by 'omnes eodem cogimur', which can apply equally
to both. We are apt to find such switches of imagery disconcerting; mixed metaphor is
characteristic, however, of the imaginative density and complexity of serious poetry; only
incongruously mixed metaphors are bad; see on 1. 4. 16-17 and 2. 5. 8-12. — eodem] to
the same end or destination'. — omnium urna] 'in the universal urn'; for the image cf.
3. 1. 14-16. — serius ocius] With *exitura.* — sors] In cases like this where there is one
each, Latin idiom prefers the singular, English the plural. — in aeternum . . . cumbae]
'that will load us upon the craft which will transport us into everlasting exile'; *cumbae*
is dative with *inpositura, in* denotes the goal or purpose of the action; the irony of
aeternum is more plangent to the Roman ear because, for a Roman, exile (a recognised
punishment or political expedient) was usually of limited duration; Cicero's exile, e.g.,
lasted less than a year and a half; the last syllable of *aeternum* is elided, as in 3. 29. 35;
cumbae] the usual designation in Roman poetry of the craft in which Charon ferries
the dead across the Styx; see Austin on *Aen.* 6. 303; the word seems vaguely pejorative
rather than emotionally charged, perhaps because of Charon's association with comedy
(e.g., in Aristophanes' *Frogs*); the ironic picture in *Aen.* 6. 298-304 and 410-14 suggests
something more like 'tub' than 'skiff' (the usual dictionary equivalent).

2. 4

Introduction: The first of three odes about love in Book 2 (the others are 2. 5 and 2. 8).
Xanthias is in love with a slave girl: 'Nothing to be ashamed of in that,' says H.; 'there
are illustrious precedents; and, who knows? — she may have rich parents, may be a
princess even; if I sing her praises, it is as a disinterested observer; I am too old for that
sort of thing myself.'

Structure: Stanzas 1-3 form a single block: the opening injunction is followed by an elegant structure of three cola in asyndeton (2 'prius insolentem . . .', 5 'movit Aiacem . . .', 7 'arsit Atrides . . .'); the first two cola, each 22 syllables in length, are linked by the repetition of *movit*; the third, introduced by the stronger *arsit*, flowers out into an independent development occupying the whole of Stanza 3. (Cf. the more elaborate employment of this technique in 2. 5. 21-4.) Then, when this exploration of a theme from myth has reached a point remote from the ostensible subject of the poem, Stanza 4 abruptly introduces the major theme: once again, three cola in asyndeton, but the tricolon is laid out on a more generous scale (Stanza 4 'Nescias an . . .'; Stanza 5 'crede non illam . . .'; Stanza 6 'bracchia et voltum . . .'); in this second block, the stanzas are heavily endstopped; rhetorical structure and metrical structure coincide and the development of the theme is argumentative, not allusive or imaginative; cf. 2. 13.

Metre: Sapphics; see 1. 2M.

1-4] Ne sit . . . pudori] 'You don't have to be ashamed of loving a servant girl'; for the construction, see on 1. 33. 1-4; ancillae amor] 'love for a servant girl'; *ancilla* is the normal word for a female slave (much commoner than *serva*); in elegy, she is usually the personal maid of the poet's mistress; Ovid *Ars* 1. 375-98 warns young men about town against affairs with such girls — without managing to keep clear of what he preached against (*Am.* 2. 7 and 8); a man could keep an *ancilla* as a sort of parlour maid — cf. the well-known anecdote about Ennius, Cicero *de Orat.* 2. 276; tibi pudori] the so-called 'double dative' (dative of the person interested + final dative). — Xanthia Phoceu] 'Xanthias from Phocis' (in NW Greece, the area of Delphi); H.'s addressee, i.e., is a Greek, not a Roman — perhaps a freed slave himself (Xanthias is the name of the slave of Dionysus in Aristophanes' *Frogs*); in any case, a snob. — prius] Best with *insolentem*, 'till then proud', i.e., until love humbled him. — Briseis] A prisoner of war awarded to Achilles; H. implies she was to begin with his servant, and only later his concubine; the second and third *exempla* follow the same pattern — a reason for supposing that Phyllis is Xanthias' servant, not somebody else's. — movit] 'stirred'.

5-8] movit] To emphasise the repetition, *movit* is moved from an unemphatic to an emphatic position. — Aiacem Telamone natum] Telamonian Ajax (so called to distinguish him from Ajax, son of Oileus); he went mad after losing a contest with Ulysses for the armour of the dead Achilles; in Sophocles' *Ajax* his concubine Tecmessa (daughter of King Teuthras of Mysia) comforts him in his madness. — forma] 'beauty'. — dominum] The man who had become her master by the rules of war. — arsit virgine rapta] = 'fell head over heels in love with the girl he had abducted'; the third precedent is even more compelling: Agamemnon, leader of the Greeks against Troy, fell victim to a sudden flaring passion in the middle of his triumph for Cassandra, daughter of King Priam (not wholly reassuring, since the outcome was Agamemnon's murder by his wife Clytemnestra); with *arsit* cf. 3. 9. 6, 4. 9. 13; rapta] not 'raped' but 'seized', 'abducted', as in the legendary Rape of the Sabine Women. — triumpho] Following the common practice of Roman historians, H. uses for foreign institutions terms familiar to his Roman audience; Agamemnon is thus spoken of as if he were a Roman general taking part in a triumphal procession in honour of his victory, in which it was the custom for kings, princesses and the like to be led in chains behind the victor's chariot — the fate eluded by Cleopatra in 1. 37. 31-2.

9-12] As often, the third member of a tricolon flows over into an ornate amplification. Paraphrased, Stanza 3 adds only the statement 'after the fall of Troy'. H. is fond of allowing the poetry to take over, as it were, in order to add richness to the line of statement and to permit a relaxation of the tempo; cf. 3. 5. 50-56. — barbarae turmae] The Trojan cavalry. — Thessalo victore] 'the Thessalian (i.e., Achilles) their conqueror'; ablative absolute. — ademptus Hector] 'the loss of Hector' (i.e., Hector's death); cf. 2. 9. 10 'Mysten ademptum'. — tradidit . . . Grais] 'handed over to tired Greeks a Troy that was easy to conquer'; the fall of Troy and the capture of Cassandra did not take place of course until both Achilles and Hector had been killed.

13-24] The first theme of the ode is thus an elegantly ironical poetic exploration of the theme 'great men in the past have fallen for a slave girl'. The second theme introduces a practical note: unlike Achilles, Ajax and Agamemnon, Xanthias did not win his girl, so to speak, on the battlefield — as Iccius hopes to do (if we may believe H.) in 1. 29. 5-6, or as the young Roman cavalry officer seems likely to do in 3. 2. 1-12; he cannot be sure, therefore, of her antecedents. Stanzas 4-6 consist of a series of reassurances, all offered tongue in cheek; if none of H.'s assertions or conjectures about Phyllis is wholly impossible (her parents may be rich, she may be a princess, she may be completely uninterested in money), it is unlikely, despite the conviction with which they are put forward, that all are true. To match the practical tone, the assertions are thrown out in a series of endstopped stanzas.

13-16] The banter now follows the lines of 1. 27. 14-17. — **Nescias an**] = 'How can you tell she isn't . . .?'; the model is *haud scio an,* = 'I rather suspect'; for *an* in place of *num* or *-ne* in such expressions, see Ernout-Thomas, *Syntaxe latine* § 319. — **generum**] Sets the tone; it is unlikely that Xanthias has married the girl, or intends to; he could only do so (assuming she is his slave) by first giving her her freedom. — **beati**] As often, an emotionally charged word for 'rich'. — **Phyllidis flavae**] Phyllis, like Pyrrha in 1. 5, is a blonde; the name again in 4. 11. 3. —**regium . . . iniquos**] = 'undoubtedly, she's a princess down on her luck'; not, of course, impossible, given the flood of refugees who found their way to Rome during the upheavals in the Middle East following the campaigns of Pompey and, more recently, Mark Antony; but that H. doesn't believe it is clear from 'maeret iniquos', which fixes the tone at the level of mock-heroic.

17-20] **crede . . . delectam**] = 'believe me you've picked a girl who wasn't born in the gutter'; the order emphasises *illam*; *dilectam* (= 'the girl you're fond of'), the reading of the major MSS, is awkward and a fairly obvious intruder. — **neque . . . fidelem**] 'the fact that she's so faithful to you, so uninterested in money, is proof she hasn't a mother to be ashamed of'; about her father H. preserves a tactful silence; H.'s confidence in heredity is no more to be taken seriously than the rest; Xanthias, we may suppose, has reason to know the second statement isn't true, and perhaps cause to suspect the first isn't true either; even if all were true, it would not alleviate Xanthias' embarrassment at being in love with an *ancilla*.

21-4] After the patent irony of 13-20, H.'s protestations of disinterestedness hardly reassure either. — **teretesque suras**] 'shapely calves'; by Roman standards, already verging on the risqué; contrast *Sat.* 1. 2. 94-5 'matronae praeter faciem nil cernere possis,/cetera, ni Catia est, demissa veste tegentis'; for *teres*, see Quinn on Catullus 64. 65. — **integer**] Literally, 'untouched'; cf. 3. 7. 22. — **fuge suspicari**] Cf. 1. 9. 13. — **cuius . . . lustrum**] = 'a man who's forty — the last five years have gone so quickly'; H.'s assertion that being forty removes him from suspicion may convince Xanthias, if he is very young; *trepidavit* and the assertion that H. was forty before he realised it do not suggest a man who feels his age; **trepidavit**] see on 2. 3. 12; **lustrum**] cf. 4. 1. 6, 4. 14. 37.

2. 5

Introduction: Advice to an impatient husband: he should develop a more sympathetic understanding of his young wife. Cf. 3. 11. One of the subtlest of H.'s poems about love. A counterpart to 1.5 (experienced woman, inexperienced boy) and a corrective to 1. 23 (which sees a comparable situation in terms of hunter and pursued); no addressee is named.

For H.'s sympathy with the woman's point of view, see on 3. 12. On young wives, see Balsdon, *Roman Women,* 1962, 173:

> . . . a girl was held to be ready for marriage at the age of twelve, a boy at the age of fourteen. Though marriage did not always take place so early . . . , the evidence of literature and of inscriptions alike establishes that fourteen was the average age of a girl at her first marriage. By Augustus' stern legislation the ages at which men and women were penalised for not being married were twenty-five and twenty respectively; and it was certainly the case that many women were in their late teens when they married, and many men in their early twenties.

Balsdon writes of course of arranged marriages — not, i.e., of consensual marriages between partners of comparable age marrying for love; cf. Pliny's account *Epist.* 5. 14 of the charming, talented girl of thirteen, cut off by death just before her marriage day. The partnership in 2. 5 is presumably of this kind; the husband is clearly older and more experienced than the girl; for Lalage's likely age, see on 6 *iuvencae*; cf. the young wife of 1. 1. 26.

Structure: Stanzas 1-2 are opposed rhetorically in asyndeton. This initial exploration of a
poetic idea (with no clue to the 'real' subject of the poem) carries us through to the
middle of the first line of Stanza 3. Stanza 3 is linked to Stanza 4 rhetorically by the
anaphora of the triple *iam* in asyndeton (*iam distinguet, iam sequetur, iam petet*); the
last member of the tricolon crescendo spills over (as in 2. 4. 9-12) into an elaborate
poetic development, in its turn structured as a tricolon crescendo (*quantum non Pholoe
. . ., non Chloris . . ., Cnidiusve Gyges . . .*), the third member of which likewise spills
over into an image (occupying the whole of the final stanza) with no ostensible relevance
to the main theme. (With this flowering-out of a concluding image cf. 3. 5. 53-6, 4. 2.
57-60 and 4. 6. 9-24).
    Metrical structure, syntactical structure and rhetorical structure weld the poem into a
single whole, in which the turning point is at line 9, where H. passes from assertion
(*nondum . . ., nondum . . ., nunc . . ., nunc . . .*) via exhortation (*tolle cupidinem . . .*)
to prediction (*iam distinguet . . .*, etc.). The poem is further held together by the
imagery: the two basic metaphors (heifer, grapes) form a chiasmus which straddles the
switch at line 9 from present to future: 1-9, heifer; 9-10, grapes; 10-12, grapes; 13-16,
heifer.

Metre: Alcaics; see 1. 9M.

1-9] H. speaks in metaphors until the decoding of the heifer metaphor begins at 15-16
'iam . . . petet Lalage maritum'. The metaphors of a young girl as a frisky, rebellious
animal that has yet to be tamed, or as a bunch of grapes ripe for picking are both found
in Theocritus 11. 21, where the Cyclops describes Galatea as 'more skittish than a calf,
sleeker than unripe grapes'. Anacreon (*LGS* 335) works out in detail the related metaphor
of a girl as a skittish filly (cf. *Odes* 3. 11. 9-12). But in Anacreon the metaphor is archly
ambiguous; H.'s metaphor is at first bluntly hortatory, then modulates into something
approaching free association. Catullus' use of the metaphor of grapes (in conjunction
with a metaphor of a young, frisky goat) of a girl who is (17. 15-16) 'puella tenellulo
delicatior haedo/adservanda nigerrimis diligentius uvis' provides the clearest hint to the
reader — H.'s addressee, i.e., like the elderly *municeps* of Catullus 17, has in his possession
'viridissimo nupta flore puella'.
    No addressee is named; it is unlikely, however, that H. is addressing himself (see on 16
maritum); cf. 2. 18 (where the unnamed addressee is clearly not H.) and 3. 24. No hint
that the metaphor is a metaphor; no subject even until 5-6 *animus tuae iuvencae*. —
Nondum valet]'Isn't yet up to'; the first word strikes the key note: the husband must
bide his time. — **subacta . . . cervice**]The primary image is the animal fleeing from the yoke
as the symbol of a life of bondage, as in Catullus 63. 33 'veluti iuvenca vitans onus indomita
iugi'; but the yoke is also the symbol, not so much of submission to the goddess of love
(as in 1. 33. 11-12, 3. 9. 18) as of sexual partnership and submission to marital duties;
the decoded meaning is something like 'submit to her husband's expectations of her as a
wife'. — **nondum munia conparis aequare**]'can't yet match up to the obligations of a
mate'. — **nec tauri . . . pondus**]Emphasises the physical obligations; the husband's
expectations are expressed in deliberately loaded language, rather as the language in
1. 8. 3-12 loads the scales against the *cultus virilis*. — **circa**]'occupied with'. — **animus**]
'thoughts'; a first hint that H. is speaking of a special kind of heifer. — **iuvencae**]In
2. 8. 21 *iuvenci* are young, sexually mature males; Lalage, therefore, is not a child bride;
she is sexually mature, but not yet emotionally or physically prepared for marriage. —
nunc . . . nunc]Amplifies the asyndetical pattern of *nondum . . . nondum,* though the
double *nunc* is adversative ('sometimes' . . . 'at other times') rather than anaphoric;
aestum]the primary sense is 'summer heat'; but a hint too, perhaps, that the *iuvenca* is
sublimating an ardour whose nature she does not yet understand. — **ludere cum vitulis**]
ludere, of a girl, = 'have fun', 'gad about' (as in Catullus 17. 17 'ludere hanc sinit ut
lubet'; cf. 3. 15. 5 and 12; see on 4. 13. 4; for H. the girl's unpreparedness isn't so much
virginal innocence as emotional immaturity, which makes her unable to endure the
physical demands of an unsympathetic husband (as opposed to casual flirtations);
vitulis]either masculine or feminine; the *vitulus* is a younger animal than a *iuvencus*;
Lalage, herself a *iuvenca*, still prefers the company of *vituli* to her *taurus*-husband. —
praegestientis]'wanting more than anything'; an echo of Catullus 64. 145 'animus
praegestit apisci', as is perhaps Cicero *Cael.* 67 'praegestit animus iam videre' (the verb
is quoted only from these three passages in *OLD*); for H.'s fondness for ending a section
with a long, precise word cf. 1. 5. 5 *munditiis*.

9-16] For the switch to precept in mid-line cf. 2. 9. 17; the change of metaphor at first
surprises; 'mixed' metaphors are common enough in serious poetry in English —
only obviously incongruous mixed metaphors are inherently ridiculous: the denser and
more allusive the style, the more a mixture of metaphors seems an acceptable device for
expressing the ultimately ineffable; what is unusual (to our ear) is the abandonment
of a metaphor which has been explored at some length in favour of a second metaphor
but (1) the change of metaphor is a hint to the reader that the heifer of 1-9 is a
metaphorical heifer, (2) since both metaphors are traditional, they can coexist, (3) the
metaphor of the heifer is only temporarily suspended, forming the final arm of a
chiasmus; see Introduction; cf. the abrupt change of metaphor in 2. 2. 13-16;
3. 20. 11, 4. 1. 4-7. — cupidinem] The resonances of *cupido* (frequently of sexual desire)
secure the appropriate overtones. — iam tibi . . . colore] 'soon Autumn, rich in colour,
will pick out'; lividos] the colour of a bruise (1. 8. 10), a fully ripened grape, as here, a
badly discoloured tooth (*Epodes* 5. 47); for *lividus* of the emotions, see on 4. 9. 33;
purpureo colore] syntactically ambiguous, (1) with *varius*, as an expansion of
Autumnus, (2) with *distinguet,* to secure the sense 'will pick out in bright colour'; like
other Roman terms of colour, *purpureus* denotes intensity or degree of saturation;
colour in our sense (hue) is a secondary consideration; thus *purpureus,* the adjective
from *purpura* (purple-dyed cloth, as 2. 16. 7, etc.), denotes heavily saturated colour
in the red-indigo-violet range — a rose (3. 15. 15), the lips of the divine Augustus (3. 3. 12),
the sea stained with blood (2. 12. 3), the swans of Venus (4. 1. 10) as well as the colour
of the cloth, whence overtones of regal spendour, arrogance, etc. (1. 35. 12, etc.). —
iam te sequetur] The metaphor of the heifer is resumed as abruptly as it was suspended;
but the statements can now be felt to apply more directly to Lalage and her husband;
sequetur] 'pursue', instead of running away; not, i.e., a wife who meekly follows her
husband, but one whose aroused desire makes her seek her partner out; cf. for this sense
of *sequi* Catullus 8. 10 'nec quae fugit sectare'. — currit . . . annos] Hard; the basis seems
to be the language of bookkeeping; the years during which an individual is in his prime
constitute a credit to his account; the passage of time will effect a transfer of credit from
the husband to Lalage; at the moment her credit is nil, in a year or so it will be a different
matter; but her husband's balance will have shrunk correspondingly; cf. *Epist.* 1. 20. 22;
the logic of this is not to be pushed; the implication is that Lalage is on the verge of her
prime, her husband near the end of his; cf. 2. 16. 31-2; for other metaphors of the passage
of time, 3. 30. 4-5, *AP* 175-6. — iam . . . maritum] 'soon Lalage will come brazenly
nudging her husband with her horns'; the metaphor of the heifer now persists as an
overtone to explicit prediction about Lalage (now named for the first time) and her
husband (now assigned his role for the first time); the two key words mark the climax
of the rhetorical structure; proterva fronte] a final assertion of the heifer metaphor;
proterva, 'provocative', i.e., taking the initiative sexually, as in 1. 25. 2, 3. 11. 11 (of the
male), *Epist.* 1. 7. 28 (of the girl); cf. 1. 19. 7; petet] for *petere* of seeking out a partner
in love cf. 1. 33. 13, 3. 19. 27, 4. 11. 21; the present *petit* (*OCT* and others) is clearly
wrong; the unmetrical present 13 *sequitur* found in the same MSS shows how little the
MSS are to be relied on in such matters; see on 3. 21. 10 *negleget;* Lalage] the Greek name
(='prattler') does not mean she is not a Roman — see on 1. 5. 3 *Pyrrha;* nor can it be taken
for granted she is the Lalage of 1. 22; maritum] the word can be used of any sexual
partner (including goats, 1. 17. 6-7); but the data of the poem (a girl over whom the man
feels he has a claim but who is too young to respond, for whom he will come to feel
affection) virtually require the hypothesis of a regular marriage; to assume H. is advising
a would-be seducer of a teenager to bide his time offends common sense; by the same
token, since H. never married (or asks us elsewhere to imagine him as married, or
marrying), it is implausible that H. is addressing himself.

17-20] Stanza 5 introduces a key modulation (see on 1. 8. 13-16); the message of the
poem now becomes something more than 'bide your time, the girl is too young';
dilecta extends the prediction: affection will take the place of lust; the husband will
feel for Lalage as he has felt for none of the other girls (or boys) in his life. — dilecta]
The syntax is extremely compact; = 'and when that happens, you will feel for her . . .';
dilecta is opposed by implication to *amata* (affection as opposed to simple desire) as
in Catullus 72. 3-4 and 7-8; H., i.e., extends the distinction between affection and desire
to a fresh area of experience. — fugax] 'elusive', i.e., not timid and inexperienced like
Lalage, but hard to keep; see on 2. 14. 1; Pholoe forms the first of an expanding series

of three. — **albo ... mari**] The concluding *rallentando* begins with the second colon of
the tricolon; Pholoe and Chloris are mistresses, past or present, of the husband; he will
come to feel for a wife as he never felt for them. — **Cnidiusve Gyges**] The serenely ample
syntax acquires an ironical note as the husband's experience is contrasted with his
wife's innocence; the husband's tastes are also, it seems, ambivalent; see on 1. 4. 19.

21-4] A final stanza devoted to Gyges completes the slackening of the tempo; with the
boy who might easily be taken for a girl cf. the beautiful creature who is the object
of conflicting attentions in 3. 20; also Lycidas, 1. 4. 19-20, Achilles, 1. 8. 15-16; that
the groom must now put aside homosexual interests was perhaps a traditional theme for
wedding banter; cf. Catullus 61. 119-43.

2. 6

Introduction: An ode which has been strangely interpreted by some: see, e.g., the
commentary of Gow, usually among the sanest of commentators on H.
   We have to remember that, in the circle in which H. moved, an obvious, to us
patently insincere, flattery was obligatory in personal relationships even among close
friends. Cf. the compliments lavished upon Pollio in 2. 1. H. can reconcile this habit
of social flattery with the independence he claims for himself because the flattery is
not fawning: there is no attempt to deceive; what is involved is a social ritual understood
by all; to fail to observe that ritual would be as uncouth as it would be simple-minded
to take what is said as a statement of views seriously held or intentions seriously
entertained. To penetrate the flattery and extract the kernel of the compliment is
something all have to learn. The journey on which H. declines to accompany Septimius is
almost certainly no more to be taken seriously than the picture of H. ending his days
in Septimius' arms. The object of the ode is to offer Septimius an elegant poem which he
can be flattered to have connected with his name; likewise, the enthusiastic description
of the Tarentine countryside can be taken as for Septimius' benefit.
   Septimius is most likely the mutual friend referred to by Augustus in a letter to H.
quoted by Suetonius *Vita H.* 30-34 R.; *Epist.* 1. 9, a formal letter of introduction
commending a Septimius to the young Tiberius perhaps refers to a son.
Structure: Stanza 1, opening hypothesis — the proposed journey. Stanzas 2-3, H.'s reply:
he has lost his taste for travel; he hopes he will be able to grow old in Tibur; but if that is
not to be his lot, then let him end his days in Tarentum. Stanzas 4-6 sing the praises of
the countryside around Tarentum. Three heavily endstopped stanzas form the first half
of the poem, three lightly endstopped stanzas the second half. Stanzas 4-6 constitute a
single sentence, the basis of which is the anaphora 13 'ille angulus ...', 21 'ille locus ...';
ille angulus is expanded by 14 and 17 *ubi, ille locus* by 22 *ibi*.
Metre: Sapphics; see 1. 2M.
1-4] The ode opens with a clear echo of Catullus 11 (also in Sapphics). The context opened
by the echo is that of old friends prepared to go anywhere together. But, where Furius
and Aurelius are prepared to go to the ends of the earth, Stanza 1 speaks only of
Spain and Mauretania ('and', not 'or'): 'Cantabrum indoctum iuga ferre nostra' sounds
like active service rather than business; a tour of duty in some of the less attractive
parts of the Eastern Mediterranean seems implied; since lines 7-8 make it plain that H.
has no intention of going, the proposal, if there was a proposal, would have had to come
from Septimius. A more likely reading, probably, is to take the ode as an elaborately
polite refusal to retire with Septimius to Tarentum: the decoded message, i.e., is 'you
would go to Spain and Mauretania with me if I asked you, but I am too old and tired even
to think of joining you in Tarentum (delightful place though it is) unless something
happens to prevent my staying here in Tibur'. — **Gadis**] A Phoenician outpost in Spain,
the modern Cadiz; the symbol of a place that is remote or difficult of access; cf.
2. 2. 10-11 'remotis Gadibus'; accusative plural, like 3 *Syrtis*. — **aditure**] No actual
journey need be intended; thus 'moriturus' commonly has the sense 'willing or wanting
to die'; cf. 4. 3. 20 *donatura*; for the formal vocative, see on 1. 7. 1-2. — **Cantabrum**]
An inhabitant of Cantabria in NW Spain; singular for plural, like 'Romanus', 'Poenus',
etc.; *adire* with the simple accusative is less common than with a preposition, but
Cantabrum naturally assimilates itself to *Gadis* and *Syrtis* (where the accusative without
preposition is the normal construction); for the Spanish war, see on 2. 11. 1-5. —

indoctum] i.e., 'who has yet to learn'. — **barbaras Syrtis**] The symbol of dangerous
parts; see on 1. 22. 5. — **aestuat unda**] Cf. Catullus 11. 4 'tunditur unda' (the concluding
line of the stanza in each case); with *aestuat*, 'boils', contrast 1. 22. 5 'Syrtis aestuosas'.
5-8] H.'s answer to Septimius' proposal is in effect a polite 'No'. The ode, i.e., belongs to
the genre represented by Propertius 1. 6, Tibullus 1. 3, etc.; see Cairns, *Generic
Composition*, 1972, 3-33. H., who was perhaps forty, represents himself as already
thinking of retirement with his days of travel and active service behind him. — **Tibur**]
The fashionable holiday and retirement place in the Sabine hills; H.'s farm was some
distance further up the Anio, but no doubt he often stayed in Tibur on his way to and from
his farm; see on 1. 7. 13; for the Sabine farm see also 1. 17; no doubt too there were
occasions when he preferred to speak of Tibur but really meant his Sabine farm,
Tibur being a more socially acceptable symbol of the life of relaxed retirement (cf.
Catullus 44. 1-4). — **Argeo colono**] The Argive farmer-colonist and founder of Tibur
is Tiburtus, who is said to have come from Greece with Evander; for *colonus*, see on
2. 14. 12; dative of the agent. — **meae senectae**] 'advancing years', not necessarily 'old
age'; for *senecta/senectus* opposed to *iuventa/iuventus*, see on 2. 11. 5-8; cf. 2. 14. 3. —
modus]'end', 'limit'; cf. 1. 16. 1. — **lasso maris, etc.**] 'for a man who is tired of the sea',
etc.; the genitive primarily with *lasso* but also with *modus*; there is no evidence that
H. ever left Italy after his return in the late forties (the journeys spoken of in 1. 22 are
fantasy); or much evidence of extensive travel within Italy apart from the journey to
Brundisium (*Sat.* 1. 5) and travel between Rome and his Sabine estate. — **militiae**]
H.'s status as an ex-serviceman was incontestable, if not to be taken very seriously; see
2. 7 and *Sat.* 1. 6.
9-12] H.'s refusal to accompany Septimius, or to join him, is softened by a concession:
if Tibur (i.e., the Sabine farm) has to be ruled out as a place of retirement, nothing will
please H. better than to spend his days in the south with his friend. — **Parcae**] See on 2. 3.
15-16 *sororum*, etc. — **prohibent iniquae**] 'malignantly forbid'; the present because the
matter is already settled (though H. cannot know what decision the Parcae have taken);
a Latin adjective often corresponds to an English adverb. — **dulce Galaesi flumen**] A
river near Tarentum; the genitive usually follows in such cases; cf. 3. 13. 1 'fons
Bandusiae'. — **pellitis ovibus**] The region was famous for its sheep; the wool was so
valuable, the sheep were covered with skins to protect the fleece; so Varro *RR*
2. 2. 18, etc.; best taken as dative with *dulce*. — **regnata . . . Phalantho**] 'I will
head for the countryside once ruled over by Spartan Phalanthus', founder of
Tarentum c. 700 BC; *Laconi Phalantho* is dative of agent with *regnata*, past participle
of the deponent *regnari* treated as passive; cf. 1. 1. 24-5, etc.; **petam**] implies a second-
best and an unwelcome journey (all journeys now being unwelcome to H.).
13-16] **Ille terrarum angulus**] 'That little corner of land'; clearly a particular place near
Tarentum, presumably Septimius' estate; for *angulus* cf. *Epist.* 1. 14. 23. — **mihi ridet**]
'attracts me'; the second syllable of *ridet* counts as long; see on 1. 3. 36; the *angulus*
meant is ̣rticularised in the following *ubi*-clause. — **non . . . decedunt**] = 'the honey does
not take second place to that from Hymettus'; *Hymetto* (the mountain near Athens)
is dative with *decedunt* ('give precedence to', as a mark of respect); this compact form
of comparison (in which nothing corresponds to English 'that of') is the normal
Latin idiom; so 'virido Venafro', cf. 2. 14. 28, 3. 6. 46. — **viridique . . . Venafro**] = 'the
olives hold their own with those from green Venafrum' (in Campania); cf. 3. 5. 55;
note that where *mella* is plural, suggesting different varieties, *baca* is singular; *viridi*
indicates the berry meant is the green olive; strictly, the epithet is transferred from
baca to *V. nafro*, but it is of course the olives which give the fields of Venafrum their
characteristic colour.
17-20] **ver longum**] Like *brumas*, object of *praebe*̣. — **Iuppiter**] God of the weather; see on
1. 2. 2. — **amicus . . . Baccho**] 'Aulon (a moun ain valley near Tarentum), fertile
Bacchus' friend', because of the grapes it produces. — **minimum . . uvis**] = 'has no cause
to envy the grapes from Falernum' (in Campania); for Falernian wine, see on 1. 20. 10;
H.'s praise of the locality (it ranks, he would have us believe, among the best honey-,
olive-, and wine-producing areas of the ancient world, as well as being known for its wool)
is best taken as a compliment to Septimius: H. is not writing a guide book.
21-4] Not so much, probably, a hint to Septimius to abandon plans for travel, but part of
the edifice of polite fiction accompanying H.'s refusal of Septimius' invitation. —
ille locus] Picks up 13-14 *ille angulus*. — **te mecum**] 'you as well as me'. — **beatae arces**]

The prosperous hilltop villages of the region around Tarentum; their prosperity comes from the produce of the lands below; in this context of retirement, *beatae* perhaps suggests the *beatae Insulae* and the more permanent retirement accorded those specially favoured. – **postulant**]'expect', 'urgently invite'. – **ibi ... amici**] i.e., 'we will retire there together, and when I am dead ...'; **calentem**] i.e., when the ashes have been removed from the funeral pyre; **debita**]'due (to our friendship)'; **vatis amici**] 'your poet friend'; this touching picture depends naturally, like H.'s promise to retire to Tarentum, on the hypothesis that fate has for some reason denied him continued possession of his Sabine farm; it is not necessary to assume that H. is older than Septimius – politeness requires the assumption that he will predecease his friend; for *vates* in H. see on 1. 1. 35.

2. 7

Introduction: If the hints of foreign travel in 2. 6 suggest an inverse propempticon (see on 1. 3), 2. 7 is a welcome-home poem like Catullus 9; cf. the simpler 1. 36 and the longer 3. 14, both of which end in a party; for a Greek model, see Alcaeus 350 LP.

Pompeius' return provides an opportunity for H. to say in effect (on behalf of others as well as Pompeius and himself) 'it's no use pretending we weren't on the wrong side in the Civil Wars'. The fact is admitted with disarming frankness; at the same time H. manages to suggest that his personal contribution to the cause of Brutus was negligible. The name Pompeius could not fail to have ominous overtones for an Augustan ear. The Pompeii, though not an ancient family, were a numerous one; a Pompeius had even been consul in 35 BC; but the return to Rome of a Pompeius who had fought under Brutus at Philippi was not an event likely to pass unnoticed. Which of the bearers of the name was H.'s friend is unknown; he can hardly be the Pompeius Grosphus of 2. 16 and *Epist.* 1. 12. 22; some MSS bear the heading 'Ad Pompeium Varum'. Many suppose an early ode and a date within a few years of Actium; if so, it is a striking testimony to Augustus' policy of forgive and forget. But the poem seems too sophisticated to be early: in the years since Actium, Pompeius perhaps redeemed himself? See on lines 18-19.

Structure: The seven stanzas are grouped 2 + 2 + 3. Stanzas 1-2, 'Old friend, are you back?' Stanzas 3-4, 'We were at Philippi together, but I was luckier than you'. In Stanzas 5-7 the welcome-home party is imagined as already in progress (cf. 1. 36).

Metre: Alcaics; see 1. 9M.

1-4] **O saepe ... deducte**] = 'Many's the tight corner we were in, you and I'; a cliché of old soldiers' talk; but paraphrase misrepresents the tone; the opening lines establish a rhetorical level which H. exploits as the poem increases in subtlety and dextrously manipulated ironic grandiloquence; the spontaneity appropriate to a welcome-home poem (cf. Catullus 9) is a carefully calculated illusion; *tempus in ultimum* invokes the high style (an English equivalent might be 'often death stared us in the face') when little more is meant than that H. and Pompeius were lucky more than once to escape alive; the formal vocative 'O deducte' expanded into a whole phrase is likewise a device of the high style (a prose writer might say 'nam tu ...' or 'tu qui ...'); cf. 1. 32. 5, 2. 6. 1, etc. – **Bruto ... duce**] H. joined the army of Brutus while a student in Athens after the triumphant arrival of the tyrannicides in August 44 BC; he served for something like two years, rising (according to his own account, *Sat.* 1. 6) to command an entire legion as military tribune (= perhaps something like 'lieutenant acting-colonel'). – **quis ... Quiritem**] = 'who has restored you to civilian life and your native Italy?'; for *Quiris* in the sense 'civilian' cf. the story that Caesar quelled a mutiny of the Tenth Legion by addressing his men as 'Quirites' (Tacitus *Annals* 1. 58, cf Suetonius *Jul.* 70, Lucan 5. 358); lines 3-4 maintain the rhetorical grandiloquence of the opening vocative; most assume that Pompeius has been returned under a pardon; *quis* in that case expresses H.'s surprise that Pompeius is back (= 'how has it come about?') rather than doubt about the source of the pardon; see however on 18 'longaque fessum militia latus'.

5-8] Stanza 2 is more intimate in tone. – **meorum prime sodalium**] Cf. Catullus 9. 1-2 'omnibus e meis amicis/antistans mihi milibus trecentis'. – **morantem ... fregi**] Perhaps 'often wore down the stubborn day's resistance', as one conquers an enemy not easily flouted; with *fregi* cf. 11 *fracta; saepe* picks up 1 *saepe*, suggesting an alternative to the heroic terms in which the military career of H. and his friend is evoked in the opening lines; following his arrival in Athens, Brutus, nominally governor of Crete, spent most of his time building up an army for the inevitable confrontation with Antony and Octavian; through Cicero's efforts he was appointed proconsul of Macedonia, Illyricum and Achaea by the Senate (the anecdote of *Sat.* 1. 7 belongs to this period); H. and Pompeius probably saw no action until Philippi (October-November 42 BC). — **coronatus ... capillos**] We seem to be a long way from active service as understood today; H. is perhaps thinking of his student days in Athens — more likely, preparing the transition from the grandiloquence of the opening lines to the mock-heroic account of the battle of Philippi which follows; for the accusative with the passive participle, see on 1. 1. 21-2 'membra stratus'; **malobathro**] a scent made from a species of laurel leaf; for scent at parties, see on 4. 12. 17.

9-12] **Tecum**] Picks up 1 *mecum*, while preparing the way for the fresh contrast with 13 *sed me*. — **Philippos ... fugam**] Hendiadys, 'the headlong rout of Philippi'; the second engagement is meant, which ended in an overwhelming victory for Antony and Octavian. — **sensi**] 'experienced'. — **relicta ... parmula**] = 'when I hardly distinguished myself by leaving my little shield behind'; to leave one's shield on the field of battle was the traditional mark of the coward; cf. the story of the Spartan women who made their menfolk return from battle *with* their shields or *on* them (Plutarch *Lacaenarum Apothegmata* 16, = *Mor.* 141 F); poets, however, were always losing their shields in battle, and H. was not too proud to follow in the footsteps of Alcaeus (428 LP); cf. Herodotus 5. 95. 1, Archilochus 5 West and Anacreon 51 D (= *PMG* 381); Wilkinson remarks (page 60) 'as a matter of fact, being a tribune, he may not even have had a shield'; **relicta non bene**] the offence is suitably underplayed — *relicta* (= Archilochus' κάλλιπον, not *abiecta*; *non bene* where some might say *turpiter*. — **cum ... tetigere mento**] Inverted cum; **fracta virtus**] i.e., brave men were crushed (because outnumbered); **minaces**] Brutus' men had been confident of victory; **turpe**] = *turpiter*, as Catullus 42. 8; **tetigere mento**] perhaps just 'bit the dust' in Homeric style; but more likely a reference to the fact (reported by Appian 4. 135) that some of the leaders came after the battle in supplication; ironically opposed in that case to *minaces* — those who had been full of threats prostrated themselves before the victors like Orientals.

13-16] H. and Pompeius escaped, however, the ignominy of surrender — H. by divine intervention, while Pompeius was swept away and engulfed in fresh fighting. — **me ... aere**] As Paris was wrapped in a mist and whisked from the battlefield by Aphrodite, *Il.* 3. 380-82, and Aeneas by Apollo, *Il.* 5. 344-6; H.'s saviour is naturally Mercury, patron of poets (see 1. 10; cf. 2. 17. 29); the occasion is recalled in 3. 4. 26; **paventem**] 'terrified', whether by the battle or the rescue we are left to imagine. — **te aestuosis**] 'sucking you back into a sea of fighting, the wave carried you through the boiling surf'; the image is that of a man who is struggling ashore to escape drowning and is swept off his feet and carried out to sea again; **fretis aestuosis**] either instrumental or locative.

17-20] Most editors assume Pompeius was among what Syme, *Roman Revolution* 206, calls the 'irreconcilable or hopeless' who 'made their escape and joined the admirals of the Republic'; among these was Cicero's son. Did Pompeius then fight to the bitter end, and has he returned only now 'longa militia fessus', some time after Actium (twelve years after Philippi)? If so, it hardly seems tactful of H. to stress, at the moment of Pompeius' return, that his friend fought on the losing side until the last. (He can make light of his own involvement with the Republican cause since it was all a long time ago, but Pompeius is surely in a more delicate position.) The ode must, moreover, be assigned in that case an uncomfortably early date, most likely some time after the amnesty of 29BC (Velleius 2. 86), unless we assume drastic foreshortening of historical events in Stanza 5. A better solution is to assume that Pompeius, while not abjectly surrendering (like the *minaces* of 11-12), was among those officers of Brutus who made an honourable capitulation to Antony and were permitted to serve under him (Syme 206); among them was Messalla Corvinus (see 3. 211); or else that he entered the service of Antony and later Octavian at some subsequent date, as did many former Republicans. If he thus redeemed himself by long service on the winning side (perhaps continuing to serve with Octavian's legions in the East after Actium), his involvement with Brutus becomes as easy to make light of as H.'s. In that case, a date around 25 BC (when Pompeius would have been forty, if he were the same age as H.) becomes plausible.

At any rate, he is back and a dinner party is in order. It will begin with a formal sacrificial offering which Pompeius has to make to Jove in gratitude for a safe return;

or perhaps it is an offering by a retiring soldier to the god of battles; cf. Ovid *Her.*
13. 50, where Laodamia prays on her husband's behalf 'sua det reduci vir meus arma
Iovi'. One need not take H. too seriously; it may be suspected the offering to Jove
belongs to the same world as H.'s lost shield. The sacrifice seems, however, to suggest the
right context for Pompeius' return — the conquering hero home at last, not the
pardoned traitor. — **longaque ... destinatis**] The formalities over, H. and his friend
can settle down to drinking (as in the old days — cf. lines 6-8); an open-air scene seems
suggested as in 2. 3; **fessum latus**] 'weary flank'; **sub lauru mea**] an appropriate tree
for a poet's garden; **nec parce**] 'show no mercy to'; appropriate advice to an old soldier;
the negative with the present imperative is frequent in all forms of verse; **tibi destinatis**]
'awaiting your return'; the party is represented as by now in progress.

21-8] The drama and excitement of the occasion are heightened by a series of commands,
questions, etc., presumably directed to slaves; cf. 2. 3. 14, 2. 11. 18-24, 3. 14. 17-24;
the realism aimed at is psychological and dramatic rather than in the language used; hence
pictorial or descriptive terms (*levia, capacibus, udo*) remain. — **oblivioso Massico**]
'heady Massic'; from the Mons Massicus in Campania; see on 1. 1. 19. — **levia** 'smooth',
i.e., 'polished', perhaps also not adorned by figures in relief. — **ciboria**] Large cups. —
exple] 'fill to the brim'. — **unguenta**] For scent at parties, see on 4. 12. 17-20. — **conchis**]
Shells, or vessels made to resemble shells. — **quis ... curatve?**] 'who's looking after ...?';
for *curatve = curat, curatve,* see on 1. 30. 6 and 2. 19. 28; **udo**] either 'damp', because
celery grows in damp places, or 'limp', 'flexible' (as opposed to dry and brittle);
apio] for celery garlands, see 1. 36. 16, 4. 11. 3. — **myrto**] For myrtle garlands, see
1. 4. 9. — **quem Venus ... bibendi**] H. turns from the slaves to his guests and we learn
that the party is not a *tête-à-tête*; **Venus**] i.e., the *iactus Veneris*, the throw of the dice
which determined the *arbiter bibendi* (see on 1. 4. 18). — **non ego ... Edonis**] 'I shall
worship Bacchus more madly than the Edonians' (a people of Thrace, chosen for the
association of Thrace with the cult of Dionysus and the Thracian reputation for heavy
drinking; see 1. 27. 1-2). — **recepto ... amico**] 'when I've got a friend back again I find
acting crazy agreeable'; for the motto ending cf. 4. 12. 28; for the idea cf. 3. 19. 18.

2. 8

Introduction: A lighthearted attack (however ostensibly indignant) upon that notorious liar,
Barine ('the girl from Bari'). The ode is a variation upon the familiar theme that lovers
are not punished by the gods whom they have called upon as witnesses if they break their
promise of undying love; cf. Plato *Phil.* 65 c, Callimachus *AP* 5. 6, Propertius 2. 16. 47,
Tibullus 1. 4. 21-2. etc.
   Here, as in 3. 15, the fiction of direct address is maintained: there is no suggestion
of a soliloquy — the poet's thoughts unwinding in a scene, as in 1. 5 or 4. 13. But the
reproaches levelled at Barine are levelled publicly (just as the advice given in 3. 15 is given
publicly), not privately (e.g., in a verse epistle). Such poems seem to fall within the
tradition of personal invective represented by Catullus 32, 41 and 43, or H.'s imitation of
the genre in the *Epodes*. But if that tradition is a formative influence, it is being put to a
new purpose (towards which Catullus was already advancing). There is no reason to
suppose Barine a real person, attacked under her real name or under a pseudonym. She
is more likely to represent a type. The personal attack is thereby depersonalised and the
poem which results acquires a new status and interest as social comment.
Structure: Stanzas 1-2 set out the facts of the case. These are followed by four endstopped
stanzas, each of which adduces fresh evidence of Barine's scandalous success.
Metre: Sapphics; see 1. 2M.
1-8] **Ulla ... nocuisset umquam**] 'If ever punishment for an oath falsely sworn had done you
harm'; i.e., 'if ever you had been hurt as you deserved for making solemn promises you
had no intention of keeping'. — **dente ... ungui**] 'if you were now showing signs of being
one black tooth, or even a single fingernail, the uglier'. — **crederem**] i.e., 'I'd believe your
solemn promises of fidelity to me'. — **simul**] = *simul atque*, as 1. 4. 17, etc. — **obligasti**]
'staked', 'put at risk'. — **enitescis**] 'you begin to shine out'; see on 1. 5. 13 *nites*. —
pulchrior multo] *pulchrior* picks up 4 *turpior; multo* balances the ablatives in lines 3-4.
— **prodis ... cura**] When Barine goes out for a walk, she is the object of universal attention;
for the renowned beauty surrounded by her admirers cf. Cicero *Cael.* 34 (of Clodia,

ODES 2.9   213

Appius Claudius speaking) 'ideo viam munivi ut eam tu alienis viris comitata celebrares?';
prodis] the word used of the emergence of the bride in the wedding procession; so
Catullus 61. 92 and 96 'prodeas nova nupta'; cf. 3. 14. 6.

9-12] **Expedit fallere**]'You thrive on swearing falsely by . . .'; the person invoked (here
Barine's dead mother) is regarded as accepting responsibility for the promise; hence
fallere = 'let down'. — **opertos**]'buried'; cf. Propertius 2. 20. 15-16 'Ossa tibi iuro per
matris et ossa parentis/(si fallo, cinis heu sit mihi uterque gravis!)'. — **signa**]The stars
and planets. — **gelida . . . carentis**] 'the immortal gods'; H.'s elegant rhetoric suggests the
eloquent, imaginative nature of Barine's promises.

13-16] The goddess of love and her retinue naturally find this great fun. — **Venus ipsa**]
ipsa not because Venus would be the first one would expect to take action, but because
she extends her personal approval to Barine; see on 3. 27. 67. — **simplices Nymphae**]
Along with the 'Gratiae decentes' the Nymphae form the retinue of Venus in 1. 4. 5-7;
simplices because their laughter is guileless — they find it all good, innocent fun,
whereas Venus is more crafty. — **Cupido . . . cruenta**] Cupid laughs because business is
brisk when Barine is around; he has to keep resharpening his arrows and his whetstone
runs red with the blood of his victims (not Barine's of course, but that of the men who fall
for her); for Cupids sharpening their arrows, see Philodemus *AP* 5. 124. 3; **ardentis**]so
called because of the burning wounds they inflict.

17-20] **adde quod**]'add to this the fact that . . .'. — **pubes . . . omnis**] = 'an entire new
generation is just reaching the age to be your victims'; i.e., not only is Barine an old hand,
she is likely to last a while yet. — **servitus crescit nova**] = 'soon they will be your slaves';
in Roman elegy, the lover is regularly cast in the role of slave of his mistress (*domina*);
Barine has not just one or two such slaves, but a whole household — and is about to restaff
with a new generation of lovers. — **nec priores . . . minati**]Their predecessors (Barine's
current victims) show no sign of moving out — for all their repeated threats to do so;
household slaves often lived on close terms with their masters or mistress and might well
threaten to run away if ill-treated — or out of fear of living under the same roof as a
perjurer (cf. 1. 35. 21-4); for a popular beauty's salon filled with admirers, see Propertius
2. 6.

21-4] Barine is the dread of three groups in Roman society: timid mothers, tight-fisted fathers,
anxious newly-weds. — **iuvencis**]The steer is the symbol of lusty youth; *iuvencus* is
interchangeable with *taurus* in this sense, according to age or the point of view of the
speaker; in the story of Jove and Europa as retold by H., Europa's lover is described by
her as *iuvencus* (3. 27. 45), by H. and by Venus as *taurus* (ibid. 26 and 72); cf. the imagery
of 2. 5. 1-8 (which introduces a third term, *vitulus*, for the as yet sexually immature).
— **te senes parci**]The *senex* anxious for his money when his son gets embroiled with a
girl is a stock figure of comedy. — **miseraeque . . . nuptae**]The third member of the series
introduces a key modulation (see on 1. 8. 13-16); young girls just married have a claim
on our sympathy not shared by mothers solicitous for their sons and tight-fisted
fathers; they fear not only alienation of affection, but that their husbands will keep up
old habits; for the former idea, see Catullus 61. 144-6 'Nupta, tu quoque quae tuus/
vir petet cave ne neges, /ni petitum aliunde eat', for the latter ibid. 97-101 'Non tuus
levis in mala/deditus vir adultera,/probra turpia persequens,/a tuis teneris volet/secubare
papillis'; *nuper* with *nuptae*; *virgo* is used of a young girl whether married or not. —
tua . . . maritos]They fear that their husbands, meeting Barine in the street (see lines
6-8), may fall victim to her irresistible attraction; for *aura*, see on 1. 5. 11.

                                    2. 9

Introduction: To Valgius, a minor elegiac poet, on the need to keep grief for lost love within
bounds. Ostensibly, the object, as in 1. 24, is to console. In fact, the ode is an urbanely-
worded rejection of the basic assumption of love elegy that love matters more than all
else. The method is less that of direct argument than that of controlled association of
ideas: the ode works within the frames of reference of elegy in order to undermine their
validity.
    Stanza 6 fixes the tone of the whole — not that of an intimate, personal note, but that
of a public letter in verse, urging Valgius to change from one style of poetry to another.

The ironic stress laid on the longwindedness and the narrow range of themes in elegy naturally reflects H.'s own critical position. Contrast Propertius 1. 6, in which opposite advice (abandon mythological epic for love elegy) is offered. We may of course suspect that H.'s attempt to persuade Valgius to undertake a task H. was not willing to undertake himself (see on 19 *cantemus*) is not without an element of tongue in cheek.

C. Valgius Rufus, *consul suffectus* 12 BC, is listed in *Sat.* 1. 10. 82 among the friends whose approval of his work H. values. He was something of a scholar as well as a poet: he translated the *Rhetorica* of Augustus' teacher Apollodorus and left an uncompleted treatise on medicinal plants. Of his elegies only a few battered fragments remain; see Bardon, *La littérature latine inconnue*, vol. 2, 19-22.

Structure: The ode is built on the model of 1. 7. 15-18:

> Albus ut obscuro deterget nubila caelo
> saepe Notus neque parturit imbris
> perpetuos, sic tu sapiens finire memento
> tristitiam vitaeque labores.

Let us call 'albus . . . perpetuos' A, 'sic tu . . . labores' B. To an expanded version of A (Stanzas 1-2) H. adds (1) a statement of the nature of Valgius' grief (Stanza 3); (2) supporting illustrations from myth (Stanza 4, spilling over into Stanza 5). An expanded version of B then follows (Stanzas 5-6).

Metre: Alcaics; see 1. 9M.

1-8] Rain, tempest, gales, as well as not lasting for ever, can be taken as a surrender by the natural world of self-control; *glacies iners* symbolises the prostration that results from that surrender. In H.'s usual manner, the natural phenomena are particularised geographically. Though the primary force of the examples chosen is that, even in the wildest places, extremes of weather are not permanent, they are chosen to symbolise also the two extremes of human grief: surrender to wild, uncontrolled emotion and the opposite, extreme prostration and reduction to helpless inactivity; at the same time the imagery carries the implied suggestion that protracted surrender to either of these extremes is uncivilised and barbarous. — **Non semper**] 'Not eternally'; cf. 2. 11. 9, 3. 10. 19, 3. 29. 6; the ode is held together by a pattern of repetition of the key ideas: 1 'non semper' + 4 'usque' + 6 'mensis per omnis' contrasted with 9 'tu semper', 13-15 'at non . . . omnis . . . annos', 16-17 'aut . . . semper'. — **imbres**] The stock translation 'shower' misrepresents *imber*, which suggests steady, pelting rain; cf. 3. 30. 3, 4. 2. 5, *Aen.* 5. 695-6 'Ruit aethere toto/turbidus imber aqua densisque nigerrimus Austris'. — **hispidos**] Proleptic. — **mare Caspium**] Between Astrakhan and Tehran, beyond the Caucasus, the sea into which the Volga flows; for a Roman, the home of the Scythae and a symbol of a wild, remote, uncivilised region; cf. *Aen.* 6. 798-9 'Huius in adventum iam nunc et Caspia regna/responsis horrent divum'; see on 1. 19. 10 *Scythas*; even in such places, storms do not last for ever. — **inaequales**] (1) 'gusting', (2) 'making uneven' (cf. *Epist.* 1. 1. 94, of an incompetent barber), perhaps also (3) 'lacking in *aequibilitas*' ('self-control'), as in *Sat.* 2. 7. 10 'vixit inaequalis'; cf. 2. 3. 1-2 'aequam mentem'; for the idea, 3. 30. 3 'Aquilo impotens'. — **usque**] 'all the time'; delayed for emphasis and to form a chiasmus with 1 *semper*. — **Armeniis in oris**] Chosen to symbolise extreme cold; many of Mark Antony's troops perished of the cold during the expedition into Armenia of 35 BC. — **stat glacies iners**] 'does the ice lie rigid and lifeless'; cf. 4. 7. 12 'bruma iners', 3. 5. 35-6 (of a cowardly prisoner of war); *iners* is here predicative. — **Aquilonibus . . . orni**] The third example brings us nearer home, to the oak forests of Mount Garganus in Apulia; **Aquilonibus**] = 'northerly gales'; either dative with *laborant* (on the model of the dative with *pugnare*, etc.) or instrumental; **laborant**] 'stuggle'; cf. 1. 9. 3; **orni**] cf. 1. 9. 12.

9-12] **urges**] = 'won't leave in peace'; a word H. is fond of (it occurs 29 times in his works, 9 times in the *Odes*); the predominant sense is something like 'pester', 'plague', with connotations of persistent, unwelcome attention — most often, hostile or aggressive (1. 15. 23-5, etc.), but the attention can also be well-meaning, as in 1. 5. 2; the sense in which Valgius will not leave Mystes in peace is that he keeps writing elegy after elegy (probably addressed to Mystes), lamenting his loss. — **flebilibus modis**] 'in mournful numbers'; cf. 3. 30. 14. — **Mysten ademptum**] Mystes was clearly a *puer delicatus*, possibly a slave; cf. Cicero *Att.* 1. 12. 4 'Puer festivus, anagnostes noster

Sositheus, decesserat, meque plus quam servi mors debere videbatur commoverat';
but the Greek name need not imply the bearer was a Greek; see on 1. 5. 3 *Pyrrha*;
the most likely sense in which Mystes is 'lost' is that he is dead (cf. 2. 4. 10 'ademptus
Hector'); but *ademptus* need not mean more than that Mystes has been lost to another
admirer, like Corydon's Alexis in *Eclogue* 2. — **nec tibi decedunt amores**] 'love won't
leave you alone'; but also (by the idiom which identifies the Roman poet with the
activity he writes about — an epic poet is 'durus', a love poet 'mollis', etc.) 'you won't
leave love poetry alone'. — **vespero . . . solem**] = 'neither with the appearance of the
evening star . . . nor at his retreat before the hastening sun'; i.e., Valgius, having written
all day, then proceeds to write all night; the fact that the planet Venus is visible sometimes
in the morning (= Lucifer), sometimes in the evening (= Hesperus/Vesper) was
frequently made use of by ancient poets; e.g., Cinna, in his *Zmyrna* (possibly alluded to
here): 'Te matutinus flentem conspexit Eous/et flentem paulo vidit post Hesperus idem';
H. (like Cinna) was mistaken if he thought the evening star could reappear the following
day as the morning star; **surgente**] as often, not of the apparent motion of the star, but
of its brightening as day dies.

13-17] **ter aevo functus** 'he who lived his life three times over'; Homer makes Nestor outlive
two generations to rule over a third, *Il.* 1. 250-51 (i.e., he lived perhaps into his nineties);
H., ironically mythologising, can be more fanciful. — **amabilem Antilochum**] His son,
killed by Memnon; *amabilem* = 'a son to be loved', i.e., inspiring love; cf. 1. 5. 10. —
inpubem Troilon] Son of Priam, killed by Achilles; his death is among the scenes
represented on the walls of Dido's temple at Carthage, *Aen.* 1. 474-8. — **parentes**] Priam
and Hecuba. — **Phrygiae sorores**] Cassandra and Polyxena are the best known.

17-24] **Desine**] For the switch to precept in mid-line cf. 2. 5. 9. — **mollium querelarum**]
'from soft lamentations'; *querela* often of love elegy, as in Propertius 1. 17. 9, 1. 18. 29,
etc,; cf. 2. 13. 24 'querentem' (of Sappho); *mollis*, the stock epithet of the elegiac
poet, here with overtones of 'effeminate', 'self-indulgent'; the genitive is a Grecism
(cf. 3. 27. 70); the normal construction with *desinere* is the infinitive (e.g., 1. 23. 11).
—**tandem**] (1) 'at length' (i.e., 'it is high time'), (2) (as often with an imperative) 'please',
'for goodness' sake'; cf. 1. 23. 11, 3. 15. 2. — **nova cantemus . . . campis**] A complex
hendiadys: 'nova Augusti tropaea Caesaris' forms the first arm, 'rigidum . . . campis' the
second arm (joined to the first by 20 *et* and subdivided by the two -*que*'s); **nova
tropaea**] 'recent victories', *tropaea*, 'trophies' (a feature of heroic warfare), being a
metonomy for *victorias* (cf. the more usual metonomy *triumphos*); **cantemus**] = 'let
us compose historical epics on the theme of . . .'; since H. has proclaimed his incapacity
for epic (see 1. 6), the first personal plural is presumably hortatory (as one says, in
encouraging a friend, 'let's try this, shall we?', meaning 'you try this'); the rhetoric of
Stanza 6 is perhaps to be taken as a gesture in the appropriate direction; **Niphaten**]
in Armenia, a mountain according to Strabo, a river according to Lucan; Armenia
was handed over after Actium by Augustus (following its recovery) to Tigranes, a
vassal of Rome (*Res Gestae* 27. 2); **Medumque flumen**] the Euphrates; **gentibus
additum victis**] i.e., the river god is added to the list of peoples vanquished by
Augustus — and behaves accordingly; **minores volvere vertices**] cf. *Aen.* 8. 726
'Euphrates ibat iam mollior undis' (one of the scenes on the shield of Aeneas);
Augustus' much publicised reconquest of the East after Actium amounted in fact
to a series of political compromises aimed at holding the frontier against Parthia (the
Euphrates formed the boundary between Parthia and Syria) until Augustus was in a
position to negotiate a settlement with Parthia and secure the return of Crassus'
standards (finally restored in 20 BC); see *Res Gestae* 29. 2 and Brunt-Moore thereon;
Gelonos] a Scythian tribe; cf. 2. 20. 19, 3. 4. 35; H. contents himself with the claim
that they have been prevented from incursions into the Roman sphere of influence
and their nomad habits brought under control; cf. 3. 8. 24 and contrast 3. 24. 9-16.

2. 10

Introduction   A poem in praise of the Golden Mean. What one makes of it depends on the
man to whom it is addressed.
Who is Licinius? He is usually identified as Licinius Murena, also known as Terentius
Varro, brother-in-law of Maecenas and half-brother to the Proculeius of 2. 2 — very much

a member of the circle in which H. moved. But if the common view is correct, he was also a public figure — consul in 23 BC, a leading figure in the conspiracy against Augustus of 23 or 22 BC. Syme, *Roman Revolution* 325 claimed: 'it is pretty clear that the consul of 23 BC "A. T[erentius] . . . V[ar]ro Murena" (CIL I², p. 28) is the same person as the Terentius Varro in Dio (53, 25, 3) and Strabo (p. 205), and the Licinius Varro in Dio 54, 3, 3. Suetonius calls him "Varro Murena" (*Divus Aug.* 19, 1; *Tib.* 8), Velleius "L. Murena" (2, 91, 2). Similarly, the "Murena" of Horace, *Odes* 3, 19 may be identified with the "Licinius" of *Odes* 2, 10, 1. Perhaps his full name was A. Terentius Varro Licinius Murena.' Not all historians accept this synthetic personage; at least one other Licinius is available as H.'s addressee — M. Licinius Crassus, grandson of M. Crassus, who, to judge from what we know of him, may have stood in need of H.'s advice; nothing we know, however, links him with H.

Most likely, publication of *Odes* 1-3 was planned to fall in the period between Augustus' return to Rome from Spain late in 24 BC and his anticipated Eastern campaign (foreshadowed in 3. 1-6 and elsewhere, postponed as a result of Augustus' illness in mid-23). That illness resulted in the appointment (with effect from 1 July 23) of L. Sestius as *consul suffectus* in place of Augustus. Since *Odes* 1. 4 is dedicated to Sestius (forming the last of a series of four honorific odes), it seems reasonable to suppose that at the time of publication Sestius' appointment had been announced, if it had not already taken effect. Murena's removal from the consulship in favour of Cn. Calpurnius Piso clearly preceded Augustus' retirement. It thus seems a reasonable assumption that 2. 10 reflects the situation at the time of publication about the middle of 23 BC: Licinius has been removed from office, but there is as yet no hint of the larger disaster which is impending. If, as some suppose, the conspiracy was Augustus' invention, Licinius' involvement in the events leading to its alleged discovery may well have been unknown to H. Or is he dropping a hint, the full import of which was unclear, even to H. himself, at the time? The argument of the ode, that those in high places need to act with courage and caution (but not excessive caution) in times of crisis can be read, i.e., as intended *ad hominem* — sound advice from a loyal friend, in no position to know his advice would be disregarded. Some such context seems necessary to justify what, in the absence of context, must seem elaboration of the obvious. The connection, however, of the consul of 23 BC with the conspiracy of that year (or the following year) is disputed by some historians.

There is a curious echo of H.'s opening lines in Seneca *Epist.* 19. 9: after quoting with approval a passage from Maecenas' *Prometheus* ('Ipsa enim altitudo attonat summa', 'there's thunder even on the loftiest peaks'), Seneca remarks 'hic te exitus manet (i.e., 'you will end like Maecenas'), nisi iam contrahes vela, nisi — quod ille (i.e., Maecenas) sero voluit, terram leges'.

Structure: Not all commentators have observed the subtlety of the rhetorical structure — H. proceeds with calculated caution in advising Licinius. There are two principal themes, each introduced by a comparative adverb: theme A ('Rectius vives') is hortatory; theme B (9 'Saepius ventis agitatur ingens pinus') appeals to evidence from the world of nature. A stanza is devoted to the statement of each theme (Stanzas 1 and 3); Stanza 2 restates the precept of Stanza 1 in different terms; Stanzas 4-5 expand the statement of theme B; Stanza 6, after a recapitulation of theme A (21 'Rebus angustis animosus atque fortis adpare'), returns to the imagery of the opening lines. A series of supporting syntactical pairs lends perceptible shape and organisation to the argument: the concluding future indicative 23 'contrahes' corresponds to the opening 'vives' and is supported by the echo of 3 'nimium premendo' in 23 'nimium secundo'; the intervening precepts are expressed either as generalisations (5 'quisquis diligit . . . ', 13 'sperat bene praeparatum pectus') or by a simple imperative (22 'adpare'); 6 'tutus caret' is paired with 7-8 'caret sobrius'; 13 'sperat' is balanced by 13 'metuit', 15 'reducit' by 17 'submovet'; 17 'nunc' by 17 'olim'; 22 'idem contrahes' echoes 16 'idem submovet'. Except for the spillover from Stanza 4 to Stanza 5 (which throws into prominence the assurance that crises always pass), the stanzas are heavily endstopped.

Metre: Sapphics; see 1. 2M.

1-4] **Rectius vives**] 'You will live more honestly'; i.e., Licinius' course of conduct will be more morally commendable (*rectus* is used by writers on ethics almost as a synonym of *honestus*); the image from sailing justifies only some such precept as 'tutius navigabis'; the middle course is not, however, urged on Licinius on grounds of safety; 'rectius navigabis', though comprehensible ('you will behave more honestly if you steer your

ship ... '), would sound strained; hence the plain precept 'rectius vives', with no attempt
to adapt the precept to the metaphor which illustrates it. — **altum semper urgendo**]
'making always for deep water' (i.e., the open sea) — and thus demonstrating, by Roman
ideas, rash seamanship; 'altum urgere' was perhaps a sailors' term; for *urgere*, see on 2. 9.
9; the phonetically prominent forms *urgendo* and *premendo* establish an opening
polarity. — **dum ... horrescis**] 'in your timid apprehension of squalls'. (i.e., always
fearing a sudden squall). — **litus iniquum**] = 'the treacherous coast' — because of rocks,
shoals, etc.

5-8] Stanza 2 reverts to the explicit moralising tone of the opening 'rectius vives'; the
advice now shifts from counsel of the middle course between foolhardiness and
timidity to advocacy of a middle course between ostentatious contempt of riches and
ostentatious display of them (these two extremes forming along with the first two a kind
of chiasmus). The doctrine of the mean goes back to Aristotle (see especially *Nic.
Ethics* 2. 6. 15 ff.). — **auream mediocritatem**] H. is perhaps the first to apply the adjective
'golden' to the mean, though 'golden' is common as a term of approval in Greek; *aureus*
is a word H. likes (1. 5. 9, 2. 13. 26, 4. 2. 23, 4. 3. 17); cf. Lucretius' 'aureā dicta' of the
precepts of Epicurus. — **quisquis**] For the preceptual force of general statements with
quisquis, see Daube, *Forms of Roman Legislation* 4-36. — **tutus caret ... tecti**] 'abstains
from the squalor of a worn-out dwelling and is safe'; the sensible man, i.e., does not live
like a miser when he does not have to; for the risk that your house will fall down on your
head (apparently appreciable in ancient Rome), see Catullus 23. 9, Propertius 2. 27. 9,
etc. Bentley's punctuation 'diligit tutus,' (instead of 'diligit, tutus') is almost certainly
wrong. — **invidenda aula**] The sort of mansion which is the envy of others; H. proclaims
his dislike for such in 2. 18; cf. 3. 1. 45-6. — **sobrius**] Displaying the moderation which
makes him avoid extravagance.

9-12] The imagery and precepts of Stanzas 1-2, though expressed in general terms, obviously
apply only to the few: the captain of a ship is the symbol of an élite of power; the
choice between miserliness and extravagance arises only for an élite of wealth. Stanza
3 stresses the greater risk to which those prominent in the State are exposed; if we are
right about the identity of Licinius (see Introduction), the argument now becomes
more plainly *ad hominem*. — **Saepius**] More often than the tree of average height, which
is protected by the mass of trees around it while the tall tree is exposed to every gale;
as with the image of navigation, the moral application of the towering tree is not
entirely happy; no need, however, to emend to *saevius*, as occasionally suggested. —
feriuntque ... montis] As far as we can judge, the lightning has already struck in Licinius'
case; Stanza 3 is intended, i.e., less as a warning than as a consolation for being removed
from the consulship; **summos montis**] 'the tops of mountains'.

13-20] **sperat ... pectus**] The matter is again put in general terms; **infestis, secundis**]
ablative rather than dative; neuter, not masculine; **alteram sortem**] = 'the opposite state
of affairs'; **bene praeparatum pectus**] = 'the mind that is well prepared', but with over-
tones of courage and fortitude supporting reason; for *pectus*, see on 1. 3. 10. — **informis
... submovet**] Fairly plainly, what H. wishes to convey is that the storm which now
rages round Licinius' head will not last; this is made explicit in lines 17-18; **informis**]
because the true shapes of things are destroyed by the storm; **Iuppiter**] as in 20 *Apollo*,
a veiled reference to Augustus is no doubt intended; for Jupiter as the god of the weather,
see on 1. 2. 1-4. — **quondam ... Apollo**] Though at the moment Apollo manifests himself
as the angry archer-god of *Il.* 1. 43-9, etc., he is also the god of the lyre (see on 3. 30. 15,
cf. 4. 6. 25-30, 4. 15. 1-4); the availability of Apollo as a symbol of Augustus is enhanced
by the use in Augustan poetry of Apollo the archer as the god who gave victory at
Actium (*Aen.* 8. 704, Propertius 4. 7. 31-4 and 55-6) and Augustus' assumption of the
role of patron of the arts by building the Temple of Apollo on the Palatine (commemor-
ating the victory at Actium, and housing a library, etc.); **cithara**] with *suscitat*: Apollo
gives the signal to the Muse by a twang on his lyre; cf. 4. 15. 2 'increpuit lyra'; the
genitive (i.e., *citharae Musam*, 'Muse of the lyre') has good MS authority, but gives weak
sense.

21-4] H.'s concluding advice takes us back to Stanza 1. Licinius is advised to act
courageously and with spirit during the present crisis (i.e., he should not run for the
coast like the timorous captain of Stanza 1); equally, when the wind changes, he will, if
prudent, not run before it with all sails set; presumably, the advice was not taken;
possibly H., in publishing the ode, wished to be seen as wise before the events which

brought about Licinius' overthrow; whether he would have published the ode after
Licinius' death is another question. — **Rebus angustis**] = 'in rebus angustis', 'when
opportunities are limited'; *angustis* is not necessarily pejorative (cf. 3. 2. 1). — **idem**]
= 'likewise', 'equally'; nominative masculine; cf. 16 'idem submovet'. — **vento nimium
secundo**] 'too favourable a wind'.

2. 11

Introduction: 'Forget about threats of war. Let us relax and enjoy ourselves before it is
too late. Ask Lyde to come and sing to us.' A dramatic monologue on the lines of 2. 3
and 2. 14, employing similar thematic material but with less sombre overtones.

How typical were Quinctius' anxieties? Did the members of the circle in which H.
moved really fear that the situation in Spain or the Far East might get out of hand? Is
Quinctius represented as a friend who has to be teased out of absurd anxieties? Or is H.
prescribing also for himself, perhaps for an entire generation? Constant allusions in the
Odes to the Cantabri and Scythae as a menace to Rome (or, in more optimistic mood, as
a menace no longer) suggest the latter view. Quinctius and H. were probably contempor-
aries (see on lines 6-8) — both survivors of the Civil Wars; Actium (which we tend to
think of as the final victory) had been followed by Augustus' campaigns in the East
(31-29 BC); then came the Spanish war (it had dragged on for some five years by the
time of publication of *Odes* 1-3 and was to continue for five years more); much of this
time Augustus had been abroad on active service; at one stage in the Spanish campaign
he had fallen ill and nearly died; he was seriously ill again in 23 BC after his return to
Rome. In the East there had been little actual fighting, but the Eastern menace loomed
large, or was represented as looming large by official propaganda (see, e.g. 1. 12. 53
'Parthos Latio imminentis'); as Syme observed (*Roman Revolution* 301), 'Crassus and
the national honour clamoured for a war of revenge'. No doubt the disgrace of Carrhae
and the threat to Rome were exaggerated (see on 3. 5); but for a ruling class sick to
death of fighting and now entering middle age, nagging thoughts of fresh wars which
might flare up at any time must have been hard to dispel; the relief expressed in 4. 5
(perhaps ten years later than 2. 11) was no less real for being in conformity with official
propaganda. The younger generation were apt to look at things differently (e.g., Iccius
in 1. 29 — or Sybaris in 1. 8). Nor was H. himself always innocent of inculcating right
ideas on the subject (see 3. 2 and 3. 5).

Structure: The ode consists of two contrasting structures (Stanzas 1-3 and Stanzas 4-6),
each comprising an opening stanza which spills over into the first line of a second
stanza; this second stanza is then followed by a syntactically independent third stanza.
The theme of Stanzas 1-3 is 'stop worrying about things which are not your concern
when life is precious': the opening exhortation 3 'remittas quaerere, nec, trepides . . .'
is backed up by the expository 5 'fugit retro levis iuventas'; this first structure is then
rounded off with the question 11 'quid . . . fatigas?' in which the opening exhortation is
rephrased in more general and grandiloquent terms. Stanzas 4-6 propose an alternative
— 13 'Cur non . . . potamus uncti?' and proceed with practical steps to make the most
of time; the theme of this second structure is summed up in 17 'Dissipat Euhius curas
edacis', which separates the opening 'Cur non . . . potamus uncti?' from the more ani-
mated instructions which pour out (18 'quis . . . restinguet?', 21 'quis . . . eliciet?', 22
'dic age . . . maturet') as H. puts into practice what he has been preaching.

Metre: Alcaics; see 1. 9M.

1-5] Cantaber] In NW Spain; a stubborn mountain people who, in the confusion of the
Civil Wars, had spread southwards threatening the more highly civilised parts of Spain;
Augustus launched a campaign against them in 26, but, despite official claims of complete
victory, it was not until 19 BC that 'Agrippa, patient and ruthless, imposed by massacre
and enslavement the Roman peace upon a desolated land' (Syme, *Roman Revolution*
333); see 2. 6. 2, 3. 8. 22, 4. 14. 41. — **Scythes**] For H., the symbol of a remote barbarous
people on the Eastern frontier; see on 1. 19. 10; cf. the Geloni, 2. 20. 19. — **Hirpine
Quincti**] Probably, the 'optime Quincti' of *Epist*. 1. 16. 1; the family, once distinguished,
had fallen into obscurity; a L. Quinctius was Pollio's father-in-law, a T. Quinctius was
consul in 9 BC. — **cogitet**] 'has in mind'; agreement with the nearer element of a multiple
subject. — **Hadria divisus obiecto**] As well as the Adriatic, a good part of Asia Minor

stood between the Scythae and Quinctius; presumably, the argument is that, even if the
worst comes to the worst and the Scythae overrun Asia Minor, there was still the Adriatic
between them and Rome (as an Englishman could say, of the Germans, 'There's always
the Channel between us', or an American 'there's always the Atlantic'); i.e., Quinctius'
anxieties are needless; the threat of war may be real enough, but it is not a matter for a
man whose claims on life are sensible and modest to worry his head about continually;
cf. H.'s advice to Maecenas, 3. 29. 25-8; for the exaggeration cf. 1. 12. 53; **Hadria**]
regularly masculine in the *Odes* (2. 14. 14, 3. 3. 5, 3. 9. 23) and elsewhere in poetry (in
prose *Hadriaticum mare*); the town name is feminine. — **remittas quaerere**] 'give yourself
a spell from asking', 'forget about for a while'; contrast the more peremptory *desine*,
1. 23. 11, etc.; cf. 1. 11. 1 'ne quaesieris'. — **nec trepides . . . pauca**] = 'the things you
need in life are few, don't get all worked up about them'; **trepides**] used absolutely, as
3. 29. 31-2; **in usum**] 'to meet the (practical) needs'; **poscentis aevi pauca**] i.e., most
anxieties are about non-essentials; the doctrine of the simple life was common to several
schools, but particularly associated with the Epicureans; Cicero, e.g., says of them, *Tusc.*
5. 97 'Extenuatur magnificentia et sumptus epularum, quod parvo natura contenta sit';
H. regularly represents himself as an adherent of the simple life; see, e.g., 1. 31. 15-20,
1. 38.

5-8]   The argument is not 'you are only young once', but 'your best years are already
behind you', as 6 'arida . . . somnum' suggests and 15 'canos odorati capillos' confirms;
for the age span denoted by *iuvenis*, see on 1. 2. 41; cf. 1. 16. 23, 1. 30. 7, 3. 2. 15,
3. 14. 27, *AP* 115 'maturusne senex an adhuc florente iuventa fervidus'; for *iuventus*/
iuventa, see 1. 2. 24, 1. 4. 19, 1. 35. 36, 3. 4. 50, 3. 6. 33. — **fugit retro**] The basis of this
and similar metaphors is that the future lies ahead of us as we advance, then becomes the
past as we leave it behind; so *AP* 175-6 'multa ferunt anni venientes commoda secum, /
multa recedentes adimunt'; cf. *Epist.* 2. 2. 55 'anni euntes' ('the years as they pass by')
H. perhaps had in mind the passenger on a boat travelling down river; objects ahead seem
to rush towards him, then flee from him into the distance behind; for the metaphor of
flight cf. 2. 14. 1, 3. 30. 5; here it is our physical characteristics which flee from us. —
levis iuventas] A man in the prime of life is 'smooth-faced' — not beardless (the mark
of the boy on the threshold of puberty, like Ligurinus in 4. 10), but with a face free from
wrinkles (*rugae*); *iuventus*, as usual, covers the period from the assumption of the *toga
virilis* until the onset of *senectus* in the early forties (our concept of 'middle age' was not
known to the Romans). H., now in his forties, sees his *iuventus* receding into the distance;
see on 2. 14. 3; for *rugae* as the symbol of *senectus*, see *Epodes* 8.3 'cum tibi rugis vetus
frontem senectus exaret', cf. 2. 14. 3, 4. 13. 11. — **arida pellente . . . somnum**] Middle
age intervenes to drive off 'lascivos amores' as an angry father might intervene to break
up a party; the natural reading of the phrase is that H. is speaking of himself as well as
Quinctius (cf. 15 'canos odorati capillos'); **arida canitie**] whitening hair is an alternative
symbol of advancing years and the limitation of life's pleasures; cf. 4. 13. 12 'capitis
nives'; H. perhaps exaggerates for effect — in *Epist.* 1. 20. 24 (about 20 BC), in a more
strictly factual mood, he describes himself as 'praecanus' ('prematurely white'); for
arida, 'dried out', i.e., no longer lithe and supple, cf. 1. 25. 19 'aridas frondes', 4. 13.
9-10 'aridas quercus'; *arida* is applied to *canitie* by the figure called 'metonomy', whereby
a noun (here *senectute*) is replaced by the name of a thing associated with that noun,
which is then treated as synonymous with it; **lascivos amores**] sexual adventures; H. and
Quinctius, i.e., have reached the age at which it is no longer seemly (or easy) to keep a
mistress — not the age at which loss of desire has to be philosophically accepted (as in
the anecdote told of Sophocles, Plato *Repub.* 329 e, repeated Cicero *De Senec.* 39);
facilemque somnum] 'untroubled sleep'; insomnia is likewise an ill of middle age; cf. for
the phrase 3. 21. 4.

9-12]   **non semper . . . vernis**] = 'the bloom of spring flowers does not last for ever'; for
non semper cf. 2. 9. 1; **honor**] = 'beauty', 'attractiveness', *OLD* 6. — **neque uno . . . voltu**]
= 'nor is the moon always ruddy-faced'; a ruddy-faced moon meant stormy weather
according to *Georgics* 1. 430-31 'at si sanguineum suffuderit ore ruborem, / ventus erit,
vento semper rubet aurea Phoebe'; the second of two contrasting images of transitoriness
in nature, the one attractive, the other menacing; the implication is 'even though the
moon is ruddy now (i.e., even though a crisis seems to be threatening — see lines 1-2),
the crisis will pass; so let us make the most of life's simple pleasures (symbolised by the
spring flowers) before it is too late'. — **quid . . . fatigas?**] 'why do you weary with never-

ending plans for the future a mind unequal to the strain? Quinctius keeps trying to decide what he will do if this or that disaster now threatening eventuates; such *consilia* are *aeterna*, both because there is no end to them, and because Quinctius allows them to stretch endlessly into the future (as if he were going to live for ever; but life is short and precious); cf. for the phrase *Aen.* 1. 229-30 (of Jove) 'qui res hominumque deumque / aeternis regis imperiis'.

13-17]   sub alta platano] The plane tree was cultivated for the shade of its broad-spreading leaves; as a result of its choice by Plato for the dramatic setting of the *Phaedrus* (229 a; cf. 230 b), it is also the symbol of relaxed discussion; as in Plato, we are to imagine the speakers walking along to begin with, and then settling down to talk; what follows, however, is not a philosophical discussion but a *déjeuner sur l'herbe.* — **hac pinu]** Deictic, like 2. 3. 13 *huc,* 2. 14. 22 *harum;* the speaker makes a gesture as he speaks and the décor of the dramatic monologue begins to take shape; cf. 1. 19. 13, 3. 26. 6. — **sic temere]** = 'just as we are'. — **rosa canos odorati capillos]** Roses in the hair suggest carefree extravagance; the juxtaposition 'rosa canos' is designedly ironical; *canos* picks up 8 *canitie;* cf. 3. 14. 25 'albescens capillus'; for the accusative with the past participle, see on 1. 1. 22 'stratus'. — **dum licet]** 'while we can'; i.e., 'before it is too late'; so 4. 12. 26; cf. 2. 3. 15-16 'dum res ... patiuntur'. — **uncti]** The Assyrian nard-oil, like the rose petals, are for the hair; see on 1. 5. 2.

17-24]   Euhius] Bacchus. — **curas edacis]** 'gnawing anxieties'; cf. 3. 30. 3; for the idea, 1. 18. 4 'mordaces sollicitudines'; for *curas,* see on 1. 7. 31. — **quis ... restinguet?]** Like 21 *'quis eliciet?',* equivalent to a command addressed to the slaves who have accompanied them; **ocius]** i.e., with more than ordinary speed; **restinguet]** the fiery Falernian needs to be diluted with water; for the Falernian, see on 1. 20. 10. — **praetereunte lympha]** The passing stream forms the final detail of the décor; cf. 2. 3. 11-12; an echo in Tibullus 1. 1. 28 'ad rivos praetereuntis aquae'. — **quis eliciet domo?]** Again a command to the slaves; **domo]** either 'from the house' (the farmhouse, perhaps, on H.'s Sabine estate; in that case Lyde is staying with H.: cf. Tyndaris in 1. 17); or 'from her house' (presumably her town house; in that case, the décor is perhaps a public garden or something of the sort in Rome itself). — **devium]** Predicative with *eliciet,* 'entice off the beaten track', i.e., away from indoors, which she prefers, out of doors (cf. 3. 25. 12), but with moral connotations 'away from the path of moral rectitude', as 1. 17. 6 — Lyde, i.e., like Tyndaris, has a husband or steady lover from whom she is to be enticed away; less likely that *devium* is attributive, 'living in seclusion', though this is the common sense (*OLD* 1 b) — **Lyden]** Also 3. 11 and 3. 28. — **eburna dic age ... maturet]** Addressed to the slave who is to go to fetch her, 'tell her to hurry and bring her ivory lyre'; *age* supports *dic,* making the command more urgent. — **in comptum ... nodum]** 'her hair bound back in a neat knot, Spartan style'; H.'s characteristic decrescendo ending, focused on a visual detail, cf. 4. 2. 55-60; for the idea cf. 3. 14. 21-2; **Lacaenae more]** suggests a severely plain hair style, and perhaps serves also to identify Lyde (= i.e., 'like the Spartan she is' — despite the name Lyde); some editors, Bentley among them, have found fault with the passage; see Brink, *Proc. Camb. Phil. Soc.* 1971, 25-7.

2. 12

Introduction: A carefully-worded *recusatio* (see on 1. 6; cf. 4. 2): whereas in 1. 6 H.'s claim that his competence as a poet does not extend beyond the themes of love and parties is little more than a polite excuse, his warmly passionate, elegantly-phrased depiction of himself in 2. 12 as the poet in love is obviously intended to disarm criticism.

We have to remember that epic was the prestige genre (it occupied in Augustan Rome the place the novel occupies today); the pressure exerted on H. by Maecenas need not have been exclusively political in its motivation; H.'s preference for what was, to conventional eyes, a minor genre must have seemed eccentric. As was customary on such occasions, H. ironically deprecates his chosen form, though he can hardly have failed to hope that Maecenas would appreciate the new, serious use H. was making of that form. Comparison with Propertius 2. 1 is instructive.

Structure: Stanzas 1-3 are controlled by the opening *nolis*; Stanzas 4-5 oppose what the Muse has decided (14 *voluit*) to what Maecenas, or H., might or might not want; in

Stanzas 6-7, 21-3 *num tu velis . . .* ? picks up the opening *nolis*: surely, on consideration, Maecenas wouldn't want matters otherwise than they are?

Metre: Asclepiad (c) — the first break in the alternation of Alcaics and Sapphics in this book; for the metre, see 1. 6M.

1-12] 'You wouldn't want a lyric poet to attempt historical or mythological themes; as far as history is concerned, and the recording of Caesar's victories, you will do a better job in prose.' The argument is disingenuous. Plainly, it is an epic poem Maecenas wants H. to attempt. Or perhaps we should say this is the view Maecenas is obliged to take; privately, he may have been more sympathetic. H., in replying, takes it for granted that for him lyric is the only possible form; a narrative poem on a historical or mythological subject is therefore plainly out of the question ('you wouldn't want me,' he says to Maecenas, 'to attempt such a poem in lyric metre').

1-4] **longa bella**] The very scale of the Numantine war precludes lyric treatment. — **Numantiae**] in NW Spain; the city was the leader of Spanish resistance to Rome, successfully repelling attack after attack (Cato in 195 BC, M. Fulvius Nobilior in 153, Marcellus in 152, Q. Pompeius in 141, Pompilius Caenas in 139-8) until finally reduced after an eight-month siege by Scipio Aemilianus in 133; in this and the succeeding examples in this stanza, H. is careful to choose possible themes at a decent distance from the present. — **nec**] Because *nolis* is equivalent to *non velis*. — **durum Hannibalem**] Symbolises the Second Punic War, 218-201 BC; many change *durum* to *dirum*; cf. 3. 6. 36 and 4. 4. 42; *durum* is probably to be opposed, however, to 3 *mollibus*; cf. the ironic opposition of these two epithets in Propertius 1. 7. 4-6. — **Sicu̇lum mare . . . sanguine**] The Roman naval victories of the First Punic War (that of C. Duilius at Mylae in 260 and that of Lutatius Catulus at the Aegates Insulae in 242); the three rejected historical themes are arranged in reverse chronological order; all are major historical themes obviously beyond the scale of lyric form. — **mollibus**] 'gentle', 'soothing', with overtones of 'effeminate', 'unwarlike'.

5-9] **nec**] See on 2 *nec*. — **saevos . . . Hylaeum**] For the battle of the Lapithae and the Centaurs, see on 1. 18. 8; *et* links the two components of a single legend; Hylaeus was one of the Centaurs; **nimium mero**] 'given to excessive drinking'; *nimius* in the sense 'transgressing the limits of correct behaviour' (*OLD* 3) is constructed both with *in* + ablative and the simple ablative. — **domitosque . . . iuvenes**] The myth of the Titans (children of Sky and Earth) who helped Cronos (= Saturnus) against Jove is constantly conflated by the poets with the myth of the Giants (sons of Jove and Earth) who rose against Jove; cf. 2. 19. 21-4; H. retells one version in 3. 4. 49-64; the second rejected mythological theme is connected to the first by -*que* (not *nec*, as in Stanza 1); **Herculea manu**] 'with the aid of Hercules'; his assistance was enlisted because of a prophecy that no Giant could be killed by a god; for the adjectival form see on 1. 3. 36.

9-12] The theme Maecenas undoubtedly would have preferred H. to tackle (in an appropriate metre) is coolly handed over to Maecenas himself — to treat in prose; cf. Propertius' less barefaced evasion (2. 1. 17-37):

> quod mihi si tantum, Maecenas, fata dedissent   17
>   ut possem heroas ducere in arma manus,
>   non ego Titanas canerem . . . :
> bellaque resque tui memorarem Caesaris, et tu   25
>   Caesare sub magno cura secunda fores.

— **tuque . . . proelia Caesaris**] As for recent history, 'you will deal with that'; H. uses the vivid *dices* (which stresses performance of the literary work rather than composition) to prepare the contrast with 14 *voluit dicere*; contrast 2. 1. 7 *tractas*; **pedestribus**] *pedester* translates Greek πεƺόs; the usual terms are 'soluta oratio' (Cicero) and 'prosa oratio' (Quintilian); Servius on *Georgics* 2. 42 says Maecenas wrote a history of the rule of Augustus; cf. Pliny *NH* 7. 148; Bardon, *La littérature latine inconnue* vol. 2, 102 is inclined to allow that Maecenas may have composed '*Mémoires*' (i.e., *commentarii*, like those of Caesar); that a full-scale historical work was planned, let alone executed, seems improbable; **historiis**] cf. the *Historiae* of Tacitus. — **melius**] The obvious sense is 'better than I could'; cf. 4. 2. 33; but we should not deny H. the insight that the point had been reached in the development of Roman literature where history was better written in prose, because prose, not verse, had become the natural form for continuous

rational exposition; the conventions of epic made it difficult to give a proper account of
complex events, and actually precluded truth; cf. Cicero's remark about his *Marius,
De Legibus* 1. 4-5. — **ductaque colla**] The triumphs which followed the victories,
adorned by the foreign princes who had been captured; H. has no doubt in mind the
triple triumph of Augustus in 29 BC (see Virgil's version *Aen.* 8. 722-6); for triumphs
accorded Augustus' proconsuls, see Syme, *Roman Revolution* 303; for a foreign
monarch who did not grace a triumph, see 1. 37. 31-2; for projected triumphs, see
1. 12. 53-6. — **per vias**] Through the streets of Rome, in particular the *via Sacra.*

13-16]   H. turns from what Maecenas 'wouldn't want' him to do (and which Maecenas
can do better) to what the Muse has commanded him to write about: he must write love
poetry; as usual, a concrete example is preferred to abstract generalisation. — **Me dulcis
dominae Musa Licymniae cantus**] *dulcis* qualifies *cantus,* 'the sweet singing of my
mistress Licymnia' (object of *dicere*); **dominae**] originally, 'mistress of the household',
especially in her relationship to household slaves (as in 2. 8. 19, 3. 27. 65, *Sat.* 1. 5. 55
and 67, *Epist.* 1. 2. 25); hence the sense 'mistress of a lover whom she treats as her
slave'; this latter sense, common in Augustan elegy, is not found elsewhere in H.,
though obviously present as an overtone in 2. 8. 19; **Licymniae**] like others of H.'s
Greek pseudonyms (e.g., Lalage in 1. 22; see on 1. 8. 2 Sybaris) chosen as etymologi-
cally appropriate (λιγύς, 'clear-voiced' + ὕμνος, 'song'); apparently a servile name
(cf. *Aen.* 9. 546 'serva Licymnia'); **cantus**] H.'s current mistress is a talented girl;
cf. Propertius' mistress in his *recusatio,* 2. 1. 9-12 'sive lyrae carmen digitis percussit
eburnis, / miramur, facilis ut premat arte manus'; similarly, Tyndaris, 1. 17. 16-20, and
Lyde, 2. 11. 21-4; a talent for music was not confined to professionals and women of
dubious respectability (like Sallust's Sempronia, *Cat.* 24-5): Pliny's third wife Calpurnia
set his verses to music and sang them herself (*Epist.* 4. 19. 4). — **voluit**] 'has decided',
i.e., left H. no choice in the matter; H. is head over heels in love and can write only of
his mistress (cf. 1. 19. 9-12, where a different mistress similarly precludes writing on
themes 'quae nihil attinent'); cf. his preoccupation with Lalage in 1. 22. — **lucidum
fulgentis oculos**] 'her bright shining eyes'; *lucidum fulgentis,* like 1. 22. 23 'dulce
ridentem, dulce loquentem'. — **bene . . . amoribus**] = 'her heart properly faithful to the
one who returns her love'; **mutuis amoribus**] dative with *fidum*; cf. 3. 9. 13, 4. 1. 30.

17-20]   Nor was dancing, though apt to be associated with decadence (cf. 3. 6. 21), in
itself inconsistent with respectability — unless, like Sallust's Sempronia, one danced
'elegantius quam necesse est probae'; H.'s mistress, however, is more likely to be a
libertina than a *matrona*; dancing was probably part of her training, a talent expected
of her at parties and on other festive occasions as much as singing; cf. Propertius 2. 3.
17-18 (of Cynthia) 'posito formose saltat Iaccho, / egit ut euhantis dux Ariadna choros'
and 2. 28. 60 (of the festival of Diana!) 'munera Dianae debita redde choros'. — **nec
dedecuit**] 'she has never disgraced herself'; i.e., by the licentiousness of her dancing,
rather than by incompetence. — **sacro . . . die**] Apparently, the Ides of August (see
Martial 12. 672 'Augustis redit Idibus Diana'); according to Plutarch (*Quaest. rom.*
100), it was an occasion when 'all slaves, male and female, kept holiday'; **celebris**] with
Dianae, 'thronged with worshippers', the goddess being supposed to be present for the
festival.

21-4]   **Num tu . . . velis**] *tu* is emphatic, following the emphatic 13 *me* ('surely *you*
wouldn't want . . . would you?'); the unexpected appeal to Maecenas led to the
interpretation (known already in antiquity) that Licymnia stands for Terentia, the wife
of Maecenas (pseudo-Acron on *Sat.* 1. 2. 64, invoking the principle that metrically
equivalent pseudonyms are substituted in such cases for the real names); this inter-
pretation has become traditional; if it makes easier sense of Stanza 6, it makes nonsense
of the poem and hardly merits the attention which it has received: whatever the
character of Terentia, it was surely impossible for H. to write of a Terentia to a
Maecenas as he goes on to write in Stanza 7 — even more impossible if Terentia's
character was (as rumour suggested — see Suetonius *Aug.* 66) not above reproach; it
need hardly be added that, if the defence 'I am infatuated with Licymnia and cannot
write of anything else' is acceptable and consistent with 1. 19. 9-12, the defence that
inspiration will allow H. to write only in praise of Maecenas' wife, even if not meant
seriously, will hardly pass; for a vigorous rebuttal, see Morris and Williams, *Philological
Quarterly* 42, 1963, 145-60; so (more cautiously) NH; **quae**] neuter plural accusative;
Achaemenes] the legendary ancestor of the Persians; cf. 3. 1. 44, 3. 9. 4; **pinguis . . .**

opes] 'the riches of wealthy Phrygia's Mygdon', a legendary prince of Phrygia, see
3. 16. 41. − **crine Licymniae**] 'a hair of Licymnia's head' (less likely that *crine* is
singular for plural, as in 1. 32. 12).
25-8]   **flagrantia ad oscula**] 'toward my burning kisses'. − **detorquet cervicem**] Licymnia,
i.e., turns her head to receive H.'s kisses; cf. Catullus 9. 9 'applicansque collum iucundum
os oculosque suaviabor'. − **facili saevitia**] 'with a cruelty that is easily overcome'. −
quae . . . gaudeat eripi] Generic: 'kisses of the sort that give her greater pleasure to give
than it gives me to claim them'. − **interdum rapere occupat**] 'and sometimes she steals
the kisses first'; the indicative puts *occupat* on the same syntactical footing as *detorquet*
and *negat*; the MSS have *occupet* (parallel in that case with *gaudeat*), but this is less
natural and less effective (as well as logically questionable).

2. 13

Introduction: 'Curses on the man who planted that damned tree: it was nearly the death
   of me.' This and the following ode represent two explorations of the traditional
   imagery of the underworld; in each case, the known unreality of the subject lends the
   exploration an imaginative freedom which transforms commonplace idea into poetic
   fantasy; 2. 13 operates throughout at the level of elegant, ironic whimsy − death was
   an opportunity for H. to see his illustrious predecessors, Sappho and Alcaeus, in action,
   holding the inhabitants of the underworld in thrall by the beauty of their verse; 2. 14
   will strike a more serious note. The incident of the tree is alluded to again in 2. 17. 27,
   3. 4. 27 and 3. 8. 7.
Structure: Stanzas 1-3 constitute an elegantly structured exercise in the rhetoric of
   invective built around a triple *ille* (1 'ille et posuit et produxit', 5 'illum et crediderim
   fregisse et sparsisse', 8 'ille tractavit'). Stanzas 4-5 develop the cliché 'one never knows
   when or how death will strike' and mark the transition from anger to reflection. In
   Stanzas 6-10 reflection becomes fanciful and poetically creative, while adhering strictly
   to traditional material.
Metre: Alcaics; see 1. 9M.
1-12]   **nefasto**] Sets the tone at the level of mock-heroic. − **quicumque primum**] 'whoever
it was that planted you originally'. − **sacrilega manu**] The hand of a man who was
sacrilegus; any action, therefore, of his was likely to prove accursed; the frame of
reference opened up is the cultivation of trees for the *benefit* of posterity; see, e.g.,
Cicero *Sen.* 24-5, quoting a line from Caecilius Statius: 'serit arbores, quae alteri saeclo
prosint'; cf. with the action of the unknown *sacrilegus* the piety with which H. conse-
crates a tree overhanging his villa in 3. 22. − **pagi**] The small community in which H.'s
Sabine farm is situated; see on 3. 18. 12. − **crediderim**] 'I can well believe'; parricide
and the murder of a guest under your own roof were regarded as particularly atrocious
crimes. − **penetralia**] His domestic shrine; that part of the house which is under the
protection of the Penates. − **venena Colcha . . . tractavit**] i.e., witchcraft and the magic
concoctions associated with Medea of Colchis; we pass now from what H. 'can well
believe' to direct assertion; **nefas**] picks up 1 *nefasto*. − **te, te**] Repetition for
emphasis, but also part of the formal rhetorical pattern. − **triste lignum**] = 'evil timber',
because destined to bring ill luck (not the happiness one hopes for in planting a tree);
cf. Catullus 36. 8 'infelicibus lignis'.
13-20]   A variation on the cliché that death when it comes is always unexpected;
cf. Seneca *Epist.* 30. 16 (quoting the historian Bassus) ' "Sed consideremus", inquit,
"tunc, cum aliqua causa moriendi videtur accedere, quanto aliae propiores sint quae
non timentur": hostis alicui mortem minabitur, hunc cruditas ('indigestion')
occupavit'. Propertius makes elegant use of the cliché (Propertius 2. 27) to advance the
paradox that only the lover knows when he will die and whence death will come
('quando periturus et a qua morte'). − **numquam . . . in horas**] = 'a man is never at
any given moment sufficiently on his guard'; i.e., one danger dominates his vision to the
exclusion of others; **homini**] dative of agent with the impersonal 'cautum est'. −
Thynus] Bithynian ships were famous; the MSS have *Poenus*; *Thynus*, Lachmann. −
timet] The second syllable counts as long; see on 1. 3. 36. − **miles, Parthus**]
Alternative subjects to 16 *timet*. − **sagittas . . . Parthi**] Hendiadys = 'the arrows of a
fleeing Parthian'; this, i.e., is the way a Roman soldier around 23 BC might expect to

end his days; the reference is to the Parthian reputation for wheeling around while apparently retreating in order to resume the attack; for the Parthi, see on 1. 2. 22 'Persae'. — **catenas et Italum robur**] A second hendiadys = 'dying a prisoner of war in an Italian dungeon'; the *robur* was a traditional name for the Tullianum, an underground execution cell of the prison on the Capitoline; execution after being led in a triumph was a fate usually reserved for distinguished prisoners of war such as Jugurtha and Vercingetorix; **Italum**] = *Italicum*; 'Italian' rather than 'Roman' perhaps to suggest death in a remote, foreign land; Heinze's insistence that *Italum* excludes the sense *Tullianum* for *robur* in favour of the sense 'pick of Italian troops' is misconceived.

21-8]   The picture of the afterlife evoked is that described in detail in *Aen.* 6; for the conventional imagery, see on 1. 4. 16. The individual scenes are, this time, connected by *et, -que* connecting the parts of a scene. — **furvae Proserpinae**] Wife of Pluto and Queen of the Underworld; the gods of the underworld are always depicted in sombre colours. — **Aeacum**] Along with Minos and Rhadamanthus, he judged the shades of the dead upon arrival and allocated to each his place of eternal abode. — **sedesque discretas**] 'the dwelling places apart' are the Elysian fields; cf. 1. 10. 17; the MSS vary between *discretas* and *discriptas* or *descriptas* ('assigned', favoured by NH). — **Aeoliis**] Sappho and Alcaeus both wrote in the Aeolic dialect. — **Sappho**] Accusative. — **puellis de popularibus**] = 'about the girls of her native Lesbos'. — **et te, Alcaee**] The switch from narrative to apostrophe marks a climax, as often. — **plenius aureo plectro**] 'striking a more resonant note with your golden plectrum'; his poetry, i.e., has a wider emotional range; the golden plectrum is the symbol of the master-post; cf. Pindar *Nem.* 5. 24, Euripides *Herc.* 351. — **dura . . . belli**] 'the hardships of his life at sea, as an exile and in war'; cf. the fuller statement of the idea in 1. 32. 5-8; for the repetition of the dissyllable *dura,* see 1. 9M.

29-40]   The last of the scenes H. so nearly saw now becomes an actual scene, related (30 *mirantur*, 32 *bibit*, 34 *demittit*, 36 *recreantur*, 38 *decipitur*, 39 *curat*) as though it were all happening before H.'s eyes; cf. the switch from what H. could well believe (lines 5-8) to the plain assertion of lines 8-10. — **sacro digna silentio**] 'songs deserving to be heard in reverent silence', accusative after *dicere*; *sacro* because the poet is the priest of the Muse (cf. 3. 1. 1-4). — **magis**] Equally with 'densum umeris' and with 'bibit'. — **exactos tyrannos**] 'the expulsion of tyrants'; Alcaeus spent much of his life fighting and writing against successive tyrants of Mytilene; two at least were expelled, Melandros and Myrsilus; see on 1. 37. 1. — **densum umeris**] = 'packed shoulder to shoulder'. — **volgus**] Contrast 3. 1. 1-2. — **Quid mirum . . . angues**] An ironical expansion of the cliché according to which the inspired poet (especially Orpheus) holds wild beasts enthralled with his music; see on 3. 11. 13-24; **demittit atras auris**] Cerberus, being a watchdog, can normally be expected to prick up his ears on hearing an unfamiliar sound (cf. 2. 19. 3-4 'auris acutas'); here he is lulled into less than his usual alertness; **centiceps**] in 3. 11. 17-20 H. gives Cerberus three heads (three tongues at any rate) and 100 snakes (on each head?), but that stanza is suspect; Hesiod *Theog.* 312 gives him fifty; H. perhaps follows Pindar *fr.* 249a; the tone is plainly ironical; **recreantur**] 'relax'. — **quin et, et**] Ironically emphatic. — **Prometheus**] This version of the legend which has Prometheus still undergoing punishment in Tartarus is not found outside H.; cf. 2. 18. 35, *Epodes* 17. 67 (from which it appears H. thinks of him as still tormented by the eagle). — **Pelopis parens**] Tantalus; his punishment was to suffer eternally from hunger and thirst in the presence of food and drink. — **laborem decipitur**] = 'is made to forget his torment'; the accusative with a passive finite verb is rarer than the accusative with a passive past participle; see on 1. 1. 22 *stratus*; the genitive *laborum* is an inferior variant found in some MSS. — **nec curat Orion**] Orion is the great hunter, but while listening to Alcaeus he forgets about hunting; to suppose that H. imagines him as normally hunting lions and lynxes in the underworld is not necessary but consistent with the ironic logic of H.'s description of the afterlife; cf. 3. 4. 70-72. — **aut timidos agitare lyncas**] H.'s characteristic preference for a concluding rallentando; cf. 3. 5. 55-6, 4. 2. 59-60.

2. 14

Introduction: The third and most ambitious of three dramatic monologues in this book

(the others are 2. 3 and 2. 11 — also in Alcaics). In all three, one thought dominates
the speaker's mind — the need to enjoy life before it is too late. The related theme of
the inevitability of death, which forms the climax of 2. 3, is absent in 2. 11; here, it is
explored at greater length (Stanzas 2-5, which stand in sombre contrast to the light-
hearted treatment of similar imagery in 2. 13). For the ideas about death of educated
Romans in H.'s day, see Cicero *Tusc.* 1. 10-12:

> 'Num te illa terrent, triceps apud inferos Cerberus, . . . tum illud
> quod —
>
> Sisyphus versat
> saxum sudans nitendo neque proficit hilum? . . .
>
> fortasse etiam inexorabilis iudices, Minos et Rhadamanthus?' . . .
> — 'Adeone me delirare censes, ut ista esse credam?'

Structure: Stanzas 1-3 comprise a single complex sentence: after a brief statement of the
two themes of the poem (old age is upon us, death is inevitable), the sentence spills
over into an impassioned expansion of the second of these themes. Stanza 4 represents
a more emphatic restatement of the same theme, which is then explored at length in
Stanzas 5-6 (each stanza a variation on the theme, the two variations being linked by
the anaphora of the opening gerundive — 17 'visendus', 21 'linquenda'). Stanza 7
brings us back to the themes of Stanza 1 with a hint from the speaker to his host to
take practical steps before it is too late.

The reader accustomed to prose rhetorical structure is apt to feel H. overargues his
case, or to expect a final stanza that he can accept as crowning the rhetoric of Stanzas
4-6. In fact, the ode is a sophisticated exploration of feelings touched off by ideas
which are in themselves commonplace (however sincerely held); it is this exploration
of feelings within a carefully organised rhetorical structure of theme and variation and
the suggestion of a dramatic context which make the poem what it is, not its ideas.

Metre: Alcaics; see 1. 9M.

1-4]   The gentle melancholy and wistful pathos often introduced into these lines
(e.g., by Wickham, 'the fleeting years slide by') are a misreading. The tone is more
urgent and more brutal. — **Eheu**] 'Alas!'; cf. 3. 2. 9, 3. 11. 42; in the form *heu*, 1. 15.
9, 1. 35. 33 — **fugaces**] 'in headlong flight'; *fugax* is a strong word; cf. 2. 1. 19 (of
cavalry horses turned in flight), 3. 2. 14 (of the panic-stricken flight from battle of the
coward), 4. 6. 33 (of lynxes fleeing before the huntress Artemis), *Sat.* 2. 7. 115 (where
H. is likened to a runaway slave); see on 2. 11. 5 'fugit retro levis iuventas'. — **Postume**]
The repetition, following the initial *eheu*, (1) makes it clear that the ode is dramatic in
form (not a verse epistle), (2) sets the appropriate level of emotional incitement; see
Leumann-Hofmann 374 § f; cf. 3. 3 18, 4. 1. 2 and 33, 4. 13. 18; Postumus seems
unidentifiable. — **labuntur**] The speaker and his host are of the age when the passage
of the years seems to get out of control — they are like an army which loses discipline
and turns and flees (*OLD* 6 c); both *fugaces* and *labuntur* personify. — **pietas**]
(Scrupulous) observance of one's obligations to one's gods (as in 1. 17. 13) and one's
father, etc. (as in 3. 27. 35), or to one's fellow-men, especially the first of these;
cf. 4. 7. 24; Epicureanism necessarily rejects the concept of a just world, as implied,
e.g., in Catullus 76. 26 'O di, reddite mi hoc pro pietate mea'; cf. *Aen.* 1. 603-5 'di tibi,
si qua pios respectant numina', etc. — **rugis et instanti senectae**] Hendiadys, 'the
wrinkles which the years in their relentless advance implant upon us'; for *rugae* as a
symbol (like white hair) of the loss of the best years of life, see 4. 13. 11, *Epodes*
8. 3-4 'rugis vetus / frontem senectus exaret'; **instanti**] not just 'advancing' (as we
speak of advancing years), but 'pressing home the attack'; cf. 3. 3. 3 'voltus instantis
tyranni'; middle age is the advancing general before whom the routed years turn and
flee; **senectae**] better rendered 'age' or 'middle age' since 'old age' suggests to us the
sixties onwards; the turning point for a Roman is in his forties (H.'s age at the time
of publication of *Odes* 1-3); cf. 2. 11. 5-8; H. uses the form *senecta* in the *Odes*
except in 2. 16. 30; the form *senectus* occurs in his hexameter verse. — **indomitaeque
morti**] = 'death, that enemy who has never been subdued'; *indomitae* continues the
military metaphor; for this sense, see *OLD* 2; cf. *Il.* 9. 158 ' ' Ἀίδης ἀδάμαστος.'

5-12]   **trecenis tauris**] A sacrifice three times as lavish as the traditional hecatomb; Livy

22. 10 records such a sacrifice at Rome (to Jove) in 217 BC during the Second Punic War. — **quotquot eunt dies**] = 'every day of your life'. — **places**] 'were to placate'. — **inlacrimabilem**] 'not given to tears'; contrast 4. 9. 26 (where the sense is 'unwept'); cf. for the idea 2. 3. 24. — **ter amplum Geryonen**] A giant with three heads or three bodies, believed to live on an island in the river Oceanus, killed and his oxen carried off by Hercules; called 'τρίσωματος' by Euripides *Herc.* 423, 'tergeminus' in *Aen.* 8. 202. — **Tityonque**] Another monster; killed by Apollo and Artemis while attempting to rape their mother Leto; Odysseus saw him bound in Hades with two vultures tearing at his liver, *Od.* 11. 576-81; cf. *Aen.* 6. 595-7 'nec non et Tityon, Terrae omnipotentis alumnum, / cernere erat, per tota novem cui iugera corpus / porrigitur'; also 3. 4. 77, 3. 11. 21, 4. 6. 2. — **tristi conpescit unda**] 'imprisons with gloomy waters'; i.e., the Styx, which encircled Hades: cf. the flat contradiction (for ironic effect) 2. 20. 8 — **quicumque terrae munere vescimur**] An echo of the Homeric formula, *Il.* 6. 142, etc. 'οἳ ἀρούρης καρπὸν ἔδουσιν'. — **enaviganda**] 'to be sailed across to their journey's end'; the first of three striking gerundives (cf. 17 *visendus*, 21 *linquenda*). — **sive . . . coloni**] For the idea cf. 1. 4. 13-14, 2. 3. 21-4; for the rhythm and the repetition of *sive*, see 1. 9M; **reges**] 'merchant princes'; see on 1. 4. 14; **erimus**] i.e., when death comes; **coloni**] 'husbandmen' (small-scale farmers), symbolising the class which has to struggle for existence; cf. 1. 35. 6.

13-16] The second theme of the ode begins with an adaptation to the present argument (that death strikes all equally) of the cliché 'no man knows when and how death will strike', from which it follows that all attempts to avoid death are futile. — **frustra, frustra**] Repetition in anaphora for emphasis. — **carebimus**] 'abstain from'; cf. 2. 10. 6-7. — **fractisque . . . Hadriae**] Avoiding travel by sea in stormy weather is equally idle (if you are not destined to die, you will survive; if you are, fate will find another way); H. as usual particularises; *fractis fluctibus* suggests the waves breaking against the coast (cf. 1. 11. 5); **rauci Hadriae**] i.e., in a howling gale; see on 1. 3. 15; for the gender of *Hadria*, on 2. 11. 2. — **corporibus**] Equally with *nocentem* and *metuemus*. — **Austrum**] The hot, sultry south wind of Autumn, traditionally an unhealthy season; cf. *Sat.* 2. 6. 18-19, *Epist.* 1. 7. 5-9.

17-20] The repetition *frustra . . . frustra* is now caught up on a larger scale by the opposing pair (identified by the sonorous *-endus* ending) *visendus . . . linquenda*, also in anaphora; where *frustra . . . frustra* share a stanza, the two gerundives link successive stanzas. — **ater**] The colour of death; all is sombre and sinister in Hades. — **flumine languido errans**] 'slowly meandering'. — **Cocytos**] The river of lamentation, tributary of the Styx. — **Danai genus, Sisyphus**] Another mythical pair, like 8 *Geryonen Tityonque*; the 'ill-famed brood of Danaus' are his fifty daughters; for the story, see on 3. 11. 23-52; Sisyphus was a lengendary king of Corinth. — **damnatusque longi laboris**] 'condemned to long torment'; meiosis, since the torment is eternal; when Death came to claim Sisyphus, he chained Death up instead; his punishment in Hades was to roll a stone up a hill for ever; when he reached the top, the stone tumbled down again; for the conventional imagery, see on 1. 4. 16-17; for Sisyphus as a mythical personage not to be believed in, see Cicero *Tusc.* 1. 10 (quoted in Introduction).

21-4] The stanza begins with an echo of a famous passage in Lucretius (3. 894-6):

> iam iam non domus accipiet te laeta, neque uxor
> optima nec dulces occurrent oscula nati
> praeripere et tacita pectus dulcedine tangent.

This is capped by the variation 'neque harum . . . sequetur' (cf. 2. 3. 17-20); at the same time *harum* gives the first hint of the décor of the monologue (made clearer in Stanza 7). — **harum arborum**] Deictic; the speaker points in the direction of the trees as he speaks; cf. 2. 3. 13 *huc* and 2. 11. 13 *hac*; presumably, in view of Stanza 7, the ornamental trees in the formal garden surrounded by the *peristylium* (see on 3. 10. 5-6 'nemus satum'); the scene, i.e., is the dining-room of a large Roman town house; see on 27 'pavimentum'. — **invisas cupressos**] Hated because of their association with death; a cypress branch was placed over the door of the house in which a dead man lay and funeral pyres were surrounded by cypress boughs; it is in this latter sense that the cypress follows its temporary owner when he has to leave all else behind. — **brevem dominum**] See on 2. 3. 17 (and *Sat.* 2. 2. 129-32, quoted there).

25-8]   At death, your temporary possessions pass to your heir; cf. 2. 3. 19-20, 3. 24. 61-2.
— absumet heres Caecuba dignior]   'your heir will drink up your Caecuban wines — and
with more right to them than you' (because he shows by drinking them that he knows
how to make proper use of them; a hint to Postumus to treat his guests more liberally);
for Caecuban wine, see on 1. 20. 9; cf. *Epist*. 1. 5. 12-14:

> quo mihi fortunam, si non conceditur uti?
> parcus ob heredis curam nimiumque severus
> adsidet insano.

— servata centum clavibus]   Suggests absurd precautions against theft; see on 1. 37. 5-6.
— mero]   Wine unmixed with water; suggests a drunken party. — tinguet pavimentum]
'will splash the paved floor' — presumably, of the dining-room where the conversation
is now taking place. — superbo]   (1) Because it is a 'proud vintage', (2) because the
extravagance with which good wine is splashed about is a symbol of contempt for
worldly possessions. — pontificum potiore cenis]   'more potent than dinners served by
the Pontifices'; i.e., than the wines (by implication, choice wines) served at such
dinners; a final rhetorical flourish to show the speaker waxing eloquent in his cups;
for priestly feasts, see on 1. 37. 2-4; for the contracted comparison, see on 2. 6. 14-15;
some favour *superbis*, a conjecture based on the Vatican codex *superbi*.

2. 15

Introduction: A sermon, closer to satire than to lyric, contrasting the extravagance of
Rome's merchant princes with the simple way of life of Rome's great men of the past.
   In this ode, H. is principally concerned with the decay of the old Roman practice
of owning a small country estate. Originally, the *villa* was no more than a farmhouse.
Such no doubt was H.'s own Sabine *villa* (3. 22. 5). A Roman in H.'s position could
count on his estate, most likely, for olive oil, vegetables, wine; see *Sat*. 2. 6, *Epist*. 1. 14.
But by H.'s day the *villa*, instead of serving as a powerful symbol of a traditional way
of life, had become a source of sterile ostentation. See White, *Roman Farming*, 1970,
418-20 ('Evolution of Farm Buildings'). Compare H. on this subject with Varro *RR*
1. 13. 6-7, where the speaker Scrofa complains 'Illic laudabatur villa, si habebat
culinam rusticam bonam', etc. . . . . 'Nunc contra villam urbanam [the technical term
for the main house on an estate] quam maximam ac politissimam habeant dant
operam . . . . laborant ut spectent sua aestiva triclinaria ad frigus orientis, hiberna ad
solem occidentem, potius quam, ut antiqui, in quam partem cella vinaria aut olearia
fenestras haberet. . .'. H.'s criticisms of extravagance are no doubt in part inspired by
official austerity programmes. But the ostentatious *villa* was to remain a stock theme
of moralistic writing: see, e.g., Seneca *Epist*. 86 (in which he contrasts the simplicity
of the *villa* of Scipio Africanus with modern luxury buildings). For a (non-ironic)
description of the *villa* of a rich Roman 100 years after H., see Pliny *Epist*. 2. 17 on
his *villa* at Laurentum, and 5. 6 on his *villa* in Tuscany. H. reverts to the theme in 2. 18;
cf. 3. 1. 33-40; also 3. 6 (where the contrast is between modern moral corruption at
Rome and the simple rural way of life of former days).
Structure: Two sections, each a complex sentence: lines 1-10, modern ostentation; lines
   10-20, the simple way of life of the great men of the past.
Metre: Alcaics; see 1. 9M.
1-5]   The inroads on agricultural land made by the *villae* of the rich and the ornamental
gardens which surround them; cf. 2. 18. 23-8, 3. 24. 1-4, also 3. 1. 32-40 (of seaside
villae built out on to the water). — Iam . . . relinquent]   Soon there will be no land
left to plough; the decline in the number of small estates and the disappearance of the
free agricultural labourer were serious economic problems; regiae]   'princely', i.e., such
as a king might build; but the wealthy at Rome are often described as *reges* — our
'merchant princes' is an appropriate equivalent since the very wealthy at Rome in
H.'s day mostly owed their wealth to business; the word stresses the power and the
arrogance of the wealthy, especially of the *patronus* in his relation to his *clientes* (see
Epist. 1. 17. 43 and Kiessling thereon); this sense is already in Plautus (see Fraenkel
18); for the polarity rich—poor cf. 1. 4. 13-14, 2. 18. 32-4; moles]   suggests the

sprawling, shapeless mass of these pretentious *villae*; cf. 3. 1. 34, 3. 29. 10 (ironically, of Maecenas' mansion on the Esquiline). − **undique latius extenta stagna**] = 'bigger and bigger ponds'; used for raising fish for the rich man's table. − **Lucrino lacu**] Close to Baiae, famous for its *villae*; ablative of comparison with *latius*; the *rex*, instead of living easily and simply off the produce of the land, goes to great trouble to secure exotic and expensive foods. − **platanusque caelebs**] The plane, an ornamental tree imported from Greece and Asia, is called *caelebs* because it was not used (like the elm) for supporting vines (a process called 'marrying' the tree to the vine; see *OLD maritare* 4, Catullus 62. 54, White, *Roman Farming* 236); cf. 4. 5. 30; the plane serves thus as the symbol of the sterility of the rich man's ostentation; contrast 8 *fertilibus*. − **evincet**] 'supplant'; the juxtaposition *caelebs-evincet* emphasises the subversion of the right order of things.

5-10] **violaria**] 'violet beds', condemned by Varro as unprofitable, *RR* 1. 35. 1 'violaria in fundo facere non est utile'; Virgil, *Georgics* 4. 32 commends them to beekeepers. − **myrtus**] Grown as a source of garlands for parties (1. 4. 9, 2. 7. 25, etc.). − **omnis copia narium**] = 'everything catering for the nostrils'; i.e., flowers grown for their scent, instead of crops; ornamental flowerbeds are probably meant, not flowers used for manufacturing scent (the best scents were imported). − **spargent . . . priori**] = 'will pervade with scent what under the previous owner were productive olive groves'. − **tum**] Picks up 5 *tum* (anaphora in asyndeton). − **laurea**] sc. *arbor*; another feature of an ornamental garden; called *spissa ramis* because it can be cut to provide a dense mass of branches and foliage. − **fervidos ictus**] The 'burning darts' of the summer sun, against which the bay tree serves as a shield.

10-12] Romulus symbolises Rome at its foundation; the elder Cato, the stern old morality of Rome at the height of its glory (and before it had surrendered to foreign decadence); their way of life served as an example ('praescriptum auspiciis') which was adopted and became the 'norma veterum'; for Romulus, see Ovid *Fasti* 3. 183-6; for Cato on *villae* and their construction, see *De Agr.* 4 and 14; Gellius 13. 24. 1 reports 'M. Cato . . . villas suas inexcultas et rudes ne tectorio quidem praelitas (i.e., left with their walls unplastered) fuisse dicit'. − **Non ita**] 'Very different' (*litotes*). − **intonsi**] 'bearded'; for a full beard as the symbol of old-fashioned austerity, see Cicero *Cael.* 33 on Claudius the censor: 'si illo austero more ac modo aliquis mihi ab inferis excitandus est ex barbatis illis − non hac barbula qua ista delectatur sed illa horrida quam in statuis antiquis atque imaginibus videmus'. − **auspiciis**] 'lead', 'example' (*OLD* 4). − **veterumque norma**] The practice of the leading men of old.

13-20] **census**] The official list of an individual's possessions drawn up by the censors. − **commune magnum**] 'the common interest was the big thing' (sc. *illis*); i.e., the thing that mattered (not 'the public fund was large' − hardly true, and not the point here); a phrase chosen to impress rather than to be pinned down; the idea, however, is a commonplace; see Cicero *Flac.* 28, *Mur.* 76; cf. Demosthenes *Olynth.* 3. 26. − **nulla. . . arcton**] i.e., the porticoes of former times were attached to public buildings (like that of the Theatre of Pompey); instead of simply saying no such porticoes were 'erected by individuals', H. substitutes the more vivid 'decempedis metata privatis'; **decempedis**] the symbol of the *architectus*, suggesting large-scale construction (cf. Cicero *Mil.* 84); **metata**] the passive sense is not uncommon; **privatis**] ablative with *decempedis* rather than dative of the person interested; **opacam arcton**] the shady northern light; the portico would be built to lie open to the north as a protection from the summer sun (cf. lines 9-10). − **fortuitum caespitem**] 'chance turf'; i.e., though not cultivated for the purpose, turf was put to service where abundant − presumably (in view of what follows) for the construction of walls; later, apparently, used only as a roofing material (cf. *Eclogues* 1. 68 'pauperis et tiguri congestum caespite culmen'). − **leges sinebant**] H. does not mean that in former times *villae* were built only of turf, but that the laws, by restricting the use of expensive materials, prevented people from turning up their noses at even the simplest of building materials. − **oppida . . . saxo**] 'while decreeing that public buildings were to be constructed at public expense and enjoining the use of fresh-cut stone for the decoration of temples'; H. has in mind that in his day *villae* were often faced with marble slabs (cf. 2. 18. 17 'tu secanda marmora locas sub ipsum funus'), whereas in former times this was restricted by law to temples; in those days, rough-hewn stone (*caementum*) plastered with stucco, or at most faced with second-hand marble, was enough for a private house (let alone a country *villa*); cf. Cato *De*

Agr. 14 'Parietes omnes . . . calce et caementis, pilas ex lapide angulari . . .'; Scipio
Africanus' *villa* was 'exstructam lapide quadrato' (Seneca *Epist.* 86. 4); H.'s lines have
been much misunderstood by those who have taken *decorare* as 'build' (e.g., by *OLD*,
which takes *oppida* as direct object of *iubentes* with the sense 'the inhabitants of
towns').

2. 16

Introduction: Everybody wants *otium* — the word is on everybody's lips; but most do not
know how to achieve it. Wealth and power do not ensure peace of mind: that goes
with a simple, traditional way of life and with acceptance of what you have. You,
Grosphus, are a wealthy farmer; my farm is small, but I am a poet.

Though highly thought of by Fraenkel (211-14), the ode tends to degenerate into a
series of moral commonplaces. The tone is too much that of the middle-aged poet
speaking to a young friend — Grosphus is, pretty clearly, the Pompeius Grosphus who
is commended to Iccius (the addressee of 1. 29) in *Epist.* 1. 12. 22-3: 'utere Pompeio
Grospho et, siquid petet, ultro / defer: nil Grosphus nisi verum orabit et aequum'.
Stanzas 3-4 are a reminiscence of a well-known passage in Lucretius (2. 20-39; see on
lines 9-12 and 13-16).

Structure: Stanzas 1-2 formulate a graphic first statement of H.'s case, structured by the
threefold *otium* (anaphora in asyndeton), each time in the emphatic position. Stanzas
3-4 represent a transposition to a more explicit statement of the same case. Stanzas 5-6
introduce a further transposition to a more impassioned rhetoric. Stanzas 7-10 are a
kind of appendix on the cheerful acceptance of one's lot.

Metre: Sapphics; see 1. 2M.

1-8] The word *otium* changes its meaning considerably from Catullus to H. In Catullus,
the man who is *otiosus* (10. 2, 50. 1) has time on his hands, nothing better, or more
urgent, to do than what he is doing; *otium* is 'leisure' (44. 15, 51. 13, 14 and 15);
Catullus and the young elegant *urbani* with whom he associates take it for granted;
mutatis mutandis, this is Cicero's concept of *otium* in the famous passage in his
defence of Sestius in 56 BC (*Sest.* 98): 'Quid est igitur propositum his rei publicae
gubernatoribus quod intueri et quo cursum suum dirigere debeant? Id quod est
praestantissimum maximumque optabile omnibus sanis et bonis et beatis, cum
dignitate otium'; it is still perhaps the sense in *Epode* 1. 7 and *Sat.* 1. 4. 138. But for
H.'s generation *otium* acquires almost neurotic overtones of escape from a way of
life which is actively unpleasant; see, e.g., the picture H. draws of Maecenas constantly
obsessed with cares of state in 3. 28.

The sense now is one more appropriate to men in their forties — something like
'retirement', either temporary (1. 1. 15-17) or permanent, as implied here (cf. 4. 15.
18). It is not simply that H. is older than Catullus. Nor need we suppose life more
unpleasant in Augustan Rome than a generation earlier. The explanation is rather the
emergence of a professional class for whom *negotia* do not interrupt leisure, but
actually preclude leisure; *otium* thus becomes something that has to be looked forward
to as a release. Cf. H.'s picture of a day in Rome and the escape to the country to which
he looks forward eagerly in *Sat.* 2. 6. — **Otium divos rogat**] The word, i.e., is on his
lips, but he does not understand that *otium* is an attitude to life, a state of mind — not
something to be saved up for; in 1. 1. 15-17 the *mercator* likewise looks forward to
otium — but is quickly bored by having nothing to do. — **in patenti prensus Aegaeo**]
'the man who is caught in mid-Aegean'; not the sailor, but the *mercator* or the soldier-
administrator who has to travel by sea to increase his fortune or to further his
ambitions; cf. *Georgics* 4. 421 'deprensis olim statio tutissima nautis'; for *prensus*
used as a noun equivalent cf. 3. 20. 16 *raptus.* — **bello furiosa Thrace**] = 'the war-
crazed Thracians'; the Thracians and the Parthians are represented as fighting to amass
riches and power as a means to securing a life of comfort and leisure (not for political
freedom or because they were naturally warlike); there were of course Eastern
monarchs who became immensely rich by war, but we may doubt whether their
minds were dominated on the battlefield by longing for *otium*; contrast 4. 15. 18,
where *otium* = something like 'freedom from war'. — **Medi**] = the Parthians, as in
1. 2. 51, etc. — **pharetra decori**] = 'a striking sight with their quivers'; the Parthians'

chief asset in battle was their armed cavalry. — **gemmis . . . auro**] The rewards of
victory; *gemmae* and *aurum* are symbols of wealth, *purpura* ('purple cloth', metonomy
for 'purple robes') the symbol of both wealth and authority; but the wearing of the
purple is more a Roman than an Eastern symbol and helps to prepare the way for the
return to the Roman scene in Stanza 3; Julius Caesar attempted to restrict the use of
purple to those entitled to wear it (Suetonius *Jul.* 43); cf. 2. 18. 8; **venale**] for the
word-division cf. 1. 2. 19, 1. 25. 11.

9-12] An Epicurean commonplace; cf. Lucretius, who also speaks of ornamental
ceilings, purple cloth and *gazae* (2. 20-39). — **gazae**] = 'oriental riches'; cf. 1. 29. 2. —
submovet] The technical term for pushing a crowd aside. — **miseros**] 'that reduce to
despondency'. — **tumultus**] The sense 'public disturbance', 'rioting crowd' is secured
by 'consularis lictor submovet' and is thus available as a metaphor for disturbances of
the mind. — **curas**] A strong word, 'anguishes'; cf. 2. 11. 18; it is clear from Stanza 6
that H. does not so much have in mind business worries or cares of state as the
morbid condition of mind of those who are unable to come to terms with the human
condition and keep trying to dispel the anguishes of maladjustment by a life of luxury,
the excitement of travel or active service, etc. — **laqueata tecta**] Ceilings divided into
squares and adorned with gold and ivory.

13-16] **vivitur parvo bene**] i.e., the simple life is the good life; cf. the fuller, less
epigrammatic statement in Lucretius 2. 20-21: 'Ergo corpoream ad naturam pauca
videmus / esse opus omnino, quae demant cumque dolorem'; the application of this
ad hominem appears in Stanza 9. — **paternum . . . salinum**] *paternum* emphasises
continuity and tradition (the man who carries on the way of life of his father),
splendet emphasises the decent dignity of the simple life (as opposed, e.g., to the
sordes of the poverty-stricken), *salinum* symbolises simplicity (the one adornment of
his table is the salt-cellar inherited from his father); probably, a silver salt-cellar, kept
clean and shining by constant use (unlike the useless glitter of the rich man's house;
cf. Catullus 23. 19 'culus tibi purior salillo est'); cf. the picture of H.'s simple table in
Sat. 1. 6. 114-18 and contrast the affected longing for the simple life of the singer in
Sat. 1. 3. 13-15, for whom a shell of salt and a dirty toga symbolise renunciation of
wealth: 'sit mihi mensa tripes et / concha salis puri et toga, quae defendere frigus /
quamvis crassa queat'; **in mensa tenui**] the small table suggests the slender repast it
carries; cf. the praise of the *victus tenuis* in *Sat.* 2. 2. 70 ff.; for H. playing the part of
modest host, see *Epist.* 1. 5. 1-7. — **levis somnos**] His sleep each night is light and
easy (unlike the man exhausted with fatigue, whose sleep is deep, or the man
consumed by cares, who cannot sleep at all; so 3. 1. 21-2, cf. 2. 11. 8 and 3. 21. 4; for
the plural, see on 2. 18. 16 *lunae*. — **timor**] Probably, fear of death and the gods (a
constant theme in Epicurean moralising). — **cupido sordidus**] Greed for material
possessions — a thing to be ashamed of; *cupido* is always masculine in H.

17-24] Further Epicurean commonplaces: why do we set ourselves many objectives
when life is short? Why do we attempt to escape when our anxieties travel with us?
With the former cf. 1. 4. 15 'vitae summa brevis spem nos vetat inchoare longam'; with
the latter *Epist.* 1. 11. 27 'caelum, non animum mutant, qui trans mare currunt' and
Lucretius 3. 1060-70. — **quid iaculamur multa?**] Why so many far-reaching ambitions?
(the ambitious man is like the hunter who casts javelin after javelin instead of confining
his hunting to sure shots and practical needs). — **brevi fortes aevo**] i.e., given the short-
ness of human life, stout-hearted ambition is misguided. — **quid . . . mutamus**] i.e., in
place of our native land. — **fugit**] Perfect; the tourist who travels to get away from it
all is a familiar figure in the late Republic and Augustan Rome. — **scandit . . . Euro**]
This stanza is omitted by Klingner and others on the assumption that it is a re-write
(or a draft) of 3. 1. 37-40 which has somehow found its way here; if it belongs, it
must represent an amplification of 18-20 — active service aboard a battleship or as a
cavalry officer likewise does not release us from the cares which plague us; **aeratas**]
'bronze-prowed'; i.e., clad with bronze plates, to reinforce the bow for ramming (if
warships are meant), or for decoration (if a private yacht, or something of the sort),
the former being the more likely; **vitiosa Cura**] 'morbid anxiety'; **cervis**] traditional
symbol of speed; **Euro**] symbol of storm; see on 1. 28. 25.

25-8] A bridge passage, leading to the theme 'no man has everything he wants in life'. —
laetus . . . curare] Two ideas are run together: our *animus* should (1) be content with
what we have, accept the present situation cheerfully, (2) dispel anxieties about the

future; **oderit**] jussive subjunctive, 'let it refuse to have anything to do with. . .';
cf. 1. 8. 4, etc. — **amara . . . risu**] = 'let it make the best of misfortune, with a gentle
smile'.

29-32] Amplification of 'nihil est ab omni parte beatum': Achilles was famous but died
young; Tithonus (husband of Aurora) was granted immortality but not eternal youth.
Time may change our lot — take from me to give to you. — **hora**] The passage of an
hour; for the idea of time as redistributing possessions or qualities, see 2. 5. 14-15.

33-40] The general statement of lines 31-2 is now spelled out. — **te**] Picked up by 34 *tibi*,
35 *te*, in preparation for the juxtaposition with 37 *mihi*. — **greges**] Flocks of sheep. —
circummugiunt] Sheep bleat, cattle moo; *circummugiunt* fits the latter, not the former
(the figure called 'zeugma'); cf. *Eclogue* 2. 21 'Mille meae Siculis errant in montibus
agnae'; Grosphus possessed large estates, presumably, in Sicily, which are contrasted
with the 'parva rura' of H.'s Sabine farm; for the division *circum- / mugiunt*, see on
1. 2. 19. — **hinnitum**] The final syllable is elided; cf. 2. 2. 18, 4. 2. 22-3, *CS* 47. — **apta**
quadrigis equa] = 'the mare in training for chariot-racing', a symbol of an extravagant
way of life; see on 1. 1. 3-6; mares were preferred for racing; the singular for a more
vivid image. — **te . . . lanae**] The best cloth was subjected to dyeing in two separate
stages; **Afro**] because the *murex* was found off the African coast. — **parva rura**] H.'s
Sabine farm; for a description, see *Sat.* 2. 6. 1-3. — **spiritum tenuem**] H. likes to
maintain that his inspiration is for slender themes only (not epic, not Pindaric ode,
etc.); cf. 1. 6, 4. 2. 27-32; but *tenuem* also with moral overtones as in line 14; with
spiritum cf. 4. 3. 24 *spiro*. — **Parca non mendax**] 'Fate that does not lie'; but also a pun
on *Parca* ('she who is sparing in her gifts'); H. had early been led to hope that this is
what life held in store for him and had not been disappointed. — **malignum spernere**
volgus] Cf. 3. 1. 1; *malignum* = (1) 'envious', (2) 'niggardly'.

2. 17

Introduction: To Maecenas: 'Stop pestering me with complaints about your health. You
and I will die together: this is no idle promise; the fates have decided thus. Look how we
were both snatched recently from death. Let us offer appropriate thanks.'

A witty poem on a solemn theme (cf. 2. 13). H. has plainly no intention of dying
(though it would be ill-omened for him to say so in as many words): to assure his friend
of their common fate is equal, therefore, to telling him his fears of imminent death are
groundless. Not a very convincing reassurance if Maecenas were, or believed himself to
be, in actual danger of dying. Maecenas was, however, a notorious hypochondriac (and
well aware of the fact) who affected a willingness to cling to life, however afflicted with
infirmity:

> Debilem facito manu, debilem pede coxo,
> tuber adstrue gibberum, lubricos quate dentes:
> vita dum superest, bene est; hanc mihi, vel acuta
> si sedeam cruce, sustine. . . .

Despite the indignant, long-winded and somewhat humourless strictures of Seneca
(*Epist.* 101. 10-14), the lines are hardly to be taken seriously. H. at any rate does not
take his friend seriously, as the opening line of his poem shows. Nor is he heartless: the
poem, despite the wit, serves as an eloquent testimony to genuine friendship; H.'s hope
that their friendship will last as long as he lives shines through the persiflage. In fact,
H. died in 8 BC, 59 days after Maecenas (assuming the usual reconstruction of the text
of Suetonius' biography is right) and was buried 'iuxta Maecenatis tumulum'.

For Maecenas' health, see Pliny *NH* 7. 54 ('Perpetua febris. . . .Eidem triennio supremo
nullo horae momento contigit somnus'); for a fragment of his verse expressing loftier
principles, see Seneca *Epist.* 92. 35 ('Nec tumulum curo: sepelit natura relictos'); for an
estimate of his character by Seneca (who abominated him), see *Epist.* 114. 4-8, cf. *Epist.*
19. 9.

Structure: Stanza 1, impatient reassurance; Stanzas 2-4, 'we will die together'; Stanzas 5-8,
'it is in the stars, as recent events have shown'.

Metre: Alcaics; see 1. 9M.

1-4] **exanimas**] The primary sense is 'frighten me to death' (with your lamentations) as in
3. 12. 2; cf. *Sat*. 1. 4. 126-7 'avidos vicinum funus ut aegros / exanimat mortisque metu
sibi parcere cogit'; senses *OLD* 2, 'you're killing *me*' (with your fears of death) and *OLD*
1, (your lamentations) 'leave me out of breath' are present as overtones, to secure a
challenging, paradoxical opening. — **nec dis amicum est**] The gods disapprove because
Maecenas' fated end has not arrived; *amicum* = *gratum*. — **nec mihi**] H. disapproves
because he does not want to lose his friend; but the logic of the poem's wit suggests
more urgent grounds for disapproval: if Maecenas dies, H.'s death must also be imminent,
as Stanza 2 proceeds to argue. — **mearum . . . rerum**] Cf. 1. 1. 2 'dulce decus meum'.

5-8] Stanza 2 toys with an ironic paradox for which *exanimas* has prepared the way: 'If
you are really dying, then I must be doomed too, since we have only one *anima* between
us.' — **meae partem animae**] For the idea cf. 1. 3. 8 'animae dimidium meae' (of Virgil);
partem = 'half'; *animae* picks up *exanimas*. — **si rapit maturior vis**] = 'if you are the first
to be snatched away'; i.e., if, as Maecenas maintains, he is already dying; *rapit* cannot,
like an English present, refer to the future; cf. 3. 9. 17-20; for the sense cf. 2. 13. 20;
maturior] quicker to act than the *vis* which awaits H. — **quid moror altera**] 'why do I,
your other half, linger on?'; H. is not threatening to commit suicide (as Stanza 3
confirms) but using the logic of the poem's hypothesis (that he and Maecenas share a
single *anima*) to reassure his friend: if Maecenas is dying, how is it that H. shows no
signs of being at death's door? **altera**] i.e., 'I who am the other half'; appositional
expansion of the unexpressed subject of *moror*, as *partem* expands *te*; NH favour
alteram ('why do I worry about the other half' — i.e., 'myself'). — **nec carus aeque**] sc.
'alteris', 'I who am a poor thing without you', 'who will want me without you?' — **nec
superstes integer**] = 'a maimed survivor with no expectation of life'.

8-12] **ille dies**] The day of Maecenas' death — when it comes. — **utramque ducet ruinam**]
= 'the overthrow of both of us'; the future *ducet* rejects the present *rapit*. — **Non ego . . .
sacramentum**] i.e., H.'s words are not the sort of promise people make (and then back
out of) that they will commit suicide when their friend dies; H. will not be able to help
himself; **sacramentum**] properly, the military oath of allegiance sworn on enlistment,
here as a metaphor of the two-man expedition Maecenas will lead to the underworld. —
ibimus, ibimus] 'we', not 'I'; the repetition for solemnity and pathos (see on 2. 14. 1) —
a rise in the level of plangency in preparation for the grand imagery of Stanza 4. —
utcumque praecedes] *utcumque* is frequentative (as elsewhere in H.; cf. 3. 4. 29, see on
1. 17. 10) and here spatial ('wherever') rather than temporal ('whenever'); when the
day of their common death comes, Maecenas will lead the way (as befits his greater
dignity) and they will make their way together — wherever the journey takes them. —
supremum . . . parati] Echoes of Catullus 11. 1 and 13-14.

13-16] **Chimaerae**] A mythical monster (a lion in front, a dragon behind) who prowled
the entrance of Hades, breathing fire. — **spiritus**] 'breath'. — **nec . . . Gyges**] 'not 100-
handed Gyges, supposing he were to rise to his feet again'; Gyges was supposed to lie
spreadeagled in Hades beneath the weight of a mountain; the MSS have *gigas*; *Gyges*
(also called *Gyas* and *Gyes*) is due to Muret; the same confusion in 3. 4. 69. — **divellet**]
i.e., from Maecenas' side; future indicative despite the preceding subjunctive *resurgat*;
in such 'illogical' conditional sentences, the unlikelihood of the hypothesis does not
diminish the certainty of the outcome; cf. lines 28-9 'sustulerat . . . levasset', 3. 3. 7-8
'inlabatur . . . ferient', 3. 16. 3-7 'munierant . . . risissent'.

17-22] Stars in the ascendant at the hour of one's birth were believed to influence one's
fate; H. substitutes signs of the zodiac for planets — perhaps to indicate his ignorance of
the subject; at any rate, by making clear he has not informed himself on the matter
(i.e., had his horoscope cast), he implies a proper scepticism; cf. 1. 11; it is not necessary
to assume that Maecenas was a believer, though this is probable. — **adspicit**] Present
because the planet presiding over your birth continues to preside over your destiny. —
pars . . . horae] i.e., a more stormy influence than Libra in one's hour of birth. —
tyrannus . . . undae] Because the sun enters Capricorn at the winter solstice, a season of
storms; **Hesperiae undae**] = 'in Italian waters'. — **utrumque . . . astrum**] As *uterque
nostrum* = 'both of us', so 'utrumque nostrum astrum' = 'both your star and mine';
though H. knows nothing of the subject, he can assert the 'incredible correspondence' of
their stars because of the clear evidence (adduced in the following lines) of a parallel
destiny; some take 'pars violentior natalis horae' with all three signs; we may suspect
H.'s astrological lore is intended to sound vaguely absurd, as is the conclusion so

confidently drawn from it; for the absence of caesura in line 21, see 1. 9M.

22-32] The common destiny of Maecenas and H. is pointed to by the fact that each has already had a narrow escape from death. For H.'s escape, see 2. 13, 3. 4. 27 and 3. 8. 6-12. For the attitude of thinking Romans to such matters, see Cicero *de Div*. 2. 92, who ridicules the belief 'eadem omnibus qui eodem statu caeli et stellarum nati sint accidere necesse esse'; cf. on 1. 11. 1-3. There is no need to assume both escapes occurred the same day or even the same year: indeed, it would be more in common with the ironic logic of the poem if they did not — Maecenas, i.e., was saved from death because he was destined to die along with H.; similarly, H. did not die when the tree fell on him because he was destined to die along with Maecenas. — **te . . . eripuit**] 'the protection of Jupiter, all resplendent, snatched you from dastardly Saturn'; Jupiter and Saturn are of course the planets, but the idea of a cosmic conflict between the gods Jupiter and Saturn (reminiscent of their legendary conflict) is obviously present as an overtone. — **tardavit alas**] Cf. Herodotus 1. 91, where Apollo claims to have delayed the death of Croesus by three years, and *Aen*. 8. 398-9, where Vulcan remarks that the fall of Troy could have been delayed a further ten years. — **cum . . . sonum**] Presumably, the occasion is that alluded to in 1. 20. 4-8; **ter crepuit sonum**] = 'gave three rounds of applause'; cf. 1. 20. 3-4. — **me . . . sustulerat**] 'a tree trunk, collapsing on my brain would have carried me off'; for the indicative, see on 15 *divellet*. —**nisi Faunus . . . levasset**] For Faunus as protector of H. on his farm, see 1. 17. 1-4, 3. 18. 1-8; cf. 1. 4. 11-12; *dextra* stresses the personal intervention of the god. — **Mercurialium custos virorum**] = 'protector of poets'; for the idea, see 2. 7. 13-20; cf. 1. 10. 1-4, 3. 11. 1-8; for the phrase cf. Catullus 3. 2 'hominum Venustiorum'; *Mercurialium* is perhaps deliberately chosen as (in the sense 'under the influence of the planet Mercury') a technical term of astrology. — **reddere . . . agnam**] A lavish expression of thanks from Maecenas, a humble offering from H., as befits each; **victimas**] a number of beasts is indicated, if not a hecatomb; H. will content himself with a 'modest lamb'; cf. 4. 2. 53-60, where ten bulls and ten cows are suggested as an appropriate sacrifice for Antonius on the return of Caesar, and a heifer for H.; for the animals used in sacrifices, see on 3. 23. 4; **aedemque votivam**] a temple to Jove is not something that can be put in hand overnight; Maecenas is to bind himself by a vow to construct it; cf. 4. 1. 19; **feriemus**] H. will carry out the sacrifice with his own hands (Maecenas' sacrifice will presumably be carried out by attendants).

2. 18

Introduction: A follow-up to 2. 15, on the misguided extravagance of those who build themselves elaborate houses and villas. Compare the views of Cicero *Off*. 1. 139-40:

> Ornanda est enim dignitas domo, non ex domo tota quaerenda. . . . Cavendum autem est, praesertim si ipse aedifices, ne extra modum sumptu et magnificentia prodeas; quo in genere multum mali etiam in exemplo est. Studiose enim plerique praesertim in hanc partem facta principum imitantur, et L. Luculli, summi viri, virtutem quis? at quam multi villarum magnificentiam imitati!

H. speaks throughout from the point of view of one who is 'libertino patre natus' (*Sat*. 1. 6. 6, etc., *Epist*. 1. 20. 20) in a society where the meteoric rise of freedmen to wealth and power was common: 'the commercial class profited in the Revolution, by purchasing the land of the prescribed' (Syme, *Roman Revolution* 354). In the Rome of Augustus, the great *patronus* may be a social parvenu, ostentatiously wealthy in his style of life at Rome, oblivious, in the development of his country estates, of his obligations to his newly-acquired *clientes*. H. prefers his own humbler way of life.

Structure: Two basic themes, each occupying 14 lines, are followed by a 12-line tail-piece. Theme A asserts the simplicity of H.'s personal way of life: the four negative statements of lines 1-8 are followed by the two positive statements of lines 9-14; the former reject, the latter affirm. The passage to theme B is marked by the abrupt 'Truditur dies die . . .': where H. has the sense to limit his ambitions (11-12 'nihil supra / deos lacesso'), his unnamed addressee's extravagance is limited neither by thoughts of human mortality (lines 15-22), nor by consideration for the innocent victims of his extravagance (lines 23-8). The two themes are drawn together in lines 29-40: death awaits rich man and poor man alike. The internal organisation of the three sections of the poem is tight, enjambment between couplets being unusually marked. The ode differs, i.e., from other odes written in distichs where a conflict between 2-line metrical structure and 4-line syntactical structure seems clearly intended (see 1. 3M) and is for that reason printed in couplets rather than 4-line stanzas.

Metre: Hipponacteans (named after the Greek iambic poet Hipponax, famed for his invective verse and traditionally the inventor of the limping iambic metre, also called scazons). The short lines consist of 3½ trochees ('trochaic dimeter catalectic'):

$$— \cup — \cup — \cup \underset{\smile}{\cup}$$

The long lines are normal iambic lines (with the usual permitted substitutions) minus the last syllable ('iambic trimeter catalectic'):

$$\bar{\cup} — \cup — \bar{\cup} \wedge — \cup — \bar{\cup} — \bar{\cup}$$

1-8] Non ebur neque aureum lacunar] Cf. 1. 31. 6 'non aurum aut ebur Indicum'; **ebur]** impressionistic rather than specific; either ivory furniture or ivory ornamentation may be implied; **aureum]** i.e., gilded; **lacunar]** cf. 2. 16. 11-12 'laqueata tecta'. — **mea]** Contrasted with 17 *tu*. — **renidet]** 'shines' (i.e., reflects the light); often of a flashing smile or grimace (as 3. 6. 12) but not necessarily pejorative, as 2. 5. 19 shows. — **domo]** Suggests a town house rather than a country *villa*. — **trabes Hymettiae]** Architraves of marble from Hymettus, fulfilling the function of wooden rafters. — **columnas . . . Africa]** Numidian marble was equally famous; nothing but the best, in short, however tasteless the combination. — **neque Attali . . . occupavi]** = 'nor have I set myself up in a princely mansion, like an heir of King Attalus whom nobody knew about'; a complex pattern of ambiguities, building up a striking satirical phrase: the negative negates the whole statement and therefore each item in it — H. is not 'Attali ignotus heres', he has not taken up residence in a *regia*; cf. 3. 12. 11; Attalus III of Pergamum symbolises the rich Eastern monarch (cf. 1. 1. 12); he bequeathed his kingdom to Rome, so in a sense all Romans were his heirs; 'ignotus heres', therefore, of the nonentity, equally unknown to Attalus and to his fellow-Romans, whose suddenly-acquired fortune enables him to live as if he had personally inherited Attalus' riches; **regiam]** if he were indeed heir of Attalus in the legal sense, the *nouveau riche* would perhaps be entitled to live in a palace; but *regia* is the word also for the 'princely mansion' at Rome of the wealthy merchant, etc. (cf. 2. 15. 1-2 'regiae moles'); **occupavi]** 'appropriated', 'taken possession of', always with the sense of taking by force, or taking what does not belong to you, or beating others to something to which you have no more right than they have — as an unknown rogue might turn up, fraudulently representing himself as the heir to a rich man's fortune, and then set himself up in the rich man's house. — **Laconicas purpuras]** Most likely, purple dresses made from wool (called 'Spartan', but actually from Tarentum, a Spartan colony); according to Pliny *NH* 8. 190, the most highly-prized wool is 'what in Italy is called Greek, but elsewhere is called Italian'; cf. Columella *RR* 7. 2. 3 (the best wool is that from Tarentum) and Griffin, 'Augustan poetry and the life of luxury', *JRS* 76, 1976, 92; for 'Spartan' Tarentum cf. 3. 5. 56; for purple dress, see on 2. 16. 7. — **trahunt]** 'trail' because respectable *matronae* wore *stolae* reaching to the ground; see Balsdon, *Roman Women* 252-3; the word is chosen for its satirical effect, but also to evoke the Homeric ἑλκεσίπεπλοι; H.'s object is to build up the scene in the rich parvenu's *atrium* during the morning *salutatio*; the interpretation, therefore, of *trahunt* as 'spin', favoured by some, is less likely; moreover, wool is dyed after spinning, not before. — **honestae clientae]** Oxymoron: the parvenu lives in such style that his *atrium* is filled with elegantly gowned respectable *matronae* (the wives of his *clientes*, come to pay their respects — or, possibly, the widows of proscribed *nobiles* seeking his protection), not, e.g., *libertinae* or *meretrices* — proof positive that he has arrived; the wearing of the purple by those not entitled to it was a controversial issue (for its adoption by women, see Balsdon 33-7) and not in itself proof of social status (4. 13. 13), but the context makes it clear that the *honestae clientae* are the real thing, however dubious the status of their new-found *patronus*.

9-14] fides] = 'honesty' — the feeling people around H. have that he is to be trusted. —
ingeni benigna vena] 'an unstinting vein of talent'; *vena* suggests a vein of precious
metal. — **pauperemque . . . petit]** 'though my way of life is modest, the rich man
comes to visit me' (instead of expecting H. to call on him). — **supra]** 'beyond what I
have'. — **lacesso]** 'importune'. — **potentem amicum]** 'my influential friend'; the
primary reference is to the *dives* of line 10, though allusion to Maecenas is easily
felt. — **largiora flagito]** 'pester for more generous gifts'. — **satis . . . Sabinis]** = 'well
enough off and happy enough with my Sabine farm and nothing else'; cf. *Sat.* 2. 6. 4
'nil amplius oro', *Epodes* 1. 31-2 'satis superque me benignitas tua ditavit'; for the
Sabine farm, see 2. 6. 5-8 and 3. 16. 33-8; H. implies it was the only property he
owned; presumably, when in Rome he lived in a rented apartment — or stayed with
Maecenas; his farm, i.e., was not a holiday place, but his real home; see on 1. 7. 10-14;
Sabinis is masculine plural, the name of the people of the district serving to designate
an estate there; cf. 3. 4. 22; thus in Pliny's letters, 'in Tuscos' regularly = 'to my
Etruscan estate'.

15-28] Truditur dies die] Each day is thrust aside by the day following, like a member of
an impatient crowd who elbows his way past the man in front of him. — **novaeque . . .
lunae]** Each new moon proceeds remorselessly to the completion of its cycle; with the
plural cf. 4. 7. 13 and Catullus 5. 4 'soles occidere et redire possunt' and 8. 3 'fulsere
quondam candidi tibi soles'; also 2. 16. 15 'somnos'. — **tu]** Emphatic, 'and yet *you*
(though time keeps passing by) . . .'; H.'s addressee is not named; cf. 2. 5; we might
suppose from hints in lines 10 and 12 that Maecenas is meant here also, but lines
23-8 preclude that; presumably, the unspecified adversary of satirical writing. —
secanda marmora locas] 'let out a contract for cutting marble'; see on 2. 15. 20. —
sub ipsum funus] 'right up to the hour of your death'; cf. 1. 8. 14-15. — **inmemor]**
'with no thought for'. — **struis domos]** town houses at Rome or elsewhere. — **marisque
. . . litora]** 'you are all eagerness to push forward the shore of the sea that breaks on
Baiae' (the famous luxury resort between Cumae and Puteoli on the Bay of Naples);
cf. 3. 4. 24; with *obstrepentis* cf. 3. 30. 10, 4. 14. 48 — **parum . . . ripa]** 'not wealthy
enough so long as the shore hems you in'; i.e., unless you can demonstrate your wealth
by building out from the shore on reclaimed land (naturally more expensive than
building on solid ground); cf. 3. 1. 33-7, 3. 24. 1-4. — **quid . . . avarus?]** Not content
with invading the sea, the *nouveau riche* builds himself a huge *villa* with surrounding
gardens, appropriating the land of tenant farmers and evicting them in the process;
cf. the 'regiae moles' of 2. 15 which will leave no land left for agriculture; **quid quod?]**
'what shall I say of the fact that'; **usque . . . terminos]** = 'you even rip up your
neighbours' boundary stones'; the neighbours are tenant farmers; the *nouveau riche*
has acquired their land in order to redevelop it as a single estate in whose elegant
grounds there is no place for the *clientes* he has taken over with the land acquired;
to remove a boundary stone was a crime, to dispossess a *cliens* worse still; the Laws
of the Twelve Tables provided 'Patronus si clienti fraudem fecerit, sacer esto'; cf. *Aen.*
6. 609 (among the blackest crimes punished in Tartarus is 'fraus innexa clienti');
ultra . . . salis avarus] behaviour recalling that of Remus, who arrogantly jumped
over the walls being built by his brother Romulus and was killed by him with the
words 'sic deinde, quicumque alius transiliet moenia mea' (Livy 1. 5. 2); for H.'s
own tenant farmers, see *Epist.* 1. 14. 2-3. — **in sinu ferens . . . natos]** i.e., clasping
them to their breast; the wife perhaps carries the gods, the father the children; the
picture of the dispossessed farmer with his household gods, his wife and children
recalls the Roman archetypal image of the refugee, Aeneas fleeing from Troy; see,
e.g., *Aen.* 2. 717-25; for a more realistic picture of the dispossessed farmer, see
Eclogue 1; **sordidosque natos]** the graphic final touch which shows H.'s characteristic
sympathy with the underdog; cf. the foreign princess in 3. 2. 6-12, Neobule in 3. 12;
the plural *natos* covers both sons and daughters.

**29-32] The arrogant *nouveau riche* may not live to see his mansion built; the only
palace he can be sure of occupying is that of Orcus. — **Nulla . . . manet erum]** 'No
more certain palace awaits the rich master than the destined goal of greedy Orcus'; for
aula of a rich man's palace cf. 2. 10. 8; since *finis* is masculine elsewhere in the *Odes*
(though feminine in *Epodes* 17.36), some take *destinata* with *aula*, but this is less
natural; **rapacis Orci]** Orcus is greedy too, but his greed is exercised in snatching us
away from life in the midst of plans for the future; for Orcus, see on 1. 28. 10; **divitem**

erum] *erus*, the slave's word for his master, here represents the *nouveau riche* in relation to his *familia*; in addition to his slaves, the *liberti* of a rich *patronus* often continued to live under his roof, and might continue to refer to him as *erus*, especially in speaking to slaves; NH take *erum* as object of *tendis*.

32-40]   quid ultra tendis?] = 'why are you always reaching out in fresh directions?'; cf. *Aen*. 12. 938 'ulterius ne tende odiis'); though the reference is to the *nouveau riche*'s insatiable ambitions, the phrase recalls the constant impulse to extend the land he controls satirised in lines 17-28. — **aequa tellus recluditur]** Two levels of meaning, the obvious and the imaginative, mingle in an effective ambiguity: (1) an equal expanse of earth is opened up (i.e., to receive the ashes of rich man and poor man alike); (2) 'an impartial earth unlocks its doors to admit each alike to the Underworld'; for the idea cf. 1. 4. 13-14, 2. 3. 21-4, 2. 14. 9-12, 3. 1. 14. — **regumque pueris]** Recalls 5 'Attali ignotus heres'. — **satelles Orci]** Most likely, Charon; possibly Mercury (favoured by NH); *satelles* suggests the sort of attendant who can usually be bribed, but there is no hope of bribing Charon. — **callidum Promethea]** 'wily Prometheus'; for Prometheus in the underworld, see on 2. 13. 37. — **revexit]** i.e., ferried back across the Styx to life. — **hic, hic]** Charon, not Orcus; he is represented as a sympathetic minor official who does what he can to alleviate the lot of the deserving poor among his passengers, while keeping a close watch upon the undeserving rich; Orcus on the other hand is merciless (cf. 2. 3. 24 'nil miserantis Orci'); a rallentando image, to slacken the tension at the end of the ode. — **levare . . . vocatus atque non vocatus audit]** 'when called upon to lighten the poor man's lot now that his life of trials is over, answers the entreaty — and even if not entreated, acts just the same'; illogical but effective anacoluthon; *laboribus* equally with *levare* and with *functum*.

2. 19

Introduction: In 2. 13. 21-40 H. asks us to imagine he 'almost saw' Sappho and Alcaeus performing their poetry to an enraptured underworld audience. We are now asked to imagine he saw Bacchus 'in remotis rupibus' instructing an attentive class of nymphs and satyrs. In 2. 13 the fantasy is explored, in an ironic pretence of the narrative mode, for its poetic possibilities; 2. 19 affects (like 3. 25) a dithyrambic fervour — H. represents himself as still in an inspired trance (Stanza 2), in which he declaims a hymn of praise to Bacchus. The dominant note is, as in 2. 13, one of sophisticated irony; there are evident similarities with Callimachus (cf., e.g., *Hymn* 2, to Apollo), which perhaps explains the interruption of the dithyrambic flow by the curiously rational and prosaic Stanza 7; this is not to say of course that H. did not believe in the reality of his inspiration.

Structure: Stanza 1, introductory; Stanza 2, bridge to hymn; Stanzas 3-6, hymn; Stanza 7, lucid interval; Stanza 8, hymn concluded. The stanzas are heavily endstopped.

Metre: Alcaics; see 1. 9M. Considered by some one of the earliest of the *Odes* because it departs (in Stanzas 3, 4 and 5) from the rules which H. later set himself with regard to the caesura after syllable 5 of line 3; see Raven, *Latin Metre* 147.

1-4]   vidi docentem] The rational tone of the description suggests a scene H. came upon by accident; Fraenkel 200-201 misses the Callimachean overtones of H.'s reconstruction of his adventure, whether we take it as a transposition of some quasi-visionary experience or wholly fanciful; Bacchus (here in his Dionysiac role of patron of poetry; cf. 3. 25, see on 3. 8. 7) is represented as a *grammaticus* declaiming to his class, who repeat the declaimed text after him (line by line, or in short snatches), as part of the process of learning the right way to accent the lines, etc.; cf. *Epist*. 1. 18. 12-14 (of the sycophantic guest at a dinner party who echoes his host's every remark) 'sic iterat voces et verba cadentia tollit, / ut puerum saevo credas dictata magistro / reddere'; this was how H. learnt his Livius from Orbilius, *Epist*. 2. 1. 70-71 'memini quae [= carmina Livi] plagosum mihi parvo / Orbilium dictare'; cf. H. instructing the chorus of boys and girls for the *Carmen Saeculare*, 4. 6. 31-44. — **credite posteri]** The appeal for suspension of disbelief, in this ironic context, is a further hint that H. does not expect to be taken seriously. — **Nymphas]** Cf. 3. 25. 14-15. — **auris acutas]** Unlike Cerberus in 2. 13. 34-5, who relaxes as he listens to the poetry of Sappho and Alcaeus, so that his ears droop, Bacchus' class is alert. — **capripedum]** 'goat-footed'; so Lucretius 4. 580; properly, an attribute of Pan and Faunus; satyrs in Greek art are human-shaped, with little horns, sharp-pointed ears and short tails.

5-8] H. could not see the god without catching the Bacchic frenzy, which is still fresh as he writes, inspiring a trance halfway between awe and exhilaration. – Euhoe] Two syllables. – plenoque Bacchi pectore] The *pectus* is the site of the *mens* (as well as the *animus*); since the god is in control there, H.'s thoughts assume the frenzied eloquence of inspiration; an interpretation of the original meaning of ἐνθουσιασμός; *pleno pectore* may be taken as locative or ablative of attendant circumstances; cf. 3. 25. 1-2 'tui plenum'. – laetatur, euhoe] For the rhythm, see on 1. 16. 3. – parce] Because a touch of Bacchus' *thyrsos* caused a frenzy bordering on madness; cf. 4. 1. 2. – gravi] i.e., terrible in its consequences.

9-24] Fas est] Because the god has chosen him to proclaim his praises; H. is not divulging secret rites irresponsibly; contrast 1. 18. 11-12; the praises of Bacchus follow in Stanzas 3-6; cf. Propertius 3. 17 and Ovid *Tristia* 5. 3 for less economical employment of similar material. – pervicacis] 'unwearying', usually with pejorative overtones ('relentless', etc.); cf. 3. 3. 70, *Epodes* 17. 14. – Thyiadas] = Maenadas; cf. 3. 15. 10. – vinique . . . mella] Traditional gifts of Dionysus-Bacchus to mankind, structured as a tricolon crescendo; an echo perhaps of Euripides *Bacchae* 141 and 704-11; truncis lapsa mella] symbol of the golden age or an idyllic pastoral existence; cf. *Eclogues* 4. 30 'durae quercus sudabunt roscida mella'; iterare] the basic sense in the *Odes* is 'go over again', 'repeat'; cf. 1. 7. 32, 1. 34. 4, 3. 3. 62; here = 'sing afresh of' (i.e., in my turn). – fas] Picks up 9 *fas* (anaphora in asyndeton); cf. 17, 18, 21 *tu*. – beatae coniugis] Ariadne, saved by Bacchus from the Island of Dia (see, e.g., Catullus 64. 251-3); she is described as *beatae* ('fortunate', 'blessed') because of her subsequent deification. – honorem] In Ovid *Fasti* 3. 509-16 Bacchus personally transports Ariadne to heaven and changes into a new constellation ('Corona') the jewelled crown given her by Venus. – tectaque Penthei disiecta] For the destruction of the palace of King Pentheus of Thebes, see Euripides' *Bacchae*; *Penthei* counts as three syllables. – Thracis . . . Lycurgi] Lycurgus, king of the Edonians, denied the divinity of Bacchus and drove him from his kingdom; for this he was struck blind by Zeus (*Il.* 6. 130-40; there are varying versions of the legend). – flectis] Literally, 'turn in their course', but often = little more than 'control', 'command' (*OLD* 7); a reference to legends that Dionysus in his Eastern travels was able to cross rivers by stopping them in their course and to cross the Red Sea by a magical parting of its waters; cf. Ovid *Tristia* 5. 3. 23-4, Propertius 3. 17. 27. – separatis] = 'remote'. – uvidus] = 'in your cups'; the word effectively undercuts any note of piety. – nodo . . . crinis] 'bind snakes in the hair of the women of the Bistones (in Thrace) without hurt'; i.e., inspire them to do this when they worship Bacchus; sine fraude] 'with no evil intent', i.e., not intending them harm; an archaic and legal expression. – tu, cum parentis . . . mala] For the Giants and their assault on Jove (already alluded to 2. 12. 6-9), see 3. 4. 49-75; parentis regna] the kingdom of Jove, the father of gods and men; per arduum scanderet] = 'were scrambling up to heaven' (by piling one mountain-top on another); cf. 3. 4. 51-2; a different version in *Georgics* 1. 278-83; Rhoetum] cf. 3. 4. 55; elsewhere called Eurytus (Rhoetus is elsewhere the name of a Centaur who fought with the Lapithae); retorsisti . . . mala] i.e., Bacchus, on joining in the fray, assumed the form of a lion; this version only here, but *Homeric Hymn* 7. 44 has Dionysus assuming lion shape to defend himself against pirates; perhaps, however, we are meant to think of Dionysus attacking with the aid of a lion under his command, as on a vase found at Spina (so Pöschl, *Hermes* 101, 1973, 218-21); horribilique mala] 'with terrible jaw'; the adjective as usual agrees with one noun, but goes in sense with both; cf. 3. 12. 12 *segni*.

25-8] This oddly matter-of-fact stanza interrupts the simulated lyric flow. – quamquam] Introduces a qualifying afterthought equivalent to a separate statement; see *L&S* II, Leumann-Hofmann 737 ('quamquam correctivum'); common in Cicero. – aptior] With *dictus*. – et iocis ludoque] Like *choreis* with *aptior*. – non sat idoneus pugnae] = 'not really a god for a fight'; cf. 3. 26. 1 'puellis idoneus'. – sed idem . . . belli] = 'but despite that, as in peace, so too in war, you were in the midst of things'; for *idem*, 'you, the same person' (*OLD* 3) cf. 2. 10. 16, 3. 4. 67, etc.; mediusque] = 'pacis medius mediusque belli'; cf. 1. 30. 6, 3. 1. 12, 3. 4. 11, (with *-ve*) 2. 7. 25.

29-32] Not so much a resumption of the praises of Stanzas 3-6 as an explanatory footnote, justifying the statement of Stanza 7 and serving as a concluding rallentando (cf. 2. 18. 36-40). Dionysus went down to the underworld to fetch back his mother Semele. – insons] i.e., offering no harm to the visitor when he saw his golden horn. – Cerberus]

Cf. 2. 13. 33-5, 3. 11. 16-24. — **aureo cornu**] An ancient symbol of strength or power; cf. 3. 21. 18; in Euripides' *Bacchae* Dionysus is ταυροκέρως; cf. Propertius 3. 17. 19; Tibullus 2. 1. 3. — **leniter atterens caudam**] 'gently rubbing his tail against you'. — **recedentis pedes**] 'your feet as you departed'. — **trilingui ore**] Presumably, the tongues of Cerberus' three mouths; cf. 3. 11. 20. — **tetigitque**] = 'tetigit tetigitque'; cf. 28 *mediusque*.

2. 20

Introduction: A provisional ironic assertion of the poet's immortality, in anticipation of the definitive statement of claim (with details of the basis for it) in 3. 30; cf. the more modestly-stated claim *Epist.* 1. 20. 20-23:

> me libertino natum patre et in tenui re
> maiores pinnas nido extendisse loqueris,
> ut, quantum generi demas, virtutibus addas;
> me primis urbis belli placuisse domique.

Where 3. 30. 6-7 'non omnis moriar multaque pars mei / vitabit Libitinam' assumes a tone of sober confidence (tinged with characteristic Horatian deprecating irony), 5-8 'non ego . . . obibo / nec Stygia cohibebor unda' is intended as a paradox which H. proceeds to sustain by a witty conceit.

Ennius in a well-known epigram (quoted by Cicero *Tusc.* 1. 34) had proclaimed:

> Nemo me lacrumis decoret nec funera fletu
> faxit. Cur? Volito vivus per ora virum.

Where Ennius spoke metaphorically, H.'s conceit requires us to toy with the consequences of taking literally what Ennius implied. If H. is to fly, he must be a bird. There must, therefore, be a metamorphosis, whose imminence the poet can sense and describe with that matter-of-fact attention to detail which will be characteristic of Ovid (see, e.g., the triple metamorphosis of Procne, Philomela and Tereus, *Meta.* 6. 667-73). There is equally a tacit improvement on Ennius' vision of himself in the proemium of the *Annals* as transformed after death into a peacock — a symbol of apotheosis or resurrection. In H.'s case the swan, the bird traditionally famous for its voice, is the obvious choice. H. is in process of becoming a swan, therefore. His funeral can thus be treated as an empty ceremony.

The essence of a conceit is a persistent, detailed assertion of the unbelievable: our minds reject the metaphorical meaning, but gradually a 'real' meaning penetrates to our consciousness without ever being plainly asserted. E.g., Propertius 2. 26A argues the conceit that the lover is exempt from death: we know it is not true, but gradually we are brought round to the view that the lover's case is different from everybody else's. Equally, there is a sense in which H. will be immortal.

A short statement in the poet's name is a traditional form, called *sphragis* by Greek critics; see H. Thesleff, 'Some remarks on literary sphragis in Greek poetry', *Eranos* 47, 1949, 116-28; Roman examples are *Georgics* 4. 559-66, Propertius 1. 21, Ovid *Am.* 3. 15. To a developed form of this, in which the poet speaks to his audience in his own person (instead of simply naming himself), H. adds in 2. 20 a concluding stanza which is his version of 'the poet's testament' (a transposition to literature of the burial instructions often contained in a will); cf. Propertius 2. 13. 17-58, *Elegia in Maecenatem* 2 (in *OCT Appendix Vergiliana*, ed. Kenney) and Cairns on 'mandata morituri', *Generic Composition* 90-91.

Structure: Stanzas 1-3 proclaim the poet's imminent metamorphosis; Stanzas 4-5, his prediction that he will make his way to the limits of the Roman world. Stanza 6 is a footnote, dispensing with the usual 'mandata morituri'.

Metre: Alcaics; see 1. 9M.

1-5] H. is about to be airborne ('ferar per liquidum aethera') but not after the usual manner of aviators such as Daedalus and Icarus (cf. 13 'Daedaleo notior Icaro'), half man and half bird — a 'biformis vates': actual metamorphosis is imminent. — **Non**

usitata nec tenui pinna] = 'not relying on the customary puny apparatus of feathers'
(which got Icarus into trouble); cf. 2. 2. 7 'pinna metuente solvi'; parallel to the obvious,
ironic meaning is an implied, serious, symbolic meaning: where others have been mere
poetic Icaruses, H.'s total metamorphosis symbolises the completeness of his poetic
success and the certainty of his immortality (see on 17-20); a complex of half-implied
overtones of meaning (the swan is no ordinary bird, etc.) supports and enhances the
'real' meaning; **pinna**] the use of the singular as a collective, characteristic of popular
speech (Leumann-Hofmann 370) and thus common in the *Epodes* and *Satires*, is here
pejorative; contrast 2. 2. 7, cf. 1. 13. 12 and 4. 3. 16 *dente, Epodes* 17. 33 *cinis, Sat.*
1. 6. 32 'quali sit facie, sura, quali pede, dente, capillo'. — **in terris morabor**] The
'obvious' metaphorical sense 'remain alive' is contradicted by the unexpected literal
sense 'remain on the ground'. — **longius**] i.e., 'unduly long'. — **invidiaque . . . relinquam**]
A further ironic contradiction: a normal victim of *invidia* may be forced into exile and
solitude; H. will leave the cities of men by soaring above them; moreover, his departure
will not be because he has been defeated by *invidia*, but because he has overcome *invidia*;
as before, the 'real' meaning (that H.'s reputation when he dies will be above carping
criticism) runs parallel to the ironic meaning; for H.'s malicious critics, see *Sat.* 1. 6,
1. 10 and 2. 6. 47-9, *Epist.* 1. 14. 37-8; in 4. 3. 16 he claims 'iam dente minus mordeor
invido'.

5-8] 'The Horace whom you know so well is going to elude mortality.' — **Non ego, non
ego**] The repetition is mock-solemn (contrast 2. 14. 1) and also an affectation of
'serious' structure (anaphora in asyndeton). — **pauperum sanguis parentum**] H. never
sought to conceal his humble origin; see *Sat.* 1. 6; cf. 3. 30. 12 'ex humili potens',
Epist. 1. 20. 20 (quoted in Introduction). — **quem vocas**] = 'the man you know as a
regular guest at your table'; H. stresses his status as a *scurra* at the great man's table to
emphasise the unexpectedness of his imminent metamorphosis; cf. Volteius at the table
of Philippus, *Epist.* 1. 7. 75 'mane cliens et iam certus conviva' (a parable of H.'s rela-
tionship with Maecenas) and Augustus' letter to Maecenas, *Vita Horat.* 24 'Veniet ergo
ab ista parasitica mensa ad hanc regiam'; the passage has been much misunderstood
(some have constructed 'whom you call *dilecte*', others 'whom you address in the
funeral ritual'); for *vocare* = invite to dinner (*L&S* B 2) cf. Catullus 44. 21; an invita-
tion to dinner is called a *vocatio* (Catullus 47. 7). — **nec Stygia cohibebor unda**] A flat
contradiction of 2. 14. 7-11; in a book where the inevitability of death has been so
prominent a theme, the note of ironic paradox is evident; with *obibo* cf. 2. 17. 3.

9-12] The metamorphosis is already beginning; to intensify the conflict in the reader's
mind, H. describes the symptoms in terms which common sense can only reject. The
reader must struggle to reduce what is asserted to a humorous description of the physical
symptoms of middle age — scaly shanks, white head, hairy body. (Contrast H.'s more
considered, more modest description of himself in 4. 2. 25-32.) — **asperae pelles**] i.e.,
patches of hard, scaly skin. — **superne**] Sufficiently vague to include anything from the
head of the real H. to the upper part of the body of the emerging swan.

13-16] Stanzas 4-6 proceed to work out the consequences of the metamorphosis
asserted in Stanza 3. Stanza 4 predicts that as a swan H. will be able to fly to the
furthest limits of the Roman world (a metaphor of his posthumous reputation, as we
say 'throughout the civilised world'); cf. for the idea *AP* 345-6 'hic meret aera liber
Sosiis, hic et mare transit, / et longum noto scriptori prorogat aevum' and *Epist.* 1. 20.
23; to judge from passing remarks by the younger Pliny and Martial (cited on line 20),
by the end of the first century AD at any rate, books of well-known authors were to be
had throughout the Roman world; Martial 11. 3 asserts he is read from Britain to Dacia.
Certainly, in modern times H.'s prediction has been more than realised. — **Iam . . . visam**]
'soon I shall visit'; *iam* is not correlative with 9 *iam iam*, as the change of tense shows;
Daedaleo notior Icaro] see on 1-5; Icarus now becomes, as it were, the symbol of one
whose transformation into bird will be less celebrated because less complete — and less
successful; cf. 1. 3. 33-4, 4. 2. 1-4. — **gementis litora Bosphori**] i.e., Bithynia; the NE
limit of the Roman world, as opposed to the expanses beyond, which were known about
but not regarded as civilised; cf. 3. 4. 29-31; **gementis**] because pounded by the waves
breaking on the shore; cf. 2. 18. 20, Catullus 11. 3-4 'litus et longe resonante Eoa /
tunditur unda'. — **Syrtisque Gaetulas**] i.e., Roman Africa, the limit of the civilised
world to the SW; for the Syrtes (in a similar context), see on 1. 22. 5-8. — **canorus ales**]
The periphrasis for 'swan', a familiar literary device ('kenning'), emphasises the point of

relevance; in their wild state swans are migratory birds; Virgil's beautiful simile is a useful
corrective to our modern image (*Aen.* 7. 699-702):

> ceu quondam nivei liquida inter nubila cycni
> cum sese e pastu referunt et longa canoros
> dant per colla modos, sonat amnis et Asia longe
> pulsa palus . . . ;

cf. *Il.* 2. 459-64; the swan is also the symbol of poetic genius in 4. 2. 25-7 (of Pindar);
cf., e.g., Lucretius 3. 6-7, 4. 181-2; *Eclogues* 8. 55, 9. 29 and 35. — **Hyperboreosque
campos**] The extreme north, traditionally imagined both as a land of happiness and
bliss and as a land of cold and solitude; the point here is probably that swans did
migrate to the far north in summer; perhaps also that H. fancies himself as a second
Orpheus, who, according to *Georgics* 4. 417-19, ranged through 'Hyperboreas glacies
Tanainque nivalem' in his search for Eurydice.

17-20]   An even rasher prediction: 'My reputation will penetrate in time to the uncivilised
world.' — **me . . . noscent Geloni**] Though applicable to H. the swan, the phrase pre-
pares the way (consolidated by 20 *discet*) for the transition from metamorphosed bard
to his poetry; **Colchus**] an inhabitant of Colchis, the homeland of Medea, east of the
Black Sea; in 4. 4. 63, a land of monstrosities; plural for singular; **et qui dissimulat . . .
Dacus**] for the Daci, a tribe of the lower Danube, see on 3. 8. 18; **metum Marsae
cohortis**] for Rome's yeoman soldiery as the strength of her army, see 3. 6. 37-44;
for the Marsi in less favourable light, 3. 5. 9; **Geloni**] a tribe of the Scythae, inhabitants
of what is now the Ukraine; see on 1. 19. 10; with 'ultimi Geloni' cf. Catullus 11. 11-12
'ultimos Britannos', 29. 4 'ultima Britannia'. — **peritus Hiber Rhodanique potor**] The
'able Spaniard and Provençal' are distinguished from the savage tribes of the East; their
longer contact with Rome had shown them apter for the arts and crafts of civilised life,
if not yet for things of the mind; *peritus* equally with *Hiber* and *potor*; see on 4. 15. 21.
— **discet**] The Eastern tribes will merely be acquainted with H.'s poetry (19 *noscent*),
the inhabitants of Spain and Provence will learn it in school; with *discet* cf. 2. 19. 3
'discentis'; **Rhodanique potor**] H. no doubt has in mind the Rhone between Lyons and
Marseilles as the symbol of Gallia Narbonensis (the modern Provence), as distinguished
from the more remote parts of Gaul; for bookshops in Provence, see Pliny *Epist.* 9. 11. 2,
cf. Martial 7. 88; with the expression cf. 3. 10. 1, 4. 15. 21.

21-4]   A final extravagance of wit. In the case of an apotheosis, there is normally a body
to bury, though the real hero is elsewhere. In H.'s case, as is clear from Stanza 3, there
won't even be a body. Given the circumstances, the normal expressions of grief can be
dispensed with; likewise, there will be no need for a tomb. Underpinning the conceit is
the characteristic Roman belief that immortality in the minds of posterity was all that
mattered. Maecenas expresses a similar unconcern for his mortal remains in a hexameter
quoted by Seneca *Epist.* 92. 35 'Nec tumulum curo: sepelit natura relictos'. — **Absint
inani funere neniae**] Echoes the epigram of Ennius quoted in the Introduction, but
within the framework of the conceit which the ode has built up, the request 'let us have
no dirges sung at a pointless funeral' suggests the sense 'let there be no funeral at all'
(just as there is to be no tomb) rather than the sense 'let there be no expressions of grief
at my funeral'; **inani**] both 'empty' because the funeral would have to take place at a
cenotaph with no body to bury (cf. the 'tumulus inanis' of Hector at Buthrotum, *Aen.*
3. 304) and 'idle' because H. will not in fact be dead; for the ambigiuty cf. *Aen.* 5. 673.
— **turpes**] Because H.'s friends should instead be celebrating his metamorphosis. —
clamorem] The uproar of grief; for the phrase, see on 1. 16. 22 'compesce mentem'. —
mitte] 'dismiss', 'dispense with'; cf. 1. 38. 3, 3. 8. 17, 3. 27. 74. — **supervacuos honores**]
The tributes are 'more than usually empty' because the tomb would be empty, no death
having in fact occurred; *supervacuos*, an emphatic synonym of *inanis*, only here in the
Odes, commoner in prose, especially in the form *supervacaneus*.

Book Three

3. 1

Introduction: The first of six long odes, all in Alcaics, usually known as the 'Roman Odes', clearly intended as an inspiration and a challenge to the generation born in the concluding years of the Civil Wars and now reaching maturity; the emphasis on the contemporary political scene at the time of publication of *Odes* 1-3 is evident. The unity of the group is not to be pressed too closely: if 3. 1 and 3. 2 are addressed particularly to the younger generation, 3. 3 and 3. 5 show the poet as moralist in more general terms; 3. 4 clearly differs from the rest; many hold that 3. 6 is several years earlier in composition than the others.

In the social upheaval of the Civil Wars, men of all conditions had found their way to places of rank and influence, while many distinguished Romans had perished or suffered political humiliation or financial ruin. The advice so solemnly proclaimed by Horace to the young is to renounce the pursuit of political power (because success and failure in politics are dependent on arbitrary factors beyond our control, so that even the power of the tyrant is illusory, while wealth destroys peace of mind) in favour of the simple life. The Epicurean overtones are obvious, as are the verbal echoes of well-known passages in the *Georgics* in which Virgil sets the farmer's life above that of the city-dweller (see on 41-8). Tibullus proclaims his adoption of a similar way of life in his opening elegy (1. 1. 5 'Me mea paupertas vita traducat inerti'). It is a commonplace that the new regime favoured a return to older, simpler ideals. H. speaks, however, more as the disillusioned individualist of the older generation reflecting his own experience than as the propagandist of Augustus. The ode is close in theme to 2. 18; cf. 2. 15, 3. 16, 3. 24, 3. 29.

Structure: After a dramatic opening stanza and an oracular second stanza, the rhetorical structure is unusually discursive, reaching a first climax after Stanza 4. Line 21 marks the transition from the opening theme (the illusory nature of power) to a second theme (the superiority of the simple life over the life of luxury). These two themes are then linked in Stanzas 11-12.

Metre: Alcaics. See 1. 9M.

1-4] A situational metaphor: Situation A (the poet addressing his chosen audience) is spoken of in terms appropriate to Situation B (the prophet prophesying to the initiate). The poet's audience is the young generation — of both sexes. — **odi ... arceo]** = 'I will have nothing to do with the uninitiated herd'; the ritual proclamation of the officiating priest; cf. the Sibyl in *Aen*. 6. 258 (at the moment of Aeneas' entry into the underworld) 'Procul este profani'; Tibullus 2. 1. 11 'Vos abesse procul iubeo'; H.'s tone is frankly élitist (it is the young of the families of influence and wealth to whom his message is addressed — the sons and daughters of his chosen friends and associates; cf. 2. 16. 39-40). — **favete linguis]** Another religious formula, commanding silence among the initiate; cf. Tibullus 2. 1. 1 'Quisquis adest faveat'. — **carmina non prius audita]** (1) 'prophecies not before heard', (2) 'poetry of a new kind' (i.e., different from the odes of Books 1 and 2, as well as from the poetry of other poets); for *carmen* 'prophecy' see *OLD* 1 c; cf. 3. 25. 7-8. — **Musarum sacerdos]** In ordinary prophecy it is the *sacerdos* who is the mouthpiece of the god; the Sibyl in *Aen*. 6, e.g., is regularly referred to as *sacerdos*; the poet in his function as *vates* is the mouthpiece of the Muses. — **virginibus puerisque]** The situational metaphor allows H. to speak as though his audience were actually assembled before him, like the choir of *virgines* and *pueri* in

1. 21. 1-2, 4. 6. 31 and *CS* 6, who sing (or are imagined as singing) their hymn under the poet's direction; cf. 3. 4. 5 *auditis*, 3. 14. 10-12; given the ritual and traditional nature of the occasion, too much should not be made of the presence of young women in H.'s audience; 3. 6, however, though not addressed to women, has a good deal to say about them (see 3. 6. 21-32); for H.'s interest in the woman's point of view, see on 3. 12. — **canto**] Equally appropriate to the prophesying *sacerdos* (*OLD* 7 c, though *canit* commoner in this sense) and to the poet performing his work.

5-8] For his *carmina non prius audita* H. adopts an oracular tone reminiscent of Pindar, strengthened by a characteristic irony — H.'s attitude is conveyed by discreet hints, not openly stated; thus, the impressive opening *regum timendorum* is progressively undercut (1) by *in proprios greges* (the awful *imperium* of kings, thus circumscribed by the traditional image of the shepherd guarding his flock, sounds less impressive), then (2) by comparison with the *imperium* of Jove, which is (i) *reges in ipsos*, (ii) as effortless as it is universal (*cuncta supercilio moventis*). — **clari Giganteo triumpho**] Jove's legendary victory over the Giants (see 3. 4. 41-80) is evoked in terms appropriate to the victory ('crowned' by the formal award by the Senate of a *triumphus*) of a Roman general; *triumpho* thus continues the process initiated by *imperium* by which the power of kings and the power-structure of the universe are conceptualised in Roman terms — as though Jove were a Roman proconsul on a vaster scale; the result is to make mortal *triumphi* sound petty by comparison, a reaction reinforced by the striking polysyllable *Giganteo* placed at the metrical climax (see 1. 9M) of the stanza. — **supercilio**] The awesome nod of Jove, the traditional symbol since Homer (*Il.* 1. 528, rendered more vivid by the reference to Jove's 'shadowy brow'; cf. Catullus 64. 204-6), becomes, in H.'s ironic rephrasing, little more than a flicker of an eyebrow; contrast the more formal, grander assertion of Jove's omnipotence in 3. 4. 45-8.

9-16] When we come to mere mortals, such trivial supremacies as they acquire or inherit are of little consequence. H. expresses his truism with oracular detachment, but the formulation is designed to bring out his ironic assessment of the illusory nature of wealth and power. — **est ut**] = 'no doubt'; four factors commonly reckoned an advantage in seeking political power are considered and dismissed: (1) wealth, (2) noble birth, (3) character and reputation, (4) influence; the owner of a large estate is put first; to him are successively opposed (*hic . . . hic . . . illi . . .*) three other typical candidates, each briefly delineated in equally ironic terms. — **hic generosior . . . petitor**] Though linked grammatically only with *generosior, descendat in Campum petitor* applies to all four types of candidate; **descendat in Campum**] i.e., down from the hills where the best people live, to the Campus Martius where the elections for office take place; the two words *in Campum*, being closely linked in sense, are not considered to break the rule prohibiting caesura after the 4th syllable; **petitor**] the technical term for a candidate for office. — **meliorque**] For the position of *-que*, see on 2. 19. 28. — **turba clientium**] i.e., the ability to support his candidature by the exercise of *potentia*, legal or illegal. — **aequa . . . nomen**] H.'s point is that the factors determining rise to power have nothing to do with our merits or supposed merits; Fate, i.e., conducts her own election; **aequa lege**] the *lex* is *aequa* because all are subject to it, not because it is 'fair'; cf. 1. 4. 13, 2. 18. 32; **Necessitas**] cf. 1. 35. 17-20, 3. 24. 5-8; election, i.e., is a lottery — the normal procedure at Athens, resorted to at Rome only for special purposes (e.g., the allocation of provincial commands); cf. for the idea 3. 29. 49-52 (of Fortuna), for the image 2. 3. 25-8; cynicism about politics was to be increasingly the note of the Augustan age; cf. 3. 2. 17-20, 4. 9. 39 and see on 1. 1. 7-8; **movet**] i.e., causes to mix with all the others.

17-21] A first climax, pointing the moral of Stanzas 2-4; cf. 37-40; power is not worth having. To make the point more forcibly, H. chooses the traditional symbol of absolute, arbitrary power, the tyrant. — **Destrictus ensis**] The famous sword of Damocles; in Cicero's version (*Tusc.* 5. 61) Dionysius I, tyrant of Syracuse, in order to illustrate the precariousness of his enjoyment of wealth and power, surrounds a courtier, Damocles, with all possible magnificence — and then suspends a sword by a horsehair from the ceiling so that it is poised over him, thus effectively destroying his enjoyment; H. reinterprets the story to his own moral purpose. — **inpia cervice**] i.e., that of the tyrant (not Damocles), the symbol in Roman eyes of the greedy misuse of power; the perfectly wise ruler would remain indifferent to wealth and therefore to the risk of losing it. — **Siculae dapes**] Sicily under the great tyrants is always represented as a place of wealth and luxury. — dulcem . . . saporem] i.e., will not make the banquet agreeable by the culinary refinement applied to it. — avium cantus] Implies captive birds, kept for the tyrant's pleasure as a background to the music of the lyre — an example, like the banquet, of sophistication in the pursuit of pleasure. — somnum reducent] i.e., will not restore the ability to sleep at night; for sleep as the symbol of freedom from care cf. 2. 11. 8, 2. 16. 15, 3. 21. 4.

21-4] The switch from the opening theme (the illusory nature of power) to the main theme (the superiority of the simple life) gathers momentum, as if by a natural transition from the insomnia of the tyrant to the untroubled sleep of simple country folk. — Somnus lenis] cf. 2. 16. 15. — agrestium virorum] cf. the idealised country folk of 3. 6. 37-44. — non fastidit] 'does not scorn' (i.e., turn its nose up at) his humble abode. — umbrosamque . . . Tempe] Scenes of natural beauty inducing peaceful sleep, opposed to the artificiality of the tyrant's way of life; umbrosamque ripam] for the delayed caesura cf. 31; Tempe is a Greek neuter plural; cf. 1. 7. 4, 1. 21. 9.

25-32] Explicit contrast of the simple life with the cares and fears of the wealthy. — desiderantem quod satis est] 'The man whose wants are equated to his needs'; cf. 2. 18. 14, 3. 16. 43-4. — tumultuosum mare] the 'storm-tossed sea' does not bring him anxiety because he does not have to cross it in pursuit of wealth; the life of the humble farmer is similarly contrasted with that of the mercator in 1. 1. 11-18; cf. 2. 16. 1-4, 3. 29. 57-61. — saevus . . . Haedi] Arcturus, the brightest star of the constellation before the Great Bear (evening setting, end of October); Haedus, better Haedi, a pair of small stars of the constellation Auriga (evening rising, early October). — non verberatae . . . iniquas] The hazards to which the large estate owner is exposed; vineae and fundus are, like 26 mare, subjects of sollicitat. —fundusque mendax] The farm, i.e., instead of keeping to its promise of a rich harvest, is full of excuses; contrast 3. 16. 30; the personification is continued by arbore culpante, which refers especially to the olive harvest; the singular asks us to fancy the owner interrogating tree after tree and getting a different answer from each.

33-7] H. passes from the overseas trader and the farmer and their troubles to the rich man who is apparently successful; despite his lavish expenditure to secure a life of pleasure, his fears and anxieties pursue him relentlessly; H. permits himself at the climax of his ironic portrayal of the cares of the rich an openly satirical tone. — contracta . . . sentiunt] 'the fish feel the sea shrink'. — iactis . . . molibus] i.e., great sprawling villas built out on to the sea at Baiae and such pleasure resorts; see on 2. 15. 2; cf. 2. 18. 19-22. — frequens redemptor] i.e., the busy contractor, rushing back and forth. — caementa] Broken stone and masonry dumped in the sea as foundations; cf. 3. 24. 1-4. — terrae fastidiosus] 'for whom dry land is not good enough'; cf. 3. 29. 9.

37-40] A second climax, pointing the moral of Stanzas 7-9; the pursuit of wealth, like the pursuit of power, is self-defeating; cf. 17-21. — scandunt] i.e., into his palazzo raised high above the waves of the sea. — aerata triremi] His pleasure yacht (cf. Epist. 1. 1. 93 priva treremis) with its bronze-plated prow; cf. 2. 16. 21-4; contrast H.'s modest two-oared skiff 3. 29. 62. — post equitem] i.e., when he goes riding. — atra Cura] cf. 3. 14. 13; with H.'s picture of the rich man hounded by Cura cf. Lucretius' picture of the rich man who seeks to run away from boredom with life and the fear of death 3. 1053-75.

41-8] H. sums up, applying the argument to himself. If power and wealth are an illusion, why should he change his way of life? Cf. 2. 18. 1-8, 3. 29. 13-16. The imagery of Stanzas 11-12 knits together the twin themes of Stanzas 3-10; the symbol of power and wealth is the great man receiving his clientes in his grand atrium during the morning salutatio and at his table at dinner; H. seems to have in mind Georgics 2. 458-74. — dolentem] i.e., the victim of the mental anguish described in 17-21 and 37-40. — Phrygius lapis] 'Phrygian marble'. — purpurarum usus] The 'wearing of the purple', the symbol of rank and power, especially the toga with its broad band of purple (latus clavus) worn by those of senatorial rank (frequently affected by those not entitled to it) rather than purple hangings, etc.; H.'s point is that the wearer gets used to his splendid clothes and no longer derives comfort from them. — sidere clarior] The hyperbole and the transferred epithet accentuate the rhetorical flourish, as does the 5th-syllable caesura after usus; cf. 3. 9. 21 sidere pulchrior. — Falerna vitis] See on 1. 20. 10; vitis, like lapis, for pejorative effect. — Achaemeniumque costum] 'scent worthy of an Achaemenes' (see on 2. 12. 21); costly wines and scent are symbols of the dinner party at which the great man presides over his friends and clientes. — invidendis . . .

atrium] = 'an *atrium* (in which to receive his guests) with a great lofty doorway in the latest style for people to envy'; *novo ritu*, like *postibus*, ablative with *sublime*. − **valle Sabina**] = 'my farm in the Sabine hills'; with *valle* cf. 1. 17. 17. − **divitias operosiores**] 'riches that will bring me more trouble'.

3. 2

Introduction: H. begins by extolling the simple, tough life of the soldier on active service as a training for the young; it can bring glory too, and bring out that true courage of which immortal heroes are made. As in 3. 5, H.'s message to the young has an evident relevance to the contemporary political scene − the much publicised final showdown with the Parthians. The reference is to what we should call commissioned rank in the *militia equestris*, open to sons of senators and knights; see Dio 52. 26, quoted 1. 8I. A young Roman of suitable status might pass directly from the sort of officer training corps in which we see Sybaris training in 1. 8 (or Hebrus in 3. 12) to junior officer rank on active service (like Iccius, presumably, in 1. 29). Throughout the Roman Odes the Parthians and the situation in the East are treated as an emergency with which the younger generation will have to deal on the battlefield; see 3. 5I and on 3. 6. 9-16. Augustus' imminent visit to the Eastern provinces (22-19 BC) is no doubt foreshadowed; Agrippa had been made commander in the East in 23 BC.

The change of theme in Stanzas 7-8 is abrupt. The sequence of thought is most often taken as a reversion to the theme of lines 1-6 after the imaginative expansion of that theme in lines 6-12: military service, i.e., is not advocated as a way of life (H.'s chosen audience are not to be thought of as all, potentially, professional soldiers), but as a preparation for life (a spell of active service will teach them 'angustam amice pauperiem pati'); the army may indeed provide a career (Stanzas 4-6); but 'est et fideli tuta silentio merces': the new regime needs as well men of stern moral fibre who can be trusted to hold their tongue; H.'s audience, i.e., may also look forward to a career in Augustus' growing civil service, where the qualities most requisite are reliability and discretion. An alternative interpretation is proposed by Pasquali 668 (who regards this ode as 'the most difficult, perhaps the only difficult ode, in the cycle of Roman Odes'): according to his tentative reading of Stanzas 7-8, H. breaks off his inspired message to the young on the verge of revealing to them the secrets of immortality, contenting himself with no more than a hint at the ultimate reward of true *virtus*; the conclusion of 3. 2 thus anticipates the theme of 3. 3. 9-16. The advantages of this reading are that it restores unity to the ode and provides a more satisfactory explanation of the mysterious avoidance of explicit-ness in the concluding two stanzas, which otherwise seems pointless (and confusing); moreover, a two-stanza afterthought on the responsibilities of a senior civil servant after the climax of line 24 falls rather flat.

Structure: Stanza 2 continues the sense of Stanza 1 almost without pause and in its turn spills over into Stanza 3. The abrupt gnomic line 13 ('Dulce et decorum est pro patria mori') is thus thrown into prominence. Stanzas 4-6 are heavily endstopped, though 5 and 6 are linked by the anaphora in asyndeton of *virtus*. Stanza 7 then spills over into Stanza 8.

Metre: Alcaics; see 1. 9M.

1-6] Angustam . . . pati] = 'to endure the simple life in extreme form and come to welcome it'; the key word is *amice*; the typical young officer is of wealthy family background, and active service his first taste of the simple life; like the *mercator* of 1. 1. 16-18, he is apt to be 'indocilis pauperiem pati', but it is a lesson he must learn if he is to be a true Roman in the old tradition; 3. 2 thus picks up the theme of the concluding stanza of 3. 1, the superiority of the simple life followed by H. to the ostentatious luxury of the rich; for *pauperies* 'the simple life' (not 'poverty'), see on 1. 1. 18; cf. 4. 9. 49. − **robustus . . . condiscat**] i.e., when he 'learns properly' to welcome the simple life, he will be *robustus*, having been made so *acri militia* (the tough life of the *militia equestris*); idea and language are traditional; cf. Cicero *Cael.* 11 'Nobis quidem olim . . . erat, si statim [i.e., immediately after assuming the *toga virilis*] mereri stipendia coeperamus, castrensis ratio ac militaris . . . . Cum is iam se corroboravisset ac vir inter viros esset. . .'; with *acri militia* cf. 1. 29. 2; **puer**] the officer training corps of Augustus was for youngsters of perhaps 15-18; at the moment of joining the army on active service, the young officer can still be regarded as a *puer*; see on 1. 5. 1; **Parthos . . . hasta**] because he is mounted, he can pursue the Parthians (noted for their horseman-ship), to whom he will appear, for all their savagery, a formidable figure with his spear; for the Parthians cf. 2. 13. 18, see on 1. 12. 53; 3. 2 is thus linked to 3. 5. — **vitamque . . . rebus**] The third member of the tricolon crescendo is, as often, double-barrelled; **sub divo**] i.e., out in the open, beneath the stars; cf. 2. 3. 23; **trepidis in rebus**] 'sur-rounded by excitement'.

6-12] **ex moenibus hosticis**] Women watching while the battle rages is a common topic in Greek poetry; cf. *Aen.* 11. 476 etc. — **matrona bellantis tyranni**] Cf. 3. 3. 3. — **adulta virgo**] The fiancée of the tyrant's son; she is imagined as *adulta* to heighten the pathos (this was to be no child marriage); the flash of sympathy for her is genuine, if quickly followed by appropriately Roman attitudes in the following stanza. — **suspiret**] 'catch her breath'; agreement with the nearer; the mother is anxious for her son, the girl for her fiancé; cf. 1. 29. 5-6, where Iccius is represented as bringing such an Eastern princess home as his slave; for H.'s sympathy with the loser, see also 2. 18. 26-8. — **eheu, ne . . . lacessat**] As though reporting the thought in their minds; for *eheu* cf. 2. 14. 1; **rudis sponsus**] H. perhaps imagines a young successor to Pacorus, the prince-general of the previous generation (see on 3. 6. 9); to reinforce the pathos, the young prince is represented as a mere tiro, no match for the young Roman already *robustus acri militia*; contrast the picture of the noble savage in 3. 24. 9-24. — **asperum . . . leonem**] The simile graphically represents the princess's thoughts: for her, the young Roman is a savage lion, about to attack her fiancé; the lion is the traditional symbol of savagery; cf. *Aen.* 12. 4-8 etc.; the caesura after syllable 5 (less common in Books 3-4) marks a distinct pause. — **cruenta ira**] The epithet is transferred for rhetorical effect from the lion to its rage; the relative clause can thus be more easily referred to the young Roman, though the formal antecedent is the lion; the lion attacks because provoked, the young Roman out of righteous anger; the blood is that of earlier victims (no suggestion the boy/lion has been wounded). — **per medias caedes**] cf. 1. 8. 15-16.

13-16] **Dulce . . . mori**] cf. 3. 19. 2, 4. 9. 51-2; the sentiment is traditional, a reformula-tion of Tyrtaeus:

τεθναμέναι γὰρ καλὸν ἐνὶ προμάχοισι πεσόντα
ἀνδρ' ἀγαθὸν περὶ ἧ πατρίδι μαρνάμενον

H. adds *decorum*, which perhaps recalls *Il.* 22. 71-4 (Priam to Hector) 'νέῳ δέ τε πάντ' ἐπέοικεν; does he intend his words to apply to the young Parthian as well as to the young Roman, or is the sympathy extended to the loser in the previous stanza now withheld? Logic suggests the former; H. can hardly ask us to assume that it is the *robustus acri militia puer* who will be killed; in either case, line 13 marks a transition from the glamour of military service to the theme of Stanzas 5-6 — the rewards open to those killed (as some must be) on active service: the consolation of dying bravely for one's country, glory, even immortality; **dulce**] the brave soldier finds satisfaction in giving his life; Virgil deals more honestly with the heroic impulse *Aen.* 2. 316-17 (of Aeneas):

furor iraque mentem
praecipitat, pulchrumque mori succurrit in armis;

see Quinn, *Virgil's Aeneid, a Critical Description*, Chap. 1. — **mors . . . virum**] Also traditional; cf. Simonides fr. 12D (= *LGS* 358) ὁ δ' αὖ θάνατος ἔκιχε καὶ τὸν φυγόμαχον, though H. is as usual more specific; H. forgets that he was himself at Philippi, if not a φυγόμαχος, at least a ῥιψασπίς (see 2. 7. 9-12). — **nec parcit . . . tergo**] True, and perhaps intentionally bathetic; **poplitibus**] the back of their knees (more strictly the hamstrings).

17-24] **virtus**] 'manly courage', but increasingly in Stanza 6 with mystical overtones (tinged with Stoicism) of the true courage (an attitude of mind in addition to physical bravery) by which immortality (in the strictest sense) may be achieved. — **repulsae**] The technical term for defeat at an election; cf. Cicero *Tusc.* 4. 54 (of Laelius) 'cum sapiens et bonus vir . . . suffragiis praeteritur, non populus a bono consule potius quam ille a populo repulsam fert?' — **intaminatis honoribus**] Opposed to the *tergemini honores* of political life, which are *contaminati*. — **securis**] i.e., the *fasces*, the symbol of authority of the *magistratus.* — **arbitrio . . . aurae**] = 'at the popular whim'; the *magistratus*, i.e., owes his reputation to election, the soldier to his own *virtus*; cf. 3. 1. 14-16, 3. 3. 2. — **recludens inmeritis mori**] 'opening up to those who do not deserve to die'. — **caelum**] = Olympus; apotheosis among the gods of Olympus, traditionally assigned to Hercules, etc. and conventionally extended to Augustus (3. 3. 9-12) is promised the heroic warrior by an extravagance of propaganda poetry. — **negata . . . via**] 'attempts the journey by a forbidden road' (i.e., one denied to others); cf. 1. 2. 45-9, 3. 3. 9-12, 3. 25. 5-6; Propertius 2. 27. 16 (of the lover returning to life) 'concessum nulla lege redibit iter'. — **coetusque volgaris**] i.e., contact with mere mortals; the language in this and the following line is deliberately vague and oracular in tone. — **udam humum**] As opposed to the *arces igneae* (3. 3. 10) of the Stoic *aether*; cf. Cicero *Tusc.* 1. 27. — **fugiente pinna**] The hero's *virtus* now becomes identified with his departing *anima*.

25-32] Stanzas 7-8 are usually taken as referring to a career in Augustus' civil service, with its obligations of secrecy. But see Introduction. — **Est . . . merces**] Apparently a version of a traditional saying 'ἔστι καὶ σιγῆς ἀκίνδυνον γέρας', attributed in various forms to Simonides (see Page, *Poetae Melici Graeci* 582), said by Plutarch to have been quoted by Augustus to his teacher Athenodorus the Stoic, and perhaps a favourite saying; **tuta**] 'certain' rather than 'safe'. — **vetabo . . . phaselon**] The man who has broken his oath of secrecy and is attempting to escape is spoken of as if he were a refugee from divine justice, whose company the prudent man will avoid; according to the usual interpretation, a situational metaphor (see on 3. 1. 1-4) in which the oath of secrecy taken by those admitted to Augustus' civil service is equated with the mystic rites of Demeter at Eleusis and elsewhere; if we follow Pasquali, a reference to H.'s role of poet-prophet assumed in 3. 1. 1-4 — there are secrets, i.e., regarding the nature of immortality which the true hero will learn in due course, but which it would be sacrilegious (and dangerous) for H. to reveal, even to his audience of initiates; note that this section of the ode, like the first, ends with flight and punishment; **vetabo . . . sit**] i.e., *ne sit*; **sub isdem trabibus**] = 'under the same roof'; i.e., give him shelter (or remain if others give him shelter); **phaselon**] a light, fast ship, like that in Catullus 4. — **Diespiter**] The sky-god; the old form of *Iuppiter*; for Jove as the god of the thunderbolt, see on 1. 2. 2. — **neglectus**] 'not reckoned with', as would be the case if an oath involving his *numen* were broken. — **antecedentem**] i.e., fleeing from justice; for the emphatic polysyllable straddling the 3rd line of the Alcaic stanza, see on 1. 9M. — **pede Poena claudo**] That divine justice is slow but sure is a commonplace (cf. our proverb of the Mills of God); cf. 4. 5. 24; the idea of making *Poena* ('Retribution') limp in pursuit of the fugitive seems to be due to H.

3. 3

Introduction: In 3.3 H. turns from the young warrior of 3. 2 to the soldier-statesman, to take up the theme hinted at in 3. 2. 21-4, the promotion of the hero to the place he has won by his *virtus* among the immortal gods. The apotheosis of Augustus is confidently predicted as the culmination of a historical process which began with the fall of Troy and the apotheosis of Quirinus; the speech made by Juno to the assembled immortals on that occasion.

Structure: Stanzas 1-4 constitute a vigorous, fast-moving statement of theme in preparation for the formal set-piece, the speech of Juno, which takes on a status comparable to the myth in a Pindaric ode (cf. the myth of Regulus in 3. 5 and the myth of Hannibal in 4. 4). The speech falls into two parts: in Stanzas 5-9 Juno absolves Quirinus from his ancestral guilt; Stanzas 10-17 predict Rome's future greatness and lay down, as a condition of that greatness, that the Romans must never attempt to refound Troy. For the stanza following Stanza 17, see on 69-72.

Metre: Alcaics; see 1.9M.

1-8] The hero destined to win immortality is now more openly than in 3. 2. 21-4 the Stoic hero, the man of moral courage. There are obvious resemblances to Virgil's Aeneas (just as Juno's prophecy resembles that of Jove to Venus in *Aen.* 1); but where Virgil's story requires a founding hero of another race, H. focuses on the true Roman, Romulus, son of Mars. The qualities emphasised are characteristically Roman (and Stoic) virtues: justice and tenacity of purpose. — **civium iubentium**] The true leader must be able to stand aloof from the misguided passions of those he leads; cf. 3. 2. 17-20. — **voltus . . .**

tyranni] Ordinary bravery is also necessary; the true leader must be able to face up to any foreign menace; the phrase is perhaps intended as a variation on 3. 2. 9-12 – there, young Roman meets young foreign prince, here, the leaders on each side confront one another; *voltus* touches off the image; with *instantis* ('advancing menacingly') cf. 2. 14. 3. – **mente solida]** The mind of the Stoic hero is an impregnable stronghold of detached courage. **Auster . . . Hadriae]** The first, perhaps, of a series of echoes – or anticipations – of *Aen*. 1, here of 1. 92-101, where Virgil shows his hero (at his first appearance in the poem) caught in a storm at sea and unable as yet to attain true Stoic detachment; *dux turbidus* personifies; the Adriatic becomes an opponent to be confronted like the *tyrannus*, one whose ill-controlled violence is contrasted with the hero's detachment; for the Adriatic as a sea of storms, see on 1. 3. 15; *inquieti* likewise personifies. – **fulminantis . . . Iovis]** Because of his conviction of his own *virtus*, the hero can face unperturbed even the thunderbolts of Jove, serenely confident they are not meant for him; cf. *Aen*. 5. 687-92 (Aeneas is less sure); for the thunderbolts of Jove, see on 1. 2. 1-4, 3. 4. 44. – **si fractus . . . ruinae]** 'though the firmament were to be shattered and fall upon him, the fragments will strike him unafraid'; i.e., were the crack of Jove's thunderbolt to tear the firmament apart (the poetic equivalent of the Stoic cataclysmic conflagration which periodically destroys the universe; the Epicureans also believed in the eventual destruction of the universe – see Lucretius 5. 95); the illogical form of the condition (future indicative following present subjunctive) emphasises the certainty of the outcome; for *orbis*, the circle or arch of the firmament, see *OLD* 7 c; the delayed caesura throws the polysyllable *inlabatur* into greater prominence (see on 1. 9M).

9-16] Five heroes who won immortality are cited, three traditional, two Roman; cf. 4. 8. 29-34. – **hac arte]** i.e., by being *iustus et tenax propositi*; picked up by 13 and 15 *hac*. – **Pollux]** Like his brother Castor, son of Jove and Leda; they are often referred to as *Dioscuri*; Helen of Troy was their sister; their cult was traditionally introduced to Rome in 484 BC after the battle of Lake Regillus, in which they were believed to have taken part on the side of Rome; they are linked with Hercules in 1. 12. 25, 4. 5. 35, 4. 8. 31, cf. the list of immortals in *Epist*. 2. 1. 5; for their other role as protectors of those in peril on the sea, see on 1. 3. 2, cf. 1. 12. 25, 4. 8. 31-2; according to one form of the legend, Pollux was killed in battle and subsequently accorded immortality. – **vagus Hercules]** 'much-travelled Hercules'. – **enisus]** 'by his efforts'; with Hercules (agreement with the nearer), but applying also to Pollux. – **arcis igneas]** i.e., the *aether*, traditionally a blaze of fire and light; cf. 1. 3. 29 and 33-4 *lucidas sedes*; an immortal abode more congenial to Stoic ideas than the Homeric Olympus. – **Augustus]** In 1. 2 Augustus is a god on earth, destined to return to the heavens (45 'serus in caelum redeas'); cf. 3. 5. 2-3, 4. 5. 31-2, also 3. 25. 3-6. – **purpureo ore]** 'with bright red lips'; the visual detail makes this the most audacious assertion in H. of Augustus' divine status. – **bibet]** The reading *bibit*, adopted by some, is a clear mistake. – **nectar]** cf. 34. – **te . . . vexere]** Implies that Bacchus, like Quirinus, earned immortality and was rescued from death; **merentem]** i.e., in return for Bacchus' gifts to mankind – poetry as well as wine. – **tigres . . . trahentes]** The yoked tigers are the traditional symbol of Bacchus as the god who brings civilised restraint and refinement to the passions of mankind. – **Quirinus]** An ancient Roman god, the god of the Quirinal, after whom the Romans on formal occasions called themselves *Quirites*; the identification with Romulus belongs to the late Republic; cf. *Epist*. 2. 1. 5. – **Martis equis]** i.e., rescued by the personal intervention of Mars, father of Romulus (cf. 33). – **Acheronta fugit]** = 'eluded death'.

17-36] Juno grants Quirinus immortality, absolving him from the guilt of Troy. For Virgil, Juno is the future protectress of Carthage and thus committed to war with Rome; her enmity with Troy was traditionally attributed to her defeat in the beauty contest presided over by Paris (*Aen*. 1. 25-8). H. goes deeper. Troy and Paris are condemned as morally corrupt. The Roman Juno is above all else the goddess of marriage and the sexual life of women; see Rose in *OCD*; cf. 3. 4. 59 *matrona Iuno*; similarly Pallas Athena is recast in Roman terms as *casta Minerva* (contrast the Homeric Pallas of 1. 15. 11-12). In the speech he allots Juno here, as in his moral reinterpretation of the battle of the Giants in 3. 4, H. shows himself in the role of creative mythologiser. For the myth of Paris and Helen, see also 1. 15. – **gratum . . . divis]** 'Juno's words having won approval from the gods in council'; H. adapts the Homeric council of the gods (cf. *Aen*. 10 init.) to his purpose. – **Ilion, Ilion]** Object of *vertit*; with the repetition cf. 2. 14. 1, 4. 13. 18. — **fatalis incestusque iudex**] Paris is *fatalis* because destined to be the instrument of Troy's destruction, *incestus* because of his adultery with Helen, which brings the destruction about (contrast 23 *castae*); the latter adjective is ironically set alongside *iudex*, which recalls his role in the 'Judgement of Paris'; see on 1. 15. 13. — **mulier peregrina**] 'the foreign woman'; ironically pejorative for Helen, emphasising her status at Troy. — **vertit in pulverem**] The Stoic doctrine that 'fate will find its way', that men are the instruments of their own destiny, willing or unwilling; Troy had been handed over for its fated destruction (*damnatum, OLD* 4+5) to Juno and Minerva ever since the original deceit of the gods by Laomedon (*ex quo . . . Laomedon*); the adulterous union of Paris and Helen, by the revulsion it arouses in Juno and Minerva, precipitates the destruction; the implication is clear that moral degeneration may bring about the destruction of Rome also — a first adumbration of the theme of 3. 6. 17-20; **vertit**] present indicative ('has been consigning' to destruction), agreement with the nearer. — **ex quo destituit**] With *damnatum* rather than with *vertit*; see on 4. 6. 21-4. — **Laomedon**] Father of Priam; he first cheated Apollo and Neptune over the building of Troy, then cheated Hercules (to whom he had promised his horses in return for killing the monster sent by Neptune). — **mihi castaeque Minervae**] Dative with *damnatum*; *castae* picks up 19 *incestus*; in order to adapt the myth to his purpose, H. eliminates Neptune from the final destruction of Troy (in *Aen.* 2 Neptune first sends the sea monster to destroy Laocoon, then joins forces with Juno and Minerva in the physical destruction of the city). — **cum . . . fraudulento**] An ironic version of such formulae as Virgil's 'cum patribus populoque Penatibus et magnis dis' (*Aen.* 8. 679); condemnation involves people and ruler alike; the *dux* is Laomedon (king at the time Troy was handed over to Juno and Minerva for destruction) rather than Priam (though he cannot escape the collective guilt — cf. 26 *Priami domus periura*; *fraudulento* equally with both nouns. — **iam nec**] 'no longer', because at the time of Juno's speech Paris, Helen, Priam and Hector are all dead. — **Lacaenae . . . hospes**] The Spartan adulteress is Helen; her guest is Paris; *adulterae* is dative with *splendet* rather than genitive with *hospes* (for the word, see on 1. 25. 9); *hospes* looks to the inception of the affair at Sparta rather than to Troy, where the roles of guest and host were reversed; *famosus* because of the scandalous nature of the affair rather than its consequences. — **nec Priami . . . refringit**] i.e., Trojan resistance (of which Hector was the kingpin) has long since ceased. — **nostris . . . resedit**] 'and the war which was protracted by our quarrels has come to an end'. — **protinus**] 'at once', i.e., without hesitation, *OLD* 3. — **invisum nepotem**] Quirinus-Romulus, son of Mars, grandson of Juno; hated because of his Trojan ancestry. — **Troica sacerdos**] Rea Silvia, the Vestal Virgin, mother of Romulus and Remus, is identified in one version of the legend with Ilia, daughter of Aeneas; see on 3. 9. 8; cf. 1. 2. 17, also 4. 8. 22; contrast Livy's dry, rationalistic version, Livy 1. 3. 11-4. 3. — **Marti redonabo**] 'I shall return to Mars'; i.e., forgive him for his father's sake; cf. 2. 7. 3. — **adscribi . . . deorum**] The language echoes that of Roman administrative practice ('enrolled in the divine order'); *quietis* suggests the serene detachment of Epicurus' gods more than the Homeric Olympus; though the Stoics kept Jove (as the executive of fate), they showed little interest in the traditional pantheon. — **discere**] Some prefer *ducere*.

37-44]   Stanzas 10-11 constitute a first statement of Juno's conditional prophecy of Rome's future greatness; cf. the prophecy of Jove to Venus, *Aen.* 1. 223-304. There is to be no question of resettling Troy. In Virgil it is ruled out by fate (*Aen.* 4. 340-46). In H.'s myth the prohibition rests on moral grounds. — **qualibet . . . regnanto beati**] The dramatic moment is the death of Quirinus-Romulus; though born in Italy, Romulus and his generation can still be thought of as refugees (*exsules*); they must cut themselves off from the past and look to the future; for H.'s myth to serve its moral purpose, considerable historical foreshortening is necessary; see on 1. 2. 13-16; like Virgil's Jove, Juno sets no limit to Roman rule (cf. 'qualibet in parte regnanto' with Aen. 1. 279 'imperium sine fine dedi'), so long as Rome remains the seat of power. — **dum . . . inultae**] A vivid image of a city that has ceased to exist (*armentum* suggests a pastoral way of life, *ferae inultae* harmless, undomesticated fauna such as deer); **inultae**] passive, 'unpunished' for what would have been desecration as long as the city stood. — **stet Capitolium**] For the image cf. 3. 30. 8-9; with *stet* cf. 1. 9. 1. — **fulgens**] The roof of the temple of Jupiter Capitolinus in historical times was covered with gilt. — **triumphatisque Medis**] i.e., the Parthians, after they have been conquered and made the subject of a Roman triumph; for the delayed caesura, see on 1. 9M.

45-56] Structurally, Stanzas 12-14 form an expanded variation, built around the epithets
45 *horrenda* and 50 *fortior*, of the theme of Stanzas 10-11. — **horrenda late**] i.e., a
force to be reckoned with, unlike the morally effete Troy. — **medius liquor**] 'the sea in
between', the straits of Gibraltar, the Western limit of empire and the known world
(marked also by the Pillars of Hercules). — **Afro**] 'the African'. — **tumidus Nilus**] 'the
flooding Nile', symbolising Egypt, under Roman rule since the defeat of Cleopatra at
Actium; Rome's outer frontiers are dealt with in Stanza 14. — **aurum ... dextra**]
Imposes a further restraint upon which the world dominion of Stanza 14 is conditional:
the Romans are not to resume the luxurious way of life of the Trojans; the allusion to
contemporary conditions and Augustus' attempts at reform is evident; **aurum ... situm**]
cf. 2. 2. 1-4; **cum terra celat**] as it does in the Trojans' new home in Italy; **cogere**] both
'collect' and 'force'; **omne ... dextra**] suggests, not the mining of gold, but the rifling of
conquered shrines, etc.; cf. Sallust *Cat.* 11. 6 (of Sulla's troops) 'Ibi primum insuevit
exercitus populi Romani ... privatim et publice rapere, delubra spoliare, sacra profan-
aque polluere'. — **quicumque terminus**] i.e., in any given direction. — **tanget armis**]
'reach with her armies'. — **visere gestiens**] A more innocent motive than conquest. —
qua parte ... ignes] i.e., the limit of the torrid zone; **debacchentur**] intensive of
bacchari; the delayed caesura emphasises the word.
57-68] The formal prohibition of a second Troy emphasises the break with what is, at the
dramatic moment of Juno's prophecy, the recent past. But no doubt the contemporary
reader is intended to see in Troy a symbol of the Eastern empire of Antony (easily
identified as a second Paris), whose moral corruption condemns it to destruction, while
the rule of Augustus is destined to survive (provided Rome recovers her respect for the
gods and resists moral degeneration — the theme of 3. 6); for talk in H.'s day of a
second Troy, see Suetonius *Jul.* 79 'Fama percrebruit [Iulium Caesarem] migraturum
Alexandream vel Ilium, translatis ... opibus imperii' and Syme, *Roman Revolution* 305;
cf. *Aen.* 12. 828 (Juno to Jove) 'Occidit, occideritque sinas cum nomine Troia'. —
bellicosis Quiritibus] = 'the martial descendants of Quirinus'. — **fata dico**] Juno assumes
(like Jove speaking to Venus in *Aen.* 1) the role of interpreter of fate. — **nimium pii**]
i.e., out of misplaced *pietas* for the land of their origin. — **rebusque fidentes**] i.e., out of
hybris. — **Troiae renascens ... fortuna ... iterabitur**] = 'if Troy is rebuilt, history will
repeat itself'; **alite lugubri**] with *renascens*, 'an ill-omened rebirth'; cf. 4. 6. 24; **iterabi-
tur**] cf. 2. 19. 12. — **victrices catervas**] Presumably the Argives of line 67. — **coniuge ...
sorore**] cf. *Aen.* 1. 46-7 'Iovisque et soror et coniunx'. — **ter**] i.e., even if the Romans,
undeterred by a second disaster, were to try a third time. — **auctore Phoebo**] As hap-
pened the first time when Apollo played his lyre as the walls rose. — **meis Argivis**] Argos
was the chief seat of Juno's worship; the implication is that the Argives would again be
the instruments of Troy's destruction, rather than that Juno is taking sides. — **uxor ...
ploret**] = 'a wife would weep for sons and husband killed', as Hecuba wept for Hector,
etc. and for Priam; the theme of Euripides' *Trojan Women*; cf. Aeneas' last glimpse of
Troy, *Aen.* 2. 766 'Pueri et pavidae longo ordine matres'.
69-72] These lines are traditionally printed as part of 3. 3, forming a self-admonitory
tailpiece, like 1. 6. 17-20, 2. 1. 37-40, perhaps 3. 2. 25-32. Taken at all closely, however,
with Juno's speech, they constitute an improbably bathetic conclusion. The stanza
seems more in keeping with the tone of the opening of 3. 4, and perhaps should be so
printed; *desine pervicax referre sermones deorum* would then act as a cross-reference to
the preceding ode, as 3. 2. 1-4 picks up the theme of the simple life from the concluding
stanza of 3. 1 and 3. 3. 9-12 picks up 3. 2. 21-4; for the abandonment of a theme which
threatened to get out of hand cf. 4. 15. 1-4. — **sermones deorum**] Generalising plural,
though only one divinity has been speaking, a common idiom. — **magna ... parvis**] cf.
4. 2. 27-32.

3. 4

Introduction: The longest and most ambitious of the Odes. In it, H. appeals to the Muses
for inspiration as their elect from childhood, before launching into the myth of the
battle of Jove against the Titans, which is told as an illustration of the triumph of order
over chaos. Cf. 2. 19, 3. 25.
Structure: Stanzas 1-2 appeal for inspiration. Stanzas 3-9 proclaim the special protection H.

has enjoyed since birth. Lines 37-42 form a bridge passage, asserting the role of poetry
as a civilising force and leading into the myth of Stanzas 11-16. In Stanzas 17-20 the
poet comments on the moral significance of his myth.
  See on 17-18 *ut ... dormirem*, etc.
Metre: Alcaics; see 1. 9M.
1-4] **Descende caelo**] 'come down from the heavens'; in a hymnal context, the words
  suggest an appeal for an epiphany — a personal appearance of the divinity before the
  suppliant; the Muses of course live on Helicon or on Parnassus, not in the heavens, and
  in fact (as in 3. 21. 7) this meaning is suggested only to be rejected in favour of a more
  matter-of-fact appeal by the poet to the Muse to abandon the heavens (the scene of the
  sermones deorum of the previous ode) in favour of a more terrestrial theme; the opening
  lines of 3. 4 are thus closely linked with the concluding Stanza of 3. 3 (see on 3. 3.
  69-72). — **dic longum melos**] H. bends to his ironic purpose the traditional convention
  according to which the Muse is the source of poetic inspiration, the poet being forced,
  as it were, to write as the Muse dictates; cf. 1. 24. 2-4, 1. 32. 3-4, 3. 11. 7; see on 3. 25.
  3-5; in the present case, H. is content for the inspiration to take the form of a melody on
  the *tibia* or the lyre (as in 1. 12. 1-2) or a sung text; by stating these three possibilities,
  he implies that inspiration provides only a starting point for a poem which must then be
  given shape by the conscious effort of the composing poet; for a first possibility followed
  by a series of others introduced by *seu*, cf. 22-4. — **regina Calliope**] 'queen of the Muses';
  Hesiod *Theog.* 79 calls her the 'noblest of the Muses'; in post-classical writers she be-
  comes the Muse of epic poetry; she figures only here in the *Odes*; cf. 1. 24. 3, 3. 30. 16,
  4. 3. 1 Melpomene, 1. 12. 2 Clio, 1. 1. 33 Euterpe and Polymnia. — **nunc**] 'on this occa-
  sion'. — **acuta**] 'clear', 'high-pitched'. — **citharave**] The *-ve* supports the preceding *sive*; no
  separation of lyre from strings is intended; cf. *Aen.* 6. 120 'Fretus cithara fidibusque
  canoris'. — **Phoebi**] For Apollo as a god of lyric poetry (a role he shares with Mercury),
  see 1. 32. 13-14, 4. 6. 29, 4. 15. 1, etc.
5-8] The poet enters into an inspired trance. — **Auditis?**] Best taken as addressed to H.'s
  chosen audience, the *virgines puerique* of 3. 1. 4, in preparation for the reassertion
  which follows of H.'s role as *Musarum sacerdos*. — **audire**] Picks up *auditis*; the poet
  hears in his trance the inspiration he sought in Stanza 1 (and appeals to his audience for
  confirmation); cf. *Eclogue* 10. 58-9. — **subeunt**] 'enter softly' (cf. *L&S* B 1).
9-20] H.'s inspired song begins with an oracular assertion of his status as the poet born to
  be *Musarum sacerdos*; cf. 4. 3. 1-2. — **fabulosae palumbes**] The woodpigeons are *fabu-
  losae* (1) in that they were destined to become the subject of a local legend (cf. 13-16),
  (2) in the sense that what occurred lay outside ordinary experience, perhaps also (3) in
  the sense that they were full of *fabulae* (had the power to foster the mythical imagina-
  tion of the young H.); cf. 1. 22. 7, also 1. 4. 16. — **Volture in Apulo**] Mt Voltur in
  Apulia, some 8 km west of H.'s birthplace Venusia, and near the point where Apulia,
  Samnium and Lucania meet. — **nutricis . . . Pulliae**] = 'outside the door of my nurse
  Pullia'; some have found it hard to accept that H. should want to tell us the name of his
  nurse, but the detail is consistent with the circumstantial tone of the following line; that
  the nurse's name should echo the name of the district seems less implausible once we
  accept that H.'s mood is fanciful (even playful) rather than wholly serious; the reading
  Apuliae has rather better authority, but the variation between *Apulo* and *Apuliae*,
  though not without parallel, is fussy and out of keeping with the context; the assertion,
  moreover, that the miracle actually occurred outside the limits of H.'s native Apulia is
  (despite *Sat.* 2. 1. 34) incredible. — **ludo . . . somno**] = *ludo fatigatum, fatigatumque
  somno*; see on 2. 19. 28; **fatigatum somno**] = 'tired out and asleep', rather than 'sleepy';
  cf. 18 *dormirem*. — **puerum palumbes**] Repeats in more emphatic form the juxtaposi-
  tion *me fabulosae*. — **mirum . . . Forenti**] i.e., a local miracle; Aceruntia, Bentia and
  Forentum are neighbouring towns, the first 'nestling in the hills', the second on the
  slopes (*saltus*), the third on the plains in rich farming country (cf. 3. 16. 26 and see on
  3. 6. 37-44); for H. as the local boy who made good, cf. 3. 30. 10-14. — **ut dormirem . . .
  ut premerer**] = 'how I slept . . . beneath the bay leaves, etc., piled on top of me'; the
  first of a series of repetitions (anaphora in asyndeton) designed to give rhetorical
  amplitude to this long ode; cf. 21, 25 *vester*, 26, 27 *non*, 33, 35 *visam*, 29, 37, 41 *vos*,
  45 *qui*, 53, 54, 55 *quid*, 58, 59 *hinc*, 61, 62 *qui*. — **sacra . . . myrto**] = *et sacra lauro et
  collata myrto*; for *-que . . . -que*, see on 1. 26. 12, for delayed *-que* on 1. 12. 11; in sense,
  both epithets with both nouns; the bay symbolises the protection of Apollo, the myrtle

that of Venus; together, they foreshadow H.'s future status as a poet of love. − **non . . . infans**] = 'though yet too young to speak, divinely inspired' (oxymoron); the context draws out the etymological sense of *infans*; for *animosus* 'filled with the breath of inspiration', cf. *Aen.* 6. 12 'Magnam cui [i.e., sacerdoti] mentem animumque / Delius inspirat vates'.

21-4] The formal hymn to the Muse which now begins continues until line 42. The transition from the magical infancy of the child destined to be a poet to the matter-of-fact account of the way of life of the grown H. is an indication of how seriously we should take the miracle just recounted; cf. for the list of favourite haunts *Epist.* 1. 7. 10-12; for the repetition of the personal pronoun (*vester . . . vestris, vos . . . vos*) as a structural device, see on 18 *ut dormirem*, etc. and on 1. 35. 5. − **in arduos Sabinos**] = 'to my farm in the Sabine hills'; see on 2. 18. 14. − **Praeneste**] 32 km east of Rome on a spur of the Apennines facing the Alban hills; a cool place in summer. − **Tibur**] See on 1. 7. 13. − **supinum**] 'sloping'. − **Baiae**] On the Bay of Naples; cf. 2. 18. 20.

25-8] The theme of divine protection now supplants that of absorption with poetry. − **vestris . . . choris**] = 'I who am welcomed at your springs and your dancing'; cf. 1. 1. 29-34; for *amicus* (*OLD* 5) cf. 1. 26. 1 'Musis amicus'; the springs are Hippocrene and Aganippe on Mt Helicon (cf. 3. 13. 13), Castalia on Mt Parnassus (line 61). − **non . . . retro**] See on 2. 7. 9-16 (where H.'s rescue is attributed to Mercury). − **devota arbor**] 'the accursed tree'; see 2. 13I. − **Palinurus**] A promontory in SW Lucania at the toe of Italy (see *Aen.* 6. 381); H. nowhere else mentions escape from shipwreck (except for the metaphorical shipwreck of 1. 5. 13-16).

29-32] H. passes from past protection to future protection; cf. 1. 22. − **utcumque**] Frequentative, 'whenever'; see on 1. 17. 10. − **libens . . . temptabo**] Cf. 2. 20. 14; **navita**] 'as a traveller by sea'; see on 1. 28. 23. − **urentis . . . viator**] *viator* balances *navita*; a land journey is meant, apparently, to the shores of the Persian Gulf (ancient Babylon and Assyria), an area known chiefly from the campaigns of Alexander, here a symbol of the remote East.

33-6] A variation on the theme of Stanza 8; see on 77-80. − **Britannos**] Symbol of the remote North; see on 1. 35. 30. − **laetum . . . Concanum**] The Concani were a tribe of the Cantabri in NW Spain; for the legend that they drank horses' blood, cf. *Georgics* 463 (of the Geloni) 'Lac concretum cum sanguine potat equino'. − **Gelonos**] A Scythian tribe; see on 2. 9. 23, cf. 2. 20. 19. − **Scythicum amnem**] The Don; see on 1. 19. 10. − **inviolatus**] The key word is delayed for emphasis.

37-42] The panegyric of the Muses continues; 37 and 41 *vos* lock on to 29 *vos*; a bridge passage preparing the transition to the myth. − **Caesarem altum**] 'great Augustus'; for *altum*, see *OLD* 11. − **militia simul . . . oppidis**] *simul* (= *simul ac*, as often) is best taken as frequentative: no sooner has Augustus disbanded his legions (after each campaign) or, perhaps, dispersed them in garrison towns throughout Italy, than, etc.; unlikely that H. means the resettlement of veterans after Actium (as in *Sat.* 2. 6. 55-6); *abdidit* has been doubted in favour of the *addidit* and *reddidit* found in some MSS (the latter an obvious 'correction') but is supported by *Epist.* 1. 1. 4-5. − **Pierio recreatis antro**] The power of poetry to restore mental health after the stresses of war is meant; Augustus is complimented as a man of peace ('finire quaerentem labores') and a patron of literature; the *Pierium antrum* ('cave of the Muses'), if not fanciful, may refer (in suitably poetic terms) to performances by writers in Augustus' Temple of Apollo or elsewhere under Imperial patronage; cf. 3. 25. 3-6, *Epist.* 2. 2. 91-101; see on 2. 1. 39. − **lene . . . gaudetis**] The *lene consilium* ('gentle counsel') refers to the power of myth to instruct when handled by a poet with a moral objective; *lene* because the instruction is (1) unobtrusive, (2) conducive to civilised (rather than violent) action; cf. Aristotle's well-known observation that poetry (i.e., myth as treated by the epic or tragic poet) is more 'philosophical' than history (*Poetics* 9.3); **consilium**] contracted to 3 syllables, of which the 3rd is elided; **dato gaudetis**] i.e., 'rejoice when the inspired poet imparts the *lene consilium* contained in his poetry'; cf. the echo in 3. 5. 45-6. − **almae**] Traditional epithet of goddesses, especially Venus; see Bailey on Lucretius 1. 1 ('the idea of creation and nourishment seems always to be presen:').

42-8] **Scimus ut . . . caduco**] The ground is now laid for the transition to the myth; cf. 3. 27. 25; H. has already alluded to the myth of the Titans (whom he identifies with the Giants) in the concluding stanza of 1. 3 and in 3. 1. 7; here, their rebellion against the authority of Jove and their defeat by him are made to point the moral that 'vis consili expers mole ruit sua' (line 65) — an obvious allusion to the Civil Wars and the overthrow of the 'mindless' might of Antony by the disciplined authority of Octavian; traditionally, the revolt of the Giants was against the gods in general; here, as in 3. 1. 7, the revolt is against Jove; **immanemque turbam**] the Giants (unlike the Titans) were monstrous in appearance (serpents for feet, etc.); **fulmine caduco**] for the thunderbolt of Jove, see on 3. 3. 6; the more picturesque details of their punishment are eliminated (see on 73-6). — **qui . . . regit aequo**] An impressive assertion of the omnipotence of Jove; contrast the compact statement of 3. 1. 7-8; *qui = is qui* (defining relative); **inertem**] i.e., unlike the sea; cf. 1. 34. 9 'bruta tellus'; **regnaque tristia**] i.e., the underworld.

49-52] Having launched himself 'medias in res' (*AP* 148), H. now retells the story of the revolt as a fill-in or flashback. — **Magnum terrorem**] Appears inconsistent with the assertion of Jove's omnipotence; the *magnus terror* is, however, the alarm and confusion of a state thrown into panic by sudden uprising — a situation with which Jove found himself confronted and with which he had to contend, though not himself sharing in the fear; H., i.e., recasts his version to make it fit more easily the events of the Civil Wars. — **fratresque . . . Olympo**] Otus and Ephialtes; cf. Virgil's version *Georgics* 1. 28-82; the traditional form of the legend was that they tried to pile Ossa on Olympus and Pelion on Ossa, as a means of climbing from earth to Heaven; **opaco**] implies that the peak of Olympus was shrouded in mist; **posuisse**] a rare example in H. of a common mannerism of the Augustan elegiac poets (traces already in early Latin); the perfect infinitive was perhaps felt as 'aoristic', stressing the completion of the action.

53-64] The Stoic view of the world, as interpreted by Virgil and Horace, involves the paradox that, though Jove can do anything he likes (3. 1. 8 'cuncta supercilio moventis'), he chooses to act through others. The gods in H.'s myth, like ordinary men in the Stoic view, are represented as the agents of their own destiny. Thus, Jove achieves victory through the collaboration of Minerva, Vulcan and Juno, though he does not need their collaboration, just as the Giants, by their action, become the reluctant agents of their own destruction: 'ducunt volentem fata, trahunt nolentem' (Cleanthes, in Seneca *Epist.* 107. 11). This is the doctrine worked out here in suitably picturesque form (the function of myth in the hands of a sophisticated poet is to stimulate its own interpretation). — **Typhoeus, etc.**] Giants rather than Titans. — **minaci statu**] i.e., inspiring terror by his gigantic stature. — **evolsisque . . . audax**] i.e., 'and Enceladus firing his gigantic javelins undaunted'; H.'s Giants are individualised figures standing out from a background of battle. — **sonantem aegida**] In Homer, the *aegis* is a shield made for Zeus by Hephaestus, sometimes used by Athena; in art, a goatskin worn by Athena, sometimes as a shield; it was fringed with snakes and the Gorgon's head was fastened to the middle; *sonantem* either because it thundered when Zeus struck it, or because of the snakes; cf. 1. 15. 11. — **avidus Volcanus**] Obscure; perhaps an allusion (so Porphyrio) to the jealousy with which he kept fire to himself (cf. 1. 3. 27-8). — **matrona Iuno**] Hints at the Roman Juno of 3. 3. 17-68; note the delayed pause. — **numquam . . . arcum**] 'he who ever has his bow slung over his shoulder' — i.e., never puts it aside but is always ready to draw and shoot. — **rore Castaliae**] 'in the pure water of Castalia'; see on line 25. — **lavit**] Present of the 3rd-conjugation form; cf. 4. 6. 26. — **Lyciae dumeta**] Apollo was worshipped in Lycia in Asia Minor, particularly at Patara; the first member of a chiasmus (*Lyciae dumeta, natalemque* [i.e., on Delos] *silvam : Delius, Patareus*), the god's name following as a climax.

65-8] A gnomic stanza, pointing the moral of the myth. — **Vis consili expers**] 'mindless force'; contrast 41 'lene consilium, etc.'. — **mole ruit sua**] 'collapses under its own weight'. — **vim temperatam**] 'controlled (disciplined) force'. — **di quoque . . . in maius**] 'the gods too advance'; i.e., the disciplined efforts of mankind are made more successful by the gods' assistance. — **idem**] Cf. 2. 19. 27. — **odere viris . . . moventis**] = 'detest force when aimed at every conceivable sinful objective'; for the idea cf. Euripides *Helen* 903 'Brute force is hateful to God'; delayed caesura after *odere*.

69-76] The ode concludes with a series of illustrations of violence (varying greatly in scale) eternally punished. — **centimanus Gyges**] See on 2. 17. 14. — **Orion**] The giant hunter; cf. 2. 13. 39-40. H.'s version of the myth, according to which he attempted to rape Diana, is also found in Cicero *Arat.* 672; Hygin. *Astra.* 2. 35 attributes it to Callimachus. — **iniecta . . . suis**] 'Earth piled on her own monstrous offspring grieves'; some of the defeated Giants were imprisoned under the earth (or had mountains piled on top

of them); Terra is cast in the role of the grieving mother who has lost her sons. — **fulmine
. . . Orcum**] Others of the Giants were despatched with a thunderbolt; cf. line 44;
Orcum] see on 2. 3. 24; the strong caesura after syllable 5 is unusual. — **nec peredit . . .
Aetnen**] 'nor has the darting fire (from the Giant's mouth) eaten through Aetna placed
over him' (the fate of Enceladus); i.e., though fire belches forth from the volcano, the
Giant does not escape.

77-80] A picturesque concluding stanza, continuing the theme of Stanza 19 (as Stanza 9
continues that of Stanza 8), slackening the tension at the end. — **incontinentis . . . iecur**]
'the liver of the lecherous Tityos' (another Giant, killed by Apollo and Artemis for
attempting to rape their mother Leto — cf. 2. 14. 8); for the liver as the site of the
passion of love, see on 1. 13. 4. — **ales**] The vulture destined to tear at Tityos' liver for
eternity as he lay in Hades. — **nequitiae**] See on 3. 15. 2. — **amatorem Pirithoum**] 'the
lecher Pirithous', king of the Lapithae; along with Theseus he went down to Hades in an
attempt to kidnap Persephone; both were imprisoned there (Theseus until rescued by
Hercules); cf. 4. 7. 28; for *amator*, see on 3. 18. 1.

3. 5

Introduction: In 3. 5 H. reverts to the theme of 3. 2 and 3. 3, the *virtus* of the fighting
soldier; as in 3. 4 a myth retold to bring out its contemporary relevance occupies a
major place. This time, a myth from Roman history: the soldiers of Crassus who surren-
dered to the Parthians at Carrhae in 53 BC deserve no more consideration than the
soldiers of Regulus who surrendered to the Carthaginians in Africa in 255 BC. Regulus'
speech in the Senate is rhetorically effective, however great our reservations about the
tough, practical sentiments attributed to him ('disgraceful way for soldiers to behave',
'waste of money to ransom them'); the series of vignettes following the speech are as
imaginatively exquisite as they are models of economy. H.'s object seems to be to lend
support to Augustus' hard-line policy with regard to Parthia. Syme, *Roman Revolution*
388: 'in the East, prestige was his object, diplomacy his method. The threat of force
was enough. The King of the Parthians was persuaded to surrender the captured stan-
dards and Roman soldiers surviving from the disasters of Crassus and Antonius.' See on
3. 2. 1-6 and 3. 6. 9-16; cf. also 1. 29. Negotiations were not completed till 20 BC. H.'s
interest is probably less in the immediate situation than in upholding, in a poem which
is one of a series reaffirming traditional attitudes for the benefit of the new generation,
the old Roman view, attributed by Livy to M. Torquatus in the Second Punic War, that
Roman soldiers do not surrender — or deserve no sympathy if they do (Livy 22. 60. 7);
see on lines 13-18.
Structure: Stanza 1, gnomic opening; Stanzas 2-3, indignant denunciation of the survivors
of Carrhae, leading into Stanzas 4-14, the myth of Regulus. As in 3. 3, the myth includes
a long set speech; here, however, the myth concludes with a dramatic evocation of the
scene following Regulus' speech — one of the finest passages in the *Odes*, comparable in
the Roman Odes only with 3. 6. 33-44.
Metre: Alcaics; see 1. 9M.
1-4] A fine, sonorous opening, to justify the extravagant compliment to Augustus; at the
same time, a clear, concise statement of theme. — **Caelo . . . regnare**] i.e., the clap of
thunder which marked the final victory of Jove over the Titans, 3. 4. 42-4 and 74-5:
'we believed in Jove as King in Heaven when he thundered in the sky'; *caelo* equally
with *tonantem* and *regnare*. — **praesens . . . habebitur**] Augustus' coming victories over
the Britons and the Parthians, i.e., will proclaim the presence of the god here on earth;
for the historical situation see 1. 35I; for the divinity of Augustus, see 3. 3. 11-12; for
the Britons (symbol of the remote, rebellious North), see on 1. 35. 30; for the *Persi*
(= *Parthi*), see on 1. 2. 22; they first appear in the Roman Odes in 3. 2. 1-4.
5-12] **Milesne . . . vixit**] i.e., the survivors of M. Crassus' disastrous defeat at Carrhae in
53 BC (more than a quarter of a century before), when 20 000 Roman soldiers were said
to have surrendered; *turpis* both with *coniuge barbara* ('soldier disgraced by a barbarian
wife' and with *vixit* ('lived a husband and disgraced', instead of dying as a soldier). —
hostium . . . in armis] = 'lived to become a veteran in the service of the foreign enemy to
whom he had allied himself in marriage'; *miles*, at its first occurrence a collective singular
(= 'have the soldiers of C . . .'), now focuses on an individual ('has the soldier who . . .');

hostium socerorum] generalising plural; the action is placed in context, as in 4. 3. 8, 4. 12. 7-8, etc.; **pro**] exclamatory ('alas', 'the shame of...'); **inversi mores**] 'values turned upside down'; i.e., no longer brave but cowards; a first hint of the theme of 25-36. — **sub rege ... Apulus**] Indignant juxtaposition; cf. 22; the *Marsus* and the *Apulus* should represent tough Sabellian stock; see on 3. 6. 37-44. — **anciliorum**] The sacred shields, dating from the time of Numa, preserved in the Temple of Mars. — **nominis et togae**] i.e., their status as Roman citizens, of which the toga is the symbol. — **Vestae**] Cf. 3. 30. 9. — **incolumi Iove**] Refers probably to the Temple of Jove on the Capitol; the fact that it still stands symbolises the continuing role of Jove and the soldier's neglect of his true allegiance.

13-18] M. Atilius Regulus, *cos. iterum* 256, attempted an invasion of Africa during the First Punic War; he was initially successful, but then defeated and captured along with large numbers of his troops. H.'s account follows the version in Cicero *Off.* 1. 39 (expanded 3. 99, followed by a long discussion of the moral problems involved) with an interesting exception: in the traditional version the emphasis is laid on Carthaginian generals held by Rome, rather than on Roman soldiers held by the Carthaginians. H. seems to have adapted to his purpose the speech made in the Senate by T. Manlius Torquatus in 216, attacking the ransoming of the prisoners of Cannae; much of what H. makes Regulus say corresponds to Livy's account (22. 59-61) of what Torquatus said; Torquatus is described as 'pristae ac nimis durae, ut plerisque videatur, severitatis'; the mythologising H., i.e., does not scruple to adapt history to his purpose; see H. Kornhardt, *Hermes* 82, 1954, 101-23. — **condicionibus foedis**] The Carthaginian terms for ransoming their Roman prisoners which Regulus had been released on parole to present to the Senate. — **exemplo trahenti perniciem**] 'a precedent that spelled disaster'; the MSS have *trahentis*. — **si non ... pubes**] i.e., if the Roman troops which had been captured were not allowed to die, as deserving no pity, at the hands of their captors, instead of being ransomed; **periret**] the final syllable counts as long; see on 1. 3. 36.

18-24] Regulus' speech begins in mid-stanza at the same point as Juno's speech in 3. 3. 18. — **Signa**] The Roman standards, like those captured at Carrhae; cf. 4. 15. 6-8. — **arma ... derepta**] i.e., prisoners disarmed without resistance. — **civium ... libero**] Indignant juxtaposition, as in 9; *civium* because, even if no soldiers, they should have remembered their status as Romans. — **portas**] The gates of Carthage. — **Marte ... nostro**] i.e., laid waste by earlier Roman victories.

25-30] Regulus' argument is that ransoming soldiers demoralised by surrender is a waste of money — they will never make good soldiers again. — **acrior ... redibit**] i.e., will return a braver soldier than when he surrendered. — **flagitio ... damnum**] i.e., the proposed ransoming is a disgrace as well as a waste of money. — **neque amissos colores ... deterioribus**] 'wool doctored with dye does not recover its lost colours' (i.e., the colours produced by the original dyeing process once these have faded); similarly, true *virtus*, once lost, resists restoration in those who have been demoralised (by surrender); the comparison of the soldier's training to the dyeing of cloth goes back to Plato *Repub.* 429 b-430 a (the training of the Guardians must be so inculcated as never to fade, as dyed fabrics sometimes fade); cf. Quintilian 1. 1. 5 (early speech habits, once inculcated, do not fade); Regulus, however, is dealing with a situation not contemplated by Plato or Quintilian — what to do when training *does* fail; his argument is that it is as futile to retrain such soldiers as to redye cloth — it won't work; **amissos colores refert**] 'takes again its lost colours'; **medicata fuco**] pejorative, 'though doctored with dye'; as usually interpreted, the argument is that wool, once dyed, can never be made white again; but (1) who would want to un-dye wool? (2) H., like Plato, clearly regards the trained soldier, like dyed cloth, as the outcome of a process undertaken to that end; his argument is that, if something goes wrong (as in the case of his soldiers who abjectly surrendered), it is useless to repeat the process; **vera virtus**] 'true courage', which, like the 'true colours' of the original dyeing, cannot be restored once lost; the argument implies that Regulus' soldiers (like those of Crassus) fought bravely enough until demoralised by defeat, courage being a state of mind (a 'colouring' of the mind) produced by training — the theme of 3. 2. 1-24; but *vera virtus* probably also echoes the 'true virtue' of the Stoics — it was a debated point whether this true virtue could be recovered if lost; **deterioribus**] the demoralised soldiers who cannot be reprocessed.

31-6] A further illustration; the point is not the timidity of the deer before capture, but the certainty that it will emerge from capture with no fight left in it; the soldier, i.e., whose failed courage allowed him to surrender will be further demoralised by captivity.

— **extricata**] Delayed caesura. — **Marte altero**] A second campaign; not a second war (the First Punic War is still in progress). — **iners**] Implies the prostration of defeat and also the resourcelessness of the soldier whose training (*ars*) has deserted him.

37-40] **unde vitam sumeret**] Safety for the soldier, i.e., lies in his sword, not in negotiation. — **altior ruinis**] Ironical juxtaposition: the rise of Carthage is at the expense of the disgrace and collapse of her opponent; **Italiae ruinis**] Regulus foresees, i.e., the literal collapse in ruins of Italy at the hands of the invader (a prophecy that nearly came true in the Second Punic War).

41-50] Cf. with H.'s imaginative expansion Cicero *Off*. 3. 99 'Regulus utilitatis speciem videbat, sed eam, ut res declarat, falsam iudicavit. Quae erat talis: manere in patria, esse domi suae cum uxore, cum liberis': H. is economical and vivid, passing from one scene to the next — Regulus pushes wife and children aside (i.e., on his way to the Senate); he is a remote, unapproachable figure until it is his turn to speak; he hastens to depart as soon as the debate is over. — **ut capitis minor**] 'like a man deprived of his status as a citizen'; Regulus, i.e., regards himself as disgraced along with his soldiers; his courage now is that of a man who accepts his fate; for *capitis* see on 1. 24. 2; genitive of respect. — **virilem . . . voltum**] The attitude of a man who refuses all contact with those around him. — **donec . . . dato**] = 'until he strengthened the resolution of the wavering senators and got them to adopt his unprecedented proposal'; *donec* ('until') is rare in Cicero, frequent in Horace, Virgil and the historians; usually in H. with the subjunctive; **consilio dato**] the echo of 3. 4. 41 is probably not unintentional; instrumental with *firmaret*. — **egregius exul**] A climactic oxymoron — exile is normally a humiliation; those exiled, normally reluctant to depart. — **atqui**] 'and yet'; cf. 1. 23. 9, 3. 7. 9. — **quae . . . tortor pararet**] Cf. Cicero *Off*. 3. 103 'Conservandi iuris iurandi causa ad cruciatum revertisse', ibid. 105 'Qui retinendi officii causa cruciatum subierit voluntarium'.

50-56] A memorable simile concludes the ode with a calculated slackening of the tension. Regulus' departure is as calm and detached as that of the great lawyer off for a break in the country at the conclusion of a drawn-out case. — **dimovit . . . propinquos**] 'pushed his way through the relatives who blocked his path'; cf. the thrusting-aside of wife and children in 41-3. — **et populum . . . morantem**] The succinctly-evoked scene widens to take in the crowd beyond. — **clientum longa negotia**] i.e., a long case undertaken by a *patronus* on behalf of his *clientes*; the image implies patience and lack of personal involvement. — **relinqueret**] 'were leaving behind him'. — **Venafranos in agros**] i.e., an estate near Venafrum, in Campania; cf. 2. 6. 16. — **Tarentum**] founded by Sparta; cf. 2. 6. 9-12.

3. 6

Introduction: The last of the Roman Odes takes up the theme of moral decline already hinted at in 3. 5. 5-12: as in 3. 5 (and 3. 2), the context is the need for a nation morally strong enough to undertake the conquest of its foreign enemies. H. argues that only a return to religion and the god-fearing humility of the past can arrest the decline.

Stanza 1 alludes to Augustus' policy of rebuilding the temples ravaged during the Civil Wars, proclaimed *Res Gestae* 20. 4 'Duo et octaginta templa deum in urbe consul sextum [28 BC] ex auctoritate Senatus refeci, nullo praetermisso quod eo tempore refici debebat'; cf. Suetonius *Aug*. 30; Livy 4. 20 calls Augustus 'Templorum omnium conditor aut restitutor'. It is unlikely that so ambitious a programme was carried out in a single year ('refici' probably refers to the decree authorising the work of reconstruction); the common assumption that the ode must have been written in 28 BC is, therefore, not justified. See 1. 35I.

Structure: Three groups of four stanzas. Stanzas 1-4 develop the theme 'di multa neglecti dederunt Hesperiae mala luctuosae'; Stanzas 5-8 castigate the decline in sexual morality as the prime cause of Rome's military defeats; Stanzas 9-12 build up a picture of the healthy home background of Rome's heroic soldiers of the past — the product of the stern, simple discipline of Italian rustic life and good Sabellian stock. Stanzas 1-4 are heavily endstopped; this pattern is continued in the second group until Stanza 7, where there is a lighter pause; at Stanza 9 a more flowing movement begins (light pause at the end of Stanza 9, Stanza 10 spills over into Stanza 11); this movement stops abruptly at

the end of Stanza 11: the damning judgement of Stanza 12 is thrown into emphasis by
its syntactical isolation.

Metre: Alcaics; see 1. 9M; the incidence of delayed caesura in line 3 of the stanza is unusual
(11, 15, 19, 27).

1-4] **Delicta ... lues**] The notion that the slaughter of the Civil Wars represents the
working-out of ancestral guilt occurs in several forms in the Augustan poets. In *Georgics*
1. 501-14 Virgil traces the curse back to Troy ('Satis iam pridem sanguine nostro /
Laomedonteae luimus periuria Troiae' — cf. 1. 2. 29-30, 3. 3); in *Epode* 7. 17-20 H.
dates the curse from Romulus' murder of his brother Remus — a more audacious
formulation:

> ... acerba fata Romanos agunt
> scelusque fraternae necis
> ut immerentis fluxit in terram Remi
> sacer nepotibus cruor;

see on 2. 1. 1-16; here, H. retreats to a position more compatible with official propa-
ganda: the opening *delicta maiorum* is left undefined; the *delicta* are spoken of, not as
a curse, but as a symptom of something more socially acceptable, neglect of the gods, as
expressed by the neglect or destruction of their shrines; **inmeritus lues**] though they
have no personal share in the *delicta maiorum*, the new generation, to whom H. again
addresses himself, will continue to pay for them (by continuing defeat in battle) until
they commit themselves to a positive demonstration of *pietas* by carrying out and com-
pleting the programme of rebuilding. — **Romane**] A form of address associated with
oracular pronouncements, e.g., Livy 5. 16. 9 'Romane, aquam Albanam cave lacu
contineri'; see Austin on *Aen*. 6. 851 (Anchises so addresses Aeneas); H., i.e., resumes
the persona of 3. 1. 1-4.

5-8] **dis ... imperas**] i.e., the young generation, by acknowledging the power of Jove, has
saved Rome from destruction; the power of Rome still stands, but is gravely threatened;
cf. 3. 1. 5-8. — **hinc ... exitum**] Emphatic general statement: the gods start and end all
things, the fact must be accepted. — **multa mala**] Such as the defeats instanced in
Stanza 3. — **Hesperiae luctuosae**] Italy is spoken of as 'plunged in grief' to magnify the
calamity of past defeats.

9-16] As in 3. 2 and 3. 5, the situation in the East is treated as a national emergency. —
Iam bis ... impetus] Pacorus, a Parthian prince, had invaded Syria at the time of the
Perusine War; after a series of victories (especially over the troops of L. Decidius Saxa in
40 BC), he was killed in 38 BC (Florus 2. 19. 3; Syme, *Roman Revolution* 223);
Monaeses is most likely the Parthian commander who defeated Oppius Statianus in 36
(rather than the commander who defeated Crassus at Carrhae in 56); the comparatively
recent defeats of the forces of Mark Antony, i.e., are intended in both cases (Carrhae
being treated as past history — and not in any case an *inauspicatus impetus*), these being
contrasted by implication with a fresh military confrontation which is imminent; cf. on
1. 2. 21-30; **manus inauspicatos**] i.e., not protected by prior consultation in proper form
of the will of the gods. — **adiecisse renidet**] Cf. Livy 23. 12. 1 (Mago, reporting the
victory at Cannae, pours before the Carthaginian Senate a huge pile of captured gold
rings) 'Adiecit neminem nisi equitem, atque eorum ipsorum primores, id gerere insigne';
here the reference is to the individual soldiers of Pacorus and Monaeses who wear the
captured rings as personal loot. — **Dacus**] The Dacians (area of lower Danube) sided with
Antony in the first confrontation with Octavian (Dio 21-2); cf. *Sat*. 2. 6. 53 (just after
Actium) 'Numquid de Dacis audisti'; they continue to be represented as a menace; see
on 3. 8. 18. — **Aethiops**] i.e., the Egyptian naval forces of Cleopatra at Actium; cf. 1.
37. 6-12; for their huge ships, *Epode* 1. 1-2. — **missilibus sagittis**] The normal weapon
of nomad cavalry.

17-20] In Stanza 2 the defeats and near-defeats suffered by Rome are represented as due
to Rome's neglect of the gods; in Stanza 5 they are traced to their source in the corrup-
tion of family life — a further instance of H.'s Stoic dualism: the gods decide our fate in
general terms, we are the instruments of our salvation or destruction; cf. on 3. 3. 17-36,
where the destruction of Troy is represented as the working-out of a curse, and finally
brought about (as here) by a moral decline. — **Fecunda culpae saecula**] = 'an age fertile
in sin', i.e., instead of producing healthy soldiers; ironic oxymoron; *culpae* especially of

ODES 3.6

257

sexual misconduct, *OLD* 3 b; genitive of respect. — **nuptias . . . domos**] = 'first polluted
the institution of marriage and the traditional purity of family life'. — **hoc fonte . . .
fluxit**] = 'the stream led off from this source became a disastrous flood, overwhelming
our country and its people in defeat' (*clades* is the word for defeat on the battlefield);
the vivid metaphor prepares the transition to the second and more important theme of
the ode, for which the imminent campaign against Rome's Eastern enemies is perhaps
no more than a convenient topical pretext.

21-4] H.'s typical modern woman of Stanzas 6-8 recalls Sallust's Sempronia, *Cat.* 25; seen
through different eyes, she is the mistress of the elegiac poets (see, e.g., Propertius 2. 3.
9-22, Ovid's composite picture *Am.* 2. 4. 24-30); addressing himself to the élite of the
new generation, H. concerns himself only with women of that class. — **motus . . . Ionicos**]
Cf. Sallust's dry 'psallere, saltare elegantius quam necesse est probae', Propertius' 'posito
formose saltat Iaccho, egit ut euhantis dux Ariadna choros', Ovid's 'illa placet gestu
numerosaque bracchia ducit / et tenerum molli torquet ab arte latus', and see on 2. 12.
17-20; for where this leads cf. the pathetic Lyce of 4. 13. 5-8; Ionian dances, like the
Ionian mode in music, were said to be especially voluptuous and lascivious. — **matura
virgo**] = 'the girl of marriageable age'; cf. 1. 23. 12, 3. 11. 11-12. — **fingitur artibus**] i.e.,
learns how to behave in order to make herself attractive to men and the accomplish-
ments that go with this (singing, lyre-playing, what in 1. 19. 7 H. calls 'protervitas'; see
on 4. 13. 21. — **iam nunc**] With both *fingitur* and *meditatur*. — **incestos amores
meditatur**] i.e., she is planning a career of adultery before she is even married. — **de
tenero ungui**] i.e., 'while she is still a mere child'; for the age at which girls married, see
2. 51; an adaptation of Gk ἐξ ἀπαλῶν ὀνύχων; a second sense, 'down to the last detail',
is perhaps also present (see Williams 66-7).

25-32] We pass now from daydreams to the sordid reality. — **mox . . . adulteros**] i.e., after
she is married; all too soon, she is past her prime and has to take the initiative with
lovers younger than herself; cf. Lydia 1. 25. 9-10 and Sallust's Sempronia — her 'libido'
was 'sic accensa ut saepius peteret viros quam peteretur', also Cicero's picture of Clodia,
Cael. 38 and 49; **adulteros**] see on 1. 25. 9 — **inter mariti vina**] i.e., at a dinner party; the
husband is more interested in his cups than in his wife, indifferent to, rather than
oblivious of, her misconduct — both, i.e., are equally depraved; for the complaisant
husband (a stock figure of Roman love poetry), see, e.g., Catullus 17, Ovid *Am.* 2. 19;
contrast the sterner morality of the Scythae, 3. 24. 17-24. — **neque eligit . . . remotis**]
i.e., as she becomes more and more desperate, it is no longer a matter of the hasty,
secret affair in the dark; instead, she rises from the dinner table with the full knowledge
of her husband, to give herself to the first bidder; cf. Cicero *Cael.* 47 (of Clodia) 'Huc
unius mulieris libidinem esse prolapsam, ut ea non modo solitudinem ac tenebras . . .
non quaerat, sed . . . clarrissima luce laetetur'. — **sed iussa coram**] i.e., in response to an
invitation openly offered in her husband's presence. — **institor . . . magister**] The small-
time businessman and the Spanish ship's captain are instanced as vulgar men whom her
husband has to entertain, perhaps, by way of business, beneath the notice of a respect-
able *matrona*; a similar pair are singled out *Epode* 17. 20 'amata nautis et institoribus'.
— **dedecorum pretiosus emptor**] = 'a purchaser of misconduct too good to be missed',
i.e., in the market for illicit sex and able to pay a stiff price; the phrase, which applies
to both *institor* and *magister*, forms an appropriate climax in preparation for the
abruptly introduced picture in Stanza 9.

33-6] In 3. 24 H. contrasts the superior sexual mores of the Scythae; here he develops
the more conventional theme 'how different things were in the days of Rome's great-
ness!'. (Even then, as we saw in 3. 5, deplorable lapses could occur.) — **Non his
parentibus**] Not, i.e., an *adultera* for a mother, an *institor* or a ship's captain for a
father. — **iuventus**] = 'men'; see on 1. 2. 41. — **infecit . . . Punico**] i.e., in the naval
battles of the First Punic War; cf. 2. 1. 34-5. — **Pyrrhumque**] King Pyrrhus of Epirus,
who invaded Italy in 280 BC; his costly victories perpetuated the phrase 'Pyrrhic
victory'. — **Antiochum**] Antiochus III, defeated by Scipio Africanus at Magnesia in
190 BC. — **Hannibalemque dirum**] The Carthaginian leader in the Second Punic War;
some MSS have *durum*; see on 2. 12. 2.

37-44] Hannibal, etc. were defeated by the soldier-sons of soldier-farmers, especially the
Oscan-speaking peoples of the SE (see below on 41-2); *Sabelli* (not synonymous with
'Sabine') is the Roman name for speakers of Oscan, including among others the Marsi
and the Apuli (cf. 1. 2. 39, 3. 5. 9, 2. 20. 18); see Salmon, 'Sabelli' in *OCD*. Even if it is

not a fact that the brunt of the fighting was borne by the Sabellian peoples of the SE,
it is true that much of the fighting in the war with Pyrrhus and the Second Punic War
was in that area; apart from local patriotism (Venusia, H.'s birthplace, had been strongly
pro-Sabellian in the Social War), H.'s assertion is justified by the increasing role played
by Sabellian troops in the Roman army since the time of the Social War and the emer-
gence of the concept of Italy as a single nation. — **rusticorum mascula militum proles**]
A series of implied polarities: farming stock, not city folk; virile, not effeminate;
soldiers' sons, not sons of *institores* and ships' captains. — **Sabellis . . . glaebas**] Stresses
their hard upbringing; **ligonibus**] 'mattocks', 'hoes'. — **severae . . . arbitrium**] 'at a stern
mother's bidding' — i.e., a mother unlike the promiscuous *matrona* of 25-32. — **recisos
portare fustis**] 'to gather cut wood' for the fire; they do this at the end of their day's
work under the farmer's direction in the fields; at home, his wife commands. — **Sol . . .
umbras**] i.e., as the shadows projected by the mountains lengthen and become
distorted at the end of the day; we are, i.e., on the eastern side of the Apennines, in
Apulia or Calabria, where the ranges run at right angles to the setting sun; cf. 4. 5.
29-30; **mutaret**] the subjunctive is probably frequentative, 'whenever' (common from
Livy onwards, Leumann-Hofmann 767; cf. *demeret*). — **iuga . . . fatigatis**] The oxen,
tired from their day in the fields, are unharnessed at evening. — **amicum tempus agens**]
For both man and beast the end of the day is 'the welcome hour'; for this sense of
amicus, see *OLD* 5. — **abeunte curru**] The sun now becomes the Sun god departing in
his chariot.

45-8] A surprise ending after the tranquil rallentando of Stanza 11. Pessimism was
conventional in the ancient world. It finds its most familiar expression in the myth of
the Golden Age (followed by ages of Silver and Bronze and then by the corrupt Iron
Age in which we now live). But if conventional, the pessimism is also sincere and
characteristic of the Roman cast of mind. Though committed in Book 5 to something
approaching a doctrine of progress by his account of the development of civilisation
from primitive times, Lucretius regards our world as irredeemably corrupt (5. 199
'tanta stat praedita culpa') and doomed to eventual destruction (5. 95-7 'Tris species
tam dissimilis . . . [land, sea, sky] una dies dabit exitio, multosque per annos / susten-
tata ruet moles et machina mundi', cf. 2. 1146). The moral depravity of progress is a
constant theme of the Augustan elegists; Ovid's enthusiasm for the new, affluent,
permissive society is plainly tongue-in-cheek. Augustus' efforts were directed ostensibly
to restoring the past — a policy as congenial to the Roman as it was politically expedient.
We might expect H. to round off his case by arguing that, given regular training and
discipline, the process of moral degeneration can be slowed down, as Virgil argues that
the natural degeneration of the physical world (*Georgics* 1. 199-200 'Sic omnia fatis / in
peius ruere ac retro sublapsa referri') can be held in check by the determined efforts of
the farmer; tight, logical argument is not, however, in the manner of the *Odes*. —
damnosa dies] 'the passage of time that destroys all things'. — **peior avis**] Contracted
comparison, = 'worse than the age of our grandfathers'. — **nos nequiores**] H. identifies
himself with his audience. — **mox . . . vitiosiorem**] Chill comfort for the new generation:
if they give up their disregard of the gods (Stanzas 1-2), they can hope to escape from
the curse of the past, but can never rival the heroes of the past; H. follows the doctrine
of the Stoic Poseidonius, who dated Roman degeneration from the destruction of
Carthage in 146 BC; cf. Livy's picture, *Praefat.* 8-9, of a steady decline in morality,
'donec ad haec tempora, quibus nec vitia nostra nec remedia pati possumus perventum
est'.

3. 7

Introduction: Asterie's faithful young husband or lover won't be back till the spring. For
the present he's held up in Oricum, where he is successfully resisting temptation;
Asterie is well advised to do likewise.
Structure: Stanzas 1-2, hypothesis; Stanzas 3-5, the temptation to which Gyges is exposed;
with Stanza 6, the transition begins from Gyges to Asterie; the turning point is at 22
At tibi in mid-line and mid-stanza (cf. 2. 5. 9); Stanzas 7-8, friendly advice to Asterie
not to get too involved with Enipeus.
Metre: Asclepiad (d); see 1. 5M.

1-5] Quid fles?] The most natural assumption is that Gyges has just left and the tears are for his departure (see, however, on 5-8). — **candidi Favonii**] The westerly winds which mark the resumption of navigation in the early spring; cf. 1. 4. 1-4; **candidi**] 'fair', 'bright'; cf. 1. 7. 15, 3. 27. 19; storm winds are black (1. 5. 7). — **Thyna merce beatum**] The Thyni occupied the coast, the Bithyni the hinterland; Gyges may be an overseas trader (*mercator*), here treated by H. with more sympathy than usual, though irony is to be suspected regarding the extent and certainty of his prosperity; or perhaps just a member of the *cohors* of a provincial governor, like Catullus in Poem 10, etc., and the *merces* gifts for Asterie (cf. 4. 12. 21-2); Gyges is assumed in that case to be likely to fare better than Catullus did in Bithynia (Catullus 10. 9-11). — **constantis iuvenem fide**] Perhaps a hint of irony here too; the genitive *fide* is a rare by-form (said by Gellius 9. 14. 24-5 to have been favoured by Caesar).

5-8] Oricum (or Oricus) is a port in Epirus at the entrance to the Adriatic, a little south of Brundisium (Gyges' likely port of departure) and about 130 km distant in a straight line. Gyges has thus completed only the first stage of his journey — and is already in trouble; *post insana Caprae sidera* (the rising of the constellation of the Goat) fixes the time as following the autumnal equinox (late September); a southerly storm in this season of storms has prevented his continued passage south — ancient ships could not put to sea in anything approaching a head wind. Most editors assume Gyges is on his way home and will have to spend the winter in Epirus. But (1) though the Romans avoided travel by sea in the winter, there is plenty of evidence for crossing the Adriatic later than September: in 3. 1. 25-8 we hear of the worries of merchants who put to sea in October; in 3. 27. 17-20 Galatea is planning to cross the Adriatic in November; the fleets of both sides operated in the Adriatic before and after the second battle of Philippi in late October; H.'s assumption in Stanza 1 would thus be unjustified; (2) if navigation has been suspended, how does H. (or Asterie) know where Gyges is and what he is doing? (See on 9-22.) The most natural assumption is that Gyges has set out from Rome at the end of the summer, intending to spend the autumn and winter in Bithynia and to return to Italy (like Catullus in Poem 46) the following spring. The situation of the *iuvenis* in 4. 5 is different: he has extended his stay in the East overlong ('cunctantem spatio longius annuo') and has been held up at the beginning of his journey home, but his mother still expects him. — **frigidas noctis . . . insomnis agit**] Gyges, i.e., is new to the experience of sleeping alone, finds the night cold and lies in bed weeping for his absent beloved (as she weeps for him); familiar clichés of Roman love poetry (the chilly bed of the deserted lover, his inability to sleep) lurk in the background; cf. Catullus 68. 29 'Frigida deserto membra cubili', Ovid *Am*. 3. 5. 4 'Frigidus in viduo toro'.

9-22] Again, the temptations to which Gyges is exposed are better taken as a foretaste of things to come. How can H. know all this? He need only have heard that Gyges has been forced to delay his journey at Oricum — or have inferred this from a recent storm; we can easily suppose that the storm is now over and a letter has come back to Rome from Gyges, the contents being reported by H. in the present tense because they represent for H. and Asterie the latest news of Gyges; we can easily suppose that much or all of Stanzas 3-5 is intended to be taken by the reader as H.'s ironical elaboration of the bare fact of Gyges' forced stay in Oricum — an exercise in fantasy and/or fancy intended to tease a young wife who is only too prepared to believe the worst about foreign parts. — **atqui**] 'and yet'; interprets *frigidas noctis* as proof of Gyges' constancy (cf. 4 'constantis iuvenem fide') — so far (22 'audit adhuc integer'); cf. 1. 23. 9, 3. 5. 49. — **sollicitae hospitae**] Chloe is presumably (see on 13-20) the wife of a resident of Oricum whose custom, or duty, it is to provide hospitality for visiting Romans. — **tuis**] 'like yours, Asterie'; the word reminds us H. is addressing Asterie. — **mille modis**] Some examples follow; in both the Bellerophon and the Peleus stories the hero (innocent and young, as we are to suppose Gyges) is staying with a friend and is subject to the unwelcome attentions of his host's wife. — **Proetum**] Sthenobaea, in love with Bellerophon, denounced him to her husband Proetus when he did not respond to her advances. — **maturare necem**] Proetus' plans to have Bellerophon killed once no longer under his roof in fact went astray. — **refert, narrat**] Chiasmus. — **Pelea**] Hippolyte, wife of King Aeastus, fell in love with Peleus, who repulsed her and was denounced by her; like Proetus, Aeastus laid elaborate plans (which failed) for doing away with his guest once departed; for the banter involved in applying these illustrious precedents to everyday affairs cf. 1. 29, 2. 4, etc. — **Magnessam**] To distinguish her from the Amazon Hippolyte, wife of Theseus. — **peccare**] With sexual overtones, like *culpa*, etc. — **movet**] 'brings to bear'; the variant *monet* is clearly weaker. — **frustra**] The superflux (unexpected continuation of the sense in the line following) for surprise effect; cf. 3. 13. 6. — **surdior audit**] = 'turns deafer ears to'; — **scopulis Icari**] Icarus is here the island; see on 1. 1. 15 and 4. 2. 2-4. — **adhuc integer**] Doesn't so much imply that he may yet give in to Chloe, but that this is Gyges' first port of call and further temptations can be counted on to follow.

22-32] We turn from Gyges to Asterie. — **Enipeus**] The name of a river in Thessaly (cf. 3. 12. 6 Hebrus); but perhaps intended to recall ἐνίπτω — = 'the reproacher' (i.e., one who reproaches Asterie for her constancy to Gyges). — **quamvis . . . alveo**] Cf. 3. 12. 9-12 and (for the abandonment of the same manly virtues) 1. 8. 5-8; Enipeus, i.e., is cast as a Roman of good family; **gramine Martio**] i.e., the green expanse of the Campus Martius where the members of the *militia equestris* trained; cf. 1. 8. 4. — **prima nocte**] Emphatic, 'as soon as night begins to fall'; cf. 1. 9. 19-20. — **sub cantu . . . tibiae**] Enipeus, it seems, has been courting Asterie; for the lover's serenade (paraclausithyron), see on 1. 25. — **vocanti**] i.e., to Asterie, reproaching her for her cruelty; cf. 1. 25. 7-8. — **difficilis**] 'uncooperative'; cf. 3. 10. 11; contrast 1. 25. 5 *facilis*.

3. 8

Introduction: Like 1. 20 and 1. 36, a conversation piece rather than an invitation: Maecenas arrives for dinner to find H. making unexpectedly elaborate preparations. It turns out it is a special occasion — the anniversary of H.'s narrow escape from death. A celebration is called for; let Maecenas put cares of state aside. Cf. the concluding lines of 2. 17. The urbane, nonchalant tone reflects (intentionally) the mood of a Rome now at last virtually free from the threat of foreign wars; even the Parthians can be left to quarrel among themselves.

Structure: An opening question (1-5) sets the scene; H. explains (6-12); a series of exhortations (13 *Sume*, 15 *perfer*, 15 *esto*, 17 *mitte*, 26 *parce*, 27 *cape*) follow, interrupted by a reassuring glance at the international situation (18-24).

Metre: Sapphics; see 1. 2M.

1-5] **Martiis kalendis**] The Matrimonalia, a festival celebrated by married women in honour of Juno Licinia. — **quid . . . vivo**] The three subjects of *velint* form a tricolon crescendo; *miraris*, the verb which controls both indirect questions, is placed after the second member of the tricolon; **positusque . . . vivo**] i.e., charcoal burning on an altar of fresh-cut turf; cf. 4. 11. 6-8. — **docte . . . linguae**] Maecenas, i.e., an expert on both Greek and Roman cultural lore, is racking his brains to guess the occasion; **sermones**] = λόγοι, i.e., writings on ritual.

6-12] **Voveram**] i.e., the explanation for the preparations is that H. 'had made a vow'. — **dulcis epulas**] A feast of rejoicing (as opposed, e.g., to a funeral feast). — **album caprum**] Because Bacchus is one of the Di Superi; to the Di Inferi a black victim is appropriate; see on 3. 23. 4 — **Libero**] H.'s protector in his role as a god of poetry; see 2. 19 and 3. 25; in 2. 17. 28 H. attributes his escape to Faunus; in 3. 4 he claims the special protection of the Muses. — **prope funeratus**] For the story, see 2. 13. — **hic dies**] i.e., March 1st. — **anno redeunte festus**] = 'a day to celebrate each year'; cf. *Sat.* 2. 2. 83 'Sive diem festum rediens advexerit annum' and Cicero *Rep.* 6. 24; the natural inference is that this is the first anniversary of H.'s escape and that he proposes to celebrate the anniversary every year (not necessarily with the same wine); cf. 3. 22. 6. — **corticem . . . dimovebit**] See on 1. 20. 1-3; **adstrictum pice**] 'sealed with pitch'. — **amphorae . . . Tullo**] For the *amphora*, see on 1. 9. 8; either L. Volcacius Tullus *cos.* 66 or his son *cos.* 33 is meant, more likely the former (i.e., a very special wine); wine thirty years old and more sounds improbable to us, but see 3. 21. 1 for a wine laid down in 65 BC, the year of H.'s birth, and 3. 28. 8 for a wine of 59 BC; **fumum bibere**] the wine was stored over the hearth or bathroom in a special *apotheca* or *horreum* (3. 28. 7, 4. 12. 18; cf. 1. 37. 6), also called *fumarium* (Martial 10. 36. 1); the smoke was believed to assist the ageing process (see Columella 1. 6); hence *depromere* (1. 9. 7, 1. 37. 5) and 3. 21. 7 *descende*), the wine being brought down from this chamber for drinking. [The suggestion of some that the escape occurred in 33 and that H. has been marking the event ever since with a wine laid down that year is implausible: apart from difficulties about the wine, Maecenas would have known by now what to expect.]

13-16] The drinking begins. — **cyathos centum]** The *cyathus* is a ladle used for filling a *canthara*, etc. or (as here) for measuring the wine to be drunk; cf. 1. 29. 8; for the procedure, see on 3. 19. 11-12; here one *cyathus* for each year of life Maecenas is to wish H.; cf. Ovid *Fasti* 3. 532-3 'Annosque precantur / quot sumunt cyathos'. — **amici sospitis]** 'in honour of your friend's escape'; genitive of respect. — **vigiles . . . ira]** i.e., an all-night party (cf. 3. 21. 23-4) — but not a wild one (like that of 1. 27).

17-24] The review of the political situation is to show that H.'s exhortation to put cares aside is not irresponsible (Maecenas hardly needs H. to brief him); at the same time H. puts on record the current official version of Rome's policy of peace on the frontiers; cf. 2. 11. 1-5, 3. 29. 25 ff. — **civilis curas]** 'cares of state', *OLD* 5. — **occidit . . . agmen]** = 'the forces of Dacian Cotiso have been defeated'; the Daci (area of the lower Danube), like the Getae (with whom they are often confused), symbolise the NE frontier; a Cotiso is mentioned by Suetonius *Aug.* 63 as 'rex Getarum'; for the Daci cf. 1. 35. 9, 2. 20. 18, 3. 6. 14; for the Getae, 3. 24. 11 (where, along with the Scythae, they are unexpectedly idealised), 4. 15. 22. — **Medus]** = the Parthians; see on 1. 2. 22 *Persae*; the feud between Tiridates (Augustus' puppet-king) and his rival Phraates is meant. — **servit . . . catena]** See on 2. 11. 1-4. — **iam . . . campis]** After three areas where there is now little cause for concern (tossed off in confident asyndeton), *iam* introduces an even more confident note; for the Scythae, see on 1. 19. 10; for their nomad habits, 3. 24. 9-16; according to H. they plan to retreat eastwards across the Don.

25-8] The ode ends on a somewhat more irresponsibly Epicurean note. — **neglegens]** = 'relax'. — **ne qua . . . cavere]** = 'get out of the habit of worrying so much in case anything goes wrong with our country's affairs; after all you are only an ordinary citizen'; the emphasis falls on *ne qua* and on *nimium cavere*; for *parce* ('think twice', 'hesitate') cf. 1. 28. 23, 3. 28. 7; Maecenas, though one of Augustus' chief advisers, and in effect his regent when the Emperor was abroad on active service, held no office; it is reasonable, therefore, to urge him to relax at a time when there is really nothing to worry about. — **linque severa]** = 'give yourself a holiday from serious thoughts'; cf. the concluding lines of 4. 12 and 2. 7.

3. 9

Introduction: An ironical exercise upon the theme of a lovers' reconciliation. Both the man and the girl have found fresh partners since their separation; both are now ready, after some cautious sparring, to make things up and start afresh.

Structure: H. takes over the traditional form of amoebean pastoral, in which two singers exchange snatches of verse, each trying to outdo the other within the same number of lines and following the wording and structure of his rival as closely as possible; cf. Theocritus 5 and 8, Virgil *Eclogues* 3 and 7; see Gow on Theocritus 5. H. clearly is indebted to Catullus' ironic study of two young lovers (Poem 45), but adheres more closely to the conventions of amoebean form.

Metre: Asclepiad (b), the first of six odes in Book 3 in this metre; the others are 15, 19, 24, 25 and 28. See on 1. 3M.

1-4] **Donec . . . tibi]** = 'so long as you found me attractive'; the manoeuvring for position which must precede reconciliation begins on a low key. — **nec . . . dabat]** i.e., there were other men of course, but I was the one you preferred; **nec quisquam potior]** 'and none with greater authority than I'; **bracchia . . . dabat]** i.e., 'took you in his arms'; the emotional level rises as the man proceeds, and at the same time H. moves away a step from conversational realism to something closer to ironic idealism; **iuvenis]** 'man' rather than 'youth'; see on 1. 2. 41 and on 16 *puero*. — **Persarum . . . beatior]** A conventional image of wealth and therefore, in popular belief, of happiness; though *beatior* leans towards the sense 'happier', the sense 'wealthier' (i.e., possessing a truer wealth than the riches of the King of Persia) is secured by context; cf. 2. 12. 21; **vigui]** the perfect, following the imperfects *eram* and *dabat* (which stress the duration of the affair) put the affair firmly in the past, as something now over and done with.

5-8] Lydia is encouraging, but not without a tinge of malice. Her response to her ex-lover's suggestion that she has other lovers is to attribute to him the blame for breaking off the affair. — **Donec . . . magis arsisti]** i.e., 'until you became more infatuated with another girl'; tense and image (the fire of passion bursting into flame) stress the sudden onset of infatuation; cf. 2. 4. 7; **alia**] instrumental with *arsisti*. — **neque . . . Chloen**] 'and as long as I didn't have to take second place to Chloe'; the *alia* of line 5 is now named; note *alia*, not *altera* — Chloe was only one in a series; Lydia also 1. 8, 1. 13, 1. 25; Chloe 1. 23, 3. 7, 3. 26. — **multi Lydia nominis**] = 'Lydia, a name much spoken', i.e., 'my name was on everybody's lips'. — **Romana Ilia**] The most famous of Roman women, Rea Silvia, mother of Romulus and Remus; cf. 1. 2. 17, 3. 3. 32, 4. 8. 22; Lydia caps the man's 'Persarum vigui rege beatior' with a more patriotic variant on the same model; **clarior**] as in the previous line, Lydia stresses the fame the liaison brought her, rather than the happiness; if we are to assume her lover was H. (the man is not named), she perhaps means poetry H. wrote about her.

9-12]   **Me**] Emphatic; picked up by Lydia in line 13. — **Thressa Chloe**] 'Thracian Chloe'; i.e., she is a resident alien; perhaps also to distinguish her from the Chloe of 3. 7. — **regit**] As usual in H., the girl, despite her modest social status (Chloe is, we may assume, a *libertina*), is not only free to do as she likes, but 'rules over' her lover (H.'s version of the *domina*-and-her-slave cliché); cf. 3. 24. 19, 4. 1. 4 and the *libertina* of 1. 33. 14 who has made H. her ready prisoner ('grata detinuit compede'; cf. 4. 11. 23-4). — **dulcis . . . sciens**] Observe there is no reference to Chloe's looks (which might be tactless at this stage); instead, her accomplishments are praised; we learn in line 19 that she is a blonde; singing and lyre-playing are common accomplishments in a mistress; cf. 1. 17. 17-20 (Tyndaris), 2. 11. 21-4 (Lyde), 4. 11. 33-6 (Phyllis), 4. 13. 4-8 (Lyce, Chia). — **pro qua . . . superstiti**] The conventional protestation of life-long love; **animae**] = 'darling' (*OLD* 7 b) — as Chrysalus says in Plautus *Bacch*. 193 'Animast amica amanti ('his mistress is life itself to a lover'); si abest, nullus est'; cf. Catullus' use of *lux* (68. 132, etc.) and *vita* (45. 13, 68. 155, etc.).

13-16]   Lydia proceeds to cap each point made by her ex-lover: (1) in her case (i.e., in her new affair with Calais), love is mutual, not one-sided; (2) Calais belongs to a respectable family (Chloe is only a lyre-player); (3) she will die *twice* over the Calais. — **face mutua**] i.e., a single torch has set them both on fire. — **Thurini . . . Ornyti**] 'Calais, son of Ornytus of Thurii'; Chloe's antecedents are presumably unknown; cf. 3. 12. 8 'Liparaei nitor Hebri'. — **puero**] Protective; contrast the neutral *iuvenis* of line 3; implies also that Lydia is older (and more experienced) than Calais; see on 1. 5. 1.

17-20]   The climax of the sparring process has now been reached, and the time come for direct negotiation. Note the present tense in *redit, cogit, excutitur, patet*. — **si prisca redit Venus**] The change of heart is presented as already happening — something, as it were, over which they have no control; cf. 2. 17. 5 for this use of *si* with the present indicative (a formula inviting agreement), see on 3. 18. 5; *prisca* is an emotionally charged word, 'love as it was in the old days'. — **diductosque . . . aeneo**] Revives the latent personification of the previous line: Venus is now the sardonic, all-powerful goddess of 1. 33. 11-12. — **flava**] A blonde, like Pyrrha in 1. 5 and Phyllis in 2. 4. — **excutitur**] 'is being shaken off'. — **reiectaeque . . . Lydiae**] = 'and the door which was once shut in her face now stands open to receive Lydia'; the context indicates *Lydiae* is dative, not genitive (it is not Lydia's door, i.e., which stands open): it is the man who is making the proposal, he is in no position to speak for her; cf. Lydia's response 'tecum vivere amem'; a lover spending an occasional night with his mistress is perhaps more likely to go to her (cf. 1. 25, 3. 10, but contrast 3. 15. 9); if the liaison is semi-permanent, the girl is more likely to take up residence with her lover; cf. Propertius 3. 6. 21-2 'Ille potest . . . / . . . qualem nolo dicere habere domi'; no doubt much depended on whether the man was master in his own house (i.e., unmarried, not living with his father), or in a position to keep a separate establishment.

21-4]   Lydia is no less ready to make things up, but cannot resist a final dig. The three vivid comparative phrases put up a show of resistance before the surrender of the last line. — **sidere pulcrior**] 'prettier than a star'; the phrase reinforces the patronising note of 16 *puero*; cf. 3. 19. 26, 3. 1. 42. — **levior cortice**] = 'more fickle than cork'; a pun of course on the two senses of *levior* (lighter in weight, lacking in moral *gravitas*). — **inprobo . . . Hadria**] 'worse-tempered than the bullying Adriatic'; *inprobo*, a word which might be used of a lover, is transferred to the sea.

3. 10

Introduction: A variation on the theme of the paraclausithyron (a serenade by the excluded lover before his mistress's street-door). The night is wild and wintry, Lyce's aloofness is unnatural and out of keeping with her social status; she should relent before it is too late. The speaker is the seasoned lover, accustomed to love's discomforts, but mildly (and wittily) indignant at his present failure to add to his conquests. The wit lies in the subversion of normal moral standards: for an attractive married woman (as Lyce must be presumed to be) to remain faithful to her husband is treated by her would-be seducer as behaving with unreasonable cruelty. The form is as conventional as that of 3. 7, H.'s exploitation of it no less witty. Cf. 1. 25, 3. 26 and the final stanza of 3. 7; for different views on wifely virtue see 3. 15; for Lyce in 4. 13 see on 19 *non semper*.

Structure: Stanzas 1-2 provide the basic data and set the tone (Lyce's victim is a coolly witty lover, able to argue his case with ingenuity); Stanza 3 reproaches; Stanza 4 spills over into Stanza 5 as the entreaties gain momentum, passing via supplication (16-17 'supplicibus tuis parcas') to veiled threat (lines 19-20).

Metre: Asclepiad (c); see 1. 6M.

1-4]   Extremum . . . biberes] The elaborately poetic rhetoric of the opening makes it clear that no attempt at verisimilitude is intended; the traditional form merely provides the starting point for a witty denigration of female virtue as seen through the eyes of a professional Don Juan; **Tanain]** the river Don, the furthest limit of the Scythae, the symbol for H. of a remote barbarous people of the NE frontier (see on 1. 19. 10); **biberes]** cf. 4. 15. 21. − **Lyce]** The name perhaps = 'she-wolf' (from λύκος, 'wolf', i.e., *lupa*, 'whore'); only here and in 4. 13. − **saevo nupta viro]** i.e., a husband who watches over her and stands no nonsense; Lyce *is* married, but her husband is absent (see on 11 *Penelopen*), perhaps spending the night with the *Pieria paelex* of line 15; the domestic virtue of the Scythae, praised by H. in 3. 24. 17-24, is stood on its head for rhetorical effect: even a Scythian wife would let him in if she dared (women, if we are to believe the professional seducer, are everywhere the same); only Lyce behaves unnaturally (line 9). − **me . . . foris]** The traditional posture of the *exclusus amator* (Lucretius 4. 1177); **asperas porrectum ante foris]** H. conveniently forgets what he will stress in 3. 24. 9-10 − that the Scythae are a nomad people. − **obicere plorares]** The Scythian wife, i.e., because she fears her husband, would have to leave him exposed to the elements, but would weep to think of him suffering outside; traditionally, it is the excluded lover who weeps (Lucretius 4. 1177). − **incolis Aquilonibus]** The bitter NNE wind of winter which originates there, but is now blowing outside Lyce's door; the plural = 'blasts of Aquilo'.

5-8]   A graphic picture of a winter's night at Rome in a howling NNE wind. − **quo strepitu ianua]** Some such verb as *crepitet* might be expected; instead, *ianua* becomes, along with *nemus*, a subject of *remugiat* by the figure known as zeugma. − **nemus satum]** Most probably, the trees in the formal garden enclosed by the *peristylium* of an elaborate Roman house. − **remugiat ventis]** The trees roar in answer to the howl of the wind. − **positas . . . Iuppiter]** It is a clear night and the snow which had fallen earlier is turning to ice; for Jove as the weather god, see on 1. 2. 2; **puro numine]** the epithet *puro* is transferred from the bright, clear night sky to the *numen* of the weather god.

9-12]   **Ingratam . . . superbiam]** Venus (according to Lyce's would-be lover) does not approve of faithful wives (their uncooperativeness is a sign of arrogance). − **ne . . . rota]** If the strain on a rope becomes too great, it snaps; or if the person pulling on it gives up, it flies back; *rota* implies some kind of windlass; in other words, if Lyce tries her lover too hard, she will lose him (the first hint of a threat; the possibility that his attentions are unwelcome is not considered). − **non . . . parens]** i.e., 'you are no Penelope, nor are you the daughter of a Tuscan father' (i.e., of aristocratic birth, cf. 3. 29. 1); *non*, as often, negates the whole statement; Penelope (the prototype of the wife who is faithful to a husband whose back is turned) denotes a class; the rhetoric follows the model of Catullus 60; cf. *Aen.* 4. 365-7 and Austin thereon; **difficilem procis]** as was Penelope; the would-be lover promotes himself to the rank of suitor; with *difficilem* cf. 3. 7. 32; for the plural, see on 14 *amantium*.

13-20]   **quamvis]** = *quamquam*; with the indicative, as usual in H. − **neque munera nec preces]** The usual devices of lovers. − **tinctus . . . amantium]** i.e., pale and turning violet; the pallor of unrequited lovers is a commonplace of Augustan love poetry; Lyce's lover is turning blue with cold as well; **amantium]** perhaps a generalising plural, but more likely the plural, following up the hint of 11 *procis*, implies that Lyce's present

suppliant is not her only unsuccessful admirer; cf. 16 *supplicibus*. — **nec vir . . . saucius**]
i.e., 'the fact that your husband is having an affair with a foreign girl'; if Lyce were
sensible, i.e., she would seek revenge; in any case, the husband is, it seems, not at home
and the coast is clear; **Pieria**] = 'Macedonian'; or does H. imply the *paelex* is a singer?
see on 3. 9. 10. — **supplicibus tuis parcas**] The high point of the lover's rhetoric; for the
plural, see on 14 *amantium* (Lyce's lover appeals to her in the common interest of the
class to which he belongs). — **nec rigida . . . anguibus**] A further rhetorical flourish
before the blunt hint of 19-20; **animum**] accusative of respect. — **non semper**] The
obvious meaning is 'not all night'; but more probably an allusion to the commonplace
that woman's beauty is quick to fade; hence a hint to Lyce to make the most of her
looks before it is too late; cf. the ageing flirt of 1. 25; if the Lyce of 4. 13 is the same
woman (which involves assuming that H. is the speaker here), H. has the last word. —
hoc latus] *hoc* is deictic, 'this flank of mine'. — **liminis**] Lyce's door-step. — **aquae
caelestis**] i.e., it is raining as well as blowing.

3. 11

Introduction: An ironic marriage hymn for a reluctant bride, beginning (as is appropriate on
   a special occasion) with an appeal for inspiration. The inspiration, when it comes, takes
   the form of a Pindaric myth on the nobility of marriage. The myth's status as a caution-
   ary tale with direct personal relevance to Lyde is as transparent as in 3. 27; in both cases
   the principle 'mutato nomine de te fabula narratur' (*Sat*. 1. 1. 69) applies; in both cases
   too the myth becomes an important structure in its own right (cf. the myth of the
   Titans in 3. 4, the myth of Regulus in 3. 5) for which the way has to be planned with
   care, as though H.'s narrative were unpremeditated.
      The relevance to Lyde of the myth of Hypermnestra is plain: H. wants Lyde to see
   marriage as a noble ideal, symbolised by that paragon among the daughters of Aegyptus
   who put loyalty to her husband above all else. The ode, i.e., is another of H.'s studies of
   the young woman who is on the threshold of sexual experience. In 3. 12 Neobule is an
   innocent girl who has fallen in love; in 1. 23 Chloe, though 'tempestiva viro', is too
   timid to respond to H.'s advances; in 2. 5 Lalage, though she has a husband, is too young
   to measure up to the expectations of her husband. Here the emphasis is on marriage as a
   revision of loyalties.
Structure: The invocation to Mercury in Stanzas 1-6 (he is asked to grant the poetic
   eloquence necessary to overcome Lyde's reluctance to listen to advice) constitutes an
   elaborate build-up for the myth which follows in Stanzas 7-13.
Metre: Sapphics; see 1. 2M.
1-8] H. is to be assumed as appealed to for a poem in honour of Lyde's marriage or
   betrothal; hence the joint evocation of Mercury and the lyre; for Mercury and the
   lyre cf. 1. 32. 1-4; for Mercury as the god of poets cf. 1. 10. 1-4, 2. 7. 13-14,
   2. 17. 29; contrast 4. 3. 17-20. — **te magistro**] 'with you to teach him'. — **movit . . .
   canendo**] As Amphion played, the stones leaped into place of their own accord to
   form the walls of Thebes; if Amphion could do that with Mercury's assistance, H.
   should be able to penetrate the *obstinatas auris* of Lyde; cf. *AP* 394-6. — **testudo**] A
   tortoise shell formed the sounding-board of the first lyre; for Mercury as the inventor
   cf. 1. 10. 6; for different types of lyre, see on 1. 12. 1; in 4. 3. 17-20 it is Melpomene
   who inspires the poet's lyre. — **nec . . . grata**] i.e., before Mercury made his lyre from it,
   the tortoise shell was despised; with *loquax* cf. 3. 13. 15. — **nunc . . . templis**] cf. 1. 32.
   13-14. — **dic modos**] 'inspire strains'; cf. 1. 32. 3 'dic Latinum, barbite, carmen', 3. 4. 1;
   the lyre invoked is the lyre H. asks us to imagine him taking up as he seeks inspiration
   for a song for Lyde; but that lyre is addressed as though it were the archetypal lyre of
   Mercury and thus representative of all lyres (hence lines 5-6); cf. 4. 4. 1-4, 4. 12. 5-8;
   dic] imperative singular though two vocatives precede, an extension of the common
   idiom of agreement with the nearer of two nouns; so Catullus 4. 13-17 and 26,
   Georgics 2. 101-2, *Aen*. 10. 185-6; cf. Cicero *Ver*. 5. 185 'teque, Latona et Apollo et
   Diana' (several similar examples follow in this formal concluding invocation). — **Lyde**]
   Also 2. 11. 22, 3. 28. 3. — **quibus . . . auris**] = 'at which Lyde may prick up the ears
   which till now have refused to listen'; Lyde, i.e., till now has turned, as we say, a deaf
   ear to all who speak in favour of marriage; H. needs assistance if he is to overcome her

resistance and persuade her to see marriage in a different light; common sense suggests
a particular husband is in view and a marriage imminent (in which, as often in Roman
marriages, the bride has little say).

9-12]   A pen picture of Lyde. — **equa trima**] 'a three-year-old filly'; a traditional symbol
(like the *iuvenca* of 2. 5) of a girl who is fond of fun; so, e.g., Anacreon 88D, Aristo-
phanes *Lys.* 1308-9; cf. *Aen.* 11. 492-7. — **ludit**] The word used of the gay young wife
of Catullus 17. 17; the sexual overtones present there and in similar passages derive from
the context; cf. 3. 15. 5. — **exsultim**] Only here; connotes high spirits as much as the
actions which result. — **metuitque tangi**] The subject is Lyde, but the metaphor con-
tinues: the filly who resists attempts by her owner to lay hands on her to tame her for a
life of usefulness is the symbol of the girl who rebels at marriage; the implication that
Lyde is a virgin (as well as unmarried) is not to be rejected out of hand — even if she is
the Lyde of 2. 11. 21-2 (*scortum* need not be taken too literally) and 3. 28. 3; for the
construction cf. 2. 2. 7, 3. 9. 11, 4. 5. 20. — **nuptiarum expers**] Not just 'unmarried',
but 'with no experience of marriage' (and what it involves). — **adhuc protervo cruda
marito**] 'unripe till now for a lusty husband', i.e., temperamentally immature, like
Lalage in 2. 5 (who *is* married); with *cruda* (the word used of unripe fruit) cf. 2. 5.
9-12, 3. 6. 22; the emphasis falls on *adhuc* ('till now', *OLD* 1 c, rather than 'as yet');
Lyde, i.e., has reached the time when she is, like Chloe in 1. 33, 'tempestiva viro'; but
where Chloe is simply shy, Lyde won't hear a good word said for marriage (7-8 'obstin-
atas auris'); and where Chloe is afraid of sex and is told a man won't hurt her, Lyde has
to be induced to think of marriage as a noble ideal.

13-24]   **tu potes**] The invocation continues; as in 7 'dic modos' the singular is to be
thought of as embracing both the god who grants the inspiration and the *testudo* which
symbolises the lyric form which the inspiration assumes. — **tigris . . . morari**] An allusion
to the miraculous playing of Orpheus; cf. 1. 12. 7-12, *AP* 392-3. — **cessit . . . aulae**] The
reference is to Orpheus' descent to the underworld in pursuit of his dead wife Eurydice;
immanis] equally with *ianitor* and *aulae*; **aulae**] the palace of Pluto. — **Cerberus . . .
trilingui**] The stanza has been objected to because (1) *eius* is rare in serious poetry (only
once elsewhere in the *Odes* — 4. 8. 18, also a suspect passage), (2) the expression is
obvious and clumsy; neither argument is conclusive and the stanza seems needed to
prepare the way for 21-4, though the similarity with 2. 13. 33-40 (a stanza describing
Cerberus followed by a stanza beginning with *quin et* expanding the description) is
remarkable; **quamvis**] in the sense 'although', usually in the *Odes* with the indicative,
as in 3. 10. 12-16; see on 1. 28. 11; **furiale**] like that of the Furies; **manet**] present
subjunctive of *mānare*; agreement with the nearer, as in 22 *risit*; **ore trilingui**] see on
2. 19. 31. — **Tityos**] Cf. 2. 14. 8. — **stetit . . . mulces**] The daughters of Danaus form the
final tableau in H.'s picture of an underworld charmed by Orpheus (cf. the picture in 2.
13. 21-40); at the same time they provide the transition to the myth which follows;
Danaus, forced to marry his 50 daughters to the 50 sons of his brother Aegyptus,
arranged with them to murder their husbands on their wedding night; only Hypermn-
estra put love for her husband before loyalty to her father; the other 49 were con-
demned as their punishment in the underworld to fill forever with water an urn riddled
with holes; the legend was depicted upon the ill-fated *balteus* of Turnus in the *Aeneid*
and formed one of the frescoes upon Augustus' Temple of Apollo; the elements of the
myth which serve H.'s purpose are reluctant marriage, love with marriage and the
reversal of loyalties which ensued (we may assume Lyde is marrying out of obedience
to her father; H.'s hope is she will be another Hypermnestra).

25-9]   **Audiat**] Picks up 7 *dic modos*; the abruptness with which H. abandons his descrip-
tion of Orpheus in the underworld suggests the inspiration he sought has now come to
him. — **notas**] 'well-known'. — **dolium**] A large earthenware jar. — **Orco**] See on
1. 28. 10.

30-36]   **inpiae**] Because *pietas* to a husband must take the place of *pietas* to a father. —
potuere] The perfect frequently has the sense 'brought oneself to'. — **una**] Emphatic.
— **periurum**] Because he had betrothed his daughters and then entered into a conspiracy
with them against his sons-in-law. — **splendide mendax**] Oxymoron, as in 1. 5. 5.
'simplex munditiis', 3. 21. 13 'lene tormentum'. — **in omne aevom**] 'for all time to
come'. — **virgo**] 'girl' (not necessarily 'virgin'); cf. 3. 15. 5.

37-44]   **iuveni marito**] His name was Lynceus. — **unde non times**] Cf. 1. 28. 28 'unde
potest'. — **falle**] 'cheat' (by eluding them). — **singulos eheu lacerant**] i.e., each of her

sisters is already murdering the man she has just married; with *lacerant*, the word used
of a mauling wild beast, the simile becomes a metaphor; with *eheu* cf. 2. 14. 1. —
mollior] Hypermnestra excuses her weakness instead of protesting her nobility; *mollis*,
however, implies the gentleness of the lover as opposed to the soldier, who is *durus*. —
nec ... tenebo] 'nor will I keep you in the trap'; i.e., she will let Lynceus escape instead
of letting her harder-hearted sisters despatch him.

45-52]   In most versions of the story, Hypermnestra is imprisoned by her father, but
ultimately rescued (by Lynceus or by the intercession of Aphrodite) and reunited with
her husband. H. prefers to have her imagine she will never see her husband again. —
me ... me] Anaphora in asyndeton. — **classe releget**] i.e., send her off by sea into exile.
— **i ... i**] Opposed to *me ... me*, more graphic than the more obvious *tu ... tu*. — **pedes
et aurae**] Symbolises travel by land and sea. — **i secundo omine**] = 'go and godspeed to
you'. — **nostri ... querelam**] All she asks is that, when she dies, Lynceus will set up an
inscription on her grave relating her 'sad story'; in Ovid *Her.* 14. 128 she dictates her
own epitaph.

3. 12

Introduction: A monologue expressing H.'s sympathy with Neobule, who has fallen in love
with a young man she has no more than seen: society is indulgent towards the young
man in love, whether he takes a mistress or drowns in drink the sorrows of unrequited
love; a respectable girl risks the sharp edge of an uncle's tongue — all Neobule can do is
sit and follow her radiant lover in her thoughts as he goes about his manly pursuits.
Like 2. 5, these sensitive lines show H.'s insight into the mind of a young innocent girl;
they form an interesting corrective to 1. 5 and 1. 8, where it is the girl who is the exper-
ienced partner; for a less indulgent view, see 3. 6. 21-32.
Structure: Stanza 1, general statement; Stanzas 2-4 (a single sentence) apply the general
statement to Neobule.
Metre: Ionicus a minore. The basic unit is ∪ ∪ — —. Most editors print in stanzas of ten
units each, variously arranged. The most obvious arrangement, in 4-line stanzas alter-
nately 2 and 3 units in length, will only work if division of a line in mid-word is admitted;
the arrangement adopted here is 2 + 2 + 4 + 2.
1-4]   The construction is 'Miserarum est (a) neque dare neque lavere, aut (b) exanimari'. —
Miserarum] Sets up a class, 'poor girls, it is their fate . . .'; for *miser*, the stock word for
the (male) victim of love, esp. frustrated love, see on 1. 5. 12; for the genitive, 1. 27. 2,
3. 13. 13, cf. Plautus *Capt.* 583 'Est miserorum ut malevolentes sint'. — **neque amori
dare ludum**] What the members of the class have in common is their inability to do
anything; they cannot 'let love have its fling' — or otherwise console themselves; the
phrase echoes Cicero's vigorous statement in defence of Caelius Rufus of the need for
young men to be allowed to sow their wild oats, *Cael.* 28. 'Datur enim concessu omnium
huic aliqui ludus aetati, et ipsa natura profundit adulescentiae cupiditates', etc.; cf. 42
'Detur aliqui ludus aetati . . . ; cum [iuventus] paruerit voluptatibus, dederit aliquid
temporis ad ludum aetatis . . .' (Cicero thinks only of young men). — **dulci mala vino
lavere**] The frustrated lover drowning his sorrows is a cliché of Roman love poetry; see,
e.g., Propertius 3. 17. 3-4 (in an elegy in praise of Bacchus) 'Tu potes insanae Veneris
compescere fastus / curarumque tuo fit medicina mero', Tibullus 1. 2. 1-4 and 3. 6. 1-4,
Ovid *Remed.* 803-6; H. avoids the cliché except in ironic contexts such as 1. 27. 9-12,
Epode 11. 13-14; **dulci**] 'pleasure-giving', 'agreeable' (not 'sweet'), as 1. 9. 15, 1. 16. 23;
drowning one's sorrows in drink, i.e., has its agreeable side. — **aut**] i.e., 'or, if they do'. —
exanimari] 'to be frightened to death'; cf. *Sat.* 1. 4. 127; see on 2. 17. 1. — **metuentis**]
Accusative plural. — **patruae verbera linguae**] 'the lash of an uncle's tongue'; the cen-
sorious uncle is the Roman equivalent of our mother-in-law; see Catullus 74. 1-2, Cicero
Cael. 25 (in rebuttal of one of the prosecuting speakers who had attacked Caelius'
morals) 'Fuit in hac causa pertristis quidem patruus, censor, magister'; cf. *Sat.* 2. 2.
96-7 'Adde / iratum patruum', *Sat.* 2. 3. 88 'Ne sis patruus mihi'; the uncle places
Neobule: she is a respectable girl who can plausibly be thought of as having an uncle
at her elbow — not a slave, who would be more summarily dealt with.
5-8]   The construction is 'tibi puer [aufert], tibi nitor aufert'. — **tibi**] Opposed by its
position to *Miserarum, tibi* particularises; at the same time, Neobule is placed in the

class of respectable girls who have to behave. — **qualum . . . aufert**] The love-sick girl
unable to pursue her tasks is another cliché; cf. Sappho 102 LP; **qualum**] The wicker
basket containing the wool which it is Neobule's daily task to spin; see Balsdon,
Roman Women, 1962, 270: 'in richer families [girls] were generally educated at home.
A part of their upbringing, spinning and weaving, they learnt working with the slave-
girls under the supervision of their mother'; cf. the epitaph of Claudia *CIL*^{2} 1211, which
concludes 'Domum servavit, lanam fecit', Catullus 64. 318-19; **Cythereae**] epithet of
Venus, as in l. 4. 5; **Minervae**] the goddess of arts and crafts (she presides over the con-
struction of the ship Argo in Catullus 64, over that of the wooden horse in *Aen.* 2);
Neobule passes, as it were, out of the control of one goddess into the clutches of
another. — **Neobule**] Greek for 'she who has new ideas in her head'; a Neobule fell in
love with the poet Archilochus (and eventually hanged herself). — **Liparaei nitor Hebri**]
The lover-poet regularly represents his mistress as resplendent like a goddess (see on
l. 5. 13); cf. l. 19. 5. H. transfers the cliché to Neobule's vision of the god-like creature
she has fallen for; to make the ode a monologue by Neobule, in order to put the words
in her mouth, as some do, is to miss H.'s capacity for sympathetic irony; **Liparaei**]
'from Lipara', one of the Aeoliae Insulae, a *civitas decumana*; **Hebri**] the name of a
Trojan killed by Mezentius in *Aen.* 10. 696, more familiar as the name of a river in
Thrace; cf. for the circumlocution 3. 9. 14, 1. 27. 10-11 and see on l. 5. 3; the name is
fanciful, like Sybaris in l. 8, but the boy is sharply particularised by the lines which
follow — the son, probably, of a Roman citizen resident in Lipara, perhaps the son of a
publicanus, who has come to Rome to undergo the kind of training and education suit-
able for young Romans of good family; L. R. Taylor, *JRS* 1924, 159: '[under Augustus]
the officers of the Roman army were still drawn from the sons of senators and knights,
many of whom flocked to Rome from the Italian towns'.

9-12]   The activities mentioned (swimming, horsemanship, athletics) belong to the *cultus
virilis* which Sybaris is upbraided for neglecting in l. 8; but where the experienced Lydia
was able to ensnare Sybaris, no such course is open to Neobule — she cannot even
approach her lover, only admire him from a distance. — **simul . . . in undis**] An ironic
reformulation, perhaps, of the familiar model of love at first sight, Catullus 51. 6 ff.
'Simul te, Lesbia, aspexi, nihil est super mi . . .'; cf. l. 19. 8 and Cicero's malicious ver-
sion (put on the lips of Clodius addressing his sister) *Cael.* 36 'Vicinum adulescentem
aspexisti', etc.; *simul = simul atque*, as l. 4. 7, etc.; **unctos umeros**] Hebrus' shoulders
were protected by olive oil against the sun and dust while on the race track (cf. l. 8. 8),
afterwards he refreshed himself with a swim in the Tiber; as he emerged, his bare shoul-
ders glistened unnaturally; it was at this point that Neobule first saw and fell for her
god-like lover; for attractive young men swimming in the Tiber (and Clodia's interest in
them), see Cicero *Cael.* 36 'Habes hortos ad Tiberim ac diligenter eo loco paratos, quo
omnis iuventus natandi causa venit'; the tenses *aufert . . . simul lavit* (perfect of *lavare*,
not present of *lavere*) imply something that happens regularly — as soon as Hebrus
arrives for his swim, Neobule can concentrate no longer. — **Bellerophonte**] He rode on
Pegasus; the final syllable is long. — **neque . . . neque . . . victus**] 'beaten neither through
slowness of fist nor of foot'; i.e., unbeaten as a boxer or a runner; *segni* with both nouns;
see on 2. 19. 24.

13-16]   Stanza 4 extends the daydream which began in the previous stanza while complet-
ing the contrast between two lifestyles (that of the respectable Roman girl in Stanzas
1-2, that of the young man of good family in Stanzas 3-4); the three appositional expan-
sions (1) 'eques . . . Bellerophonte', (2) 'neque . . . victus', (3) 'catus . . . aprum' form a
tricolon crescendo, each member grammatically independent of the others, each evoking
a different aspect of Hebrus' activities; Neobule can hardly have seen Hebrus hunting,
but she has heard men talk of such things and H. imagines her following him there in her
thoughts; at the same time the word-order becomes more elaborate and the syntax less
spare and economical than in the opening stanza, to suggest the expansion of the day-
dream; cf. Tibullus' advice 1. 4. 49-54 to the prospective (male) lover to join his beloved
in hunting and athletics as a strategy of courtship. — **fugientis . . . cervos**] Chiastic word
order ('framing') — adjective A, adjective B, noun B, noun A. — **celer**] Locks on to *catus*.
— **arto . . . aprum**] Adjective A, adjective B, noun A, noun B; **excipere**] i.e., 'cut off'
when the boar is driven out of the thicket; for *arto* some MSS have *alto*.

3. 13

Introduction: A dramatic monologue, reproducing the unwinding of the poet's thoughts
as he contemplates the scene before his eyes, structured syntactically as a formal
address, in the manner of a hymn to a god or goddess, to the *Fons Bandusiae* on the eve
of a rustic festival. Both the site of the spring and the occasion have been the subject of
debate. Common sense suggests H. is playing the role he plays in 3. 18 and 3. 22 of the
landed proprietor whimsically attuned to the rural scene and its traditions. If the imagi-
native continuity of the poem, which seems carefully contrived, is to be preserved, the
dramatic moment must be in mid-summer, not the *Fontinalia* in mid-October (but see
on 1 *Bandusiae* and 3 *cras*).

Structure: An adaptation of the traditional structure of a hymn of dedication. H. adds to
the formal opening address (line 1) and the list of attributes of the divinity addressed
(Stanza 3) an indication of the occasion, which develops into a digression (lines 4-8) as
H. follows a train of thought (structured as a series of images). Instead of the normal
promises of future offerings (cf. 3. 22. 6-8, 3. 26. 3-4) H. promises the best gift a poet
can offer — immortality.

Metre: Asclepiad (d); see 1. 5M.

1-3]   **O Fons Bandusiae**] Bandusia is unidentifiable; H.'s farm is more likely than boy-
hood memories of Venusia; cf. *Sat.* 2. 6. 2 'tecto vicinus iugis aquae fons', *Epist.*
1. 16. 12-13 'fons etiam rivo dare nomen idoneus, ut nec / frigidior Thraecam nec
purior ambiat Hebrus'; for the genitive see on 2. 6. 10-11. — **splendidior vitro**] 'more
brilliant', or 'more sparkling than glass'; the image is not of course of sheet glass (flat
and transparent), but of a mass of fused glass (complex in shape, a mixture of reflected
light and shadow) or a vessel or ornament made from poured glass (filled with air
bubbles, translucent rather than transparent); cf. 4. 2. 3 and *Aen.* 7. 759 'vitrea unda';
see on 1. 17. 20, 1. 18. 16. — **dulci . . . floribus**] Libations of wine form part of most
ancient ceremonies; flowers were offered to springs at the *Fontinalia* (Varro *Ling. lat.*
6. 22) and presumably other occasions; *digne* places tomorrow's festival in the context
of ceremonial offerings to springs, not so much describing what will occur as affirming
Bandusia's right to be so treated; **non sine floribus**] = 'and flowers, too'; cf. 1. 23. 3. —
cras] Emphatic position, to stress the imminence of the festival, or perhaps to contrast
what Bandusia deserves with the offering which will in fact be made. — **donaberis**] 'you
will be offered' (i.e., in sacrifice); the passive shifts the emphasis from the giver (whether
H. will conduct the service himself is left unclear) to the recipient. — **haedo**] Along with
pig (or piglet), the most modest and usual sacrificial animal (see on 3. 23. 4); cf. 1. 4. 12,
3. 8. 7-8, 3. 18. 5.

4-8]   After the simple, unadorned directness of the opening statement of occasion, the ode
gains momentum as the mention of a kid touches off a sequence of images. A first hint
also of the time of year: though goats can be born at any time, the traditional mating
period is between October and December; the kids are born about five months later; for
the image cf. the calf in 4. 2. 54-60. — **cornibus primis**] i.e., the emerging horn-tips; the
horns begin to appear within a few days of birth, and can be 5cm long in two weeks. —
et venerem et proelia] Hendiadys: 'the battles of love'; the goat is the symbol of lust in
ancient literature (see on 1. 17. 7); cf. Catullus 17. 15 and 69. 6). — **destinat**] 'marks
him out for'; cf. 2. 7. 20, 2. 18. 30. — **frustra**] For the surprise effect cf. 3. 7. 21. —
gelidos . . . rivos] i.e., the chill waters of the stream into which the spring flows will be
tinged by the ritual pouring upon them of blood from the sacrificial kid; a few drops
(at most a gobletful) would suffice to symbolise the offering of the sacrificial animal;
the animal itself is kept for consumption by H. and his household at the ensuing festival;
inficiet rubro sanguine] ironic and imaginative; the indignation of A. Y. Campbell,
Horace, 1924, 1-3 and others is misplaced; *gelidos* and *rubro* both imply their con-
traries (warm blood, clear water) in the usual Horatian manner. — **lascivi suboles gregis**]
Brings us back to the scene before H.'s eyes.

9-12]   An adaptation of the familiar recital in a hymn of the attributes of the divinity
addressed; anaphora in asyndeton of the personal pronoun is traditional; see on 1. 35. 5.
The traditional structural device is, as it were, secularised, to lend poetic form to the
description of a scene: in place of the general statements of a hymn, H. describes what
he sees before him as he stands (in fact or in imagination) by the spring. The imagery of

this stanza (like the young kid of lines 3-6) requires a mid-summer setting which precludes the *Fontinaiia* (in mid-autumn). — te . . . tangere] The spring is sheltered from the mid-summer heat by the ilex oak of line 14, perhaps by other trees as well; the constellation Canicula (the 'Lesser Dog') rose in late July; **atrox hora**] 'the cruel hour'; i.e., the heat of midday (as in lines 10-12), not 'the cruel mid-summer season'. — **frigus amabile**] The shade of the area round the spring, as in *te . . . tangere*, rather than the cool waters of the spring itself. — **fessis vomere tauris**] Oxen tired from the morning's ploughing; cf. 3. 18. 11-12; summer ploughing, in addition to ploughing in spring and autumn, was regular ancient practice; see Columella 12. 2. 53; cf. Xenophon *Oeconomicus* 16. 72, Theocritus 25. 25 (and Gow thereon). — **pecori vago**] The *lascivus grex* of line 8; whereas the oxen have work to do, the goats can wander where they will until the midday heat drives them to seek shelter.

13-16] **Fies . . . fontium**] i.e., Bandusia will join the order of distinguished springs (Arethusa, Aganippe, Egeria, Hippocrene, etc.) as a result of H.'s poem; cf. 3. 4. 25; **Fies**] i.e., as a consul, etc. is 'created', *OLD* 6 b; for the genitive, see on 3. 12. 1. — **me dicente**] 'upon my singing the praises of' (as H. proceeds to do). — **cavis . . . tuae**] Impressionistic (as often in natural description in Roman poetry): *cavis . . . saxis* suggests a rocky basin, perhaps part of some kind of rock cave or grotto; *inpositam ilicem* suggests that the rock mass is on a hillside, or on rising land, so that the *ilex* (an evergreen oak) rises directly above the spring, shading its waters — a picture reinforced by *desiliunt*: the water, i.e., tumbles down the rock basin, to form the stream (7 *rivos*) flowing down the slope from the spring (cf. 2. 3. 11-12, perhaps the same setting); **loquaces**] personifies; a more daring figure than our 'babbling brook' (H.'s spring is fully articulate); cf. 3. 11. 5.

<h1 style="text-align:center">3. 14</h1>

Introduction: An ode expressing the joy and relief of public and poet alike at Augustus' return to Rome in 24 BC after three years of active service in Spain. For the circumstances, see Syme, *Roman Revolution* 333; cf. 4. 5 written to mark Augustus' return from further campaigns in Spain ten years later.

The ode has disconcerted commentators. Page finds the transition from the 'formal and official frigidity' of the opening stanzas to the 'licentious vigour' of Stanzas 5-7 intolerable. Fraenkel 288-91 is more sympathetic, though uncompromising in his preference for 4. 5.

Structure: Stanza 1 introduces the theme of Augustus' return; Stanzas 2-3 describe some ceremony of thanksgiving; Stanza 4 bridges the transition from public to private celebration; Stanzas 5-7 issue instructions for a party.

Metre: Sapphics; see 1. 2M.

1-4] **Herculis ritu**] The parallel of Hercules (1) lends heroic stature to Augustus' achievements, (2) reminds us that Hercules too arrived in Rome (or where Rome would one day stand) from Spain covered with glory (after defeating the monster Geryon, an event celebrated by Virgil in *Aen.* 8 and by Propertius in 4. 9 and commemorated by the *Ara Maxima*), (3) introduces the idea that Augustus went to Spain, not for personal glory, but at the behest of the Roman people, as Hercules went at the command of Eurysthenes. — **o plebs**] Addressed to the assembled crowd; the first of three vocatives (cf. 10 *vos*, etc., 17 *puer*), a device aimed at securing dramatic effect, making also a gradation from the exalted expression of public feeling (both the form and the sense of *o plebs* belong to the high style) through something only slightly less formal (*vos, o pueri et puellae*) to the purely personal *i pete, puer*. — **morte . . . laurum**] 'to have sought the laurel crown (worn by the victorious general in his triumph) at the price of death'; i.e., to have gone to certain death; the danger to which a victorious commander-in-chief has exposed himself is commonly exaggerated in panegyric, though in fact Augustus did fall gravely ill during the Spanish campaign. — **repetit Penatis**] Stanzas 1-3 seem poised for Augustus' formal public appearance (see on line 11); but *hic dies* would be premature (and ill-omened) if he had not returned safely; some compression of events is likely, as commonly in commemorative poetry, for dramatic effect: the news that Augustus is on his way home, the public thanksgiving decreed by the Senate, his actual arrival, the ceremony to mark his safe return are probably run together by

the process called 'historical foreshortening' (see on 1. 37); the phrase *repetit Penatis*
(= both 'he is on his way home' and 'he is home' — offering his prayers at this moment
to the Penates) is chosen to cope with this foreshortening.

5-10]　Unico ... marito] *unico* perhaps = 'unparalleled', as in 1. 26. 5 'unice securus'; but
probably the meaning is 'wife whose only happiness is her husband' (*unico marito*
representing an extension of the idiom of *summos montes*, etc.; cf. 3. 13. 4-5 'cornibus
primis'); in either case, *unico* comes dangerously close to reminding us that Livia was in
fact a divorcee. **— prodeat]** i.e., make her public appearance at the head of the proces-
sion, following a private ceremony; cf. 2. 8. 7. **— iustis operata sacris]** 'after participat-
ing in the proper sacrifice'; for defence of the more obvious variant *divis* ('after sacrific-
ing to just gods'), see Williams. **— soror]** Octavia, the widow of Mark Antony. **— ducis]**
Stresses Augustus' role as conquering general. **— decorae matres]** sc. *prodeant*; the
mothers join the procession led by Livia. **— supplice vitta]** The headband worn while
offering prayers to the gods for Augustus' safe return; for the role of *matres* in a
national emergency, see Quinn, *Virgil's Aeneid, a critical description* 282; cf. 3. 2. 6-9;
as in *Aen.* 11. 481-5, their status is as participants in the ceremony, not as spectators.
— virginum iuvenumque nuper sospitum] The mothers are the mothers of the generation
whose safety has been ensured by Augustus' victories; their children are called *virgines*
(a term applicable to young married women as well as girls) and *iuvenes* as more approp-
riate to the high style than 'sons and daughters'; the sense 'soldiers who have returned
home safely' is excluded by context; for *iuvenis* as a synonym of *adulescens*, see on 1.
2. 41.

10-12]　vos, o pueri et puellae] Younger than the *virgines* and *iuvenes* just mentioned; H.
warns them that Augustus is about to appear and they must behave properly; the
aside prepares the transition from the formal rhetoric of lines 1-10 to the personal note
of Stanzas 4-7; the *pueri* and *puellae* are probably, like the *matres*, participants in the
ceremony rather than spectators; their role is perhaps that of a choir (like the *virgines*
and *pueri* of 1. 21, 4. 6. 32-44 and the *CS*; cf. the *virgines* and *pueri* in Catullus 34. 2. **—
iam virum exspectate]** 'watch now for the man to appear' (i.e., Augustus, whose appear-
ance is now imminent); *vir*, used absolutely in the singular, has the sense almost of
'hero'; cf. *Aen.* 6. 791-2 (Anchises to Aeneas) 'Hic vir, hic est, tibi quem promitti
saepius audes, / Augustus Caesar, divi genus', *Aen.* 12. 425 'Arma citi properate viro',
etc. and see Norden on *Aen.* 6. 174; *iam virum exspectate* is James Gow's emendation
of probably the most vexed line in the *Odes*; the MSS have *iam virum expertae* for the
first half of the line, being divided for the second half between *male ominatis* (which
requires a hiatus after *male*) and *male nominatis* (which seems meaningless); *iam virum
expertae puellae* (i.e., married girls) seems odd and inappropriate and many accept
Bentley's *non*, which seems hardly less odd; Williams's defence of the inherited text is
ingenious but unconvincing; Gow's *iam virum exspectate* (anticipated by Bücheler's
iam virum spectate) requires *male ominatis* (no hiatus); for the resultant caesura after
syllable 6 (instead of after syllable 5), see 1. 2M. **— male ominatis parcite verbis]** =
'keep quiet' (lest any unfortunate remark at a crucial moment invalidate the ceremony
of thanksgiving; cf. 3. 1. 2 'favete linguis'.

**13-16]　At this point H. abandons description of the ceremony, either as beyond his
intentions, or because he wants to dramatise his involvement in the occasion, rather as
4. 2. 45-56 anticipate (or purport to anticipate) Augustus' victorious return in 13 BC.
— Hic dies] i.e., the day of Augustus' return; cf. 3. 8. 9; it had become Augustus'
practice to decline triumphs for his numerous victories, contenting himself with formal
salutation as *imperator*; see Brunt-Moore on *Res Gestae* 4. **— atras exiget curas]** cf. 3. 1.
40; **exiget]** 'will drive away' (var. *eximet*). **— tumultum]** The technical term for civil
uprising within Italy. **— mori per vim]** (= 'ne per vim moriar') 'death by violence'. **—
tenente Caesare terras]** 'while Caesar is here on earth' (i.e., not yet a god; cf. 3. 3.
11-12).

**17-28]　Instructions for a party to follow the ceremony; cf. 1. 36. 10-16, 1. 38, 2. 11.
17-24; the plural *coronas* and the *cadus* of special wine imply the presence of guests at
H.'s private celebration. **— unguentum]** For scent at parties, see on 4. 12. 17. **—
coronas]** For garlands at parties, see on 1. 38. 1. **— cadum]** Probably to be purchased
for the occasion, like that in 4. 12. 17-20; see on 1. 9. 8. **— Marsi duelli]** Dating from
the Marsian War (usually called the 'Social War' by modern historians) of 90 BC and thus
over 65 years old; the Marsi (see on 3. 6. 37-44) were the strongest supporters of the

rebellion of Rome's *socii*; Latium was one of the principal wine-producing areas; cf. the *testa* of *Massicum* dating from 65 BC in 3. 21. 1 and the *amphora* of *Caecubum* of 59 BC in 3. 28. 8. — **Spartacum**] The leader of the slave rebellion of 73-71 BC; this is the second allusion to past upheavals (*tumultus*), the ode concludes with a guarded allusion to the Civil Wars; the allusions serve as a reminder that the confidence expressed in lines 14-16 reflects a state of affairs which, till Actium, had been the exception rather than the rule for several generations. — **vagantem**] i.e., in his marauding raids; the revolt began in Capua and resulted in widespread plundering of southern Italy. — **testa**] Smaller, or less grand, than *cadus*; H. would like to buy a whole *cadus* but doubts if as much as a *testa* of this rare wine survives; *testa* also 1. 20. 2, 3. 21. 4. — **dic . . . crinem**] Neara is to sing and play for the company, like Lyde in 2. 11. 21-4 (not invited *en tête-à-tête*, like Phyllis in 4. 11 or Tyndaris in 1. 17) and therefore dispensable; **argutae**] 'clear-voiced'; cf. 4. 6. 25; **murreum**] fragrant with myrrh (rather than Porphyrio's 'inter flavum et nigrum'); **nodo cohibere**] similar instruction to Lyde in 2. 11. 21-4. — **si . . . fiet**] i.e., if Neaera's *ianitor* makes difficulties about admitting H.'s messenger (perhaps because his mistress is otherwise occupied); cf. Catullus 32.9. — **abito**] 'let him not wait'. — **albescens capillus**] Cf. 2. 11. 15; H., i.e., is no longer the man to fuss about a girl. — **protervae**] The stock epithet for the love-partner of either sex who is in an aggressive mood; see on 1. 26. 2; cf. 1. 25. 2. — **consule Planco**] Plancus, the addressee of 1. 7, was consul in 42 BC, the year H. fought at Philippi; a good example of H.'s trick of the quiet ending at a little distance from the point — and a final hint that times, like H., have changed.

3. 15

Introduction: Ironic advice to an ageing flirt: it is time she retired and let her daughter take over. No suggestion, as there is in 4. 13, of a dramatic context; all the same, they are hardly lines intended for Chloris' ear.

With Chloris, the notoriously promiscuous (3 'famosis laboribus') wife who is past her prime (the type castigated by H. in 3. 6. 25-32) cf. Lydia in 1. 25; for the 'like mother, like daughter' motif cf. 1. 16; for H.'s *moechae*, see 1. 15I.

Structure: Lines 1-6 are connected by the imperatives 2 *fige* and 4 *desine*. Lines 7-16 by 7-8 *non te decet* and 13-14 *te non decent*; in these lines Chloris is opposed to her daughter Pholoe. The ode concludes with a tricolon crescendo 14 *non citharae . . . nec flos . . . nec . . . cadi.*

Metre: Asclepiad (b); see 1. 3M

1-6] Lines 1-3 place Chloris (though her name is held over to line 8): she is a poor man's wife (and therefore potentially respectable, a proper object for H.'s concern) who has given herself over to a life of *nequitia*; her efforts to keep up the pace are notorious, it is time for her to stop. — **pauperis**] The word implies humble circumstances, not poverty (the type of Volteius in *Epist.* 1. 7. 55-9) — obviously not a husband to keep his wife in the style to which Stanza 4 shows her accustomed. — **Ibyci**] The name of a Greek poet of Rhegium, noted, according to Cicero, for his passionate love poetry (*Tusc.* 4. 71 'Maxime vero omnium flagrasse amore Rheginum Ibycum apparet ex scriptis'); possibly, therefore, a clue to the social status of Chloris' husband. — **tandem**] Though often *tandem* does little more than emphasise an imperative, it here prepares the way for H.'s complaint that Chloris has gone on too long. — **nequitiae**] 'loose-living'; normally pejorative, of conduct which is criminal or depraved (e.g., 3. 4. 78, of Tityos' attempt to rape Latona); but the word is adopted by the elegists as connoting a lifestyle that renounced traditional values (Ovid styles himself *Am.* 2. 1. 2 'nequitiae poeta meae'): promiscuity on the part of a mistress was a matter for indignation if you were the victim (Propertius 2. 5. 2), but could be viewed more indulgently if you were the beneficiary, or an uninvolved observer of the human comedy (Propertius 1. 6. 26, 3. 10. 24, Ovid *Am.* 1. 3. 32, 3. 1. 7). — **fige modum**] i.e., 'make a definite end'; cf. 1. 16. 2. — **famosisque laboribus**] 'infamous exploits'; *labores*, as the 'labours of Hercules', of prodigious, celebrated feats; cf. 4. 13. 15. — **maturo funeri**] i.e., a death that will not be untimely. — **propior**] Nearer than the *virgines* of line 5. — **inter ludere virgines**] Some kind of dance is perhaps implied like the *chorus puellarum* of 2. 5. 21; but the usual connotations of *ludere* ('play around') with sexual overtones are of course present as in line 12 (see on 2. 5. 8; cf. 3. 11. 10, 4. 13. 4); **virgines**] 'young girls', not necessarily virgins; cf. 3. 11. 35. — **stellis . . . candidis**] i.e., putting a damper on proceedings by her presence; Chloris perhaps spoils the *virgines'* dancing act.

7-8] Chloris is contrasted with her own daughter, as Lyce in 4. 13. 6-8 is contrasted with Chia. — **Non siquid . . . decet**] = 'not everything that suits Pholoe well enough suits you'; **Pholoen**] perhaps the *adultera* of 1. 33. 6-9; **satis decet**] H., i.e., has reservations about Pholoe's conduct too; but she is young and society is tolerant.

8-16] **Filia**] The most economical assumption is that the daughter is Pholoe (who is otherwise left undefined and the daughter left nameless); that Chloris has a daughter old enough to take the field herself adds weight of course to H.'s case for pressing retirement on Chloris; for the idea 'like mother, like daughter' cf. 1. 16. — **expugnat . . . domos**] The daughter, i.e., does not wait to be vanquished by her admirers; she mounts the attack herself, and sweeps all before her like a conquering general (unlike Barine in 2. 8. 17-20 who keeps her enthralled lovers under her own roof, like Homer's Circe); for the idea cf. Seneca *Q. Nat. 4 praefat.* 8 'Crispus Parsienus saepe dicebat adulationi nos opponere, non claudere, ostium, et quidem sic quem ad modum opponi amicae solet; quae si impulit, grata est, gratior si effregit'. — **pulso . . . tympano**] 'aroused like a Bacchant at the beat of the drum'; cf. 2. 19. 9; for the 'mixed metaphor', see on 2. 5.

9-12. — **amor Nothi**] 'her love for Nothus' (= 'the Bastard', a name chosen for ironical effect); he is presumably her current lover; the daughter, i.e., though promiscuous (line 9), is the type to fall passionately in love (lines 10-12), if not for long with the same man. — **lascivae capreae**] The metaphor changes again; for the proverbial friskiness and lustiness of young goats, see on 3. 13. 5. — **te . . . Luceriam**] Spinning wool is the symbol of domestic respectability; the words also place Chloris: the role of the respectable *matrona* is hers to play, but she has forsaken it; cf. the formula found on tombstones 'domum servavit, lanam fecit' and Balsdon, *Roman Women*, 1962, 270; Augustus is said to have attempted to restore the custom (threatened by large-scale manufacture), Suetonius *Aug.* 73. 1; **lanae**] the plural implies the weighed-out parcels of wool (*pensa*) allotted each day by the *matrona* to her *ancillae*; **prope nobilem Luceriam**] in Apulia, called *nobilis* because the best Italian wool came from there, Pliny *NH* 8. 190; presumably H. means Chloris would do well to devote herself to making high-quality cloth for sale (or barter), not for her own use. — **citharae**] i.e., singing at parties and accompanying herself on the lyre; cf. 1. 17. 18-20, 2. 11. 22, 3. 28. 9-16, 4. 11. 34-6, 4. 13. 6-8; the instrument becomes the symbol of the activity, as often; the plural to suggest repeated performance; for the cithara, see on 1. 12. 1. — **flos purpureus rosae**] = 'bright-red roses', likewise a symbol of parties, or the luxurious *tête-à-tête* (see on 1. 5. 1; cf. 4. 10. 4); the singular *flos* has a collective force (see on 1. 4. 10) and can thus be matched up with the plurals *citharae* and *cadi*. — **poti . . . cadi**] 'jars drained to the dregs'; a final cruel image, rendered more cutting by the delayed, measured thrust of *vetulam*; cf. 4. 13. 25 and, for the general picture, 4. 13. 4-5.

3. 16

Introduction: An ode to Maecenas, expressing H.'s satisfaction with the way of life he has adopted, of which the Sabine farm (a gift from his patron) is the symbol. Wealth corrupts and the power it gives is illusory. In different terms and in a more personal style (the tone of which is set by the opening exercise in ironic heroic) 3. 16 thus reiterates the moral stance of 3. 1.

Structure: Stanzas 1-4 develop the minor theme: wealth is a source of corruption: Stanzas 1-2, the conspiracy of Jove and Venus against Acrisius; Stanzas 3-4, bribery and corruption more generally; the style is abrupt and oracular, the tone plainly ironic. Stanzas 5-7 introduce the major theme: 'money brings trouble, the quiet, retiring life of self-denial for me'; the tone is now more earnest. Stanzas 8-11 develop the major theme: H.'s Sabine farm and the way of life that goes with it are extolled to the accompaniment of a series of defences of the paradox 'the poor man content with his lot is richer than the rich man who is not'.

Metre: Asclepiad (c); see 1. 6M.

1-8] Acrisius kept his daughter Danae locked up in a tower of bronze because it had been prophesied that she would bear a son destined to kill him; but Jove, descending in a shower of gold, added Danae to his conquests; their son Perseus later accidentally fulfilled the prophecy. — **turris aenea**] the 'tower of bronze' (a traditional detail) establishes the appropriate level of rhetoric and mythical fantasy. — **robustaeque fores**] 'and doors of stout oak'. — **vigilum . . . excubiae**] The poetic rhetoric of the high style is adopted almost in a spirit of mock-heroic; **tristes**] 'surly', 'menacing'. — **munierant**] For the indicative instead of the pluperfect subjunctive (also a feature of the high style), see on 2. 17. 14-15. — **nocturnis ab adulteris**] 'nocturnal seducers'; *adulterium* involves a woman whose status (as a virtuous wife, as a marriageable daughter or widow) suffers as a result of the seduction (hence the traditional right of the aggrieved husband to take the law in his own hands for the loss suffered); *adulter*, therefore, normally of a man who has an affair with a married woman (see on 1. 25. 9 *moechos*); its extension here to the would-be seducers of Danae is possible since the essence of the crime committed by the *adulter* is the offence against *pudicitia* (Cicero *Cael.* 49 'expugnare pudicitiam'); the phrase introduces none the less overtones of ironic realism which prepare for the undercutting of the opening rhetoric: Acrisius is assimilated by implication to the typical husband of Augustan love poetry who resorts to locked doors to protect his wife's virtue; Jove, well known for his adulterous affairs, to the typical man about town who knows how to bribe his way past any door. — **virginis . . . pavidum**] The rhetoric is now openly undercut: we see Acrisius through the mocking eyes of Jove and Venus who laughingly enter into a conspiracy to deceive him (rather as Virgil makes Jove and Venus conspire against Dido, *Aen.* 4. 115-28); H.'s rationalistic interpretation of the legend now begins. — **risissent**] A plural agreement is normal when persons are involved, agreement with the nearer almost always with a multiple inanimate subject. — **fore, etc.**] The *oratio obliqua* represents what Jove and Venus said to one another as they laughed at Acrisius' precautions; **converso in pretium deo**] 'with the god metamorphosed into a bribe'; Jove, i.e., by turning himself into a shower of gold, overcame all resistance; the opening myth thus ends on a suitably bathetic note; for *pretium* 'bribe' cf. Cicero *Caec.* 29 'Utrum gravius aliquid in quempiam dici potest, quam ad hominem condemnandum adactum esse pretio?'

9-16] **Aurum**] Limited by context to the sense 'gold used as money' and lent pejorative overtones ('money used for corrupt purposes') by H.'s retelling of the legend of Danae. — **per medios ire satellites**] Picks up 7 *tutum iter.* — **saxa**] i.e., of a fortress, etc. — **ictu fulmineo**] Jove's usual method of clearing obstacles in his path. — **concidit . . . domus**] Amphiaraus' wife was bribed to persuade him to take part in the fateful expedition of the Seven against Thebes; upon his death she was killed by her son, who was then pursued by the Furies for the murder; the original bribe thus brought ruin on the whole line (*concidit domus*). — **diffidit**] 'split open' (from *diffindo*). — **vir Macedo**] 'a man from Macedon', pejorative for Philip II, father of Alexander the Great, famous for his bribes. — **muneribus, munera**] The chiasmus, by breaking the series of verbs (*concidit, diffidit, subruit*) each in the initial position in its clause (anaphora in asyndeton), marks a quickening tempo at the climax. — **navium . . . duces**] Apparently an allusion to Menas, a *libertinus* who served as commander of the fleet of Sex. Pompeius and twice deserted to the other side; see Suetonius *Aug.* 74, Dio 48. 45 and 49. 1; some see an allusion to him in *Epode* 4. 15-20; a generalising plural in that case; **inlaqueant**] indicative.

17-28] **crescentem . . . fames**] Surprise transition from minor to major theme, continuing the oracular abruptness which characterises Stanzas 1-7; at the same time the scope of H.'s moralising widens; till now his subject has been the use of money to corrupt in the strict sense; he now shifts the emphasis to wealth as destroying the peace of mind of the possessor generally. — **iure perhorrui**] = 'my distaste was justified'. — **late conspicuum . . . verticem**] 'to raise my head high where it could be seen on all sides', as does the man whose luxurious lifestyle makes him conspicuous. — **Maecenas, equitum decus**] Usually printed as part of the preceding clause, but the initial position gives a better rhythm to sentence and stanza — H. turns to Maecenas to emphasise the increase in earnestness which marks the shift from ironic moralising to the explicit tone of what now follows; **equitum decus**] 'ornament of the Order of Knights', points to Maecenas' own (relative) self-effacement — the descendant of Etruscan kings (1. 1. 1) who is content with the title of *Eques*, the chief adviser of Augustus who seeks no official title. — **quanto . . . feret**] The first of a series of paradoxes in the Stoic manner which characterise the development of the major theme. – **nil cupientium . . . gestio**] H. is anxious (*gestio*) to desert the cause (*partis*) of the rich; indeed, he asks us to imagine him, like one who changed sides in the Civil Wars (*transfuga*), on his way unarmed (*nudus* – i.e., having abandoned his arms; cf. 3. 27. 52) to join the camp (*castra peto*) of those who 'desire nothing' (*nil cupientium*); those, in other words, who have learnt to be content with what they have, unlike the rich man, whose besetting sin is *avaritia*, the urge to keep adding to the wealth he already possesses; 'unarmed' in the sense that he has abandoned all encumbering forms of wealth; no suggestion that H. wants to join a sect of those who renounce material possessions altogether; for the military metaphor cf. Seneca *Epist.* 2. 5 'Soleo enim in aliena castra [the Epicurean camp], non tamquam transfuga sed tamquam explorator . . .'; for *nudus*, 'unarmed', see *OLD* 4. – **contemptae . . . rei**] = 'more distinguished as the proprietor of an estate men despise'; a second paradox (a variant of the Stoic model 'only the philosopher is king'), rejecting conventional distinction in men's eyes (based on wealth) in favour of true distinction (based on spiritual worth and philosophical insight). – **quam si . . . horreis**] i.e., the sort of wealthy speculator about the extent of whose wealth others talk with envy – in this case, rumours that he has bought up the whole Apulian grain harvest (with a view to selling later at a profit); **quidquid arat**] i.e., 'produce by ploughing', *OLD* 2; for the tough farming stock of the SE, see on 3. 6. 37-44; **arat**] the final syllable counts as long (see on 1. 3. 36), – **magnas . . . inops**] A further Stoic paradox, though the idea is found also in Epicurean writers (e.g., Epicurus Frag. A25B; for the idea cf. 1. 1. 9-10.

29-32] The ode concludes with 4 stanzas in praise of H.'s 'contempta res' – his Sabine farm and the simple lifestyle which it permits and of which it is the symbol. – **Purae . . . paucorum**] Cf. *Sat.* 2. 6. 1-3 (the first mention of H.'s farm?):

> Hoc erat in votis: modus agri non ita magnus,
> hortus ubi et tecto vicinus iugis aquae fons
> et paulum silvae super his foret.

For the farm, see on 2. 18. 14. – **segetis . . . meae**] 'a crop I can rely on'; unlike, i.e., the *fundus mendax* of 3. 1. 30-32; for the farm and what it produced, see *Epist.* 1. 16. 1-10 and *Epist.* 1. 14. 23. – **fulgentem . . . beatior**] A fourth paraxox: H.'s farm represents a lifestyle which is happier (and more truly wealthy) than that of a governor of Africa, though *he* cannot see it; **fulgentem imperio Africae**] 'the man who is resplendent in the command of Africa', the most coveted Roman province after Asia; **sorte**] 'as one's lot', literally in the case of the governor of Africa, who was chosen by ballot for provincial commands (*sors provinciarum*), metaphorically in the case of H.; **beatior**] as usual, balanced between the two senses 'happier' and 'wealthier'; H. is literally happier, but can consider himself also as wealthier in terms of the paradox developed in the previous stanza; *beatior*, like *fallit*, agrees with the nearest.

33-8] **Calabrae apes**] Cf. 2. 6. 14, 4. 2. 27. – **Laestrygonia in amphora**] i.e., from Formiae, said to be the Laestrygonia of *Odyssey* 10.82; see on 3. 17. 5-9; cf. 1. 20. 11-12. – **Bacchus**] = wine. – **languescit**] Cf. 3. 21. 8. – **Gallicis**] i.e., Cisalpine; cf. Pliny *NH* 8. 190 'alba [lana] circumpadanis nulla praefertur'. – **inportuna pauperies**] i.e., H. was *pauper*, but not to the extent that his *pauperies* was *inportuna*. – **nec . . . deneges**] The qualification, though obviously intended as a compliment to Maecenas, renders suspect the sincerity of H.'s self-denial (see Stanza 6): he can enjoy his simple lifestyle at no real risk.

39-44] **contracto . . . continuem**] A fifth paradox, 'by reducing my greed for material possessions, I shall increase my income more effectively than if I were to add untold riches to untold riches'; **contracto cupidine**] picks up 21-22; **vectigalia**] i.e., the income from his estate; cf. for the idea Cicero *Rep.* 4. 7 (= *Parad.* 6. 3) 'Magnum vectigal parsimonia'; *Att.* 12. 19. 1 'Equidem iam nihil egeo vectigalibus et parvo contentus esse possum'; **porrigam**] 'stretch', 'expand'; **quam si continuem**] i.e., than if I were to add the kingdom of Alyattes to the dominion of Mygdon – two traditionally wealthy areas of the Roman province of Asia; **continuem**] 'extend'; **Mygdoniis campis**] dative, 'the plains (i.e., territories) of Mygdon', legendary prince of Phrygia (cf. 2. 12. 22); **Alyattei**] father of Croesus. – **multa . . . multa**] A concluding paradox, 'those who want a lot are those who are conscious of needing a lot'; i.e., 'the more you want, the more you need'. – **bene est . . . manu**] 'he is well-off to whom the god, with sparing hand, has offered what he needs' – provided, i.e., he has learnt, like H., to content himself with *quod satis est*, a recurring theme, cf. 3. 1. 25-32, *Epist*. 1. 2. 46; for H.'s contentment with his Sabine estate, see *Epode* 1. 31, *Sat*. 2. 6. 4, *Odes* 2. 18. 14.

3. 17

Introduction: A birthday poem (the poet's response, according to a likely reading, declining an invitation to spend his friend's birthday with him) ironically complimentary about Aelius' distinguished ancestry, before descending to the casual tone appropriate between friends who pride themselves on their *urbanitas*.

Structure: An ironic adaptation of hymn form: opening vocative, long aside dealing with the attributes of the divinity addressed, concluding prayer or entreaty. Here, in place of the prayer or entreaty, some advice to H.'s friend (lines 14-16), preceded by a discursive, mock-solemn explanation of the circumstances which make the advice appropriate. There is no pause between stanzas.

Metre: Alcaics; see 1. 9M.

1-9] **Aeli**] Identified by Syme, *Roman Revolution* 535 as the L. Aelius Lamia who was Augustus' *legatus* in Spain 24-22 BC (still abroad in that case at the time of publication of *Odes* 1-3); presumably the Lamia of 1. 26. 8 and *Epist*. 1. 14. 6. – **vetusto . . . Lamo**] i.e., a *nobilis* by descent from that Lamus who is mentioned in *Odyssey* 10. 81; Aelius belonged to a distinguished family and such families were in the habit of tracing their descent from remote ancestors, divine (e.g., the Iulii from Venus) or heroic (see, e.g., *Aen*. 5. 117-23); the tone of the ode suggests the pedigree is not to be taken very seriously, and may be invented by H. for the occasion; **vetusto**] 'of old'. – **priores**] probably accusative with Lamias, 'the Lamias before you', not nominative with *ferunt*; if *ducis*, the reading of the MSS, is retained in line 5, *priores* and *genus* become successive subjects of *ferunt*, and *auctore . . . originem* becomes a separate statement, but this gives weak sense and poor rhythm. – **hinc ferunt denominatos**] = 'take, people say, their name from here'. – **nepotum genus omne**] i.e., the descendants of the original Homeric Lamus, without exception. – **per memores fastus**] = 'as is recorded in official documents'; for the *Fasti*, see *OCD*; for the accusative plural *fastus* (as in the same phrase 4. 14. 4, contrast 4. 13. 15 *notis fastis*) see *OLD*. – **auctore . . . tyrannus**] i.e., describe themselves as descended from the founder of Formiae; they could hardly do that in the *Fasti*; H. probably means no more than that the branch of the Aelii to which his friend belonged describe themselves as *Aelii Lamiae*, thus by implication claiming descent from Homer's Lamus on the grounds that Homer's city of Lamus in the land of the Laestrygonians was Formiae; in H.'s day Formiae was a fashionable city on the Via Appia where it touches the coast about 65 km N of Naples and 130 km S of Rome, better known as the home of the Mamurra family; H. spent several days getting there in *Sat*. 1. 5; **moenia**] with *tenuisse* (i.e., 'built and inhabited'); **innantem . . . Lirim**] = 'the Liris that joins the coast at the point made famous by the nymph Marica'; the Liris is personified as the river-god who swims down between (i.e., meanders among) the marshlands at the mouth of the Garigliano; **late tyrannus**] a suitably impressive conclusion to the pedigree.

9-16] **cras**] The honorific preamble over, H. turns to talk of the morrow. – **foliis . . . sternet**] H.'s prediction of a SE storm is graphically transposed into poetic description: the open land between the trees (*nemus*) will be a carpet of leaves; the beach will be covered with seaweed. – **aquae . . . cornix**] H.'s authority for his forecast; for the crow as weather sign, see *Georgics* 1. 388; such weather lore was traditional, but *annosa* is a hint that H. is no more serious here than he is in 3. 27. 7-12. – **dum potes**] i.e., today. – **aridum conpone lignum**] 'gather dry wood', for a good fire tomorrow; cf. 1. 9. 5-6. – **cras genium curabis**] *cras* picks up 9 *cras*; the *genius* is especially worshipped on one's birthday; a hint, therefore, to the reader that tomorrow is Aelius' birthday (hence the talk of how the day is to be spent, the importance of the weather that day); the future indicative, as often, instructs rather than predicts. – **mero et porco**] i.e., a libation to the *genius* and a sacrifice; in other words, a good dinner with plenty to drink; for pigs as sacrificial animals, see on 3. 23. 4. – **cum famulis operum solutis**] i.e., a holiday for the staff on the master's birthday; for the simple country practice of dining with one's slaves, cf. *Sat*. 2. 6. 65-7; for the idea cf. 3. 18. 9-12.

In all this, H. is conspicuous by his absence. A natural assumption is that Aelius has invited H. to spend his birthday with him and the ode is H.'s polite refusal. Whether the birthday party was at Formiae or on some country estate nearer Rome (in *Sat.* 1. 5 H. spends several days getting to Formiae), how in any case H.'s note declining the invitation was to reach Aelius in time are matters the reader is not expected to scrutinise. What we have is not the text of a verse epistle, but a poem which has taken shape out of a set of circumstances, real or imagined. The only legitimate requirement is that H.'s poem, while not to be pressed in detail, should retain, as something expressed or easily inferred, its motivating hypothesis.

3. 18

Introduction: Ostensibly, a hymn to Faunus; in fact, a charming description, tinged with sophisticated irony, of a holiday scene on H.'s farm; cf. 3. 13 and 3. 22.
     On such an occasion it was H.'s duty as *dominus* to officiate; see Cato *RR* 143. 1, quoted 3. 22I; contrast the more realistic, more diffuse treatment of the same theme in Tibullus 2. 1.
Structure: Stanzas 1-2 address the god and announce the sacrifice which marks the holiday; Stanzas 3-4 describe the scene.
Metre: Sapphics; see 1. 2M.
1-4]   **Faune**] Also 1. 4. 11-12 (of a spring sacrifice to Faunus), 1. 17. 2 (spoken of as the protector of H.'s farm), 2. 17. 27-9 (mentioned as saving H. from death when the tree fell on him). — **Nympharum . . . amator**] The appositional expansion of the opening vocative is conventional hymn form (cf. 1. 10. 1, 3. 22. 1, Lucretius 1. 1-2, etc.); but the solemnity of the form is ironically undercut by the sense; *amator* in this sense (*OLD* 1) is pejorative, closer to 'lecher' than to 'lover' (cf. 3. 4. 79, *Sat.* 1. 2. 55, 1. 3. 38, 2. 3. 259, *Epist.* 1. 1. 38). — **lenis . . . alumnis**] The god is imagined as attending the festival in his honour; H. prays that he will arrive in a good mood and remain well-disposed during his visit; the traditional material (gods were held to be present on such occasions, their benevolence had to be sought and could never be counted on) is handled with the urbane irony of a poet who finds the persona of the small landowner honouring his gods congenial; **parvis alumnis**] the piglets and kids (perhaps also lambs) reared on the farm; *parvis* suggests their vulnerability.
5-8]   The circumstances and the sacrifice promised Faunus to secure his goodwill are specified. — **si tener cadit haedus**] A formula inviting agreement (it is for Faunus to decide whethei the *haedus* is *tener*), but not expressing doubt or proposing a bargain; cf. 3. 9. 17-20; for the sacrifice of a kid, see on 3. 23. 4; for *tener* = young, cf. 4. 2. 54. — **pleno anno**] 'at the year's end'; the occasion is specified in line 10. — **larga nec desunt vina**] = 'if ample quantities of wine are available'. — **Veneris sodali creterrae**] 'in (lit. 'for') the *creterra*' (the large bowl in which the wine is mixed for general consumption and from which the libations are being poured); the bowl is described as 'Venus' boon companion' because of the role of wine on such occasions in relaxing sexual inhibitions — an aspect which Faunus can be supposed as regarding with approval. — **vetus . . . odore**] As before, it is for the god to decide whether the smoke from the sacrifice is sufficiently abundant; **vetus ara**] suggests the continuity of worship on H.'s farm.
9-16]   The holiday scene is described in tones of ironic realism (the irony lies in attributing the emotions felt by the human revellers to the animals on H.'s farm); contrast the idyllic tone of 1. 17. 1-12. — **Ludit . . . campo**] The opening word fixes the mood. — **nonae Decembres**] December 5. — **festus vacat pagus**] The inhabitants of the little community in which H.'s farm is situated are in holiday mood; cf. 2. 13. 4; in *Epist.* 1. 14. 1-3 H. tells us that his little estate comprised five homesteads and five heads of family (each probably a tenant-farmer, like Tityrus, etc. in Virgil's *Eclogues*); in *Sat.* 2. 7. 118 he speaks of his *familia rustica* as comprising eight *operae* (i.e., probably the hands who worked the home-farm under H.'s *vilicus*; cf. *Sat.* 2. 6. 65-7; **in pratis**] i.e., (1) out in the fields as opposed to at home; (2) (with *vacat*) rejoicing in the fields instead of working. — **otioso cum bove**] Released from the labour of ploughing, etc.; cf. 3. 13. 10-12. — **inter . . . agnos**] The lambs enter into the spirit of the occasion; we may, if we choose, regard them as under Faunus' protection, and H. perhaps alludes to a belief linking Faunus with the *Lupercalia* (see *OCD* s.v. *Lupercalia*); but the suggestion

of divine protection need be taken no more seriously than the suggestion of a sympathising nature in line 14. − **spargit . . . frondes**] The trees shedding their autumn leaves are spoken of as if spreading a carpet to honour the advancing god, thus introducing just the right hint of a participating nature ('pathetic fallacy'). − **gaudet . . . terram**] To conclude the holiday scene the spotlight falls on the ditch-digger (the humblest of agricultural workers), whose dance is ironically interpreted as a dance of triumph over his inveterate enemy; hence *pepulisse*, which suggests more violent beating than the *quatiunt* of l. 4. 7 and the *quatient* of 4. 1. 28 and in addition the notion of defeating an enemy (*OLD* 5).

3. 19

Introduction: A dramatic monologue; as in 1. 27, the scene is a symposium. There the party is at its height and H. intervenes to restore order; here H. cuts in to interrupt one of the company (whose learned conversation he finds misplaced) in order to prescribe, as host or as *magister bibendi*, a midnight toast in honour of Murena's entry upon his augurship. For the symposium scene cf. 2. 14.
Structure: Lines 1-8 set the stage for the toast proposed in lines 9-17; lines 18-28 add some more general reflections.
Metre: Asclepiad (b); see on 1. 3M.
1-4] It is clear from Stanza 3 that H. is running the party and fairly obvious that the party is a large one (not, i.e., a foursome, as might be supposed from Stanza 7); unnecessary, therefore, to assume the speaker teased by H. in Stanzas 1-2 is the Telephus of line 26 (for an unnamed addressee cf. 2. 5 and 2. 18). − **Quantum . . . Codrus**] Inachus was the first king of Argos, Codrus the last king of Athens. − **pro patria . . . mori**] For the story, see Lycurgus *in Leoc.* 84-5; for the phrase, 3. 2. 13, 4. 9. 51-2. − **narras**] The man H. interrupts is perhaps a chronologist and/or historian, like Cornelius Nepos, or an encyclopaedist, like the great Varro (see on 'pugnata . . . Ilio'); these being topics he knows and writes about, they keep intruding at inordinate length into his party conversation. − **genus Aeaci**] 'the descendants of Aeacus', father of Peleus and hence grandfather of Achilles and ancestor of the kings of Macedon in historical times (cf. *Aen.* 6. 839 'Aeaciden' of Perseus, son of Philip V). − **et pugnata . . . Ilio**] The 'fighting at Troy' might in a different context suggest an epic poet; here, probably, the reference is to the exploits of the *Aeacidae* Achilles and his son Pyrrhus (= Neoptolemus) at Troy; **sacro**] Troy in Homer is ἱρή.
5-8] H. urges more practical considerations. The questions put are those to which the seasoned partygoer (*scurra*), on the alert for an invitation (*vocatio*), should have a ready answer. − **quo . . . mercemur**] 'What's the price of Chian wine?' − the only reference to this prized wine in the *Odes*; for buying wines (as opposed to wines grown on one's own estate) cf. 4. 12. 16-20; the price of a really good wine is given as the sort of practical information a partygoer should know. − **quis . . . ignibus?**] 'Who has water on the fire?' (to mix with wine); i.e., where is a party imminent? − **quo . . . frigoribus?** = 'Who is putting on a party where one can escape from this terrible cold weather, and when does the party start?'; with 'quo praebente domum?' cf. *Sat.* 1. 5. 38 'Murena praebente domum' (where by an odd coincidence H.'s host is a Murena); **quota?**] = *quota hora?*; **Paelignis . . . frigoribus**] i.e., cold like that in Paelignum (in the Apennines) − presumably it is a bitter winter's night outside; **caream**] cf. 3. 26. 10. − **taces**] 'these are points on which you are silent' (contrast 3 *narras*).
9-12] H. turns to the wine waiter with instructions for a toast; it was the privilege of the *magister bibendi* (who might of course be the host himself − cf. 3. 8. 13) to impose upon the company such rules as he chose regarding what was drunk and how (cf. Catullus 37; in *Sat.* 2. 6. 67-70 H. tells us that at dinner on his Sabine farm each guest was free to drink what he liked, 'solutus legibus insanis'). − **Da lunae . . . Murenae**] A toast to the new month, to the new day which begins at midnight, to Murena as *augur*; i.e., a toast in three stages (timed to begin at midnight) to celebrate Murena's assumption of office on the first of the month (probably January 1st in view of 8 'Paelignis frigoribus'); not the beginning or the end of the night's drinking (for all-night parties, see 3. 8. 14-15, 3. 21. 23-4); the duty of the *puer*, it seems, was to distribute the cups as instructed and to call the toasts; cf. 1. 29. 7-8; **Murenae**] generally presumed

to be the Licinius of 2. 10; nothing is known of his appointment to the College of
Augurs. — **tribus ... commodis**] 'cups are mixed with the appropriate 3 or 9 ladlefuls',
or perhaps '3 or 9 good ladlefuls'; guests, i.e., were free to choose a modest cup or a
bumper (nothing in between); therefore, for a toast in three parts the minimum is 9
cyathi, the maximum 27 *cyathi*; cf. 3. 8. 13-16 where H. calls for a toast of 100 *cyathi*
to celebrate his escape from death.

13-17]   **qui ... vates**] i.e., 9 Muses, therefore 9 *cyathi* (an example of the logic resorted
to on such occasions to justify one's choice); 8, 10, etc. are not available as a result of
H.'s decree imposing either 9 or 3; 3, though an odd number, has no appeal for the
attonitus vates; **attonitus**] 'crazy', madness being, along with drunkenness, the tradition-
al popular image of the poet; see *Sat.* 1. 4. 33-5, *AP* 455-76; cf., on a more serious level,
the 'amabilis insania' of 3. 4. 5; **vates**] see on 1. 1. 35. — **tris prohibet supra tangere**]
'forbids taking more than three' (at a time). — **rixarum metuens**] With the genitive of
respect cf. 3. 24. 22, *Sat.* 2. 2. 110, *Epist.* 2. 2. 15. — **Gratia**] Any one of the 3 Graces.
— **nudis iuncta sororibus**] Cf. 1. 4. 6, 4. 7. 5-6.

18-24]   Further instructions, aimed perhaps at giving fresh life to a party which shows
signs of flagging. — **Insanire iuvat**] = 'I'm in the mood for a wild party'; cf. 2. 7. 27-8,
4. 12. 28. — **cur ... tibiae?**] For the *tibia* (a kind of oboe), see on 1. 12. 1; cf. Catullus
63.22 'tibicen ubi canit Phryx curvo grave calamo'; for *tibiae* at parties cf. 4. 1. 22-4,
4. 15. 30, Tibullus 2. 1. 86; **cessant**] might imply either that the *tibicen* is tiring or is
slow to begin; the latter seems to fit better what follows. — **cur pendet ... lyra?**] For
the *fistula* (reed pipe) and the *lyra*, see on 1. 12. 1; **pendet**] hanging up, i.e., not in use;
tacita] with *lyra*. — **Parcentis ... odi**] Instructions to the appropriate *puer* to sprinkle
the rose petals with a free hand; cf. 1. 38. 1-4. — **sparge rosas**] For roses as a symbol of
extravagance, see on 1. 5. 1. — **audiat ... Lyco**] For the party that keeps the neighbours
awake cf. Propertius 3. 15. 26 'Publica vicinae perstrepet aura viae'; for an all-night
party cf. 3. 21. 21-4; **invidus**] 'ill-natured', not one to approve of such goings-on; **vicina
non habilis**] 'our neighbour (Lycus' wife) ill-matched to a husband past his prime'.

25-8]   A final aside to one of the guests (possibly the guest addressed in 1-8) on their
respective standings in the matter of love; the girls named are presumably there to
perform on the instruments mentioned in lines 18-20, but Glycera, at any rate, is well-
known to H.; for the girl invited for her company as well as her skill as musician cf.
Tyndaris in 1. 17. 17-20, Lyde in 2. 11. 21-4, Phyllis in 4. 11. 33-6. — **spissa nitidum
coma**] i.e., hair that is thick (as opposed to thinning) and sleek (black and glistening) as
opposed to grey; cf. H.'s white hair in 2. 11. 15, 3. 14. 25; Telephus in short is a *iuvenis*,
H. middle-aged. — **puro similem Vespero**] i.e., radiant like the evening star in an un-
clouded sky; cf. 3. 9. 21. — **tempestiva petit Rhode**] i.e., Rhode takes the initiative;
with *petit* cf. 1. 33. 13, 2. 5. 16, 4. 11. 21; for falling in love at parties, see on 3. 21. 3;
tempestiva suggests both Rhode's readiness (cf. 1. 23. 12) and that her attentions are
opportune (cf. 4. 1. 9). — **me ... meae**] While Telephus is about to embark on a new
affair, H. continues to nurse his smouldering passion for Glycera; for her, see 1. 19. 5,
1. 30. 3, 1. 33. 2; with *lentus* cf. 1. 13. 8; with *torret* cf. the livelier *urit* of 1. 19. 5 and 7.

3. 20

Introduction: A showdown is imminent between Pyrrhus, who has attempted to alienate
the affections of young Nearchus, and the 'lioness' who regards Nearchus as belonging
to her. The beloved is manifestly indifferent to the outcome.

The young male attractive to both sexes is a traditional variation on the theme of the
eternal triangle. The range of possibilities is represented by the myth of Hylas, kid-
napped by the water-nymphs from his admirer Hercules (see, e.g., Propertius 1. 20, but,
as Virgil remarks, *Georgics* 3.6 'cui non dictus Hylas?') and Petronius' Giton, stolen by
Encolpius from Tryphaena. The situation was clearly familiar to H.'s contemporaries
and accepted by them in a mood closer to tolerant amusement than reprobation. H.'s
combination of whimsy, fantasy and acute psychological realism is superbly executed —
a further study in experience and inexperience, with an unexpected reversal of sympa-
thies. See on 1. 4. 19-20; cf. 2. 5. 20-4 and 4. 10.

Structure: Stanzas 1-2 (loosely connected by the inverted-*cum* clause) set up the metaphor;
in Stanzas 3-4 the principal clause spills across the stanza junction as the spotlight shifts
from Pyrrhus and the lioness to the coolly indifferent object of their affection.

Metre: Sapphics; see 1. 2M.

1-8] The starting point is a simile in *Il*. 18. 318-23, in which Achilles grieving over the body of Patroclus and about to launch himself in pursuit of Hector is likened to a lion setting out in angry pursuit of the hunter who has stolen his cubs during his absence. By a process of ironic reversal, H. substitutes for Achilles grieving for the death of a male lover a powerful, aggressive woman angry at the loss of a youngster of the opposite sex; at the same time the simile becomes a metaphor. For the dominant female and her young protégés cf. Cicero's Clodia, *Cael*. 36 (Clodia has gardens by the Tiber where the young men come to swim, and she takes her pick) and 37 (she maintains some of her youthful lovers at her own expense − 'quae etiam aleret adolescentes et parcimoniam patrum suis sumptibus sustentaret'). − Non vides?] For the conversational opening cf. 1. 1. 9; also 1. 14. 3, 3. 27. 17. − moveas] 'meddle with'. − Pyrrhe] Suggests perhaps that his present conquest is a 'Pyrrhic victory'. − Gaetulae catulos leaenae] Generalising plural (only Nearchus is involved); with the Gaetulian lioness cf. the 'Gaetulus leo' of 1. 23. 10. − Dura . . . raptor] The prediction is clear: when the showdown comes, Pyrrhus will be no match for the lioness; inaudax raptor] 'timorous predator'; the oxymoron anticipates Pyrrhus' behaviour when the showdown comes; *raptor* ironically overstates: Nearchus has forsaken the company of the lioness for that of his new admirer, but it is clear that the seduction has made little progress. − cum . . . ibit] Inverted-*cum* clause, a feature of epic narrative, here mock-grandiloquent; per obstantis iuvenum catervas] (1) expands the metaphor (the *iuvenum catervae* are Pyrrhus' fellow-hunters who attempt to confront the charging lioness), (2) suggests some public confrontation in which Pyrrhus' male friends will attempt to keep the lioness and Pyrrhus apart; the diction is mock-heroic. − insignem Nearchum] i.e., he catches the eye, like Gyges with his 'ambiguos voltus' in 2. 5. 20-24; the name Nearchus is probably chosen to suggest the sense 'youthful commander'. − repetens] 'claiming back'. − grande certamen] 'a battle royal'; the implication of lines 3-4 is that the brunt of the battle will be borne by Pyrrhus' friends. − tibi praeda cedat, maior an illa] '(to decide) whether the booty goes to you, or she is the stronger'; *illi*, the reading of the MSS, is clearly wrong (Nearchus is *praeda* only for Pyrrhus); *illa*, Peerlkamp.

9-16] Interim] i.e., while waiting for the confrontation. − arbiter pugnae] Initiates the withdrawal from the metaphor and the substitution of an alternative metaphor, as in 2. 5. 9-12; it is Nearchus himself who will decide the outcome; the battle to come for which the preparations are ironically described in *dum . . . timendos* is to be no more than a battle of words: Nearchus is a free agent. − nudo . . . fertur] The alternative metaphor represents the rival lovers as about to be engaged in some organised encounter (a boxing match, or a wrestling match); Nearchus, the judge of the forthcoming contest, is, 'according to report' (*fertur*), supremely indifferent to the outcome; nudo sub pede] for visual effect and to emphasise childlike innocence; palmam] The palm of victory; Nearchus plants his foot on it, perhaps to prevent either contestant from snapping it up till Nearchus has made his decision; the sense 'palm of the hand' is a potential meaning excluded by context; fertur] while Pyrrhus and the lioness are in the limelight, information about Nearchus is hard to come by. − recreare] 'fan'. − sparsum capillis] For long hair see on 1. 32. 11-12. − Nireus] The handsomest of the Greeks at Troy after Achilles. raptus] Ganymede, carried off by Jove as Nearchus has been by Pyrrhus; cf. 4. 4. 4; *raptus* picks up 4 *raptor*; for the participle used as a noun equivalent cf. 2. 16. 2 *prensus*.

3. 21

Introduction: An ode, promising a very special wine for his guest M. Valerius Messalla Corvinus, cast in the form of a hymn to the *testa* in which the wine has been stored; cf. Rabelais' poem (with its ironic echo of the *Ave Maria*) '*O bouteille pleine de grâce*'.

Messalla was an old friend and contemporary (b. 64 BC). He and H. had been together in Athens; like H., Messalla joined the army of Brutus; after Philippi he went over to Octavian, commanding the centre of the Roman fleet at Actium. In later years he became well-known for his interest in literature; he was the patron of Tibullus, perhaps also of Ovid, the guardian of the girl-poet Sulpicia; he is listed among the friends whose judgement H. values in *Sat*. 1. 10. 81-8. It appears from Servius on *Aen*. 8. 310 that Maecenas wrote an imaginary conversation (called *Symposium*) in which Messalla was

represented as extolling the virtues of wine. *Catalepton* 9 (probably not by Virgil) cele-
brates his exploits (mainly military).

For the occasion of the present party, see on 7 *Corvino iubente*.

Structure: A sophisticated *contaminatio* of familiar components of hymn structure: (1) the
aside following the opening vocative (lines 2-6; cf. Catullus 11. 2-14 for a similar re-
capitulatory formula following the anacoluthon); (2) the prayer or entreaty (lines 7-8);
(3) the recital of the attributes of the divinity, here forming a tricolon crescendo, each
member introduced by *tu* (lines 13, 14 and 17 — the familiar structure of anaphora in
asyndeton). Usually (3), if present, follows (1); here (1) and (3) are separated by (2) and
the bridge passage, lines 9-12. A concluding stanza sketches in the scene at the party
which is imminent.

Metre: Alcaics; see 1. 9M.

1-4] **nata mecum**] To facilitate the hymn parody, the *testa* is identified with its contents.
— **consule Manlio**] L. Manlius Torquatus, cos. 65 BC; a rare wine, therefore; so *Epode*
13. 6 'Tu vina Torquato move consule pressa meo'; cf. the 65-year-old wine in 3. 14. 18,
the Caecuban of 59 BC in 3. 28. 8; H. was not always so ostentatious — see on 1. 20. 1,
cf. 4. 11. 1-2. — **seu . . . seu . . . seu**] i.e., 'whatever the destiny you have in store for us';
the formula sets up the hymn form which is simultaneously undercut by the content;
three stages of drunkenness seem to be suggested and the thought 'who can tell how the
party will end?'; Messalla is the guest of honour, not the only guest; the wine, therefore,
is likely to affect different guests differently; **seu querelas sive iocos**] the first possibility
(the maudlin stage) is subdivided: a little drink makes some depressed (so that they
lament their ill luck), but puts others in a mood for joking; **seu rixam et insanos amores**]
the second is the aggressive stage, expressing itself in fighting or unrestrained amatory
behaviour; for fights at parties cf. 1. 27; for love at parties cf. 1. 36. 17-20, 3. 19.
25-7; **seu facilem somnum**] the third stage; for the phrase cf. 2. 11. 8.

5-8] **quocumque nomine**] The ritual formula (used to avoid offending a god by naming
him wrongly — cf. *Sat*. 2. 6. 20) is used ironically with the sense 'on whatever account',
'on whatever score' (*OLD* 24, 26). — **lectum Massicum**] 'choice Massic', as in the epic
formula *lecti iuvenes*, etc.; Massic was a Campanian wine (also 1. 1. 19, 2. 7. 21). —
moveri] As the image of a god is brought out in a procession; the sense 'handle',
'tamper with' (cf. 3. 20. 1) is also present. — **descende**] (1) 'descend to earth' (of a
divine epiphany — cf. 3. 4. 1); (2) 'come down' (from the wine-loft — see on 3. 8. 11);
a calculated ambiguity. — **Corvino . . . vina**] The reader is to assume that Messalla has
dropped a hint that something special in the way of wine will be appreciated; the
formula *Corvino iubente*, 'at the direction of Corvinus', probably parodies the language
of administrative procedure (*OLD* 5, 6); **languidiora**] 'mellower'; i.e., having matured
longer; cf. 3. 16. 35; **vina**] generalising plural.

9-12] Stanza 3 provides the transition to the formal encomium of Stanzas 4-5. The logic
of the transition is that the *testa* requires assurance that so stern-minded a guest of
honour as Messalla will show (by partaking freely) the divinity the respect due to her. —
quamquam . . . sermonibus] 'though soaked in Socratic talk', i.e., his habitual form of
intoxication is with the sort of talk Socrates is represented as engaging in in Plato's
dialogues; probably also = the topics discussed in the Academy at Athens where H.
and Messalla had been students (for H.'s time there, see *Epist*. 2. 2. 43-5); with
Socraticis cf. 1. 29. 14; *madet* is chosen to suggest both metaphorical (*OLD* 5) and
literal intoxication (*OLD* 3). — **te negleget horridus**] 'will not be so uncouth as to deny
you the respect due to you'; cf. for the sense *Epist*. 1. 7. 63-4 'te neglegit et horret'; the
MSS are divided (as often) between the future and the present (cf. 2. 5. 16 *petet*); but,
though the encomium develops into praise of the divine properties of wine in general,
the formal addressee is still the *testa* which Messalla has, as yet, had no opportunity of
spurning; the statement, i.e., is particular, not general (so Williams). — **et prisci Catonis
virtus**] = 'even old Cato with his uncompromising moral standards'.

13-16] The encomium which now follows represents a transition from the particular
instance of Messalla and Cato to a general statement of the power of wine to mellow
the sober-minded. The transition is permitted by the ancient belief that the divinity, if
properly evoked, inhabits as a *praesens divus* any particular *simulacrum*; cf., e.g., the
epiphany of Minerva in the shape of the *Palladium* in *Aen*. 2. 172-5; the transition in
3. 11. 5-16 from the original lyre of Mercury to the power of lyres in general to enthral
mankind is similar. — **lene . . . admoves**] 'you bring to bear a gentle rack'; *admoves* draws

out the sense of an actual instrument of torture brought to bear on the victim; with the
oxymoron *lene tormentum* cf. 1. 5. 5 'simplex munditiis', 3. 11. 35 'splendide mendax'.
— **ingenio plerumque duro**] 'those who are normally tough-minded', like Messalla and
Cato; suggests that the philosopher, though able to stand up to physical torture, is
powerless against the more insidious assault of drunkenness. — **iocoso Lyaeo**] Probably
dative ('for a jesting Bacchus') rather than ablative; *Lyaeus* = 'the loosener'.

17-20] The encomium becomes even more general — and increasingly ironic (the 'power
and might' lent to the poor man is illusory). — **virisque**] With *reducis*, not *addis*. —
cornua] Horns are an ancient symbol of power; Bacchus himself is 'aureo cornu
decorum' in 2. 19. 19-30. — **apices**] 'diadems' or 'tiaras', as worn by Eastern monarchs;
the poor man, i.e., in his drunken fantasy, likes to think of himself as facing up to the
great of the earth.

21-4] The encomium is now brought back into the context of the all-night party which is
about to begin. The stanza depends for its relevance on the ambiguity of 23 *producent*:
(1) 'will lead forth' (as the statue of the divinity is led forth in a procession); (2) 'will
make last' (through to the end of an all-night drinking session); with (1) Bacchus, Venus,
etc. represent the attendants in the procession; with (2) they represent the powers
presiding over the party; Bacchus' presence is assured, but the success of the party will
also depend on Venus' cooperation; if she comes in lighthearted mood (*laeta*, predica-
tive with *aderit*), all will be well; but if she shows herself the *saeva Venus* of 1. 19. 1 and
4. 1. 5, or the *perfidum ridens Venus* of 3. 27. 67, it will be another matter; see on 3
insanos amores. — **segnesque ... Gratiae**] The Graces dance naked (3. 19. 16-17,
4. 7. 5-6), but they are shy girls and slow to strip; **nodum solvere**] i.e., to untie their
zona, the first step towards undressing; cf. 1. 30. 5-6 'solutis Gratiae zonis'; a girl with
her *zona* off was said to be *recincta* (see Barsby on Ovid *Am.* 1. 5. 9); for this sense of
nodum, *OLD* 2 c. — **vivaeque ... lucernae**] The touch of realism, interposed between
the ironic fantasy of lines 21-2 and the final fantasy of Phoebus putting the stars to
flight, has much to do with the charm of this stanza; for *lucernae* as the symbol of
parties, see 1. 27. 5, 3. 8. 14; cf. *Aen.* 1. 726-7. — **dum ... Phoebus**] 'until Phoebus
(i.e., the Sun) puts the stars to flight'; cf. the all-night party in 3. 8. 14-15.

3. 22

Introduction: A dedicatory hymn to Diana, in which H., with conscious irony, acts out
the traditional role of *pater familias*. Cf. 1. 21 (a choral hymn of supplication to Diana
and Apollo); for H. as *pater familias* cf. 3. 18; for the role of the *pater familias* in
religious matters, see Cato *Agri.* 143. 1 'Scito dominum pro tota familia rem divinam
facere'.
Structure: One of 5 odes 8 lines in length; the others are 1. 30 (a hymn to Venus, also in
Sapphics), 1. 38 (Sapphics), 1. 11 and 4. 10 (both Asclepiad (e)). The 8 lines form a
single sentence: Stanza 1, formal address of the deity; Stanza 2, *votum*.
Metre: Sapphics; see 1. 2M.
1-4] The opening stanza covers, in condensed form, the traditional roles of the Roman
Diana (cf. Catullus 34) — the goddess of the wilds, the goddess of childbirth, the god-
dess who is *triformis*; it is the second of these which is given prominence. — **Montium
... virgo**] i.e., Diana the huntress (= the Greek Artemis); *montium custos* stresses the
divinity, *nemorum virgo* the personality (young, active, ferociously chaste) of the
goddess; the punctuation of Klinger and others with a comma after *nemorumque* is
artificial. — **quae ... leto**] Like Catullus, H. identifies Diana with Lucina, goddess of
childbirth (a role also attributed to Juno, the goddess of marriage); the Romans no
doubt connected *Lucina* with *Luna* as symbolising woman's subjugation to the monthly
cycle; perhaps also because of the role of Luna as goddess of death. — **ter vocata**] 'thrice
summoned', three being a magic number. — **audis**] 'answereth'. — **diva triformis**]
Because Diana (her name on earth) is also Luna, the moon goddess, and Hecate, the
goddess of the underworld; hence the name *Trivia* (Catullus' 'potens Trivia') because her
statue was placed at a crossways where three roads met to symbolise her threefold status.
5-8] H. dedicates a pine tree to Diana and promises a boar once a year; the pine is a tribute
to her as *nemorum virgo* (cf. Catullus 34. 1-2 'domina silvarum virentium'), the boar to
her as the huntress goddess. The pine is obviously a *quid pro quo*, and the promise of a

boar each year a request for continued protection; but what has been received and what is the protection asked for? The answer lies, probably, in the emphasis placed in the previous stanza on Diana as goddess of childbirth (whereas her other roles are only briefly alluded to). A natural assumption is that a child has been born to one of the women on H.'s estate and H. as *pater familias* is making an offering to Diana for preserving the mother and child from death (cf. 2-3 'laborantis . . . leto') and promising an annual sacrifice if she protects the child; for children born on H.'s estate cf. the 'vernae procaces' of *Sat.* 2. 6. 66; H.'s solicitude and the tender note of 2 *puellas* perhaps hint that H., like Martial's Quirinalis (Martial 1. 8. 4) could claim more than token status as father. — **imminens villae**] i.e., the pine dedicated to Diana is one which is fully grown and 'hangs over the farmhouse', not a tree planted for the ceremony. — **quam donem**] Final relative clause; the pine, as it were, represents Diana and receives the offering made to her; **per exactos annos**] = 'on each anniversary' (each birthday of the child just born?); cf. 3. 8. 9; contrast 3. 18. 5 *pleno anno*; **laetus**] 'gladly'; **verris sanguine**] naturally, a wild boar is appropriate to the huntress goddess, but we may suspect ironic grandiloquence — what Diana will actually get will probably be a modest *haedus* granted the status of a wild boar for the sake of the ceremony; for the animals used in sacrifices, see on 3. 23. 4; **obliquom meditantis ictum**] 'getting ready for a sidelong sweep', a concluding image to slacken the tension, as frequently in the *Odes*; H., i.e., asks us to imagine him confronting the 'wild boar' and striking it down as it takes aim for a charge at him; cf. the equally whimsical image in 3. 13. 4-5.

3. 23

Introduction: Instructions to Phidyle (φαιδύλη = 'the thrifty housewife') for honouring the Lares; she is perhaps the wife of H.'s *vilicus*, whose special concern this is (Cato *Agri.* 143. 2 'Focum purum circumversum cotidie, priusquam cubitum eat, habeat; Kalendis, Idibus, Nonis, festus dies cum erit, coronam in focum indat, per eosdemque dies lari familiari pro copia supplicet'), all other religious matters being the responsibility of the *dominus* (ibid. 1, quoted 3. 22I).

Structure: Stanzas 1-2, instructions for the ceremony; Stanzas 3-4, an elaborate sacrifice is unnecessary; Stanza 5, a simple ceremony has proved effective before now.

Metre: Alcaics; see 1. 9M.

1-8] **Caelo**] = *ad caelum*, as often in the common style of verse. — **supinas**] 'upturned' (i.e., palms uppermost). — **nascente Luna**] i.e., at the new moon. — **horna fruge**] 'with this year's corn'. — **avida porca**] Greedy, therefore fat; after the goat (or kid), the pig (or piglet) is the most usual sacrificial animal, both being cheap and common as food; cf. the pig sacrificed to the Lares in *Sat.* 2. 3. 165, the *porcus bimenstris* offered to the *genius* in 3. 17. 15 and Cato *Agri.* 134 on the *porca* to be offered at harvest time; for kids, see 1. 4. 12, 3. 13. 3, 3. 18. 5; cf. the goat of 3. 8. 7-8 and the 'boar' of 3. 22. 7; for lambs, see 2. 17. 32 and 4. 11. 8; to sacrifice a calf (1. 36. 2 and 4. 2. 54) was more ostentatious (not every farmer owned cattle — see Tibullus 1. 1. 21-2); more ostentatious still (and usually reserved for public occasions) was an ox or even a number of cattle (4. 2. 53). — **Lares**] Cf. 19 *Penatis*, with whom the Lares are closely associated. — **pestilentem Africum**] A hot, sultry SW wind (the 'Scirocco'), likely to bring disease to the vines in late summer just as they are bearing fruit (*fecunda*). — **sterilem**] i.e., bringing sterility. — **robiginem**] 'mildew'. — **alumni**] i.e., the young lambs and kids. — **pomifero grave tempus anno**] = 'oppressive autumn weather'; cf. 2. 14. 15-16; *pomifero anno* is Keats's 'season of mellow fruits'.

9-20] Specially reared and fattened victims are all very well for the public sacrifices of the Pontifices; there is no call for lavish sacrifices where Phidyle's humble gods are concerned; even when you have had no victim to offer at all, the ritual offering of flour and spelt has appeased the anger of the Penates. — **devota victima**] i.e., the animal which has been specially bred for sacrificial purposes; *devota* = marked off for sacrifice while still young. — **nivali Algido**] 'on snowy Algidus' (= 'Frozen Peak'), in the Alban Hills, S of Rome; cf. 1. 21. 6, 4. 4. 58; perhaps pastoral land reserved for fattening animals for public sacrifice. — **quercus inter et ilices**] Evocative of mountain scenery. — **herbis**] i.e., pastures. — **victima**] The word suggests a large animal, such as an ox; cf. 2. 17. 30; Varro *RR* 2. 1. 20 'sic boves altiles ad sacrificia publica saginati dicuntur opimi'. — **te**

nihil attinet] 'it is inappropriate for you', given, i.e., the humble nature of the ceremony
over which Phidyle presides. — **temptare**] 'importune'. — **multa caede bidentium**] i.e., a
sacrifice involving large numbers of sheep; for attempts to explain the term *bidens*, see
Gellius 16. 6. — **parvos . . . myrto**] 'the humble gods whom you crown with rosemary
and fragile myrtle sprigs'; i.e., the Lares of line 4; cf. Evander in *Aen.* 8. 543-5 (his
household gods, too, are modest; but, being a king, he offers *bidentes*); *deos* both with
temptare and with *coronantem*; for the *corona*, see Cato (quoted in Introduction);
fragili] that snaps when broken, unlike the softer rosemary. — **inmunis, etc.**] H.
clinches the argument with the extreme case in which no sacrifice at all is offered to
the Lares, thus proving that Phidyle's humble sow will be more than sufficient; the
stanza has puzzled commentators and widely differing interpretations have been
offered; **aram**] the household altar; **non sumptuosa blandior hostia**] i.e., 'though not
assisted in its appeal to the Lares by a lavish sacrifice'; *hostia* implies a smaller animal
than *victima*; **mollivit . . . mica**] i.e., the ritual act of scattering flour and salt has
appeased the Penates; the perfect *mollivit* has a gnomic force (= 'there are cases on
record'); it does not follow, because there are cases on record, that the Penates will
always be mollified — on a different occasion H. will take a different view (cf. 1. 19. 16
'mactata veniet lenior hostia'); the suppliant's circumstances must be taken into account
(cf. Cato's 'pro copia supplicet', quoted in Introduction); in the present case, H. recom-
mends a sow; **Penatis**] see on 4 *Lares*; **saliente mica**] salt which crackles when tossed on
the fire.

3. 24

Introduction: A further attack on the pursuit of luxury and the decline in moral standards
which accompanies it. Except for the metre, very much in the manner of the Roman
Odes; cf. 2. 15 and 2. 18. A noticeable innovation is the encomium of the noble savage
in Stanzas 3-6.

Structure: Stanzas 1-2 state the major theme: a life of ostentatious luxury will not confer
either peace of mind or immortality. Stanzas 3-6 develop a contrasting minor theme:
the superior lifestyle of the nomads of the NE frontier (9 'melius vivunt', etc.); they
have no attachment to material possessions (Stanzas 3-4); their way of life is superior
morally (Stanzas 5-6). Stanzas 7-11 bring an impassioned resumption of the major
theme, this time on a national level (as opposed to the individual level of Stanzas 1-2)
and in explicitly moralising terms: the attack is now not on extravagance as such, but on
the lack of moral restraint (29 *licentiam*) of which extravagance is both the symptom
and the cause. Stanzas 12-16 are a call for action: if Rome is to return to moral health,
wealth must be renounced and a programme introduced of moral education of the
young, who at present learn only vicious ways from their elders.

The unnamed wealthy Roman of Stanzas 1-2 (3 *occupes*, 4 *tuis*, 8 *expedies* — the
'ideal' second person singular of the moralist) is succeeded by the *quisquis* of Stanza 7;
Stanzas 12-13 adopt the form of a harangue of the Roman people (*nos . . . vel nos . . .
mittamus*).

Metre: Asclepiad (b); see 1. 3M.

1-8] **Intactis opulentior thesauris**] 'wealthier than the untapped treasures'; the Arabes,
i.e., are so rich, they have treasure-houses upon which they never draw; cf. 1. 29. 1-2;
contracted comparison. — **caementis tuis**] Rubble filling upon which to build a luxury
villa out into the sea, e.g., at Baiae; cf. 2. 15. 1-2, 2. 18. 19-22, 3. 1. 34-6; the phrase is
ironical (as though all that the wealthy man contributes to what he seizes possession of
is a heap of rubble). — **licet occupes . . . publicum**] = 'though you seize the whole
Tyrrhenian sea and take possession of that which belongs to all'; **licet occupes**] for the
second person singular, see Introduction; the subjunctive without *ut* with concessive *licet*
is frequent; **Tyrrhenum omne**] i.e., the sea bordering that part of the Mediterranean
coast which extends N of Rome; cf. 1. 11. 5-6; **mare publicum**] an ironic extension of
ager publicus, as though the rich man who builds his villa out into the sea were asserting
squatter's rights; *Tyrrhenum omne et mare publicum* thus forms a kind of hendiadys;
the reading *terrenum*, favoured by German editors since Lachmann against the evidence
of the MSS, gives pedestrian sense and is almost certainly to be rejected; Porphyrio's
gloss 'aedificiis novis non terram tantum, verum etiam maria occupantem', whence

terrenum is derived, is plainly an interpretation intended to bring out the sense of the passage, not a rephrasing of it (with *terrenum, caementis* refers to the walls of the villa, constructed from pebbles, gravel, etc. mixed with cement); with regard to *publicum* the testimony of the MSS is confused; however, *Apulicum,* the most plausible variant, though justifiable as a rhetorical exaggeration, spoils the point of *occupes.* — si . . . clavos] Variously interpreted; most likely, driving nails into the topmost points of the villa under construction is a way of asserting legal ownership (as writs are nailed today to the mast of a ship to assert taking legal possession); i.e., 'you assert your ownership over the sea which is not yours, but Necessitas asserts *her* ownership over the villa you build'; it appears from 1. 35. 17-20 that nails (*clavis trabales*), like other builder's materials, are part of the traditional symbols of Necessitas; **adamantinos**] where an ordinary claimant would use iron nails, Necessitas as an eternal force uses nails of a material regarded as everlasting and unbreakable; cf. 1. 6. 13 and the adamantine chains with which Prometheus is bound to the Caucasus in Aeschylus; for Necessitas, see on 1. 35. 17; cf. 3. 1. 14, where Necessitas is also represented as a divinity of death; cf. Cicero *Tusc.* 3. 59 (a version of a passage from Euripides' *Hypsipyla* on the inevitability of death) 'mors est finita omnibus; sic iubet Necessitas'. — **animum . . . caput**] Chiasmus.

9-24]   The Scythae (see on 1. 19. 10) and the Getae (see on 3. 8. 18 *Daci,* with whom the Getae are often confused) usually symbolise the remote, primitive, warlike tribes of Rome's NE frontier; here they are represented in terms more akin to those used of the simple, unspoiled Italians of 3. 6. 37-44; the effect aimed at (especially in Stanza 5) seems more than paradox; the 'noble savage', an obvious candidate for a binary opposition in which the corrupt, overcivilised Roman forms the opposite member, appears in Sallust's *Jugurtha* and in Tacitus; cf. for other sympathetic glimpses of Rome's traditional enemies 1. 29. 5-10, 3. 2. 9-12; the Augustan cult of the pastoral represents a similar revulsion from civilised decadence; contrast the picture in Lucretius 5. 925 ff. of primitive man as a 'genus durius tellus quod dura creasset'. — **Campestres**] 'living on plains' (instead of towns), i.e., 'nomad'; cf. Livy 39. 53. 13 'campestres barbaros'; see 2. 9. 24, 3. 8. 24. — **rite**] 'regularly', i.e., as a way of life. — **rigidi**] 'hard-living'. — **liberas**] Always an emotionally-charged word in the Augustan age. — **Cererem**] = 'grain', or 'bread'; see Quinn on Catullus 63. 36. — **nec cultura . . . vicarius**] Caesar was perhaps the first Roman writer to be intrigued by this way of life; on the Suevi he wrote *BG* 4. 1 'Quotannis singula milia armatorum bellandi causa educunt. Reliqui qui domi manserunt se atque illos alunt. Hi rursus invicem anno post in armis sunt, illi domi remanent, . . . neque longius anno remanere uno in loco incolendi causa licet'; **aequali sorte**] = 'for an equal period'. — **illic . . . innocens**] Cf. H.'s picture of the Sabellian farmers 3. 6. 33-40. — **nec dotata . . . adultero**] Cf. 3. 6. 25-32; **regit**] cf. 3. 9. 9; for *adultero,* see on 1. 15. 19. — **dos . . . castitas**] 'the *virtus* of their parents is (i.e., takes the place of) a great dowry, as is a chastity that guarantees fidelity and will have nothing to do with another man'; with the genitive cf. 3. 19. 16; **certo foedere**] cf. Catullus 76. 3, 87. 3-4 and 109. 6. — **peccare**] i.e., taking a lover. — **aut pretium est mori**] = 'or if she does, the penalty is death'; for *aut* cf. 3. 12. 3.

25-32]   The theme of Stanzas 1-2 is now expanded and treated in a national context and on a more impassioned level. Licentia (anything from 'lack of self-control' to 'lawlessness') is made responsible by H. for all Rome's ills, including civil war; this is the problem any national leader must deal with. — **quisquis volet**] The future tense precludes any actual leader; cf. 27 *quaeret.* — **inpias . . . civicam**] Hendiadys, 'the national madness which led to civil war'; *inpias* echoes the normal expression *bellum inpium,* a war which has not been properly declared, or which is embarked upon without proper taking of the auspices, especially a civil war. — **pater urbium**] The plural to suggest that statues with this subscription might be set up in many places; again H. is careful to avoid implying he has any actual leader (e.g., Augustus) in mind. — **refrenare**] Picks up the latent metaphor of *indomitam.* — **clarus postgenitis**] i.e., destined to be famous in the future (because of the statues which will be set up). — **quatenus**] 'in so far as'. — **invidi**] = 'being the malevolent people we are' (i.e., toward the living).

33-44]   **querimoniae**] i.e., complaints at the state of the nation. — **reciditur**] 'pruned back'. — **quid leges . . . deserit arduae?**] An expanded variation on the model of *quid . . . reciditur,* in which the *si* clause, after a double negative (36 *neque . . .* 38 *nec*), makes two positive statements (*horrida . . . navitae, magnum . . . arduae*), the second of these a double-barrel statement (42 *iubet,* 44 *deserit*); **fervidis . . . caloribus**] = the torrid zone (i.e., the tropics); **Boreae ... nives**] i.e., the frozen region near the pole; *Boreae* is dative; **mercatorem** for the overseas trader as an object of satire, see on 1. 1. 16; **horrida ... navitae**] for navigation by sea as sinful, see on 1. 3. 9-24; for *navitae*, 'travellers by sea', see on 1. 28. 23.

45-50] In contrast to the vague *quisquis volet* of Stanzas 7-11, Stanzas 12-16 contain a positive call to immediate action; H. speaks as if he were addressing the Roman people in a *contio*; see Fraenkel 55-6 on *Epode* 7. − **Capitolium**] The principal public treasury, the *aerarium Saturni*, was situated in the Temple of Saturn below the Capitol. − **quo ... faventium**] i.e., the shouts of approval of H.'s imaginary audience. − **summi materiem mali**] i.e., 'the source (lit. 'that out of which we make') of our misfortune'. − **mittamus**] 'cast'.

51-64] **eradenda ... elementa**] i.e., re-education must begin with the young, in whom the earliest traces of greed must be eradicated; **cupidinis pravi**] *cupido* is regularly masculine in H. − **tenerae nimis mentes**] i.e., minds too exposed to corruption. − **asperioribus studiis**] Such as those whose absence is deplored in 54-6. − **equo ... haerere**] i.e., stay in the saddle; see L. R. Taylor, *JRS* 1924, quoted 1. 8I. − **Graeco trocho**] sc., *ludere*; apparently, some kind of hoop; *Graeco* is of course pejorative. − **mālis**] From *malle*. − **vetita legibus alea**] For gambling in Augustan Rome (prohibited, but flourishing), see J. Griffin, *JRS* 1976, 94-5. − **cum**] 'at a time when', 'whilst'. − **consortem socium**] 'business partner'. − **indignoque ... properet**] Cf. 2. 3. 19-20, 2. 14. 25. − **scilicet ... rei**] Explains *properet*: accumulated wealth always grows; that is part of its evil nature (*inprobae*), but to a wealthy man his fortune always seems 'crippled' *(curtae)* i.e., needing still some addition to give it proper stability; the dry conclusion slackens the tension in H.'s manner, but hardly helps the unity of an ode too much of which reads like satire only casually transposed into lyric form.

3. 25

Introduction: An impassioned address of Bacchus as god of poetry. H. asks us to imagine we are present at the moment when an ode in praise of Augustus is about to take shape. An attempt, shorter and more effective than 2. 19, to represent, within the conventions of traditional imagery, the onset of poetic inspiration; cf. 1. 12, 1. 32, 3. 4, 3. 11, 4. 3; contrast 1. 6. 17-20.
  It seems unlikely that 3. 25 foreshadows any particular poem (as 4. 6. 29-44 foreshadows the *Carmen Saeculare*); probably the ode is to be taken as a suitably dramatic announcement of H.'s willingness (phrased in general terms) to celebrate the apotheosis of Augustus (as he does in 1. 2, 3. 3. 11-12, 3. 5. 2-3, 4. 5. 31-2).
Structure: The principal junctures are in mid-stanza. Lines 1-6, the excitement produced by the onset of inspiration; lines 7-14, the poet proclaims his confidence in the power of his inspiration; lines 14-20, his promise to the inspiring god that the poem he will write will be worthy of the inspiration.
Metre: Asclepiad (b); see 1. 3M.
1-6] Dionysus, the god of dramatic poetry, was also for the Greeks the god of the dithyramb: the term, first found in Archilochus 120 West, denotes an impassioned form of choral ode for which the poet literally sought inspiration in drunken frenzy. H., as usual, adapts: he adopts the note of excited immediacy appropriate to the dithyramb, while simplifying the traditional dithyrambic structure to fit into his repertoire of lyric metres and adapting the conventions to fit into the framework of a collection of personal poems which recognise the reality of inspiration but preserve at the same time a stance which is consciously rational and dominated by a cool, critical self-awareness. The inspiration proclaimed is what later writers (at least since Plato) have recognised as the special poetic frenzy. (For Bacchus in Roman poetry, see P. Boyancé, *Fondation Hardt, Entretiens 2*, 1956, 200-209). − **Quo ... quae aut quos ... quibus ... ?** A series of rhetorical transformations (forming a tricolon crescendo) of the model 'where am I', etc., common, in both Latin and English, in situations where the speaker feels intellectual awareness threatened (or imperfectly restored after loss of consciousness); here used to structure an imaginative representation of the onset of poetic frenzy; **quo ... plenum?**] the poet, i.e., in the frenzy of inspiration, is literally carried off and can only follow the god; cf. 19 *sequi deum*; *tui plenum* recalls the original concept of Dionysiac inspiration

through drunkenness, in order to reject it; for a satirical treatment of the theme of drunkenness as inspiration, see *Epist.* 1. 19. 1-11; cf. *AP* 453-76; here the traditional cliché is used as a symbol of the exalted state of mind in which the form his poem is to assume comes to the poet as the result of something mysterious transcending rational decision; **quae nemora aut quos specus**] symbols of the different forms which the poem, as yet formless, may take; the pastoral analogue thus gives visual expression to the different areas of poetic territory (i.e., the different genres) in any one of which the inspiration can be expected to locate itself; with *nemora* cf. 13 *nemus*; for the cave (*specus*) as poetic haunt cf. *Eclogue* 6 (the cave of Silenus), the *spelunca* of the Muses in Propertius 3. 3. 27-36; cf. also 1. 5. 3; **quibus antris**] continues the pastoral image of *quos specus?*, but, by suggesting an audience (*audiar*) as well as a setting, H. implies, suitably transposed into pastoral terms, an actual performance, perhaps in the *Collegium Poetarum* (see on 3. 4. 40 'Pierio antro' and 2. 1. 39); **Caesaris aeternum decus**] the phrase softens the positive affirmation of the apotheosis of Augustus in the following line; **audiar**] i.e., heard declaiming as he composes; **meditans**] the word used of rehearsing a part in a play, working over a poetic text (as in *Sat.* 1. 9. 2, etc.); conventionally, a performance of a lyric poem is overheard rather than heard, the poet being thought of as working at his text, filling out the inspiration which provides only the starting point (see on 3. 4. 1-4), rather than performing a definitive text; every performance is thus, in theory, provisional; **stellis inserere et concilio Iovis**] i.e., proclaiming the apotheosis of Augustus; cf. 1. 2, 3. 3. 11-12, 3. 5. 2-3, 4. 5. 31-2; the phrase neatly avoids deciding between actual assertion of apotheosis and apotheosis within some form of inspired poetic fancy; for *decus* of a person cf. 1. 1. 2, 2. 17. 4 (Maecenas in each case); **concilio Iovis**] i.e., representing Augustus as participating in the Council of the Gods; for the Council cf. 3. 3. 17-18 'consiliantibus divis'; the MSS are divided between *concilio* and *consilio* (the commoner word; if right here, 'stellis et consilio Iovis' becomes a zeugma).

7-8] **Dicam . . . ore alio**] The inspired poet proclaims his power; his poem will be 'striking, fresh, unlike the work of any poet before him'; cf. 12 *devio* and 17-18 *nil parvum . . . loquar*; that which will be new will be the form and/or the manner of its expression, rather than the theme (H. can scarcely claim to be the first poet to sing the praises of Augustus); cf. 3. 1. 2-3 'carmina non prius audita'; **dicam, indictum**] for *dicere* (the regular word for poetic composition), see on 1. 6. 5; *dicam* is future indicative (see on 18 *loquar*).

8-14] The Bacchic dance symbolises the combination of frenzy and organised form which will characterise H.'s poem; thus, lines 1-8, though proclaiming surrender to Bacchus, have a carefully organised formal rhetorical structure. — **exsomnis stupet Euhias**] H. imagines, as representing his surrender to inspiration, an individual Bacchant on her way to join the Bacchic dance; she is *exsomnis* because the urge to join the dance (which takes place by night) will not let her sleep; **stupet**] she gazes in wonder at scenery she would never approach in her normal rational life. — **Hebrum**] The principal river of Thrace; cf. 1. 25. 20. — **prospiciens**] Implies looking at what lies in the distance; cf. Catullus 64. 61 and 62. — **nive candidam Thracen**] Cf. 1. 9. 1-2. — **pede barbaro . . . Rhodopen**] 'Mt Rhodope, traversed by barbarian foot'; the dance takes place in the mountains (8 *in iugis*); **lustratam**] of ritual dance, the movements of which conform to a pattern, despite the frenzy of the dancers (*OLD* 1 + 3). — **ut**] Picks up 8 *non secus*. — **devio**] 'off the beaten path'; cf. 1. 17. 6, 2. 11. 21; here, the symbol of poetry which is unprecedented; cf. Lucretius 1. 926-7 (= 4. 1-2) 'avia Pieridum peragro loca nullius ante trita solo' (echoed by H. *Epist.* 1. 19. 21-22 'libera per vacuum posui vestigia princeps, / non aliena meo pressi pede'. — **vacuum nemus**] Picks up 2 *quae nemora* and reinforces the idea of poetry which is without precedent. — **mirari libet**] Cf. Lucretius 1. 927 'iuvat integros accedere fontis'.

14-20] **O Naiadum potens**] 'O you who control the River Nymphs'; i.e., Bacchus; cf. 2. 19. 3. — **Baccharumque . . . fraxinos**] The power of the Bacchants to uproot grown trees symbolises violence which is inspired and therefore controlled (as opposed to brute violence, which is merely destructive — cf. 3. 4. 65-8); a reference to Euripides *Bacchae* 1109. — **nil . . . loquar**] Picks up 7 *dicam . . . alio*; future indicative (a jussive subjunctive would require *ne quid loquar*); **mortale**] = 'uninspired'. — **dulce periculum est**] i.e., surrender to the power of the god is dangerous, but exhilarating. — **Lenaee**] Traditional title of Dionysus, from λῆνός, 'wine vat'. — **cingentem . . . pampino**] The Bacchant placing round her head the garland of wine leaves is the symbol of the poet's surrender to inspiration (so Heinze); to take *cingentem* of Dionysus gives weaker sense; 3. 30. 15-16, where the garland is the symbol of victory, is not parallel.

3. 26

Introduction: A wryly-worded announcement of retirement by the poet from his career as a professional lover. As tends to happen in such cases, H. would like us to believe he can face the fact with equanimity that he is not the man he was, but does not quite convince us.

Like Ovid in a famous elegy (*Am*. 1. 9 'Militat omnis amans et habet sua castra Cupido'), H. compares the regular lover to the regular soldier; cf. 4. 1. 16. In 3. 26, H. is an engineer rather than an infantryman; his years of active service over, he dedicates the equipment for which he has no further use to his patron divinity; cf. the retiring gladiator *Epist*. 1. 1. 4-5 'Veianius armis / Herculis ad postem fixis latet abditus agro'; similarly, the old boxer in *Aen*. 5. 483-4 proclaims his retirement and dedicates his gloves to Eryx ('caestus artemque repono'); many such dedicatory epigrams in the *Greek Anthology*; e.g., in *AP* 6. 1 (attributed to Plato) the courtesan Lais dedicates to Aphrodite the mirror for which she has no longer any use; cf. *AP* 6. 70 (a ship), 6. 178 (a shield), etc.

Structure: In form, a dedicatory address to Venus, leading up to a final request (cf. 3. 22). The sense is organised around three temporal adverbs: 1 *nuper* and 3 *nunc* sketch in the hypothesis as a simple binary opposition of recent past and the future that now lies ahead; 12 *semel*, separated from these two by the aside of lines 6-8 (which transforms the dedicatory epigram into a dramatic monologue), lends an unexpected twist to the concluding request (lines 9-12).

Metre: Alcaics; see 1. 9M.

1-6] The hypothesis we are asked to concede is that H. has been serenading Chloe, lyre in hand, with unprecedented lack of success. For H., the failure is a warning that his womanising days are over, and he affects to lay down arms with the businesslike resignation of the old soldier no longer fit for active service who commends himself to his patron divinity, identifying himself as he does so by a brief statement of his past record. The opening is ironically matter-of-fact. — Vixi ... idoneus] 'till recently I was up to standard as a ladies' man'; *vixi* places his career firmly in the past, but *nuper* emphasises the recentness of its conclusion; **idoneus**] the word which might be used of a soldier passed fit for service, adds overtones that can perhaps be rendered 'till recently I was classed as an able-bodied lover'; cf. 4. 1. 12. — militavi ... gloria] Draws out and particularises the overtones latent in line 1, 'and my years of active service were not without distinction'. — nunc habebit] Wrenches us out of the recent past across the razor-edge of the present into the future. — arma] The word for a soldier's equipment, or 'equipment' ('tackle', 'gear') in general; cf. 1. 8. 10. — defunctumque bello barbiton] Extends the conceit of the soldier-lover, but with an increasingly ironic tension, 'and my lyre which has completed its service in the war'; the lyre, the symbol of H.'s status as a lyric poet, has of course no more real existence than the more down-to-earth equipment of 6-8; see on 1. 12. 1-2. — hic paries] The deictic *hic* establishes the dramatic context: the wall upon which the now useless lyre will hang as a dedicatory offering is before our eyes; cf. the 'sacer paries' of 1. 5. 13-16 upon which the 'vestimenta' of H., the shipwrecked sailor on the seas of love, are suspended. — laevom ... latus] 'the left flank of Venus of the sea'; 'left' and 'right' have complicated and confusing connotations in Greek and Roman ritual (see on 3. 27. 15); suspicion that (in fact or in H.'s fiction) the left side is appropriate for the offerings of those who have lost their dexterity is probably justified; for *Venus marina* cf. 4. 11. 15, also 1. 3. 1. — custodit] 'protects', as the warrior's shield protects his left flank in battle; here, from the elements, perhaps; or because Venus is imagined as facing to the right (i.e., seen in profile or half-profile) so that her gaze is averted from *arma* no longer blessed with success.

6-8] The directions (to slaves accompanying H.) fill out the dramatic hint of 4 *hic paries* (we realise we are listening to a dramatic monologue, not reading an inscription) and prepare the way for the prayer of 9-12; cf. 1. 19. 13-15, Catullus 36. 18-20 and see on 2. 11. 13. Interpretation depends on the sense attributed to 6 *lucida*: is the epithet ornamental or are the torches still flaring? If the latter, why? Is the symbol of passion still burning but about to be quenched? Or are we to imagine that H., having encountered unexpected resistance in his night assault upon Chloe, has gone off forthwith (accompanied by his slaves) to some nearby temple of Venus (the Temple of Venus Erycina, e.g., in the *Horti Sallustiani*), torches still flaring? It seems more likely that the reality which H.'s poem transposes into traditional fanciful imagery is that H., acknowledging defeat, dumps the torches (used to light his way through the streets) beside his mistress's door; the wall of Chloe's house thus becomes (within the fantasy of the poem) the shrine at which H. makes his prayer to Venus; see on 1. 30. 3-4, cf. 1. 19. 13-16. — **funalia**] Torches made of twisted hemp impregnated with pitch, fat, etc. (as opposed to *faces*, torches of resinous pine); see Austin on *Aen.* 1. 727; they seem to have been used out of doors, or when a stronger, more intense light was required. — **et vectis et arcus**] Reference to crowbars and bows (because the lover-soldier presses home the attack with an armed escort — or is some kind of bow-saw or bow-drill intended?) corrects any impression that H. is attempting realistic description; violent assault by the lover on the locked street door of his mistress is spoken of by Roman poets from Terence to the Augustan age as a matter of course; see, e.g., Terence *Adel.* 101-2 'Non est flagitium, mihi crede, adulescentulum / scortari neque potare, non est; neque fores ecfringere' (in a scene where the matter is discussed at length), Tibullus 1. 1. 73-4 'Nunc levis est tractanda Venus, dum frangere postis / non pudet'; see K. F. Smith on the latter passage; common sense suggests such talk was as conventional as the theme of the paraclausithyron itself (see on 1. 25), of which it constitutes the *reductio ad absurdum*; cf. Plessis on the passage in Tibullus: '*croit-on vraiment que, dans la Rome d'Auguste, les amoureux s'en allaient le soir avec des leviers faire sauter les gonds et qu'ils entraient, en brisant la porte, chez une femme, cette femme fût-elle une courtisane?*' H. (1) explores and extends the conventional material for ironic effect; (2) uses it as an 'unreal' (conventional) or fantastic objective correlative for a study in psychological realism (see on Stanza 3). — **foribus**] The twin leaves of the *ianua*. — **minacis**] i.e., used (in the past) in the assault upon doors that barred the lover's path to victory.

9-12]   The dedicatory prayer. As usual, the goddess is identified by reference to well-known shrines; cf. 3. 28. 13-15 and the parody of this convention in Catullus 36. 11-15. — **Memphin**] In Egypt; for the Temple of Aphrodite, see Herodotus 2. 112, Strabo 17. 1. 31. — **carentem Sithonia nive**] Parodies the elaborate formula of invocation usual on such occasions; *Sithonia* = 'Thracian'; if Chloe is the 'Thressa Chloe' of 3. 9. 9, the snow perhaps symbolises her cold heart (from which Venus is dissociated). — **sublimi flagello**] 'with raised whip'; i.e., before driving Chloe beneath the yoke which symbolises the subjection of her victims (cf. 1. 33. 11, 3. 9. 18); a further ironic extension of conventional imagery. — **tange Chloen semel arrogantem**] A variation on the Catullan theme of 'at tu dolebis' (Catullus 8. 14): Chloe is to regret her coldness when it is too late; *tange* = 'bring into line' with a flick of the whip; Chloe needs disciplining; she shows signs of escaping from the ranks of Venus' subjects; at the same time, *tange* suggests the degree of involvement H. feels entitled to expect — a twinge rather than a searing fire of passion; if the prayer is answered, H. will be able to enjoy the reversal of roles when Chloe wants him and he is no longer to be had; **semel arrogantem**] 'for once uncooperative'; a dismissive insult; i.e., it takes only one snub from Chloe for H. to know he has lost his grip; for *semel* 'once and once only', see 1. 24. 16, 4. 2. 50, 4. 9. 18, etc.; with *arrogantem* cf. 1. 25. 9; to take *semel* with *tange* on the assumption that H. is asking Venus to make Chloe 'fall in love for once' (and with him) is implausible; equally unlikely that H. prays that Chloe should find out for once what love is like by falling in love with some successor to H.; we may of course suspect (as many have) that H. is bluffing and that the proclaimed retirement is no more than a strategic withdrawal.

3. 27

Introduction: A propemptikon or *bon voyage* poem (see on 1. 3). When farewelling a friend, a warning of dangers is only natural (cf. 1. 3. 9-16); here, that theme becomes the occasion for retelling the myth of Europa, who set off on her journey across the sea trusting rather too blindly in her handsome new lover. H.'s Galatea seems in danger of making the same mistake.

Structure: Stanzas 1-6 constitute the propemptikon proper; Stanzas 1-3 are taken up with omens (favourable and unfavourable), 4 with good wishes, 5-6 express concern at the possibility of a stormy crossing of the Adriatic; Stanzas 7-19 are H.'s sophisticated retelling, *ad puellam*, of the myth of Europa; more than half this section (lines 34-66) is devoted to Europa's lament on arrival in Crete (see on line 34).

Metre: Sapphics; see 1. 2M.

1-7] Talk of unfavourable omens to accompany the *inpii* on their journey is hardly calculated to reassure a mistress about to run off with a new lover, though H. eventually promises to conjure up a favourable omen (lines 7-12). The reason for the ambiguity of his feelings becomes clearer in lines 13-16. — **Inpios]** Clearly a disconcerting note on which to begin (Galatea, as we shall see, has good reason to suppose the generalising plural includes her), even if what follows fixes the tone at the level of elaborate irony. — **parrae recinentis omen]** The Iguvine tables, like H., name particular birds and directions of flight: see, e.g., Table VIa Poutney, 'Demand that I may observe a *parra* in the west, a crow in the west, a woodpecker in the east, a magpie in the east'; cf. Plautus *Asin*. 260 'picus et cornix ab laeva, corvus, parra ab dextera consuadent' (i.e., the same four birds as mentioned by H. in Stanzas 1-4); to what extent Umbrian and Roman rules coincided is unknown; Roman practice is complicated and confusing (see 15 *laevos picus*); it seems a safe assumption, however, that H.'s intention is to create an atmosphere of hocus-pocus, not to make a parade of recondite knowledge or provoke research; the context makes it clear that the omen which would be invoked in the present case is unfavourable; **recinentis]** a recurrent hoot, repeated at intervals to accompany the traveller as he starts on his journey, like a refrain or chorus (as in *Epist*. 1. 1. 55 'haec recinunt iuvenes dictata senesque'); cf. 1. 12. 3; see on 3. 28. 11. — **ducat]** i.e., send on their way. — **ab agro Lanuvino]** 20 km from Rome on the W side of the via Appia, along which Galatea would most naturally make her way to join ship at Brundisium in order to cross the Adriatic (see Stanza 5). — **rumpat]** i.e., cause to abandon. — **per obliquom . . . sagittae]** i.e., slanting across the path of the horses at high speed.

7-12] H. turns from unfavourable to favourable omens. — **ego . . . auspex]** i.e., 'I, a providential augur, if I have a person's welfare at heart'; for the future *timebo*, see on 13-16. — **antequam repetat]** 'before it can regain'. — **stantis paludes]** The Pomptine Marshes; the Appia ran through the marshes, flanked by a canal used by barges; see H.'s journey in *Sat*. 1. 5. — **imbrium . . . imminentium]** See on 3. 17. 12-13; if the crow were to be seen first from the direction of the Pomptine Marshes, that would indicate rain; to sight it flying in the reverse direction nullifies (if we may believe H.) the rain-warning. — **prece suscitabo]** In the case of *inpii*, H. contents himself with expressing a wish (2 *ducat*, 5 *rumpat*); in the case of those he wishes well he is prepared to promise he will personally produce (*suscitabo*) a favourable omen; the confident prediction dispels, i.e., any lingering suspicion that H.'s bird lore is to be taken seriously.

13-16] **Sis . . . mavis]** 'you are entitled to happiness wherever you prefer to be'. — **memor . . . vivas]** = 'I hope you'll remember me in your new life'; the coming parallel of Europa is a sufficient clue: Galatea is deserting H. to accompany her splendid new lover to the East; H.'s attitude is irreproachably correct, but the formal good wishes, if not double-edged, are not over-enthusiastic. — **teque . . . cornix]** At first sight lines 15-16 seem otiose (why further talk of omens?); they are, however, essential to the strategy of the poem; in Stanzas 1-3 it seemed Galatea was on her way and all H. could do was wish her godspeed; now the true force of the futures 7 *timebo* and 11 *suscitabo* becomes apparent — Galatea has yet to set out; the possibility exists, therefore, of a last-minute hitch (H. politely hopes one won't occur), or a last-minute change of heart; from this point the poem assumes the character of an oblique deterrent; **laevos picus]** 'ill-omened wood-pecker'; for the woodpecker, see on 1 'parrae recinentis omen'; the sense 'ill-omened' triumphs in *laevos* and *sinister* over the fact that in Roman augural practice (as opposed to Greek) the left was considered the lucky side (Roman and Greek augurs faced opposite directions); cf. 3. 26. 5.

17-24] The strategy of H.'s attempt to deter Galatea is to begin on a note of common-sense concern: 'this is no time of year for a journey; take it from me, the Adriatic can be treacherous.' — **vides]** Cf. 1. 9. 1, 1. 14. 3, 3. 20. 1. — **pronus Orion]** Sets early November; cf. 1. 28. 21. — **ater]** = 'stormy'; cf. 23 *nigri*; contrast 19 *albus* and 3. 7. 1 *candidi*. — **albus Iapyx]** = 'what tricks a fair Nor'westerly can play'; the traveller, i.e., may set out on a fine day with the Iapyx (the favourable wind for travellers from Brundisium across the Adriatic to Greece — cf. 1. 3. 4) behind him, and then be over-taken by a storm (like Gyges in 3. 7). — **hostium . . . ripas]** i.e., 'it's not a time when I want those dear to me to be at sea'; caecos motus] = 'the blind fury'; orientis Austri] 'a rising Southerly'.

25-8] H. slips, as if the story had just occurred to him, into the myth of Europa and her elopement with Jove disguised as a bull; cf. the transition at 3. 4. 42 and 3. 11. 25. The second part of H.'s strategy of oblique dissuasion now begins. His object is not just to warn Galatea against precipitate departure, but to suggest to her that the whole venture is misguided and that she will live to regret it. − Sic] Suggests an immediate relevance of myth to reality − the terror Europa felt as she crossed the Adriatic; but it quickly becomes clear the relevance is more far-reaching; see Quinn, *Latin Explorations*, 1963, 253-66. − niveum doloso] As frequently, each adjective implies a binary opposition (snow-white girl, black bull; guileful bull, guileless girl); see on 2. 3. 9. − scatentem . . . pontum] 'the sea teeming with monsters' (or so it appeared to Europa). − mediasque fraudes] 'the treachery all around her'; again the scene is seen through Europa's eyes. − palluit audax] Not so much an oxymoron (like 3. 11. 35 'splendide mendax') as 'paled at her audacity' (in setting out with her bull-lover).

29-32] Flashback following the dramatic opening (an illustration of H.'s precept *AP* 148-9 that the good poet 'in medias res auditorem rapit'. − studiosa florum] 'all occupied with flowers'; cf. 43-4 below and 1. 26. 6-8. − debitae . . . coronae] = 'working at a garland which she had promised to the Nymphs'; i.e., she was thus engaged when the bull appeared before her; cf. Ovid's version of the rape of Proserpine *Met.* 5. 391-5. − nocte sublustri] i.e., the near-darkness of a clear night (stars, but no moon).

33-4] The lovers are no sooner in Crete than Europa is abandoned by her bull-lover; in H.'s version, events are foreshortened to stress the brief duration of Europa's happiness. − simul] = *simul atque*, as in 1. 4. 17, etc. − centum . . . Creten] Crete (in some legends the birthplace of Zeus) is called 'hundred-citied' by Homer *Il.* 2. 649 (an example, repeated from *Epode* 9. 29, of H.'s adherence to the Callimachean tradition of the learned detail − 'οὐδὲν ἀμάρτυρον ἀείδω').

34-44] Europa's lament resembles that of Ariadne (deserted by Theseus, with whom she had eloped, after one night of love) in Catullus 64. The lament begins and ends at the same point in the stanza (and could thus be removed without damage to the narrative structure). It begins on an impassioned level with a string of exclamations and rhetorical questions. − Pater] Europa was the daughter of King Phoenix of Tyre (in modern Lebanon), from where her flight-path would have taken her across the SE Mediterranean to Crete. − relictum . . . pietas] i.e., she has abandoned the right to call herself daughter and abandoned her loyalty to her father; *relictum* with both nouns. − victa furore] 'overcome by madness'. − unde quo veni?] The double question (a Grecism characteristic of the high style) stylises the time-honoured 'where am I' of the mentally distraught; see on 3. 25. 1-6. − una mors] 'a single death'. − virginum culpae] 'for girls who sin'; *virginum* is a generalising plural; culpae] dative with *levis*; as often, of sexual misconduct, *OLD* 3 b; for the idea cf. Propertius 4. 4. 17. − vigilansne . . . ducit?] = 'do I wake or dream?'; porta . . . eburna] in *Od.* 19. 562-7 Penelope remarks that deceptive dreams pass up from the underworld to earth through a gate of ivory (true dreams through a gate of horn); cf. *Aen.* 6. 893-8, Propertius 4. 7. 87-90. − recentis . . . flores] i.e., flowers that have just bloomed; cf. 29-30 above.

45-8] A more rational, angrier interlude separates the opening outburst from the fresh outbreak of 49-66. − iratae] = 'in my present anger'.

49-56] 'I was shameless to do what I did, I deserve an appropriate death'; picks up the theme of 37-8 'levis . . . culpae'. − Orcum moror] = 'delay death'; for Orcus, see on 1. 28. 10. − deorum siquis] 'whatever god'; in a strange land Europa does not know what god to appeal to. − utinam . . . nuda leones] She is perhaps, like Catullus' Ariadne, almost *nuda* already (though she has her *zona* with her still − see 59), but the context draws out the sense 'unarmed', 'defenceless', *OLD* 4 (cf. 3. 16. 23); only the lions are needed. − antequam . . . tigris] Tigers, i.e., are an acceptable alternative; if she is consumed by them while still young and beautiful, the punishment (she implies) will better fit the crime; tenerae praedae] she will also provide a tastier (and more attractive) meal if she dies young..

57-66] She fancies she can hear her father, who has more practical suggestions to make. − Vilis] 'worthless', as opposed to *cara* (cf. Catullus 72. 6), but also as not deserving the spectacular kinds of death Europa has been contemplating. − quid mori cessas?] i.e., 'why not get on with it?' − potes . . . collum] = 'you can easily hang yourself';

hanging seems to have been regarded by the Greeks and Romans as an especially
degrading form of death or suicide; **pendulum laedere collum**] = 'hang yourself by the
neck', but with overtones something like 'break your pretty neck' (*laedere* in the
sense 'disfigure', *OLD* 1 b); **zona**] symbolic of maidenhood, as in Catullus 2. 13 'zonam
soluit diu ligatam'; see on 3. 21. 22; **bene te secuta**] heavily ironical. − **sive . . . veloci**]
i.e., 'if jumping off a cliff appeals to you, jump'; *rupes* is the cliff-face, *saxa* the rocks
below; **acuta leto**] 'sharp for death'; **age te procellae crede veloci**] ironic mock-heroic.
− **nisi . . . paelex**] i.e., 'unless you, a princess, prefer to end your days as a slave and a
concubine'; **erile carpere pensum**] the *pensum* is a measured weight of wool given out
to slaves by their mistress (*era*) each day for spinning; *carpere* denotes the plucking of
the wool from the distaff; **paelex**] i.e., some barbarian potentate will make Europa his
concubine; she will thus pass under the control of his wife for household duties; Europa,
being an Asian, naturally thinks in Oriental terms; an ironic reversal of the usual cliche
(usually the deserted mistress prefers life as a household slave to loss of her lover; cf.
Catullus 64. 160-63).

66-76] The dénouement by divine intervention favoured by Athenian tragedy − the *dea
ex machina* who foretells how the story will end. − **Aderat querenti**] Venus has been
standing beside Europa, but she has been too busy lamenting to notice her. − **perfidum
ridens Venus**] 'Venus with her shifty smile'; Venus is regularly represented as smiling;
cf. 1. 2. 33, 2. 8. 13, 3. 21. 21; H. prefers to see the smile as sardonic rather than charm-
ing; cf. 1. 33. 12 'saevo cum ioco'; for Venus as the gay intriguer cf. *Aen*. 4. 128 'dolis
risit Cytherea repertis'; for the construction cf. 1. 22. 23. − **remisso filius arcu**] Cupid;
the slackened bow indicates his work is accomplished. − **mox**] It is at this point that we
are to imagine Venus interrupting Europa's lament. − **Abstineto . . . rixae**] 'You will
refrain from hot and angry brawling'; the future imperative suggests majesty − and adds
a hint that the bull's return is a remote contingency; contrast the more businesslike 74
mitte, 75 *disce*; **irarum . . . rixae**] genitive of separation (a Grecism favoured by the high
style; cf. 2. 9. 17); for the *rixae amoris* see on 1. 13. 11. − **invisus taurus**] 'the bull you
hate'. − **laceranda cornua**] Ironically picks up 46 *lacerare*. − **uxor . . . nescis**] 'you do
not know how to be the consort of almighty Jove'; the sense 'you do not know you are
the consort . . .' (nominative and infinitive − a Grecism) is probably also present as an
ambiguity adding to the shiftiness of Venus' consolation; to assume that Venus
seriously means to console Europa is to miss the relevance of the Europa myth to
Galatea − she too, we may presume, has a distinguished lover (a Roman official off to
his province, or a rich *mercator*); she too will be deserted by her lover, with only the
honour of being known to have been his mistress to console her. − **mitte singultus**]
'stop your sobbing'; see on 1. 38. 3. − **bene ferre . . . ducet**] i.e., 'behave as an ex-
mistress of Jove should − you are going to be famous'; **tua . . . ducet**] 'one half of the
world will bear your name'; **sectus orbis**] a section of the *orbis terrarum* cut off from
the rest; H.'s myth ends, i.e., with a proclamation (ironically adopting the oriental point
of view) of the discovery of Europe; *sectus orbis*, 'a section of the world', follows the
model of *ab urbe condita*, 'from the foundation of the city'.

3. 28

Introduction: Preparations for an afternoon with his mistress to celebrate the festival of
Neptune: a vintage wine, some songs, a night to follow. As in 1. 11 and 1. 17, the party
seems to be a *tête-à-tête*, close *mutatis mutandis* to 3. 8 or 1. 20; 4. 11 seems a grander
occasion (servants rushing everywhere, talk of other guests).
Structure: A conversational fragment structured as four heavily endstopped stanzas.
Metre: Asclepiad (b); see 1. 3M.
1-4] The poet is talking to his mistress; we join them in mid-conversation (as we come in
upon H. talking to Maecenas in 3. 8); the tone is brisk, relaxed (contrast the more formal
2. 11, where the preparations for the party begin only at Stanza 4); no indication of
scene, though in mid-July H. is more likely to be on his Sabine farm, as in 1. 17, than in
Rome; cf. the mid-July party, pretty clearly at the farm, in 3. 29. − **Festo die Neptuni**]
The *Neptunalia*, on 23 July. − **quid potius faciam?**] i.e., rather than spend the day with
Lyde? − **prome reconditum Caecubum**] Most likely, 'let's have that Caecuban we've got
stored up'; a guest will sometimes call on his host to produce a vintage wine (cf. 3. 21.

7-8); here, context and the fact that H. is able to specify the wine before it is produced (line 8) suggest he is the host, but leaves the work to the girl; see on 1. 9. 6-7; cf. 11. 6; *promere* = 'serve', 'produce', *depromere* (1. 9. 7, 1. 37. 5) more particularly of fetching the jar down from the storeroom (7 'deripere horreo'); for Caecuban as a wine kept for special occasions, see 1. 37. − Lyde] Also 2. 11. 22, 3. 11. 7. − strenua] 'and look sharp about it'; implies Lyde is to fetch and serve the wine herself (i.e., there are no servants present; cf. 1. 9. 6-7, 1. 11. 6 'vina liques'; contrast 4. 11. 9-12). − munitae . . . sapientiae] = 'assault the fortress of philosophy'; for similar imagery cf. 3. 21. 13-16; for the idea cf. 4. 12. 27-8.

5-8] inclinare meridiem] 'it's past midday'; H., i.e., is in the frame of mind of the man in 1. 1. 19-21 'qui nec veteris pocula Massici / nec partem solido demere de die / spernit'. − veluti . . . dies] 'as though the fleeting day stood still'; with *stet* cf. 1. 9. 1. − parcis] 'you hesitate'; cf. 1. 28. 23, 3. 8. 26. − horreo] 'wine-loft'; see on 3. 8. 11. − cessantem . . . amphoram] The amphora is called 'sluggard' because it has lingered so long in the *horreum*; for *amphorae*, see on 1. 9. 8 *diota*; Bibuli consulis] Caesar's colleague in 59 BC, chosen here for his name; i.e., a wine some fifteen years old; for even older wines, see on 3. 21. 1-4.

9-12] Nos cantabimus invicem . . . comas] 'You and I will take it in turn to sing of Neptune and the green-haired Nereids'; any singing on the *Neptunalia* must obviously begin with songs in praise of Neptune and his suite of Nereids; an informal competition in the amoebean tradition of *Eclogues* 3 and 7, etc. seems indicated; cf. 3. 9; viridis comas] the colour appropriate to sea-dwellers. − tu . . . Cynthiae] H. proposes, i.e., after the exchange of hymns to Neptune, etc. to leave the singing to Lyde; cf. 1. 17. 17-20, 2. 11. 21-4, 4. 11. 33-6; curva recines lyra] Lyde, i.e., will sing her song accompanied by the lyre; cf. 1. 12. 3; for the lyre, see on 1. 10. 6; celeris spicula Cynthiae] i.e., Diana the huntress (daughter of Latona) armed with her spears; cf. 3. 22. 1; a hint, perhaps, of a rural setting.

13-16] The symbolic strategy of H.'s musical programme now becomes clearer. Venus is obviously involved at the conclusion of the programme in order that she may favour the nocturnal celebration which is to follow. − summo carmine] sc., 'recines', 'you will end your singing with . . .'; cf. Catullus 64. 116 'a primo digressus carmine' ('digressing from where I began my song'); in such contexts *carmen* is a collective ('singing', 'poetry') and may denote, as here, several individual songs or poems; cf. 1. 7. 6, 3. 30. 13. − quae . . . oloribus] Venus, identified by her shrine at Cnidus in Asia Minor, the islands of the Cyclades (cf. 1. 14. 19-20), Paphus in Cyprus and by the swans which draw her chariot; cf. 4. 1. 10; with the formula cf. 3. 26. 9-10. − dicetur . . . nenia] a well-deserved *nenia* to night will also be chanted, perhaps by both after Lyde's performance is concluded; *nenia* = 'any plaintive or melancholy song'; in 2. 20. 21 a 'dirge', here some 'sad, haunting melody'; but the passive *dicetur* is perhaps a hint that the *nenia* is a symbolic euphemism for the night that H. and Lyde will spend together; cf. Propertius 3. 10. 28-32.

3. 29

Introduction: The last ode of Book 3 (apart from the concluding *sphragis*) and, like 1. 1, addressed to H.'s patron Maecenas; the third ode to Maecenas in this Book (the others are 3. 8 and 3. 16); cf. 1. 20, 2. 12, 2. 17 and 2. 20.

The theme is an expansion of 3. 8, a further invitation to put cares of state temporarily aside and join H. on his farm. But where 3. 8 tended to assume a note of facile confidence, the tone of 3. 29 is more sombre − perhaps a reflection of the uncertainty in Rome in the summer of 23 BC (see on 25-6 'tu . . . curas').

Structure: Stanzas 1-3, invitation; Stanzas 4-7, a change is usually welcome, and now is just the time. Except for Stanza 1, all the stanzas in this opening section are heavily endstopped. Stanzas 8-12 adopt a flowing tempo, each stanza spilling over into the stanza following, with the transition in mid-line: lines 29-41, the future is unpredictable; lines 41-8, the wise man takes each day as it comes. Stanzas 13-16 represent a variation on the theme of Stanzas 8-12 and a return to a more staccato movement of the sense: Stanza 13, Fortune comes and goes; Stanzas 14-16, I make myself independent of Fortune. See on 29-48.

Metre: Alcaics; see 1. 9M.

1-12] H.'s invitation to leave Rome behind in mid-July (see on 19 'stella vesani Leonis') and join him in the country is pressing (*iamdudum*) but unspecific, since the time must be of Maecenas' choosing. Lines 2-4 suggest lavish but not extravagant preparations (no promise, i.e., of a special vintage wine); contrast the austere tone of H.'s first invitation to Maecenas, 1. 20. 1-2 and the sacrificial feast of 3. 8. 1-4. — **Tyrrhena regum progenies**] Recalls 1. 1. 1 'atavis edite regibus'. — **non ante verso cado**] i.e., an unopened jar (to make it a special occasion); the vintage is unspecified; for *cadus*, see on 1. 9. 8 *diota*. — **cum flore rosarum**] = 'along with a supply of roses'; for *flos* as a collective, see on 1. 4. 10; for roses as a symbol of extravagance, see on 1. 5. 1 (here, as there, probably rose petals, not blossoms). — **balanus**] An Arabian nut from which a fragrant oil was pressed; for hair oil, see on 1. 5. 2; cf. 4. 12. 14-20. — **iamdudum**] The implication is that the invitation has already been made and that H. now sends Maecenas a reminder or perhaps Maecenas has a standing invitation but has not availed himself of it for overlong); cf. *Epist.* 1. 5. 7 (also an invitation) 'iamdudum splendet focus'. — **apud me**] i.e., the Sabine farm. — **eripe te morae**] i.e., 'stop putting it off'; the first of a series of exhortations (cf. 6-7 *ne semper contempleris*, 9 *desere*, 11 *omitte*); *morae* is dative. — **ne semper ... parricidae**] 'don't go on gazing at Tibur, etc. (i.e., admiring them from a distance) for ever'; i.e., 'get away from Rome'; Maecenas' house on top of the Esquiline commanded a panoramic view extending from NE to SE; Tibur is about 26 km from Rome, H.'s farm (not visible from Rome) a few km further into the hills; **udum Tibur**] The air of Tibur is moist and there is water everywhere, unlike the dry heat of Rome in mid-July (see on 19 'stella vesani Leonis'); see on 1. 7. 13; cf. 4. 3. 10; for H.'s farm, see on 2. 6. 5-8; **Aefulae declive arvom**] between Tibur and Praeneste (to the SE); **Telegoni iuga parricidae**] = Tusculum, in the Alban hills, SE of Rome, said to have been founded by Telegonus, son of Odysseus (by Circe), whom he killed unwittingly. — **fastidiosam ... arduis**] Hendiadys; first the striking abstract generalisation ('fastidiosam desere copiam'), then the concrete precept 'quit your palace in the clouds'; **fastidiosam copiam**] 'boring abundance', opposed by implication to the attractive simplicity of H.'s farm; cf. 3. 1. 37; **desere**] both literally ('leave behind') and figuratively ('forsake'); **molem**] Maecenas' mansion on the Esquiline; cf. the 'regiae moles' of 2. 15. 1; pejorative in both cases. — **omitte ... Romae**] Ironical; the apparently approving *mirari beatae* is contradicted by *fumum et opes strepitumque* (so different from the clear air, the unpretentious peace and quiet of H.'s farm); cf. the picture of Rome in *Sat.* 2. 6. 23-59.

13-28] **Plerumque ... frontem**] i.e., a change is often a tonic — especially if it means escape for the rich man from 'fastidiosa copia' to the simple life; **mundae ... cenae**] the basic sense of *mundus* is 'neat', 'attractive', whence the sense 'trimmed of superfluities'; cf. *Epist.* 1. 5. 7 'iamdudum splendet focus et tibi munda supellex', *Odes* 1. 5. 5 'simplex munditiis'; **parvo, pauperum**] the emphasis is on the simple lifestyle of ordinary folk (which H. affects on his farm), not on poverty; cf. line 56 and the similar opposition in 3. 1. 45-8, 2. 18. 1-14; **lare**] metonomy for 'home', as in Catullus 31.9 'larem ad nostrum', etc.; **sine aulaeis et ostro**] Hendiadys, 'without purple (i.e., expensive, elaborate) hangings'; **explicuere**] i.e., dispelled the wrinkles of care; gnomic perfect. — **iam ... iam ... iam**] The three *iam*'s (anaphora in asyndeton, forming a tricolon crescendo) structure the theme 'now is the time of year to be in the country' by means of three symbols of mid-summer — the first two emphasising the heat and dryness of Rome (from which all who could escaped), the third building up a contrasting cluster of pastoral imagery (cf. 2. 5. 10-20); **clarus ... ignem**] King Cepheus of Ethiopia, placed after his death among the stars; the constellation Cepheus begins to appear in mid-July; *clarus* = both 'famous' and 'bright'; **Procyon**] principal star of the Lesser Dog (a forewarning of the 'dog days'); cf. *Epist.* 1. 10. 15 'ubi gratior aura / leniat et rabiem Canis et momenta Leonis'; **stella Leonis**] the constellation Leo; **iam pastor ... quaerit**] i.e., even in the country it is hot, but one can seek relief from the heat; **horridi dumeta Silvani**] i.e., what shade he can, even that of a clump of bushes; sheep are grazed in poor, open country, not in forests (where there is no pasture); Silvanus (the god of forests, etc., but here especially the god of thickets) is appropriately represented as a shaggy, bristly fellow; **caretque ... ventis**] i.e., the bank of a stream, normally an attractive resting place, is too hot when there is not a breath of air; **taciturna**] silent on a mid-summer's day — no longer any babbling of water (the stream has dried up) or rustle of leaves (no wind). — **tu ... curas**] i.e., as if this were a time to worry about constitutional reform; after the triple *iam* the continuing asyndeton sets up an abrupt, unexpected binary opposition (three appropriate summer activities: what Maecenas does); the effect approaches ironic bathos, emphasising the unseasonableness of Maecenas' continuing preoccupation with cares of state; H. possibly hints at Augustus' ill-health which caused him to relinquish the consulship on 1 July 23 BC. — **urbi ... discors**] We pass to Maecenas' preoccupation with external affairs; **Seres**] = the Chinese; since the conquests of Alexander, the symbol of the eastern limit of the known world; **regnata ... Bactra**] the capital of Bactrea (= Parthia), once ruled over by King Cyrus of Persia; **Tanaisque discors**] for 'the unruly Don', symbol of the NE frontier, see on 1. 19. 10.

29-41] Stanza 7, the climax of the rhetorical structure of lines 13-28, serves also as a bridge passage preparing the way for the second main section, in which H. develops, at a different tempo (see Structure), the central theme of the ode — that the wise man resigns himself to the unpredictable uncertainty of the future: 29 *futuri temporis exitum* is opposed to 32 *quod adest*, which is opposed in its turn to 33 *cetera*. The ground is thus laid for an expansion of 32-3 *quod adest memento conponere aequos* in 41-8 'Ille potens sui laetusque deget', etc. — **trepidat**] Pejorative, = 'concerns himself needlessly'. — **quod adest**] 'what is present and at hand'. — **conponere**] 'arrange', i.e., 'make the best of'. — **aequos**] 'unruffled'; cf. 2. 3. 1. — **cetera ... feruntur**] = 'the rest (all that is not *quod adest*) is like a river in its course'. — **nunc ... delabentis**] 'sometimes peacefully gliding down in the middle of its bed'; the last syllable of *Etruscum* is elided (only here and in 2. 3. 27 in this position). — **nunc ... volventis una**] i.e., at other times in flood and sweeping all before it; **adesos**] 'eroded' by the flood waters; **stirpisque raptas**] i.e., 'whole trees uprooted'. — **cum ... amnis**] i.e., a flood that swells all streams far and wide — the symbol of a general calamity.

41-8] **Ille ... deget**] Hard on the climax of the simile in mid-line comes the abrupt contrast of the man who can remain detached from the swirl of events; the sentiment is both Epicurean and Stoic, though the philosophical basis is different — Epicurean concentration on the pleasures of the present enhanced by memories of the past in one case, Stoic resignation to fate in the other; **potens sui**] 'in control of himself', the opposite of 'impotens sui'; like *laetus*, predicative with *deget*. — **cui licet dixisse**] 'who is in a position to have said each day'; *licet* is present because the wise man's right to say this lasts throughout life; *dixisse* is perfect because the saying is past with reference to *deget*. — **vixi**] Not 'I have survived another day' (as in 1. 9. 14-15), but 'I have enjoyed life'; cf. Catullus 5. 1 'Vivamus, mea Lesbia, atque amemus'; some carry the direct speech through to 56 or even 64, but a monosyllabic hedonist suggests resignment and contentment better than one so prolix. — **cras ... vexit**] H. resumes and expands his statement of faith; cf. 1. 9. 13-15; **polum**] 'the heavens'.

49-56] At 49 the tempo changes once more (see Structure): Stanzas 13-16 seem designed, along with Stanzas 4-7, to serve as a frame for the more fast-moving Stanzas 8-12 — a concluding section, in which the vivid portrait of the man who lives happy and unruffled is given a more general philosophical context. — **Fortuna**] Cf. 1. 34. 12-16. — **ludum ... pertinax**] i.e., 'relentlessly and contemptuously treating us as her playthings'. — **transmutat incertos honores**] 'redistributes her temporary favours'. — **resigno**] 'renounce'. — **mea virtute me involvo**] Plato *Repub.* 5. 457 a (of the wives of the Guardians, stripped for exercise) 'they will put on *arete* in place of clothing', quoted by editors, is hardly a parallel; the image H. wishes to suggest is perhaps that of the man who draws his cloak over his head to protect him from the elements; cf. Cicero *Fam.* 9. 20. 3 (46 BC) 'litteris me involvo' ('I immerse myself in reading and writing'). — **probamque pauperiem ... quaero**] = 'I espouse an honest, simple life and demand no dowry'; cf. Stanza 4.

57-61] Having espoused the simple life, H. is liberated from the anxieties of the *mercator* caught in a storm at sea; cf. 1. 1. 15-18, 2. 16. 1-4, 3. 1. 25-8. — **non est meum**] = 'I don't have to ...'. — **si mugiat ... procellis**] = 'whenever the mast creeks in a bit of a Sou'westerly'; frequentative subjunctive. — **avaro mari**] Cf. 1. 28. 18.

62-4] Why should H. rely on Castor and Pollux to keep him safe? The explanation that he is free from *avaritia* and a poet will hardly do. More likely, H. means the *mercator* and his cargo are in no great danger ('si mugiat ... procellis' hardly suggests a real storm), but the *mercator* is already worrying about his precious cargo — as Maecenas keeps anticipating disasters for Rome which may never eventuate. — **biremis scaphae**]

Apparently, a kind of lifeboat, as in Plautus *Rudens* 75 'De navi timidae desiluerunt in scapham'; but the 'two-oared skiff' is metaphorical, symbolising the security of H.'s 'proba pauperies' rather than a mode of transport seriously contemplated; cf. Cicero *Att.* 10. 10. 5. — **geminusque Pollux**] = Castor and his twin brother Pollux; cf. 1. 3. 2 'fratres Helenae'.

3. 30

Introduction: An epilogue or *sphragis*, in which H. states his claim to immortality: his *Odes* will last longer than *monumenta* of bronze or stone, as long as Rome itself. Cf. 2. 20.

Structure: Lines 1-5, statement of claim (1-2), amplified by a tricolon crescendo (3-5). Lines 6-14, assertion of immortality in the form of a further tricolon crescendo: 'Non omnis moriar . . .' (6-7), 'postera crescam laude recens . . .' (7-9), 'dicar . . . princeps Aeolium carmen ad Italos deduxisse modos' (10-14). Lines 14-16, the poet's coronation by the Muse.

Metre: Asclepiad (a), the same metre as the opening ode to Maecenas, 1. 1; this metre again in 4. 8.

1-2] **Exegi monumentum**] A poem claiming immortality should exemplify some of the qualities of the collection — wit, irony, structural complexity; **exegi**] the primary sense is 'I have completed', *OLD* 5 (with overtones suggesting perfect form achieved after long revision, as in *Epist.* 2. 1. 72); a secondary sense, 'I have established my claim to', *OLD* 8-9, contributes to the complexity of the opening phrase; **monumentum**] = anything that 'brings to mind' or 'records', especially an inscription in bronze or stone, or a natural feature or man-made structure associated with a famous name; in H.'s case, the 88 poems which constitute Books 1-3 of the *Odes*, published together in 23 BC (for the date, see on 2. 10); the earliest surviving inscription of this kind belongs to a consul of 298 BC; Augustus set up *eclogia* of Rome's great men in his new Forum dedicated in 2 BC (one recorded the career of Marius); the most famous is the statement of Augustus' own achievements drawn up by himself (Suetonius *Aug.* 101. 4 'indicem rerum a se gestarum, quem vellet incidi in aeneis tabulis') which has survived in a stone version found at Ankara (*monumentum Ancyranum*); cf. 4. 8. 13-20. — **aere perennius**] One hears a literary work, or has it by heart; it can therefore outlast, not only the roll of papyrus on which it was first recorded, but even bronze (the material chosen for *monumenta* to ensure their permanence); H. is less concerned, however, with this fairly obvious truth than with placing literary achievement in a context that challenges the convention which accords first place, in the history of a nation, to political achievement. — **regalique . . . altius**] 'loftier than the Pyramids' royal rubble'; H. speaks of the Pyramids as if they were already mouldering into decay — a notion fostered, perhaps, by the thought that Egypt's day, as an independent kingdom, had come to an end with the overthrow of Cleopatra (though the Pyramids commemorated, of course, the pre-Hellenistic Kings of Egypt); cf. the imitation in Martial 8. 3. 5; **altius**] in the case of the Pyramids, of physical height, in that of the *Odes*, of moral or intellectual stature; the phrase is a hint of the witty or ironic stance adopted by H. toward his theme which will become clearer as the poem progresses (see on lines 6-7, 14-16).

3-5] **quod . . . temporum**] A tricolon crescendo graphically evoking the sources of decay (rain, wind, the passage of time) to which ordinary physical *monumenta* are exposed; a sophisticated recasting of Simonides' lines on the dead at Thermopylae, 'the tombs of men such as these neither decay nor time, that masters all things, will tarnish'; cf. Pindar *Pyth.* 6. 10; **imber edax**] 'the greedy rain'; for *imber*, 'steady, pelting rain', see on 2. 9. 1; *edax*, like *impotens*, personifies; **Aquilo impotens**] 'the North wind, raging out of control'; for *impotens*, see on 2. 1. 26; **possit diruere**] 'could tear apart', generic subjunctive; H.'s *Odes*, i.e., are exempt from the ultimate destruction by the elements which is the fate of all purely physical *monumenta*; **aut . . . temporum**] the third member of the tricolon is of a different order from the previous two and is not assimilated to the anaphora in asyndeton; consequently, the first two cola (*non imber . . . non Aquilo . . .*) combine with the third in a kind of large-scale hendiadys (= 'the destructive action of the passage of time'); **fuga temporum**] for the notion that the past recedes into the distance, see on 2. 11. 5-6; for its 'headlong flight' cf. 2. 14. 1-2 'fugaces anni';

the plural *tempora* suggests a complex entity (cf. *castra, viscera,* etc.), 'time in its pas-
sage'; cf. 4. 2. 40, 4. 7. 18, 4. 12. 13; closely related is the sense 'days gone by', 1. 28.
12, 4. 13. 14.

6-7] **Non omnis moriar**] 'I shall not wholly die'; on first reading, a reiteration of the
commonplace that the only immortality a thinking man can hope for is to live on, through
his achievements, in the minds of those who come after him; see on 4. 8. 13-15. —
multaque pars . . . Libitinam] A witty transposition of the same thought: *multaque pars
mei,* 'a substantial part of me' (i.e., the *Odes*), picks up *omnis* and imposes a reassess-
ment (the poet 'will live on in his works' in more than one sense — because he is the
author, because of their intensely personal character); **vitabit Libitinam**] Libitina,
goddess of corpses and funerals, a rather unliterary divinity, is probably chosen to
produce an effect of self-depreciatory casualness (something like 'will give Old Nick
the slip').

7-9] The second member of the second tricolon. — **usque**] Emphasises the continuing
nature of the process. — **postera . . . recens**] *crescam* and *recens* emphasise that the *ego*
meant is exempt from the normal fate of corpses, *postera laude* indicates the sense in
which the dead H. 'will grow in stature, uncorrupted by decay'; as in 2. 20, the paradox
depends on the common idiom by which a Roman poet identifies himself with his
work, so that statements appropriate to his poetry can be made of the poet himself and
vice versa; such a statement is not put forward as argumentatively valid, but as a rhetori-
cal structure, offering a semblance of logic, which can serve as the vehicle of a statement
acceptable to the reader as fundamentally, if not literally, true. — **dum . . . pontifex**]
Chosen as a (suitably modest) symbol of the continuity of Roman culture and institu-
tions; cf. 3. 3. 42-3, 3. 5. 11; H.'s *Odes* will be as much a part of Roman life as the
ceremonies of her state religion.

10-14] The third member of the second tricolon (lines 10-14) represents the *sphragis*
proper: a carefully worded, appropriately subtle statement of H.'s achievement as a
poet is encapsulated in an autobiographical context; at the same time, the imagery
suggestive of the leading figure in political life is picked up in a final challenge to the
reader to accept poetic achievement as comparable to that of the statesman. — **dicar**]
= 'it will be said of me'. — **qua . . . populorum**] With *dicar*; the nominative and infini-
tive *princeps . . . deduxisse modos* thus expresses the pride of future generations in the
local boy who made good (*ex humili potens*); H. exploits a convention of the *sphragis*
favouring circumlocution in naming one's place of birth (cf. Propertius 1. 22. 9-10,
Ovid *Am.* 3. 15. 3) as an ironic corrective to the rhetorical flourish of the nominative
and infinitive; **Aufidus**] now the Ofanto, about 16 km from H.'s birth-place Venusia;
cf. 4. 9. 2 'natus ad Aufidum', also 4. 14. 25, *Sat.* 1. 1. 58; **pauper aquae**] 'short of
water', because the SE, compared with Latium, has a hot, arid climate; cf. *Epode*
3. 16 'siticulosae Apuliae', *Sat.* 1. 5. 97-8; *aquae* is genitive of respect (cf. 3. 6. 17,
etc.); **Daunus**] legendary first king of Apulia; cf. 4. 14. 25-6, also 1. 22. 14, 4. 6. 27;
to be distinguished from the father of Turnus in the *Aen.*; **agrestium regnavit populorum**]
'ruled his rustic peoples'; *agrestium* undercuts the grandiloquence of the poetic plural
and the genitive (a Grecism, characteristic of the high style). — **ex humili potens**] 'a man
of humble birth risen to power'; for H. on his humble origin, see *Sat.* 1. 6; cf. 2. 20.
5-6; *potens* picks up 3 *impotens*; cf. 4. 8. 26. — **princeps . . . deduxisse modos**] H.'s
claim to fame operates on two levels of meaning: (1) the primary sense assigns to
princeps the sense of leader and invokes the metaphor of the founding hero (such as
Aeneas, Diomede and the founders of Greek colonies in Southern Italy and Sicily) who
'leads down' his people to the ships in which they are to embark for their new home
across the seas (whence *deducere coloniam,* etc., *OLD* 9; cf. *Aen.* 2. 799-800 [the
Aeneadae are] 'parati / in quascumque velim pelago deducere terras'); poetic achieve-
ment is thus (as in the opening lines) spoken of in terms appropriate to political
achievement; the title *princeps* which H. claims for himself echoes that officially
accorded Augustus himself; (2) running parallel with this primary sense is a secondary
sense of *deducere* which invokes the metaphor of spinning (*deducere filum,* etc.) to
denote the poetic process (*deducere versus,* etc., *OLD* 4), favoured especially by the
Roman disciples of Callimachus; with this sense of *deducere, princeps* assumes the
sense 'he who was first in time' (or 'he who outstripped others') in refining the old
Aeolic poetry and gave it a new elegance; H., i.e., is the innovator of a new kind of
poetry at Rome (Catullus' experiments with the Sapphic stanza, being of limited

extent, are ignored); cf. Lucretius 1. 926-30 (= 4. 1-5) and H.'s restatement of his status as innovator in *Epist.* 1. 19. 21-34 (where he claims recognition as the Roman Alcaeus) 'libera per vacuum posui vestigia princeps', etc.; **Aeolium carmen**] i.e., poetry of the kind traditionally associated with Sappho and Alcaeus (who wrote in the Aeolian dialect), especially poetry in Sapphics and Alcaics (22 and 33 odes respectively in *Odes* 1-3 out of 88), but not excluding the Asclepiad metres, which belong in the same · tradition; cf. 4. 3. 12; for the singular *carmen*, 'poetry', see on 3. 28. 13; cf. *Epode* 14. 7 'promissum carmen' (of the *Epodes*); **ad Italos modos**] with both senses of *deduxisse*, = 'took over [Aeolian poetry] and made it the basis of metrical form in Latin, adapting and refining the original metres in the process'; *ad* to reinforce the metaphor of migration secured by *deduxisse*; for H.'s innovations in the Alcaic stanza, see 1. 9M; in the Sapphic stanza, 1. 2M; in the Asclepiad metres, 1. 1M and 1. 3M; **Italos**] not 'Roman' or 'Latin' (1) to support the primary sense of *deduxisse* ('to Italian metres', as if 'to Italian shores'), (2) to identify himself with his fellow-Apulians.

.4-16] The ode ends, as it began, on a note of irony, to offset the magnitude of H.'s claim and to reinforce the ingenuity and wit with which the claim is formulated. The Muse is imagined as standing with the garland of bay leaves (a symbol of poetic achievement) ready. H. bids her get on with the job. − **Sume . . . meritis**] i.e., 'assume the majestic, haughty look my achievements call for'. − **Delphica lauro**] = 'Apollo's bay'; Apollo, god of the oracle at Delphi, is also god of lyric poetry; cf. 1. 21. 12, 2. 10. 19-20, 4. 2. 9; for the garland as the reward of poetic innovation see on 1. 1. 29; cf. Lucretius 1. 929-30 (= 4. 4-5). − **volens**] i.e., 'let there be no show of reluctance'. − **Melpomene**] Also 1. 24. 3, 4. 3. 1; see on 1. 12. 2.

Book Four

4. 1

Introduction: The opening poem of Book 4 reintroduces the poet of love. It is a role H. finds congenial (cf. 1. 6. 17-20), and with it goes the tone of ironic self-depreciation adopted here. Venus at war again is the symbol of a new book of poems, but in this campaign H. is a reluctant combatant, too old for active service — or can he be mistaken? For the urbane, bantering tone with which H. addresses Venus cf. 1. 30; contrast 1. 19.

In fact, only three of the fourteen odes which follow have love as their subject: 4. 10 is a wistful trifle which picks up the theme of the concluding stanzas of 4. 1; in 4. 11 H. *is* in love, but for the last time; 4. 13 looks to the past rather than the present. The important odes of the book are those in which H. plays, with a new confidence (all the old reservations gone), the role of laureate and propagandist.

As well as introducing the book, 4. 1 serves as a compliment to H.'s friend Paullus Maximus, usually identified as the Paullus Fabius Maximus who was consul in 11 BC, best remembered for the cruel epigram of Cassius Severus (quoted Seneca *Controv.* 2. 4. 11) 'Quasi disertus es, quasi formosus es, quasi dives es; unum tantum es non quasi, vappa'; he was to become an intimate friend of Augustus; Ovid appeals to him, *ex Ponto* 1. 2 and 2. 3.

Structure: Stanzas 1-2 entreat Venus to spare H. and turn her attention elsewhere. Stanzas 3-7 recommend Paullus Maximus. Stanza 8 brings us back to H. Stanzas 9-10 introduce the carefully-planned unexpected ending.

Metre: Asclepiad (b), the metre of the propemptikon for Virgil (1. 3); used in twelve odes in all, in Book 4 only here and in 4. 3.

1-8]   **Intermissa . . . moves**] Venus is in the mood for war again and expects H. to turn out as before; but the old campaigner has had enough and begs off; Book 4 thus picks up the metaphor of 3. 26. 2 'militavi non sine gloria' (cf. 16 'late signa feret militiae tuae'); **intermissa diu**] in the ten years or thereabouts which separate Book 4 from Books 1-3 there has been no activity on this front (H. has written no poems about love); for the generation which survived the Civil Wars, the opening word sets the tone (despair at a fresh outbreak of fighting, not jubilation); H. casts himself in the role of Don Juan *malgré lui* (the plural *bella* suggests, not an isolated affair, but a way of life H. has not the heart to resume); **rursus**] for the idea cf. Propertius 2. 3. 2-3 'Vix unum potes, infelix, requiescere mensem, / et turpis de te iam liber alter erit'; **moves**] cf. 1. 15. 10. — **parce, precor, precor**] Cf. 2. 19. 7-8; for the repetition, see 2. 14. 1. — **non sum . . . Cinarae**] 'I am not the man I was . . . '; explained in the next sentence; Cinara again 4. 13. 21-2 (where she is spoken of in similarly affectionate terms), also *Epist.* 1. 7. 28, 1. 14. 33, not in *Odes* 1-3; **regno**] cf. 3. 9. 9, 3. 24. 19. — **Desine . . . imperiis**] 'Stop' in the sense 'give up the attempt you are making'; *flectere* suggests the taming or breaking-in of a horse (cf. *Aen.* 9. 606, *OLD* 7); for the change of metaphor, see on 2. 5. 9-16; **dulcium . . . Cupidinum**] picks up 1. 19. 1, with the addition of *dulcium*; for the oxymoron, see Quinn on Catullus 68. 17-18; the concept of love as bitter-sweet is as old as Sappho; **circa lustra decem**] = 'about 50'; if *Odes* 4 was published in 13 BC, H. was 51 or 52; cf. 2. 4. 23-4; already some years earlier, probably, H. had written, *Epist.* 2. 2. 55-6 'singula de nobis anni praedantur euntes: / eripuere iocos, venerem, convivia, ludum'; **mollibus . . . imperiis**] a double oxymoron: *mollibus* (the stock epithet of love and lovers, 'young', 'supple' as well as 'responsive', 'easily aroused') is opposed both to *imperiis* (maintaining the sweet-bitter polarity of *dulcium — saeva*) and to *durum*

('stiff with age', 'unresponsive'; cf. the related imagery of 1. 25. 16-20 and 4. 13. 9-12);
imperiis] 'commands', *OLD* 8; dative with *durum*, or ablative with *flectere*. − **abi** . . .
preces] = 'go where you will be welcome'; **blandae preces**] prayers to Venus flattering
her and enlisting her aid, as H. does 3. 26. 9-12; **iuvenum**] see on 1. 2. 41; H., still (if
only just) a *iuvenis* in *Odes* 1-3, is now a *senex.*

9-12] Clearly, Paullus is among those who beg Venus' help. For Venus taking up residence
in the house of a favoured suppliant cf. 1. 30; there, the suppliant is a woman, for whom
worship of Venus' 'ture multo' is a matter of business; here, Paullus is cast in the role of
the Don Juan who will have need of Venus as his ally, presumably in his struggle with
the generous rival of line 18 (and will be in a position to reward her handsomely). −
Tempestivius] 'More appropriately'; cf. 1. 23. 12, 3. 19. 27. − **purpureis . . . oloribus**]
'on the wings of your dazzling purple swans'; cf. 3. 28. 15. − **comissabere**] 'you will
transfer your revels'. − **si . . . idoneum**] For the liver as the site of passion cf. 1. 13. 4, 1.
25. 15; Paullus presumably will prove a willing victim; for *idoneum* cf. 3. 26. 1.

13-16] Paullus commended to Venus' attention. − **pro sollicitis . . . reis**] = 'an eloquent
defender of those in trouble in the courts'; cf. the terms in which Ovid appeals to him to
intercede with Augustus *ex Pont.* 1. 2. 67-8 and 115-16. − **centum puer artium**] = 'a
most talented young man'; the new dispensation of Augustus permitted election to the
consulship at age 32; thus, in 13 BC (the likely date of publication of *Odes* 4) Paullus
was at least 30; *puer* usually implies one much younger (see on 1. 5. 1; cf. line 29);
circumstances alter cases, but perhaps it is better to take H. to mean 'he who was *centum
puer artium* will now . . . '. − **late . . . tuae**] = 'will advance deep into enemy territory
while fighting under your standards'; the metaphor of the opening couplet is now
resumed; for *signa* (the emblems carried by Roman legions into battle) cf. 3. 5. 18; H.
clearly means to flatter Paullus, representing him as an irresistible charmer and heart-
breaker, not as a ruthless womaniser, though so long as the conqueror avoided respectable
matronae, conquest (e.g., of a charming *libertina*, even if it meant ousting a rival) was
socially acceptable.

17-20] Stanza 5 extends the metaphor of 16 *militiae.* The victorious general eventually
overcomes his enemy, and when he does so he gives his thanks to the divinity who has
brought him victory − may even set up a statue to the divinity as an *ex voto* offering;
similarly, when eventually (*quandoque*) Paullus overcomes his rival, he will set up a
shrine to Venus on his estate, complete with a marble statue of the goddess who has
granted him success. − **quandoque**] = *quandocumque*, 'when eventually', as in 4. 2. 34
(in *AP* 359 'quandoque bonus dormitat Homerus', *quandoque* is frequentative). −
largi . . . aemuli] The 'generous rival' is the familiar *dives amator* of Augustan elegy −
though one assumes that Paullus, when it came to generosity, was (unlike Tibullus) able
to hold his own; **muneribus**] with *largi*; **riserit**] 'has had the laugh over'. − **Albanos prope
lacus**] The Alban lake proper and the adjacent *lacus Nemorensis*, in the Alban hills about
20 km SE of Rome, destined to become a favourite place for villas of the rich under the
Empire; Paullus presumably had an estate there. − **marmoream . . . citrea**] A marble
Venus under a protective roof of cedar beams, forming an *aedes votiva* like that in 2. 17.
31; for the idea cf. 4. 8. 8.

21-8] **Illic**] i.e., when Venus takes up residence in Paullus' house (9 *domum*), not in the
shrine just referred to. − **plurima tura**] Cf. 1. 30. 3. − **Berecyntia . . . fistula**] The kind of
music that goes with a really good party; cf. 3. 19. 18-20; such parties, it is implied, will
be a regular feature of life with Paullus; for the instruments, see on 1. 12. 1-2; **delectabere**]
the distinctive form picks up 11 *comissabere.* − **bis pueri die . . . humum**] The formal
dance in Venus' honour by a team of boys and girls twice a day contributes further to
the picture of a way of life beyond the resources of normal devotees; for the dance, see
on 1. 36. 12; cf. 2. 5. 21-4; nothing of course like modern ballroom dancing is intended;
numen] with *laudantes*; **candido**] points to the youth of the dancers.

29-32] 'I am getting too old for love and parties' (the way of life proclaimed 1. 6. 17-20).
− **Me**] For the emphatic *me* at the turning point of an ode, see on 1. 1. 29. − **nec femina
nec puer**] The stark, simple language of one who has come to terms with reality; with
femina cf. 4. 11. 34 (the only other instance of the word in the *Odes* is 1. 15. 14); **puer**]
while H. occasionally hints at the homosexual interests of others in *Odes* 1-3 (1. 4. 19,
2. 5. 20, 3. 20), he has not confessed his own interest since *Epodes* 11. 23. − **spes . . .
mutui**] Cf. 2. 12. 15, 3. 9. 13. − **certare mero**] i.e., trying to outdrink others at a party.
− **vincire . . . floribus**] For garlands at parties, see on 1. 38.

33-40] H. began by telling Venus he is too old to be her champion — she would do better to turn elsewhere; he has just told her that love and the way of life that goes with it bring him no pleasure any more, he can no longer delude himself about love; why then does she not leave him alone? The ode concludes, not so much with a surprise ending (a cheap effect which H. has learnt, since *Epode* 2, to avoid) as with a reversion to the opening lines. One might expect Book 4 will be about Ligurinus, but adherence throughout a book to a single theme is not H.'s manner: in fact, we meet Ligurinus again only in 4. 10. — cur heu ... , cur ... cur ... ?] Exclamation and repetition mark a reversion to the emotional level of the opening lines; similarly, the direct address ('apostrophe') is a sign of emotion, not a change of addressee. — manat ... genas] For tears as evidence of passion cf. 1. 13. 6-7. — facunda ... silentio] Pent-up emotion causes H. to lose the thread in conversation; *cadit*, like the other present tenses in Stanzas 9-10, is to be taken as frequentative (there are things which keep happening; facunda] with *lingua* rather than with *verba*; parum decoro silentio] 'in unseemly silence'; the last syllable of *decoro* is elided — a rare effect (only here in the *Odes* in Asclepiads) — to suggest the trailing off of H.'s speaking voice. — nocturnis ... volubilis] Vain pursuit is one of the commonest of dream fantasies; H.'s dreams place Ligurinus in familiar contexts: he sees him taking part in a race on the Campus Martius, swimming — no doubt in the Tiber, like Hebrus in 3. 12. 7 (cf. Sybaris in 1. 8. 8) — but reinterprets the normal activity in accordance with the private fantasy of his dream; volucrem] 'speeding'; dure] 'cruel boy'; volubilis] the waters that swirl around the head of the swimmer; word and image are a carefully calculated expression of emotion (desire verging on despair).

4. 2

Introduction: 'Anyone who tries to compete with Pindar is doomed to meet with disaster. Pindar's verse, whatever the subject, surges forward like a raging torrent. My talent is for slender themes, my poems are the result of hard work. You, Jullus, will make a better job than I of a poem in honour of Augustus' return from Gaul. My contribution will be modest and personal. You can be expected to sacrifice ten oxen and ten cows: in my case, the young calf I am fattening for the occasion will be enough.'

H.'s ode is easily summarised, its rhetorical strategy less easily grasped by the modern reader. The situation is not unlike that of 3. 14: there, victorious Caesar is just back from several years in Spain, his appearance at a public ceremony of thanksgiving imminent; here, Caesar's return (after several years' absence in Spain and Gaul) to celebrate his triumph over the Sygambri (a German tribe) is still in the future (34 *quandoque*) but sufficiently assured for preparations to be taken in hand. As in 3. 14, H. proposes to content himself with the role of bystander.

Was it expected that H. might continue to play the role of official laureate which he had assumed with the performance of the *Carmen Saeculare* in 17 BC? Did Jullus propose a victory ode likewise designed for public performance by a choir on the Pindaric model? He was praetor in 13 BC, the year of Augustus' return, and may have had a hand in organising the ceremony. When H. declined, did Jullus write the victory ode himself, as H. suggested? We know that he wrote a mythological poem in twelve books about Diomede. It seems more likely that H.'s flattery was received in the spirit in which it was intended. It is a reasonable guess that *Odes* 4 was not published until after Augustus' return; indeed, publication of both collections may have been timed to coincide with the Emperor's return to Rome (1-3 in 23, 4 in 13 BC). H.'s disclaimer, by being published, fulfils the function of the formal victory ode he did not write, more modestly and more sincerely. In the published collection 4. 2 is backed up by other poems (especially 4. 4 and 4. 14) in which H. comes close to the role of laureate. It is, however, a good guess that the *Carmen Saeculare* pleased him less than it has some modern critics; that he disliked the constraints imposed by a public occasion, as he disliked the constraints of encomiastic epic (see 1. 6 and 4. 15. 1-4); the modesty of Stanza 7, if tongue-in-cheek after the Pindaric pastiche of Stanzas 2-6, need not be wholly insincere; Stanzas 14-15, in which we see H., the personal poet, relaxed and in full control of his chosen form, show his instinct was sound.

The ode is the first of a series in this book dealing with poetry and the poet's role: cf. 4.3, 4. 6, 4. 9, 4. 15.

Structure: Stanza 1 states the minor theme, 'Pindar has no rival'. Stanzas 2-6 sing the praises of Pindar in a creditable imitation of the Pindaric manner (a grand tricolon crescendo is built around the anaphora in asyndeton of 10 and 13 *seu*, 17 *sive*); the structure of this section is more loosely accumulative, relying heavily on appositional expansion and a string of verbs of equal grammatical status (contrast 1. 2. 1-12, 3. 2. 6-12, 3. 6. 33-44), but the metre and the stanzaic organisation of the syntax remain characteristically Horatian. Stanzas 7-8 sum up and contrast H.'s own modest procedure. Stanzas 9-13 introduce the major theme: 'You, Jullus, will write a better victory hymn than I can; I shall be content to take no official part.' The contrasting roles of Jullus and H. will be symbolised by their respective sacrifices (Stanzas 14-15) — Jullus', a grand affair, as befits his official role; H.'s in keeping with his humble, private status.

Metre: Sapphics; see. 1. 2M.

1-4] As in his disclaimer to Agrippa (1. 6), H. is somewhat disingenuous: he has attempted the grand, public manner of Pindar a number of times (1. 2, 1. 12, the Roman Odes) and will again in this book (4. 4), to say nothing of the *Carmen Saeculare*, though always confining himself to the simpler metres of Sappho and Alcaeus and avoiding the more complex metrical structures of Pindar's choral odes. — **Iulle**] Jullus Antonius (cf. 26 *Antoni*), consul 10 BC, second son (by Fulvia) of Mark Antony, brought up in Rome by Octavia (Augustus' sister, who succeeded Fulvia as Antony's wife in 40 BC), married 21 BC to Marcella (Octavia's daughter by her previous husband) and brother-in-law, therefore, to Augustus' favourite nephew (the Marcellus of 1. 12. 45-6), educated by the famous *grammaticus* Crassicius; praetor 13 BC; became a close personal adviser of Augustus; executed 2 BC for adultery with Augustus' daughter Julia; for his *Diomedea*, see Introduction. — **ceratis pinnis**] 'on wings fixed with wax'. — **ope Daedalea**] With *ceratis*, 'with his Daedalean apparatus'; cf. 1. 6. 15; the would-be Pindar is destined, like Icarus, to soar too high for his borrowed apparatus, and will crash into the sea; presumably Daedalus has to be equated with Pindar and the apparatus of wings and feathers with Pindar's complex metrical and syntactical structures (it takes a Pindar or a Daedalus to manipulate so complex a structure, lesser men and disciples are bound to fail); H., i.e., has a different interpretation of the story in mind from Ovid (*Met*. 8. 183-235), whose Icarus is foolhardy (he flies too high and the wax melts), not incompetent; cf. 2. 20. 13. — **vitreo**] See on 3. 13. 1. — **daturus nomina**] For the *mare Icarium*, see 1. 1. 15.

5-8] Having proclaimed that to rival Pindar is to court disaster, H. offers his own modest pastiche. — **monte ... amnis**] Pindar is like a mountain torrent in flood; cf. Quint. 10. 1. 61 'Novem vero lyricorum longe Pindarus princeps ... beatissima rerum verborumque copia et velut quodam eloquentiae flumine'. — **imbres**] = 'heavy continuous rain'; see on 2. 9. 1. — **fervet**] Denotes the swirl of water, air or flame; by extension, rapid, confused movement; cf. 1. 13. 4; for the adjective *fervidus*, see on 1. 9. 10, 4. 13. 26, etc.; cf. *aestus* (1. 17. 18) and *aestuosus* (1. 22. 5, 2. 7. 16). — **inmensusque ruit**] The forward thrust of Pindar's style suggests incalculable energy. — **profundo ore**] Both instrumental with *ruit* and descriptive with *Pindarus*; *profundo* revives the metaphor of the river (Pindar's style suggests, as we might say, the deep-throated roar of a river in flood) while depending also on the easily-evoked notion (for a Roman) that the roar of the river is the roar of the river god himself.

9-16] The sentence continues for four more stanzas — one of the longest in H.; the sense flows on, wave after wave, in a series of appositional expansions, the waves of sense coinciding with the stanzas — with a distinct pause at the end of each stanza; only at the end of Stanza 3 does 10 *seu* create an expectation of more to follow; contrast H.'s own more syntactically sophisticated practice in, e.g., 1. 37. 5-32, 3. 29. 33-41, 4. 4. 1-28. — **laurea**] See on 3. 30. 15-16; the forms *laurus* and *laurea* are interchangeable in this sense; for the adjective see on 1. 3. 36. — **donandus**] 'deserving'; cf. 20 *donat*. — **nova verba**] Fresh coinages; for H.'s views on neologism, see *AP* 49-72. — **devolvit**] Continues the image of the river. — **numerisque ... solutis**] 'is borne along on numbers which are subject to no law'; H. has in mind the dithyramb, the most animated and spontaneous of the lyric forms (Pindar's dithyrambs have not survived). — **seu deos ... canit**] H. now refers to Pindar's hymns (also lost); the kings are not those of Pindar's day, but the demi-god kings of mythology. — **Centauri**] Slain by Pirithous. — **Chimaerae**] Slain by Bellerophon.

17-24] **Elea palma**] Victory at the Olympian games is taken as representative of Pindar's epinicean poetry (the only body of his verse to survive, apart from fragments), celebrating victory at the Olympian, Pythian, Nemean and Isthmian games, at Olympia in Elis, at Delphi, at Nemea in Argos and at Corinth respectively. — **caelestis**] Cf. 1. 1. 5. —

pugilemve equomve] 'whether boxer or horse'; boxing and horse-racing are (like the selection of Elis) taken as representative (Pindar also celebrated victory in chariot-race, wrestling and running contests, etc.); cf. 4. 3. 4-5, (in a different context) 1. 12. 26; the double *-ve* (on the model of *et . . . et*) and the appositional expansion are intended to suggest the Pindaric manner. — **dicit**] 'celebrates'; see on 1. 6. 5. — **centum . . . munere**] 'a gift worth more than a hundred statues' (i.e., a victory ode). — **flebili . . . plorat**] 'or laments the hero snatched away from his weeping bride'; Pindar's dirges are meant; for the form, see *OCD*; **iuvenemve**] the delayed *-ve* (equivalent to a further *sive*) is an artificial mannerism of the high style. — **viris . . . aureos**] = 'and the virtues of the deceased (*viris* is accusative plural of *vis*), his courage and his exemplary character'; **aureos**] for 'golden' = 'best of all' cf. 2. 10. 5, 4. 3. 17. — **educit . . . Orco**] For the immortality conferred by poetry cf. 4. 9. 25-8; for Orcus, see on 1. 28. 10.

25-32]   For the comparison of Pindar with himself, the image of the torrent is abandoned in favour of that of the swan and the bee; cf. H.'s own predicted metamorphosis 2. 20. 9-12. — **Multa aura**] The mass of air swept by the swan's wings at take-off — a dramatic spectacle. — **Dircaeum**] After Dirce, a fountain in Thebes. — **Antoni**] The second vocative and the change from *praenomen* to *nomen* suggest a second beginning and a key modulation (to a more serious tone, perhaps, after the *tour de force* of lines 5-24). — **tractus**] 'regions'. — **Matinae**] See on 1. 28. 3. — **more modoque**] Alliterative hendiadys. — **grata thyma**] = 'the thyme it seeks so eagerly'. — **carpentis**] See on 1. 11. 8; the word used for picking flowers (3. 27. 44), of cattle grazing, etc.; H. uses the word ten times in all. — **laborem**] Always *hard* work, effort (see on 1. 7. 18). — **circa . . . Tiburis ripas**] See on 1. 7. 13. — **operosa**] Cf. Petronius' famous 'curiosa felicitas'. — **parvos**] 'a small creature'. — **fingo**] 'shape', 'work at'; regularly of poetic creation (*OLD* 6 a).

33-44]   Stanza 9 introduces the major theme: when Augustus returns from Germany, the appropriate person to celebrate his achievement in a formal victory ode is Antonius — no one can hope to do as well as Pindar, but Jullus will make a better job of it than H.; cf. 1. 6 — poetry treating martial themes adequately is impossible, but Varius is the man for Agrippa. — **Concines . . . Caesarem**] = 'It is you, who are a greater lyric poet than I, who should perform the poem in honour of Caesar'; **concines**] the compound usually implies a song sung to an accompaniment or in unison; here, however, the sense seems to be 'compose and perform', 'perform in its totality' (cf. *conscribere, componere, condere*); **maiore plectro**] better taken as descriptive with *poeta* than instrumental with *concines; plectro* (the quill used to strike the lyre) implies some kind of lyric poem (written for public performance) — not, i.e., an epic; cf. 2. 1. 40. — **quandoque trahet . . . Sygambros**] = 'when the time comes for him to lead the savage Sygambri down the Via Sacra in his triumph with the hard-earned garland of laurel leaves on his head'; cf. 4. 14. 51-2; for *quandoque* (= *quandocumque*, 'when eventually') cf. 4. 1. 17. — **quo . . . dabunt**] To describe victory over a German tribe as the greatest benefaction of mankind by the gods of all time is perhaps the lamest concession to propaganda in the *Odes*; it rather seems from 4. 14. 52 that Augustus eventually agreed to terms with the Sygambri — probably, therefore, no triumph was in fact awarded; **bonique divi**] cf. 4. 5. 1. — **quamvis . . . priscum**] = 'even if the golden age of old were to return'; **tempora**] for the plural, see on 3. 30. 5. — **concines . . . ludum**] The anaphora in asyndeton and the 'poetic' *-que . . . et* (= *et . . . et*) are an attempt to give appropriate rhetorical shape to pedestrian sense; **urbis publicum ludum**] = 'a city rejoicing'; most probably, games specially proclaimed for the occasion. — **super inpetrato reditu**] 'at the return which we had prayed for'; there are coins of 16 BC with the inscription V • S • PRO • S • ET • RED • AVG • ('vota suscepta pro salute et reditu Augusti'). — **forum . . . orbum**] On a public holiday the normal business of the courts is suspended.

45-8]   H.'s role on the day of Augustus' triumph will be that of loyal private citizen; cf. 3. 14. 13-28. — **si . . . audiendum**] = 'if I say anything at all worth paying attention to'; for *loquar* cf. 3. 25. 18. — **vocis . . . pars**] = 'there will be added (to your hymn of praise) my hearty cry'; *bona pars* implies the ringing tones of a loyal subject. — **'o sol pulcer'**] = 'o happy day'. — **'o laudande'**] i.e., Caesar. — **canam**] Emphasises the formal, ritual character of H.'s cries; cf. Ovid *Am.* 1. 2. 34, quoted on line 50.

49-52]   **Teque**] The god of triumph is addressed as in *Epodes* 9. 21 — a formula probably based on the last line of the ancient hymn of the Arval brotherhood, where the repeated 'Triumpe!' is an imperative ('jump!'); cf. Varro *Ling. Lat.* 6. 68 'Cum imperatore milites redeuntes clamitant per urbem in Capitolium eunti: Io Triumphe!', Tibullus 2. 5. 118

'Miles "Io" magna voce "Triumphe" canet'; many find the emphatic opening *te* of
Stanzas 13 and 14 directed to different addressees intolerable, especially after the ana-
phora of 33 and 41 *concines*; a common repair is *terque*, but *ter* followed by *non semel*
is clumsy and *dum procedis* addressed to Augustus (instead of to Triumphus, as in *Epodes*
9. 21) hardly an improvement. — **dum procedis**] Triumph is imagined as personally leading
the procession. — **dicemus . . . civitas omnis**] Subject is separated from verbs by a second
cry, as if to reproduce the shout and answering shout of the crowd; for the crowd taking
up the cry, originally addressed to the general by his soldiers (see Varro, quoted above)
cf. Ovid *Am*. 1. 2. 34 'Volgus "Io" magna voce "Triumphe" canet'.

53-6] After the triumphal procession will come the time for sacrifices in discharge of *vota*
undertaken for Augustus' safe return. Antonius, as a rich man (and, no doubt, in his
capacity as praetor, perhaps also as the poet designated to perform the hymn of welcome),
will make a grand sacrifice; H., a poor man and a *privatus*, will make a humbler offering.
— **decem . . . vaccae**] For the animals offered in sacrifice, see on 3. 23. 1-8; for the
contrast cf. 2. 17. 30-32. — **tener**] 'young' (see on 1. 1. 26); cf. 3. 18. 5. — **vitulus**] Cf.
1. 36. 2. — **largis . . . herbis**] = 'is growing fast on the abundant grass'; the natural assump-
tion is that the calf is being fattened on H.'s Sabine estate; cf. the kid of 3. 13. 3-5; cf.
Epist. 1. 3. 36 'pascitur in vestrum reditum votiva iuvenca'; **iuvenescit**] almost a play
upon words: the *vitulus* is becoming an *iuvencus*. — **relicta matre qui**] The relative
pronoun falls to the second position in order to emphasise *relicta matre*; for the idea cf.
1. 23. 14. — **in mea vota**] With *iuvenescit*, 'to discharge the *vota* I have made'.

57-60] A further appositional expansion of 54 *vitulus*. For the flowering-out of a con-
cluding image cf. 2. 5. 21-4 and 3. 5. 50-56, the effect in each case being to secure a
slackening of tension at the conclusion; as often, Greek models can be pointed to (*Il*. 23.
454-5, Moschus 2. 84), and, as usual, H.'s reformulation is more detailed, more allusive;
cf. Ovid *Ars* 1. 290-92, where the image is expressed with characteristic Ovidian wit,
'taurus erat / signatus tenui media inter cornua nigro; / una fuit labes, cetera lactis erant'.
— **fronte . . . ignis**] = 'bearing on its forehead what looks like a blazing crescent . . . '; the
plural *ignis* suggests (as often) a complex unity. — **tertium . . . ortum**] The new moon at
its third rising. — **qua notam duxit**] 'where it took the imprint'. — **niveus videri**] 'like
snow to look at'; one of H.'s daringly compact combinations of adjective + infinitive.
— **cetera fulvos**] Accusative of respect; see on 1. 1. 22; cf. *Epist*. 1. 10. 50 'cetera laetus',
Aen. 3. 594 'cetera Graius' and see Austin on *Aen*. 4. 558, *OLD* on *ceterus* 4.

4. 3

Introduction: After 4. 2, in which H. disclaims the role of official laureate, comes an ode
in which he states with calm confidence that Rome has accepted him as its leading lyric
poet. Cf. 1. 1, 3. 4, 3. 30.
Structure: Stanzas 1-3, the chosen poet can follow no other career. Stanza 4, Rome now
accepts me as a poet. Stanzas 5-6, H. thanks the Muse for her gift.
Metre: Asclepiad (b); see 1. 3M.
1-6] H. takes up the theme of 1. 1, but the tone is very different. What was spoken of
there with appropriate modesty, as an obsession to be forgiven like other men's obsessions,
is now spoken of in the language traditionally applied to inspiration: the poet is chosen
at birth by the Muse, no other career is open to him; cf. 3. 4. 9-20. — **Melpomene**] Cf.
3. 30. 16; for the Muses in H., see on 1. 12. 2. — **semel**] With *placido lumine videris*:
'once and for all'; cf. 4. 7. 21. — **placido lumine**] 'with favourable eye'; contrast *Epist*.
1. 14. 37 'obliquo oculo'. — **illum . . . pugilem**] = 'he will never win the boxing contest
at the Isthmian games' — because he is destined to be a poet; H., as usual, names a
particular event and a particular set of games; **labor Isthmius**] see on 1. 3. 36; **pugilem**]
cf. 4. 2. 18. — **non equos . . . victorem**] For the charioteer cf. 1. 1. 4-6 (in 4. 2. 17-18 the
reference is to the horse-race); **Achaico**] = *Graeco* (as opposed to the Roman chariot in
which the victorious general rides in triumph).
6-9] In 1. 1 H. had not dared, perhaps, to include the victorious general among his harm-
less eccentrics (the reference to military life in 1. 1. 23-5 is tactfully framed); here he
speaks more boldly. — **res bellica**] 'a military exploit'; the phrase has an odd ring; the
plural is commoner, though it tends to be confined to the dative ('rebus bellicis praefectus',
etc.) and ablative ('de rebus bellicis'); the singular is perhaps a Horatian coinage and is

possibly pejorative. — **Deliis . . . foliis**] = 'adorned with Apollo's crown of bay leaves'. — **regum . . . minas**] i.e., taught some upstart of an Eastern tyrant a lesson; *regum* is best taken as a generalising plural; again the phrase is not framed to suggest an outstanding victory; with *minas* cf. 4. 8. 16 and 2. 12. 12. — **ostendet Capitolio**] The triumphal procession started there; for the Capitol as symbol of Roman power, see on 1. 37. 6.

10-12]   In opposition to the heroes of the games and the military life, H. sets up his own way of life, stressing not (as often) the simple, humble routine of the Sabine farm, but the idyllic surroundings of Tibur; see on 1. 7. 13. — **praefluunt**] = *praeterfluunt*. — **spissae . . . comae**] = 'and the thick foliage of the trees which enclose the glades'; cf. for the idea 1. 21. 5; for *comae* cf. 4. 7. 2; for *spissa coma* in the literal sense cf. 3. 19. 25; for the *nemus* as a poetic haunt, see on 1. 1. 30 (here evocative, perhaps, of the lyric mode, whereas the Sabine farm suggests the philosophical H.). — **Aeolio carmine**] See on 3. 30. 13; the phrase makes clear that, though Stanzas 1-3 are put in general terms, H. means himself. — **nobilem**] = 'a hero'; cf. 1. 1. 5.

13-16]   To be a born poet is one thing, to be accepted as such by one's contemporaries is another. We can imagine that poetry so novel, so ambitious and so difficult as the *Odes* was not at once accepted; the jealousies to which H. fell victim were, to begin with, the consequence of the support received, while still an unknown poet, from Maecenas; see *Sat.* 1. 6, 2. 6. 47-58. With success came animosities of a different kind, those of the literary establishment: see *Epist.* 1. 19. 39-49. A few years before the publication of *Odes* 4 he had made up his mind to give up writing: see *Epist.* 2. 2. 49-66 (about 20 BC). We may suppose that H.'s selection to write the *Carmen Saeculare* did much to restore his confidence. Following the death of Virgil (19 BC), he becomes Rome's leading poet (Propertius his only possible rival); his open letter to Augustus in defence of poetry (*Epist.* 2. 1, about the time of publication of *Odes* 4) shows the confidence which came with general acceptance. — **suboles**] The word seems chosen to suggest the new generation — the 'virgines puericue' to whom H. addresses the Roman Odes; Ovid, e.g. (born 43 BC), belonged to this generation (for his memories of H., see *Tristia* 4. 10. 49-50). — **amabilis . . . choros**] = 'the ranks of the poets whom they love'; for *amabilis*, 'lovable', cf. 1. 5. 10; *choros* suggests the poets of the lyric canon whom H. aspires to join in 1. 1. 35 (cf. Cicero *Fin.* 1. 26 'Epicurum e philosophorum choro sustulisti'; *OLD* 5), while evoking the traditional connection of the lyric poet with song and dance. — **dente**] For the tooth of envy cf. *Sat.* 2. 1. 75-8.

17-24]   Stanzas 5-6 weld together the themes of Stanzas 1-3 and 4: H. acknowledges his indebtedness to the Muse, not only for inspiration, but also for his success with the public. — **testudinis . . . temperas**] For the sense cf. 3. 11. 1-6; the tortoise-shell sounding-board stands, by the figure known as synecdoche, for the lyre, in its turn the symbol of lyric poetry; see on 1. 12. 1; **aureae**] for 'golden' = 'best of all', 'supreme' cf. 2. 10. 5, 4. 2. 23; **Pieri**] = Muse, from Mt Pierus in Thessaly. — **donatura**] = 'you who would give'; cf. 2. 6. 1. — **cycni**] Symbolises the most songful of birds; cf. 4. 2. 25. — **totum . . . tui est . . .**] = 'it is wholly within your power to grant . . . '; cf. 1. 26. 9-10. — **Romanae fidicen lyrae**] = 'as Rome's lyric poet'; Quintilian was to confirm the claim a century later (10. 1. 96 'lyricorum Horatius fere solus legi dignus'). — **quod spiro et placeo**] Sums up Stanzas 1-3 and 4: 'in so far as I am inspired and have success'; with *spiro* cf. 4. 6. 29 *spiritum*.

4. 4

Introduction: A formal laureate ode celebrating the victory in 15 BC of Augustus' stepson Drusus over the Raeti and Vindelici (Alpine tribes occupying an area corresponding roughly to the modern Tyrol and extending also into Switzerland). Drusus, who was 23 at the time, shared the command with his elder brother Tiberius (the future Emperor), whose exploits are commemorated separately in 4. 14.

Structure: Lines 1-18, the double simile of the eagle and the lion. This is followed by a more relaxed, discursive passage (lines 18-28) in which appropriate credit is paid to the Emperor for the training and fatherly guidance given his stepsons. This leads to further reflections on the equal importance of heredity (Stanza 8) and proper upbringing (Stanza 9). The remainder of the ode is devoted to a panegyric of the Claudii Nerones, the major part of which (lines 50-72) is put on the lips of the defeated Hannibal.

Metre: Alcaics; see 1. 9M. The first of four Alcaic odes in this book (also 4. 9, 4. 14, 4. 15).

1-12] The sustained simile sets the ode on an appropriate stylistic and rhetorical course. —
Qualem . . . alitem] H. does not trouble to distinguish between the particular eagle of his
simile and the archetypal eagle of Jove (in careful prose we should say 'like *an* eagle, the
bird to which Jove . . . '); similarly, the *testudo* of 3. 11 is both the archetypal *testudo* of
Mercury and the lyre in general; the 'winged plyer of the thunderbolt' of Jove provides a
suitably grand analogue for Drusus as the intrepid warrior harrying the enemies of
Augustus (the eagle of Jove is sometimes represented in art as grasping the thunderbolt in
its talons); for *minister*, 'he who attends upon and supplies with . . .', see *OLD* 1 b; for the
idea cf. *Aen.* 5. 255 and 9. 563 'Iovis armiger' (of the eagle — in the latter passage, in a
comparable simile). — **cui . . . permisit**] Cf. 3. 1. 5-6. — **expertus . . . flavo**] The reference
to Ganymede (snatched away to be his cup-bearer; cf. 3. 20. 16) and the assertion that
the eagle was rewarded by being made king of the birds represent H.'s whimsical expansion
of his simile. — **olim**] 'once' (i.e., when the eagle was first fully fledged; opposed to 9 *mox*.
— **iuventas**] See on 2. 11. 6 and 1. 2. 41. — **patrius vigor**] = 'the strength inherited from
his father'; that part of the simile which applies more particularly to Drusus now begins. —
laborum inscium] 'with no knowledge of the hardships ahead'; cf. 45 *laboribus* and see
on 1. 3. 36. — **(vernique . . . paventem)**] A further imaginative expansion; the 'winds of
spring' and the 'cloudless sky' suggest an idyllic picture of an unusually favoured eagle;
insolitos nisus] the young eagle's first attempts at flight; **paventem**] a nice touch: the
young bird is as yet frightened by its own new-found power of flight. — **mox**] 'before
long'. — **in ovilia . . . vividus impetus**] It is in the eagle's intrepid nature to attack; the
sheep gathered in their folds suggest the Vindelici gathered (equally defenceless against
Drusus) in their mountain strongholds; for the conqueror as (as it seems to us) a merciless
assailant cf. 1. 37. 17-18. — **nunc**] = now that the eagle is fully grown. — **in reluctantis
dracones**] Suggests worthier opponents and the hand-to-hand combat of leader against
leader of heroic warfare; **reluctantis**] 'fighting back'.

13-16] A second simile: the lion cub about to make his first kill symbolises the young
Drusus leading his troops into battle for his first victory. Cf. the young Roman subaltern
in 3. 2. 10-12; in both cases the lion-like hero is seen through the eyes of a frightened
enemy. — **laetis pascuis intenta**] 'intent on rich pastures'; the goat is taken by surprise (cf.
Europa, 3. 27. 29-30). — **fulvae . . . depulsum**] i.e., freshly weaned and sent out by his
mother to fend for himself — as Livia (Drusus' mother and the wife of Augustus) had sent
Drusus off to the wars; the detailed, sympathetic picture of the lioness is no doubt inten-
ded as a compliment to Livia, and also a hint (building on 5 *patrius vigor*) of the course
the ode will take at Stanza 10; **ab ubere lacte**] *ubere* is adjectival.

17-28] The climax of the double simile is followed by a brief statement of the relevant facts
(Stanzas 5-6) which leads into the major theme — the victory of Drusus interpreted as a
triumph of heredity + right upbringing. — **videre**] i.e., *talem videre* (sc. Vindelici). —
Raetis . . . Vindelici] Actually two peoples: the Vindelici were, it seems, defeated by
Tiberius, the Raeti by Drusus; H. gives Tiberius (who was four years older and had
already served under Augustus in the East) an ode to himself (4. 14), in order to concen-
trate here on the hero victorious in his first battle; *Raeti* (*OCT*), though better supported
by the MSS, is less likely than *Raetis* (Heinze, Klingner). — **Quibus . . . omnia**] Pindaric
pastiche rather than misplaced pedantry; presumably the Vindelici carried battleaxes and
either claimed descent from the Amazons or, more likely, had such descent ascribed to
them by an obliging Greek historian or antiquarian. — **diu . . . catervae**] = 'those squadrons
which had long enjoyed victory over a wide area'. — **consiliis . . . revictae**] = 'conquered
in their turn by a youthful strategist'; for *iuvenis*, see on 1. 2. 41; Drusus, at 23, was, by
any standards, a young man; *iuvenis*, however, casts him in the role of able-bodied hero
leading his men (the typical Republican army commander was a pro-consul in his mid-
forties — already a *senex*) more than it stresses his tender years. — **sensere**] 'realised', i.e.,
learnt to their cost. — **quid mens . . . posset**] = 'what intelligence and character can do
when properly nurtured by a sheltered and propitious environment'; Drusus, born just
before Livia's remarriage to Octavian, had been brought up as a member of what was to
become the Imperial household. — **quid Augusti . . . Nerones**] = 'what Augustus'
fatherly influence can do for boys who are of Neronian stock'; Stanza 7 shows the
tactful course the laureate must sometimes steer: H. has planned his ode as a compliment
to Livia and her younger son (concentrating on him, perhaps, because he had been wholly
brought up by Augustus); but Augustus must get as full a share as possible of the credit,
nor can Tiberius be wholly passed over; **Nerones**] the word is prominently placed, to

prepare the way for the panegyric of the Claudii Nerones in Stanzas 10-19; Drusus' father was Tib. Claudius Nero; Livia belonged to a different branch of the same family (see on 73 'Claudiae manus').

29-36]   Stanzas 8-9 elaborate the theme of lines 25-8, the equal importance of heredity and upbringing. — fortibus et bonis] The instrumental ablative without *ab* puts the aphorism in general form: 'strong begets strong when the stock is good'; according to Suetonius *Tib.* 2, the name Nero means 'fortis ac strenuus' in the Sabine language. — aquilae] Allusion to the eagle of Stanzas 1-3 is probable. — doctrina] 'training', 'education'. — rectique . . . roborant] 'right habits produce strength of character'; for *cultus*, see on 1. 8. 15-16 'virilis cultus'; for *pectora*, see on 1. 3. 10; roborant] the verb is less common than the noun *robur* (1. 3. 9) and the adjective *robustus* (3. 2. 2, etc). — utcumque . . . culpae] The theme of 3. 6.17 ff.; reference to Augustus' campaign for moral reform may be assumed; *utcumque* is frequentative (cf. 1. 17. 10); indecorant] the form is rare (elsewhere only in a fragment of Accius); H. perhaps intended it as a forceful archaism in preference to *dedecorant* (found in some MSS); bene nata] no need to take with *pectora*.

37-49]   The ground is now laid for the myth which will form the centrepiece of the ode (cf. the myth of the Giants in 3. 4, the myth of Regulus in 3. 5, etc.; see 1. 15I). The myth begins with an encomium of Drusus' ancestor, C. Claudius Nero, who in 207 BC marched the length of Italy with his army to join his fellow-consul M. Livius Salinator in defeating Hasdrubal at the battle of the river Metaurus (the traditional turning point of the Second Punic War). — Neronibus] Picks up 28 *Nerones*. — testis . . . Hasdrubal] sc., *sit* or *erit*; for the formula, see Quinn on Catullus 64. 357. — Hasdrubal devictus] 'the rout of Hasdrubal'. — Latio] Dative of advantage with *pulcer*. — adorea] An archaism, characteristic of the high style. — dirus Afer ut . . .] 'ever since the dread African (Hannibal) . . . '; *ut*, with *primus risit*, = *ex quo*, as in *Epodes* 7. 17-20 'fata Romanos agunt . . . ut . . . fluxit in terram Remi . . . cruor'; cf. Cicero *Brutus* 19, *Att.* 1. 15. 2. — ceu flamma per taedas] 'like a flame through the pine forest'; *taeda*, the pitch-pine, from which torches were made. — Eurus equitavit] The SE gale roaring across the sea is personified as a horseman riding at full gallop; the subject of *equitavit* is of course 42 *Afer*. — secundis . . . laboribus] = 'successful struggle following successful struggle'. — pubes] Cf. 1. 25. 17, 2. 8. 17, 3. 5. 18. — inpio . . . rectos] The picture of the younger generation successful in war and restoring (while the war still raged) the temples ravaged by the enemy sounds like grafting current propaganda (cf. 3. 6) on to past history. — perfidus Hannibal] H. focuses on the moment (3-4 years later) when Hannibal is forced to admit defeat and withdraw from Italy (passing over in silence the grim legend that Hasdrubal's severed head was tossed into Hannibal's camp by the victorious Romans); *perfidus* is the Roman stock epithet for the Cathaginians in general and Hannibal in particular; cf. 3. 5. 33 and Livy 21. 4. 9 (of Hannibal) 'perfidia plus quam Punica'.

50-52]   For the set speech at the climax of a myth cf. 3. 3. 18-68, 3. 5. 21-40. — sectamur ultro] 'we actually keep pursuing'. — quos opimus est triumphus] Victory for the Carthaginians is out of the question; to get away with their lives counts as a signal triumph; if they were to engage the Romans in battle, it would be like deer attempting to fight wolves; in fact, after the defeat of Metaurus, Hannibal withdrew to Bruttium and held on, like a lion at bay, till ordered home; earlier Roman disasters (particularly Cannae) are conveniently ignored; triumphus] H., like Livy, attributes characteristically Roman institutions, etc. to foreigners.

53-68]   The tribute to Roman greatness is put on Hannibal's lips for rhetorical effect — the conventions of H.'s form do not require a historically plausible Hannibal. — gens . . . ad urbis] A neat summary of the theme of *Aen.* 2-3 (published about five years before *Odes* 4, and consecrating the myth of the Trojan origin of the Romans); cremato . . . Ilio] with *pertulit*, but the position of *fortis* suggests the sense 'undaunted by the burning of Troy'; iactata] cf. *Aen.* 1. 3 (of Aeneas) 'multum ille et terris iactatus et alto'; here *iactata* probably with *sacra* (cf. *Aen.* 6. 68 'errantisque deos agitataque numina Troiae'); Tuscis aequoribus] the sea off the west coast of Italy; sacra . . . patres] cf. *Aen.* 3. 12 'cum sociis natoque penatibus et magnis dis'; Aeneas himself is the best-known of those who brought sons and aged fathers with them. — duris . . . Algido] First image of triumphant victory over what would destroy others: the holm-oak, though brutally pruned, grows stronger than ever; nigrae frondis] refers of course to the dark green foliage of the holm-oak, but depends on *feraci*, 'productive of', 'which produces in

abundance'; Algidus is a mountain in Latium (also 1. 21. 6, 3. 23. 9). – **per damna . . .
ferro**] The subject is *gens*, but *ferro* (which can be applied equally to the sword, etc. of
the battlefield and the woodman's axe) binds simile and main subject closely together;
ducit opes animumque] 'gathers strength and courage'. – **non hydra . . . Thebae**] A
second and third image making the same point: the hydra was a many-headed water-snake
whose heads grew again as fast as Herclules cut them off; at Colchis, Jason was confronted
with two fire-breathing bulls and a dragon from whose teeth, when planted in the ground,
armed warriors sprang up; Cadmus had to contend with a similar dragon before he could
found Thebes; H. makes Hannibal admit he is no Hercules, no Jason and no Cadmus;
vinci dolentem] = 'angry at being defeated'; **submisere**] 'confronted (Jason) with';
Colchi] nominative plural; **Echioniaeve Thebae**] sc. *submisere*; Echion was one of those
killed by Cadmus. – **merses profundo**] = 'plunge in the sea' (a traditional way of
disposing of an unwanted enemy); the *gens Romana* is treated as though it were a single
creature you could take in your hands; with *profundo* cf. *Aen.* 12. 263 'profundo vela
dabit'. – **pulcrior**] Unlike any normal corpse. – **luctere**] 'wrestle with it'. – **proruet**]
'will throw down'. – **integrum victorem**] i.e., an opponent fresh from victory over others.
– **coniugibus loquenda**] 'for their wives to talk about'; i.e., boast about, instead of
lamenting the loss of sons and husbands; contrast 1. 1. 24-5 'bella matribus detestata'.

69-72] Hannibal is made to sum up on a note of despair. – **Carthagini**] Dative, *nuntios
mittere* being equivalent to 'report'; similarly, *litteras mittere* can take the dative (as well
as *ad* + accusative). – **Hasdrubale interempto**] i.e., 'there was no hope for us once
Hannibal was dead'.

73-6] Editors are divided on whether to give the last stanza to Hannibal, or to have H.
resume his encomium of Drusus; the former interpretation, though hotly defended by
Page, involves capping the simple dignity of Stanza 18 (Hannibal *could* feel his brother's
death spelled the end of hope) with a wholly implausible prophecy. The myth of
Hannibal illustrates Rome's debt to the Nerones (line 37): the final stanza brings us back
to that theme; a prophecy from H. holding out hopes for the future achievements of
Drusus and Tiberius is clearly what is needed. – **Claudiae . . . manus**] i.e., the hands in
battle of the Claudii Nerones. – **curae sagaces**] 'wise concern', sc., 'Iovis'. – **expediunt**]
'give quick and easy passage'. – **per acuta belli**] = 'the emergencies of war'; for the phrase
cf. 2. 1. 23 'cuncta terrarum'.

4. 5

Introduction: An affectionate appeal (warm, yet respectful) to Augustus not to delay longer
his return to Italy: the country misses its benefactor.

Clearly, H. preferred the informal, personal stance to the grander rhetoric of laureate
panegyric. It enables him to play his favourite role, that of the small landed proprietor
attuned to the simple, pious routine of Italian rural life. He speaks to Augustus, one is
tempted to say, with the same ease as to his patron Maecenas: the tone is more serious,
however (there is no trace of the irony which his more genuine intimacy with
Maecenas permitted).

The occasion is that of 4. 2 – Augustus' imminent return from Gaul; he had been
absent on active service for about three years, and that absence had been preceded by
similar absences; of the first two decades of his reign the greater part had been spent
outside Italy. Cf. 3.14.

Structure: The stanzas are endstopped throughout. The first six stanzas are grouped in pairs.
Stanzas 1-2 plead for Augustus' return. Stanzas 3-4 introduce the simile of the mother
who anxiously awaits the return of her son. Stanzas 5-6 build up (in a remarkable
sequence of eight one-line statements) a picture of Italy at peace and restored to moral
decency and the rule of law. Stanza 7 lists the threats to Rome removed by Augustus'
long absences. Stanzas 8-10 build up a picture of a countryside at peace and devoted to
its ruler.

Metre: Asclepiad (c); see 1. 6M.

1-8] The formulae recall those used, according to Ennius (quoted Cicero *de Repub*. 1. 41.
61), of the dead Romulus:

O Romule, Romule die,
qualem te patriae custodem di genuerunt!
O pater, o genitor, o sanguen dis oriundum!

H., by picking up Ennius' lines, gives his poem at the outset the note of simple, traditional piety which will pervade it. — **Divis orte bonis**] As the adopted son of Julius Caesar, Augustus was the descendant of Venus and therefore related to the Olympian hierarchy; in consequence of the officially proclaimed apotheosis of Julius, he was also *divi filius* (and so styled himself on coins as early as 42 BC); with *divis bonis* cf. 4. 2. 38 'boni divi'. — **Romulae custos gentis**] Cf. Catullus 34. 22-4 (to Diana) 'Romuli . . . bona sospites ope gentem'. — **abes iam nimium diu**] The simple directness of these four words is to be the keynote of the poem. — **patrum . . . concilio**] The Senate. — **redi**] By echoing *reditum*, the simple word takes on an urgent tone. — **lucem**] 'the light of day'; (1) as the symbol of life (as opposed to death); cf. Cicero *de Dom.* 75 'me patria sic accepit ut lucem salutemque redditam sibi . . . accipere debuit'; (2) 'light' as the radiance of the *praesens divus* (the sense picked up in the lines following). — **Instar**] Uncommon and a mark of the high style; see Austin on *Aen.* 2. 15; *instar veris* is a daring appositional anticipation of *voltus tuus*, justified by the lyric, almost pastoral, conceptual framework within which the poem moves. — **ubi**] Frequentative, 'whenever' (i.e., each time Augustus returns from abroad). — **adfulsit**] see on 5 *lucem*. — **soles melius nitent**] Effusive, but expressive of the simple countryman's piety which infuses the ode; for the plural, 'the sun each day', cf. Catullus 5. 4 and 8. 8, *Eclogues* 9. 52; similarly, *lunae*, 2. 18. 16, 4. 7. 13.

9-16   The mother anxious for her son's return is undisguised emotional incitement. — **iuvenem**] See on 1. 2. 41; Augustus is about 50. — **quem . . . cunctantem**] the *mare Carpathium* is the Mediterranean east of Crete; the image is, as usual, particularised; a Roman in the position of Catullus, say, returning to Italy after his tour of duty in Bithynia (see Catullus 46) and hoping to sail due south through the Aegean, would not be able to put to sea in a strong southerly; see on 3. 7. 5-8; **invido flatu**] 'with its unwelcome (lit. 'envious') blast'. — **spatio . . . annuo**] With *cunctantem*; the normal tour of duty for a young man who had taken a position on the *cohors* of a provincial governor (a typical case, and very possibly the one H. has in mind) was from one spring to the next; the common view that the son will have to spend the winter abroad is based on a mistaken interpretation of 3. 7; nor does it fit the present case — the son, like Augustus, is overdue but is still expected any day (line 14); in the ancient world, there was no way in which news of delay could precede the traveller — if one ship was held up by unfavourable winds, all were held up. — **votis . . . vocat**] The mother, i.e. does everything she can to speed her son's return ('votis et precibus vocat'), and keeps trying to find omens that promise his speedy return (rather as Virgil makes Dido keep sacrificing to the gods to get the answer she wants, *Aen.* 6. 62-3). — **quaerit patria Caesarem**] One of H.'s more memorable phrases, disarming by its combination of simplicity and emotional intensity.

17-24]   The picture of an Italy transformed by two decades of Augustan rule is hard to resist (though we may ask whether H. really thought in such simplistic terms): the assertions follow one another (attempting no argument, anticipating no rebuttal) in the most sustained deployment of parataxis in the *Odes*. — **Tutus . . . perambulat**] The ox is safe (if we care to examine the assertion) from warfare or marauding bands; but the ox shambling through the countryside suggests a picture of pastoral felicity; cf. 3. 18. 11-12. — **nutrit . . . Faustitas**] Adds to the picture of idyllic rural prosperity; *Faustitas* (something like 'Felicity') seems to be a word coined by H. — **pacatum . . . navitae**] Again a phrase which can be defended at the level of literal truth (there is no longer war at sea, no danger from pirates — cf. Augustus' own statement, *Res Gestae* 25.1 'mare pacavi a praedonibus'), but it suggests a magical new dispensation in which the very seas are stilled; **navitae**] 'travellers by sea' (not necessarily sailors); see on 1. 1. 14 *nauta*. — **culpari metuit Fides**] Fides, i.e., is anxious to be seen as above reproach; for this divinity, see *Aen.* 1. 292. — **nullis . . . stupris**] Contrast 3. 6. 17-32; *stupris* suggests not so much adultery as the more heinous crimes alluded to by Catullus in his picture of a corrupt society, 64. 401-4. — **mos et lex . . . nefas**] Augustus' moral and religious reforms of 18-17 BC are alluded to; *mos* suggests that what had been enacted by law had become the moral standard of a reformed society; cf. 3. 24. 35-6; **edomuit**] the only clear perfect (20 *metuit* is ambiguous) in this string of presents. — **laudantur . . . puerperae**] i.e., the remark 'how like his father!' can now be made again with safety; cf. Catullus 61. 214-18 'Sit suo similis patri / Manlio et facile insciens / noscitetur ab obviis / et pudicitiam suae / matris vindicet ore'. — **culpam . . . comes**] Cf. 3. 2. 31-2.

25-8]   The modern reader finds the propaganda stereotypes of this stanza hard to take; it seems, moreover, to spoil the otherwise natural transition from Stanza 6 to Stanza 8. For the fears, now dispelled, of foreign wars, see 2. 11I. The anaphora in asyndeton of the quadruple *quis*? is structured as a tricolon crescendo (built around 25 *paveat*), spilling over into a fourth question (*quis curet?*), longer than the first two but shorter than the third. — **Quis Parthum . . . Scythen?**] i.e., as a result of Augustus' campaigns in the East in 22-19 BC; for the Parthians, see on 1. 2. 22, for the Scythae on 1. 19. 10. — **quis . . . fetus?**] Augustus has been in Gaul since 15 BC; his major concern there has been to protect the frontier from German incursion. — **quis ferae . . . Hiberiae?**] Augustus had been in Spain in 27-24 BC and again in 16 before going to Gaul.

29-36] H. reverts to the pastoral imagery of lines 17-20. He seems to have in mind the veterans of Augustus' campaigns — always conventionally represented as soldier-farmers who return to the land (or for whom land has to be found) when the fighting is over; it is a class with which he can sentimentally identify himself. His *quisque* blandly ignores the fact that the majority of Romans do not live (or even pretend, like himself, to live) the life of farmers. — **Condit . . . collibus in suis**] Cf. 3. 6. 41-4; with *condit diem* cf. *Eclogues* 9. 52 'condere soles'. — **vitem . . . arbores**] The process of 'marrying' the vines to the trees which support them is meant; see on 2. 15. 4, cf. *Epodes* 2. 9, White, *Roman Farming* 236. — **hinc . . . laetus**] The wine he drinks with his evening meal. — **alteris mensis**] At the second course, because drinking and libations did not begin till then. — **te adhibet deum**] Worship of the living Augustus as a god was officially frowned upon, though his apotheosis could be confidently predicted (see, e.g., 3. 3. 11-12); simple countryfolk can be represented as not making such fine distinctions; cf. Virgil's tenant farmer, *Eclogues* 1. 6-10; Dio 51. 19 records, however, that in 24 BC the Senate decreed that libations could be poured to Augustus in both private and public banquets; **adhibet**] 'invites your presence'. — **uti Graecia . . . Herculis**] So worshipped after their apotheosis; cf. 3. 3. 9-12.

37-40] H. identifies himself with the simple countryfolk of the previous stanza. — **Longas . . . ferias**] Compared with what it had been before Augustus, life has become one continuous holiday: long may it remain so! — the phrase attempts to reproduce the habit of thought of the farmer who sees the world in terms of a limited range of concepts; *dux bone* likewise expresses the simple devotion of the farmer to the leader of his country; for the title *dux*, see Syme, *Roman Revolution* 311. — **dicimus, dicimus**] The dexterity with which H. passes himself off as the spokesman of those who matter is not without audacity, however congenial the simplification to Augustus, which no doubt reflects the mood of the age to identify peace with the farmer's life (cf., e.g., Virgil's *Eclogues* and *Georgics*, Tibullus 1. 1, 1. 10, 2. 1; contrast Propertius and Ovid, whose sophistication may be more exceptional than we tend to think). — **sicci . . . uvidi**] The farmer's head is clear when his day's work lies ahead of him, at sunset he can relax, his day's work done; cf. 3. 6. 41-4.

4. 6

Introduction: A hymn to Apollo, asking for his support on the occasion of the performance of the *Carmen Saeculare* (17 BC), followed by a short address to the chorus. Cf. 1..21.

Structure: In 1. 21 (a much shorter poem), the hymn to Apollo and Diana follows the address to the chorus; here the hymn comes first. Stanzas 1-7 reproduce the typical hymn structure: opening vocative, praise of the god (flowering out for the description of Apollo's third and most distinguished victim, Achilles). The address to the chorus occupies Stanzas 8-10; in a final stanza (Stanza 11) H. addresses himself to one member of the chorus. Stanzas 1-7 form a single complex sentence. Stanzas 8-11 begin and conclude with relatively short sentences framing the address to the chorus in lines 31-40. The stanzaic structure is clearly marked throughout by the syntactical structure.

Metre: Sapphics; see 1. 2M.

1-4] Apollo is cast in the role of the god who strikes down those carried away by success or pride in their achievements. It is in keeping with H.'s manner that some reappraisal is called for before we can see his trio of victims as sharing (and deserving) a common fate. Their relevance to H. is nowhere made explicit, though it is clear, when we set lines 27-8 alongside 9-12, that H. is anxious lest the *Carmen Saeculare* (by conventional standards the work which marks the highest point of his poetic career and about the performance

of which he feels such obvious pride) prove *his* downfall. — **Dive**] The god is identified
allusively and not named till line 26. — **proles Niobaea**] The seven sons and seven daugh-
ters of Niobe were shot down by Apollo and Artemis to punish Niobe for boasting that
her children set her as a mother above Leto (mother of Apollo and Artemis); for Ovid's
version, see *Met.* 6. 146-312. — **Tityosque raptor**] Killed by Apollo and Artemis for
attempting to rape their mother; see on 2. 14. 8; *raptor* identifies the crime, but the
context invites us to see Tityos as led by conceit (his boastful pride in his sexuality) to
commit the crime that led to his downfall. — **Troiae . . . Achilles**] H. alludes to the post-
Homeric legend according to which Achilles is killed, shortly before the fall of Troy, by
Apollo, disguised as Paris (cf. *Il.* 21. 278).

5-8] The modern reader who knows best the glamorous, if wilful, hero of the *Iliad*, finds it
hard to accept Achilles as the third in H.'s trio. H.'s Achilles is closer to the Achilles of
the *Aeneid* — the ruthless ancestor of the Macedonian kings of Roman history. — **ceteris
maior, tibi miles inpar**] Makes clear Achilles' role in H.'s trio of those who went too far:
repeated success in combats with mortal opponents led him to match himself against
Apollo himself; whether Achilles knew his opponent was the god (disguised as Paris) or
was led unwittingly to his doom by fate is irrelevant to H.'s purpose — to provide a
heroic context for his own possible foolhardiness; the parallels are not intended to
convince, but as a witty challenge to see familiar material in a fresh light (the equivalent,
at the level of myth, of what, at the verbal level, H. calls [*AP* 47] 'callida iunctura'). —
filius Thetidis marinae] For the phrase cf. 1. 8. 13-14. — **quamvis quateret**] Sets the
scene of Achilles' death: he is struck down at the moment when he threatens Troy itself.
— **tremenda cuspide pugnax**] The vivid detail; the ablative both with *quateret* (instru-
mental) and with *pugnax* (descriptive).

9-20] A Pindaric parenthesis, in which H. turns aside, as though spontaneously, to evoke
Achilles in the moment of his death (Stanza 3), following this with an appraisal of his
character in terms relevant to the present context (Stanzas 4-5). — **mordaci . . . Teucro**]
For the image cf. the Homeric model *Il.* 13. 389-93 (Idomeneus kills Asius); with re-
grouping or expansion of the elements this becomes the typical heroic death scene in the
Aeneid; cf. Catullus 64. 105-11. — **ille non inclusus . . . aulam**] Achilles, i.e., was no
Ulysses — if he had lived to take Troy, it would not have been by guile; for the wooden
horse, built under Minerva's direction and purporting to be an offering to her, see *Aen.*
2. 15-32; for the dancing and the holiday mood in which the Trojans drag the horse
within their walls, see *Aen.* 2. 234-49; for the 'pictorial' use of *ille* in the second of two
clauses with a common subject, see Williams on *Aen.* 5. 186 and 457, Austin on *Aen.*
1. 3; **sacra mentitio**] 'that made lying pretence of a sacrifice'; **falleret**] the imperfect
subjunctive (instead of the pluperfect) has an effect similar to the use of the historic
present indicative, representing as still actual what in fact belongs to the past; cf. 19
ureret; the apodosis is 21-2 *ni adnuisset*. — **sed palam . . . alvo**] Achilles, i.e., would have
acted even more ruthlessly than Virgil represents his son Pyrrhus as acting (*Aen.* 2. 469-85;
cf. 2. 766-7); **palam captis gravis**] = 'cruelly, in the presence of those whom he had taken
prisoner'; *captis* both with *palam* (for *palam* as preposition, see *OLD* 4) and with *gravis* —
ablative in the first instance, dative in the second; H. implies that Achilles would have
taken the men and women off into slavery (the usual ancient practice with prisoners-of-
war), after consigning their young children and pregnant mothers to the flames of the
burning city before their parents' eyes — a gratuitous act of cruelty and a crime against
the gods (*nefas*) by Roman standards, if not offensive to Homeric sensibility (Agamemnon,
in reproaching Menelaus for sparing Adrastus, *Il.* 6. 55-60, calls for the destruction of the
whole male population, even 'the male child whom his mother bears in the womb');
Achivis] with *flammis*.

21-4] **ni tuis flexus . . . muros**] Apollo and Venus (mother of Aeneas) intercede with Jove
and save — not Troy, but the Trojan race, destined to found a greater Troy in Italy;
Achilles is thus represented as eliminated by Apollo because he stood in the way of fate's
plan for the rise of Rome; for this Stoic doctrine of fate as stronger than the human
participants, supporting those who make themselves the agents of fate, eliminating those
who oppose it, cf. on 3. 3. 17-36; it is of course the theme of the *Aeneid*; **ni divom pater
adnuisset rebus Aeneae**] 'if Jove had not granted to the fortunes of Aeneas'; **potiore . . .
muros**] 'walls raised under more potent auspices'; the need for Rome to rise prevailed
over the need for Troy to fall; for the ill-fated building of Troy (Laomedon cheated
Neptune), see on 3. 3. 21-2.

25-8] It would be ill-omened for H. to spell out the parallel his *exempla* foreshadow (that
the *Carmen Saeculare* may prove too ambitious and be denied Apollo's favour). — **doctor
... Thaliae**] 'you, the lyre player who taught clear-voiced Thalia'; the lyre implies the
song which it accompanies; for Apollo as the god of the lyre, see on 2. 10. 18-19; for the
Muse Thalia, see on 3. 4. 2 *Calliope*; **argutae**] cf. 3. 14. 21. — **qui ... crinis**] The Xanthus
is a river in Lycia, connected with Apollo in his role as leader of the dance by Virgil, *Aen.*
4. 143-6; for the image cf. 3. 4. 61-2. — **Dauniae ... Camenae**] 'protect the Daunian Muse
from disgrace'; Daunian = Apulian (see on 3. 30. 11 *Daunus*) and hence Italian (as opposed
to Greek), but especially Horatian (after H.'s birthplace; see on 3. 4. 9-10); cf. 4. 8. 20
'Calabrae Pierides' (= 'the poetry of Ennius'); as the logic of his poem requires, H. does
not ask for the success of the *Carmen Saeculare*, but only that the performance will not
disgrace his reputation; *Dauniae Camenae* is dative rather than genitive. — **levis Agyieu**]
= 'eternally youthful Apollo'; *levis*, 'smooth-faced', is the opposite of *rugosus* (not 'beard-
less', as many editors); see on 2. 11. 6.

29-40] H. now turns to the chorus, speaking to them as though at a rehearsal. — **Spiritum
... poetae**] = 'It is to Apollo that I owe my inspiration, my skill as a poetic craftsman
and recognition as a poet'; with *spiritum* cf. 2. 16. 38, 4. 3. 24; *artem* is technical skill as
opposed to *ingenium*, or (as here) to inspiration; with *nomen poetae* cf. *Sat.* 1. 4. 43-4
'ingenium cui sit, cui mens divinior atque os / magna sonaturum, des nominis huius
honorem'. — **virginum ... orti**] i.e., boys and girls of leading families; the formula is
varied, but the sense is the same; cf. 1. 21. 1-2. — **Deliae ... deae**] = 'you who are under
the protection of Diana'. — **fugacis ... arcu**] The appositional expansion (*cohibentis*
depends on *deae*) identifies Diana as the huntress goddess (the 'montium custos
nemorumque virgo' of 3. 22. 1), always represented as fiercely chaste, and the protec-
tress, therefore, of the young and chaste. — **Lesbium ... ictum**] The ode becomes a
drama in which we see H. rehearsing the chorus who will sing the *Carmen Saeculare* (in
Sapphic stanzas, like the present poem); we are invited to imagine him, not beating time,
but giving the tempo or the rhythm by plucking the lyre with his thumb (armed with a
plectrum); no doubt, an element of ironic fantasy enters into the picture, which it would
be ingenuous to take seriously — H. probably entrusted so important a task to an expert;
it is clear, however, from numerous references to the subject (e.g., *Epist.* 1. 1. 55, 1. 18.
12-14) that the normal procedure of the *grammaticus* was to perform the text (giving, by
his reading, his interpretation of the text) line by line with the class repeating each line
after him. — **rite Latonae ... mensis**] The *Carmen Saeculare* invokes the protection of
Apollo and Diana for Rome: H. as usual particularises — Apollo is alluded to as 'Latona's
son', Diana in her role as moon goddess ('she who lights up the night with her brightening
torch'); **crescentem face**] more fanciful and poetic than the prosaic and logical *crescenti
face*; **prosperam frugum**] genitive of respect; **celeremque ... mensis**] 'swift to set rolling
by the headlong months'.

41-4] The final stanza functions as a kind of *sphragis* (see 2. 20I), identifying, not the poet,
but the occasion which has been referred to throughout the ode; note, however, that the
last words are 'vatis Horati'. — **Nupta iam dices**] = 'Before long you will be married and
will say ... '; the switch from speaking to the chorus as a whole to speaking to a single
member is unexpected and successful, reinforcing the suggestion of a dramatic context;
for the age at which girls belonging to respectable families married, see 2. 5I. — **dis amicum
reddidi carmen**] H. anticipates the approval of Apollo (and Artemis) which he solicited in
Stanza 7; *reddidi*, 'performed', reinforces the idea of performance as an interpretation
('dictated' by the poet himself) of the text; the performance on 2 June 17 BC by a
chorus of 27 boys and 27 girls is recorded in an extant inscription (*CIL* 6. 32323; see
Fraenkel 367-8); for the *Ludi saeculares* (a festival revived by Augustus), see *OCD* (under
'Secular Games'); it seems to have been on this occasion that *saeculum*, which previously
denoted a period closer to our 'three score years and ten', came to be fixed as denoting a
period of a hundred years. — **luces**] = *dies*. — **docilis ... Horati**] = 'having been taught my
lines by the poet Horace'; **modorum**] genitive of respect.

4. 7

Introduction: H.'s second spring ode inevitably invites comparison with the first (1. 4).
There are important differences. First, time: in 1. 4, spring is just beginning; it is the

moment of the thaw; in 4. 7, the thaw is over, spring is well advanced. Next, mood:
1. 4 reflects the ambivalence of spring, the uneasy balance between joy and thoughts of
human mortality; in 4. 7, the joy is gone, the mood is more sombrely philosophical.
Third, structure: 4. 7 is longer, its rhetorical structure simpler, more controlled; the
couplets are arranged in seven heavily endstopped quatrains (a structure more like that of
modern lyric — as in Housman's well-known imitation); at the same time, the counter-
point between long and short lines is more marked. Cf. also 4. 12.
Structure: See above. The syntactical structure provides the vehicle for an increasing com-
plexity of mood: Stanza 1 consists of four simple statements; Stanza 2 begins with a
fifth, longer statement, and ends with a syntactically more complex couplet which epito-
mises the theme of the poem: 'inmortalia ne speres', monet annus et almum quae rapit
hora diem'; Stanzas 3-4 elaborate this theme, distinguishing between the passage of the
seasons and human mortality; at the same time the syntax becomes increasingly compli-
cated and the thought more rhetorical and emotionally charged; this progression continues
in Stanza 5, which juxtaposes the notion of the uncertainty of human life ('you may not
live to see tomorrow') with a hint to make the most of time; Stanzas 6-7 develop the
commonplace 'death is final and irrevocable'; the tone is one of open emotional incite-
ment, supported by the plangent rhetoric of Stanza 6, succeeded by the wrier, ironical
imagery of the final stanza.
Metre: Archilochean (c): a dactylic hexameter is followed by a half-hexameter (up to the
3rd-foot caesura). In the hexameter, the usual variations between dactyl and spondee (and
therefore in syllable count) occur, as in Archilochean (b) (1. 7 and 1. 28); cf. Archilochean
(a) (1. 4); the short lines are invariably dactylic, the final syllable being either long by
nature or a closed syllable with the single exception of line 22. Enjambment at the end
of the hexameter is common, and not uncommon at the end of the first couplet in each
group of four lines; the quatrains are invariably endstopped.
1-4]   The thaw is over: description of the natural scene, a first hint of a philosophical theme
(mutat terra vices). — mutat . . . vices] 'the earth runs through her changes'; cf. 1. 4. 1
'grata vice'.
5-8]   As in 1. 4, H. shifts from the natural scene to the imaginary world of sophisticated
fancy. — Gratia . . . choros] A fusion of 1. 4. 5-6 and 3. 19. 15-17; for the Nymphs and
Graces, see on 1. 4. 6; audet] because it is now warm enough to venture forth unclad. —
inmortalia . . . diem] Picks up the hint of 'mutat terra vices'; the fact that the seasons
keep changing is nature's warning; annus] the cycle of the seaons, as is made clear in
Stanza 3; almum . . . diem] = 'the swift passage of time'.
9-16] Frigora . . . Zephyris] The cold of winter is mellowed by the warm West Wind of
spring; cf. 1. 4. 1 'grata vice veris et Favoni', 4. 12. 1-2; Zephyris is instrumental, as
though mitescunt were passive; cf. Catullus 46. 2-3 'caeli furor . . . / iucundis Zephyri
silescit aureis'. — proterit] 'tramples on'; the first hint of a personification. — pomifer
autumnus] Reinforces the personification. — effuderit] Future perfect after interitura.
— mox . . . iners] Before we know where we are, winter is back again; the present
recurrit is more dramatic than a future; at the same time it establishes the notion of
repeated recurrence in preparation for Stanza 4; recurrit iners] ironic oxymoron ('torpid
winter rushes back'), sharpened by alliteration; for iners, see on 2. 9. 5. — damna . . .
lunae] 'yet the swift moons make good the wastage of the sky'; each new moon as it
comes proceeds to make good the losses it suffered during the previous month; the
hexameter represents a variation on Catullus' simpler, more direct 'soles occidere et
redire possunt'; for H., the phases of the moon are the symbol of the cycle of change in
the natural world (whereas Catullus' suns stand for simple recurrence); contrast 2. 18.
15-16, where the 'new moons hastening to their destruction' are the symbol of the swift
passage of time; for the plural, see on 4. 5. 8 soles. — nos ubi decidimus . . . umbra sumus]
Cf. Catullus 5. 5-6 'Nobis cum semel occidit brevis lux, / nox est perpetua una dormienda';
again the different form and the more serious mood dictate a grander rhetoric; the MSS
are divided between pius Aeneas and pater Aeneas (the former perhaps supported by
24 pietas) — in either case a compliment to Virgil's poem, recently published; Tullus
Hostilius and Ancus Marcius were the third and fourth of the legendary kings of Rome;
with 'pulvis et umbra sumus' cf. 1. 4. 17 'domus exilis Plutonia'; decidimus, sumus]
perfect + present secure the general statement 'we mortals' ('we' = 'you and I' would
require future perfect + future).
17-20] Stanza 5 attempts the transition from reflection to spelling out the warning

implicit in the cycle of the seasons (7 'inmortalia ne speres, monet annus'). The moral is that of 1. 11. 8 'carpe diem, quam minimum credula postero', but to the idea 'make the most of time', is added the idea 'make the most of your worldly goods'. Circumstances alter cases — one does not express advice to a wealthy friend in the same terms as to the girl one is in love with. The modern reader finds it hard, however, to avoid the feeling that H.'s Epicureanism is weakened by an intrusive cynicism which lacks the dramatic justification it possesses in 2. 14. 25-7. — **hodiernae summae**] 'to today's total'. — **tempora**] For the plural, see on 3. 30. 5. — **amico ... animo**] = 'that you have spent on yourself', but *amico animo* (= φίλη ψυχῇ) softens the phrase by lending it literary overtones.

21-4] Stanza 5 introduced the idea that death might come any day. Stanza 6 retreats to the idea of death as final, building on the imagery of lines 14-16 in a more plangent variation on the same theme. — **Cum semel occideris**] An echo of Catullus, 'Nobis cum semel occidit brevis lux' (5. 5); but where Catullus is general (*nobis* = 'us mortals', as the tense of *occidit* shows), H. is now specific ('you, Torquatus'). — **et de te ... arbitria**] For Minos as the judge of the dead in Hades (he was one of three, the others were Rhadamanthus and Aeacus [2. 13. 23]), see *Aen.* 6. 431-3, cf. 1. 28. 9; note the awful solemnity of the three heavy monosyllables *et de te* following the caesura; **splendida arbitria**] 'his resplendent decision'; *splendida* in the figurative sense ('magnificent'), but the sense 'shining' is not to be excluded — as though the judgement of Minos (about the fate that awaits Torquatus in Hades) will flash out through the gloom of the *lugentes campi*. — **non genus ... pietas**] If we exclude the vocative *Torquate*, a tricolon crescendo, with anaphora in asyndeton; **genus**] 'birth'; Torquatus, known to us otherwise only as the addressee of *Epist.* 1. 5 (an invitation to dinner) was perhaps a son of the L. Manlius Torquatus who was consul in 65 BC, the year of H.'s birth (see 3. 21. 1); **facundia**] 'eloquence'; it appears from *Epist.* 1. 5. 9 that Torquatus was an orator; **pietas**] cf. 2. 14. 2-4.

25-8] The Roman concept of *pietas* involves *inter alia* loyalty to one's friends, and in his final stanza H. concentrates on this aspect in illustrating from myth the hard truth that loyalty is subject to the limitations of the human condition. For the slackening of tension in the concluding lines cf. 1. 4. 17-20. — **Diana ... Hippolytum**] Diana, conspicuous for her chastity among goddesses, would rescue that model of chastity (and fellow-devotee of hunting) Hippolytus from death if that were possible; **liberat**] present because, in the imaginary world of myth, the gods still live (and the dead are forever consigned to Hades). — **nec Lethaea ... Pirithoo**] For 'the lecher Pirithoos' ('amatorem Pirithoum'), see on 3. 4. 79-80; H.'s concluding conceit needs care in elucidation; the clue lies in the present *valet*: after the failure of their joint mission to the underworld to kidnap Persephone, both Theseus and Pirithoos were thrown into chains; Theseus was subsequently rescued by Hercules (always a law unto himself); following Theseus' death, he came again (H. asks us to imagine) to the underworld — and is there now; his old friend Pirithoos still languishes in chains; Theseus would 'strike off' (*abrumpere*) those chains if he could but he has not the power; the chains are called 'Lethaea' to conjure up a picture of Pirithoos chained by the River of Forgetfulness: he has forgotten his friend; Theseus still remembers.

4. 8

Introduction: An odd poem. First, because of its length (see below). Then, because of its manner: it is the least lyrical of all the odes; even more than 4. 9, it reads like an epistle (the metre slightly altered); much of it, indeed, reads like prose — limpid, logical, but pedestrian.

Lines 1-12 are best taken as a note in verse to accompany a presentation copy: H. is in no position to offer expensive works of art; nor does Censorinus need such gifts; nor is he over-devoted to them: he likes poetry (lines 9-10). Form and content are perfectly adequate to the neat, witty statement of these ideas. We might expect an encomium of Censorinus to follow. Instead, H. proceeds to 'set a price upon his gift' (12 'pretium dicere muneri'). Lines 13-34 make the case (by argument and illustration) that the poet is supremely able to commemorate the deeds of men. It is hard to regard these lines (disjointed and sometimes jejeune as they stand) as more than a first version of the theme of which the ode to Lollius which follows is a fully worked-up version. How they could have been included in their present form unless H. somehow thought them good enough to stand is not clear; that this particular ode should have suffered corruption by an interpreter's hand as extensive as some maintain seems improbable.

The poem is also the only one of the odes which is not a multiple of 4 lines in length. That an ode so unsatisfactory in other respects should also violate Meineke's canon (see 1. 1M) has seemed to most editors to justify emendation: the passage 15 'non celeres . . .' to 19 '. . . lucratus rediit' is easily condemned (see on these lines), but that is no help with the problem of length; two lines more, at least, must go; Klingner's solution, to bracket lines 28 and 32, is arbitrary.

It is tempting to see the whole poem as an intruder: did H. draft it to accompany a copy of *Odes* 4, intending, perhaps, to have it serve also as an introduction – and then abandon the draft, only to have it restored by some editor of *Odes* 4 after H.'s death? The case argued in the poem, that poetry is the most effective commemoration of the deeds of great men, is fully relevant to *Odes* 4 (more so than any other book); but perhaps H. shied at so plain a statement of the book's intentions and replaced 4. 8 by the blander 4. 1. Or did Censorinus (if it is the consul of 39 BC who is addressed) die while H. was still working on his introductory poem to him?

Structure: Lines 1-12 form a single, elegant sentence. Lines 13-22 (with or without interpolation) a similar sentence. The structure of lines 22-34 (a series of *exempla* adduced in support of H.'s thesis) is more disjointed.

Metre: Asclepiad (a), the metre of 1. 1 and 3. 30.

1-8]   **Donarem**] We are perhaps to assume an occasion requiring a gift (a birthday, one of those occasions when the Romans customarily exchanged gifts – the Saturnalia [cf. Catullus 14], or the Calends of March); 2 *meis sodalibus* is in that case a generalising plural; alternatively, we may suppose that H. is in the process of distributing copies of *Odes* 4 (if that is what the gift is) to his friends with an apologetic note, Censorinus being one of the recipients (the sense supported by 4-5 'neque tu . . . ferres'). – **grataque commodus**] A neat juxtaposition: the gifts would be ones the recipients would gladly receive, the giver would give them freely, without reluctance. – **Censorine**] Probably C. Marcius Censorinus, consul 39 BC, possibly his son, consul 8 BC (the easy, urbane tone suggests the latter, but lines 21-2 point to the former – see below); a distinguished, wealthy family. – **aera**] 'bronzes'; i.e., (small) bronze statues, especially from Corinth. – **donarem**] Repetition for emphasis, 'I'd not hesitate to give'. – **tripodas . . . Graiorum**] Tripods (ornamental three-footed cauldrons), originally offered as prizes at the Olympic games, etc., and now prized as works of art by collectors. – **divite me scilicet**] 'assuming of course I was well endowed with . . . '; H. now proceeds to undercut his grand opening. – **artium**] 'works of art'; the plural commonly denotes instances of the abstraction denoted by the singular. – **Parrhasius, Scopas**] The famous Greek painter and sculptor respectively. – **liquidis coloribus**] 'in flowing colours'. – **ponere**] Cf. 4. 1. 20.

9-12]   **sed non . . . vis**] 'but I have no supply of these'; *vis = copia* (cf. 4. 11. 4); *haec = harum rerum* is an extension of the idiom found in such models as *Aen.* 4. 347 'hic amor, haec patria est' (= 'hoc amor, hoc patria est'). – **nec tibi . . . egens**] 'nor are your circumstances such that you need, nor is your disposition such that you feel the lack of, such sophisticated frivolities'; for *deliciarum*, see Quinn on Catullus 2. 1. – **gaudes carminibus**] 'you enjoy poetry'. – **carmina . . . donare**] Hardly suggests a single poem with Censorinus as addressee; more likely, a book or books (*Odes* 4, *Odes* 1-3?); *donare* picks up 1 and 3 *donarem*. – **et . . . muneri**] 'and set a price upon the gift'; H. is hardly speaking seriously; he is perhaps mocking more conventional givers of gifts who cannot resist the temptation to tell the recipient what the gift has cost; at the same time the phrase leads into the defence of poetry which follows.

13-22]   In 3. 30 H. maintained that his odes would bring him more lasting fame than a plaque of bronze ('exegi monumentum aere perennius'). He now develops a related argument: poetry (or at any rate literature) can bring greater fame for the statesman or general than the official record of his achievements or the deeds themselves – indeed, such recognition is the only recognition that counts. The theme is taken up at length in 4. 9. To commemorate the achievements of the great had long been the duty of poets; at Rome it became the chief function of historical epic, the *Annals* of Ennius being the most famous example of the genre. In H.'s day this kind of poetry was already losing ground to prose history: the future lay with Livy and his successors, not with the imitators of Ennius. – **notis publicis**] Inscriptions upon tombs, etc., set up in the name of the state;

see, e.g., Cicero *Phil.* 14. 33 'Erit igitur exstructa moles opere magnifico incisaeque litterae, divinae virtutis testes sempiternae'; Livy 6. 29. 9 'tabula . . . his ferme incisa litteris fuit'; for the idea cf. 4. 13. 15 'notis condita fastis'. — **per quae . . . post mortem**] They are restored to life when the inscriptions bring back the memory of their achievements in the minds of suceeding generations — the only immortality hoped for by most educated Romans in H.'s day; see on 3. 30. 6-7. — **non celeres . . . lucratus redit**] This passage is rejected by Klingner and others on logical and stylistic grounds (*eius* is suspect as the only instance of the pronoun *is* in the *Odes* and *Epodes* except in the equally suspect line 3. 11. 18); the arguments from style cannot be conclusive (3. 11. 18 is not manifestly corrupt, H. does use *eius* twice in the *Satires*), particularly in an ode whose style is so different throughout from other odes; but the logic of lines 13-22 is almost impossible to defend if the passage is retained; on the other hand, it is hard to see how the passage could have come to be grafted into H.'s text; see Introduction; **non celeres fugae . . . minae**] presumably, a reference to Hannibal's change of fortunes after the battle of the River Metaurus (the theme of 4. 4. 37-72); with *minae* cf. 4. 3. 8; **incendia**] the destruction of Carthage after the Third Punic War in 146 BC; **eius qui . . . rediit**] *eius* (dependent on *incendia*) is very clumsy; the reference is to the *cognomen* 'Africanus' assumed by Scipio Aemilianus, 'the conqueror of Africa'; **nomen lucratus**] 'having earned the title'. — **laudes**] 'one's merits'. — **Calabrae Pierides**] The poetry of Ennius, who came from Calabria; his *Annals* included an account of the Second Punic War. — **neque . . . tuleris**] A somewhat lame afterthought; **sileant, tuleris**] the subjunctives are best taken as equivalent to the normal imperfect and pluperfect ('nor, if there were no mention of you in literature, would you have got your due reward of fame'); the present and perfect subjunctive in this sense are common in early Latin, occasionally found in classical Latin; cf. *Aen.* 2. 599-600 'Ni mea cura resistat, iam flammae / tulerint inimicus et hauserit ensis'; the implication is that Censorinus has already had his achievements celebrated in an epic poem.

22-9] Two *exempla* are adduced as proof of the assertion of lines 13-22. H., however, seems to be shifting his ground. He began with a defence of poetry; 21 *chartae* was already vaguer (the natural assumption is that verse is meant, but *chartae* could denote any written record). If 22 ff. are to be taken seriously, the argument must be extended to cover all forms of *litterae* (e.g., prose history). This position is not inconsistent with lines 1-12 (and, indeed, it is perfectly sensible to praise poetry as commemorating achievement in the wider implied context of a defence of all forms of *litterae*), but it means adopting a rather different position from that taken in 4. 9. — **Quid foret . . . Romuli**] = 'What would Romulus be now if he had suffered from a conspiracy of silence?' H. stops short of denying the immortality of Romulus which the subsequent development of his argument requires him to allow. — **Ereptum . . . Aeacum**] Aeacus is familiar as one of the judges in Hades (cf. 2. 13. 22); H. seems to mean that, as a result of what the poets have written about him, Aeacus is, to all intents and purposes, promoted to the Islands of the Blest; but there can be suspicion that H. has confused Aeacus with Rhadamanthus, whom Homer in one place (*Od.* 4. 564) places in the Islands of the Blest. — **virtus et favor et lingua**] 'his own courage, his popularity and the eloquence of poets'; H.'s point is that *virtus* alone is not enough. — **Dignum . . . mori**] A neat, forceful line, summing up H. 's argument. — **caelo Musa beat**] The Muse grants immortality by inspiring poets to proclaim it; H. comes dangerously close to admitting that immortality is a fiction of the poetic imagination.

29-34] H. concludes with three instances of immortality granted by poetry. Those promoted to immortality are represented as engaged in an appropriate activity in each case (Hercules eating, Castor and Pollux rescuing men from shipwreck, Bacchus, suitably garbed, granting *vota*); cf. 3. 3. 9-15. — **Sic**] 'It is in this sense that'. — **clarum Tyndaridae sidus**] 'the sons of Tyndareus, that bright constellation'; see on 1. 3. 2 and 3. 3. 9. — **ornatus tempora**] 'his brows adorned with . . . '; for the construction, see on 1. 1. 21-2 'membra stratus'.

4. 9

Introduction: An ode in honour of M. Lollius, consul 21 BC.

We may suspect from H.'s opening stanza that Lollius would have preferred (like

Agrippa before him in 1. 6) an epic poem celebrating his achievements (he had been proconsul in Macedonia in 19-18 BC, governor of Gallia Comata in 17-16 BC) and has to be assured that the *Odes* will take their place alongside the poetry of Homer and Pindar and the great lyric poets of the past. After further assurances that poetry has the power to confer immortality, Lollius is told that political success is transitory, that wisdom and integrity are the mark of the truly great mind and that they, not riches, make for true happiness. In 16 BC Tiberius had taken over Lollius' command in Gaul; it was important that credit for victory over the Vindelici (the subject of 4. 4) should be seen to belong to Tiberius; advantage seems to have been taken, indeed, of a minor defeat suffered by Lollius in 17 BC to make his replacement appear motivated by military necessity (see Syme, *Roman Revolution* 429). It is easy to read 4. 9 as perfunctory praise; it is perhaps intended as a cautious rehabilitation.

   In either case, the ode is apt to strike the modern reader as an example of H.'s failing powers. It reads more like the hexameter essays of his book of *Epistles* (published 20 BC) than the poetry of *Odes* 1-3. The language is vigorous, the illustrations abundant and effective; but the imagery is less spontaneously evocative, the sentences are argumentative rather than challenging, the syntax logical and prosaic. We feel H. is merely stating his views, not discreetly arranging things so that we seem to be making up our minds for ourselves. Stanzas 1-8 are not without rhetorical merit, but we are disconcerted to find them used as a preamble for the vague rhetoric which follows.
Structure: Stanzas 1-3 state a first proposition: 'Rest assured, my poetry will last; there are other poets beside Homer.' Stanzas 4-7 introduce a second proposition, related to the first rhetorically rather than logically: 'Helen is the great adulteress, the heroes of the Trojan War have survived because they had a poet to celebrate their achievements.' Lines 29-34 represent the transition to the major theme, the encomium of Lollius. The encomium proper continues to the end of Stanza 11, and is then capped with the general statement of Stanzas 12-13 on the nature of true happiness.
Metre: Alcaics; see 1. 9M (the same metre as 4. 4, 4. 14 and 4. 15).
1-4] **Ne forte credas**] For the construction ('lest you suppose . . . ' = 'don't suppose . . . '), see on 1. 33. 1-4; the formula *ne forte*, found only here in the *Odes* and once in the *Satires*, is characteristic of H.'s later hexametric style (four times in the *Epistles*, twice in the *Ars Poetica*). — **quae verba loquor socianda chordis**] = 'my lyric poetry'. — **longe . . . Aufidum**] Cf. 3. 30. 10. — **non ante . . . per artis**] Cf. 3. 30. 13-14; H. speaks here more in the laureate role he adopts in 3. 1. 2-4.
5-12] **si tenet**] = 'if, as is the case'; no doubt is implied by this idiom. — **Pindaricae latent . . . Camenae**] = 'has the poetry of Pindar, etc. fallen into obscurity'; **Ceae**] evokes Simonides of Ceos; **minaces**] refers to the public poetry of Alcaeus — his war songs and his attacks on tyranny; **graves**] i.e., possessing the quality of *gravitas*; the opposite is *leves* (applied by H. to his own poetry in 1. 6. 20); **Camenae**] of Greek poetry also 2. 16. 38. — **nec . . . puellae**] We come now to the poets not traditionally ranked as serious; observe that H. puts the love poetry of Sappho on a different level from the political poetry of Alcaeus; a similar distinction in 2. 13. 24-32; **lusit**] the word implies lightness of theme and of treatment; cf. *Sat.* 1. 10. 37 'haec ego ludo'; for the sexual overtones of *ludo*, see on 2. 5. 8; **vivuntque . . . puellae**] 'and Sappho's love affairs still live today because she entrusted them to the strings of her lyre'; **calores**] milder than *ignes* (Ovid *Tristia* 4. 10. 45 'saepe suos solitus recitare Propertius ignes'); cf. 1. 4. 19 'calet'.
13-24] The emphatic *non sola* picks up the *non* of line 5. Helen and the heroes of the Trojan War were not unique: there were other adulteresses and other heroes, but they have perished, whereas these live on in the pages of Homer. The *exempla* which follow are arranged in a loosely-structured tricolon (lines 13-18, lines 18-21, lines 21-4). — **comptos crinis**] See on 1. 15. 14 'caesariem' and 19-20 'adulteros crinis'; with *mirata* — not with *arsit*. — **arsit**] Cf. 2. 4. 7, 3. 9. 6. — **adulteri**] See on 1. 25. 9 'moechos'. — **comites**] The members of Paris' entourage during his visit to Sparta. — **Teucer**] Ajax' brother, described *Il.* 13. 313 as the best archer of the Achaeans. — **Cydonio**] = 'Cretan'; stock epithet of bows. — **non semel . . . vexata**] 'not once only was Troy attacked'; i.e., there had been previous attacks. — **non pugnavit . . . proelia**] Idomeneus and Sthenelus are taken, by a natural rhetorical figure, as representative of Homeric heroes who fought in single combat, these being opposed, as a group, to those whose achievements have gone unrecorded. — **Hector, Deiphobus**] Both Trojans; the others are Greeks; Deiphobus figures prominently in *Aen.* 6. 494-534; oddly enough, the only wife of his we hear of is

ODES 4.10 317

Helen, whom Deiphobus married after the death of Paris.

25-8] Stanza 7 draws the conclusion pointed to by Stanzas 4-6 in preparation for the transition to Lollius in Stanza 8. — **Vixere . . . multi]** Cf. *Sat.* 1. 3. 107-8 'fuit ante Helenam cunnus taeterrima belli / causa'. — **inlacrimabiles]** 'unwept'; contrast 2. 14. 6.

29-34] A bridge passage. — **Paulum . . . virtus]** = 'Little separates a hero's deeds, if covered up, from those of the man who achieved nothing and now lies buried and forgotten'; the encomium of Lollius which follows will, in short, not merely honour him in life (ensure that he is not 'meis chartis inornatum'), but will preserve his memory for future generations. — **chartis]** Cf. 4. 8. 21. — **totve tuos . . . obliviones]** 'nor will I allow envious oblivion to gnaw unchecked at your great deeds'; for *labores*, see on 1. 7. 18; for *carpere*, see on 1. 11. 8; **lividas]** the colour of a bruise (yellow-blue, rather than our 'black and blue') as in 1. 8. 10 or a ripe grape (2. 5. 10) or a decayed tooth (*Epodes* 5. 47); here, of the face discoloured by spite or malice (contrast our 'livid with anger'); the phrase suggests some pack of evil monsters (cf. the Furies, etc.).

34-44] The formal encomium of Lollius is conspicuous for its generalities; H. concentrates on Lollius' upright character and his wisdom as an administrator (though his consulship is now a thing of the past) and his uncorruptibility; the hint of a military career in lines 43-4 is so vague as to be innocuous; the things said might be said (on an appropriate occasion) of almost any public figure — with an equal ring of truth. The adjectives 35 *prudens*, 36 *rectus* and 37 *vindex et abstinens* all define 34 *animus*, of which 39 *consul* is also an appositional expansion (as though *Lollius*, not *animus*, had preceded); 41 *praetulit*, 42 *reiecit*, 44 *explicuit* are all to be taken with 40 *quotiens*. — **animus]** 'Character' is a convenient translation, but the sense implied by the context is the *animus* of the Stoic philosophers — a kind of guiding intelligence strengthened by reason and understanding. — **rerumque prudens]** = 'noted for its practical wisdom based on experience'; *rerum* suggests something like 'the affairs of life', as opposed to theoretical wisdom; *-que* links *rerum prudens* with *et secundis . . . rectus* (= *et . . . et*, a variation favoured by the high style). — **rectus]** 'upright'. — **vindex . . . fraudis]** 'quick to punish the frauds of avarice' (i.e., the avarice of others). — **abstinens . . . pecuniae]** = 'keeping clear of wealth that attempts to gather all things into its clutches'. — **consulque non unius anni]** The normal span; Lollius had been consul in 21 BC; for the implied disparagement of politics and politicians, see on 3. 1. 9-16; cf. 3. 2. 17-20. — **sed quotiens . . . utili]** The subject is *animus, bonus atque fidus iudex* functioning as an appositional qualifier; *quotiens* follows on *non unius anni*: Lollius, i.e., is to all intents and purposes consul when he acts like one — an expansion of the Stoic paradox that the philosopher is king, not by virtue of the position he holds, but by his moral supremacy; similarly, Lollius is the *bonus atque fidus iudex* whenever he so acts (whether he holds any position conferring judicial functions or not); by making his encomium depend throughout on *animus*, H. is able to make Lollius appear as realising the Stoic ideal while saying nothing of the offices actually held by Lollius. — **reiecit . . . voltu]** '(whenever the *animus* of Lollius) disdainfully rejected the bribes of men of nefarious intent'; the rhetoric is impressive but hard to pin down. — **per obstantis . . . arma]** Likewise hard to pin down, coming as it does at the climax of this structure of figurative and allusive rhetoric; *per obstantis catervas* suggests, however, the routing of the serried ranks of a metaphorical opposition rather than a victory on the battlefield.

45-52] The concluding stanzas continue the increasingly abstract and philosophical note of the encomium proper. — **Non vocaveris]** = 'one cannot call'; i.e., the mere fact of possessing great wealth is not enough. — **rectius . . . beati]** 'he has a better claim to the title "beatus" . . . ' (only the true Stoic saint can with full accuracy be called 'beatus'). — **duramque . . . pati]** See on 3. 2. 1-4. — **peiusque . . . timet]** 'and fears as something worse than death'. — **non pro patria timidus perire]** Cf. 3. 19. 2 (also 3. 2. 13).

4. 10

Introduction: Ligurinus again (cf. 4. 1. 33-40): he will live to regret his present indifference. The ode is commonly misunderstood (e.g., Fraenkel 414-15): the opposition is not between youth's missed opportunities and the denial of love's pleasures which old age brings, but between Ligurinus as he is now (a young boy attractive to men but not interested) and as he will be soon (too old to be attractive any longer to men but with his own interest in

homosexual relationships quickening). With Ligurinus cf. Nearchus in 3. 20. The ode is
close in subject and manner to Hellenistic epigram, but the situation it explores is Roman.
Structure: The 8 endstopped lines form a single sentence.
Metre: Asclepiad (e); see 1. 11M.

1-5] The first 5 lines concentrate on Ligurinus' present attractiveness (1 *adhuc*, 3 *nunc*, 4
nunc) and the imminent loss of those charms which make him 'Veneris muneribus potens'.
The events predicted represent three successive stages in the loss of Ligurinus' boyish
attractiveness; the three stages are structured as a tricolon crescendo (1 line + 1 line + 2
lines). — **crudelis]** i.e., to H. — **insperata]** 'unexpected'; often 'of neutral or undesirable
events' (*OLD* 2). — **tuae superbiae]** The arrogance that makes him indifferent to H.'s
attentions; dative. — **pluma]** The down on the cheeks which is the first sign of coming
manhood; needlessly obelised in *OCT*. — **et quae nunc . . . comae]** 'when the hair that
now falls over your shoulders has been cut off'; the next stage; cf. Nearchus, 3. 20. 13-14
and Lycus, 1. 32. 11-12. — **nunc et qui . . . hispidam]** The third stage is the beard of the
fully-grown *adolescens*; **nunc et]** the postponement of *et* is a mark of the high style; cf.
1. 12. 11, etc.; **color . . . rosae]** cf. the 'cervicem roseam' of Telephus, 1. 13. 2; **flore]**
see on 1. 4. 10; **prior]** 'superior to'; **in faciem . . . hispidam]** the bearded face of a grown
man (whether the beard is worn long or not); *hispidam* is pejorative; **verterit]** the intran-
sitive use (in the sense 'change') is not uncommon.

6-8] We might suppose that Ligurinus, on reaching this last stage, would be eager to turn
his attention to finding himself a mistress (like Marathus in Tibullus 1. 8). H. represents
him as not yet ready for the future, disturbed instead by thoughts of lost opportunities.
— **quae mens est hodie]** = 'the way I feel today' (about homosexual relationships); for
mens = 'frame of mind' cf. 1. 16. 22, *Epist*. 1. 1. 4 'non eadem est aetas, non mens', *Aen*.
5. 812 'mens eadem perstat mihi'. — **his animis]** 'feeling the way I do'. — **incolumes . . .
genae]** = 'why can't I be again the attractive boy I was?'

4. 11

Introduction: An invitation to a party in honour of Maecenas' birthday, addressed to the
last woman in H.'s life. A variation on the theme of 3. 28 — longer and more elaborate
in structure, but lacking the spontaneity and simple elegance of its model. The first of
three odes about parties.
Structure: Stanzas 1-3, the preparations for the party described. Stanzas 4-5, the occasion?
It's Maecenas' birthday. Stanzas 6-8 (to line 31), 'forget about Telephus — you're not in
his class'. Lines 31-6, 'come, a song or two will dispel our cares'.
Metre: Sapphics; see 1. 2M.

1-12] The scale of the preparations precludes a *tête-à-tête* (contrast 3. 28); we may assume
that Maecenas will be present as guest of honour and that there will be other guests; H.,
however, will have eyes only for Phyllis, just as at the party in honour of Murena his
passion for Glycera smoulders away while he talks (3. 19. 28 'me lentus Glycerae torret
amor meae'). No indication (except, perhaps, 2 *in horto*) whether we are to think of the
party as taking place on H.'s farm or in town; references to H.'s farm, like praise of
the simple life, are, however, conspicuous by their absence in *Odes* 4. — **Est mihi . . .
cadus]** A respectable but not a rare wine; for the ages at which wines were drunk, see on
3. 21. 1-4; for Alban wine, see *Sat*. 2. 8. 16; for the *cadus*, see on 1. 9. 8 *diota*. — **in
horto]** A kitchen garden adjacent to the place where the party is to take place. —
nectendis . . . coronis] 'celery for weaving garlands'; cf. 2. 7. 23-4; for garlands, see on
1. 38, 1. 7. 23, 1. 17. 27; for celery, see also 1. 36. 16; for the construction (final dative),
see 1. 28. 18. — **vis multa]** 'a large supply'; cf. 4. 8. 9. — **qua . . . fulges]** = 'and when you
have an ivy garland in your hair, you look divine'; for *fulges*, see on 1. 5. 13 *nites*; the
present indicative indicates that for H. Phyllis in her party attire is a familiar sight; **crinis
religata]** probably, as in 1. 5. 4, 'with your hair bound back in a knot', the garland of ivy
being superimposed, not interwoven; cf. 2. 11. 23-4; for the construction, see on 1. 1. 21-2
'membra stratus'. — **ridet argento domus]** A neat simplification of such descriptions of
luxury as Catullus 64. 43-6; H.'s way of life has changed since 2. 18 and his ideas since 2.
16. 13-14. — **ara . . . agno]** The altar and the sacrifice preceding the meal are a feature of
parties; cf. 3. 8. 3-4; **verbenis]** cf. 1. 19. 14; **spargier]** the old ending of the passive infini-
tive (five times in the *Satires* and *Epistles*, only here in the *Odes*); **agno]** for the animals

offered at sacrifices, see on 3. 23. 4. – **cuncta manus**] 'the whole household'. – **huc et illuc . . . fumum**] H. describes the scene before his eyes; the ode purports to be a written invitation to Phyllis who has yet to arrive (cf. 2, 11. 21-4, 3. 14. 21-4); **sordidum . . . fumum**] 'the curling flames (of the kitchen fire) send their filthy smoke spiralling upwards'; *sordidum* because greasy; cf. the kitchen fire that got out of hand in *Sat.* 1. 5. 73-4.

13-20] **Ut . . . noris**] Illogical and conventional; cf. our 'if you'd like to know . . .'. – **Idus . . . agendae**] 'you are to celebrate the Ides'; the formula includes Phyllis as one of the guests, not as a mere entertainer. – **qui dies . . . Aprilem**] The date is 13 April; April was connected with Venus marina by deriving *Aprilis* from ἀφρός) (the foam of the sea, from which Aphrodite was born); see Ovid *Fasti* 4. 61-2. – **iure . . . mihi**] 'for me a truly festive occasion'. – **ex hac luce . . . annos**] 'from this day my Maecenas reckons his increasing years'; Maecenas was perhaps 2-3 years older than H. – in his mid-fifties; this is the only reference to him in *Odes* 4.

21-4] The invitation seems complete at the end of Stanza 5. We now learn the matter is not as simple as it appeared. As in 1. 17, accepting H.'s invitation to come and sing for him implies a choice between lovers: Cyrus was a brute, Tyndaris need have no compunction; Phyllis can forget about Telephus – another girl has got in first; for Telephus, see 1. 13 and 3. 19. 25-7. – **petis**] Cf. 1. 33. 13, 3. 19. 27. – **non tuae sortis iuvenem**] Telephus, i.e., was 'not destined' to be Phyllis' lover; that Phyllis has set her sights too high is made clear in Stanzas 7-8; Telephus might have fallen just the same for Phyllis, as H. remained infatuated with Myrtale 'melior cum peteret Venus'; but that was not the way it was to be. – **puella dives et lasciva**] A sly ironic reversal of a cliché of elegiac poetry – the poet-lover who has his mistress stolen from him by a *dives amator*. – **grata compede**] Cf. 1. 33. 14.

25-31] A short sermon for Phyllis' benefit on the dangers of aiming too high. – **Terret . . . spes**] = 'The burning of Phaethon serves as a deterrent to greedy hopes'; Phaethon, son of Helios, lost control of his father's horses and had to be destroyed by Zeus to prevent the destruction of the earth; while *avaras* can apply to Phyllis, it is hard to see the relevance to Phaethon. – **exemplum . . . Bellerophontem**] After killing the Chimaera, Bellerophon attempted to fly to Olympus and immortality, but was thrown by his mount; **terrenum . . . gravatus**] 'finding his terrestrial rider burdensome'; a hint that the parallel is not intended very seriously. – **ut . . . sequare**] 'that you should always aim at goals appropriate to your station'. – **disparem**] 'a mate who is no mate'; cf. 1. 33. 10-12.

31-6] That Phyllis will accept H.'s invitation is taken for granted (contrast 3. 14. 21-4, where difficulty is anticipated); her role at the party and her relation to H. are now defined. – **meorum finis amorum**] 'last of my loves'. – **calebo**] Implies something less than searing passion; cf. 1. 4. 19, 4. 9. 11; contrast 4. 1. 29-32. – **condisce modos**] = 'let me teach you some songs'; H., i.e., will rehearse Phyllis, as he rehearsed the chorus of the *Carmen Saeculare* in 4. 6. 31-44, perhaps providing the words, as he did then; cf. 1. 17. 17-20, 2. 11. 21-4, 3. 28. 9-16. – **amanda . . . reddas**] 'which you can sing with that voice I can't help loving'. – **minuentur . . . curae**] The sombre ending suits the ageing H., for whom love is only a not-wholly-successful distraction; with *atrae curae* cf. 3. 1. 40, 3. 14. 13; also 4. 12. 19-20.

4. 12

Introduction: An invitation to Virgil: 'Spring is here; let's have a party; I'll provide the wine; you can bring some scent as your contribution.' The light-hearted tone has led many to suppose the Virgil meant is not the poet; the banter of Stanza 4, in particular, has been felt inappropriate in a poem published after the death of H.'s distinguished fellow-poet and intimate friend. It is unlikely, however, after two poems in *Odes* 1-3 addressed by common consent to the poet (1. 3 and 1. 24), that H. should add a poem addressed to an unknown Virgil: 4. 12 reads like an early poem; it lacks the poetic seriousness and the depth of feeling of the two more famous spring odes, 1. 4 and 4. 7; probably, H. intended it to be recognised as an early poem, published after Virgil's death to recall the easy intimacy that had existed between old friends – perhaps around 30 BC, when H. was beginning his collection of *Odes* and Virgil about to embark upon the *Aeneid*.

Structure: Seven heavily-endstopped stanzas. Stanzas 1-3, a series of variations upon the theme 'spring is here'. Stanzas 4-6, invitation. Stanza 7, tail-piece.

Metre: Asclepiad (c); see 1. 6M.

1-4] Stanza 1 sets the scene: not the early spring scene of 1. 4, but more that of 4. 7; the frozen fields of winter and the thaw of early spring are already a thing of the past. — **Iam, iam**] The repetition creates a note of excitement; cf. Catullus 46. 1-2; but the anaphora is also structured; cf. 2. 5. 10-16, 3. 29. 17-24. — **veris comites**] The warm spring winds that bring the world to life again and permit the resumption of navigation; cf. 1. 4. 1-4. — **quae mare temperant**] 'which soothe the sea', after the storms of winter. — **inpellunt lintea**] The spring winds 'swell the sails' of the ships now putting to sea. — **animae Thraciae**] An appositional expansion of *veris comites*; the winds are called *animae* to suggest that they breathe life into the world again; 'Thracian' perhaps because Homer *Il.* 23. 229-30 sets the home of the winds in Thrace; but the epithet is traditional in Greek poetry (cf. Sophocles *Antig.* 589), if inappropriate in the Roman poem as an epithet of the westerly winds of spring; contrast 1. 25. 11-12. — **nec fluvii . . . turgidi**] Cf. 4. 7. 3-4.

5-8] Stanza 2 transposes from the real world (imaginatively evoked) to the fanciful world of myth. Spring means the return of the swallows from warmer climes. Procne, metamorphosed into a swallow, is spoken of as though she had become each and every swallow in the world around us (as the lyre of 3. 11 becomes each and every lyre; see on 3. 11. 1-8 and 4. 4. 1-4). — **Ityn gemens**] 'grieving for Itys', her son, whom Procne murdered to punish her husband Tereus. — **Cecropiae . . . opprobrium**] Procne, daughter of Pandion, King of Athens, was the descendant of Cecrops; by her unnatural action she brought everlasting shame on her line. — **quod male . . . libidines**] Tereus had seduced Procne's sister Philomela and then cut out her tongue; to punish him, Procne served the body of Itys to him at a banquet, whereupon all three were metamorphosed into birds; for Ovid's version, see *Met.* 6. 424-674; **male**] equally with *barbaras* (= 'as was characteristic of the evil ways of barbarians') and with *ulta* (revenge being normally commendable, but not in this case); **barbaras regum libidines**] Generalising plural: Procne's action is put in the category of misguided acts aimed at avenging the barbaric lust of princes.

9-12] A further shift of scene to the pastoral world: there too spring means the renewal of activity. — **in tenero gramine**] '(sitting upon) the young spring grass'. — **pinguium**] 'fat' because they have had their fill of the new grass and can relax while the shepherds play their pipes. — **fistula**] Singular following the usual idiom; though there are several shepherds, each has one pipe. — **deum**] Pan, the god of shepherds, was especially worshipped in Arcadia (the traditional setting of pastoral poetry). — **nigri**] Because of the dark-green mountain forests; cf. 1. 21. 7.

13-16] **Adduxere . . . Vergili**] The simple, direct assertion effectively caps the description of pastoral relaxation in the preceding stanza; for the plural *tempora*, see on 3. 30. 5. — **pressum Calibus Liberum**] A good wine; see on 1. 20. 9-12. — **ducere**] Cf. 1. 17. 22. — **iuvenum nobilium cliens**] The appositional expansion first explains *sed pressum . . . si gestis* (Virgil is likely to have picked up expensive tastes at the tables where he normally dines out), then places Virgil (he has distinguished patrons); we need hardly doubt the *iuvenes nobiles* are Augustus and Maecenas; Augustus was 7 years younger than Virgil, Maecenas perhaps 5-6 years younger; both, therefore, were in their thirties when Virgil began to frequent their tables, whereas the typical Republican *patronus* is a *consularis*; for the age denoted by *iuvenis*, see on 1. 2. 41; Maecenas, if not strictly a *nobilis*, passed for the descendant of Etruscan kings (1. 1. 1); **cliens**] the normal word for the protégé of a *patronus*, covering a wide range of relationships, including that of the writer or intellectual and his patron (in our sense of the term); in the late Republic and Augustan age, the term is avoided (except in connection with the courts) in favour of *amicus*, in order to avoid the suggestion of social inequality implicit in *cliens*; thus Maecenas, *Sat.* 1. 6. 61-2, bids H. 'esse in amicorum numero'; by using the term *cliens* here, H., by implication, represents the relationship, for ironical effect, as on a par with that of the more humble retainer of the great, rather as in *Epist.* 1. 7. 46-95 he equates himself with the lowly Volteius who became the 'mane cliens et iam certus conviva' (line 75) of the great Philippus. — **nardo . . . merebere**] 'you will have to earn your wine with scent'; the future amounts to a command, as often.

17-20] For scent at parties cf. 2. 7. 7-8, 3. 14. 17. The joke seems to lie in the inequality of the bargain: a 'parvus onyx' of spikenard is going to entice out of the cellar where it reposes a whole *cadus* of a very respectable wine. There is perhaps implied an ironic reversal of the situation in Catullus 13: there, Catullus was in a position to provide only scent for his guest; here, H. is going to provide everything except the scent. — **parvus** onyx] A small onyx container. – **cadum**] See on 1. 9. 8 *diota*. – **Sulpiciis horreis**] Presumably, a wine merchant's store (according to Porphyrio the establishment later known as 'Galbae horrea'); for *horreis*, see on 3. 8. 11; the implication is that H. normally drinks cheaper wines, but will buy in a *cadus* of special wine for the party. – **spes . . . efficax**] Cf. the praises of the *testa* of 65 BC in 3. 21. 13-24; **amaraque curarum**] 'and the bitterness of our anxieties'; see on 4. 11. 35-6.

21-4] The insistence on the commercial nature of the transaction indicates H. is joking (one does not invite a real merchant in these terms). – **merce**] Ostensibly, 'merchandise', as in 1. 31. 12 'vina Syra reparata merce'; there, however, the *mercator* is able to buy wines out of the profits of his trade; here Virgil is asked to bring the merchandise with him, as though the dinner party were a business transaction and the deal one to be effected on the spot; Virgil is to buy the scent, as H. will buy the wine (no need to suppose he has brought the scent himself from abroad); the suggestion that *merce* means 'a poem' is attractive but is ruled out by 'tinguere poculis' which clearly refers back to Stanza 5. – **plena dives ut in domo**] Picks up 15 'iuvenum nobilium cliens': a shameless *parasitus* like Terence's Phormio might arrive empty-handed at his rich patron's table with nothing to offer except his company (*Phormio* 339-40 'tene asymbolum venire unctum atque lautum e balneis, / otiosum ab animo quom ille et cura et sumptu absumitur'); H., however, has no intention ('non ego meditor') of letting Virgil get away with such behaviour; a decent guest was supposed to help out; see Terence *Andria* 88-9 'symbolam / dedit, cenavit'; contrast 3. 29. 1-5 (to Maecenas) where it is clear that H. is going to provide everything.

25-8] The final stanza represents, as often (cf., e.g., 1. 8. 13-16), a modulation of key – here, from somewhat heavy-handed persiflage to something closer to expression of an attitude to life. – **studium lucri**] Continues the persiflage. – **nigrorum ignium**] The fires of the funeral pyre. – **memor dum licet**] 'bearing in mind while you can' (before it is too late to do anything about it); cf. 2. 11. 16; *dum licet* anticipates *misce*, but grammatically it modifies *memor*. – **misce stultitiam . . . in loco**] Cf. 2. 7. 27-8, 3. 19. 18, 3. 21. 13-16, 3. 28. 4; **in loco**] 'on occasion'.

4. 13

Introduction: The last of H.'s love poems is, like the first, a dramatic monologue – the poet's thoughts unwind as he watches the scene before his eyes; the ode is a study in the emotions of the speaker as he looks at Lyce and voices his thoughts to himself, not a poem abusing Lyce. Where 1. 5 showed Pyrrha in calm control, the Lyce of 4. 13 is a pathetic figure whose attempts to exercise the attraction she once possessed are met by her audience with indifference or derision.

The ode belongs among H.'s studies in the ageing flirt (see 1. 25I). Stanzas 1-2 place Lyce fairly conclusively: her status is that of the women who appear at parties as professional entertainers; sometimes, they are already the mistress of the host (like Phyllis in 4. 11, or Glycera in 3. 19. 28) or of one of the guests; but they keep an eye open for fresh conquests (like Rhode in 3. 19. 25-7); while they are young and beautiful, they are the centre of attraction (like Damalis in 1. 36. 16-20, or Chia here). The time comes, however, when they would do well to retire (like Chloris in 3. 15). Lyce has gone on too long. Such women have a husband (like Chloris in 3. 15) and may (again like Chloris – see 3. 15. 9) lead an active love-life outside the party context, but their status is different from the upper-class *moecha* such as Lydia (probably) in 1. 25.
Structure: Stanzas 1-3 set the scene and sketch in the background. Stanzas 4-7 represent the unwinding of H.'s thoughts as he reflects on days gone by, then reverts (Stanza 7) to the scene before his eyes. The variation between endstopped stanzas (Stanzas 2, 3, 4) and stanzas in which the sense carries over into the stanza following (Stanzas 1, 5, 6) follows H.'s more mature practice.
Metre: Asclepiad (d); see 1. 5M; 1. 5 and 4. 13 are the first and last odes using this metre.
1-6] **Audivere di mea vota**] 'The gods heard my prayers'; at the time he could not be sure, now he knows; *vota* implies repeated supplication, *audivere* views it all as a single past occasion; H. presumably prayed that Lyce would live to regret her treatment of him – and is now startled to see how amply (and unexpectedly) the gods have granted his prayer. – **Lyce**] A punning name: λύκη (a made-up form from λύκος) = *lupa*, 'whore'. – **di**

audivere] With the repetition cf. 1. 2. 4-5, 2. 3. 17, 2. 14. 1 and, below, lines 17-20; the effect aimed at is usually one of pathos. — **fis anus**] 'you're getting old'; the translation 'you are becoming an old woman' misleads; *anus*, like *senex*, includes what we call middle-age (see on 2. 11. 6 *iuventas*); cf. 1. 25. 9. — **formosa**] 'a beauty'; an emotionally charged word in Roman love poetry; see Quinn on Catullus 86. — **ludisque**] A word always hard to pin down; here, something like 'play around'; pursuit of party life and all that goes with it is implied — the area covered by our 'having a good time'; see on 3. 15. 5. — **cantu tremulo pota**] = 'and in a shaky, tipsy voice'. — **Cupidinem lentum sollicitas**] 'you importune a reluctant Cupid'; i.e., by her song-and-dance act Lyce seeks to arouse the sexual desires of her male audience; the modern editor has to print *Cupidinem* with a capital since the clause following refers to Cupid, thus spoiling the ambiguity.

6-12] H. plays with the fancy that Cupid is present in the party scene, reacting to Lyce's act as the men react — it is Chia who holds his attention, for Lyce he has no more than a passing glance. — **virentis**] = 'young'; cf. 1. 9. 17, 1. 25. 17-20. — **psallere**] Cf. Chloris, 3. 15. 13-14 'te . . . non citharae decent'. — **Chiae . . . in genis**] = 'keeps his eyes fixed on Chia's pretty cheeks'; the metaphor is from the sentry on guard at night who is alert while others sleep, his gaze on one point; cf. for *excubat* Sophocles *Antigone* 784; for the idea, Propertius watching Cynthia with fixed gaze like Argos guarding Io, 1. 3. 19-20 'sed sic intentis haerebam fixus ocellis, / Argus ut ignotis cornibus Inachidos'; **Chiae**] = 'the girl from Chios'; the name is frequent in inscriptions. — **inportunus**] = 'in his unmannerly way'; the predicative adjective where English idiom prefers an adverb; for the sense cf. 3. 16. 37. — **transvolat**] (1) literally, because Cupid has wings; (2) 'skips', 'passes over'; cf. *Sat.* 1. 2. 107-8 'meus est amor huic similis; . . . / transvolat in medio posita'. — **aridas quercus**] dried-out (and ancient) oaks; picks up the metaphor of 6 *virentis*; with *aridas* cf. 2. 11. 6 'arida canitie'. — **refugit**] Present. — **te, te**] Cf. the repetitions of Stanza 5.— **rugae**] The mark of advancing years; cf. 2. 14. 3; contrast 2. 11. 6 'levis iuventas'. — **capitis nives**] = 'the snow-drifts in your hair'; the third member of the tricolon suggests the first hint of sympathy in the picture of Lyce.

13-16] A bridge passage, marking the transition in H.'s thoughts from the scene before his eyes to memories of another Lyce. — **Coae purpurae**] Expensive dresses of Coan cloth dyed purple; Coan cloth was famous for its delicate weave, which rendered it virtually transparent; cf. *Sat.* 1. 2. 101-2 'Cois tibi paene videre est / ut nudam'; for the wearing of purple as a social affectation, see on 2. 18. 8. — **cari lapides**] 'precious stones'; see on 1. 5. 5. — **tempora**] For the plural, see on 3. 30. 5. — **semel**] 'once and for all'. — **notis condita fastis**] = 'which are now part of the public record'; the names of Lyce's lovers, i.e., are as much public property as the names of the magistrates recorded in the official *Fasti*, her conquests as familiar as the triumphs of Rome's generals recorded in the *fasti triumphales*; cf. 3. 17. 4, 4. 8. 13, 4. 14. 4. — **inclusit**] 'stored up', 'recorded'; but the word suggests also finality — that which is part of the public record is over and done with.

17-22] The questions, structured to strike an increasingly pathetic note, are addressed by H. to himself. — **quo? quove? quo?**] All with *fugit* (perfect). — **venus**] The special charm that makes a woman attractive. — **color**] 'complexion'. — **decens motus**] The ability to move with unobtrusive grace, especially while dancing; cf. 3. 6. 21. — **quae spirabat amores**] 'whose very breath was love'; i.e., who inspired love by her very presence. — **surpuerat**] = *surripuerat*; cf. for the sense Catullus 86. 6. — **felix post Cinaram**] = 'who succeeded Cinara as my mistress'; *felix* in the sense 'enjoying good fortune', 'lucky' (*OLD* 3 a); for Cinara cf. 4. 1. 3-4. — **notaque et . . . facies**] = 'a familiar figure, famous for her accomplishments'; *facies* denotes the appearance in general, not just the face; *artium* suggests her talents as a singer, musician and dancer, *gratarum* being added to exclude the sense 'wiles', 'tricks' (as in 3. 6. 22); equally with *nota* (genitive of respect) and with *facies* (descriptive genitive).

22-8] The end of the poem brings us back to the present and the answer to H.'s prayer. — **parem . . . Lycen**] 'Lyce, a match in years for a little old crow'; *temporibus* is dative with *parem* ('contracted comparison'), *cornicis* is genitive; for the longevity of the crow cf. 3. 17. 13. — **iuvenes fervidi**] Cf. 1. 25. 2 'iuvenes protervi', 1. 25. 9 'moechos arrogantis'; *fervidi* denotes aroused desire (but not aroused by Lyce); the metaphor prepares the way for the final image of Lyce as a burnt-out torch, no longer able to set off the flame of passion. — **visere**] 'to look upon'. — **dilapsam . . . facem**] 'the torch collapsed in its own ashes'; Lyce, i.e., who used to inspire passion in others, has now been consumed by the fire of her own passion; the concluding phrase is the culmination of the mood of detailed, objective realism which characterises the stanza – and the poem; H. is taken aback on seeing Lyce again, not vindictive: their quarrel is too much a thing of the past for vindictiveness.

4. 14

Introduction: Book 4 ends with two laureate odes, though in the second H. ostensibly declines the laureate role. In 4. 14, the formal occasion is the defeat of the Raeti by Tiberius; Augustus, however, gets the lion's share of the glory. H. is clearly anxious Augustus should not feel Tiberius (never, it seems, his favourite stepson) is allowed too much of the limelight (contrast the lavish praise of Drusus in 4. 4). For the Alpine campaign, see 4. 4I.

Structure: Stanzas 1-6 place Tiberius' victory in context: it is a further demonstration of the military might of Augustus (9 'quid Marte posses'); the six stanzas form a single unit (the sense carries over from one stanza to the next, several times without pause; the only strong pause is that after 9 'quid Marte posses' in mid-line). Stanzas 7-8 contain the formal encomium of Tiberius, followed, within the same sentence, by a further attribution of the victory to Augustus (33-4 'te copias, te consilium et tuos praebente divos'). Lines 34-40 proceed to link the victory with Augustus' victory, just fifteen years earlier, at Alexandria. Stanzas 11-13 commemorate Augustus' victories throughout the Roman world.

Metre: Alcaics; see 1. 9M; the absence of caesura in line 17 is unusual.

1-6] The construction is 'Quae cura . . . tuas, Auguste, virtutes . . . aeternet?': how can the normal procedures for rewarding military victory preserve for ever the achievements of a leader whose victories extend over the habitable world (5-6 'qua sol habitabilis inlustrat oras')? – Quae cura?] = 'What action taken by . . .'. – patrum, Quiritium] The twofold entity of the Senatus Populusque Romanus. – plenis . . . muneribus] = 'by according official honorific distinctions'; instrumental ablative, the first of a series of modifiers of *aeternet*; the *munera* are rewards offered Augustus by decree of the Senate, etc.; these might confer on him all manner of *honores* (official titles and distinctions). – tuas virtutes] 'your deeds of valour'. – in aevum] 'for all time to come'; a second modifier of *aeternet*. – per titulos . . . fastus] A third modifier of *aeternet*; the *honores*, once conferred, would be recorded in the usual way on official inscriptions. – o qua sol . . . maxime principum] The implied answer to H.'s opening question is that normal procedures for commemorating military success cannot cope with preserving the memory of Augustus' victories; H. now explains why this is so: the extent of his victories is unprecedented, he is the greatest of Rome's leaders.

7-13] The proof of the assertion that Augustus is *maximus principum* is twofold: the recent victory over the Vindelici, the victory which followed over the Raeti; 14 *mox* picks up 8 *nuper*; but before dealing with Tiberius' victory (the formal subject of the poem), H. turns aside ('milite nam tuo . . . plus vice simplici') for a brief recapitulation of Drusus' victory over the Vindelici (dealt with at length in 4. 4). The construction 'quem dedicere quid posses' follows the normal idiom by which the subject of the dependent clause is first made the direct object of the main verb. – legis . . . Latinae] = 'to whom the benefits of the rule of law characteristic of our way of life had yet to be extended'; i.e., they were barbarians, on whom the benefits of civilisation have been conferred; for *Latinae* instead of *Romanae*, see on 2. 1. 29. – milite tuo] 'commanding your troops'; the ablative without *cum* is usual in this and related expressions. – Genaunos, Breunos] Neighbours of the Vindelici – arces . . . tremendis] The Alpine strongholds of both the Genauni and the Breuni; tremendis] 'daunting', 'inspiring fear' by their height, etc. – plus vice simplici] = *plus quam vice simplici* (*quam* frequently omitted in comparative expressions with *plus*); with *deiecit*, 'overthrew with interest'; i.e., for every reverse suffered, Drusus inflicted a more crushing defeat.

14-24] maior Neronum] Drusus' elder brother, Tiberius (the future Emperor), son of Tib. Claudius Nero, adopted son of Augustus. – spectandus . . . Martio] = 'a striking figure on the battlefield'; the line is unusual in rhythm, lacking a caesura after syllable 5. – devota . . . ruinis] The indirect question expands *spectandus* in the same way as 9 'quid Marte posses' expands 'quem didicere'; morti liberae] the Raeti preferred death to living as slaves (enslavement being the normal fate of prisoners of war); H. is thinking of individuals, not of nations; contrast Livy 2. 1. 1 'Liberi iam hinc populi Romani res . . . peragam';

but the sympathy extended to a vanquished enemy still catches us by surprise; cf. Cleopatra 1. 37. 21-32; **quantis fatigaret ruinis**] = 'how he first wore down and then routed ... '. — **indomitas** ... **Auster**] The picture of the South Wind engaged in battle with the waves of the untamable sea and driving them back scarcely fires the imagination and is not improved by the unusual and unexpectedly gauche *prope qualis*; for the idea of the winds doing battle on (if not with) the sea cf. 1. 9. 10-11; **exercet**] 'harasses', *OLD* 2 b. — **Pleiadum** ... **nubis**] The light of the stars of the constellation Pleiades (rising and setting: early spring and autumn) cutting through the clouds provides the backdrop for an equinoctial gale. — **inpiger** ... **per ignis**] An appositional expansion of *fatigaret*; **vexare, mittere**] the infinitives depend on *inpiger*; **medios per ignis**] if not pure rhetoric, presumably refers to flaming torches, timber, etc. hurled down by the Raeti from mountain strongholds like those of the Genauni and Breuni in lines 11-12 — a vivid and plausible touch, however improbable.

25-34] **Sic**] Picked up by 29 *ut*. — **tauriformis Aufidus**] For the Aufidus, the river of H.'s boyhood, see on 3. 30. 10; rivers are commonly identified with the god thought to dwell in them, such gods being often represented in art in the form of bulls; see on 4. 2. 7-8 'profundo ore'. — **Dauni**] See on 3. 30. 11. — **saevit, meditatur**] Continue the personification of the river as an angry god. — **Claudius**] i.e., Tiberius. — **ferrata**] Refers to their protective armour; formidable opponents, therefore. — **primosque et extremos**] i.e., rank after rank. — **metendo**] For the image of the reaper cf. Catullus 64. 353-5. — **stravit humum**] The leader is identified with his army, as though he alone did the fighting. — **sine clade victor**] 'victor without loss', i.e., without casualties to his own troops. — **tuos divos**] The gods who had granted favourable auspices to Augustus and under whose protection Tiberius therefore fought.

34-40] **quo die**] Alexandria surrendered to the forces of Octavian on 1 August 30 BC; the Raeti, it seems, surrendered to Tiberius on the same day fifteen years later. — **vacuam** ... **aulam**] 'threw open a palace abandoned'; i.e., not defended, but a hint also at the suicide of Cleopatra (some ten days after the arrival of Octavian in Alexandria). — **lustro** ... **tertio**] = 'favourable to you just fifteen years later'; for reckoning by *lustra* cf. 2. 4. 24, 4. 1. 6. — **laudemque** ... **adrogavit**] 'added this glory and wished-for distinction to (that won by) your previous campaigns'; a bridge passage, preparing the way for the recital of Augustus' victories with which the ode concludes; *imperium*, the supreme authority of the commander-in-chief in the field, comes to be used of a particular campaign carried out in exercise of that authority; **adrogavit**] a procedural term (= to make an addition to a bill by passing a *rogatio*) used metaphorically.

41-52] The recital of Augustus' previous victories now begins. The list is structured in a series of seven cola each beginning with *te*; the first two form alternative subjects to 43 *miratur*, the next four, separated from these by the vocative 'o tutela ... Romae', serve as subjects to 50 *audit*. — **Cantaber**] NW Spain; see on 2. 11. 1. — **Medus et Indus**] The Parthians and the peoples beyond the Persian Gulf; for the Medi, see on 1. 2. 22 *Persae*; for the tendency to talk of a campaign against the Parthians in terms of an indefinite extension eastwards cf. 1. 29, 1. 35. 29-32. — **profugus Scythes**] The NE frontier; see on 1. 19. 10; cf. 1. 35. 9 'profugi Scythae'. — **tutela**] 'guardian', contrast 4. 6. 33. — **te fontium** ... **Britannis**] The peoples of Stanza 11 are separated from those of Stanza 13 by a group of four rivers (including Oceanus); the qualifier 'fontium qui celat origines', though most obviously linked with the Nile, is probably to be taken with all four, each representing, as it were, a point where Roman civilisation has made contact with the unknown vastness of a remote, outer world; **Nilusque et Hister**] 'both the Nile and the Hister'; *-que et* for *et* ... *et*, a device of the high style; the Nile is the symbol of the victory over Cleopatra; the Hister (the Danube) the symbol of the Daci; see on 3. 8. 18; **rapidus Tigris**] the 'headlong Tigris' symbolises the remote eastern frontier; **beluosus Oceanus**] the 'monster-filled Ocean' was traditionally a river encircling the *orbis terrarum*; **Britannis**] dative with *obstrepit*; cf. 2. 18. 20; to speak of the waters round Britain as 'obedient to' (50 *audit*) Augustus is something of a simplification, or an anticipation of a campaign repeatedly talked of as in the time as imminent; see on 1. 35. 29-30. — **te non paventis** ... **armis**] The final stanza brings us to Augustus' most recent campaigns (19-16 BC) in Spain and Gaul; **non paventis funera**] 'scorning death'; **Sygambri**] see 4. 2I and on 4. 2. 33-44.

4. 15

Introduction: 'I have been warned by Apollo himself not to proceed with a recital of Caesar's achievements on the battlefield, listing the cities subdued by him.' The relevance of Apollo's admonition to the poem which follows is left implicit but quickly becomes obvious: what H. was warned against was not an epic poem (a form against which no such divine warning was necessary), but against stressing in his lyric poetry the role of Augustus as conqueror to the neglect of his more important role as bringer of peace and restorer of the rule of law; it is as though, after the recital of vanquished peoples in 4. 14. 41-52, the obvious conclusion to H.'s book of Odes were an ode (on the model of 4. 4 and 4. 14) on Augustus' military achievements; H. is about to launch upon such a poem, when Apollo, the god of lyric poetry, warns him this is a theme beyond his powers (3-4 'ne parva Tyrrhenum per aequor vela darem'); cf., for the abandonment of a theme which showed signs of getting out of hand, 3. 3. 69-72.

As in 4. 2. 45-60 and 4. 5. 29-40, H. declines the formal laureate stance, preferring to represent himself as voicing the everyday thoughts of ordinary people united in the expression of heartfelt gratitude to an Emperor who had brought universal peace and re-established the rule of law; H. thus links himself with the oldest traditions of Roman poetry (see on lines 20-32).

Structure: The opening sentence (lines 1-4) serves as a prefatory apology for the poem which follows. The structure of the remaining lines is unusually elaborate, even for H. A string of five *et*'s (5 'et rettulit . . . ', 6 'et restituit . . . ', 8-9 'et clausit . . . ', 9-11 'et iniecit . . . ', 12 'et revocavit . . . ') gives shape to five major achievements of Augustus; the last of these fans out into a concluding tricolon crescendo (lines 13-16; see on these lines). The second half of the poem is constituted by a second, more extensive tricolon crescendo, built around the three futures 18 *exiget*, 22 *rumpent* and 32 *canemus*; all three members of the tricolon are subordinated logically to the opening 17 'Custode rerum Caesare'; the first two are negative ('non furor . . . exiget otium, non ira quae . . . urbis'; 'non . . . edicta rumpent Iulia . . .'), the third positive ('nosque . . . canemus').

Metre: Alcaics; see 1. 9M.

1-4] The intervention of Apollo is traditional: cf. *Eclogues* 6. 3-5 (Virgil is warned to stick to pastoral), in its turn an imitation of Callimachus *Aetia* 1 Fr. 1. 21-4 Pf.; but where Virgil was deterred from misguidedly attempting an epic poem, H. is deterred from stressing what was the traditional and obvious aspect of a great leader (his achievements on the battlefield) at the expense of Augustus' greater achievement as the leader who had banished war and the threat of war. – **loqui**] = 'write a poem about'; the term is not inconsistent with the lyric mode; cf. 3. 25. 18, 4. 9. 4; parallel, therefore, to 32 *canemus*. – **increpuit lyra**] Apollo, i.e., admonished H. by striking the strings of his lyre, thus reminding H. that he is a lyric poet; for Apollo as the god of the lyre, see on 2. 10. 18-19; cf. 4. 6. 25-30. – **ne . . . darem**] Cf. 4. 2. 27-32; with 'Tyrrhenum per aequor' cf. 1. 11. 5-6.

4-12] The opening sentence suggests a formal *recusatio*. H. instead launches upon an encomium of Augustus as a benefactor of the Roman people. – **Tua aetas**] i.e., the period since Actium, nearly twenty years before the publication of *Odes* 4; the verbs following (*rettulit*, etc.) are to be taken as true perfects ('has brought back', etc.). – **fruges . . . uberes**] By way of emphasising the contrast with the poem he did not write about Augustus' military exploits, H. begins with Augustus as the ruler who has brought about the restoration of Italian agriculture (following the devastation and neglect of the Civil Wars); the postponed *et* (a feature of the high style; see on 1. 12. 11) permits the framing of the line by noun and corresponding adjective; the position of the adjective (following its noun) gives it its full force (preceding the noun, the adjective tends to be ornamental or picturesque, or to serve an essentially structural function). – **et signa . . . postibus**] The standards of the Roman legions captured at Carrhae in 53 BC, recovered by Augustus following protracted negotiations; see 3. 5I; cf. 3. 5. 18-21; **superbis postibus**] the doorways of temples; 'arrogant' or 'boastful' because of the defeat of the Roman legions which they symbolised by hanging there; the recovery of the standards came to assume major importance and is thus placed high on H.'s list of Augustus' achievements. – **vacuum . . . clausit**] Closing the gates of the Temple of Janus Quirinus was the symbol of Rome at peace; see *Res Gestae* 13 'Ianum Quirinum, quem claussum esse maiores nostri voluerunt cum per totum imperium populi Romani terra marique esset parta victoriis pax, cum, priusquam nascerer, a condita urbe bis omnino clausum fuisse prodatur memoriae, ter me principe senatus claudendum esse censuit'; the gates were closed in 29 after the end of the Civil Wars and again in 25 after the war with the Cantabri; the third closing, the occasion of which is uncertain, was not in H.'s lifetime; for the legendary first opening of the gates after the arrival of the Aeneadae in Latium, see *Aen.* 7. 607-22. — **ordinem . . . culpas**] The moral reforms of Augustus are referred to; see Syme, *Roman Revolution* 440-58; **emovitque culpas**] to be taken closely with the words preceding; *frena iniecit* points to the legislation, *emovit culpas* to its success. — **veteres revocavit artis**] = almost 'restored our traditional way of life'; *revocavit*, like 5 *rettulit* and 6 *restituit*, emphasises the idea of an older, traditional order restored; *artis* denotes the 'arts and crafts' of a society at peace (agriculture, the industry of artisans, even good government, etc.) after the disruption of these by war; cf. *Aen.* 6. 852 (Anchises to Aeneas) 'hae tibi erunt artes'.

13-16] The first half of the poem ends with a tricolon crescendo expanding and explaining 12 'veteres revocavit artis'. — **Latinum nomen**] The three successive subjects of *crevere* are arranged chronologically, representing the geographical expansion of Roman power; first comes the group of city states in Latium, federated to Rome since ancient times and enjoying special privileges, generally known as the *nomen Latinum*. — **Italae vires famaque**] The concept of the *nomen Latinum* became obsolete following the Social War of 90-88 BC, which resulted in the extension of Roman citizenship to all Italians. — **crevere**] Plural with *vires* ('agreement with the nearest'). — **imperi maiestas**] The third subject of *crevere* represents the new Imperial concept of world power (though Roman citizenship was not extended to all Rome's subjects until much later). — **ad ortus . . . cubili**] = 'to the rising from the setting sun'; the phrase describes the extent of Roman power, not its place of origin.

17-24] For the structures of Stanzas 5-8, see above under Structure. The emphasis continues to be placed on peace (18 *otium*) and the rule of law (22 *edicta Iulia*). — **non . . . exiget otium**] = 'neither civil war nor revolution will put an end to peace'; in accordance with a common idiom, the negative negates the whole proposition; H. means, i.e., there will be no civil war, no attempt at a *coup d'état* and therefore no end to *otium*; cf. 1. 23. 9-10, 3. 10. 11-12; **furor civilis**] the madness of civil war; cf. the figure of 'Furor impius' in *Aen.* 1. 294-6; **vis**] the general term for public violence threatening the security of the state; **otium**] the relaxed way of life of a society at peace with nothing more to fear; cf. 2. 16. 5-8. — **non ira . . . urbis**] The anger of state against state that drives both to war; the third subject of *exiget* follows its verb and is then expanded by a relative clause. — **non qui profundum . . . Iulia**] Throughout the empire, the rule of Augustus will be respected and his decrees obeyed; **Danuvium**] (=the Hister of 4. 14. 46) the symbol of the NE frontier, inhabited by the Daci (see on 3. 8. 18); for *bibunt* cf. 3. 10. 1, also 2. 20. 20 'Rhodani potor'. — **non Getae . . . orti**] Four more eastern peoples from whom no further trouble need be anticipated: the Getae, like the Daci, symbolise the NE frontier (see on 3. 8. 18); the Serae the Far East (cf. 1. 12. 56, 3. 29. 27 — there linked with the peoples of the region of the Tanais); for the Persae (= the Parthians), see on 1. 2. 22; the 'peoples born by the River Tanais' (the Don) are the Scythae (see on 1. 19. 10, 3. 10. 1; cf. 3. 29. 28; contrast 3. 24. 9-24).

25-32] For H.'s modest role in this world universally at peace, see Introduction. — **nosque**] The expansion in line 27 ('cum prole matronisque nostris') makes it clear that *nos* = 'we Romans' (or, more probably, 'we Italians'); the *-que* eases the transition from negative prediction to assertion; we pass back from a vast but remote world at peace to the more intimate context of everyday family life. — **profestis lucibus**] 'working days'; cf. *Sat.* 2. 3. 144. — **iocosi Liberi**] 'Bacchus in jovial mood'. — **rite . . . adprecati**] The prayers to the gods which precede all meals, etc. — **virtute functos . . . canemus**] H. has in mind the custom of ancient times recorded by the elder Cato of celebrating the deeds of famous men in song at banquets, etc., reported by Cicero *Tusc.* 4. 3 'in Originibus dixit Cato morem apud maiores hunc epularum fuisse, ut deinceps qui accubarent canerent ad tibiam clarorum virorum laudes atque virtutes' (cf. *Tusc.* 1. 2 — both repeated from *Brutus* 75); H. thus, in the concluding lines of his book, represents himself as continuing the ancient practice of the remote past; **virtute . . . duces**] = 'those of our leaders who fought with courage like their fathers before them'; **Lydis . . . tibiis**] 'in song accompanied by Lydian flutes'; for the *tibia* as an adjunct to singing at parties, see 3. 19. 18-20;

Troiamque . . . Veneris] along with the *laudes clarorum virorum* of historical times will go song in celebration of Rome's Trojan ancestors (recently consecrated by Virgil's *Aeneid*) and the Julian house, of which Augustus is the descendant (by adoption) and the ruling representative; the fusion of recent and remote past ('historical foreshortening') is characteristic of H. and the Roman mind in general, as well as a carefully cultivated aspect of Augustan policy; see on 1. 2. 13-16; the last line of the *Odes* virtually paraphrases the opening words of the *Aeneid.*

List of Abbreviations

AP   *Anthologia Palatina*
L & S   Lewis and Short, *Latin Dictionary*
LGS   *Lyrica Graeca Selecta,* ed. D. L. Page
    (1968)
OCD   *Oxford Classical Dictionary*
OCT   *Oxford Classical Texts*
OLD   *Oxford Latin Dictionary*

Works of Latin authors are abbreviated as in the *Oxford Latin Dictionary.* Standard commentaries on Horace, etc. are referred to by the names of editors; the Commentary by Nisbet and Hubbard is referred to as NH.

I, M and S added to a reference = Introduction, Metre, Structure.

Index

References are in general to the lemma of
the Commentary where the point in
question is discussed rather than to the line
where the word or passage occurs.

Where a topic is fully cross-referenced in
the Commentary main entry, the Index
normally refers only to this entry.

Metrical and syntactical points are
gathered under 'Metre' and 'Syntax'.

adulter, etc., 1. 15I; 1. 25. 9-16; 3. 16. 1-8
adynation, 1. 29. 10-12; 1. 33. 5-9
aequos, 1. 4. 9-17
age of girls at marriage, 2. 5I; 3. 11I
Agrippa, 1. 6; 2. 11. 1-5
allegory, 1. 14I
amator, 1. 25. 9-12
amicitia of political alliances, 2. 1. 1-8
ancillae, affairs with, 2. 4. 1-4
animals offered at sacrifices, 3. 23. 1-8
anus, 1. 25. 9-12
Archytas, 1. 28
Asterie, 3. 7
astrologers, 1. 11. 1-3; 2. 17. 17-22
Augustus
  as benefactor of Roman people, 4. 15. 4-32
  expeditions to Britain and East, 1. 35I;
    2. 10. 17-24; 2. 11I; 3. 5I
  in Gaul, 4.5
  in Germany, 4. 2. 33-44
  in Spain, 2. 11I; 3. 14; 4. 21
  victories of, 4. 14. 41-52; 4. 15. 1-4
aura, 1. 5. 9-12
aureus, 2. 10. 5-8

Bacchus, 1. 18; 3. 25
Barine, 2. 8
Britanni, 1. 35. 29-32

Campus Martius, 1. 8. 1-7
Cantabri, 2. 11. 1-5
carmen, 1. 2. 25-30
  = poetry, 3. 28. 13-16
Carmen Saeculare, 4. 2I; 4. 6
Carrhae, Roman defeat at, 3. 5

Castor and Pollux, 1. 3. 1-8; 3. 29. 62-4;
  4. 8. 29-34
Cato the Elder as example of ancient virtues,
  2. 15. 11; 3. 21. 11-12
cave as poetic haunt, 1. 1. 29-34; 2. 1. 37-40;
  3. 25. 1-6
Censorinus, 4. 8
Chloe, 1. 23; 3. 26
Chloris, 3. 15
Civil Wars, 1. 2. 25-30; 2. 1; 3. 1I
Cleopatra, 1. 37
Cura, 2. 16. 17-24; 3. 1. 37-40; 3. 14. 13

Daci, 3. 8. 17-24
Damocles, sword of, 3. 1. 17-21
Danae, 3. 16. 1-8
Daunus, 2. 1. 29-36
deducere, 3. 30. 10-14
Delius, Q., 2. 3
Diana, 1. 21; 3. 22
dicere, 1. 6. 5-9
difficilis, 3. 7. 22-32
dithyramb, 2. 19; 3. 25
domina, 2. 8. 17-20; 2. 12. 13-16
Drusus, 4. 4; 4. 14. 7-13

eius, 4. 8. 13-22
elegy, H.'s attitude to, 2. 9
Epicureanism, 1. 4. 9-17; 1. 31. 17-20;
  1. 34; 2. 3I
Europa and the bull, 3. 27. 25-76

Faunus, 1. 4. 9-17; 1. 17; 3. 18
flattery, 2. 6I
flowering-out of image, 2. 5S
foreshortening
  historical, 3. 3. 37-44; *see also* 1. 2. 13-16;
    1. 37I
  of distance, 2. 3. 17-20
Fortuna, 1. 35; 3. 29. 49-56
fugax, 2. 14. 1-4
Fuscus, Aristius, 1. 22

Galatea, 3. 27
garlands, 1. 1. 29-34; 1. 38
Geloni, 2. 10. 13-17